THE "STATELY PRESIDENT LINERS"
American Passenger Liners of the Interwar Years

Part 1—The "502"s
By
Mark H. Goldberg

Volume 5
Of The American Merchant Marine History Series
The American Merchant Marine Museum
Kings Point, New York
1996

This book is for my father

THE AMERICAN MERCHANT MARINE HISTORY SERIES
by the same author

Additional titles forthcoming

Also by the same author
SHIPS OF THE LIBERA LINE
Published by A.J. Hilgersom/Navigare
Amsterdam, Netherlands 1987

LIBRARY OF CONGRESS Catalogue Number 95–083451
ISBN # 1-879 180-1-11

CONTENTS

 (A cumulative index for the entire series will appear
 in the final volume.)

A WORD OF THANKS

Upon the publication of "GOING BANANAS" 100 Years of American Fruit Ships, Volume 3 of this series, I PROMISED myself and my partner Chris Smith that I would NEVER write so big a book again. I'm afraid that though it comes nowhere near the scope of that one, the current work just about rivals "GOING BANANAS" in size. My work on the "502"s began life almost ten years ago as 67 pages of double spaced type in a proposed book on American passenger cargo ships. That possible book got far too big to be a single volume and Frank Braynard suggested to me that I turn my intended book into an entire series. So I always have to thank Frank Braynard first for it was he who told me I must write about these ships I so love. His was the initial support given my writing. Of course I thank my father, Dr. Harold S. Goldberg at the same time and in the same pride of place for all his help and guidance in so many ways for so many years. . . . NO, make that decades! My good friend Maury Newburger and the May and Morris Newburger Foundation have my thanks as they have had all along.

Thanks, too, to many of the same people who have been so willing to help me with this work throughout the series. With my project since the preparation of "GOING BANANAS" is Eric Johnson whose generous contribution of the photographic images so vital to this work is a real "guardian angel". So, too, is Bill Kooiman, accomplished gentleman and author of The GRACE SHIPS, former Grace, Prudential and Delta Purser and for quite a few years on the staff of the James Porter Shaw Library at the National Maritime Museum in San Francisco. He has helped me so often with this project, finding details and information to fill in the cracks in whatever material I was able to unearth elsewhere. He supplied a few of the photos for this book. Here in Baltimore, Ann C. House, Librarian of the Steamship Historical Society of America's collection at the Langsdale Library at the University of Baltimore deserves special thanks. She's recovering from another hip replacement as I write this, but I think she knows that I was aware of how much pain she had to endure in those last few weeks before surgery and how special I considered her help, so kindly and enthusiastically tendered whenever I needed it. From the Hawaii Maritime Center in Honolulu comes the help of my old friend Stan Melman pitched in and found me the photo of the PRESIDENT TAYLOR stranded on Canton Island.

Special thanks go to Captain Warren Leback. Master of quite a few Grace Line vessels and Maritime Administrator in the Bush Administration, he took the time to go to the trouble to provide me with copies of Captain Orel Pierson's accounts of the last voyage of the PRESIDENT HARRISON under the American flag as well as Captain Pierson's 1945 statement to American

President Lines and his later memoirs. Captain David Grover graciously allowed me to use whatever information I needed from *The Captives of Shanghai*, the book he and his daughter Cmdr. Gretchen Grover wrote about the capture of the PRESIDENT HARRISON and the wartime imprisonment of her American crew. Let me also thank Mike Skalley, whose fine book, *A Medal for Marigold*, is based on the records and memories of his father. His father, Robert Skalley, was the captain of the Marigold. Everyone at the Army Transportation Museum at Fort Eustis, Virginia seemed to want to help and they did, but I send special thanks to Carolyn Wright who found and copied a rare monograph on Army hospital ships for me.

I must add a few words about the Library at the Independence Seaport Museum, the best of its kind on the East Coast and rivalled only by San Francisco's National Maritime Museum for the title of the "best in the nation". Seeking out the names of the women who sponsored five of the "502"s turned up nothing until I turned in frustration to Librarian E. Ann Wilcox and Assistant Librarian Sarah Sullivan of that marvelous maritime museum. They put me in touch with library volunteer Joel Loeb. He got to work right away on my request and found the names of all the sponsors but one . . . the woman who launched the PANHANDLE STATE. In Philadelphia a few months later, I found that one myself in an article on the ship's delayed launching in *The Philadelphia Inquirer*. Making a list of all the London voyages of the PANHANDLE STATE I thought that I had neglected to cover the period between June and December 1921. Slightly alarmed because I couldn't find the necessary information in any of my notes or photocopies, I once more turned to the Library at the Independence Seaport for help on this one. This time volunteers Cedric Scarlett and Tom Welch stepped in and searched through every issue of *The New York Maritime Register* for a few pieces of information. Perhaps it seemed I need unconnected pieces of trivia but when I read the results of their work it came to me in a flash. The period in question is when the PANHANDLE STATE was fitted with steerage accommodations.

Let me neither forget nor hesitate to thank Reference Archivist Angie van Deredt at the National Archives for so much help with so many projects. So, too, I wish to thank the Office of Record Management of the Maritime Administration where Donald Post and Cozette Miles have been so helpful to me on so many occasions.

Then there are all my friends who put up with my periods of silence, crankiness and lethargy in the preparation of this book. I thank you all.

THE "502"S—THE NAMES

In typical Emergency Fleet Corporation fashion, planned names for the "502s" were discarded and new names given prior to launching. April 1922 brought new names for almost all U.S. Shipping Board passenger ships. By May the "502"s were renamed. All became "PRESIDENT" liners. Sold to Dollar Line in September 1923, they retained their names. With similarly named "535" type passenger and cargo liners, the first word in the names of these standard ships made AMERICAN PRESIDENT LINES the natural name of the company the Maritime Commission formed to succeed Dollar Lines in the summer of 1938. Resuming Dollar's moribund services with "PRESIDENT" liners, APL soon moved to replace the aging "502"s. Ordering at first six new C3 P type ships for 1940 and 1941 delivery, they renamed six of the old "502"s. For the sentimental reason that the PRESIDENT HARRISON made the first of voyage on the round the world service, APL allowed her to keep her name. Eventually the largest American vessel captured by the enemy in World War II, her captors renamed her twice. Beyond their second "PRESIDENT" names, some "502"s were renamed during World War II. Each surviving vessel later reverted to her second "PRESIDENT" name.

The following should make it easier to follow an individual ship through changes in name.

All seven vessels were built to United States Shipping Board Design Number 1095 to Emergency Fleet Corporation Contract 418 SC by New York Shipbuilding Corporation at Camden, New Jersey.

	EFC HULL #	NYSHIP HULL #
	2585	244
intended name	WOODBBURY	
launch name	OLD NORTH STATE	
renamed 1922	PRESIDENT van BUREN	
renamed 1940	PRESIDENT FILLMORE	
renamed 1944 (as US Army hospital ship)	MARIGOLD	
renamed 1946	PRESIDENT FILLMORE	

	EFC HULL #	NYSHIP HULL #
	2586	247
intended name	ICARIA	
launch name	PANHANDLE STATE	

renamed 1922   PRESIDENT MONROE
renamed 1940   PRESIDENT BUCHANAN
renamed 1943 (intended hospital ship name)   IRIS
renamed 1944 (as U.S. Army hospital ship)   EMILY H. WEDER
renamed 1946   PRESIDENT BUCHANAN

EFC HULL #	NYSHIP HULL #
2587	248

intended name   JAKIN
launch name   WOLVERINE STATE
renamed 1922   PRESIDENT HARRISON
renamed after capture by Japanese   KAKKO MARU
renamed 1943   KACHIDOKI MARU

EFC HULL #	NYSHIP HULL #
2588	245

intended name   IASSUS
launch name   CREOLE STATE
renamed 1922   PRESIDENT HAYES
renamed 1940   PRESIDENT TYLER
renamed 1944 (intended hospital ship name)   HOWARD McCURDY
renamed 1945   PRESIDENT TYLER

EFC HULL #	NYSHIP HULL #
2589	246

intended name   JADWIN
launch name   GRANITE STATE
renamed 1922   PRESIDENT POLK
renamed 1940   PRESIDENT TAYLOR

EFC HULL #	NYSHIP HULL #
2590	249

intended name   IDAS
launch name   CENTENNIAL STATE
renamed 1922   PRESIDENT ADAMS
renamed 1940   PRESIDENT GRANT

EFC HULL #	NYSHIP HULL #
2591	250

intended name	IDMAN
launch name	BLUE HEN STATE
renamed 1922	PRESIDENT GARFIELD
renamed 1940	PRESIDENT MADISON
renamed 1942 (as US Navy troop ship)	KENMORE
renamed 1944 (as US Navy hospital ship)	REFUGE
renamed 1946	PRESIDENT MADISON

As of Sept 10, 1918 there were still neither estimated dates for KL, L or Del for any of the seven "502"s. United States Shipping Board Statistical Section carried them on progress reports but on that date only blanks followed their hull numbers (2585 through 2591). Those charts, though, listed all the big troopers as 10,000 tonners, all troop transports besides the Type B "Hog Islander" were expected to be identical!!!!

For the "502"s, extracted here from the planning and statistical department of the USSB as of January 14, 1919:

WOODBURY (OLD NORTH STATE)	KL	expected	1/28/19
	L	"	9/ /19
	Dl	"	12/ /19
IASSUS	KL	expected	3/ 7/19
	L	"	9/ /19
	Dl	"	11/ /19
JADWIN	KL	expected	5/ /19
	L	"	11/ /19
	Dl	"	1/ /20
ICARIA	KL	expected	3/ 2/19
	L	"	9/ /19
	Dl	"	11/ /19
JAKIN	KL	expected	6/ /19
	L	"	12/ /19
	Dl	"	2/ /20
IDAS (CENTENNIAL STATE)	KL	expected	9/ /19
	L	"	3/ /20
	Dl	"	5/ /20

IDMAN (BLUE HEN STATE)   KL   expected 12/ /19
                         L   "   6/ /20
                         Dl   "   8/ /20

KL = keel laying; L = Launch; Dl = delivery

ORDER of KEELS LAID:

OLD NORTH STATE
PANHANDLE STATE
WOLVERINE STATE
CREOLE STATE
GRANITE STATE
CENTENNIAL STATE
BLUE HEN STATE

ORDER of LAUNCH:

OLD NORTH STATE
PANHANDLE STATE
CREOLE STATE
GRANITE STATE
WOLVERINE STATE
CENTENNIAL STATE
BLUE HEN STATE

ORDER of DELIVERY:

PANHANDLE STATE
OLD NORTH STATE
CREOLE STATE
WOLVERINE STATE
GRANITE STATE
CENTENNIAL STATE
BLUE HEN STATE

Introduction—
The Seven "502" Passenger
and Cargo Liners

In an earlier time in ports throughout much of the world stars and stripes hailed proudly from masts and sterns of hundreds of American sailing ships both boxy and racy. American ships and Yankee sailors were familiar sights everywhere. Unfortunately those American glory days at sea happened during the first sixty years of the nineteenth century. By 1840 American ships dominated world trade routes and foreign shipowners had long come to these shores to have American yards build their ships. Once a major exporter of merchant tonnage to the world, innovator of the fast clipper ship, America seemed to have no stomach for the ocean steamship. Those were the glory days of the American Merchant Marine and the American shipbuilder, a brilliant epoch in the development of a new and largely untried nation. Then came the Civil War and for the American Merchant Marine a fast downhill slide. With the end of the Confederacy and a short lived boom in the building of American ocean steamers fast enough to run Union blockades, the fortunes of the American Merchant Marine seemed to grow in almost reverse measure to those of the United States of America herself. Despite a strong lead in the declining age of fast sailing ships, a variety of factors saw America leave the further development and operation of ocean steam shipping to others, yielding her dominant position in merchant shipping without a fight. Overseas steam shipping held little allure for American interests. There simply wasn't enough money in it. Foremost in the mind of the investor was the outrageous cost of operating tonnage under the American flag. High grade ocean services under the American flag cost considerably more than operation under any other flag. Almost prohibitive were construction costs in American shipyards. Prices here for the construction of an important steamship was anywhere from two to five times that for comparable ships coming from a European yard. Equally effective a barrier to the development of a leading position among the world's maritime nations was Congress' unfriendly attitude and a patent unwillingness to support an American Merchant Marine.

All too quickly American ocean shipping became a laughing stock among shipping men in other maritime nations of the world. Americans didn't seem to mind. Their many coastal shipping services really satisfied the overwhelming majority of Americans and American business interests throughout the remaining years of the century. Most overseas business was conducted with the countries around the shores of the Caribbean Sea, anyway.

1

Things changed rapidly for all industrialized nations with the turn of the century, for if nothing else, the Age of Imperialism had dawned. For a player to win in this new era, ocean steamships were a requisite.

Before the century was fourteen years old the importance of having a strong merchant fleet was driven home when Europe went to war. But that was across a big ocean from the United States and Americans felt little need to pay any attention to the troubles of a Europe they or their not so distant ancestors were only too happy to leave. They were part of a different world, a new world, or so they thought. Looking back with pride on their nation's relatively short history, citizens of the United States expected nothing more than continued peace and prosperity when they celebrated their country's 138th birthday on July 4, 1914. They could, and many were, if contemporary patriotic panegyrics portrayed the true spirit of the people, be warmed by the thought of just how far the nation had come since its beginnings as a small backwater across the seas from mighty Europe. Events that took place in the mysterious and turbulent Balkans six days earlier seemed to have no connection to the American home life. No, there could be nothing to link Americans to those Serb inspired nationalists who ambushed and gunned down the presumptive heir to the throne of Austria-Hungary. America paid scant attention to these machinations, snug in the knowledge that across the seas their homeland was safe and that a war in the Balkans would have little if any effect on them. They had little reason to suspect eventual involvement in that imbroglio, it had nothing to do with them. It was just as well, for despite its riches and potential, America was no great military giant. Even if it were . . . she hadn't the ships to deliver her punch to an overseas enemy.

Blessed with seemingly inexhaustible resources and more land than its population could use, the nation's industries burgeoned with the passing of the nineteenth century to put America into a position of an economic powerhouse. By 1892 the United States outstripped all others to rank first per capita in manufacturing output. While American business and industry were expanding, the nation's population was moving westward, exploring and developing huge tracts of formerly uninhabited land (naturally, there were many instances of native Americans who were abused and deprived of their land, but at no time did their population exceed one million). By the millions, foreigners flocked to America's shores, hoping for riches but more certain of the truths of democracy, freedom and a chance for economic success that all served as a powerful draw.

As the new century dawned and the Gilded Age yielded to the Age of Imperialism, the industrialized world continued expanding. The United States already stood with the leaders of the pack in almost every area of labor intensive, capital intensive industry and business—except one—ocean shipping. The lackluster state of the American merchant marine stood in dreary contrast to America's dizzying successes in most other things. And yet, that great and mighty industrial nation attracting immigrants by the millions hadn't ships of her own to carry her produce and manufactures to buyers abroad. That country so successful at creating millionaires at home and increasing its economic importance abroad was a nation without ocean ships and was thus militarily of limited importance among the major military and industrial powers in that era when Europe was the center of the military and diplomatic world. Simply put, without a way to transport your armies and your war materiele, your country is no great power. War with Spain at the end of the nineteenth century drove that point home to some savvy Americans. There were not enough ships to go around. Fortunately America had chosen an enemy not much better off nor much better equipped to prosecute an overseas war. Spain's seagoing Navy and Merchant Marine were not materially better than their American counterparts. With America's victory in that short, tragicomic war came the problem of moving armies of occupation across the Pacific to newly won territories in the Philippines, Guam and in the Caribbean to Cuba and Puerto Rico. For a nation with but very few troopships, it was a tough task and authorities had to hustle to provide the necessary troop lift. After all, in winning the islands, America inherited an anti-Colonial guerilla war. Alas, that scramble to transport troops was quickly forgotten and the nation turned its face from the sea again.

Nothing learned from the lessons of the Spanish American War sank in as Americans took such little notice of ocean shipping that by 1914 the American Merchant Marine carried only eight per cent of the nation's overseas commerce. When Europe's decades of peace blew apart that summer, absorbing Europeans in a patriotic orgy of spilling blood, belligerent European nations could devote less time and money to ocean shipping. Neutral nations stood by ready and in the cases of Norway and Spain, able to make tidy profits carrying many of the cargoes warring nations needed. International commerce suddenly became more vital than ever. Some in the United States caught on immediately, for here was a great opportunity to make fortunes both in ocean shipping and selling of ocean going tonnage. Here was a chance to earn real money supplying either or both sides. Anything that could float and move under its own power found an eager buyer. Yet America could take little comfort in any of this, isolationist at heart, and equipped with few ocean ships of her own, she would have to stand idly by. It was really an inexcusable situation because it was the second time in less than a score of years that America found herself short of ships in time of war. Far reaching would be the implications of this endemic weakness, yet no lesson learned would not go unlearned in an America endemically short of ships. Less than twenty years after the end of the World War I era, Europe returned to war. Having grown almost neurotically isolationist as a backlash to the Great War and internalizing during the Depression, the United States was in sorry shape militarily once again. Her Merchant Marine was not much better.

While the nation grew westward and inward during the nineteenth century few Americans felt any effects of the country's diminishing presence on the world's oceans. And even though the young nation's Pacific Coast developed faster than much of the center, coastal and river shipping seemed to satisfy most of the nation's need for water transport. The lapse of American ocean shipping was no particular problem since the nation's economic base required but limited participation in overseas markets until the America of the "Gilded Age" gave way to the America of the Age of Imperialism. THAT America could not afford to ignore foreign commerce, for the nation's vastly expanded manufacturing potential and output required overseas markets. At that point, though, few were the ocean traders under the "Stars and Stripes".

Cost was the major factor in the lack of American presence in steam powered merchant shipping. Historically higher wages paid in this country corresponded to higher prices to build ships in the United States as well as amazingly higher costs for crew. America could have followed a European example and provide subsidy to steamer services but Congress felt no compunction to subsidize anxious American shipping interests. All too often Congress passed laws that were ultimately deleterious to the fortunes of American ocean shipping. Rather than alleviate the distressed situation of a lagging American industry, Congress seemed to delight either in hammering many nails into the coffin of the American Merchant Marine, or ignoring its representatives.

Only part of the blame can be traced to Congress. Their experience with subsidizing ocean shipping thus far yielded less than happy results. Two mid nineteenth century maritime subsidies yielded such scandals that Congress was wary and disillusioned if not hostile to the idea of providing American shipowners with money from the public purse. Responding to the success of Britain's Cunard Line, Congress voted to allow New Yorker Edward Knight Collins a subsidy to operate a steamship service across the Atlantic. Building and commissioning the most fabulous ships of the age (except maybe that perennial financial disaster, the GREAT EASTERN), the Collins Line performed tragically, losing two of their highly vaunted ships in horrifying accidents.

Drawn by furs and abundant land, some hearty Americans set out for the West Coast and had settled in Oregon. Taking Mexican lands in the West as spoils of war, Americans began settling the Pacific Coast in ever greater numbers. After Oregon and California were organized as territories, enterprising men looked to make their fortunes there. New York financier W.H. Aspinwall sold investors on the idea of a coast to coast steamship service via the Isthmus of Panama and in 1848 created the Pacific Mail Steamship Company. Offering his proposed steamship line to the Navy and Post Office to carry the United States mail from New York to Oregon, Aspinwall promised to provide steamship service all the way, save for the land portion from the Atlantic coast of the Isthmus of Panama to Balboa. Steamships from New York would land passenger, mails and freight at a new port where they would begin a 50 mile overland passage across the isthmus of Panama to board or be loaded aboard another steamer at Balboa for carriage in safety and speed to American possessions on the Pacific Coast. Congress granted the Pacific Mail Line a subsidy in 1848. Aspinwall's name remains clean but over the course of the next twenty years, tales of bribery tarnished the good name of the venerable enterprise and Congress' attitudes towards possible ocean subsidies hardened.

With no financial assistance, American shipbuilders and shipping men were unable to compete against those of other countries where building and operating costs were so much lower and often state subsidized. After the Civil War, ocean transport was something Congress was in no mood to consider. Spending money at sea offered legislators little return and no votes, so pleas for help unaccompanied by large gifts of cash from American shipping men went largely unheard. After the Collins and Aspinwall debacles, only one more firm won Congressional assistance and that had more to do with Department of State attentions than anything else. In three different incarnations the United States & Brazil Mail Steamship Company enjoyed financial assistance from Washington, the only one to do so during some forty years of official neglect. The first law designed to offer some relief to a desperate American industry was the Postal Aid Law of 1891. After the end of the Civil War only four small passenger liners for the North Atlantic had sailed forth from American yards for American owners. Built in 1873 for a line backed by the Pennsylvania Railroad, those ships were the ILLINOIS, INDIANA, PENNSYLVANIA and OHIO. Though they all lasted a long time, over the long run they did little to raise American prestige on the seas. As a result of the Postal Aid Law, a few ships were built for the American flag, but even those were primarily involved in domestic and off-shore trades. The only really notable ships to emerge from all Congress had wrought were the Atlantic flyers ST. LOUIS and ST. PAUL of 1895, but that pair was as much the result of the Law's permission to enroll two British flag Atlantic speedsters, the CITY OF NEW YORK and CITY OF PARIS under the American register as much as was federal assistance. Meanwhile, American financiers and railroad men, the real forces behind American shipping, concentrated either on coastal shipping or on cooperation with foreign companies. Many famous transatlantic lines and ships were actually mostly, if not wholly, American owned. Flying either British or Belgian flags, their owners saved considerable sums of money by building those ships abroad and hiring foreign nationals to man them.

Of course this lack of safe, fast, modern ships under the American flag was no major problem unless you were in the shipping business or inordinately patriotic. It was no problem at all during the "Gilded Age", nor for the few years thereafter. It wouldn't even be noticed by either masses or experts until the nation became involved in foreign wars. Smart money bet against the flag time and time again. They won every time. Then came the short semi-comic war with Spain and the Army, at least, learned of the need for a force of troop transports. With the acquisition of island colonies, the

Army worked quickly to acquire permanent peacetime troopships. It was no easy task for there really were very few suitable American ships. The Navy was no help, nor was it at all interested. With no troops of its own to move, the Navy saw no need for what they called "passenger ships" . . . they left trooping the province of the Army.

Further aid to shipping was hardly considered and one law in particular proved more detrimental to the well being of the American merchant marine than anything any enemy might have devised. The canal building at the Isthmus of Panama gave a boost to a few companies involved in the transport of men and materials to either Colon on the Atlantic or Balboa on the Pacific. Expected to be quite a boon to American shipping, Congress saw that it would benefit but a very few, passing the Panama Canal Act in 1912. Since the canal was still under construction, it would be some years before its provisions could take effect. Trying to level the playing field among American shipping operators, so many of whom were primarily railroad men, Congress passed the Panama Canal Act. Its primary effect on shipping forbade use of the canal to any ship owned by a railroad company. That was a big blow to the fabled Pacific Mail Steamship Company because it was owned by the Southern Pacific Railway Company. Other important American steamship companies were owned by railroads, especially on the Pacific, where magnate J.J. Hill was boss of the Great Northern. Then there were the Harrimans whose Union Pacific Railroad remains famous to this day. Their role in American transportation is rightfully legendary. Ships were important to them, too. Within a few years of the outbreak of war in Europe, scion Averell Harriman became heavily involved in American shipbuilding and shipping.

One further provision of the Panama Canal Act had a devastating impact on any move to quickly build the American Merchant Marine by incorporating foreign ships under the U.S. flag. The act simply forbade American registry to any foreign vessel not at least five years old. When prompted to repeal that clause in March 1914, Congress did nothing for six months until the outbreak of war in Europe brought them a shipping crisis. August 1914 brought the Shipping Act, permitting United States registry for ships excluded by the Panama Canal Act and generally making life much easier for American shipping. By June 30, 1915, no less than 148 ships of 523,361 gross tons were brought into American registry.[1] Unfortunately, American shipbuilding declined by almost the same amount. Not only that, shipbuilding on the East Coast for the fiscal year ending June 15, 1915 was one third less than it had been the previous year. Sad to say, it was the lowest output for any of the preceding sixteen years. Against this background of inaction, declining numbers of new buildings and dwindling ocean shipping capabilities came the loud voice of Missouri Congressman Joshua W. Alexander. It was

---

[1] According to several editions of the "Report of the Commissioner of Navigation" quoted by Edward N. Hurley in "The Bridge to France."

a cry in the wilderness, for his 1914 call to create a Shipping Board was ignored. America shut out ships at its and the free world's own peril, but it did shut them out.

In 1914 America's Merchant Marine was in truly sorry shape, able to attract or carry but eight per cent of the nation's overseas commerce. Besides Great Lakes and coastal shipping, only fifteen overseas cargo lines were served by American-flag vessels. To the Caribbean and South America were a few, small ships under the Stars and Stripes. The situation of American steamship interests on the Atlantic was hardly more impressive. Only a few passenger liners engaged in overseas trades flew the American flag at their sterns. Among those American ships on the Atlantic were the ST. LOUIS, ST. PAUL, NEW YORK and PHILADELPHIA.[2] All at least twenty years old, none was still a real contender for the high class trade. Other American liners on the Atlantic included the FINLAND and KROONLAND, while the Atlantic Transport Line occasionally flagged a ship in the United States.

Only on the Pacific could American shipping hold its head high, but not for long for news worse than the Panama Canal Act was on the way for the American steamship owner when Congress next meddled in 1915. Trouble came this time from a leading progressive, Senator Robert La Follette of Wisconsin. Champion of the American sailor, who was still legally considered somewhere between ward of the state and idiot savant (*sad but true!*), La Follette thought his bill would be an anchor towards the emancipation of the American mariner. But while trying to protect jobs of American season, the Senator did the American merchant marine a great deal of harm. His bill, the Seaman's Protection Act of 1915, forced American shipping companies to employ a crew of which at least 50% were fluent in English. La Follette's Act wrought further havoc on the Pacific Mail Steamship Company, at least so said flamboyant Pacific Mail president Rennie Schwerin in his vociferous denunciations of the new order. If nothing else, the Senator's good intentions provided Schwerin a viable smoke screen behind which the old firm could dump their big transpacific passenger ships to take advantage of especially good prices for ships occasioned by the European War.

Able to operate effectively because of the overwhelming preponderance of Chinese in their ship's crew, this last Act was a real blow to the Pacific Mail. Taking a big potshot at Senator La Follette and his 1915 Seaman's bill, famed Pacific Mail Line head Rennie Schwerin announced that his company could not survive under the terms of the new law and that forthwith he was suspending the nation's most important American flag service to the Far East and selling off the ships. There were two other reasons for his decision and neither of them got much play. The Panama Canal Act was one of them and an even more important factor than LaFollette's law. Having expanded to offer service across the Pacific from California, the Pacific Mail remained involved in part of its original coast to coast services and still operated be-

---

[2]Launched in 1895, let us consider the ST. LOUIS and ST. PAUL twenty year old ships in 1914.

tween Panama and California. Its history and operations inextricably linked to the development of California and the Pacific Coast, the birth of the Republic of Panama and the construction of the Panama Canal, it was certain that the company would expand the service through the Canal into the Caribbean and Atlantic. The Panama Canal Act made that idea impossible. The other reason for Schwerin's seemingly capricious act was also a very simple one. With Europe at war, prices for anything that could float rose immediately and dramatically, giving Schwerin a ready market for his big transpacific steamers. He sold them for very high prices. But what could be more convenient for Mr. Schwerin to pin the blame on Senator LaFollette and his Seaman's Protection Act for the loss of the country's oldest extant steamship line? Then among America's biggest and most important merchant ships were the four Pacific Mail passenger ships KOREA, SIBERIA, MANCHURIA and MONGOLIA. Once La Follette's bill became law, the American flag began to falter on an ocean where American ships were once the most important. Good as his word, Schwerin pulled the ships out of service and offered them for sale. The first two went to buyers in Japan who immediately put them back into transpacific service. The other pair went to the Atlantic Transport Line, a member of financier J.P. Morgan's steamship line combine, the International Mercantile Marine Company. An American company, the Atlantic Transport Line then operated most of its fleet under the British flag, giving strong testimony to the premise that under foreign flags American shipping men could and did make more money. For this among other reasons, J.P. Morgan established International Mercantile Marine on the framework of the American Line and then absorbed a number of important foreign steamship companies, particularly British.

Sale of Pacific Mail's four steamers left a big void in American shipping from the West Coast. Other than Matson Navigation Company's ships trading to Hawaii, only the SIERRA, SONOMA and VENTURA, in operation between California and Australia remained in service on the Pacific under the American flag.

The sum of the few maritime laws provided more incentive for shipowners to register ships under foreign flags than to foster the growth of the nation's Merchant Marine. Whatever La Follette's bill did, it did not make American registry any more attractive than had a Shipping Bill the previous year. Though that law allowed American registry to certain foreign built vessels, American shipbuilding for 1915 declined by almost the exact amount of vessels newly incorporated onto the American register. The European war notwithstanding, the sum of the few Maritime laws still provided more incentive for shipowners to register ships under foreign flags than to foster the growth of the nation's Merchant Marine.

Ocean shipping under the American flag did not pay, or it didn't pay enough to satisfy the typical investor. Ships are operated because they can make money, that occupation so aptly dear to the American psyche. Except in the rarest of instances, merchant ships are not operated because they are pretty or big or fast or prestigious. They are operated to make money. That and ONLY that is the bottom line, and the dreams of the romantic ship enthusiast have nothing to do with this hard, cold fact.

Flexing its muscles on the world stage under Presidents McKinley, Roosevelt and Taft, the United States was very lucky she had no serious and powerful external enemy, for had there been one (or more), America would have been hard pressed to find the tonnage necessary to move tens of thousands of men and mountains of weapons, munitions, materiele and foodstuffs to prosecute a war. After all, American flag ships then carried a dwindling percentage of the nation's overseas trade.

So when European powers considered America as a potential military ally, they had to discount her because she could not be expected to move her forces and supplies to a battlefield so many thousands of miles across the sea. The European powers did not expect America to be able to abide by any serious commitments for this reason above all. The declaration of war by Germany and Austria on the Allies in 1914 caught a neutral America off guard and with an appalling shortage of merchant ships. It still took a stupefied Congress over two years to begin to resolve this problem. America's lawmakers finally heeded Missouri Congressman Joshua Alexander and voted for ships. The nation's chronic shortage of American merchant tonnage was at long last addressed with the Shipping Act of 1916. With its enactment into law on September 7, 1916, came the simultaneous establishment of the United States Shipping Board. Congress endowed it with a budget of $50,000,000 from the sale of Panama Canal Bonds and gave it the task of the development of the American Merchant Marine. Its most pressing task was to amass the largest pool of merchant ships for the coming war in as short a time as possible.

The Shipping Board had very little time to do its appointed work. Because there was a war on in Europe and every passing day suggested an increasing likelihood of eventual American involvement, government, military and business leaders struggled with the simple fact of life that stuck in its peaceful corner of the globe . . . the United States simply did not have the motive means to transport men and material to any overseas theater of war. Time was fast running out for isolationist neutrals. Once the United States entered the war on April 6, 1917, the Shipping Board really got busy. Under wartime conditions, the Shipping Board received broad powers and authority from Congress and for the duration of the wartime emergency, all American ocean shipping came under the direct control of the United States Shipping Board. Curiously enough, most coastal ships were not included in the broad sweep of the Shipping Board's arms for the bulk of the coastal fleet was commandeered by Federal Railway authorities.

Less than two weeks after the United States declared war on the Central Powers the Shipping Board established the United States Shipping Board Emergency Fleet Corporation on April 17, 1917. Aware that any real American participation in the War rested upon the availability of a large fleet of merchant ships to carry the nation's military men and might, the Trustees of the Shipping Board geared their efforts to the acquisition of modern cargo carriers. Now troopships would be needed, and the Emergency Fleet Corporation was charged with one single overriding mission—to provide the United States of America with the merchant marine needed by a vibrant, industrial nation. Often known by the initials EFC, the Fleet Corporation was the actual entity that ordered new ships, bought existing ships and operated the fleet itself. Owner of record, the Emergency Fleet Corporation was also permitted to establish its own shipyards.

Besides taking up anything considered able to cross the Atlantic the Shipping Board looked to enemy tonnage to help prosecute the war against the Central Powers. There was a lot of it in American ports, for over a hundred German and eight Austrian vessels had taken refuge in American neutrality in 1914 and 1915. Since there was never a declaration of war against Austria-Hungary, only a rupture of diplomatic relations, the Shipping Board could, and did, buy Austrian tonnage and bought those eight ships outright. Except for a very few intermediate German vessels sold by their owners during the interim, Germany's exiled ships were seized after April 6, 1917. So, too, through the right of angary, were neutral ships fair game for American hands. Neutral Dutch ships in American ports were also soon acquired by seizure. Many other foreign vessels similarly came under American control, all to spend the coming years under the control of the Shipping Board. Some of Germany's most prestigious passenger vessels were included in the American sweep and would be instrumental in carrying American troops overseas to deal Germany a crushing defeat. Although this put a good number of ships suitable for trooping under the control of the United States, there were neither enough of those nor enough freighters to support efforts for an all out war.

The Shipping Board continued to amass a fleet by all means at hand. When the United States went to war every one of 234 building ways in the nearly 40 shipyards able to build ocean going tonnage was occupied building the 470 some-odd ocean going freighters, passenger cargo ships and tankers on order in American yards, many of these building for Britain, France and Norway. American yards employed about 5,000 men. Virtually every one of the contracts for those ships building in the nation's shipyards was soon requisitioned by the Emergency Fleet Corporation in the name of the war effort. That would help, of course, but for the scale and scope of the Great War, the number of ships acquired by seizure and requisition could not come close to the total thought necessary. Once the land war in western Europe bogged down into trench warfare, it seemed that as a war of attrition it could last for years. With the Kaiserliche Marine, Germany's Navy, practicing unrestricted submarine warfare, only new ships, lots of new ships, could stem the tide of lost tonnage. To that end the Shipping Board Emergency Fleet Corporation contracted with American shipbuilders to build a massive number of ships of nearly a hundred different types. "Build them faster than the

Germans could sink them!" That was the rallying cry—and America rose to the effort, turning its fabulous manufacturing capabilities to emergency shipbuilding for the first time in her history. With the call for the rapid construction of hundreds of thousands of tons of new ships came new shipyards and expansion of old ones, each charged with the emergency construction of "standard" types of ships, each of a specific Shipping Board design. By the time the guns fell silent on November 11, 1918 some 350,000 men and women toiled to build ships in the nation's 216 shipyards whose 970 building ways were in full operation building ships for the war effort. War surely made shipbuilding a number one growth industry! The United States Shipping Board Emergency Fleet Corporation was able to take delivery of at least 1,562 purpose built steel cargo ships alone among an amassed fleet totalling 3,720 units by the time the war shipbuilding effort ended. At one time as many as a quarter of the ships on order were to be "manufactured ships", constructed with a great many prefabricated parts. Whether built in the traditional shipbuilding manner or in the new "manufactured" style, all of these Emergency Fleet Corporation types shared several characteristics—little or no sheer, flat sides, straight stems, single, bolt upright funnels, and an overall no "frills" approach that met the immediate demand for tonnage.

The ships were hastily designed, contracts were handed out right and left, and new ships debuted within months. They were not all noble examples of the shipbuilder's art nor did opportunities to make fortunes go unnoticed. With so much money flying from Washington to shipbuilders, suppliers and designers, widespread corruption soon blighted this patriotic effort. The extent of financial shenanigans has yet to be revealed even more than seventy years after the building of this emergency fleet.

The Emergency Fleet Corporation and Shipping Board did face one enormous hurdle. With the American steel industry devoting fully 75% of its output to the Navy, there was no way to get all the steel required for the construction of the gargantuan fleet ordered by the Shipping Board Emergency Fleet Corporation. While arrangements to increase steel output were being made, some shipbuilders were instructed to build ships not only of steel, but of wood, of concrete or of combinations of all three. Those last were the composite ships and were quite a fiasco. In the emergency, it did not matter what the ship looked like—the requirements were simple. Build something that could float, and while loaded with vital war cargo—food, munitions, spare parts, livestock, men—literally anything under the sun—move under its own power—and hopefully arrive on the other side of the Atlantic. America worked hard to increase steel output. More and more miners dug out coal and iron. Blast furnaces worked overtime. The nation HAD to have steel and lots of it. America got her steel, the Army got its weapons and ammunition, and the Navy and Merchant Marine got their ships. Beyond the need to lift cargo was the congruent and equally important need to ship hundreds of thousands, maybe eventually over a million, men across the Atlantic to the battlefields.

While it seemed that immediate transport requirements could be met by existing troop transports—nearly all of them former passenger ships hastily converted to carry soldiers—a few were purpose built troop transports. It was soon obvious that ever more troop transports would be needed. Among ships building to requisitioned contracts were a number of passenger and cargo ships that were now slated to be completed as troop transports. Those included the ORIZABA, SIBONEY, SANTA ELISA and SANTA TERESA and their sister SANTA LEONOR which would remain with the military for the course of her entire career. Less familiar now were ships like the EDEL-LYN, MARICA, SOL NAVIS from Sun Shipbuilding Company at Chester, Pennsylvania and Bethlehem Shipbuilding's Alameda Yard products HEF-FRON and HEGIRA. All of those ships could be only stopgaps and were likely to be reclaimed by commercial owners after the war, so the War Department, whose own Army Transportation Service, Water Division, handled all overseas trooping, asked the Shipping Board to develop plans for permanent troopships.

In the early days of American belligerency in the First World War both the Shipping Board and War Department agreed to limit development of troop transports to two specific designs. Their construction was to greatly concern both Shipping Board and all shipyards contracted to build them. Of more than three thousand ships ordered for the emergency shipbuilding program of the First World War, less than two hundred of them were specifically laid down to be troop transports though the development and construction of troopships was in itself highly important for several reasons. They would have garnered tremendous interest if only because these transports were big ships, expensive to build. Though designed during the heat of war for military transport purposes, the Shipping Board gave tremendous weight to the possibility of rapid conversion of these transports into passenger and cargo liners for no one forecast a need for a large force of active peacetime troop transports. It turned out to be a good thing commercial uses for these ships was inherent in their planning, for almost all of these eventual ships wound up serving the American Merchant Marine.

Assigning the job to its Design Division, several plans for each size of transport were soon offered. Many observers believe that the War Department and Shipping Board wanted three distinct types of troop transports and thus developed plans for small, intermediate and large transports but that is not true. First thoughts about the carriage of troops in wartime elicited but two types of troopships, a big one and a small one. Nebulous contemporary news items soon parroted standard announcements of dozens of troopships that would soon steam forth from America's premier shipyards. Delving enthusiastically into the spirit of war production, the Shipping Board and the military finally broadcast news of two specific types—the big, fast 13,000 tonner able to carry 3,500 troops at 18 knots and an 8,500 ton transport that could carry about 2,300 men at 15 knots. Despite an occasionally heard comment from interested observers that the Shipping Board no doubt planned the construction of a large fleet of "502" type ships, only seven of them were ever planned and those ships were originally intended to be 535 foot long troop transports. Competition for the contracts to build them was limited to the nation's most important shipbuilders for only these were thought capable of building such vessels.

The smaller 8,500 ton transport was designed for mass production and only one company in the world had a shipyard able to handle fabrication of so many ships of that size. That was American International's new yard at Hog Island, Pennsylvania. Their smaller transports would be known as Type B "Hog Islanders". For the fabrication of standard ships, the American International Shipbuilding Corporation at Hog Island, Pennsylvania was awarded Emergency Fleet Corporation Contract SC#83. There were three phases to that contract. First was the construction of fifty 7,500 deadweight ton sister freighters, the fabled Type A "Hog Islander". Next on the list were seventy 8,500 ton Type B transports. Finally, there would be sixty more Type A freighters. Hog Island did build all 110 freighters but long before the transport construction scheme could advance very far the war ended, greatly curtailing the demand for such tonnage. In the wake of the Armistice, Congress forced the Shipping Board to greatly reduce the number of transports from this yard. In two stages the bulk of the class was cancelled and only twelve Type B ships were completed. Only three of them were laid down in time to claim wartime origin, and even that was an "iffy" call because the keel of the first one went onto the stocks on November 9, 1918 and the keels of the next two were laid down on Armistice Day, November 11, 1918.

Discussing the Type B transport at a meeting in March 1919, leading Shipping Board naval architects felt "some doubt regarding the general usefulness of the vessels". After considering various trade routes consensus held that a number of minor design changes would render them more serviceable, E.H. Rigg, chief naval architect of the New York Shipbuilding Corporation was asked to draw new plans. While the twelve ships built to surviving orders were still under construction, it appeared that the class would be split into two groups—one to be completed as troopships, the other as passenger cargo ships. The reason behind that plan was the War Department's intention to grab the first five of the largest type transports. Once the Shipping Board realized that the Army really had no intention to pay anything for those ships, considering the transfer simply a transfer between Government departments, the Trustees of the Shipping Board worked long and hard to divert the Army's attention in the hope of retaining those madly expensive ships for their own commercial uses. Somehow they managed to convince the War Department to make theirs an all Hog Island Type B fleet, so all twelve transports were completed for the military. At that the Army realized it didn't need that many new ships for it already operated a sizable fleet of perfectly serviceable troopships and new as the "Hog Islanders" were, it cost plenty of money to run them. Eleven of the new ships went directly into the

Army, attached to the Quartermaster Division, United States Army Transportation Service. The last ship, the WRIGHT, was assigned to the Navy and distinguished herself for her work as the first Navy aircraft mother ship. In short order the War Department realized it really did have too many passenger ships in service and didn't really need eleven new ones. Within two years of their delivery, two of them, the ARGONNE and CHAUMONT, were loaned to the Navy, a branch of the military that had only reticently agreed to operate troopships. The two Type B ships at work for the Navy, a financially strapped Army then withdrew several of their remaining new Type B "Hog Islanders" and sent them into lay up. After paying bills for idle transports for about a year, the War Department greeted a Shipping Board request for five Type "B" ships with not a little relief. Retired and released in late 1923 by the United States Army Transport Service, five of them were refitted for commercial use. Tying the story of the Type B "Hog Islanders" to that of the "502"'s, the B ships replaced the five "502"'s that had operated the New York to London passenger and cargo service. Two more sister "Hog Islanders" joined them in 1931. The others, the CHATEAU THIERRY, ST. MIHIEL, ARGONNE, CHAUMONT and WRIGHT remained in active military service, though the ARGONNE and CHAUMONT saw some periods of inactivity before the defense buildup started in 1940.

There were no beauties among the eventual 35 ships of these three classes of intended troopships but their frankly unexciting appearance was primarily a result of the emergency of their build. Even the people who designed them knew they were ugly, one of them writing of the "535"'s: "although they look like colliers ... " they were all designed without a thought to aesthetics or beauty so they were strictly functional in design, starkly utilitarian in appearance, indeed ugly ships to many eyes. Simple design features, common characteristics and standard parts made construction of these ships quick, simple and cost effective. Standardized parts for standard types facilitated prefabrication of parts in factories many miles away from the shipyards. All three classes of ship shared certain design features like plumb straight stems and upright bridge fronts. But somehow the hull lines of the "502s" were quite graceful and a hint of sheer gave the "535"'s a magnificence when viewed from certain angles. As designed and built, a split superstructure instantly distinguished the "502" from Hog Island Type B as did the "502" 's thinner funnel and short poop. A bolt upright single funnel and straight sterns, it has been said, could help confuse a possible enemy vessel by making it difficult to quickly figure out which way the standard built American ship were headed. Though a boon to their functional silhouette to be sure, but that's not why the ships were so designed. It was cheaper and faster to give the ships such features.

While the Hog Island Type B ships were among the ugliest ships ever to run in trans-Atlantic service the "502" on the London line was undeniably uglier. Quite possibly the initial appearance of the "502" remains unsurpassed for the brutality of its ungainly aesthetics. But that's OK, for a ship needn't be a beauty externally to win the warm affection of her passengers and crew. Many of today's ships are frankly externally hideous but are internally marvelous, well constructed and beautifully equipped and furnished. Through exigency and subsidy, four "502" class sisters received substantial rebuilding during the 1920's, emerging therefrom with well proportioned superstructure, a thicker funnel topped with Admiralty cap, and two partially glass enclosed promenade decks, all of which made them very handsome ships, perhaps the best looking of all thirty five steamers originating in the emergency troopship building scheme.

Then in the employ of the United States Shipping Board, naval architect Theodore Ferris worked on the production of the specification book for the proposed large transports. He also had a hand in drawing plans, but many other hands contributed both to the first and the many subsequent plans produced to build the "535"'s and their "502" relatives. The claim of any one man to have designed either class of vessel simply cannot stand. A final design for big troop transports was ready for approval by December 1917. Nicknamed for their overall length, these would be the "535"'s, steel steamers of about 8,000 deadweight tons, and carry about 3,000 men including passengers and crew, stores, fresh water and fuel oil at a mean draft of 30 feet. They should have had no problem keeping a sustained sea speed of 16 knots. Though they were conceived jointly by the Shipping Board and War Department, current thinking called for them to be operated under allocation to the Navy. In the heat of the moment, the responsible officials were ready to order construction of a fleet of at least fifty and maybe even sixty or seventy of these 535 foot long ships. It was the beginning of an inordinately long gestation for once plans were reviewed by Shipping Board, Fleet Corporation, War Department and Navy Department experts and ranking executives in the case of the first two and ranking officers of the two branches of the military, the intended ships were found lacking. Extensive changes were requested by all parties. Both War Department and Navy wanted rearrangement of accommodations for ship's crew, military officers and enlisted men. Concerned for the ships' safety, the Navy called for a material increase in armament, a feature that had a bearing on the construction of both hulls and decking. The following months brought a great many changes as all concerned parties and all involved shipyards and their design departments reviewed and revised plans. Many of those amended plans for these ships were being drawn and redrawn at New York Shipbuilding Company, one of the three companies that won contracts to build the big transports. Orders were placed through several contracts for at least fifty six big ships but a spate of cancellations eventually totalling twenty-three of them and evolution of seven more into a smaller ship left the program with but sixteen sister ships eventually building to Shipping Board Design #1029. For months, all mention of the bigger transports indicated a single type, but later it was made clear that there would be three different types of transports, not two and that is why there were both "535" and "502" types.

It could be successfully argued that the ships of both types were perhaps the only classes of passenger ship designed and built with no regard whatsoever to the particular requirements of any eventual commercial route. Who would build more of these big ships and where would they be built was a question occupying many minds throughout the American shipping and shipbuilding industry. Announcing on July 10, 1918 that the latest contract let brought the number of troopships on order to 92, Shipping Board Chairman Edward Hurley fed the hopes of Western shipyards and their suppliers, promising that a good number of these purpose built troopships would be built on the West Coast.

All indications suggest but unfortunately do not confirm the evolution of the "502" as a third type of troop transport that came about on the heels of cancellations of building contracts with the Bethlehem Steel Company whose Alameda, California shipyards were to have built twenty big 13,000 ton transports. Had the war continued, there would have been well over a hundred new troop transports. But it ended that November 11th and in its wake Congress took a dim view on the expenditure additional shipbuilding would require. Within weeks suspensions of building contracts came into shipyards all over America. Later contracts were reinstated with those shipbuilders at yards where steel and building materials had been received in sufficient quantities that cancellation would be more expensive than abandonment. At that, cancellations of planned freighters were not the extent of rescission of Congressional appropriations. Hard hit was the troop transport construction program which saw the withdrawal of $33 million previously earmarked for the building of troop ships. The plan to build the big 535 foot long transports had already been reduced by twenty ships before the Armistice was signed. Taking the brunt of cancellations this time was American International Shipbuilding Corporation. It cost their Hog Island the building of 58 Type B transports. Bethlehem would be hit again, losing contracts for three "535"s to be built at Sparrows Point. With no further urgency to get big, fast troop carriers into the water, the large number of planned troopships no longer made any sense at all. It was also immediately clear that any ships evolving from surviving building contracts better have commercial capabilities. That was also true for several vessels still building as troop transports for the War Department, which still expected the Shipping Board to build not only Type B "Hog Islanders" for the Army Transportation Service but to build at least six "535"s to their orders and specifications. It didn't take the Army long to inform the Shipping Board that they did not expect to have to pay for the big ships, advising the Shipping Board to arrange delivery without ANY transfer. The Army never did have to sort out financial arrangements for "535"s with the Shipping Board because all sixteen such ships were completed for the Merchant Marine.

As the grand troop transport construction scheme began to crash, the Shipping Board and New York Shipbuilding Corporation asked E.H. Rigg,

New York Shipbuilding Corp.'s chief naval architect, to devise several alternative plans for the large, expensive "535", asking him further to develop a version less expensive to build. Of further if not equal concern to New York Shipbuilding were material and manpower shortages and the need to execute their contractual obligations in as expeditiously a manner as possible. Scaling down plans for the "535", Rigg and his colleagues devised the "502" described as a "compromise type vessel" in their own words.[3] Unsaid by him at the time were the factors rising to the need for a compromise type—frequent alterations to building plans, availability of steel and requisite parts, even the extent of the yard's own work force. Under Rigg's direction the Design Staff of New York Shipbuilding wasted no time at all and in December 1918 turned in Rigg's approved plans for the completion of the "535"'s as commercial vessels with accommodations for 278 First and 236 Second Class passengers. In Washington, the Shipping Board took Rigg's work and ordered its own Design Department to get busy and amend building plans for the "535"'s. As yet the concept of a "502" was still nebulous. Now plans were prepared in the offices of the Chairman of the Shipping Control Committee as the big transports were now laid out as passenger ships for First and Second Class passengers. As for the seven ships New York Shipbuilding was to construct under Contract 418 SC, what emerged from the initial round of December 1918/January 1919 plan revisions was principally a big cargo vessel with high grade accommodations for a very limited number of one class passengers.

Little further note of these ships appeared in Shipping Board offices until March 11, 1919 when Shipping Board Naval Architect and Consulting Engineer H.C. Sadler wrote Daniel H. Cox, manager of Ship Construction Division regarding a March 8th conference he had had with Division of Operations manager Thomas Rosseter, E.H. Rigg and Messrs. Hague and Bruce of the Shipping Board's Construction and Repair Department of the Division of Operations regarding conversion of the 1/New York Ship and Newport News "535" Troopships; 2/New York Ship "502" Troopships; and 3/Hog Island "B" Troopships.

First type discussed was the "502". It seems the gathered men placed greater faith in the earning potential of this type than in either of the other two. According to Sadler's memo, acting on suggestions of P.A.S. Franklin's[4] Committee, plans had been prepared showing this type as a cargo vessel fitted for a maximum of 12 passengers to prevent these ships from coming under jurisdiction of requirements and laws regarding bulkhead subdivi-

---

[3]So described by them in a description of such ships prepared for the Shipping Board. Copy in the construction files of the USSB in RG 32 at National Archives.

[4]Of I.M.M. fame, P.A.S. Franklin devoted extraordinary energy to emergency shipbuilding efforts. Under his guidance a standing committee overlooked much of the construction of the big USSB passenger ships. It was Franklin who recognized the talents of William Francis Gibbs, hiring him to be I.M.M.s "in-house" naval architect, thus giving quite a boost to the career of the young Gibbs and earning him the undying enmity of colleague Theodore Ferris.

sions, etc. for passenger ships. Rosseter remained unconvinced, stating that the intrinsic design of the type would best be served should these be completed with increased passenger accommodations. Discussing general laws and requirements, the general arrangements of the type was discussed and Mr. Rigg was asked to draw new plans.

Turning to the Type B transport, those present felt "some doubt regarding the general usefulness of the vessels." After considering various trade routes consensus held that a number of minor design changes would render them more serviceable. Again, Mr. Rigg was asked to draw new plans.

Curiously enough, the "535" ships then building at the New York Shipbuilding Corporation did not initially appeal to the Division of Operations. But once Sadler suggested their eventual employment as "Intermediate" type ships on Atlantic routes, the ships began to gain in stature before the men of the operations Division. Not employed by the Shipping Board since he resigned under a cloud of scandal in November 1918, Theodore Ferris wrote to the Construction Division during the spring of 1919 asking for a look at the various plans. Enraging him were those submitted by William Francis Gibbs. Ferris lost no time before composing a letter of several pages to Chairman Hurley of the Shipping Board attacking the proposed vessel and its author on every conceivable point.[5]

After further conferences between Division of Operations and Division of Construction and Repair and the three shipyards, a modified plan based on New York Shipbuilding's most recent drawings was adopted. That plan allowed quarters for 247 First Class, 226 Second Class passengers and a crew of 194 officers and men. No provision for Third Class was made but the subject of steerage soon arose and after a number of discussions were held, Second Class in the "535"s was omitted in favor of a Third Class to accommodate about 300 passengers. Later still the number of First Class was fixed at 259 while crew was expected to number 215 officers and men.

On March 18th, the Construction Division of the Shipping Board wrote to Brigadier General Frank T. Hines, Chief of Embarkation Service of the War Department, who was eager to acquire new tonnage for the Army Transport Service. The subject this time was "TRANSPORTS FOR PERMANENT ESTABLISHMENT—WAR DEPARTMENT". The memo informed him that eleven Type B "Hog Islanders" were being constructed so that "when completed they will be arranged as troop transports, all scheduled for delivery not later than January 1, 1920".[6] The plan of the moment was to have the balance of Type B ships to be completed as passenger and cargo ships. The last "Hog Islander", the eventual WRIGHT, was not mentioned.

Continuing, the Shipping Board informed Brigadier General Hines:

Five Hundred Thirty Five Foot, Seventeen Knot Transports: Five of these ships, namely hulls 1164 and 1165, Bethlehem S.B. Corp (BERRIEN and BERTICE), Contract 182, and Hulls # 1012, 1013 and 1014, (CANONICUT, MANMASCO and KODA), New York Shipbuilding Corporation, Contract #151, will be completed as troop transports, all of these vessels being scheduled for delivery not later than January 1, 1920. The balance of these vessels will be completed as passenger and cargo vessels.[7]

International Mercantile Marine (IMM) Company now expanded its assistance to the Shipping Board, assigning their house architect William Francis Gibbs to try his hand at drawing plans for the "535"s. The results satisfied very few and all parties agreed to make further rearrangements. By late April, drafting work was distributed as follows: New York Shipbuilding Corporation was to prepare structural steel plans and modifications to general plans as well as calculations such as displacement. In addition, New York Ship handled specifications and/or plans for carpentry work, sparring and coiling of holds, masts, rigging and cargo handling gear, anchors, cables,etc, canvas gear, bilge and ballast system, insulation, steering gear, winches and windlasses. Bethlehem Shipbuilding Corporation was assigned joinery, bulkhead panelling, furniture and furnishings, deck coverings, steward's department outfitting, deck outfitting, navigating instruments, heating system, ventilating sanitary system of plumbing, fire system and deck piping. Newport News Shipbuilding and Drydock Co, handled refrigeration systems, interior communication systems and the ships' electric plant.

Each yard was instructed to handle its own side lights, scuttles, manholes, watertight doors, deck castings, rails, boats and boat davits.

April 10, 1919 brought a memorandum from James Converse, Assistant Secretary of the Board, for wide circulation among department heads. At a meeting of the Trustees of the Corporation held April 9, 1919, the matter of the transfer of the troop ships to the War Department, and the arrangement of transports as passenger and cargo vessels was discussed. It was ordered that the Director General be directed to proceed with the completion of the work on five (5) 535 ft. 17 knot transports, hulls Nos. 1164, 1165, 1012, 1013 and 1014 (eventually the HAWKEYE STATE, BUCKEYE STATE, WENATCHEE, SOUTHERN CROSS and AMERICAN LEGION—and then intended to be named BERRIEN, BERTICE, CANONICUT, MANMASCO and KODA—author's note) and on the six (6) vessels of the Class "B" Type (the eventual CAMBRAI, CANTIGNY, CHAUMONT, ST. MIHIEL, ARGONNE and SOMME, but then scheduled to be named MOUNT WOLF, MOUNT MICHAEL, MOUNT HERRELL, MOUNT PACTIO, MOUNT URAKA and MOUNT BLACK, respectively) American International Shipbuilding Corporation, and the Secretary was directed to transmit a copy of the correspondence in this docket of the United States Shipping Board Emergency Fleet Corporation, calling particular attention to the sixth paragraph in the

---

[7]March 18, 1919 letter from P.J. McAuliffe to General Hines. Copy in the Construction Files of the U.S. Shipping Board in RG 32 at National Archives.

letter of March 27, 1919, from the Chief of Transportation Service of the War Department. That memo read as follows:

> It is understood that the five 535 ft. 17 knot transports and the six Class "B" transports referred to above, will upon completion, be assigned to the War Department transport service without any special appropriation being made available for this purpose, the matter being merely one of transfer of the vessels to the War Department upon their completion. Confirmation of this understanding is requested.[8]

On the following day, P.J. McAuliffe, Manager of the Ship Construction Division informed Delaware District Manager, H.C. Higgins of the decision to complete five "535"s and six Type B "Hog Islanders" for the War Department. Not a word was said or written about the "502"s.

April 19, 1919 brought Acting Secretary of War Benedict Crowell to write to the Chairman of the Shipping Board/Emergency Fleet Corp. He said:

> Dear Sir:
>
> Referring to your latest revised estimate of the anticipated dates of delivery or the combination troop and cargo ships under construction for the War Department. You are advised that the following is the policy of the War Department with reference to the completion of those ships, and you are requested to take action accordingly.
>
> (a) It is desired that all vessels under construction at the Hog Island Plant of the Emergency Fleet Corporation, with dates of delivery during 1920, be completed as commercial vessels and not as transports, with the exception of the eleven vessels with dates of completion prior to February 1, 1920, which vessels will be suitable as permanent transports for the War Department.
>
> (b) It is desired that all requisitioned vessels now building with dates of completion prior to August 1, 1919 be completed as troop transports.
>
> (c) It is desired that the eleven vessels building as permanent transports referred to above in (a). be transferred to the War Department without transfer of funds, by simply making a corresponding charge on the books of the Emergency Fleet Corporation for such vessels. It considered that this action is justified in view of the action of Congress in striking from the estimates of the War Department an item of $93,000,000 for the construction of transports to replace old army transports now operating on the Pacific.
>
> The above policy is, of course, based upon the anticipated requirements of the War Department with reference to the return of our troops from France.[9]

---

[8]Copy in the Construction Files of the U.S. Shipping Board in RG 32 at National Archives.

[9]April 19, 1919 letter from Acting Secretary of War Benedict Crowell to Chairman Hurley of the Shipping Board/Emergency Fleet Corp. Copy in the Construction Files of the U.S. Shipping Board in RG32 at National Archives.

Chairman Ed Hurley's April 26th answer to the War Department speaks for itself. Writing to Acting Secretary Crowell, Hurley thought:

My dear Mr. Crowell:

TROOP SHIPS

In reply to your letter of April 19, on this subject, inasmuch as in certain respects this letter does not state the facts, correctly, it is thought best to review the situation:

Referring to paragraph (a) of your letter as relates to the troop ships under construction at Hog Island, it appears that you now desire eleven (11) of these class "B" vessels, which it is expected will be completed prior to February 1, 1920, to be completed as transports for the permanent establishment of the War Department.

In this connection your attention is invited to attached copy of letter from Col. Bettison to me under date of March 27, stating in effect that a total of eleven transports was desired by the War Department and that if five of the large transports are completed as originally designed, only six of the class "B" Hog Island vessels should be completed as transports.

The Fleet Corporation is proceeding along the lines indicated in the letter from Colonel Bettison except that pending further investigation as to the cost of cancellations the remaining thirty-five class "B" vessels including the six in question, have been suspended.

In paragraph (b) you state that it is desired that all requisitioned vessels now building with dates of completion prior to August 1, 1919 be completed as troop transports. It is not assumed that this paragraph should be taken literally but that it refers to requisitioned vessels arranged to be converted to as transports. In order to clear this point, there is attached hereto, a summary giving in detail the requisitioned vessels now under construction which are to be completed as troop transports with the estimated dates of delivery.

With respect to paragraph (c) relating to the transference of the eleven vessels to the War Department without transfer of funds, this matter is receiving careful consideration by the Trustees.[10]

For the record, those other vessels included the requisitioned Grace ships SANTA ELISA, SANTA LEONOR, SANTA TERESA and SANTA MALTA, then building at both New York Ship and the Cramp yards, plus the MARICA, EDELLYN and SOL NAVIS building at the Chester, Pennsylvania yards of the Sun Shipbuilding Company.

Chairman Hurley next answered the Secretary of War, Newton D. Baker, in a May 20th letter:

My Dear Mr. Secretary,

1. I am in receipt of your letter of May 10th, which has reference to Mr. Crowell's, Acting Secretary of War, letter of April 19th, outlining the

---

[10]April 26, 1919 letter from Chairman Hurley to Acting Secretary Crowell of the War Department. Copy in Construction Files of the U.S. Shipping Board in RG 32 at National Archives.

policy of the Department regarding the completion of troop ships.

2. It is my understanding that a total of eleven (11) troop ships, permanently fitted as such, is the number decided upon by the War Department, the ships selected for this service being as follows:

American International Shipbuilding Corporation:
Six (6) Class "B" Troop Ships, Hulls Nos. 669,670, 671, 672, 673 and 674.

Bethlehem Shipbuilding Corporation, Sparrows' Point Plant:
Two (2)"535" 17 knot Transports, Hulls Nos. 1164 and 1165.

New York Shipbuilding Corporation:
Three (3)535, 17 knot Transports, Hulls Nos. 1012, 1013 and 1014.

3. The following requisitioned vessels under construction, which will be completed prior to August 1, 1919, are to be fitted as transports, but are not to be part of the permanent transport fleet, these vessels to be utilized for the return of the American forces now abroad and upon completion of that duty to be redelivered to the Shipping Board.

New York Shipbuilding Corporation:
Hull No. 197, SANTA ELISA and 198, SANTA LEONORA

William Cramp & Sons Ship & Eng. Bldg. Co.
Hull No. 447, SANTA MALTA

Sun Shipbuilding Company
Hull No. 6. MARICA, 9, EDELLYN and 10, SOL NAVIS.

4. In addition to the above, at the request of the War Department, Hull 1574, HEFFRON, building by the Bethlehem Shipbuilding Corporation, Alameda Plant, is being fitted as a temporary troop ship. This will give eleven (11) regular and six (6) temporary troop ships, Hull No. 447 SANTA MALTA having been delivered May 16th.

5. With respect to Paragraph (0) of your letter, relative to the transference of the vessels to the War Department without transference of funds, this matter has been referred to the Trustees of the Shipping Board for consideration.[11]

Another letter written that month refers to these ships. On May 26, 1919 Ship Construction manager P.J. McAuliffe wrote to Vice President Ackerson regarding "troopships and passenger & cargo ships". He said:

The following is the situation regarding Troopships and Passenger & Cargo ships, of the large type:

TROOP SHIPS

1. There are five large troopships under construction in addition to 6 at Hog Island. Three are being built by New York S.B. Co. and two by Bethlehem S.B. Co. at Sparrows Point. These troopships are 535' long 17 knots. Those building by New York S.B. Co. will be equipped with Westinghouse dou-

---

[11]May 20. 1919 letter from Chairman Hurley to Secretary of War, Newton D. Baker. Copy in Construction Files of the U.S. Shipping Board in RG 32 at National Archives.

ble reduction gear turbines; and those at Bethlehem with the Curtis turbines of their own make, single reduction.

PASSENGER & CARGO SHIPS

2. (a) The New York S.B. Co. is building seven 502' 14 knot, Passenger & Cargo ships, with passenger accommodations in accordance with Mr. Rosseter's plans. These ships will be driven by reciprocating engines, with Scotch boilers.

3. (b) The New York S.B. Co. is building 6; Newport News 2, and Sparrows Point 6, Passenger Cargo Ships, 535' long. 17 knots, all of which will probably be equipped with Bethlehem S.B. Co.'s Curtis turbines, single reduction gear. The passenger accommodations for those are the result of suggestions made by Mr. Gibbs, associated with P.A.S. Franklin, of International Mercantile Marine, modified by our Engineering Section in conference with Bethlehem, New York Ship and Newport News.

4. It is apparent that Mr. Rosseter did not know we were building a 535, type. It appears he considered these troopships at New York Ship to be of the 502' type, similar to those on which he has designed the passenger accommodations. He has previously indicated that he had no need for the 535' ships, and I believe if the situation is made clear to him, he will not dare to interfere with our present arrangement.

5. The New York S.B. Co., Newport News and Bethlehem Shipbuilding Companies have divided the detail work on these plans between them and the work is proceeding very rapidly. Mr. Sadler is going to Bethlehem tomorrow with Mr. Gibbs, Mr. Rigg and a representative from Newport News in order to discuss progress and effect an agreement on all plans. The work has progressed to such a stage that immediate action must be taken if we are to save ourselves considerable expense providing the change from troopships to passenger and cargo ships is to be made.[12]

Within days plans changed again and for awhile it seemed that none of the Type B being built at Hog Island would be completed as troop transports for the War Department. Accordingly, P.J. McAuliffe passed on instructions to others. One instance was his memo to Mr. Blankenship on the subject of troopships of June 2nd:

1. Please issue instructions to Mr. Higgins to the effect that 11 of the Type B ships at Hog Island will be made into passenger and cargo ships, instead of six as previously ordered.

2. There are twelve keels laid for these Type B ships. The work on the 12th should be suspended until it is definitely decided whether it will be constructed as a passenger and cargo ship at its present dimensions or lengthened 54 feet.

3. Mr. Rosseter will be here tomorrow, and at that time we hope to receive a decision from him as to the lengthened Type B ships building at Hog Island.

---

[12]May 29, 1919 letter from McAulliffe. Copy in Construction Files of the U.S. Shipping Board in RG32 at National Archives.

4. Attached is a memorandum from Mr. Hurley to the effect that the Army will be satisfied with 11 Hog Island troopships and will give up their claims for the three "535" and two "535" troop transports, building at New York Ship and Bethlehem, respectively. Instructions should be sent to Mr. Higgins and to Mr. Martin to the effect that these five ships are to be changed into passenger and cargo ships, to be built to plans now being prepared for 535' passenger and cargo ships, and all work on the construction of these troopships should be stopped and report made to show in detail the cost of this transformation and an estimate prepared to show the length of time lost. Copies of communications should be sent to Mr. Hurley with a forwarding letter stating that these suspensions and changes were made in accordance with his memorandum of May 27th to Mr. Ackerson and his further telephone conversations.[13]

No doubt McAuliffe erred in his statement that all 11 Type B ships were to complete as passenger cargo ships for an unnamed hand has bracketed that phrase on the copy in the Shipping Board files.

On the same day Mc Auliffe wrote to Blankenship, Middle Atlantic District Manager Joseph Martin acknowledged receipt of three sets of blueprints of General Arrangement of Decks and of Profile and Hold plans for the conversion into passenger and cargo ships of the two ships building at Newport News (referred to as EFC hulls 2564–65 and Bldrs. 256–257) and six Bethlehem projects, EFC hulls 2505—10. Bldrs. hulls 4195–4200. This was in response to a May 10th note from H.C. Sadler, the Board's naval architect resident at the Philadelphia office.

McAuliffe addressed the subject of troopships to Joseph Martin on the following day. With copies to Chairman Hurley, Sanders of the Cancellation Divison, Sadler in the Engineering Section and Murfee in the records Section, the Ship Construction Manager wrote:

1. A resolution of the Board of Trustees of the U.S. Shipping Board, April 9, 1919, directed that five (5) 535 ft. 17 knot vessels, Hulls Nos. 1164, 1165, 1012, 1013 and 1014, and six (6) vessels of the "B" type, American International Shipbuilding Corporation, Hulls Nos. 669 to 674 inclusive, be completed as troop transports.
2. We are now advised by Mr. Hurley that the above program has been changed and that the Department will take over for transport service eleven (11) vessels of the "B" type. Hulls Nos. 669 to 679, inclusive, will accordingly be completed as troop ships.
3. The five (5) 535 ft. 17 knot troop ships. originally intended as permanent transports. will not be required by the war Department and the operating Department of the Shipping Board is desirous that they be fitted as passenger vessels.
4. Hulls Nos. 1164 and 1165, Bethlehem Shipbuilding Corporation, Sparrows Point, Contract 182, accordingly will not be completed as troop

---

[13]Ibid

ships, but will be changed to passenger and cargo vessels, to be built in accordance with the plans now being prepared for 535 ft. passenger and cargo ships. All work on the construction of these troop ships should be stopped. It is requested that a report be submitted giving in detail the cost of this change and an estimate prepared showing the time lost.[14]

Confirmation of these new orders were sent by Higgins on the 4th.

McAuliffe soon learned that American International and New York Ship had already been informed and ordered to stop work on those vessels in question. Reporting back to Secretary of War Baker on June 10th, Shipping Board Chairman Hurley virtually reprised his previous letter, adding only salient bits of new information like which hull was to replace those previously coveted by the military. Additionally, Hurley informed the Secretary of War that delivery of the SANTA ELISA was expected that month followed in July by the SANTA LEONOR. As for the Army's plan to acquire eleven permanent ships at no cost, Hurley repeated his earlier words verbatim: . . . "this matter has been referred to the Trustees of the Shipping Board for consideration."[15]

In this latest exchange replacing the eventual HAWKEYE STATE and BUCKEYE STATE were hulls 675 and 676, the eventual AISNE and OURCQ while the eventual MARNE, CHATEAU THIERRY and TOURS, hulls 677, 678 and 679 at Hog Island, were accepted in place of the "535" class steamers which became the WENATCHEE, SOUTHERN CROSS and AMERICAN LEGION, ships then still referred by the intended names of CANONICUT, MANMASCO and KODA. With the War Department thus mollified in regard to previous demands for "535"s by the plan to take requisitioned vessels and eleven Type B "Hog Islanders", the Shipping Board returned again to the question of the big ships. Scrapping all ideas of their completion as either transports or hospital ships, only two options remained. Complete them as first-class passenger and cargo vessels or abandon the project entirely and pay each yard hefty penalties for cancellations.

The Board was only too aware of such costs for cancellation of these big ships. Withdrawing the contract with the Bethlehem Shipbuilding Company for the construction of twenty big transports at their Alameda, California yard had already cost millions. Furthermore, America needed modern passenger tonnage if she hoped to compete for passengers and the valuable cargoes that always went in the fast passenger ships. A memorandum from Ed Hurley to New York Shipbuilding Corporation and Bethlehem Shipbuilding Company on May 27, 1919 authorized completion of the five ships (three at New York Ship and two from Bethlehem) as passenger and cargo ships.

Some divisions of the Shipping Board learned of the intention to convert the planned transports to passenger and cargo ships before others. That

---

[14]June 2, 1919 memorandum by PJ McAulliffe. Copy in the Construction Files of the U.S. Shipping Board in RG 32 at National Archives.

[15]Hurley, *op. cit.*

caused a bit of confusion and wasted time and manpower while letters and memoranda questioning what was happening were dispatched, answered and confirmed. Curiously, all through May 1919 most ships of both "535" and "502" types were still officially contemplated and publicly referred to as troop ships, though it was clear to anyone paying attention to the shipping scene that most would be completed for commercial service. It was really a matter of who knew what and when did he know it. Contemporary newspapers carried occasional stories of the progress of the construction of the Government's passenger ships but they were far better publicized in shipping trade publications whose detailed descriptions give a realistic view of the traumatic birth of these ships. So many changes to building plans for these two types of ships were made before any of them was able to steam out on her trials that frustration rose from shipyards and the Shipping Board. Someone must have thought, if he did not exclaim out loud: "Let's get these damn things built!"

The Shipping Board thought the matter settled and could rest easy on the directions given the builders to complete the "535"s as passenger and cargo liners. Then, on August 30th, like a jack in the box, Major General Hines of the Army Transportation Service sprang another surprise on the Shipping Board. All it was was another of his (by then) famous letters to the Chairman. Subject this time: "Renewal of Request for Some 18 knot Transports of the Camden 535 Foot Class." Here is how General Hines almost threw a monkey wrench into the workings of the Shipping Board:

> 4. As expressed in the former letter of this Office date August 19, it is the desire of the War Department to maintain upon the Pacific a fleet of permanent transports, the main group of which shall have a speed of 16 or 17 knots.
>
> 5. If the original six 18 knot ships now underway of the Camden 535' class cannot be made assignable to the War Department, request therefore being made again to the Shipping Board that they should reinstate the contracts for at least three more of these 18 knot Camden 535' class and make definite assignment of same for exclusive use of War Department.[16]

This request got the Army nothing.

There were eight known contracts for 56 big transports. Subtract the eventual seven "502" ships, that means there would have been forty-nine "535" class ships. Three different shipbuilders and four different yards won contracts to build them and the Government insisted on tremendous cooperation from and among all three concerns. Representing the Emergency Fleet Corporation on many design questions was H.H. Thayer who also sat for the Shipping Board's Design Department; Naval architects H.C. Sadler, E.H. Rigg, Hugo Frear and H.F. Norton represented respectively the Shipping Board's Design Department, New York Shipbuilding Corporation,

---

[16]August 30, 1919 letter from General Hines to Shipping Board. Copy in the Construction Files of the U.S. Shipping Board in RG 32 at National Archives.

Bethlehem Shipbuilding Company and Newport News Shipbuilding and Drydock Company. After various conferences between the Division of Construction and Ship Repair and the Division of Operations and the three building yards, it was decided on April 9, 1919 to split the main work among the builders. Handling all details and plans for structural steel and modifications to any general plan was New York Shipbuilding Corporation. Further assigned to that yard were the responsibility to make all calculations as to displacement, cubic capacities, etc. They were to design and handle all ship carpentry work, cargo handling gear, bilge and ballast systems, insulation, steering gear, winches, windlasses, mooring equipment and canvas gear. Given charge over joinery work on all the big transports was the Bethlehem Shipbuilding Company who also had responsibility for all deck coverings, furniture, outfitting, heating, ventilating and sanitary systems, fire control systems and deck piping. Finally, Newport News was assigned charge of the refrigerating system, interior communication and the ships' electric plants. Each yard was left responsible to develop scuttles, manhole covers and a host of other utilitarian items.

A thoroughly unexplored sidelight to the "502" class ships lies in the far sightedness of Shipping Board Division of Operations Manager John Rosseter. Like nearly every one else in the hierarchy of both the Shipping Board and Emergency Fleet Corporation, Rosseter joined the Government's shipping activities during World War I. Long versed in the steamship business, as were colleagues like Shipping Board Commissioner John Donald, P.A.S. Franklin and Robert Dollar, Rosseter apparently considered the eventual "502" type a vessel with great potential for the Latin American trades of both the Grace Line and the Pacific Mail Steamship Company. At that, only one 1920 article in the shipping trade press divulged that fact, an item both the Shipping Board and Pacific Mail promptly quashed.

The United States Shipping Board Emergency Fleet Corporation gave the first contract to build some of these big, fast transports to New York Shipbuilding Corp. In the business of building ships since 1899, it had quickly grown to prominence, latterly under the ownership of the American International Corporation and thus related to the gigantic shipbuilding endeavor underway at Hog Island. Signed on December 14, 1917, Contract 151 SC was for the construction of three 535 foot long steel troop transports. No further contracts for such ships were granted for a while. Then, during the spring and summer of 1918, the Fleet Corporation awarded a spate of them. For its Sparrows Point, Baltimore yards, the Bethlehem Shipbuilding Company won two contracts to build 13,000 ton transports. First was Contract 162 SC for two such steel steamers. Allowing the builder a $320,000 fixed profit plus certain increases in profit depending upon certain variations in the basic price, Contract 465 SC was for six more of these big sisters and Bethlehem had meanwhile won Contract 340 SC, a sixty million dollar order signed on July 5, 1918 for twenty more identical sisters to be built to the same plans at the Liberty plant of their recently acquired Alameda, California yard. In fact the Liberty plant was built specifically for the construction of "535"s. EFC hull numbers 1985 through 2004 were assigned to these projects but so far no names intended for them have surfaced. Chances are that Mrs. Woodrow Wilson had or would have chosen names for them, but they likely would not have been used, for all these once "535" and "502" type intended transports were at one time or another assigned a "State" name. Able to devote their energies to but two of these big transports was the Newport News Shipbuilding and Drydock Company which had Contract 403 SC. They finagled quite a profit from the Fleet Corporation, earning a fixed fee for profit of $425,000 per ship. Rumor has it that their two ships, the GOLDEN STATE and SILVER STATE, were actually the best of all twenty three ships to emerge from all these contracts.

By default through cancellation of twenty three of Bethlehem's intended 535's, the yard with the most surviving contracts for these big troopships was of course Camden, New Jersey's New York Shipbuilding Company. With four separate contracts, Contract 151 SC (three ships), 418 SC (seven ships), 419 SC (two ships) and 420 SC (four ships), that yard had orders for sixteen transports. Financial arrangements for their first contract are sketchy, but the other three provided the yard payment for each vessel based on actual cost plus a fixed profit for the builder. Neither provision for any variations or changes in the fixed profit was allowed. That would come to annoy the Shipping Board to no end in the spring of 1919 when they successfully renegotiated hundreds of contracts with American shipbuilders but could get nowhere with their attempts to force New York Ship to reduce prices. There was no legal reason for New York Shipbuilding to budge and the Board had foisted so many changes in plans and delayed the construction, causing backups in the yards' production schedules that the company began to treat the Shipping Board with bemused contempt and not a little hostility[17].

Though they later placed additional contracts for such tonnage, on June 22, 1918 the Shipping Board suspended orders for ten of the "535"s to come from Bethlehem's new Alameda, California plant, the "Liberty" yard, developed especially for the construction of such vessels. That move may well have signalled the evolution of the "502" class as an intermediate third type of troop transport for the contract to build seven ships that became the "502"s was signed on July 1, 1918. Curiously enough, tonnage figures given in connection with the ships covered by this contract correspond to the original 10,000 gross ton figure mentioned for "535"s. Only a shorter length and narrower beam, which began to appear in Shipping Board documents suggested any modification of the "535" type. Perhaps the "502"s owed their very existence to these lesser dimensions for even before November 11, 1918

---

[17]Several letters in the Construction files of the USSB support this contention. RG 32 National Archives.

Armistice, Bethlehem lost its orders for the ten "535"s under suspension at Alameda. The Shipping Board cancelled those ten projected ships on October 15, 1918. Those cancellations were followed by the revocation on November 23rd of Bethlehem—Alameda's remaining ten "535" contracts. Softening the blow to the corporation were various fees and penalties the Government paid Bethlehem but of course none of that was any recompense to workers whose jobs evaporated with the advent of the Armistice. With the end of the war came months of vacillation and indecision on the remaining shipbuilding program as Congress and Shipping Board hashed out further details. These delays almost wrecked the entire troopship program.

Adding to the lack of definition of building terms, the indecision over eventual deployment of the first ships delayed the construction of all the intended troopers. As early as May 10, 1918 the subject of the expected outfitting of the earliest "535" transports came up. In view of an urgent need for hospital ships, the Shipping Board directed New York Shipbuilding Corporation to complete the first two as hospital ships with the ability to carry troops when required. New York Ship had plans ready by late June. Little progress towards any real outfitting of the planned hospital ships had been made when on August 28, 1918 the Shipping Board formalized orders to complete these first two as troopships. That was not really news to New York Ship which learned as early as June that their first "535"s would be troopers. A diverting sidenote to the vacillation in deciding the eventual role of the two ships was a difficulty interpreting Geneva conventions rules on hospital ships. When no one could decide whether or not to arm them or fit them as unarmed hospital ships under the rules of the Geneva conventions, they ordered New York Ship back to the drawing boards. July and August 1918 brought new "final" building plans from New York Shipbuilding Corporation's naval architects, but once again objections were raised. Then the military delayed the process further, once more requesting definitive changes be effected in the first two ships, already on the ways. No longer to be troop transports, those two ships were again to be hospital ships. A few months later these two ships would be noted in Shipping Board files as having No.5 hold fitted with independent tanks which when filled with bunker oil would give them a steaming radius of 11,700 miles at a speed of 17 knots. That was in contrast to the first pair of "535"s building at Bethlehem's Sparrows Point yard. With no such tanks provided, they had a steaming radius of 9,800 miles. Curiously, further references in Shipping Board memos state that all remaining ships of the type were to have deep tanks fitted at No. 5 hold which, when used for bunker oil would give them a steaming radius of 14,000 miles at 17 knots.

When the second annual report of the United States Shipping Board was published on June 30, 1918, the Government was expected, on December 1, 1918, to still have under contract the construction of 94 troop transports,

The date is July 14, 1920 and at the busy Camden yards of New York Ship, workers labored to complete the big passenger ships. At right in the foreground is the CREOLE STATE. Front and center is the OLD NORTH STATE with the SEA GIRT and AMERICAN LEGION beyond her. Mostly obscured by the bigger "535" is the PANHANDLE STATE. New York Shipbuilding Collection. Courtesy of the Independence Seaport Museum Library.

This shot taken by the yard's photographer on August 16, 1920 shows how far work has progressed on the WENATCHEE, OLD NORTH STATE and PANHANDLE STATE. New York Shipbuilding Collection. Courtesy of the Independence Seaport Museum Library.

All that separates us from being there now are the smells and sounds. When the yard's cameraman clicked his shutters on September 24, 1920 the PANHANDLE STATE was away from the yard. Tightly packed into the fitting out area from left to right were the sisters WOLVERINE STATE, GRANITE STATE, CREOLE STATE and OLD NORTH STATE. New York Shipbuilding Collection. Courtesy of the Independence Seaport Museum Library.

The painters had been very busy. Already in United States Mail Line colors in this October 6, 1920 view is the OLD NORTH STATE (top). At left is the WOLVERINE STATE with the GRANITE STATE next to her and then the CREOLE STATE. New York Shipbuilding Collection. Courtesy of the Independence Seaport Museum Library.

representing an expenditure of $207,398,400.00 of public money. That did not include the cost of wireless equipment, which at a price of $6,100 per ship suggested further expenses of $573,400.00. Nothing additional in that June statement alerted the reader to the likelihood of orders for even more troopships. First of the additional orders came on July 1, 1918 with the placement of the second of four building contracts for troop transports awarded to the New York Shipbuilding Corporation as Contract 418 SC. Initially calling for 535 foot long ships, the final version of the pact specified ships of a length of 500 feet and a beam of 62 feet. A "cost plus" contract, #418 guaranteed the yard a fixed profit of $300,000.00 per ship. Though this was no sweetheart deal for the yard, actual costs included several overriding items including a) the cost of labor and materials as well as other direct charges including insurance; b) indirect charges; c) proportion of interest on debts; d) proportion of taxes; e) proportion of physical losses; f) allowance of depreciation of buildings and machinery; No provision for profit sharing was written into the pact. These seven ships became the "502"s.

Next for New York Shipbuilding was Contract 419 SC. Signed on August 10, 1918 it was an order for two 20,000 deadweight ton troopships of 535 foot length and 72 foot beam. Those projected ships were assigned hulls #2583 and 2584. Once again the contract agreed on remuneration based on actual construction costs plus a fixed fee for profit of $425,000 per ship.

New York Ship's last contract for troop transports was Contract 420 SC. Signed on August 5, 1918 it led to the construction of four more of the 535 foot troopships. These were assigned hulls #2579, 2580, 2581 and 2582. Once again financial terms called for actual cost plus a fixed fee for the yard's profit of $318,750 per ship.

Unlike contracts with Bethlehem and Newport News, these last three troopship contracts held no provision for any variations or change in the fixed profit, nor was there any base price mentioned or provided for. As a result, there was no question of revision of base prices once Congress forced the Shipping Board to curtail its wild spending during the spring of 1919. By June of that year, all pretense of a military future for the "535"s and "502" class had been dropped and the ships were listed as building as passenger and cargo ships. The first of the "502"s had been launched as WENATCHEE on May 24th. No one involved with the progress suspected how long it would take to get her or any of the other Government passenger steamers into service.

Because these were really very important ships, the Shipping Board was in a quandary of how to extract maximum propagandistic mileage from them, exuding patriotic spirit and pride while at the same time concealing the extravagance of their cost and the irrelevance of their construction. Had there been no hostilities, not a single one of these ships would be considered in her final form. Once peace returned, none of them was really needed, at least not at her building price. Contemporary newspapers carried occasional but hardly detailed stories of the progress of their construction, but so frantic was the Shipping Board when it came to reminders of their cost that most of their launch parties went ignored by the general press. Not much better coverage of them appeared in shipping trade publications though a few detailed descriptions appeared almost by accident. At best they provide an insight into the nearly traumatic birth of these ships.

More than almost any other class of ships ordered by the United States Shipping Board Emergency Fleet Corporation during the World War I era, the contracts let for the construction of troop transports generated a mountain of paperwork, plans, correspondence, telegrams, night letters and memos plus a good deal of controversy both private and public. Not surprisingly the Shipping Board gave the "502"s substantially less attention in its conferences, memos and press releases than it gave either the "535" or Type B "Hog Islanders". Even certain classes of freighters won more publicity than these intended ships. After all there would only be seven ships of the "502" type.

The Armistice of November 11, 1918 turned the whole emergency shipbuilding program on its head. Everyone had to reconsider the entire shipbuilding program with its enormous dollar cost. Orders were dispatched to naval architects, interior designers and shipyards for the "restudy of design with reference to accommodations in the intended troop transports."[18] Plans were then prepared in the offices of the Chairman of the Shipping Control Committee and the big transports were now laid out as passenger ships for First and Second Class passengers. New York Shipbuilding wasted no time at all and in December 1918 turned in suitable plans for the completion of the "535"s as commercial vessels with accommodations for 278 First and 236 Second Class passengers.

The Shipping Board's Design Department was the first to admit to many flaws in their arrangement, reminding critical observers that in the heat of war these ships were designed for military transport purposes. As far as the compromise type which evolved into the "502" type, what emerged from the naval architect's drawing boards was principally a big cargo vessel with high grade accommodations for a limited number of one class passengers. Over the course of 1919 they would be the object of occasional references, but as late as October 28th of that year New York Shipbuilding Corporation had not received the specification book for them. The final compromise type had still to evolve into its final form. All anyone really knew of them at that date was that the "502"s were "ex-standard troop ships" now being built by the New York Shipbuilding Company.

The opening words of a November 12, 1919 memo from McAuliffe suggested plenty: "The change from troop transport to passenger and cargo ship is so extensive and not covered in any clause in existing contracts . . . " Wise readers of those words knew what he really meant—building costs for the "535"s and "502"s were going to rise spectacularly and delivery dates would

---

[18]Memo in the Construction files of the U.S. Shipping Board in Rg 32 at National Archives.

not hold. It was also at about that time that references to the "502" ships's design number gained wider currency among Shipping Board staff. For the record the seven ships were finally built to Design #1095. During their long gestation many proposed plans for them were discarded. While during the winter of 1919 only the Munson Steamship Company and Shawmut Steamship Line expressed any interest in ships of the "502" type, hardly more popular at that time was Design #1029, the "535". Those intended ships appealed only to the James W. Elwell Company, known for their agency of France's Fabre Line, and the ever willing Munson firm. Among American operators, big ships still had few willing takers. That would change as the ships neared completion.

As late as July 1920 only two "535"'s were definitely assigned to specific private operators. Even the PANHANDLE STATE, fast approaching completion, was not under signed contract to be delivered to the United States Mail Steamship Company. For these passenger ships, the Shipping Board intended to extract every iota of patience from eventual operators. Not just for reasons of his own, but undoubtedly also to maintain his own sanity, Shipping Board Chairman Benson decided to keep decisions regarding allocations of these big ships private. He permitted no public announcements of the allocation of the WENATCHEE and KEYSTONE STATE to the Pacific Steamship Company for their Admiral Line's "Great Circle Route" from Seattle to the Far East, yet that news leaked out and rival firms immediately clamored for allocation of similar modern tonnage. Concurrently, the San Francisco based (but in reality owned and controlled by W.R. Grace & Co. and the American International Corporation in New York) Pacific Mail Steamship Company bombarded the Shipping Board with telegrams noting the assignment of big "535"'s to the Seattle based firm and requested similar favor. Late that month the Shipping Board began to consider the situation and decided to allocate at least two ships of the "535" type. This time the Chairman kept the decision to himself for the time being.

The second and third of the nine "535"'s built at New York Shipbuilding Corporation were the SEA GIRT and AMERICAN LEGION. They were allocated to Munson Line for service on the Shipping Board's express service to South America. This important service was eventually named the Pan American Line. At the urging of Munson Steamship Line president Frank C. Munson, the name of the SEA GIRT was changed before her completion and she entered service as the SOUTHERN CROSS. Among other names once intended for this pair were GOPHER STATE and BADGER STATE. Two others of the type, launched at Bethlehem Steel's, Sparrows Point, Maryland yard as the PALMETTO STATE and NUTMEG STATE were added to that service as the PAN AMERICA and WESTERN WORLD. These two were built from an eight ship order that was reduced to five by the cancellation of three orders. Never laid down, all that remains of these intended vessels are their EFC and yard hull numbers, cancellation numbers and intended names, BLUE GRASS STATE, COTTON STATE and SUNFLOWER STATE.

The Shipping Board was savvy enough to realize the potential of the fast "535" on the North Pacific and quickly decided to allocate three of them to the Pacific Steamship Company for their Admiral Line to run from Seattle to Japan, China and Hong Kong. The first of the clan to go into transPacific service was the WENATCHEE, first ship of the class. She among the sixteen sisters was fitting out as a troopship but converted to passenger and cargo ship before delivery. First ship of an order for two Hospital ships and one transport to be built to "535" plans, one of her first two intended names was C.M. SCHWAB.[19] The name WENATCHEE was actually the fifth name assigned to her. To conform to the "STATE" nomenclature foreseen for both the "535"s and "502"s the name BEAVER STATE was contemplated for a short while.

Very early in the design stages for these big transports, plans changed, and not only the WENATCHEE and her two contracted sisters, but the six more ships of the type contracted at New York Shipbuilding were designated for completion as troopships. The end of the war obviated the need for large numbers of big troopships, so after a few months of haggling between Shipping Board and War Department over just which ships would be completed and fitted as troop transports, all sixteen of the "535"s were delivered as passenger and cargo ships. The others of the class operated in the transPacific service from Seattle with the WENATCHEE were the SILVER STATE, BAY STATE, KEYSTONE STATE and PINE TREE STATE. In the spring of 1922, they were renamed PRESIDENT JEFFERSON, PRESIDENT JACKSON, PRESIDENT MADISON, PRESIDENT McKINLEY and PRESIDENT GRANT, respectively.

Initially, the Shipping Board had planned to allocate five ships of this class to Munson Line but the cancellation of Bethlehem Steel's last three units reduced the pool of available passenger tonnage and the Shipping Board could allocate but four. That quartette of big ships proved adequate to the demands of the Munson Line's trade between New York and the East Coast of South America. The four sisters worked the route for over fifteen years. Munson Line bought the Pan America Line and its four ships in 1926. After Munson Line collapsed in 1938, the ships were bought by the Government and became troopships, fulfilling the promise of their original design.

With more than sixteen "535"s planned, initial thinking called for a quartette of them to run in trans-Atlantic service but with the cancellation of the BLUE GRASS STATE, COTTON STATE and SUNFLOWER STATE, only two "535"s ever went to work on the Atlantic ferry. Both worked for United States Lines, and were included in a sale of the United States Lines to Paul Chapman in 1929. Those ships were the PRESIDENT HARDING, built as the LONE STAR STATE, and the PENINSULA STATE, which became famous in her time as the PRESIDENT ROOSEVELT. Getting them onto the Atlantic was a fluke, especially for the LONE STAR STATE. As an incom-

---

[19]Her first intended name is apparently lost to history.

plete liner she had been promised to Pacific Mail during 1921 and allocated to them in February 1922 for a July 1st delivery. So, too, it seemed, that the PENINSULA STATE would head off to the transPacific trade. At least that seemed to be in the works until Matson returned their two "535"s to the Shipping Board. Also once intended for service either together or with two sisters on a transAtlantic service were the HAWKEYE STATE and BUCKEYE STATE, Bethlehem Steel's first pair of "535"s. Instead of debuting on the Atlantic, where their somewhat limited steaming radius would never be noticed, those two ships were allocated to Matson Lines for a new Shipping Board service between Baltimore and Honolulu via Havana, Panama, Los Angeles, and San Francisco, to both Honolulu and Hilo. This service soon proved unsuccessful in all aspects. The HAWKEYE STATE would do a total of five round trips, including an "Orient Cruise". Actually an extension of a regular Hawaii trip to Yokohama, Shanghai, Hong Kong and Manila during her second voyage, this was made to allow a big new ship to cover for the absence of the WENATCHEE, which suffered serious engine trouble on her maiden voyage from Seattle to Japan. Thus the HAWKEYE STATE, on temporary allocation to the Pacific Steamship Company (operators of the fabled Admiral Line), interrupted her work for Matson Lines and diverted to the Far East. The BUCKEYE STATE made only three Hawaii trips. Both sisters were returned to the Shipping Board. They were both allocated to United States Lines for transAtlantic service in May 1922, just before the announcement that they were to be renamed. The HAWKEYE STATE was to be PRESIDENT WILSON, but that name went to the EMPIRE STATE and the HAWKEYE STATE became PRESIDENT HARDING. The BUCKEYE STATE was renamed PRESIDENT ROOSEVELT. Because Matson redelivered this pair at San Francisco before their names were changed, the Shipping Board reversed its decision to run them on the Atlantic. Then they cancelled their allocation to United States Lines. That decision made, the Shipping Board name game was hauled out once more and the HAWKEYE STATE was renamed PRESIDENT PIERCE, the BUCKEYE STATE became PRESIDENT TAFT. On the East Coast the PRESIDENT TAFT, the former LONE STAR STATE became PRESIDENT HARDING and the PENINSULA STATE was renamed PRESIDENT ROOSEVELT and the ships allocated to United States Lines. The two former Matson ships then went to Pacific Mail, which placed them in the transPacific trade along with three others of this type, the GOLDEN STATE, EMPIRE STATE and HOOSIER STATE. The other three were respectively renamed PRESIDENT CLEVELAND, PRESIDENT WILSON and PRESIDENT LINCOLN. To confuse this tale further, an April 18, 1922 announcement from the United States Shipping Board stated that the first two ships were to become the PRESIDENT TAYLOR and PRESIDENT CLEVELAND. At about the same time the Shipping Board changed its system of allocation of big ships. No longer was an operator awarded a ship on a voyage by voyage basis. With the May 1922 departure of the PRESIDENT JEFFERSON from Seattle, the Board made allocations an indefinite assignment.

In 1925, Dollar Line triumphed over resident operator Pacific Mail Steamship Company and despite fears of a monopoly voiced by several top executives of the Emergency Fleet Corporation, bought the five sister ships then operating between San Francisco and the Far East. Giving up its fight for the ships and California—Orient Line, Grace sold the Pacific Mail name to the Dollars and concentrated on inter-American services thereafter.[20]

---

[20]Grace Line seriously contemplated resurrecting their Far East passenger services after the end of the Second World War but nothing ever came of the idea.

THE "502" CLASS STEAMERS

Even pessimists knew that the Great War would one day end. Only the date was uncertain. One of the most important classes of vessels authorized by the Shipping Board during the war was the "502" class, that class of seven ships developed from the plans for the larger "535" class troop transport. A memo written some years after the initial order for their construction was sent from the Ship Construction division to the Chairman of the United States Shipping Board: "The '502' is a compromise type".[1] Every executive of the Emergency Fleet Corporation as well as every Commissioner of the United States Shipping Board kept an eye on the potential postwar earning capabilities of these ships. If they were to ever be able to repay any of their enormous construction costs, they would have to be suitable for commercial service and attractive to private operators so commercial considerations played a key role from the earliest stages of the development of their design and for that reason the Commissioners of the Shipping Board specifically instructed the designers to make these ships adaptable to ready conversion into passenger and cargo ships.

An inkling of their eventual existence came during Shipping Board Chairman Edward M. Hurley's July 10, 1918 announcement of contracts for the construction of 92 troop transports for the United States Army Transportation Service, Water Division. Feeding the hopes of Western shipyards and their suppliers, Hurley promised that a good number of these specially built troopers, all destined to be able to work commercially after the war, would be built on the West Coast. Of course, established East Coast yards would build these big ships, too. Soon thereafter the July 5, 1918 contract with Bethlehem Shipbuilding Corp's Alameda yards for twenty 13,000 ton transports was revealed. To facilitate their construction, Bethlehem began an expansion of that California yard. What would Eastern yards build, and which companies would build them? And to whose plans? Theodore Ferris claimed to have designed them as troopships but who has seen those plans? At the request of the Shipping Board Theodore Ferris resigned in late January. As late as March he was still publicly denying any wrongdoing, but the Board did not return him to office. He later wrote to the Board's Construction Division asking for a chance to look at the builders plans for transport types.

Those ships that became the "502"s stemmed from United States Shipping Board Emergency Fleet Corporation contract 418 SC. That contract began life as an order for thirteen 13,000 ton, 535 foot long ships. In its inimitable fashion, dating and redating, backdating and postdating, tracking down the

---

[1] Copy in the Construction files for the "535" class in RG 32 at National Archives.

initial contract is impossible and the actual contract which became Contract #418 SC is an order for seven 502 foot long passenger and cargo vessels. Perhaps it is not important, for that is the contract that actually yielded seven ships rather than any earlier pact with other intended results. In either event, the Design Department had a number for the design used. The "502" class ships were built to Emergency Fleet Corporation design number 1095. Although many sources accept Theodore Ferris' claim as their designer, and his input was no mean feat, it was limited to preliminary drawings for troop transports and the specification book. A showman very conscious of having his name up in lights before the steamship industry, even Ferris accepted the fact that many people had a hand in the design of all three transports types. Ferris was but one of many to contribute to the development of the "502" class steamer as a distinct Shipping Board design type. In any event, he thought very little of at least ONE of the other designers, penning a scathing letter of criticism of the work of one of the other designers, a young man by the name of William Francis Gibbs. The claim of any one man as designer of either the "535"s or "502"s cannot stand. Like the camel, which seems to be a horse designed by a committee, the "502"s sprang forth from the work of too many disparate hands. Credit for the design of their passenger accommodations goes to John H. Rosseter. Veteran shipping man, vice president of both W.R. Grace & Co.'s Grace Line and Pacific Mail and since 1918 also an executive with the Shipping Board, Rosseter probably knew more about ships and shipping than any man then alive.[2] Theodore Ferris eventually did improve upon the passenger accommodations Rosseter designed for the "502"s for after most of the accommodation spaces in the PRESIDENT POLK burned out in October 1924, Ferris provided the drawings, specifications and plans for the 1925 repairs and rebuilding of the ship. He also supervised the resurrection of the almost burned out liner. Four years later it was an almost identical set of figures and Ferris plans that were used to substantially upgrade the PRESIDENT ADAMS, PRESIDENT GARFIELD and PRESIDENT HARRISON. Finally, their initial and very ugly appearance reflects their origins in a committee.

Indeed, it was such a long time from the laying of the first of the "502" keels on March 20, 1919 and the laying down of the last, on March 4, 1920 that more than a few men still and quite incorrectly suspect that more than seven "502" class ships were intended. There were so many design changes, delays, deviations, uncertainties, that by the time the PANHANDLE STATE was completed, a host of other talented men had added their knowledge, talents and experience to the planning prices. Nor were postwar plans for these ships easily nor quickly derived and in fact the designs of both types of ships were a cumulative effort. As early as October 16, 1918, the Shipping

---

[2] According to a May 26, 1919 memo from P.J. McAuliffe, then manager of the Ship Construction Division to Fleet Corp. vicepresident Ackerson. Copy in the Construction files of the USSB in RG32 at National Archives.

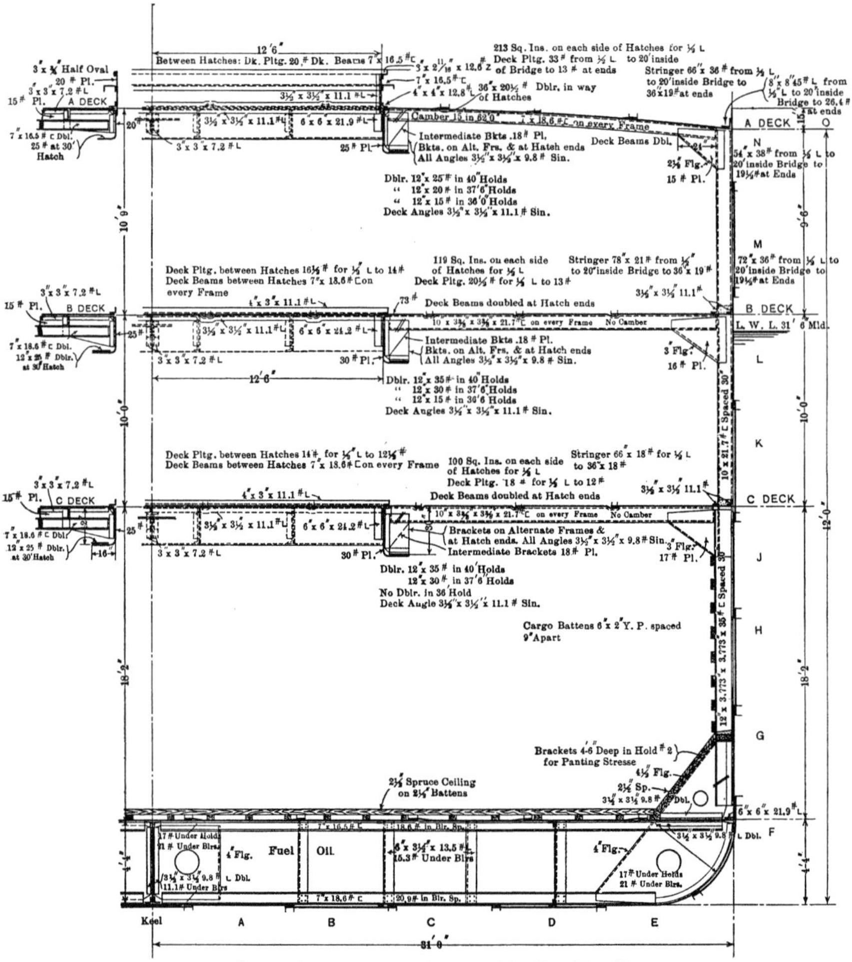

Fig. 1.—Section Through Hold of 13,000-Ton Troopship

Introducing the shipping world to the intended transports, *International Marine Engineering* showed sections through the hold and through the midships section.

Board asked P.A.S. Franklin to rearrange the "535"'s from transports to passenger and cargo ships at Emergency Fleet Corporation expense. As late as April 1919 the heavy word on the "502" class from the Shipping Board's publicity men was this: "Although these vessels were originally designed as troopships, and are being constructed as such, they can be readily converted into combined passenger and cargo ships for commercial services."[3]

---

[3] April 1919 *Marine Engineering* article on the "Twin Screw Troopship of 13,000 Tons D.W.," page 192

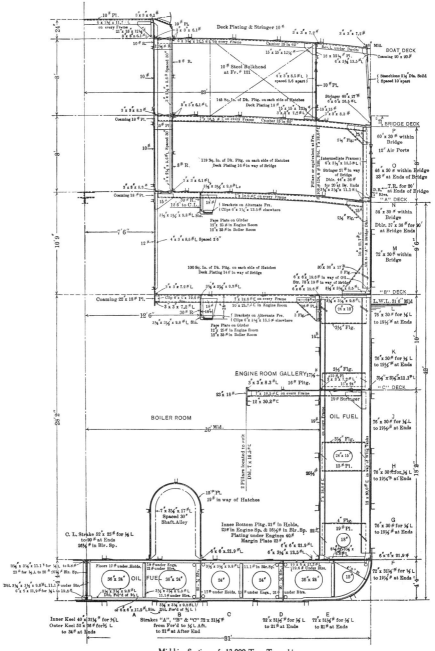

Midship Section of 13,000-Ton Troopship

Here are the principal dimensions of the "502"s as building during the early spring of 1919:

Length overall .... 522 feet, 6 inches
Length per classification rules .... 502 feet
Beam, molded .... 62 feet
Depth to A Deck .... 42 feet
Depth to B Deck .... 32 feet, 8 inches
Designed draft, full load .... 31 feet, 9 inches
Corresponding displacement .... 20,900 tons
Corresponding deadweight capacity, about .... 13,000 tons
Indicated horsepower .... 7,000 hp
Speed on trial .... 14.5 knots
Trial draft .... 24 feet
Total cubic capacity .... 655,000 cubic feet
Deadweight capacity as a trooper .... 7,000 tons
Number of passengers carried (troops) .... 2,700[4]

That number included 24 Navy officers aboard to oversee gun crews and serve Navy functions and at least 127 Troop Officers, whose intended Boat Deck Troop Office eventually showed up on deck plans as the Veranda Cafe.

For the record, a year later, by which time all pretense of military employment for the "502"s was a distant memory, a few amended figures were released:

Depth to A Deck .... 31 feet, 9 inches
Gross Tonnage .... 10,500 tons
Deadweight Tonnage (approximate) .... 12,000 tons
Service speed .... 14 knots
Indicated horsepower 6,000
Fuel oil capacity .... 3,476 tons
Boiler feed water .... 215 tons
Domestic water .... 241 tons
Bale capacity .... 465,940 cubic feet
Ship's cold storage .... 5,300 cubic feet
Cargo cold storage .... 52,300 cubic feet
Number of First Class passengers 78
Number of crew 115

Once completed the seven ships very much resembled the figures given, varying only slightly in some cases. The "502"s saw a bit less design activity than was lavished upon the larger and frankly more important "535"s but

---

[4] *ibid.*

many of the same men did the bulk of the design work for both classes of ship. H.H. Thayer represented both the Emergency Fleet Corporation and the Shipping Board's Design Department; William Francis Gibbs spoke for the IMM whose P.A.S. Franklin was virtually on loan to the Shipping Board; Hugo P. Frear represented the Bethlehem yards; E.H. Rigg did the same for the New York Shipbuilding Corp.; and H.F. Norton contributed his talents for Newport News, a yard that was so busy they accepted contracts to build only two "535"s and wouldn't even think of taking on the rather enigmatic "502"s.

Like all other contracts for "535"s and "502"s, New York Ship's contract 418 would bring the yard plenty of headaches before the ships were finally built and handed over to the Emergency Fleet Corporation. On March 11, 1919, EFC naval architect H.C. Sadler wrote to colleagues including Cox regarding all three classes of intended transports. Reporting discussions relevant to the "502"s, he informed them that addressing these particular ships, they had drawn plans for them as cargo ships with passenger spaces limited to 12 berths. Mr. Franklin's committee had further contemplated likely trade routes for these planned ships. That same day, Cox informed then Shipping Board General Manager Charles Piez that for the "502"s, a compromise plan was in the works at that time. October 28th brought a memo to the Emergency Fleet Corp's Philadelphia office about the "502"s from Robert Hague, then manager of the Construction and Repair department of the Shipping Board. At that date he had still to receive specifications for the seven "502"s, which he referred to as "ex-standard troop ships" now being built by the New York Shipbuilding Company. Having heard that the boat deck might be but a canvas covered deck instead of a laid caulked deck, he informed the Fleet Corp. that his department preferred that the deck be of Oregon pine, of 3" to 4" planking.[5] A November 12, 1919 memo from P.J. McAuliffe, then Manager of the Construction Division, enlightens: "The change from troop transport to passenger and cargo ship is so extensive and not covered in any clause in existing contracts." This was an early indication that in the case of these ships, from about that time on always were referred to as passenger and cargo ships if not by their length. Costs would rise spectacularly and that no one should count on specific delivery dates.

During the long gestation of the seven "502" sisters, the Shipping Board took the opportunity to provide American steamship operators with plans of 22 different vessel types drawn by the Board's Design Department. Polling various shipping men, the Shipping Board learned that as of winter 1919, only the Munson Steamship Company, and Shawmut Steamship Line expressed any interest in ships of the "502" type. Among American operators, big ships had few willing takers and big passenger carriers were of even less interest. Offered Government inspired tonnage, only the Coastwise Trans-

---

[5] Reference #6348 on Construction files of the U.S. Shipping Board in RG 32, National Archives.

TWIN-SCREW TROOPSHIP OF 13,000 TONS DEADWEIGHT

Designed and Built by the New York Shipbuilding Corporation, Camden, N. J.

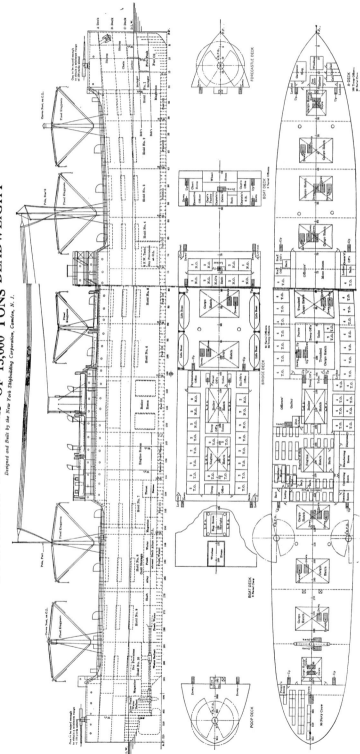

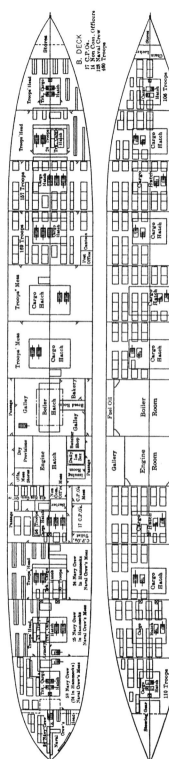

The same publication published plans of the intended 13,000 d.w.t. transports that became the "502''s. Compare this plan with later issues.

portation Company, James W. Elwell & Co.. John S. Emery & Co., Gulf Re-
fining Company, Matson Navigation Company, Munson Steamship Company, Nafra Line, Ocean Navigation Company, Pan American Steamship &
Transportation Company, Shawmut Steamship Company (eventually a com-
ponent of United American Line), Sinclair Navigation Company, Standard
Navigation Company and Sun Navigation Company expressed interest in
ships of and more than 10,000 deadweight tons. Mostly in the oil business,
most of those only wanted big tankers. Not many operators set much store
in speed either—only Elwell, Munson, Nafra, Ocean Navigating, Ocean
Steamship Company (Savannah Line), Old Dominion S.S. Co., Panama Railroad S.S. Co., San Francisco & Portland S.S. Line and the Southern Pacific
Company wanted ships able to make 14 knots or better.

Expansive articles introducing the "502"s in the shipping press to the
steamship business in the spring of 1919 reported them under construction
as originally intended, headlining the advent of big new troopships. At the
same time authors and the Shipping Board left the door open to commercial
venues reporting how readily these ships could be converted into combined
passenger and cargo steamers for commercial service. Whether they were in
the design stages as twin screw troopships of 13,000 deadweight tons or
actually building as passenger cargo ships, these intended vessels were to
be three deck combined passenger and cargo vessels of 20,900 displacement
tons on a draft of 31 feet, 9 inches. As of April 1919 these big new ships were
projected to have a service speed of 14 knots but for service in the war zone
and lightened in draft, their machinery was designed to allow the necessary
power to obtain a speed of 15 knots. Had they been completed as planned,
they would have accommodations for about 2,700 troops and still have room
to carry about 7,000 tons of cargo.

The "502" hull was designed with a straight stem and cruiser stern with
three complete steel decks, designated as A,B and C Decks, with steel deckhouses amidships and a short poop and forecastle with long bridge. Above
the tank top, the hull was subdivided by thirteen transverse watertight bulkheads, all of which extended up to A Deck and gave six cargo holds forward
and four aft of the machinery space. Separate compartments were provided
for engine and boilers. Safety of life at sea preoccupied every man working
in the design of these intended troopships. Because safety was such a vitally
important consideration, the "502" was designed as a three compartment
vessel with 30 per cent permeability for troop, cargo, boiler and engine
spaces with the ship carrying 7,000 deadweight tons of cargo and supplies.
Hulls of the seven sisters were built with transverse framing, frames spaced
30 inches center to center midships but reduced at the ends. Deck beams
stopped at the inner face of the frames. Safety concerns led officials to allow
these ships to have hulls built on the still new "Isherwood" system.[6] That

---

[6] Some sources counted 14 watertight compartments.

gave each of the ships fifteen watertight compartments and even if any three consecutive compartments flooded, the ship would not sink. Such safety features made these ships particularly attractive to commercial operators. Above the tank tops the frames were channel section except in the peaks and in way of excessive bevel, where they were built up of angles and reverse angles. Solid floors were fitted on every third frame with angle frames and reverse frames. Double frames or their equivalent were fitted on every floor from three-fifths length forward to the collision bulkhead. Above tank tops the hull was subdivided by thirteen transverse watertight bulkheads, all wing bulkheads, extending up to B Deck. They were fitted in the boiler room and formed side tanks for fuel oil. The B and C Decks had no camber, while all weather decks had a camber of 15 feet, 6 inches. Extending from the fore peak to the after end of Number 8 hold was the double bottom, divided into ten main compartments on each side by transverse bulkheads. The center keelson was continuous throughout the length of a "502" type ship. On each side were two longitudinals, intercoastal between solid floors with thickness increased under the boilers. Conforming to safety provisions for troop transports, all decks were steel plated, riveted to channels on every frame, and on B and C Decks the deck beams were toggled down with the plating worked flush. The deck beams stopped at the inner face of the frames.

A double bottom extended from fore peak to after end of No. 8 hold and was divided by transverse members into ten main compartments on each side. Compartments under the engine room were arranged to carry feed water only, while all the other compartments were arranged for carrying either fuel oil or water ballast. The staying and stiffening of the fuel oil bunkers in the boiler space rendered the fitting of web frames unnecessary and there were no web frames fitted in cargo holds though two web frames were fitted in the engine room and webs were also fitted as panting frames end. No side stringers were fitted amidships, but short stringers were fitted at the ends to resist panting.

In their original Shipping Board livery, with grey hulls and a short, thin funnel with hardly enough room for them to display the Shipping Board shield, these were particularly severe looking ships whose hulls had no sheer midships but plenty of it fore and aft. There was a pronounced knuckle at the bows and their sterns were almost perpendicular to the rest of the hull. Like the up and down bow, that stern was something of a trademark feature of Shipping Board passenger (troopship) tonnage. Long since said to be a built-in camouflage feature, it was no such thing, at least it was not the reason behind the distinctive stems and sterns fitted to the 35 ships of the "535", "502" and Hog Island "B" types. With highly pronounced fore and aft sheer and very straight stems and sterns it might well seem that one of these ships was both going and coming at the same time. Many people still believe that this unattractive feature of the ships was an inherent trap designed to make indiscernible to any potential enemy submarine captain the direction any such ship were heading because fore and aft section were so similar. Limiting sheer to fore and aft ends and giving the ships straight up and down stems and sterns was simply and purely an economic measure. The idea that the appearance of the ships could confuse possible enemies was a publicity man's coup and diverted attention to the fact that these ships were rather ugly, fully lacking the aesthetic panache of a great liner. Blithely explaining why these ships were so severely ugly fore and aft, great credence followed such statements. The old saw has been in print ever since the Shipping Board's publicity men first thought of it in 1920. Those bows and sterns were fitted because they were simple, quick and easy to build, efficient to fit and cost effective.

The "502"'s were three island ships. Aft, a short poop was topped by a small house, forward was a 42 foot long forecastle and a 200 foot long bridge topped by steel deckhouses was midships. Midships, the tops of the deck-houses were carried out to the sides of the vessel to form a boat deck which was of steel unsheathed. A wooden wheel house and chart room were placed forward on the Boat Deck, and a similar house for winches, aft. Above the bridge deck their superstructures were split. The longer, after part had two glass enclosed promenade decks. Upper promenades were glassed-in, mak-ing their midsections appear too heavy. With simplicity of construction an overriding concern, curves were supplanted wherever possible by straight lines and angles. Three island, flat sided ships with straight stems and nearly straight up and down cruiser sterns, the overall length of a "502" class ship was 522 feet, 8 inches long. Each of the seven ships was 62 feet in beam. Somehow the heavy word never reached all commentators because some sources quoted their overall length at 518 feet, while still others rounded up to 523 feet. But it was not their overall length that mattered when it came to nicknaming these sisters. Their 502 foot length between perpendiculars seemed to do the trick and the seven sisters have been known as the "502"'s since 1920. As built, their gross tonnages ranged a few tons either way from a median of 10,533 gross tons. With a deadweight tonnage of 13,100 tons, net tonnage was measured at about 6,200 tons, and on a draft of 32 feet, 3 inches, they displaced at first 20,610 tons. Once all thought of trooping ca-reers for them was abandoned and the ships completed as passenger cargo ships, they were considerably lighter than they would have been for they carried neither military equipment nor the 2,700 some-odd metal frame standee berths for troops. As a result, each one was loaded with steel rails and scrap metal as ballast to compensate for the ultimate lesser weight. The ships had a moulded depth of 42 feet, 3 inches. Once the need for their completion as troop transports disappeared, the intention of their comple-tion as big carriers of freight was assured. To compensate for less weight as a result of their commercial status the ships were ballasted with scrap steel and rails. After refits, four of them displaced 21,480 tons. Again, some sources differ, reporting a 13,000 deadweight tonnage figure.

Because of the convertability inherent in the "502" design, propulsion requirements were the cause of extensive study. Designed to steam at sustained sea speeds of 14 knots, the Shipping Board ordered these ships fitted with engines of sufficient reserve power to give them an easy 15 knots. The question of propulsion occupied the Shipping Board, marine engineers, naval architects, War Department and New York Shipbuilding Corporation for quite some time before all parties finally agreed on what motive power to fit into these important new ships. Quickly discounted were oil engines. There were no ocean-going passenger motorships to allow comparisons and American engine builders, loathe to support diesel machinery in any American ship, had no interest in retooling any of their facilities during wartime to produce innovative machinery for the Government's planned transports. The question of turbines, which had already proved themselves and were the machinery of choice for all fabricated ships building at the "Agency yards" at Hog Island and Harriman, Pennsylvania and at Newark Bay, New Jersey as well as for the big "535"s were considered, but in the end everyone settled on two sets of four cylinder triple-expansion reciprocating engines. That old fashioned machinery was designed to take steam from six single ended Scotch boilers working at 220 pounds Psi under forced draught. Each boiler was 15 feet 3 inches in mean diameter and 11 feet 6 inches long between heads, giving a total heating surface of about 16,000 square feet. For some reason the Shipping Board accepted such orthodox machinery for these important ships while providing more efficient turbine engines to scores of freighters like the 150 fabricated 5,075 deadweight ton "Sub Boats". No shortage of parts here, no limited manpower, the decision to fit triple expansion engines in these ships instead of giving them turbines relegated them forever to the middle tier among contemporary American ships, but the "502"s had the last laugh, lasting as long commercially under the U.S. flag as the best of the bigger "535"s. The "502s" worked hard for almost thirty years, "antiquated" machinery notwithstanding. Their up and down engines had four cylinders measuring 24 inches, 40.4 inches, 54 inches and 54 inches diameter by 45 inches stroke. The engine cylinders were mounted on four front and four back cast iron housings of box section. Fore and aft the cylinders were arranged as follows: low pressure, high pressure, intermediate pressure and low pressure. Only the high pressure cylinder was fitted with a liner. The high pressure and intermediate pressure cylinders each had one piston valve, while each of the low pressure cylinders had one double ported flat slide valve. The intermediate and low pressure valves had Lovekin assistant cylinders. There were two main condensers each independent and transforming.

On the question of fuel economy, the "502"s far exceeded Shipping Board expectations of their average daily consumption. Calculating operating costs on an estimate of only 37 tons of oil per day, when fully loaded, these ships averaged a daily consumption of 90 to 92 tons. It might not have been as bad as it seems for this figure allows speculation that graft and corruption extended to the engine departments as well. An old scam in the shipping business involves overpayments by the shipping company to oil companies with hefty kickbacks to the Chief Engineer. It works like this. The Chief Engineer signs for the delivery of a certain amount of oil, an amount in excess of what his ship really took. The owner or operator pays the oil company the full amount of its invoice (or risk legal action and possible arrest of the ship) which in turn shares the payment for nondelivered oil with cohorts aboard ship. Sometimes the scam extended into shoreside offices, sometimes not.

The listed cruising range of the unfinished "502"s was expected to be 12,000 miles, but figures indicated that actual range was somewhat less. The "502"s could bunker some 3,470 tons of fuel, which was fine on the North Atlantic and could carry the ship to Europe and see her home again. On the round the world service, each "502" class "President Liner" had to be re-fuelled three or four times, or as often as every forty days.

At least the Shipping Board accepted the cost of twin screws in each of the seven sister ships. Each propeller was of the three bladed, built up type, about 16 feet, 6 inches in diameter. On trials, some managed to achieve top speeds of 16.5 knots though the ships' contract speed was 14 knots, and that was the figure upon which the sisters's schedules were reckoned.

Electricity was furnished by three 50-kilowatt turbo generating sets of the latest type and an auxiliary lighting circuit, operated by a 25 volt storage battery was provided on Boat Deck to illuminate the boats and launching gear in case of emergency. The refrigerating plant was of the brine circulating system. Consisting of two machines each of about 10 ton capacity, each machine was self contained and included the compressor engine and all necessary apparatus. In connection with the steam heating system, a system of mechanical ventilation was fitted for the troop spaces. Steam coils were placed in the discharge ducts of the mechanical ventilating system, which was operated by electrically driven fans. Steam powered a "502"s windlass. Of the spur-gear type, triple geared, the windlass was located under the forecastle with the engine on the same bed.

Any good shipping man reading April 1919 descriptions of these intended transports could read between the lines and intuit that in these ships the Government was offering a series of passenger cargo vessels. Everything about the general arrangement plans of these proposed troopships looked ready for conversion to commercial purposes and converting the extant design into a serviceable merchant ship was easy. Follow the accompanying plans and see for yourself. Outside cabins topsides easily became quarters for ship's officers and passengers while the big 4 berth troop officer cabins on A Deck lent themselves into quick modification to First Class passenger cabins while their intended messroom gave way to the eventual passenger dining room. Plans for proposed troop accommodation on the lower decks suggested cargo stowage spaces given to other uses.

There could be little doubt. These ships would come available for commercial operation. With some paying passengers able to be berthed in Army officer accommodation and the rest of the troop accommodation spaces given over to freight, these ships looked to be big cargo carriers. And they were. The ruse of completing as troopships soon enough dropped, industry publications began to run articles introducing the ships while they were still incomplete. *Pacific Marine Review* wrote: "A very lavish equipment has been provided for the handling of cargo. General arrangement and deck plans showed no less than 34 winches and a similar number of booms arranged singly and at pairs on ten cargo masts"[7]. *Marine Engineering* said: "The equipment for handling cargo is unusually complete."[8] Further descriptions of the "502"'s referred to a cargo capacity in the area of 465,940 cubic feet (bale) or 496,000 cubic feet (grain). There was space for 52,300 cubic feet, or 1,200 tons of refrigerated cargo space.[9] For the use of her own passengers and crew, each "502" had 5,300 cubic feet of cold storage. Each of the seven ships carried her cargo in 8 cargo holds and tweendecks. The arrangement of the various compartments allowed the "502" six cargo holds forward and four abaft the engine spaces.

Dating back to their original conception of troopships, elaborate equipment was designed and fitted for rapid handling of cargo. Connected by heavy crossbeams were two sets of forward kingposts and one after set. Unconnected kingposts were positioned aftermost and another pair was amidships in the well space between forward and after deckhouses. Stopped to those 10 kingposts were thirty-two 6 ton booms worked by 26 winches. A heavy lift boom capable of a 30 ton lift was fitted in each ship. To facilitate cargo handling and arrange stowage, yet honor the desired safety concepts troopships needed, no less than 10 hatchways were fitted. Each regular cargo hold was reached through large hatches in all of the decks and each hatch was served by two cargo booms located at derrick posts, each boom being served by one of twenty single-drum single geared winches. Sixteen of those were 8.25 inches by 8 inches double cylinder single drum, single-geared reversible winches with one winch head on each winch, while the other four, two forward and two aft, were of the double geared, single-drum type, each with two large winch heads. Five of each "502"s' cargo hatches were 17 feet, 6 inches × 25 feet; one was 18 feet × 15 feet; another was 17 feet, 6 inches × 15 feet and two were 19 feet × 20 feet, all worked by at least two booms and winches. Each of the five larger hatches was worked by four booms and winches. Holds #6 and #7 had two hatchways each. In her deep tanks, a

---

[7] The actual number of booms and winches was rather less.

[8] April 1920 edition of *Marine Engineering*. page 265

[9] From an article from a British shipping magazine. Clipping in the ship's 901 file in RG 32 at National Archives.

"502" class steamer could carry a thousand tons of liquid cargo, and eventually coconut oil became the usual liquid commodity carried home to North America. The tanks were loaded through hatches #4 and #5, located in the split between the houses of the superstructure.

An identifying mark of Emergency Fleet Corporation/Shipping Board passenger tonnage was the lack of dedicated masts. On all three types of Government built passenger ship, the Type B "Hog Islander", the "535" and the "502"'s, whatever function a mast filled was performed by poles attached to the crossbeam connecting a pair of kingposts. On the "502", the foremast was a pole extended from the middle of the crossbeam of the second set of posts. Atop this crossbeam sat the crow's nest next to the pole extension. Unconnected kingposts were positioned midships, in the space between fore and aft houses, and aftermost. The mainmast was another pole, set atop the after connected kingposts. There was a reason behind this peculiar mast arrangement and it came from requirements of the War Department. Wartime and emergency demands for rapid cargo handling meant that cargo had to be handled as quickly as possible so a lot of hatches and a lot of gear was thought to make things go faster.

All intended accommodations for military as well as ship's officers were provided for above decks while most spaces on B and C Decks were designed to berth some 2,500 troops and a crew of naval gunners. Because of the large number of people the "502" was designed to carry, extra attention was paid to ventilation and heating. Once the Armistice of November 11, 1918 was signed, the course of their construction and eventual fitting changed to reflect the economic realities of peacetime. Thus did commercial instincts greatly alter expected passenger figures. To that end both the ships' cargo and living spaces were redesigned on orders of Shipping Board Division of Operations boss John H. Rosseter who took up a pencil and drew some of the plans himself. His plans were those ultimately chosen for the installation of First Class passenger accommodation. The results of the transition from design for war to design for peace were remarkable and the "502" ships were completed with very high class accommodations for a usual capacity of 78 First Class passengers. Initial estimates of a 92 man crew were upped substantially, and quarters were fitted for a crew of about 120 officers and men. Even that was not sufficient as crew numbers varied considerably over the years. Once the ships were downgraded to Cabin liners and passenger capacities increased, some of the "502"'s shipped crews numbering 143 officers and men. Had a 1921 scheme to employ two of them on a line to Spain worked out, each would have been required to comply with Spanish law and employ a Spanish physician, nurse, cook, assistant cook and two stewards. When the CENTENNIAL STATE was fitted to carry hundreds of Third Class passengers on the North Atlantic, several extra crew men were needed for the Steward's Department. Years later, when six of these ships worked for the military, they carried crews far larger than any commercial operator would employ.

Long before any of them was in any condition for launching or have any equipment with her name on it, the Shipping Board accepted names for these sisters. To be the WOODBURY seemed the destiny of hull number 2585, first of the class laid down. In sequential number through number 2591, subsequent hulls were to be named IASSUS, JADWIN, ICARIA, JAKIN, IDAS and IDMAN. By November 25, 1919 the Manager of the Ship Construction Division of the Shipping Board began to circulate memos advising of a new system of nomenclature. The Department of Shipping Information was informed: "In order to carry out the Corporation's desire of naming the large passenger and cargo vessels with a series of names similar to the state names used for the battleships . . . "[10] Thus did the ships gain their first new names. In honor of North Carolina, the intended WOODBURY would be christened OLD NORTH STATE. For Louisiana the IASSUS would instead be CREOLE STATE. Trading in the intended name JADWIN, hull number 2587 would honor New Hampshire as the GRANITE STATE. Instead of ICARIA, the fourth of the planned vessels would enter the water as the first of the clan, the PANHANDLE STATE, in honor of West Virginia. The intended JAKIN would go down the ways honoring Michigan as the WOLVERINE STATE. For Colorado the name CENTENNIAL STATE would stand in place of IDAS and finally Delaware would be recognized when the name IDMAN was dropped for the last of the seven ships and her name changed to BLUE HEN STATE. Accordingly, New York Shipbuilding was informed of these changed names in writing at the end of November.

Here is the order in which the ships were launched: OLD NORTH STATE, PANHANDLE STATE, CREOLE STATE, GRANITE STATE, WOLVERINE STATE, CENTENNIAL STATE and BLUE HEN STATE. That was neither the order in which they had been laid down nor was it the order in which they were completed and delivered. May 1922 brought them new names and they became PRESIDENT van BUREN, PRESIDENT MONROE, PRESIDENT HAYES, PRESIDENT POLK, PRESIDENT HARRISON, PRESIDENT ADAMS and PRESIDENT GARFIELD. The ships kept those names through December 1940. So fully associated with the round the world service had the "502"'s become on the round the world line that when six new ships were under construction to replace them, six of the "502"'s were renamed to allow the new ships to keep those familiar names on the line. Sentimental favorite because she was the first delivered to Dollar Line and made the first round the world trip, the PRESIDENT HARRISON retained her name. The other six were respectively renamed PRESIDENT FILLMORE, PRESIDENT BUCHANAN, PRESIDENT TYLER, PRESIDENT TAYLOR, PRESIDENT GRANT and PRESIDENT MADISON. Those last two names had long been carried by "535" class steamers. New names came to five of the "502"'s during the war. Captured by the Japanese, the PRESIDENT HARRISON was

---

[10] Memo Nov 25, 1919 from Manager, Construction Division. Copy in Construction files in RG 32 National Archives.

renamed KAKKO MARU before the name KACHIDOKI MARU was given her as she steamed towards an unplanned rendezvous with the American submarine PAMPANITO which sank her in 1944. Converted into Army hospital ships the PRESIDENT FILLMORE, ex PRESIDENT van BUREN and OLD NORTH STATE became MARIGOLD and the PRESIDENT BUCHANAN, ex PRESIDENT MONROE and PANHANDLE STATE became IRIS. HOWARD McCURDY was the name the PRESIDENT TYLER, ex PRESIDENT HAYES and CREOLE STATE was assigned while rebuilding for hospital service but she did not sail under that name. As the war ended she resumed service for the War Department as PRESIDENT TYLER. Becoming the Navy transport KENMORE was the PRESIDENT MADISON, the old PRESIDENT GARFIELD and original BLUE HEN STATE. When she, too, became a hospital ship, the Navy named her REFUGE. Once returned to civilian authorities, the surviving renamed "502"s resumed their "President" names—FILLMORE, BUCHANAN and MADISON.

Fully unexpected in Government owned tonnage were the extraordinary passenger accommodations in the "502"s. Of generous proportions and fitted to a very high quality were the quarters each ship had for less than 100 First Class passengers. The first five ships were delivered with only 78 First Class berths in 39 outside cabins. Every cabin was outside and had chiffoniers, wardrobes, electric fans, thermos bottles and mirrors. With beds for more were the CENTENNIAL STATE and BLUE HEN STATE which were completed with space for 82 First Class passengers.[11] With the passage of time the ship's passenger quarters were often modified and passenger capacity varied considerably at different points during the lengthy careers of the "502"s .

Cabin accommodation in all seven ships was of a very high standard, and the large number of private bathrooms was an indication of trends in American shipbuilding and standards required by American travelers. Always looking to increase possible revenues, passenger accommodations were increased when an upper berth was added to 37 cabins aboard each sister, giving the first five ships a First Class capacity of 115 passengers and the other two a capacity of 119 passengers. The reason two cabins did not get extra berths is simple. They were just too small to take any more furniture and already had an upper berth.

Hefty operating losses prompted the Shipping Board to consider ways to allow these ships additional revenue. Increasing passenger capacity was their best bet and the Board soon learned that they could add as many as 25 berths to these ships at little or no expense by berthing travelers in spare cabins on Promenade Deck in the forward house.[12] Up to nine cabins in this

---

[11] Per 1922 Annual Report of the United States Shipping Board.

[12] These rooms were not necessarily used by ship's officers and as spares because they were holdovers from the days when sufficient rooms had to be provided for senior Army officers who would be traveling in one of these ships.

section, some of them singles, all of them without facilities, and separated from the remainder of the passenger accommodation by the split in the superstructure were prepared for use by passengers in some of these sisters. Because there were sanitary facilities for men only, no women could be quartered here. Berthing only male travelers, this section was called "Bachelor Quarters". Once these rooms were given to the passenger department, berthing plans for the sisters began to differ, for not all of them offered all nine cabins to the public. As "Cabin Liners", with "Bachelor Quarters", the PRESIDENT GARFIELD, PRESIDENT ADAMS and PRESIDENT POLK offered 158 passenger berths. The first two sisters, the PANHANDLE STATE and the OLD NORTH STATE, never offered these cabins to passengers while on the London service. Because of the use of these cabins, slight differences arose among these otherwise identical sisterships and different deckplans were needed thereafter. Only later, under Dollar Line ownership, did those ships berth passengers here. The need to use cabins in this section proved that demand for passage in these ships was there, for when they began sailing for the Dollar Line, their passenger capacities were limited to their original First Class beds and numbers. Demand for space quickly outpaced availability and after a short while both "Bachelor Quarters" and upper berths were available again.

During the winter of 1922 the five sisters working on the Atlantic were downgraded to "Cabin" liners in the expectation that such a move with its congruent lowering of passenger tariffs would win the ships greater favor with travelers. Turning the ships into "Cabin" liners was easy enough. All they needed were more upper berths in the cabins that could take them. Passenger capacity in the PANHANDLE STATE and OLD NORTH STATE increased to 135 when an extra upper berth was placed in the 20 Saloon Deck passenger cabins. Giving them a Cabin Class capacity of just over 150 passengers, extra berths were added to all but the two tiny cabins in the GRANITE STATE, CENTENNIAL STATE and BLUE HEN STATE. Using every berth in "Bachelor's Quarters", the BLUE HEN STATE had as many as 176 Cabin Class berths, but she had yet to sail on a commercial voyage. Once she started trading, she never carried that many on a single voyage. Nothing else was really needed to downgrade these ship's passenger accommodations from "First Class" to "Cabin Class". Now United States Lines needed only to reissue sales and publicity literature, sailing schedules and rate folders, substituting the word "Cabin" for "First" class.[13]

Almost every author mentioning Steerage, or, Third Class, passenger accommodation in the "502" cites a different supposed capacity figure for that class and none of them jives with anything submitted by the ships' owners and/or operators. Not even the Shipping Board could get its heads together on this score, using different figures in different publications. Thus for over

---

[13] Steamship company issued berthing plans for these ships showed the various cabin arrangements available in this section and are the only way to trace these minor details.

fifty years the subject of Third Class accommodations in the "502"'s has been a mystery. Figures of 400, 450, 596, 600 and 650 Third Class passengers have all been reported by different authors, each of whom seems to have accepted a single instance and none seems to have delved deep enough into the subject to come up with the right answer. Fitted in several of the ships, it was never advertised in the United States nor was it probably much more than a temporary measure in some of these ships working the North Atlantic. Towards the end of 1920 the Shipping Board decided to withdraw the PANHANDLE STATE and OLD NORTH STATE from the London service as soon as two more "502"'s could replace them. The older ships would then be allocated to run in the Spanish trade for the New York and Cuba Mail Steamship Company. On that service they would need cheap berths so the Shipping Board's Design Department got to work and quickly developed two different sets of plans for steerage accommodations for "502"'s. At least two sets of plans for Third Class accommodations were drawn by Carl Petersen. One set of plans was for a "closed steerage" for 450 passengers, the other for an "open steerage" for 650. Thought more accepting of the less private and more spartan "open" steerage because it carried correspondingly lower tariffs, the Spanish trade might have done well with "502"'s so equipped. By early March Commander Gatewood had made the final decision about the installation of Third Class spaces in the CENTENNIAL STATE and BLUE HEN STATE. Such accommodations would be installed in those ships after delivery to the New York and Cuba Mail Steamship Company. But in April 1921, just when the last two "502"'s, the CENTENNIAL STATE and BLUE HEN STATE were nearing completion, New York and Cuba Mail withdrew from the triangular trade from New York to Spain, Cuba and Mexico. There was no longer any reason to fit "open" steerage in those ships.

Through the accident of timing, workmen were installing steerage accommodations in the CENTENNIAL STATE when New York and Cuba Mail abandoned the North Atlantic. That's why that was the only one of the seven ships to enter service with two classes of passenger accommodations, debuting on the London line with berths for 78 First and 159 Third Class passengers. Within months six more beds were added to First Class to increase her capacity to 84 in that class. While the ship was at Todd Shipyards in New York harbor her Third Class capacity was also increased. The Shipping Board need hardly have bothered to spend money to increase her Third Class capacity for she rarely carried more than a few Third Class passengers on any single voyage. For reasons neither explained nor comprehensible, the CENTENNIAL STATE was finally equipped with 596 Third Class berths. Curiously, the usual capacity figure given for that class in the "502"'s is 450. Because the BLUE HEN STATE was not ready for delivery until well after the Ward Line withdrew from the Spanish trade, no steerage fitted in her at that time.

Also frustrating any attempt to trace the history of these seven ships is the lack of accommodation plans for Third Class published by their commercial operators. However, some shipping magazines printed plans for such quarters in 1922. Reproduced in this chapter, those represent the big Third Class planned for the CENTENNIAL STATE which was at least partially fitted by the Morse Dry Dock Company. Then there was Third Class in the BLUE HEN STATE, a class of accommodations fitted at Robbins Dry Dock at Brooklyn after the ship arrived at New York from her builders' yard. A third sister fitted to carry Third Class passengers on the Atlantic was the PRESIDENT POLK. Still named GRANITE STATE when the Shipping Board withdrew her from the San Francisco—Calcutta line, she was equipped with Third Class quarters and given her "President" name before joining the London line in the spring of 1922.

It may also be argued that Third Class in the five sisters on the North Atlantic was removed in favor of cargo spaces before their September 1923 sale but since cargo offerings were usually pretty poor, the ships may well have retained but not used them. This is less a matter of conjecture than deduction since passenger figures provided in voyage reports for these ships don't mention steerage passengers in any of the London line "502"'s but the CENTENNIAL STATE/PRESIDENT ADAMS. It is truly a mystery to which must be added the effect of draconian cuts in immigration into the United States, bread and butter of the steerage carriers.

None of the three "502" sisters assigned to work on Pacific Mail's Calcutta line left the builders yard with Third Class accommodations but were so equipped before beginning their maiden voyages to Calcutta. Looking to capture a share of the "Asiatic" steerage trade to and from Manila especially, Pacific Mail suggested equipping those "502"'s with "Oriental steerage", the most elementary and spartan sort of passenger accommodation imaginable. Winning the enthusiastic support of the Shipping Board because such quarters were both inexpensive to install but able to yield a good profit, the CREOLE STATE, WOLVERINE STATE and GRANITE STATE were fitted with steerage accommodations for 246 passengers at West Coast yards shortly after their maiden arrivals at San Francisco. Limited to the most basic facilities with few permanent berths or bulkheads and no public rooms worthy of the name, "Oriental steerage" was retained aboard the ships long after Pacific Mail handed them back to the Shipping Board. There is no question that while operating for Pacific Mail Steamship Company those three ships featured both First and Third Class accommodations. Inspired by the accommodations fitted at New York into the recently completed CENTENNIAL STATE, the subject of Third Class accommodations in the three "502"'s in the Pacific was finally addressed during the summer of 1921. Would that the installation of Third Class in the sisterships working the Pacific could have resulted from the waving of a magic wand and the intonation of a few magic words. Responsible to too many voices, the Shipping Board generated enough paperwork on any question to cover itself many times over. Installation of steerage quarters yielded a good many typed and cabled words. May 5th brought the Washington headquarters of the Shipping Board and

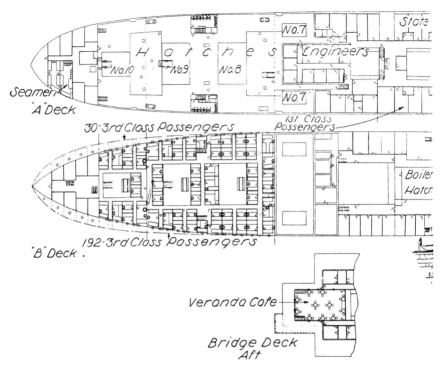

Three months after Ward Line dropped the Spanish service *Marine Review* printed this, the only known published third class plan for a "502". Such accommodations were likely the third class of the CENTENNIAL STATE. Author's collection.

the Philadelphia office of Construction and Repair a telegram from San Francisco District Manager William Chisholm who requested installation of 200 Third Class berths to be fitted into each ship's No. 8 tweendecks at a per ship cost of $29,000.00. Commander Gatewood responded on May 7th with a telegram and a set of plans for that space showing how 232 berths could be fitted in there, adding that it would take each ship three weeks to have such berths installed. Commenting that Pacific Mail, the Division of Operations and the Pacific District office in San Francisco agreed that the service then operated by the three ships required additional steerage space, Chisholm waited for the "go-ahead". That same month of May as well as June 1921 brought Shipping Board personnel plenty of paperwork on the subject of increasing Third Class accommodations in the CREOLE STATE, GRANITE STATE and WOLVERINE STATE.

Installation of 230 additional berths in tweendeck compartments at a cost

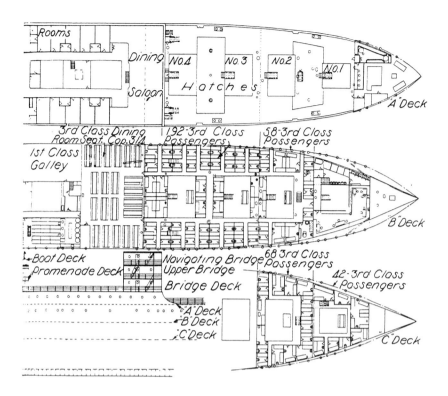

of $29,000.00 was authorized, but it seems that only the CREOLE STATE and WOLVERINE STATE had those berths added. Even now it is unclear whether or not those 230 berths would have been in addition to 246 berths installed between maiden arrival at San Francisco and their first departures for Calcutta. Records of the movements of the GRANITE STATE show that she was not in port long enough for any such work to have been undertaken, and of course, before entering service on the Atlantic, she had a modern closed steerage fitted at Brooklyn. When the Shipping Board modified the Pacific itinerary served by the CREOLE STATE and WOLVERINE STATE and limited them to an area east of Manila, they suggested an intention to increase the number of steerage berths in each ship, but financial results of each ship were so miserable the idea never proceeded beyond talk, paperwork and a few items in the shipping press.

Availability of Third Class berths was one reason two of the sisters were

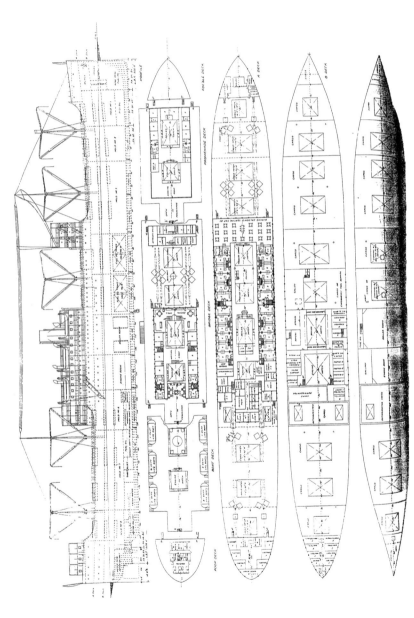

General arrangement plan of the "502"'s as built. Notice that the aft house atop bridge deck has grown taller than that intended in the original troop transport configuration. Author's collection.

allocated to Swayne & Hoyt to work the Pacific-Argentine-Brazil Line. A few tantalizing references speak of a Chinese Third Class aboard "502" class ships during their days under Dollar Line ownership, too, but no reliable confirmation has turned up to satisfy the curiosity of a scholarly observer. Any Third Class space in the "502"s was said to have been removed in favor of cargo spaces by 1924 but again, that must be considered conjecture for there is ample evidence that when operating round-trip transPacific voyages, Dollar Line "502"s brought steerage passengers to California and a few items mentioned Chinese steerage in the "502"s. Dollar Line arranged Third Class accommodations for Chinese, Japanese and Philippine passengers on ships in the transPacific service, but since the "502"s worked around the world, there would be no westbound demand for the traditional "Asiatic steerage" then common. Who can say for sure?[14] There was plenty of evidence, though, that some officers and crew in at least one of the "502"s ran a smuggling operation, providing transportation to Chinese nationals attempting illegal immigration into the United States. Discovered under the duress of a major fire that almost destroyed the PRESIDENT POLK at New York in October 1924, the men involved lost their jobs, but no one believed that was the end of such antics aboard the "502" type "President" liners.

No matter whether the "502"s cabin accommodation was labelled First or Cabin Class, cabin passengers occupied identical spaces designed by John H. Rosseter. Ranging over three decks, Upper Promenade Deck, Promenade Deck and Saloon (or "A") Deck, arrangements for passengers followed the relatively new, highly successful formula for intermediate passenger carriers. A plan perfected in the opening years of the present century by the Hamburg American Line and United Fruit Company, the all important passenger Dining Room was situated forward on the lowest of the three decks with the Lounge just above and either a veranda or Smoke Room aft. Ships with a veranda often featured a Smoke Room aft on the highest deck of the superstructure. The split superstructure of the "502"s imposed a slight variation on this standard theme.

On the ships' printed deckplans, public rooms seem small but were quite adequate for the limited numbers of passengers originally carried. Originally serving as the venue for most social gatherings aboard these sisters, perhaps the most interesting public space in these compact liners was the Veranda Cafe. Extending aft beyond the after end of the main house, the room was built with no after bulkhead, allowing it to function as an indoor-outdoor room. To afford protection in cold or rainy weather a removable screen was provided. Extending to the sides of the hull on Upper Promenade Deck, a 95 foot long and 8 foot wide glass enclosed promenade extended the full

---

[14] Nonetheless, there are a very few references to steerage in the Dollar Line "502"s. It seems to me that such spaces did exist but because they were not available for sale to Americans at any time, Dollar Line just kept quiet on this score. Grace Line is an example of a company advertising "First Class only" but in fact many of their passenger ships had at least limited numbers of steerage berths.

length of either side of the house on that deck. Abaft the house was open deck space. Enclosing port, starboard and forward thwartships promenades allowed greater advantage to be made of limited space. Unfortunately this provision of covered spaces further spoiled the appearance of these ungainly-looking ships.

Within, there were originally nine single bedded passenger cabins surrounding the forward machinery casing on three sides. Finished in white with mahogany trim, those cabins measured 9 feet 3 inches by 8 feet, with 7 feet 3 inches for headroom. Original furnishings in each included single beds of square metal tubing enameled to harmonize with other decorative touches of those rooms like their mahogany dressing tables, wardrobes and lavatory. Each room also had a sofa bed for the second passenger. All of those rooms were carpeted. Not only in this section of cabins but throughout the fleet of "502"s, all passenger blankets had the ship's name prominently stitched on. Later, under Dollar ownership, as the original blankets wore out and needed replacement, they were replaced by blankets with the Dollar Line emblem. On Upper Promenade Deck, the main foyer separated the cabin area from the Smoke Room, a room panelled in fine woods. That in the PANHANDLE STATE was panelled in fumed oak and decorated with mission style furniture. Beamed ceilings stood above tiled floor while the focal point of the masculine decor in each Smoke Room aboard the "502"s was an electric fireplace flanked by upholstered seats at the center of the forward side. Affording additional privacy to intimate groups, the sides of the room were divided into alcoves. By extending a bit forward of the machinery casing, the Smoke Room avoided an oblong shape. Just off the entrance on port side was a pantry and a storage room, spaces eventually converted into a 3 berth

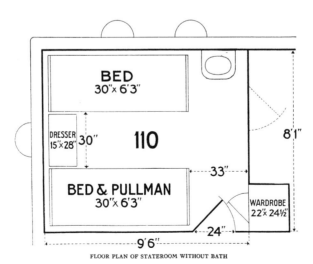

FLOOR PLAN OF STATEROOM WITHOUT BATH

Author's collection.

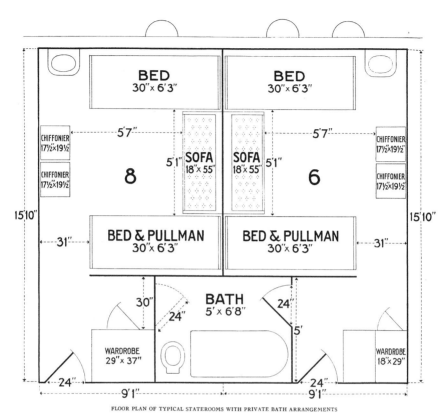

BED
30"× 6'3"

BED
30"× 6'3"

CHIFFONIER
17½×19½

CHIFFONIER
17½×19½

5'7"

5'7"

CHIFFONIER
17½×19½

CHIFFONIER
17½×19½

5'1" SOFA
18'× 55"

SOFA
18'× 55" 5'1"

8

6

15'10"

15'10"

31"

BED & PULLMAN
30"× 6'3"

BED & PULLMAN
30"× 6'3"

31"

30"

24"

BATH
5' × 6'8"

24"

5'

WARDROBE
29"× 37"

WARDROBE
18'×29"

24"

24"

9'1"

9'1"

FLOOR PLAN OF TYPICAL STATEROOMS WITH PRIVATE BATH ARRANGEMENTS

Author's collection.

cabin. The nearby Foyer was furnished to be used as a sitting room, as foyers so often were in smaller liners. A curved staircase in the foyer gave descent to the Promenade Deck where covered deck circled the house. Furnished either in Federal or Adam styles, which are very similar—one American, the other British, of generally contemporary periods, was a Social Room, forward. Although they were quite small, and not much more than extensions of staircase landings, these Lounges were splendid rooms. With walls painted ivory marked by fine woodwork and mahogany trim,architectural detail imparted a feeling of refinement unexpected aboard vessels of otherwise modest proportions. Each Social Room featured a piano and musicales on many evenings attracted a fair number of passengers.

Decorative focal point in each ship was a painted and carved ballustraded staircase leading below along the after bulkhead. Indicating an expected demand to come, the large number of cabins with attached private baths identified a trend in American shipbuilding towards fitting American passenger carriers with the equipment the high standards increasingly required by ordinary American travelers.Along either passageway were five cabins, each fitted for up to three passengers. The two forwardmost, one on either side, had private facilities. The other cabins were arranged with a bathroom between each pair, and could be booked with either, both, or neither cabin. Instead of port holes in the promenade deck house, rectangular cottage windows of novel design arranged with a narrow stationary upper sash and large movable lower sash permitted clear vision by avoiding obstruction of the old style rail.

Located at the forward end of Saloon Deck where air ports could be fitted on three sides, the passengers' Dining Saloon was a room big enough to seat 84 people at a time. A "U" shaped apartment in each ship, decorated glazed sashes varying in design among the sisterships disguised the portholes but still permitted plenty of natural light and air to enter the room. When the air outside was cold, ports remained shut and the ship's Thermotank ventilation system forced hot air into the place to keep passengers and staff toasty warm. Each a showplace of American decor, carved columns and fine marquetry set a classical architectural tone while Chippendale (or Hepplewhite, depending upon the ship) chairs around small tables set with the crispest of snow white linens topped with logoed steamship china and silver stood ready to serve any diner. In white and mahogany trim and furnishings, the passenger Dining Saloon in the PANHANDLE STATE expressed an American Colonial atmosphere while decor in Dining Rooms in the other "502"s differed mainly by nuance to afford a certain uniformity of ambiance throughout this fleet of seven ships. Served by experienced stewards, food and drink came from a nearby pantry located above the main galley, located one deck below on "B" deck.

The greater width of Saloon ("A") deck permitted larger cabins here and the twenty rooms situated aft of the Dining Room were each 9 feet 6 inches long (fore and aft) and 16 feet wide. Furnished with one lower, one sofa bed, and two upper berths for additional passengers if desired, the ten cabins on port mirrored those on starboard. Like those passenger cabins on the decks above, "A" Deck cabins were finished in white and trimmed in mahogany but the larger area of these rooms permitted furniture a bit more elaborate. The four forwardmost on either side were arranged with one bathroom for each pair of cabins. The next two each had private baths, and the after four cabins again had one bath for every pair. As opposed to the fetish today's cruise lines have of basing rates on a cabin's altitude, charging more the higher up you sleep, until the Ferris refits of 1925 for the PRESIDENT POLK and 1929 for three others, the most expensive cabins in the "502"s were these twenty outside rooms. Coming in at about 150 square feet, these were the largest of the original cabins, and carried a heftier price tag for that reason. Irrelevant was their location on the lowest passenger deck. After all, cabin size on the two decks above averaged a pretty tight 80 square feet but in fairness, furniture in every cabin was arranged to take fullest advantage of limited space.

As criticized as they were for their ugly external appearance, they were lavishly praised for the beauty and fittings of their Cabin accommodation. Countless were the "oohs" and "ahhs" of both visitor and first time passenger touring for the first time the passenger spaces aboard these American ships. No one should have been surprised for little expense had been spared in furnishing these ships. Counting on quality, the Shipping Board bought all furniture for the seven ships from New York's famed W. & J. Sloane and most furnishings from Gimbels Brothers Department Store. Opting to patronize such high-end stores did cost the Shipping Board quite a bit of money, but the results justified the added expense, for the ships' interiors were of high quality and the accommodations beautiful enough and of sufficient class to please the discriminating traveler. Officials agreed that only high grade accommodations could attract a share of the traveling public. Even choosing the furniture did not get the accommodation spaces finished on time. Frustrating the planned progress of both Shipping Board and New York Ship and jeopardizing delivery dates, joiners at the Camden yard went out on strike in June 1920.

It soon occurred to Shipping Board and ships' operators that the limited passenger accommodations of these ships was something of a mistake. As early as 1921 Shipping Board naval architect Carl Petersen drew up plans for alterations and modifications to their passenger accommodations. To further increase their passenger capacity at little or no expense to the Shipping Board, several Promenade Deck cabins in the forward house, separate from the rest of the passenger accommodation, were soon taken for passenger use in some of these ships. There were as many as nine of these cabins, though some of the sisterships offered only seven. Some of those were single cabins. Because sanitary facilities were available for men only, the cabins in this section were known as "Bachelor Quarters". These cabins were originally officers cabins. A "502" with these cabins available could take up to 25 more passengers than the other ships. Because of these cabins, slight differences arose among these otherwise identical sisterships.

Though by no means an error of the highest order, it was soon abundantly clear that though extremely well fitted, these ships were too small and too slow to compete for the true First Class trade. But officialdom works slowly and it took quite a while before the Shipping Board accepted a most obvious solution, conversion of First Class to Cabin. Credit Carl Peterson for drawing the plans for the ships' additional Cabin accommodations. His plans were also used to convert the "502"s on the Atlantic into Cabin liners during the winter of 1922. With an extra upper berth placed in the 20 Saloon ("A") Deck cabins in the PANHANDLE STATE and OLD NORTH STATE, capacity in those ships was increased to 135 cabin passengers. Soon afterwards, two extra berths were added to all but two cabins in the GRANITE STATE, CENTENNIAL STATE and BLUE HEN STATE. This gave them a Cabin Class capacity of just over 150 passengers. The only additional alterations required to downgrade their accommodation from "First" to "Cabin" class consisted primarily of reprinting sales literature, sailing schedules and rate folders, substituting the word "Cabin" for "First" class. The passenger capacity in the "502"s varied quite a bit during their careers but on the North Atlantic only the BLUE HEN STATE ever had as many as 176 Cabin Class berths. And though none of the "502"s ever had more than that number of permanent cabin berths, none of them ever carried quite nearly that many on any Atlantic voyage in either direction.[15]

Ignoring the ships' splendid accommodations to concentrate their frustrations with the ships looks, contemporary observers never shrank from voicing their opinions on the appearance of the "502"s. Even as her screws pushed her nearer by the minute to London in September 1920, British observers commented in print that the brand new PANHANDLE STATE was "perhaps the ugliest ship afloat". And though the "502"s were very ugly as built, a number of eye-catching features gave these seven sisters an undeniable appeal, even if it was only the patriotic Shipping Board shield each displayed below her bridge wing. After the PRESIDENT POLK burned out in 1925, Theodore Ferris devoted quite a bit of thought to aesthetic considerations. Awarded the contract to design the reconditioning and improvement of the damaged liner, he joined the two houses of the split superstructure together. That gave her a well proportioned upperworks dominated by two partially glass enclosed promenade decks, while a thicker funnel topped with an Admiralty cap worked to the ship's further aesthetic advantage. That did the trick. The ungainliness of her emergency origin mellowed into a handsome American combiliner with a smart contemporary flair. Using much the same plans, Dollar Line improved three more "502"s in 1929 under the terms of the Jones-White Act and would have taken one more of the remaining three for such modifications in 1930 had business been better. The refitted sisterships were certainly the best looking of all 35 of the Government standard built intended troop transports.

Without altering either the mood or the style of the ship's accommodation, Ferris' hand greatly improved passenger spaces in the refitted "502"s. Of a high standard from the beginning, Ferris modifications to the "502"s was a triumph, if only because it was so simple and logical. Joining the separated houses of the superstructure produced two long promenade decks on either side. For aesthetic reasons Ferris had them glassed in for 40% of their lengths on Upper Promenade and for half of their lengths along Promenade Deck. High grade passenger quarters in the form of a quartette of suites were built at the forward end of Upper Promenade Deck. Situated behind the thwartship promenade with views out over the bows, two were outboard and two were built on the centerline. Below was a similar arrangement of high end

---

[15]Only steamship company-issued berthing plans for these ships show the various cabin arrangements and subsequent editions indicate to the observer any changes. Such plans offer the only way to trace these minor details.

cabins, but here, the suites were only on the centerline and outboard were two doubles, each with private facilities. During repairs, cabins gutted by fire were rearranged and additional cabins built in the new midships section on Upper Promenade Deck. Six of those were large cabins of some 200 square feet in area, each of which shared a bath with another cabin. Twelve other cabins were built without facilities.

Almost totally reconfigured was Promenade Deck. A new lounge was built midships. This was a real, separate apartment—not an extension of a lobby like the original. Ten new cabins were built on that deck. Only the popular Veranda Cafe remained as before.

Relocated half a deck below its original position was the Dining Saloon, now entered by descending a prominent central staircase from a foyer above. Enlarged and reconfigured to seat 142 persons at one sitting, the new Dining Saloon was made possible when the well between the separate houses of the superstructure was filled in. Further aft, several more cabins were built abaft the original ten cabins on either side and the doctor was returned to his original cabin on portside aft. On starboard side, forward, a new pair of cabins with a shared bath were reserved for the Chief Purser and Chief Steward. All upper berths were removed during this time of repairs and reconditioning.

Redelivered by the yard after these extensive renovations to her super-structure, a refitted "502" was actually about 2,000 gross tons larger than before, but using every trick in the shipowners book, subtracting for every last possible item American rules permitted, Dollar Lines was able to register her at only 10,500 gross tons, a figure slightly less than her original gross tonnage. This lower certified tonnage saved money on registry fees and port charges. Advertising the ship's displacement rather than gross tonnage to the general public no prestige was forfeited.

Taking advantage of the ship improvement provisions of the Jones-White Act of 1928, Dollar Line applied for loans for betterments to several "502"s. Ultimately on May 29, 1929 the Shipping Board authorized loans for the reconditioning of four sisters. The Construction Loan Fund financed $257,000 of the conversion costs for the PRESIDENT HARRISON. $250,000 for the PRESIDENT GARFIELD, and $425,829 for the PRESIDENT ADAMS (both for improvements and to repair the damages suffered in her recent ground-ing). They also allowed the Dollar Line an additional $250,000 to refurbish one more sister, at Dollar Line's choice. That would probably have been the PRESIDENT HAYES, but the actual whereabouts of the three other ships at the time any refit could start would have been the deciding factor. That would leave only two "502"s in their "as built" condition and give Dollar Line five improved "502"s. Using the standard repayment formula allowed under the Jones-White Act which authorized the construction loans in the first place, repayment terms included interest at three percent, with the loan to be repaid over a period of 15 years. As late as December 8, 1930 plans to upgrade the accommodation spaces of a fifth sister were under discussion, but with two flagships building for the transPacific service, the former MAN-CHURIA and MONGOLIA on the round the world line, business didn't warrant increasing accommodations in another "502".

Using Ferris' plans of the PRESIDENT POLK as a guide, workers at the yards of the Newport News Shipbuilding and Drydock Company at Newport News, Virginia refurbished the PRESIDENT HARRISON between early February and May 1929. Externally indistinguishable from the PRESIDENT POLK but a far cry now from the PRESIDENT HAYES, PRESIDENT MONROE and PRESIDENT van BUREN, she was now a handsome liner of some 12,000 gross tons, yet like her refitted sister, was registered at some tons less than her prerefit 10,504 gross tons. Fewer suites were fitted than in the PRESIDENT POLK, but after her refit, the PRESIDENT HARRISON had very comfortable accommodations for a maximum of 158 First Class passengers. She then rejoined her fleetmates and returned to work. Refloated after a severe stranding while inbound into Cristobal in January 1929, the PRESIDENT ADAMS was sent home to San Francisco for full repairs and her refit. Before many months had passed the PRESIDENT GARFIELD was similarly rebuilt. Proud of the accommodations in their refitted ships, Dollar Line shared photographs and descriptions of the new spaces with the trade and general press. Great attention to detail marked the whole of the passenger accommodation and that in the PRESIDENT ADAMS was designed by San Francisco's A.F. Marten Company. That June *Marine Review* published seven pictures around the headline "New Passenger Accommodations on Steamship PRESIDENT ADAMS." Now in modified French style was the Lounge. Under a skylight, its walls were now painted a pale brown or cafe au lait with architectural trim highlighted in gold leaf. Hung from cornices of gold leaf were draperies of peach damask. Sparing little expense, sofas were covered in silk velvet. Decorative focal point of this room aboard the PRESIDENT ADAMS was a console table under an elaborately carved walnut mirror highlighted in gold leaf. Enlarged during the refit was the all important Smoking Room whose walls were now finished in light artichoke green around a floor of medium red brown and terra cotta Goodrich rubber tiles. As before the focal point of the room was the fire place. Flanking the "Magic Coal" grate was a handsome Nubian lion above a hand carved walnut mantle and black and gold marble facing. Invitingly placed were big, hand made chairs of carved walnut covered with soft, top-grain green morocco leather. Retaining the delicate decor of the dining room, designers of the refit wanted to create the feeling of intimacy of the dining room in a private home. In the ship's new dining room, light tan walls stood in contrast to drapes of aquamarine taffeta. Beautiful were the suites and cabins de luxe where broadloom carpeting in solid green shades lent rich tones to private quarters. Siena and gold were the principal colors of upholstery used in cabins while walnut was the preferred wood for all cabin furniture.

Passenger comfort and convenience were the keynotes in the accommodation in these seven sisterships. Nothing *outré,* nothing ostentatious, nothing out of the ordinary . . . just the good solid comfort expected and demanded in an upper class American hotel sufficed designers, builders, outfitters and Shipping Board in the execution of the living spaces for passengers in the "502"s. Laboring against the rigors of American shipping policies as well as Prohibition and the Depression itself, the "502"s made a great name for themselves. Most of their passengers were left very satisfied. While more than a few people developed a genuine fondness for their ungainly "President", goose bumps rose on the skin and hearts beat faster in others who developed strong emotional links to the first "Stately President" liners.

THE "502"'S ON THE ATLANTIC

After its 1916 inception the Shipping Board became increasingly involved in the day-to-day operation of its own tonnage. From prominent American shipowners came constant advice about Government owned tonnage in general and steady streams of advice about the unfinished seven sisterships in particular. Plenty of applications for their eventual allocation came to the Washington offices of the Board and the Philadelphia offices of the Division of Operations as well. In 1920 and 1921, no less than 97 different firms were operating ships for the Shipping Board on over 330 different services. Then heading the Division of Operations of the Shipping Board Emergency Fleet Corporation, John Rosseter, consummate American shipping man, went to great lengths to put American flag passenger ships to work on the world's seas and oceans, proposing a number of services, most of them new. Excluding none of the ships still under construction, he proposed the assignment of one of the new "502" class ships to his suggested "Route F", a service to be established from New York to North African Mediterranean ports. He proposed to partner the "502" with the NANSEMOND, formerly the Hamburg American Line steamer PENNSYLVANIA. For "Route K", to the west coast of Africa, he proposed using two of these untested "502" type ships. He called for three more of them to be placed on "Route L", a service to Cape Town. Such a three ship service to South Africa was eventually intended by the American South African Line, for which they ordered three of the finest passenger cargo ships ever conceived, the AFRICAN COMET class, through the Maritime Commission's shipbuilding scheme. The three ships were built but never sailed commercially, though the AFRICAN COMET came within days of delivery to the American South African Line. No American company ever did manage to get three passenger ships on that run at the same time. One remaining "502" could serve on any other route where her speed and capacity could be best used. Not much ever came of Rosseter's December 1919 plan. That was too bad, for implementation of his highly rational and well thought out scheme would have allowed the American Merchant Marine a real head start over the steamship operations of other nations just now returning to commercial shipping after the traumae of war. Quite possibly it might have brought the American flag to a position of predominance not known since the 1850's. At very least it might have silenced the haughty old cry "No one travels in an American ship."

Even when requisitioned ships were released to private owners the Shipping Board didn't relinquish as much as an iota of its sweeping powers over American merchant shipping, so much of which was performed with government owned tonnage, anyway. Keep in mind though that when it established the Shipping Board in 1916 to accumulate an American Merchant Marine to suit the nation's commercial transportation requirements during a time of war abroad, Congress had not intended the creation of a Government operated Merchant Marine. Once peace returned, Congress still didn't want to follow the Canadian model and get the Government into the steamship business. Congress felt that Government did not belong in competition with American citizens and corporate interests. Congress went further than having numerous members go on record in opposition to Government operation of merchant ships. It explicitly commented on the matter in its 1920 maritime legislation, the famed and often derided Jones Act. Once the emergencies of war and civilian relief were over, American shipowners wasted little time banding together to try to force the government out of the shipping business.

Against a policy mandated by Congress refuting Government ownership and involvement in commercial shipping, the Shipping Board had grown increasingly involved in the day-to-day operation of its own tonnage. Clamoring for the government to retreat from the shipping business, American shipowners banded together to lobby against the Shipping Board and soon enough prevailed, eliciting an April 1920 promise from the United States Shipping Board to discontinue management of its merchant vessels in short order. Never mind that its own Division of Operations was highly effective and a damn sight more efficient than any number of private concerns, the Shipping Board would bend to the will of vested interests. At that point the Shipping Board invited further applications from private operators who wanted to manage and operate Shipping Board vessels. This all happened while the "502" class ships were building.

Brainchild of Colonel Francis Mayer, an entrepreneur and a judge who made a fortune transporting livestock to France for the military during the late war was the United States Mail Steamship Company. For reasons perhaps forever buried under inches of dust and perhaps in exchange of occasional gratuities,[1] the United States Shipping Board had enormous faith in Mayer and his shipping ventures so far, the France & Canada Steamship Corporation. Even before America's 1917 entry into World War I, Mayer's newly established France & Canada Corporation made money transporting cattle and horses for the French government. During and immediately after the war, the France & Canada Corporation managed quite a lot of Shipping Board tonnage. Sensing profits from another direction in the shipping business in 1919, Mayer established the "Swiftsure Line" to operate tankers.

Despite winning the immediate favor of the Shipping Board, Colonel Mayer had better luck trading in livestock during wartime than in the op-

---

[1] I speak here of gratuities like a $40,000 gift given by "unnamed" donors to Shipping Board member Thomas Bolling, brother-in-law of President Woodrow Wilson. Late 1920 brought investigation of his conduct by the Shipping Board who found him innocent of wrongdoing. Curiously enough, there was no mention of impropriety.

eration of ships during peacetime. The Shipping Board made no bones about which horse they were backing: "It is the committed policy of the Board to facilitate the expansion of the US Mail Company. This can be best accomplished by getting ships in service promptly in sufficient number to assure regular and dependable sailings, and incidentally revenue to offset the large overhead and reconditioning expenses in which they are involved."[2] Thus having the ear of the Shipping Board, Colonel (or Judge) Mayer gained the support of the Commissioners for his plan to fill with American flag tonnage the void left by the absence of North German Lloyd's North Atlantic passenger fleet. Without acute mental exhaustion anyone interested in this aspect of maritime history could deduce just where he proposed to find the American passenger ships . . . from the United States Shipping Board. He reached an agreement with them to establish several trans-Atlantic passenger and freight services on May 29,1920. Highly ambitious and with a voracious appetite for tonnage, Mayer's United States Mail Steamship Company won possession and operative custody of at least thirteen ships over the next year and a quarter. Obtaining publicly owned tonnage either under charter or purchase, the new concern had an enviable relationship with the Shipping Board which granted unusually favorable terms to its "favorite" steamship company.

The bulk of tonnage coming into the company's fleet were ex-German passenger ships no longer required by the War Department for the transportation of American soldiers. The evidence shows that US Mail looked at every one of the 40 some odd "ex-Germans" before turning their covetous glances at the passenger ships building for the United States Shipping Board Emergency Fleet Corporation in American yards. With encouragement of the Shipping Board the US Mail Line planned to establish a passenger and cargo line between New York and London, expecting that moderately equipped vessels with economically priced fares could attract considerable custom. They had no particular ships in mind it seems, yet considered the incomplete "502" class ships for the proposed one class passenger and cargo service between New York and London. Since no "ex-German" liner then available was suitable for the proposed service, the Shipping Board entertained notions of allocating the first two of the "502"'s to the company and encouraged them to submit an application for them. US Mail applied for allocation of at least two, if not more of the "502"'s. No one seemed to notice that this proposed service was essentially a duplication of a Shipping Board cargo line managed since 1918 by the venerable J. H. Winchester Company. Responding to a 1924 Shipping Board invitation to resident operators to name the Government services in their hands, Winchester named their Shipping Board services the American Merchant Line. That U.S. Mail Line application was accepted but was not made official until emission of the req-

---

[2] August 14, 1919 memorandum from Director of Operations Paul Foley to Shipping Board Chairman Admiral W.S. Benson.

uisite legal documents several months after the completion of the "502" steamer PANHANDLE STATE.[3] At that time the Shipping Board was actually willing to allocate three new "502"s, delivering them upon completion to United States Mail.

Despite a heavy demand for inexpensive transatlantic space in the post World War I era, the United States Mail Steamship Company was an extraordinary failure. A line whose chief had big plans for the future, only ten ships ever actually sailed under the United States Mail Steamship Company houseflag. Blame its failure on several major factors. Inexperience in passenger and freight shipping coupled with the refusal of the Shipping Board to live up to its implied willingness to cover the costs of postwar conversion to passenger ships of the many ex-German liners promised the company could have been overcome, but the cargo slump of late 1920 that wrought a full fledged depression to shipping in 1921 hammered quite a few nails into the coffin of this upstart company. Finally, operating difficulties and bad management decisions finished off a company whose excessive ambition might well be considered fundamental causes for their corporate failure, despite scandalously favorable terms from the Board.

When the PANHANDLE STATE entered service, the United States Mail Steamship Company was operating perhaps the grandest collection of illfitting units ever assembled under a single houseflag. All of their ships belonged to the Shipping Board, and only the PANHANDLE STATE and OLD NORTH STATE were built after 1908. Yet the motley assortment of ex-German ships comprising the rest of the United States Mail Line fleet represented a large measure of prewar Germany's maritime greatness. Those ships were then among America's best and largest passenger liners. Passenger accommodations in these ships was in varying states of restoration after their years of war work and post war transport duties. Among the US Mail steamers that actually made it into service under the American flag were the former North German Lloyd liners GEORGE WASHINGTON, PRINCESS ALICE, PRINZESS IRENE, NECKAR and RHEIN and the former Hapag steamers AMERIKA and HAMBURG. Coming under American registry, only the GEORGE WASHINGTON kept her name. The other ships were renamed by the Shipping Board in 1917 and became the PRINCESS MATOIKA, POCAHANTAS, ANTIGONE, SUSQUEHANNA, AMERICA and POWHATAN, respectively. The POWHATAN was renamed RED CROSS during the term of a single round trip charter voyage between the United States and Europe. She resumed the name POWHATAN and was later renamed NEW ROCHELLE. After a short while in U.S. Mail Line service the NEW ROCHELLE was renamed HUDSON and the ANTIGONE was renamed POTOMAC.

Colonel Mayer had a very good and effective public relations man. During its short life the United States Mail Steamship Company had big plans, cast-

---

[3] A copy of the authorization is in the 1091 file for the ship in RG32 at National Archives.

ing envious eyes on almost any ocean-going passenger ship then in the hands of the United States Shipping Board. They managed to win custodial allocation of other ex-German ships including three former North German Lloyd four-stackers then surviving in American hands as MOUNT VERNON, AGAMEMNON and von STEUBEN. Famous in their day as the German four-stackers KRONPRINZESSIN CECILIE, KAISER WILHELM II and KRONPRINZ WILHELM, they had been seized in American ports in April 1917 and were all renamed during the war. There was persistent talk of converting them into well equipped modern passenger liners at Shipping Board expense, meaning, ultimately, the taxpayer would bear the expense, as the United States Mail Steamship Company was neither in a position to nor willing to pay for refurbishing projects of this magnitude. No reconditioning work began before the demise of the United States Mail Steamship Company and never would. Besides those ships the former German KÖNIG WILHELM II, SIERRA CORDOBA, KÖLN and WITTEKIND, renamed MADAWASKA, CALLAO, AMPHION and FREEDOM respectively, were all mentioned from time to time in newspaper articles as "about to be reconditioned for United States Mail Line". Each saw a turn in the company's custodial allocation, and a few of them had made a voyage or two under allocation to the related France & Canada Corporation. The United States Mail Line also set its sights on the former Hapag PRESIDENT GRANT and even the Shipping Board passenger liners AEOLUS and HURON, once the North German Lloyd's GROSSER KURFURST and FRIEDRICH DER GROSSE, were not uncoveted by the tonnage hungry United States Mail Line. Munson Line had been allocated these old ships, but would return them to the Shipping Board upon delivery of the new "535"'s, SEA GIRT and AMERICAN LEGION. Unsatisfied even with so much available older tonnage, US Mail eventually announced that the new "502" class ships CREOLE STATE and BLUE HEN STATE were expected to join the fleet upon completion, asking for the former as early as August 1920. Mayer and the men around him seemed to have had a very simple philosophy: "if it floats and can carry or be fitted to carry steerage passengers, ask for its allocation."

Inaugurating the London service of United States Mail Steamship Company was the PANHANDLE STATE which left New York on her maiden voyage on Sept. 20, 1920. The new liner was in British waters for the first time on September 30th when the Shipping Board issued Memorandum #339 reflecting the jist of a Shipping Board discussion about the 22 "535"'s and "502"'s still building. Even then there was no equanimity as to their eventual deployment on Shipping Board services. A week later the Chairman requested deferment of their actual allocations. During October 1920 the Manager of the Traffic Department proposed action on the matter of assigning the CENTENNIAL STATE and BLUE HEN STATE for allocation to the transAtlantic triangular trade linking New York with Spain and Cuba operated by the New York and Cuba Mail Steamship Company. That plan occupied too many men for too long before going nowhere.

Results of the first month of the ship's operation led US Mail to recommend certain alterations for the next ship, the OLD NORTH STATE. Addressing Commander Gatewood on September 28th, O.W. Koester, U.S. Mail vice president in charge of construction and repairs, reported the need for many minor changes and asked the Division of Construction and Repairs for betterments. Considering passenger service first, Koester suggested that the Board equip the remaining "502"'s earmarked for the London line with accommodation for 5 additional dining room waiters by reconfiguring regular steward's department quarters in the after part of the ships. Next on his wish list was his plan to fit the Doctor's waiting room to accommodate the Second Steward. This could be easily accomplished by installing a pullman berth on the extant settee. Such a change should not hamper the doctor's work, he said. The third item related to the butcher shop, which US Mail felt should be relocated to the space then occupied by the steward's messroom, a room not really necessary in Koester's opinion. That would obviate the need for men to work in the cold storage chamber, and the ships really did need a place for cutting and caring for meat before the chef cooked it. Asking for some sort of ventilator for the Chief Steward's room, Koester ended his request mentioning that provision of openable deadlights in the galley. Making the usual rounds of Shipping Board departments for comment, the original and a copy now bear handwritten notes in the left margin. While one Board executive, presumably Thayer, noted across from the request to add berths for five more waiters: "can be done have 10 waiters now for 84 passengers", a colleague was not moved, asking: "Why more than 10 waiters for 84 passengers?" Against the request to turn the waiting room into a cabin for the Second Steward, "Authorized" is all anyone wrote, but on the copy, the writer expounded: "OK + previously suggested by Farrell." The question of the butcher shop brought disagreement. One member pencilled in a simple "NO". a colleague felt: "OK, if they want it, but present arrangement preferable." Less controversial were the final items which seemed well worth the cost.[4]

On Commander Gatewood's invitation, United States Mail Steamship Company vice president George Crowley wrote the Commander a detailed report on October 1, 1920 after a careful examination of both the PANHANDLE STATE and one of the "535"'s building at Camden, probably the WENATCHEE, suggesting a variety of improvements and betterments for both classes of ship. Before moving on to specific suggestions, Crowley summarized his conversation with New York Ship's Chairman Workman whose frustration with Shipping Board, Fleet Corporation and operators slated to take delivery of these passenger carriers was abundantly clear. Learning that most of the joinery work for all of the "502"'s was complete, and that all furniture had either been made or was being made, and that all color schemes, upholstery and hangings had been chosen, the yard would oppose

---

[4] Koester's memo is in the 1091 file for the ssPANHANDLE STATE in RG32 at National Archives.

Appearing in New York City newspapers on November 10, 1920, this US Mail Line notice advertised upcoming sailings from New York. The CREOLE STATE was never delivered to them and her two sailings were taken by her sisters.

"ANY ALTERATIONS WHATEVER IN THESE SHIPS BY REASON OF THE ABOVE FACT", and also because the joinery shop on D deck was small and congested. Workman also told Crowley that New York Ship was anxious to get these ships out of the yard. Crowley predicted difficulty in modification to any panelling designs, moreso as those panels were made in the yard's joinery shop.

Nonetheless, Crowley strongly felt that the "502" class needed some specific alterations, even if they could not be effected at the builders' yard. In

```
┌─────────────────────────────────────────┐
│                                           │
│      U. S. MAIL                           │
│  STEAMSHIP COMPANY, Inc.                  │
│  ─────────────────────────────────────   │
│      MINIMUM PASSENGER FARES              │
│                                           │
│        S. S. PANHANDLE STATE              │
│        S. S. OLD NORTH STATE              │
│                                           │
│        First Class only, $180             │
│          Outward and Return               │
│                                           │
│         S. S. SUSQUEHANNA                 │
│                    CABIN   THIRD CLASS    │
│                                           │
│   To Bremen      $180        $125         │
│   from Bremen    $180        $125         │
│                                           │
│   To Danzig      $210        $135         │
│   from Danzig    $210        $135         │
│   U. S. War Revenue Tax or Head Tax additional │
│                                           │
│        S. S. PRINCESS MATOIKA             │
│                                           │
│   To Naples                               │
│   and Genoa      $150        $95          │
│                                           │
│       U. S. War Revenue additional        │
│                                           │
│   From Naples                             │
│   and Genoa      $160        $95          │
│          Head Tax Included                │
│  ═════════════════════════════════════   │
│            RAIL FARE                       │
│  Boulogne-sur-mer-Paris Fcs. 53.90 First Class; │
│        Fcs. 35.60 Second Class            │
│                                           │
│  IN FRANCE: Children between 3 and 7 years pay │
│  half fare, under 3 years free.           │
│                                           │
└─────────────────────────────────────────┘
```

From US Mail Line's January 30, 1921 sailing schedule. Author's collection.

order to render the ships more efficient, comfortable and competitive on the North Atlantic, the US Mail Line felt:

1. Exhaust ventilation should be provided in the Dining Rooms. This could be done at a very moderate cost by running shafts in the ceiling through the decks without passing through the cabins over the Dining Saloon.
2. In the service passage from the pantry to the Dining Saloon, the hatch into the hold should be narrowed by four feet as no modern ship uses a passenger passageway as a service into the Dining Room.
3. Change the seats in the Smoking Room. The original seats are fixed, narrow, hard and uncomfortable. At slight cost that could be remedied, as could a minor rearrangement of the seats which would materially add to the attractiveness of the room and comfort of the passengers.
4. The Verandah Cafe should be enclosed by an extension as sketched in diagram "A". That entailed moving the staircase from "B" to "C", or alternatively continuing the casing with patent windows where the teak rail was, and putting in doors at "E" and "F", installation of a few radi-

ators to heat the area in cold weather was also requested. In the opinion of the Line, these alterations would render the Verandah Cafe more popular and allow it used to best advantage in all weathers. Beyond that, US Mail officials considered extant "sitting out accommodation" inadequate, calling it altogether less than could be found on any other comparably graded Atlantic steamer.

5. In its present form, the Lounge was also inadequate, and US Mail recommended removal of the staircase, decking over the remaining well., and installation of a small electric fireplace in addition to the installation of more chairs and another table or two. Not a costly change, it was argued, but it would make the Lounge far more comfortable and obviate its use as a passageway.

6. US Mail wanted the galley range moved from its original fore and aft position to an athwartship position, the only practicable and safe way to position that vital piece of equipment.

7. US Mail recommended immediate installation of five hundred Third Class berths, the maximum number that "boatage", or the maximum number of lifeboats a "502" could possibly ship. US Mail was well aware that contemporary conditions did not allow profitable operation with the limited number of passengers the "502"'s could then handle. On the matter of steerage, US Mail looked to Canadian Pacific and suggested that any Third Class in these ships be as comfortable and attractive as possible. It would take several years before much of these recommendations were realized, and by then, the United States Mail Steamship Company was but a dimming, bad memory to the Shipping Board.

Before that happened, though, the OLD NORTH STATE came out of the builders yards and entered service on the London line with her maiden sailing from New York on November 16, 1920. The only other sister "502" to actually sail for United States Mail Line was the CENTENNIAL STATE which made a trip for them after her June 1921 delivery. Although the BLUE HEN STATE was delivered to the company upon completion, she never made a voyage for them. Altogether, the three new "502" ships did not make more than 20 some-odd round voyages for this unsuccessful company.

The question of employment of "502"'s on the North Atlantic was bandied about the various offices of the Shipping Board and Emergency Fleet Corporation for well over a year. Not even the presence of the first two ships on U.S. Mail Line's London service settled the matter. Indeed, the Commissioners of the Shipping Board held temporary the assignment of the PANHANDLE STATE and OLD NORTH STATE to the United States Mail Steamship Company, preferring to allocate later such units for the London line and fit this pioneering pair with steerage and send them to work on New York & Cuba Mail Steamship Company (then perhaps more commonly referred to as Ward Line)'s triangular transAtlantic trade that then linked New York with Spain, Cuba and Mexico. For months prior to May 1921 the shipping press was full of teasers, blurbs, items and articles about the impending assignment of two steerage equipped "502" to the Ward Line. By January 17, 1921 R.H. Bailey, Special Assistant to the Chairman of the Shipping Board prepared an explanation for Shipping Board Commissioner Donald and his Committee of Commissioners on Operations:

> There is transmitted to you herewith five copies of M.O.4 Agreement covering the operation of the S.S. PANHANDLE STATE and the S.S. OLD NORTH STATE, together with statements of revenues derived from the operation of these steamers (these figures are the only figures I have been able to obtain), also copy of memorandum to the Chairman from Captain Foley recommending approval of the M.O.4 Agreement, and copy of memorandum from Mr. Keene giving manifest of the OLD NORTH STATE which is scheduled to sail on Tuesday, January 18th. Please note that the Chairman has already signed these Agreements: he desires, however, that they be held up and not transmitted to the U.S. Mail Steamship Company.
>
> These two vessels were assigned to the U.S. Mail Steamship Company at a meeting of the Commissioners of the Board with Judge Mayer and other officials of his company held some two months ago. They were assigned because the steamers which were to be turned over to the U.S. Mail under their charter agreement would not be ready for operation for some time to come, and it was thought advisable to place these two vessels in the London service so that that service might be started without delay. No contract has ever been entered into with the U.S. Mail Steamship Company covering the operation of these two steamers, but the Chairman, at the time the assignment was made was under the impression that they would be operated under the same terms as the vessels which were to be chartered to the U.S. Mail—that is on a bare boat charter basis—$3.50 per net registered ton per month.
>
> These two vessels have so far been operated by the U.S. Mail Steamship Company at a considerable loss, the figure, in my opinion, will run from $150 to $250,000. The question now arises as to whether we should in accordance with the suggested recommendation made by Captain Foley, fit these two vessels with steerage accommodations at an estimated cost of about $100,000 each and continue them in their present service, or whether they should be withdrawn from the U.S. Mail Steamship Company, assign them to some other steamship company for operation in the same or a similar service, or place them in some other service which would be more suitable for the vessels as they are now constructed. When considering this question, I would call your attention to the statement in Mr. Keene's memorandum that the OLD NORTH STATE, scheduled to sail tomorrow, will have a revenue for the round trip of approximately $130,000, and that her estimated expense for the round trip will be from $80,000 to $100,000. Please note in thus connection, however, that $50,000 of the $130,000 revenue is derived from her cargo.
>
> As you are Chairman of the Committee of Commissioners on Operations, I am referring these papers to you with the request that your committee make a thorough investigation of this matter and submit definite recommendations to the Board as to what should be done, and as this Company

has a sailing of one of these two vessels approximately every two or three weeks, it is requested that action be expedited as much as possible.[5]

Had they not yet had the means to notice the sinking fortunes of the US Mail Line, the Committee on Operations had it the following morning when Shipping Board Secretary John Flaherty forwarded to them a U.S. Mail Line request for $200,000 to be used as a working fund in connection with the operation of the two ships. Money was advanced to pay bills recuperable from the Shipping Board but not much was extended to allow U.S. Mail to stay afloat. Nor was a conscious decision on the next operator of the ships really ever made.

When the game was up for U.S. Mail in August 1921 and the company went down for the count, never to rise again, the immediate future of the "502"'s on the Atlantic remained in the hands of the Commissioners of the Shipping Board who retained them on the London line. On August 22, 1921, after incredible operating losses had forced the company into bankruptcy, two Court appointed receivers examined the company's affairs in minute detail. They discovered liabilities totalling well over $1.5 million. Within five days they had their findings before a District Court. Not willing to go quietly, United States Mail Steamship Company countersued the Shipping Board, claiming their debts resulted from the refusal of the Shipping Board to repay the line for money spent reconditioning ex-German vessels. On August 27, 1921 a judge ordered the United States Mail Steamship Company to return all ships to the Shipping Board.

Thus ended a very interesting experiment but luckily for intending travelers, ocean services of the failed company were scarcely interrupted. The Shipping Board quickly substituted a new operation to take over the services of the defunct United States Mail Line. Thus was born the fabled United States Lines. The new line retained all US Mail line services, going so far as to accept the bankrupt company's passage tickets. Even funnel markings sprang from the former operator. Patriotically painted in red, white and blue, they did without the unwieldy Shipping Board shield, whose proportions rarely looked right on the tall, thin funnels still in vogue in that period.

Without missing a beat, the PANHANDLE STATE, OLD NORTH STATE and CENTENNIAL STATE continued their work on the London line service of the new United States Lines. In fact, the London office of the United States Shipping Board played a considerable role during the early days of the new line. Witness this October 5, 1921 cable from the Washington, D.C. headquarters of the Board to their London subordinates:

You are to handle GEORGE WASHINGTON AMERICA HUDSON PO-CAHANTAS PRINCESS MATOIKA CENTENNIAL STATE and PANHAN-DLE STATE just the same as you do other Shipping Board vessels operating

---

[5] Jan. 17, 1921 memo to Commissioner Donald. Copy in the PRESIDENT van BUREN's 1091 file in RG 32 at National Archives.

UNITED STATES MAIL STEAMSHIP COMPANY, Inc.
45 BROADWAY - NEW YORK
THIRD CLASS RATES
Outward and Prepaid

EASTBOUND OUTWARD				WESTBOUND PREPAID			
S. S. George Washington America	S. S. Centennial State Blue Hen State	S. S. Susquehanna Potomac Hudson Matoika	**Ports**	S. S. George Washington	S. S. America	S. S. Centennial State Blue Hen State	S. S. Susquehanna Potomac Hudson Matoika
			QUEENSTOWN		77.50	72.50	
87.50	82.50		PLYMOUTH				
	82.50		SOUTHAMPTON	77.50	77.50		
90.			LONDON			72.50	
	90.		CHERBOURG	120.	120.		
			BOULOGNE			120.	
125.		125.	BREMEN	125.	125.		125.
135.		135.	DANZIG	135.	135.		135.
			Through Bookings				
			SCANDINAVIAN POINTS				
			Arendal, Aalesund, Aalborg. Bergen, Christiania, Christiansund, Christiansand, Copenhagen, Esbjerg, Frederikshavn, Gothenburg, Helsingborg, Laurvig, Malmo, Molde, Stavanger, Trondhjem				
105.	100.			105.	105.	100.	
112.	107.		Stockholm	112.	112.	107.	
112.	107.		**FINNISH POINTS** Abo, Hango, Helsingfors	112.	112.	107.	

CONTINENTAL POINTS — For all Steamers

Basle	$127.
Belgrade	140.
Bucharest	135.
Budapest	135.
Cracow	138.
Durazzo	139.
Kovno	150.
Lemberg	138.
Ljublian	135.
Marseilles	128.
Modane	127.
Paris	122.
Prague	127.
Sofia	145.
Valona	139.
Vienna	130.
Vilna	150.
Warsaw	137.
Zagreb	135.

For Eastbound (outward) Rates to continental points add the railroad rates shown on following pages to above port rates.

U. S. Revenue Tax Additional
On tickets costing over $10 to $30 Tax $1 each passenger
On tickets costing over $30 to $60 Tax $2 each passenger
On tickets costing over $60 Tax $3 each passenger
No tax on tickets costing $10 or less

Children's Fares
Infants under 1 year $5.50 (one for family)
1 year and under 10 years Half Fare
10 years and over Full Fare

Head Tax $8.00 Additional
also following charges
Transit charges, European Visae, Polish Tax
Sanitary and maintenance expenses $25.00
U. S. Landing money to be paid passenger on arrival $25.00

under MO four agreements except at Bremen and Danzig at which ports all features their operation will be handled by agents United States Lines, you to render such assistance as they request. This modifies our 7612 your 9356 unable confirm price thirty shillings ton coal Bremen. Your 9363 our 7589 and 7593 stand except with respect repairs Bremen and Danzig where this work will be handled by agents US Lines and bills therefor paid when approved by their representatives and Atkins. Your 9400 repairs POTOMAC and AMERICA at Bremen will be handled by agents US Lines.[6]

---

[6] Oct. 5, 1921 cable from USSB headquarters to London office. Copy in 1091 file for the PANHANDLE STATE in RG 32 at National Archives. The four digit numbers refer to specific telegrams, none of which has a copy remaining in the files for that ship.

Appointed as the United States Lines agents and managers for the Shipping Board was a trio of impressive names in American shipping. First was the Roosevelt Steamship Corporation, founded by Kermit Roosevelt, a son of former President Theodore Roosevelt and incorporated in Delaware in December 1920. After leaving the Army with the rank of Captain in 1920, Roosevelt joined the Harriman's American Ship and Commerce Corporation to learn the shipping business. The United American Line, which was the outgrowth of several firms, including the Livermore-Dearborn Company, the Independent Steamship Company, the Shawmut Steamship Company and the Coastwise Transportation Company which then amalgamated with the American Ship & Commerce Company was the brainchild of W. Averell Harriman and formed at his instigation during 1920. Not only was Harriman the President of the American Ship and Commerce Company he was then also Vice-President of the American Hawaiian Steamship Company. Operating its own passenger services on the North Atlantic, the United American Lines were compelled by March 1922 to withdraw from United States Lines management. The third partner in the management of the new United States Lines was the firm of Moore & McCormack, which was incorporated in 1913. They went on to great success in American flag shipping, becoming the leading American firm in shipping to the Baltic and South America before adding to their ocean network the Robin Line, which linked the United States to South and Eastern Africa.

The Shipping Board expected to be able to quickly release all three firms from their management role in the new United States Lines as they expected to be able to make a quick sale of both line and ships to private interests. It didn't happen quite that way and the Government owned while private interests operated United States Lines for nearly eight years. The AMERICA and GEORGE WASHINGTON were retained by United States Lines, but the other old ex-German ships lasted only a short while under the new house-flag. The PRINCESS MATOIKA, formerly the PRINCESS ALICE was renamed PRESIDENT ARTHUR and the HUDSON, formerly the HAMBURG, now the PRESIDENT FILLMORE, were laid up pending eventual reallocation or sale. The POTOMAC was also laid up and never returned to service and later scrapped.

Despite an earlier plan to use one and sometimes two of the "502"'s on a route from New York to Ireland and Germany in an attempt to take advantage of whatever steerage trade still existed, the five sister "502"'s on the Atlantic enabled United States Lines to offer a weekly Cabin service on the London line. From the late spring of 1922 the five sisters offered a departure from New York every Wednesday. Just as before, eastbound ships stopped at Queenstown (Cobh), Plymouth and Cherbourg. Weekly homewards departure from London were scheduled for Saturdays. Besides Cherbourg, westbound "502" ships sometimes stopped off Plymouth and almost always called at Queenstown (Cobh). The minimum one way Cabin Class fare was $120.00. For a Saloon Deck cabin with private facilities the cost was much higher, set at $360.00 per person, based on each of two. Slightly discounted rates were posted for third and fourth passengers in a cabin. Round trip passengers enjoyed a fare discounted by five per cent.

Though serving neither wine nor spirits to comply with American Prohibition law, these ships proved quite popular for many reasons, chief among them were their low fares, comfortable cabins, decent food and competent service. Other factors drawing passengers to choose them were their American dependability, safety and engineering. Despite their popularity with travelers, these ships showed no profits, posting very heavy losses instead.

Tantalizing the observer of these ships almost half century after the Master of the last of them rang up "finished with engines" for the last time was the question of these steamers' Third Class passenger accommodations. The question of steerage in these ships originated in response to service on any or all of several routes: from Ireland, from Spain, from the Far East. Now hardly a sidebar to the story of these ships on the North Atlantic was that never realized plan to put two of them to work on the triangular line linking New York with Spain, Cuba and Mexico. It sprang up as early as 1919 when the Ward Line sent four different passenger carriers to Spain, then enjoying an unprecedented volume of trade and traffic with the United States. Of limited capacity was the HENRY R. MALLORY, one of the few real combination passenger cargo ships ever built for coastal service. Of similar cabin but extensive steerage capacity was the Shipping Board's ex-German BLACK ARROW. Pride of place on the run went to the company's own grand, new flagships ORIZABA and SIBONEY. Able to carry fair numbers of travelers in three classes, the New York and Cuba Mail Steamship Company really needed them on their New York to Havana express service and did not let them long serve elsewhere. Sometime during 1920 someone came up with the idea of using "502"'s on the run to Spain. Two things held up employment of the new ships on that run. None was yet complete and no one had planned any steerage accommodations in them, a class of accommodations then thought necessary for the Spain service. It didn't take all that long for that lack to be addressed. November 2, 1920 saw W.B. Keene, Assistant Director of Operations address his thoughts on the matter to Shipping Board Secretary John J. Flaherty: "These assignments will make it necessary to provide for steerage passengers, and in order to obtain the most satisfactory result in the arrangement of quarters at minimum expense, modifications should be undertaken before the vessels are too far advanced on lines of original (sic!) plans to have the necessary modifications effected while the ships are still in the builders' yards. This will save expense and avoid the necessity of making expensive interior changes."[7] Unmentioned are just which "502" class ships Keene had in mind but left out of consideration by virtue of being

---

[7]Memo from W.B. Keene.Copy in 1091 files for CENTENNIAL STATE, BLUE HEN STATE in RG 32 at National Archives.

at that moment elsewhere in service were the PANHANDLE STATE and OLD NORTH STATE and literally days away from completion was the CRE-OLE STATE. The four others were then in varying states of construction at Camden. A December 10th memo from Keene to Cmdr. Gatewood, Director of Construction and Repair inferred that in the opinion of the Ward Line, installation of steerage was a simple matter, unlikely to entail much expense. True enough, but under no circumstances was that company going to pay for as much as a mattress for steerage passengers . . . there was a Government agency to handle such expenditures . . .

Yet citing comments from Mr. Cabaud, then General Manager of the New York and Cuba Mail Steamship Company, the Shipping Board missed the company's hint of a planned retreat from the triangular transAtlantic service. All during the winter of 1921 the Shipping Board spoke of partnering the GRANITE STATE and the still incomplete BLUE HEN STATE on the Spanish trade. That would allow the CENTENNIAL STATE to be "claimed" by Pacific Mail, or go to yet another operator. Then talk suggested fitting steerage in the last two "502"'s and sending them to Spain. Three of the "502"'s were in service on January 6, 1921 when the Shipping Board sent New York Shipbuilding Company plans showing desired revisions to include steerage accommodation in the CENTENNIAL STATE and BLUE HEN STATE. New York Shipbuilding Corporation received this latest Shipping Board suggestion with unbridled contempt and not a little hostility in its response the following day. Here is the yard's unyielding position: " . . . the construction of the ships had advanced beyond the point where the desired revisions could be done as a matter of course" at their Camden yards. The Shipping Board would not take no for an answer and the Construction and Repair Department weighed in with a general description of Ward Line's proposed requirements on January 25, 1921. According to their figures, suggested modifications would cost the yard an estimated $219,500.00 per ship, if heated by steam, and $221,500.00 per ship if heated by the Thermotank system. Neither figure indicated any profit to the shipbuilders. According to the memo, among the work in question of interest here:

ITEM "A" Steelwork

Bulkheads to be fitted in forecastle to suit rearrangement of lamp and paint rooms, washroom, etc.

Bulkheads bounding toilets for 3rd Class Passengers at forward and after end of "A" Deck.

Steel deck to be fitted over poop deck house, sufficiently supported for housing two sets of 28' nested lifeboats.

Angle coaming to be fitted around cargo hatches on "B" Deck in 3rd Class Quarters, to form boundary for deck covering and to allow for necessary hatch cover fastenings.

ITEM "E" - Miscellaneous Fittings

16 Mechanical davits of the "Welin" type (4 type B and 12 type C) to be fitted for handling 18 additional lifeboats and stowage facilities for boats provided.

Support stanchions fitted in way of nested lifeboats on poop house.

Forged rail stanchions with pipe rails to be fitted in vicinity of lifeboats, aft.

ITEM "F" - Cabin, Galley, and Pantry Outfit

This item includes supplying the necessary linen, bedding, crockery, etc. for 690—3rd Class Passengers. 8 berths in contiguous ward and 5 extra crew.

349 pipe berths (2-tier) to be fitted for 690—3rd Class Passengers and contiguous ward.

Kettles, one 60 gallon coffee urn, One 12' section oil burning range, one complete steam table with necessary piping, valves, hangers, etc, and additional smoke pipe with revolving cowl.

ITEM "G" - Deck Outfit, etc.

The following additional lifeboats with equipment to be supplied. 4—28' nested, 2—24'. 8—20' nested and 4—18' nested. Also 695 life belts to be provided.

ITEM "H" - Rigging

Additional lifeboat falls together with the necessary blocks to be provided.

ITEM "I" - Tarpaulins and Boat Covers

Boat covers to be provided for 18 additional lifeboats, and waterproof and non-waterproof tarpaulins to be fitted on cargo hatches in way of 3rd Class Passengers on "B" Deck.[8]

Taking the estimated costs into accounts, it took the Shipping Board no time at all to decide to defer installation of steerage quarters in the two sisters. The subject of steerage in these ships just would not die and the shipyard soon heard the Board's final decision on the matter of Third Class accommodations in the last two "502"s. And as each branch of both the Shipping Board and Emergency Fleet Corp. got around to it, New York Shipbuilding Corporation kept on hearing it over and over again. On March 12, 1921 A. Conti, Manager of the Technical Department and R.A. Smith, Head of the Hull Section, sent Shipping Board Delaware District Director G.K. Nichols the following memo:

CHANGES REQUESTED BY THE WARD STEAMSHIP COMPANY ON THE S.S. 'CENTENNIAL STATE' and 'BLUE HEN STATE' BUILDING BY THE NEW YORK SHIPBUILDING CORPORATION UNDER CONTRACT 418-SC.

---

[8] From the 1091 file for the CENTENNIAL STATE, BLUE HEN STATE in RG 32 at National Archives.

1. It has been decided by Commander Gatewood to make the alterations requested by the New York and Cuba Mail Steamship Co., on the S.S. "CENTENNIAL STATE" and "BLUE HEN STATE", when the ships are delivered to the Division of Operations.
2. It is requested that you notify the New York Shipbuilding Corporation of this fact, and bring to their attention that all present construction in the way of alterations should be adjusted so that the expense of the alterations can be made with as little cost as possible in altering the items that cannot be made portable or eliminated.
3. Attached, herewith, are specifications which show where the alterations are to be made.[9]

Apparently, Shipping Board records clerks felt no need to keep a copy of the specifications in the correspondence file so this latest news could not be easily measured against existing plans. At the same time, the Washington office of the Shipping Board sent the yard specifications covering the desired changes, ordering the builder to "leave loose such work as would be effected by these modifications."

It was Commander Gatewood who once again proved himself to be an untiring source of information:

Referring your letter December first regarding proposed change cargo space into steerage passenger accommodations steamers CENTENNIAL STATE and BLUE HEN STATE and referring to Commissioner Teal's letter to me February seventh delay in submission estimates of cost due inability obtain from builders this estimate. Builders estimate finally obtained and considered grossly excessive probably because they do not desire work but prefer complete vessels in accordance original plans and get them away from their yard which is already overcrowded. Consider it essential before vessels can be profitably operated by Cuba Mail Company to which understand they are tentatively assigned and consider it entirely possible to advertise this work on competitive bids to be proceeded with immediately upon delivery and obtain prices for it at a saving of at least one hundred fifty thousand dollars total under builders present estimate and without undue delay to vessels. Specifications for this now being prepared and the whole matter will be presented to the Board for approval. Please furnish copy this wire to Commissioner Teal and Captain Foley[10]

The matter of Steerage in the last two "502" ships dragged on. From Emergency Fleet Corporation's Assistant District Manager's no-nonsense letter about the CENTENNIAL STATE and BLUE HEN STATE written on March 15th the Yard:

---

[9] ibid.

[10] Gatewood's telegram to the Board, quoted by Secretary J.J. Flaherty in his February 19th memo on this subject for the Chairman. Copies in the ships' 1091 files in RG 32 at National Archives.

1. You are hereby advised that it has been decided the necessary modifications to provide the above vessels with third class accommodations will be executed after the delivery of the vessels. All constructions in the way of these changes which will be affected by the execution of these modifications will be made portable so as to reduce the cost of removing various items to a minimum. and
2. We are attaching hereto a copy of the specifications covering these modifications, for your guidance. Plans for the same have been forwarded previously so that you could prepare the estimate which you have submitted to this office.[11]

The yard lost no time before replying:

All steel work, such as divisional bulkheads, ventilators, boom rests and the riveting of rigging pads, which may interfere with the proposed changes has been completed for months. The laundry machinery has been completely installed on the CENTENNIAL STATE and has been placed in its compartment on the BLUE HEN STATE. It was necessary that this machinery should be placed in its respective compartment during the early stage of construction of the above vessels, as certain structural bulkheads had to be left loose until the same has been accomplished. Joiner panels on both ships can be considered portable throughout the entire vessel, due to the fact the Builder has installed this work by means of wooden screws.[12]

At that juncture, the Board learned that New York Ship had followed orders of April 15, 1921 and not gone beyond any necessary work. At least the amount of work done which would have to be ripped out was limited. Meanwhile, Hull Section chief Smith addressed Technical Department Manager Conti with an April 5, 1921 memo. "Confirming telephone conversation of recent date, we are forwarding to you, today, under separate cover, nineteen complete specifications showing modifications and alterations on vessels allocated to the Ward Steamship Company, and nineteen drawings H-236251 rearrangement of quarters on bridge deck, navigating, upper bridge & "C" Deck, also drawing #H-236252 rearrangement of Quarters on "A" & "B" Decks"[13]. There was still no official allocation of the incomplete steamers to the New York and Cuba Mail Steamship Company.

Days later Ward Line dropped the Spanish trade making the extensive changes foreseen to the last two "502"'s more speculative than ever yet the matter of Third Class in ships of this type raged on. After consultations with their operator, the Pacific Mail Steamship Company, Emergency Fleet Corporation Pacific District Manager William Chisholm chimed in with his June 28, 1921 letter to Commander Gatewood, referring to his May 5th telegram #498 to the Repair Department and Gatewood's letters of the 7th and 10th.

---

[11] op.cit.
[12] April 19, 1921 memo from District Manager G.K. Nichols to T.D. Pitts. Copies in the ship's 1091 files in RG 32 at National Archives.
[13] op. cit.

Writing of increased steerage accommodations in the CREOLE STATE, WOLVERINE STATE and GRANITE STATE, he began:

1. The above three references all refer to the S.S. CREOLE STATE. The first item in reference (a) requested authority for the installation of accommodations for about 200 steerage passengers in #8 tweendeck at an estimated cost of approximately $29,000.00. Your letter of May 10th stated that specification should be prepared for this work.
2. We are enclosing blue print and specification showing proposed alterations to accommodate 232 steerage passengers on these vessels. It is estimated that the change will take about three weeks on each vessel.
3. This matter has been the subject of several conferences between the Division of Operations, this office and Pacific Mail Steamship Company and the attached bear the recommendation of all concerned. In my opinion the service in which these vessels ply requires this additional steerage space."[14]

By no means the final word on the subject of steerage was a July 12, 1921 memorandum from Secretary Clifford Smith to the Acting Director of Operations:

The Shipping Board, at a meeting today, considered the recommendations contained in your memorandum to the Board dated July 5, 1921, with reference to the installation of open steerage quarters on the S.S. BLUE HEN STATE, and authorized and directed the Director of Construction and Repairs, prior approval thereof having been first obtained from Messrs. Smull and Love, to take the necessary steps to have open steerage quarters installed on said vessel.

The Board further directed the Division of Operations to submit to the Board as soon as practicable definite recommendations for the employment of said vessel upon completion of said vessel.[15]

Two things are certain. "Open steerage" was not fitted and upon completion, the ship had no work and spent almost a year in lay up.

No matter what names were initially chosen for these ships by Mrs. Woodrow Wilson, her secretary Edith Benham and Admiral Phelps. The Shipping Board discarded them before any of them was launched and these "502" class ships all entered commercial service named with nicknames of states of the union, as did most of the "535"'s. There was no formula to identify a member of either class by her "state" name, nor was there any way to distinguish a vessel by class once they were renamed with "President" names. Towards the end of their commercial careers, all but one of the "502"'s were renamed, as were most of the "535"'s, once those ships entered military service. So many similar names makes it difficult to follow any particular vessel over the course of her career.

As they debuted the "502" class ships were eventually divided between two companies. Three were sent out to the Pacific to serve on Pacific Mail

---

[14]June 8, 1921 letter. Copy in 1091 file in RG 32 at National Archives.
[15]Copy in the ship's 1091 file in RG 32 at National Archives.

PROPOSED SAILINGS

(Subject to Change)

EASTBOUND

WESTBOUND

Due NEW YORK	Due CORK (Queenstown)	PLYMOUTH	CHERBOURG	LONDON	Due BREMEN	Due DANZIG	STEAMER	from DANZIG	from BREMEN	from LONDON	from CHERBOURG	from Southampton	from CORK (Queenstown)	Due NEW YORK
Wed. Aug. 9	Aug. 18	Aug. 19	Aug. 20	Aug. 21			Centennial State		Sat. Aug. 26	Tue. Aug. 29	Aug. 27	Aug. 31	Aug. 28	Sep. 6
Sat. Aug. 12	Aug. 25	Aug. 19	Aug. 20	Aug. 28			Lone Star State		Sat. Sep. 2	Tue. Sep.	Aug. 31		Sep. 3	Sep. 8
Wed. Aug. 16		Aug. 27	Aug. 28				Panhandle State		Sat. Sep. 9	Wed. Sep. 6	Sep.	Sep. 7	Sep. 7	Sep. 13
Sat. Aug. 19							George Washington		Sat. Sep. 16	Tue. Sep. 12	Sep. 10			Sep. 15
Wed. Aug. 23	Sep.	Sep. 2	Sep. 3	Sep. 4	Aug. 29		Blue Hen State							Sep. 20
Sat. Aug. 26	Sep. 1	Sep.	Sep.	Sep. 5			Hudson	Sep. 17						Sep. 24
Wed. Aug. 30	Sep. 8	Sep. 9	Sep. 10	Sep. 11			Old North State		Sat. Sep. 23	Tue. Sep.	Sep. 17	Sep. 21	Sep. 15	Sep. 27
Thur. Aug. 31							Potomac		Wed. Sep. 20	Sat. Sep.				
Sat. Sep. 2	Sep. 15	Sep. 10	Sep. 11	Sep. 18	Sep. 12		America		Sat. Sep.	Tue. Sep. 26	Sep. 21	Sep. 21	Sep. 26	Oct. 4
Wed. Sep. 6		Sep. 16	Sep. 16		Sep. 13		Granite State		Sat. Sep. 23	Tue. Sep. 26	Sep. 28	Sep. 28		Oct. 5
Sat. Sep. 9		Sep. 17	Sep. 17				Peninsula State							Oct. 8
Wed. Sep. 13	Sep. 22	Sep. 23	Sep. 24	Sep. 25			Princess Matoika		Sat. Sep. 30	Tue. Oct.	Oct.	Oct.	Oct. 2	Oct. 11
Sat. Sep. 16	Sep. 23	Sep. 23	Oct.	Oct. 2			Lone Star State		Sat. Oct. 7	Wed. Oct. 3	Oct.	Oct. 5	Oct. 9	Oct. 18
Wed. Sep. 20	Sep. 30	Oct. 1	Oct. 1				Panhandle State		Sat. Oct. 14	Tue. Oct. 11	Oct. 8	Oct. 12	Oct. 9	Oct. 20
Sat. Sep. 23	Oct. 6	Oct.	Oct. 7	Oct. 9			George Washington				Oct. 15		Oct. 10	Oct. 23
Wed. Sep. 27							Blue Hen State		Sat. Oct. 17					Oct. 29
Sat. Sep. 30	Oct. 13	Oct. 14	Oct. 15	Oct. 16	Oct. 12		Hudson		Wed. Oct. 25	Tue. Oct.	Oct. 23	Oct. 23	Oct. 23	Nov. 1
Wed. Oct. 4		Oct. 14	Oct. 16				Old North State		Sat. Oct. 21		Oct. 26	Oct. 30	Nov.	
Sat. Oct. 7	Oct. 20	Oct. 15	Oct. 16	Oct. 23			America		Sat. Oct. 28	Tue. Oct.	Oct. 29			Nov. 7
Thur. Oct. 12		Oct. 21	Oct. 22				Granite State							Nov. 9
Sat. Oct. 14				Oct. 23	Oct. 29		Centennial State	Oct. 29	Sat. Nov. 4	Tue. Nov.	Nov.	Nov. 2	Nov.	Nov. 12
Sat. Oct. 14	Oct. 27	Oct. 28	Oct. 29	Oct. 30			Potomac		Tue. Nov.					Nov. 15
Wed. Oct. 18		Oct. 28	Oct. 29	Nov. 6			Lone Star State		Sat. Nov. 11	Wed. Nov.	Nov. 9	Nov. 9	Nov. 6	Nov. 15
Sat. Oct. 21	Nov. 3	Nov. 4	Nov.	Nov. 5			Panhandle State		Sat. Nov. 15	Tue. Nov.	Nov. 14	Nov. 16	Nov. 13	Nov. 22
Wed. Oct. 25	Nov. 10	Nov.	Nov. 12	Nov. 13			George Washington		Sat. Nov. 18	Wed. Nov. 15	Nov. 16	Nov. 16		Nov. 24
Wed. Oct. 28		Nov. 11	Nov. 12				Blue Hen State		Sat. Nov. 21		Nov. 19	Nov. 19	Nov. 20	Nov. 29
Sat. Nov. 4	Nov. 17	Nov. 18	Nov. 19	Nov. 20			Old North State		Wed. Nov. 29	Tue. Nov.	Nov. 26	Nov. 26	Nov. 27	Dec. 6
Sat. Nov. 11		Nov. 19	Nov. 20	Nov. 21			America		Sat. Nov. 25	Wed. Nov.	Nov. 30	Nov. 30		Dec. 8
Wed. Nov. 15	Nov. 24	Nov. 25	Nov. 26	Nov. 27			Granite State		Sat. Dec. 2	Thur. Nov. 30	Dec. 2	Dec. 3	Dec. 4	Dec. 13
Sat. Nov. 18		Nov. 25	Nov. 26	Nov. 30			Peninsula State		Sat. Dec. 2	Tue. Dec.				Dec. 15
Wed. Nov. 22							Centennial State		Sat. Dec. 9					Dec. 20
Thur. Nov. 23	Dec. 1	Dec. 2	Dec. 3	Dec. 4	Dec. 10		Potomac	Dec. 10		Sat. Dec.		Dec. 10	Dec. 11	Dec. 25
Sat. Nov. 25		Dec.	Dec.				Lone Star State		Sat. Dec. 16	Tue. Dec.	Dec. 11	Dec. 11		Dec. 27
Tue. Nov. 28	Dec.	Dec. 6	Dec. 7	Dec. 8			George Washington		Sat. Dec. 16	Wed. Dec.	Dec. 14	Dec. 14		Dec. 27
Wed. Dec. 6	Dec. 16	Dec. 16	Dec. 17	Dec. 18			Panhandle State		Sat. Dec. 16	Wed. Dec. 13	Dec. 17	Dec. 18		
Sat. Dec. 9							Blue Hen State		Sat. Dec.	Thur. Dec. 21	Dec. 22	Dec. 22		Jan. 9
Tue. Dec. 12	Dec. 20	Dec. 21	Dec. 21	Dec. 24			Hudson		Thur. Dec. 28					Jan. 10
Tue. Dec. 12	Dec. 22	Dec. 22	Dec. 22				America		Thur. Jan. 3	Wed. Jan.			Dec. 31	Jan. 10
Wed. Dec. 14	Dec. 21	Dec. 21	Dec. 24				Old North State		Sat. Jan. 6	Sat. Jan.	Jan. 5	Jan. 5	Dec. 31	Jan. 17
Wed. Dec. 20	Dec. 30	Dec. 31	Dec. 30	Dec. 23			Granite State		Sat. Jan. 6	Tue. Jan.	Jan.	Jan. 8		Jan. 17
Wed. Dec. 27	Jan.	Jan.	Jan.	Jan.			Centennial State		Sat. Jan. 13	Wed. Jan.	Jan. 8	Jan. 14	Jan. 15	Jan. 24
Thur. Dec. 28	Jan.	Jan. 6	Jan. 6	Jan. 7			George Washington		Sat. Jan. 17	Wed. Jan. 17	Jan. 18	Jan. 18	Jan. 15	Jan. 26

This March 10, 1922 sailing schedule issued by United States Lines was outdated in less than two months when the "State" ships took "President" names. Author's collection.

Steamship Company's Calcutta line and four were eventually allocated to United States Mail Steamship Company. Bear in mind that US Mail Line never did manage to get all four of them into service together but that their successor, United States Lines ran five "502" sisters together on the London line. At that the gestation of a weekly sailing on the London Line was a long time coming. So was the decision that the London line was the best place for these ships.

Miserable results on the Calcutta run brought a fifth "502" to the Atlantic in the spring of 1922. That and the US Lines inspired decision to downgrade the passenger accommodation in these sisters from First to Cabin Class led to the return of the OLD NORTH STATE to service as well as the belated debut, as PRESIDENT GARFIELD, of the eternally idle BLUE HEN STATE.

With the coming of the 1922 summer season, United States Lines finally wanted to offer weekly service on the London line. With the backing of the Shipping Board they were able to do that, adding the thus far idle PRESIDENT GARFIELD to the sailing schedule for a June 7th departure. They were able to get the ship ready for service more quickly than planned and as a Cabin liner, the ship began her maiden voyage on May 31, 1922. From then until their delivery to their purchasers in early 1924, the five "502"'s on the Atlantic put in dependable service between New York and London via intermediate ports of Queenstown, Plymouth and Cherbourg. They called little attention to themselves but gained a fair share of popularity among travelers who found them a good value for money. The very size of these sister ships charmed many passengers who enjoyed the intimacy of their passenger accommodations.

Five of these sisters were still in service on the London line when R. Stanley Dollar concluded their purchase in September 1923. In the final analysis the "502"'s on the Atlantic made little impression on the bulk of the traveling or even migrating public. Nor did their charms work their way into the psyche of the average ship enthusiast. Anyone who remembers them probably fails to make the connection these ships had to the North Atlantic, identifying the sisters only with Dollar Line, their long time owners. Keep in mind that the PANHANDLE STATE had turned in some three and a half years of transAtlantic service when she was delivered to the Dollars in 1924. Maybe that is to their and the Dollar Line's credit, for the Dollars made a success with these ships that the North Atlantic never gave them. Precious few were their "heavy" sailings when a berth in one of them was not to be had and few were the positive results of their westbound cargo carriage. Other than showing the American flag, the five "502"'s on the London line made their chief mark in red ink, having cost the American taxpayer through his Government over $29 million to build and about $3.5 million to operate on the North Atlantic under public ownership. By the end of winter 1924 the ships were the property of privately held Dollar Steamship Lines. When they came off the London line to go into Dollar Line's round the world service, very few were those who were unhappy to bid them farewell.

THE "502"'S ON THE PACIFIC

◇

In concert with the Shipping Board which supplied the tonnage, W.R. Grace & Company's subsidiary Atlantic & Pacific Steamship Company began a long haul freight service from New York via Panama to India in the spring of 1919. Under the name U.S. Line, several Fleet Corporation ships did a voyage or two on that service, though by March 1921 when Grace withdrew Atlantic & Pacific from the trade for lack of business, it was handled by four Government owned freighters, the Type A "Hog Islanders" FLUOR SPAR and SEEKONK and the standard freighters ABRON and SALUDA.

Claiming a poor freight market (which was true), Grace withdrew from the rate conference and notified shippers and officials of their impending withdrawal from the trade. As usual, there was more to it than that. Part owner of Pacific Mail Steamship Company since 1915, Grace had served Indian ports since 1917 when Pacific Mail chartered Atlantic & Pacific's combination passenger and cargo ship SANTA CRUZ to run on a new service with their own combiship COLUSA between San Francisco via ports to Calcutta. In the 5,000 ton range, neither the SANTA CRUZ nor the COLUSA could carry more than 50 passengers and were more comfortable when limited to about 30. Need it be said that both parent companies, W.R. Grace & Company and the American International Corporation, had great faith in the potential of that service? Wartime importation of rubber, oils and tropical products gave this line a strong *raison d'etre*, but in peacetime such products were available from other sources, fact quickly forgotten in the free for all enjoyed by American steamship operators gluttonously adding routes, services and Government tonnage to their fleet lists in the heady years of 1919 and 1920. Both American International and W.R. Grace & Company were firms of great importance and immeasurable clout with the Shipping Board, a fact offspring Pacific Mail used to its advantage for as long as possible. With apologies to a major brokerage firm, Pacific Mail gained their clout the old fashioned way, they earned it! During the height of the wartime shipping emergency, they shared their own vice president John H. Rosseter with the Shipping Board. Thus did Pacific Mail eventually have access to the most up to date information about the Shipping Board and its many machinations. Since Rosseter himself had designed the passenger accommodations in the "502" class combination passenger and cargo ships then building at Camden, Pacific Mail carefully followed the construction of all three types of passenger ships then building under orders for the United States Shipping Board Emergency Fleet Corporation. Once unofficially assured that none of the Type B "Hog Islanders" would be completed for commercial purposes but that most, if not all of the big "535"'s would be, the Shipping Board intimated eventual allocation of some of those big "535"'s for Pacific Mail's transPacific line. When they learned that the Shipping Board had promised the first few "535"'s to the Pacific Steamship Company's "Admiral Line" for a new service from Seattle to the Far East, Pacific Mail brought out its biggest guns to lobby for cancellation of Admiral Line's good fortune. The company's protests brought assurance from the Commissioners of the Shipping Board that there were ships and business for both companies. Not only that, the Shipping Board informed Pacific Mail that no vessel allocation was official as yet.

From its San Francisco offices Pacific Mail was still close enough to keep a close watch on developments in Washington, New York and Philadelphia and when they learned that upstart United States Mail Steamship Company was collecting Government tonnage with great success, their reaction was cool. But when Pacific Mail learned that US Mail Line had won allocation of the three first "502"'s for the London line, they sprang into action. Pacific Mail's interference paid off, forcing cancellation of the plan to allocate the new CREOLE STATE to US Mail. At the last possible minute the Shipping Board allocated the third completed "502" steamer to the Pacific Mail Steamship Company for service on their run between San Francisco and Calcutta. They also won the promise of the next of the class, the WOLVERINE STATE, then fitting out at Camden.

With the delivery of so many ex-German ships in the offing US Mail was mollified by the offer of additional tonnage in the near future. All they had to do was sit back and wait for the Shipping Board to drop additional tonnage into their laps. As for the November 27, 1920 departure they had latterly advertised for the CREOLE STATE, a little bit of extra planning and some fast shuffling would cover that, too. US Mail assigned the PANHANDLE STATE to take that sailing from New York to London.

Teaming up with American Express, Pacific Mail organized a cruise from Baltimore to San Francisco for the delivery voyage of the new CREOLE STATE. With only a short time before the planned December 27th sailing date to market it to the traveling public, they did a creditable job, selling tickets to 40 people for the 19 day trip.

Pacific Mail overlooked a few things. There really wasn't enough business for ships like this on the Calcutta run. Two ships were adequate to handle the traffic . . . three were ludicrous. By January 1992 the Shipping Board pulled the plug.

Even their steerage spaces were not always what Asian passengers wanted in inexpensive transportation. As the *New York Maritime Register* told it on March 15, 1922:

> Oriental steerage passengers have been refusing to sleep on the steel spring berths assigned to them, so it has fallen to the division of construction and repair to provide canvas slings as substitutes. Pacific coast supply houses were asking $3.00 each for the slings but competitive bidding at New York brought an offer of a large quantity at 95 cents each.

Withdrawing allocation from Pacific Mail Steamship Company of both PRESIDENT HARRISON and PRESIDENT HAYES on June 9, 1922, the Shipping Board issued a statement:

> Several days ago the Pacific Mail Steamship Company informed the United States Shipping Board Emergency Fleet Corporation that the route from San Francisco to Hawaii, Manila, Hong Kong and return was far from a paying proposition, in fact the returns were so poor and the immediate prospects showed no improvement that they recommended the PRESIDENT HARRISON and PRESIDENT HAYES, both of the 502 type ships plying on the above route, be withdrawn temporarily until conditions improved. The Board considered very carefully the recommendations of the operators of these boats, and directed that the ships be laid up for the time being in San Francisco harbor. When the Board first considered the advisability of such a route for two ships of the above type, it had in contemplation the expected application of coastwise laws to the Philippine trade, as well as better all-around conditions. The coastwise laws have not yet been extended to the Philippines, and that, combined with the decreased demand for both freight and passenger accommodations, has made it necessary to lay these ships up for the time being in order to save losses on each round voyages, At the present time the Pacific Mail is operating the PRESIDENT WILSON, PRESIDENT CLEVELAND and PRESIDENT LINCOLN, all of the 535 type of ship in the Oriental trade, touching at Manila both ways. This fleet will be augmented very shortly by the PRESIDENT PIERCE and PRESIDENT TAFT, also 535 type. The original plan of the Board was for a fleet of five of these ships, but the last two were not turned over to the Pacific Mail Steamship Company until autumn, but by a re-arrangement of plans in the transAtlantic trade, it will be possible to turn the last named ships over to them in August, consequently the withdrawal of the PRESIDENT HAYES and PRESIDENT HARRISON will not affect the trade of the Pacific Mail, as the bookings of freight for these two ships are being transferred to the 535 liners now in service. The laying up of these two vessels is but a temporary expedient, and it is the intention of the Board to put them back in the route originally laid out for them as soon as trade conditions warrant.[1]

When it became known that Pacific Mail, after having attempted a Hong Kong and Manila service with these three new "502"'s (CREOLE STATE, WOLVERINE STATE and GRANITE STATE), were considering turning the ships back to the United States Shipping Board, several West Coast firms loudly proclaimed their interest in acquiring these three units. Among them was an Oregon syndicate, the Columbia Pacific Steam Ship Company, which eventually became the States Steamship Company. They got nowhere with their application to operate the two sisters retained on the West Coast, the PRESIDENT HARRISON and PRESIDENT HAYES. Both ships went from Pacific Mail custody right into lay up and stayed there for a while.

---

[1] Quoted in the June 21, 1922 issue of the *New York Maritime Register*.

Respite from indolence for the PRESIDENT HARRISON came in the wake of tragedy. Lassco's CITY of HONOLULU burned out and in a pinch for tonnage that could carry a few dozen First Class passengers, that new company settled on temporary allocation of the "502". A more permanent allocation for the idle sisters came through that same fall when both ships were assigned to Swayne & Hoyt for the run between Seattle and Buenos Aires. A long haul service with many, many intermediate ports, it almost seemed like the run was via everywhere. Most divertingly, Puerto Rico, an island quite out of the way to both Washington State and Argentina, was on the itinerary in both directions. An amended itinerary between the two terminals was eventually worked out and the line came to a certain prominence among West Coast American shipping endeavors as the "Pacific Argentine Brazil Line (or by the initials P-A-B-L)," but at that early stage its trade name was a mouthful—The Pacific West India and East Coast of South America Line. The two sisters made less than half a dozen round trips on that run before they were delivered to a new operator, their purchasers, the Dollar Steamship Lines, Ltd., Inc. which bought them for their new round the world service.

Even before the first "502" cast off from San Francisco for the voyage round the world, Dollar Line sought passengers. Aggressively marketed was the full round the world trip but realistically, few people had the time to take the 120 day sailing. Evocative advertisements appeared soon in magazines of general interest and in newspapers shortly after the consummation of the sale and a number of interesting folders and brochures were prepared, printed and distributed to steamship agents and hotels all over the United States, Canada, Europe and the Far East. Many alternatives to the full cruise were offered though for those with nothing but time and money the full circuit of the globe was just the ticket!

The "502"s Go Around the World

―――――――――――――――――――――――――――――◇

For over four hundred years many men dreamed of a sailing around the world via the isthmus of Panama, but the lack of a passageway through the 50 miles of land separating Caribbean Sea from Pacific Ocean presented a barrier virtually impassable. For almost as long as there had been Europeans aware of the "Panama Route" men dreamed of building a canal there but not until the last decades of the 19th Century did anyone make a serious effort to dig his way through. Completion of the Panama Canal in 1914 made the long desired "path between the seas" a reality and not only did it make possible a quick passage from Atlantic to Pacific, it allowed the United States Navy to establish its much desired two-ocean fleet. Business and commerce benefitted enormously since the new canal permitted vastly improved and quicker commercial sea links between East and West Coasts. But hardly anyone thought of the Canal as a short cut for long haul lines from the Northeast of the United States to either the Far East or the Antipodes nor did any Americans immediately assign steamers to an around the world run via Panama just yet. One reason for the delay to maximize the possibility of ocean services through Panama was the First World War. The history of American merchant shipping in the five decades preceding the completion of the Canal was another effective barrier to entrepreneurial thinking. No one was surprised that American steamship operators were slow to look into the possibilities of new trade routes until a proactive Shipping Board nudged hesitant shipping men to operate new routes.

By 1920 the Panama Canal had done two things for American merchant shipping—it had brought untold numbers of vessels and cargoes to both coasts of Panama during the construction of the big "Ditch" and once the canal opened for business, it made viable the intercoastal run between Atlantic and Pacific coasts of the United States. That "path between the seas" attracted so many operators that by the early 1920s American ships were making some 1,400 intercoastal voyages a year. Scores of companies both old and new chanced the new route, none as successful as those involved in carrying lumber from the Pacific Northwest to the East Coast, hauling all kinds of general manufactured goods westbound. Among the leaders was the Dollar Line which began operating intercoastal service in early 1921 by taking over the management and operation of the fleet of the Williams Steamship Company. But some far sighted shipping men aimed further than a New York to San Francisco and/or Seattle run. Of the many new lines established to operate under the American flag, perhaps none was more exciting than a round the world run.

97

Credit America's venerable Pacific Mail Steamship Company, the nation's oldest active steamship company, for scheduling and operating the first round the world sailings ever offered by an American steamship company. No one outside of the company's San Francisco headquarters had much faith in the success of the venture but Pacific Mail thought it worth a try. Maybe the shipping slump of late 1920 and its aftermath of a full scale depression in the shipping business had something to do with Pacific Mail's decision to send American ships around the world. Maybe it had something to do with cargo bookings being so few and so poor and big, fast Government owned tonnage being so many might have enticed Pacific Mail to attempt such a service. First American steamship line to California, first American steamship line to Japan, Pacific Mail was primarily under Grace ownership when it established round the world cargo service under the American flag in 1921. Of course results were unencouraging—the shipping world was in a depression and no one was making any money so to no-one's surprise, the line was quickly abandoned. Worse, though, there seemed to be no point in operating such a service under the United States flag. It was SO expensive and as was so often true in American shipping endeavors, when there was no money to be made, the steamship men and the financiers looked elsewhere to make a buck.

Enter the Dollars, father Robert and son R. Stanley. They reasoned that a round the world passenger and cargo service made sense. Canny and astute as ever, the two men thought a round the world service under the American flag could work. Self made lumber and steamship man, a millionaire several times over, Captain Robert Dollar and his second son, R. Stanley Dollar approached Pacific Mail's experience from another angle, rightly reasoning that the facts of geography would make a round the world passenger and cargo service profitable. Captain Dollar made his point proving that cargo could arrive in the Northeastern United States quicker by sailing westwards from India by water to New York than eastwards by sea to San Francisco and thence by land across America. He showed how a ship sailing on the Panama route took even longer to get Indian cargo to New York markets. He was soon convinced that frequent sailings maintained on a strict schedule would eventually lower shippers' costs by speeding up required shipping time. Robert Dollar (the title "Captain" was an honorific), also knew that the service would lose money, lots of money and lose it for as many as five years. Events would prove him right on almost every count.[1]

Even as Pacific Mail drew back from its losing round the world venture, the Dollars sent British flag freighters in the wake of the American ships that had lost so much money. Captain Dollar was so sure the service would work that he did more than put words into the plan. He went east with his Port Captain and arrived in Boston on May 26, 1922 to see if and how that port could fit into his company's round the world line.

---

[1] His multi-volume published diary, perhaps more notable for what he never said for posterity than what he did say, makes his point, plainly stated that the service cost money in the first five years.

His aggressively determined son, R. Stanley Dollar also believed in the principle of such a line. He also insisted on offering passenger service. Prodded by Stanley, patriarch Robert Dollar soon realized that the service could work and resolved to accept the financial losses the inauguration of such a line entailled. The next step was the hunt for suitable ships. They had to be modern vessels of good speed and able to carry a fair number of passengers who would bring the line tidy sums of cash in passage fares. Thus far the Dollars had no real experience in the carriage of passengers but losses in cargo carriage over the first few years were expected to be so heavy that passenger revenues might help soften the financial blow.

Rationalizing the scope of the plan, the Dollars estimated that they would need to offer sailings from every port along the way at two week intervals. At first it looked like they would need twelve ships but they quickly realized that seven sister ships could handle the line if the voyage were limited to 112 days. Of the many classes of Shipping Board vessels, only one was already fitted for the carriage of about a hundred passengers. That was the "502". They fit the bill since there was no need to send each ship for extensive modifications to fit passenger quarters. The hunt for tonnage narrowed down, father and son agreed—only the "502"'s would do and they had to have all seven of them. When the Dollars hit on the idea of buying those sisters, no one even knew if they were for sale. So far the Shipping Board had never included them among vessels advertised for sale. However, ANY ship is for sale if an intending buyer offers enough money, but the frugal Dollars were not inclined to overpay for anything.

The Dollars had to find out if they could buy these ships and had to make their inquiries very discretely, lest antagonists in the business attempt their own pre-emptive purchase of tonnage the Dollars coveted. With the staggering operating losses they posted on the important London line, the five "502"'s on the North Atlantic looked like a poor bet to most private operators. Who could contemplate buying these ships for they had yet to reward an operator, manager or agent with anything but headaches? The Dollars felt confident that if an agreement on a price could be reached, they might very well be able to buy the seven ships. As the Northeast of the United States shivered through another frosty winter, R. Stanley Dollar made his way in February 1923 from his San Francisco offices to those of the Shipping Board in Washington to do just that. Buying the seven sister "502"'s was not a matter of walking into the head office of the Shipping Board Emergency Fleet Corporation, handing over a suitcase of money or a stack of bank checks and taking titles to those steamers. It took him six months of tough negotiations to come to terms with the officers of the United States Shipping Board Emergency Fleet Corporation. In September they finally struck the bargain for the sale of the seven sisterships and the Commissioners of the Shipping Board lost no time in approving recommendations to authorize the sale. A very quiet and very private transaction thus far, a very quiet announcement of the sale was circulated in the Washington office of the Shipping Board and to the Dollar offices in San Francisco on September 12, 1923. Under the terms of the contract it would take up to six more months for the fleet of seven sister ships to be transferred to their buyer. The quest to buy the seven ships generated a tremendous pile of paperwork all of which was read, if only once. Except for the wholesale disposition of emergency built wooden steamers for scrapping, the Shipping Board had yet to make such a large bona fide sale.

As expected, news of the sale was not greeted with universal approval. Oppositionists howled in protest against Dollar's luck, detractors charging the Board with favoritism in selling these important ships to the Dollars. Some even sued the Shipping Board to halt the sale. In its defense the Shipping Board denied the allegation, reporting the vote on the sale was six in favor to one opposed, and the sole dissenter balked at the sale only because he felt the sales price was too low. Further, answered the Shipping Board, the sale was made after the public appearance of an advertisement in newspapers and trade journals and that the ONLY offer for the "502" class ships was that made by the Dollars. The suit was thrown out of court.

When the announcement of the sale was made on September 12, 1923, Stanley Dollar had yet to receive corporate authority for his action. That technicality was completed in San Francisco five days later when the Board of Directors of the Dollar Steamship Line resolved a special meeting on September 17, 1923: "That R. Stanley Dollar, Vice President of this company be, and is hereby authorized to purchase for this company the following named (*Author's note—names misspelled in the original*) steamers ss PRESIDENT HAYES, ss PRESIDENT HARRISON, ss PRESIDENT ADAMS, ss PRESIDENT GARFIELD, ss PRESIDENT MONROE ss PRESIDENT POLK, ss PRESIDENT van BUREN on such terms and conditions as he deems advisable, and that said R. Stanley Dollar be, and is hereby, authorized to execute for and on behalf of this company and in its name all agreements, notes, mortgages and undertakings necessary to effect said purchase. And be it further resolved that William J. Brush be appointed assistant secretary and be empowered to affix the duly attested corporate seal of documents necessary to effect the purchase" Signed by H.M. Lorber, Secretary Dollar Steamship Line.[2]

The paperwork was not completed nor was the sale recorded until September 25th. Purchase contract #3148–23 was the result of months of negotiations and details. It begins: "This agreement entered into this 25 day of September 1923, between the UNITED STATES OF AMERICA, represented by the UNITED STATES SHIPPING BOARD, herein after called the "seller", and DOLLAR STEAMSHIP LINE, a California Corporation, herein after called the "BUYER".

---

[2] A copy of the sales agreement, exhibits and this authorization appears in the 1091 file for each of the seven sister ships in RG 32 at National Archives.

WITNESSETH

WHEREAS, the Seller is the owner of the following steamers "PRESIDENT HAYES", "PRESIDENT GARFIELD", "PRESIDENT ADAMS", "PRESIDENT HARRISON", "PRESIDENT VAN BUREN", "PRESIDENT POLK" and "PRESIDENT MONROE"; and WHEREAS the Buyer has agreed to purchase said vessels from the Seller on the terms and conditions hereinafter set forth; and WHEREAS: the Buyer has agreed to establish with said vessels and to maintain for a period of five years a Round-the-World route and service as hereinafter set forth:

ARTICLE I

The Seller agrees to sell to the Buyer, and the Buyer agrees to purchase from the Seller, the steel vessels "PRESIDENT HAYES", "PRESIDENT GARFIELD", "PRESIDENT ADAMS", "PRESIDENT HARRISON", "PRESIDENT VAN BUREN", "PRESIDENT POLK" and "PRESIDENT MONROE", official numbers 220858, 221426, 221203, 220952, 220709, 221054, 220325 respectively, for the sum of Five Hundred and Fifty Thousand ($550,000) Dollars for each vessel, payable as follows:

(a) On delivery of any vessel by the Seller to the Buyer, Twenty Five (25%) percent in cash, or by an irrevocable letter of credit satisfactory to the Seller, payable on March 14, 1926, together with interest thereon at the rate of four percent per annum from the date of the delivery of the vessel.

(b) Five (5%) percent of the purchase price per annum on or before the Fifteenth day of March in the years 1927, 1928, 1929, 1930, 1931, 1932, 1933, 1934 and 1935. together with interest thereon at the rate of four (4%) percent per annum, Payable annually from the date of delivery of the vessel.

(c) The balance of the purchase price on or before March 15, 1936, together with interest thereon at the rate of Four (4%) per annum, payable annually from the date of the delivery of the vessel.

(d) All of said deferred payments shall be evidenced by negotiable promissory notes of the buyer bearing interest at Four (4%) percent per annum, payable annually, which notes shall be substantially in the form of Schedule "A", hereunto annexed.

ARTICLE II

Simultaneously with the delivery of any vessel by the Seller to the Buyer, and with the payment of the aforesaid first installment of the purchase price, and the execution and delivery of the aforesaid promissory notes by the Buyer to the Seller, the Seller shall execute and deliver to the Buyer a bill of sale for such vessel, in usual Government form, conveying the vessel, with warranty but not warranting the vessel as to tonnage, quality, condition or seaworthiness, which bill of sale shall be substantially in the form of Schedule "B" hereunto annexed; and immediately following the execution and delivery of such bill of sale by the Seller to the Buyer, the Buyer shall execute and deliver to the Seller a First Preferred Mortgage on the vessel to secure the payment of the deferred installments of the purchase price and the aforesaid promissory notes evidencing same, which First Preferred Mortgage shall be substantially in the form of Schedule "C", hereunto annexed, but the execution of such bill of sale shall not release or discharge the covenants contained in Articles VI and VII hereof.

ARTICLE III

The Seller shall use due diligence to deliver four of said vessels within the period of four months and the remaining three vessels not later than six months from the date of this agreement, but if such delivery is prevented for reasons which the Seller thinks justifiable, the time of delivery shall be extended until such vessels can, by exercise of due diligence, be delivered. Said vessels shall be delivered at the ports of New York and/or San Francisco, at the option of the Seller, classed at the highest classification for vessels of their type by the American Bureau of Shipping, and with certificates of the United States Steamboat Inspection Service in full force and effect, and in the condition that said vessels now are, ordinary wear and tear excepted, except that if any of said vessels shall suffer any damage by accident between date hereof and date of delivery to the Buyer, such damage shall be repaired by the Seller at its expense.

ARTICLE IV

The Seller shall also deliver with each of said vessels, as part and parcel thereof, all boats, tackle, apparel, equipment, spare parts, furnishings and appurtenances thereunto pertaining and belonging, as shown by the inventory on her last voyage before delivery, whether aboard the vessel or ashore, in the same good order and condition as they now are, ordinary wear and tear excepted, including therein all advertising matter in stock pertaining to the vessels, and all plates, cuts and one complete set of builders plans and specifications for each vessel, but Excluding fuel, consumable stores, submarine signalling apparatus and leased radio equipment on board said vessels.

ARTICLE V

The Buyer agrees to make with said vessels not less than a total of ten round voyages a year, unless prevented by any causes of whatsoever kind beyond the control of the Buyer, for a period of five successive years from and after the date of the delivery of the first vessel to the Buyer, in a Round-the-World route and service, which shall commence on the East Coast of the United States and continue through the Panama Canal to the United States and continue through the Panama Canal to the Pacific, with the Buyer's option to call at United States pacific Coast ports and Honolulu; thence to Japan, China, Philippine Islands and Straits Settlements, with the Buyer's option to call at Dutch East Indies and Indian ports; thence through the Suez Canal, with the Buyer's option to call at any African, Eastern Mediterranean and European ports: thence to the East Coast of the United States: or at the Option of the Buyer any or all voyages may be made in the reverse order. and said ports or Places may be visited in any order; provided, however, that in the event any of the vessels are not delivered to the Buyer, and/or after delivery any of the vessels is lost or destroyed, the number of voyages hereunto shall be reduced proportionately.

ARTICLE VII

In the event that the Buyer shall fail to make the number of voyages required by Article VI hereof, unless prevented by said excepted causes, or if the buyer by its act shall render it impossible to make the number of voyages required by Article VI hereof, then in such case the Seller may at once take possession of all of the vessels wherever the same may be and the Buyer shall forthwith surrender the actual possession of the vessels immediately on written demand of the Seller so to do, and the Seller may hold, lease, charter, operate or otherwise use the vessels for maintenance of said route or service, for the remainder of said five year period, or any part thereof, at its sole cost and/or to its sole profit: in the event of the Seller taking possession of the vessels; the Buyer agrees, if requested by the Seller, to place at the service of the Seller its entire organization without charge for executive salaries, and all other facilities for the operation of the vessels at current published rates, less ten percent.

The Seller shall redeliver said vessels, together with all boats, tackle, apparel, equipment, spare parts, furnishings and appurtenances thereunto appertaining and belonging, to the Buyer at the end of said five year period at the port or place at which possession was taken from the Buyer, in good order and condition, ordinary wear and tear excepted, and free and clear of all liens and encumbrances except the mortgage herein provided for, unless lost or destroyed.

In the event of the Seller taking possession of the vessels under this Article, condition surveys of the vessels and inventories of the boats, tackle, apparel, equipment, spare parts, furnishings and appurtenances thereunto appertaining and

belonging, and of fuel and consumable stores on board; both on delivery and repossession of the vessels, shall be taken and agreed upon, and all consumable stores and fuel, and, if taken, all excess boats, tackle, apparel, equipment, spare parts, furnishings and appurtenances, shall be paid for by the party taking the same at current market prices prevailing at the port or place where delivery and/or redelivery of the vessels, as the case may be, is made, unless otherwise agreed to.

During such period as the Seller may operate said vessels under the provisions hereof, the Seller agrees, at its own cost and expense, to keep each vessel insured for Five Hundred Fifty Thousand ($550,000) dollars, as required by the provisions of the First Preferred Mortgage, and to pay the cost of such insurance.

The right to take possession of and operate said vessels, as aforesaid, shall be the exclusive remedy of the Seller against the Buyer for any failure to maintain said service as hereinabove provided.

ARTICLE VIII

The Buyer shall have the right to change the name of any and all of the vessels at any time.

ARTICLE IX

If by any reason of anything beyond the control of the Seller, it is unable to deliver all of the vessels herein contracted for, the Buyer agrees to accept such vessels as the Seller is able to deliver. Upon the terms and conditions herein set forth.

ARTICLE X

The Buyer shall furnish to the Seller a financial statement of its assets and liabilities and of its profits and losses the end of each fiscal year in the five year period during which said route and service is to be maintained.

ARTICLE XI

All the covenants, stipulations and agreements in this agreement contained are and shall be binding upon the successors and of the parties hereto.

IN WITNESS THEREOF, the parties hereto have executed these presents the day and year first above written.

ATTEST: BY UNITED STATES OF AMERICA
CARL P. KREMERBY EDWARD P. FARLEY
Secretary Chairman

ATTEST:DOLLAR STEAMSHIP LINE
WILLIAM J BUSH BY R. STANLEY DOLLAR
Assist. Secretary Vice-President[3]

With that almost standard form six page contract, the machinery to turn the "502"'s over to private hands began. The reason for the detailed four month period for delivery of the first four and up to six months for the remaining three units had to do with the Shipping Board's need to retain the five "502"'s on the London line until suitable replacements could be placed in service. Indicating just how poorly the sisters were doing financially and how bad sales prices were in general, the amount the Dollars paid for all seven ships was approximately the same amount as one ship had cost just over two years earlier. Closely inspecting their purchases in taking delivery, Dollar Line discovered an alarming number of items needing correction and/or repair and felt the Shipping Board responsible to pay related costs, under terms of the original contract. Settling the matter was a further agreement between the Board and Dollar Line, a document attached to the purchase contract dated January 12, 1924.

In it, the United States of America represented by the United States Shipping Board was named First Party. Second party was Dollar Steamship Line, a California corporation.

WHEREAS, controversy has arisen between the parties hereto as to which party is obliged to bear the cost of effecting those certain repairs set forth and described in the telegram of Chisholm and Relyea dated San Francisco, January 3, 1924, a copy of which is hereto attached, to the steamship PRESIDENT HAYES, now in the port of San Francisco, California. Under the provisions of that certain purchase and sale agreement dated September 25, 1923, covering the sale and purchase of the steamships PRESIDENT HAYES,

---

[3] ibid.

PRESIDENT GARFIELD, PRESIDENT ADAMS, PRESIDENT HARRISON, PRESIDENT van BUREN, PRESIDENT POLK and PRESIDENT MONROE.

NOW THEREFORE it is hereby agreed:

1. That the Second Party shall make, and advance the funds necessary to pay for, such repairs, if any, described in said Exhibit, to said steamship as shall be necessary to enable said steamship to obtain a United States Steamboat Inspector's Certificate, so as to proceed to sea on her Round-the-World voyage, under protest and without prejudice to claim of Second Party, if any, that said repairs should be made and paid for, and that reimbursement for said expenditures should be made, by the First Party under the Provisions of the aforesaid agreement.

2. That the remaining repairs set forth and described in the aforesaid Exhibit shall be held in abeyance without prejudice to the claim of the Second Party that the same should be made and paid for by the First Party under the aforesaid agreement of September 25, 1923.

3. That a representative of the Second Party shall proceed to Washington as soon as possible for the purpose of endeavoring to adjust and settle said controversy with the First Party.

4. That if the parties hereto are unable to agree as to which of them is obligated to make and pay for all or any of the repairs set forth and described in said Exhibit, then the Second Party may complete all or any of said repairs under protest and without prejudice to any claim which it may legally have under said agreement of September 25, 1923 for reimbursement for its expenditures, in making such repairs and for its expenditures made under Paragraph 1 of this agreement, or any part thereof for which the First party does not admit liability.

5. That the acceptance of delivery of said steamer and Payment of the first installment of the purchase price and the execution and delivery of the promissory notes evidencing the balance of said purchase price and of the preferred mortgage securing the same shall be without prejudice to this agreement and the rights. if any, hereby reserved.

6. That the execution of this agreement shall in no respect prejudice the First Party in its denial of any liability for repairs set forth and described in said Exhibit hereto attached.

7. That in no event shall the First Party be liable for the making of any repairs other than those specified in the Bid under date of [this left blank in Shipping Board General Files Copy.] 1—made by Bethlehem Shipbuilding Company for the making of the repairs described in Exhibit A, nor at a cost in excess of the lowest bid received by the Second Party for the making of such repairs and Second Party agrees to submit all such repairs to not less than three responsible repair concerns in no way affiliated with the Second Party.

For the United States of America, Shipping Board Chairman Admiral Benson signed while for the Dollars, it was their attorney Ira A. Campbell whose signature inked the space for the Dollar Steamship Line.[4]

---

[4] ibid.

What were these repairs? What was "EXHIBIT A"? Exhibit A was a telegram reading:

Retel one five HAYES Competitive bids opened Bethlehem low bidders prices as follows STOP Drydocking vessel fifty two hundred sixty six dollars fifty cents renewing outer section starboard tail shaft place in lathe try for trueness and replace this includes checking and adjusting pitch on the propellor blades twenty nine hundred eighty dollars STOP If required make one section starboard tail shaft thirty five hundred sixty dollars renew one bronze propellor blade seventeen hundred twenty eight dollars STOP Renewing insulation lower refrigerating chambers twenty three thousand eight hundred fifty dollars this includes six thousand dollars cost for material to be removed from our stock in warehouse STOP Free up and put in good working condition eight lifeboat davits one hundred eighty dollars remove nuts from one hundred seventy five leaky stay nuts in main boiler furnaces burn off stay nuts and rivet over caulk one hundred thirty feet of leaky seam in back connections caulk sixty eight rivets back furnace flange caulk one hundred fifty seven leaky stay bolts in wrapper sheets remove nuts from six main stay rods remake with white lead and caulk around nuts remove nine furnace fronts caulk front seam of furnaces and replace furnace fronts three thousand two hundred thirty dollars this price covers work on five boilers only one boiler now under steam yet to be tested estimated cost of this boiler seven hundred dollars STOP Received quotation of fifteen dollars per stay for renewing stay bolts in back connections will not know exact number of stays to be renewed until after stay nuts have been removed from stays estimated cost thirteen hundred dollars STOP Renew present angle bar clips from settling tanks bulkheads in fireroom and replace with tee bars this item will require steaming and cleaning of both settling tanks forty one hundred eighty dollars renew brick arches in eighteen boiler furnaces four hundred thirty dollars STOP Life boat equipment five hundred ten dollar grand total estimated forty seven thousand six hundred twenty four dollars fifty cents STOP Completion date of repairs January twenty second STOP Shipley quotation for renewing insulation refrigerating chambers twenty four thousand five hundred dollars.[5]

Since the total for these repairs and claimed deficiencies was in the neighborhood of 10% of the total sales price, it is no wonder controversy raged between buyer and seller. Before long, lists of items to be paid for by Shipping Board, by the Dollars and others to be settled by arbitration were soon prepared.

All things considered, the purchase of the seven ships as well as the establishment of this frankly speculative round the world service was an amazingly ambitious program for a conservative American shipping man. On paper it certainly looked like the Dollars got a sweetheart deal—paying a total of $3,850,000.00 for seven still new ships that had cost the government

---

[5] ibid.

of United States of America a total of $28,604,444.22. Plus expenses the total cost of the seven ships to the Government was $29,071,000.00 and various extras brought the sale price to be paid by the Dollars to $4,200,000.00. Not obvious to the naked eye were the exorbitant costs of the operation of such ships under the American flag and the start-up nature of the venture. There was no guarantee that any shipper would rush to patronize this new service. This purchase represented a major step for the family's businesses, theretofore restricted to frequently exchanged freighters, West Coast shipping and lumber trading. Head of the conservative Dollar clan, Captain Dollar was almost seventy-eight years old when he bought the "502"'s, quite an age to have to prepare for more years of hard work and semesters of red ink. But he very much believed in the project and knew the service would eventually turn in quite a profit. To make the downpayment of about 20% of the purchase price of the "502"'s, Captain Dollar turned to the Board of Directors of his newly incorporated Dollar Steamship Company and to Herbert Fleischhacker, San Francisco banker, frequent associate of the Dollars. The new Dollar firm provided the sum of $105,000 towards the down payment. Fleishhacker arranged a much bigger sum, financing the down payment in the form of a letter of credit issued by his Anglo London & Paris National Bank in the amount $866,250.00. Those payments satisfied the Shipping Board's immediate demand for cash. Within two years the buyers were to pay 25% of the purchase price while the remaining balance due on the ships would be payable at 5% interest after the first two years and be paid off by March 15, 1936. For his part in arranging the money, Fleischhacker became an officer in the Dollar Steamship Line, Inc. His hand would stay in the Dollar Line pie for years. For masterminding the purchase of the seven sister ships and for the tremendous energy he expended travelling to Washington and personally negotiating with the Commissioners of the United States Shipping Board to buy the seven ships as well as his work in arranging the deal, R. Stanley Dollar was handsomely rewarded by his father. Captain Robert Dollar paid Stanley a finder's fee of over $200,000.00, an unseemly payment that was charged as an expense against the ships in company records.

News of the purchase of the Government steamers remained secret for less than 24 hours. In its September 13, 1923 edition, the *San Francisco Examiner* reported the sale to its readers. Two days later that paper carried a report about the planned round the world route.

Though he prevailed over other parties in purchasing the "502"'s, not all went as Stanley Dollar planned, for he really wanted a Britain to Boston and New York route at the tail end of the round the world voyage. His intention was to have the "502"'s work their way back from the Suez Canal via Italy and Gibraltar and then sail north to Britain from whence they would work their way back across the Atlantic to the United States. Certainly a longer final leg to a homeward leg of a world trip, the possible revenues on the Britain to New York, Panama, Los Angeles and San Francisco run lured Stanley Dollar every bit as much as did the rest of the round the world service. He felt that westbound cargo on the North Atlantic would produce the revenue needed to make the service pay. In his ambition to get that routing on the homeward leg, Stanley Dollar struck a nerve among both American and British shipping men who evinced a visceral contempt for the grandiose plan. Most hostile to the Dollars was the New York based management of the United States Lines . . . Moore & McCormack and the Roosevelt Steamship Company, seconded by the Harriman interests. Indeed, had United States Lines been an independent, private company at the time Dollar Line bought the "502"'s, they would have fought hard to keep them, feeling that as conditions in Europe improved, more business would come their way.

Partisan politics surely entered the picture and it must be assumed that the Dollar family were staunch Republicans. Rising ascendant under the administrations of Calvin Coolidge and Herbert Hoover, Dollar Steamship Lines later named their most important ships for those men. During the first two terms of the Democratic administration of Franklin Roosevelt, the fortunes of the line and family ebbed considerably. Stanley Dollar was unable to get a route to and from Britain. That had to wait until 1931 when he and his firm invested with the IMM and the Roosevelt Steamship Company bought United States Lines. In 1923 there was simply too much opposition from other steamship operators to permit the Dollars to get the United Kingdom to New York route. Instead, the ships were obliged to return to the United States logically and directly from the Mediterranean. Consequently Genoa became the most important European center of Dollar Line operations.

The Dollar Line retained the "President" names and the seven steamers joined the Dollar fleet in this order: PRESIDENT HARRISON, PRESIDENT HAYES, PRESIDENT ADAMS, PRESIDENT GARFIELD, PRESIDENT POLK, PRESIDENT MONROE and PRESIDENT van BUREN. Already on the West Coast when the sale was made, it was an easy matter for the Shipping Board to arrange delivery to their purchasers of the PRESIDENT HARRISON and PRESIDENT HAYES. In the right place at the right time, to these two ships fell the honor of inaugurating the heralded new American flag round the world line. On delivery, the ships were made to help pay for themselves. With Dollar luck rising ascendant, the market for scrap steel was on an upswing. R. Stanley Dollar, never one to pass up a chance for profit, sold the tons of steel rails and scrap ballasting each of the seven ships. Captain Dollar was quite aware of the financial risks involved in establishing this passenger cargo service but there were a few crutches on which he could rely if need be. Government assistance in the form of mail payments was promised if the Dollar Line offered a minimum of ten sailings per year on the round the world line. Dollar Line did better than that, providing an average of 26 sailings a year on this itinerary. Despite an expected first year operating loss, of an amount approaching $650,000, the following four years showed annual average profits of about $750,000 and Captain Robert Dollar

DOLLAR STEAMSHIP LINE
EXPRESS FREIGHT AND PASSENGER SERVICES
SCHEDULE OF SAILINGS

INTERCOASTAL WESTBOUND

PASSENGER STEAMER	Voy.	LEAVE		ARRIVE			
		BOSTON	NEW YORK	Los Angeles	San Francisco	*Seattle	*Vancouver
President Garfield - - -	3	Sailed	Oct. 2	Oct. 20	Oct. 23	Oct. 28	Oct. 30
President Polk - - - -	3	Oct. 7	Oct. 16	Nov. 3	Nov. 6	Nov. 14	Nov. 15
President Monroe - - -	3	Oct. 21	Oct. 30	Nov. 17	Nov. 20	Nov. 28	Nov. 29
President Harrison - -	4	Nov. 4	Nov. 13	Dec. 1	Dec. 4	Dec. 12	Dec. 13
President Van Buren -	3	Nov. 18	Nov. 27	Dec. 15	Dec. 18	Dec. 26	Dec. 27

FREIGHT STEAMER	Voy.	LEAVE				ARRIVE			
		Portland	Philadelphia	Baltimore	Norfolk	Los Angeles	San Francisco	Seattle	Vancouver
Margaret Dollar - - - -	7	Oct. 3	Oct. 8	Oct. 14	Oct. 15	Nov. 5	Nov. 8	Nov. 14	Nov. 15
Diana Dollar - - - - -	7	Oct. 17	Oct. 22	Oct. 28	Oct. 29	Nov. 19	Nov. 22	Nov. 28	Nov. 29
Stuart Dollar - - - - -	7	Nov. 1	Nov. 5	Nov. 11	Nov. 12	Dec. 3	Dec. 6	Dec. 12	Dec. 13
Melville Dollar - - - -	9	Nov. 17	Nov. 21	Nov. 26	Nov. 27	Dec. 17	Dec. 20	Dec. 26	Dec. 27
Stanley Dollar - - - -	8	Dec. 11	Dec. 16	Dec. 20	Dec. 22	Jan. 14	Jan. 17	Jan. 23	Jan. 24

*Via San Francisco

INTERCOASTAL EASTBOUND

STEAMER	Voy.	LEAVE				ARRIVE			
		Vancouver	Seattle	San Francisco	Los Angeles	Philadelphia	New York	Boston	Portland
Stuart Dollar - - - - -	7	Sailed	Sailed	Sept. 28	....	Oct. 21	Oct. 24	Oct. 30	Nov. 1
Melville Dollar - - - -	9	Oct. 2	Oct. 8	Oct. 13	Oct. 15	Nov. 5	Nov. 7	Nov. 15	Nov. 17
Stanley Dollar - - - -	8	Oct. 22	Oct. 30	Nov. 4	Nov. 6	Nov. 28	Dec. 1	Dec. 8	Dec. 11
Margaret Dollar - - - -	8	Nov. 22	Dec. 1	Dec. 6	....	Dec. 29	Dec. 31	Jan. 8	Jan. 10
Diana Dollar - - - - -	8	Dec. 6	Dec. 13	Dec. 18	Dec. 20	Jan. 10	Jan. 14	Jan. 26	Jan. 29

ATLANTIC COAST—FAR EAST			PACIFIC COAST—ORIENT		
VIA PANAMA			VIA HONOLULU		
EXPRESS MAIL STEAMERS			EXPRESS MAIL STEAMERS		
TO			TO		
HONOLULU, KOBE, SHANGHAI, HONGKONG, MANILA, SINGAPORE, PENANG, COLOMBO			KOBE, SHANGHAI, HONGKONG, MANILA, SINGAPORE, PENANG, COLOMBO		
STEAMER	From Boston	From New York	STEAMER	From Los Angeles	From San Francisco
President Polk - - - -	Oct. 7	Oct. 16	President Adams - - -	Oct. 7	Oct. 11
President Monroe - - -	Oct. 21	Oct. 30	President Garfield - - -	Oct. 21	Oct. 25
President Harrison - -	Nov. 4	Nov. 13	President Polk - - - -	Nov. 4	Nov. 8
President Van Buren -	Nov. 18	Nov. 27	President Monroe - - -	Nov. 18	Nov. 22
EVERY 14 DAYS THEREAFTER			EVERY 14 DAYS THEREAFTER		

SUBJECT TO CHANGE WITHOUT NOTICE

Advertising upcoming sailings on the round the world line, the Dollars appealed to those shipping freight or travelling between New York and the West Coast. Author's collection

came to regard the purchase of the "502" ships "the best large deal his company ever made."[6]

This new service made the Dollar Line a company with the world on its schedule. The voyage around the world was at first scheduled to last 120 days and passengers could book a full circuit or take passage among any ports along the way. Cargo, though, was at the heart of this service and for invaluable freight, calls were arranged at ports in 14 countries around the world. To allow fortnightly sailings, the service would need twelve ships. There were only seven of the passenger carrying "502"s, so five big, fast Dollar Line freighters were assigned to operate with them, their sailings interspersed to best advantage. A few years later saw the introduction of additional passenger tonnage on the run, but it is the "502" that remains forever associated as the Dollar Line Round the World steamer.

---

[6] op.cit.

Here is the original itinerary planned for the round the world service: The voyage from New York was originally set and for years began with a Thursday afternoon sailing from either Pier 22 or Pier 23 in Brooklyn for Havana. At first the Dollar "502"'s departed at 2:00PM but later on sailing time was set back to 5:00PM and later still to 7:00PM. The Havana call was made on Mondays between 8:00AM and midnight. Between Havana and San Francisco lay more days in the warm sun, as the ships made for a Friday transit of the Panama Canal. Ten days' steaming away was Los Angeles where the sisters showed their blunt bows on Mondays at 6:00AM. Sailing Tuesday nights at 10:00 PM gave over two full workdays to handle freight and allowed passengers a chance to head inland, perhaps for a glimpse at the homes of their favorite movie stars. After a day at sea, usually spent pitching in the usually rough waters off the California coast, the round the world Dollar liner arrived at her San Francisco home port at 6:00 AM on Thursday. From San Francisco at 5:00PM on Saturday, the "President" liners crossed the Pacific to Honolulu where most passengers and not a few crew headed for Waikiki Beach during the ship's call on Saturdays between the ship's 6:00 AM arrival and 10:00PM departure for Kobe. Twelve days away by "502"[7], the Dollar Liner arrived at 7:00 AM on Fridays, to sail on the tide on Saturday. Shanghai was next and these ships were scheduled to arrive on the tide on Tuesday and sail on the tide on Friday. Then these ships steamed on to Hong Kong, where they arrived on Monday mornings. More precise was the Tuesday sailing scheduled for noon from that Crown Colony. Southwards now the "502"'s made for Manila and arrived at that American colony at 8:00 AM on Thursdays for an overnight stay. Every second Friday at 5:00PM a Dollar "502" sailed from there for Singapore and a 6:00AM Wednesday arrival. Forty eight hours later the Dollar ship sailed at that early hour from busy Singapore for Penang to load rubber after her 11:00AM Saturday arrival. At 6:00PM the same evening the "502" cast off for Colombo, Ceylon, which she reached just two hours short of four days later at 4:00PM on Wednesday. After stocking her holds with locally grown tea, rubber and spices the Dollar ship sailed from there at noon on Thursdays. It then took her eleven days to make her way through the Indian Ocean, Gulf of Aden and the Red Sea to Suez. Arrivals of these sisters was set for Mondays at 8:00AM. Itineraries next mentioned a Tuesday departure at 6:00PM from Port Said. Once through the Canal, after a call from 7:00AM Wednesday through Thursday at 7:00AM at Alexandria, the "502"'s sailed across the blue Mediterranean for a 6:00AM Sunday arrival at Naples. That call was no more than a technical visit for the "502" departed from there at 2:00PM for Genoa. From Mondays at 4:00PM through Tuesdays 6:00PM the "502" was at Genoa. Finally the Dollar ship arrived at her last foreign port—Marseilles. Calls there were on Wednesdays between 8:00 AM and 6:00PM when the "502" cast off

---

[7] It might look like thirteen days, but heading westwards, the "502" crossed the International Date Line and lost a day.

for a twelve day run to Boston. After an overnight call there she finally headed back to New York. Later on, the ships crossed directly to New York and then made a "side trip" to Boston. Sailings from New York were eventually set for Wednesdays and towards the end of their commercial careers took sailings on Saturdays.

East Coast manager of Dollar Line operations J.F. Schumacher announced the sailing schedule of the round the world liners on December 5, 1923. Informing the shipping business that the PRESIDENT HARRISON would sail from San Francisco on January 5, 1924 and be followed from there by the PRESIDENT HAYES on February 2nd, he let everyone know that all five "New York boats" would begin their Dollar Line careers with sailings from there. First out would be the PRESIDENT ADAMS, booked for February 7th. Following her on February 21st would be the PRESIDENT GARFIELD with the PRESIDENT POLK sailing on March 6th. Then would come the turn of the PRESIDENT MONROE, expected to join the world service with her March 20th sailing from New York. Last was to be the PRESIDENT van BUREN, slated to head out to sea in Dollar Line colors on April 17th. Schumacher also announced rates ranging from $1,250.00 to $1,890.00 per person for the full voyage and ranging from $250.00 to $450.00 for the New York to California segment.

At San Francisco at the close of their unspectacular careers on the Pacific-Brazil-Argentine Line from Seattle, San Francisco and Los Angeles to the East Coast of South America, the PRESIDENT HARRISON and PRESIDENT HAYES were just where the Dollars wanted them. It was easy to take delivery and ready them to inaugurate Dollar Line's round the world service. It was also a cause for celebrations. One of the most famous was a Christmas party hosted by Captain Dollar aboard the PRESIDENT HARRISON in San Francisco harbor on December 25, 1923. Inviting a number of civic leaders, leading shipping men and other notables to join him and his family, Captain Dollar took the opportunity to present the new service in living form, introducing a series of young women, each dressed in costume typical of one of the countries on the line's itinerary. After welcoming the new ship into the fleet, Captain and Mrs. Dollar took off for Seattle on the first leg of another round the world trip on their own. Establishing and maintaining personal contact with shippers in the Far East had so far helped his steamship line's growth. Adding to his great collection of business friends could not help but to do the same for this new Dollar service. Not all were thrilled when Dollar entered the world service. Voicing strong anti-American sentiment (most famous was the cry "the Americans are fly-by-night, here today but who knows where tomorrow") were several shipping companies. Lord Inchcape, P & O's Chairman, publicly called Dollar an "interloper", adding further unkind words to his plea for shippers to ignore the new American alternative. As Captain Dollar told it in his memoirs, the two men eventually became   great   friends,   but   his   diaries   have   the   deserved   rep-

DOLLAR STEAMSHIP LINE
SERVES THE WORLD
The ROBERT DOLLAR CO. MANAGING DIRECTORS

PASSENGER FARE SCHEDULE
(Cancelling Passenger Fare Schedule of November 21, 1923)
PRINCIPAL ONE-WAY AND ROUND THE WORLD
FIRST CABIN PER CAPITA ADULT FARES ARE SHOWN BELOW
More Complete Information is Contained in Passenger Tariffs

	Rooms with Private Tub Bath	Rooms with Private Shower Bath		Rooms Without Private Bath		
	A-1	A-2	A-3	B-1	B-2	B-3
INTERCOASTAL FARES						
NEW YORK To						
Havana	$170.00	$160.00	$150.00	$125.00	$110.00	$ 85.00
Colon	235.00	220.00	205.00	185.00	160.00	145.00
Los Angeles (Port of)	450.00	425.00	400.00	325.00	300.00	250.00
San Francisco	450.00	425.00	400.00	325.00	300.00	250.00
TRANS-PACIFIC FARES						
SAN FRANCISCO To						
Honolulu	200.00	175.00	165.00	140.00	130.00	115.00
LOS ANGELES (PORT OF) To						
Honolulu (via San Francisco)	225.00	200.00	185.00	160.00	145.00	130.00
SAN FRANCISCO or						
LOS ANGELES (PORT OF) To						
Kobe	415.00	363.00	350.00	311.00	311.00	311.00
Shanghai	461.00	404.00	385.00	346.00	346.00	346.00
Hong Kong	500.00	438.00	415.00	375.00	375.00	375.00
Manila	500.00	438.00	415.00	375.00	375.00	375.00
Singapore	561.00	500.00	482.00	423.00	408.00	408.00
Penang	575.00	513.00	494.00	434.00	418.00	418.00
Colombo	729.00	656.00	632.00	552.00	520.00	520.00
Suez	1015.00	923.00	890.00	771.00	711.00	711.00
Port Said	1015.00	923.00	890.00	771.00	711.00	711.00
Alexandria	1022.00	929.00	896.00	776.00	715.00	715.00
Naples	1118.00	1015.00	973.00	849.00	789.00	789.00
Genoa	1118.00	1015.00	973.00	849.00	789.00	789.00
Marseilles	1118.00	1015.00	973.00	849.00	789.00	789.00
ROUND-THE-WORLD FARES						
WORLD TOUR No. 1—FROM NEW YORK						
Intercoastal via Panama Canal						
Trans-Pacific via Honolulu-Japan-China	1890.00	1750.00	1660.00	1425.00	1300.00	1250.00
Orient-European via Straits Settlements and Suez.						
Marseilles, Boston, New York						
WORLD TOUR No. 2—FROM SAN FRANCISCO OR LOS ANGELES (PORT OF)						
Trans-Pacific via Honolulu-Japan-China						
Orient-European via Straits Settlements and Suez.	1440.00	1325.00	1260.00	1100.00	1000.00	1000.00
Trans-Atlantic Marseilles, Boston, New York						

BAGGAGE—Free Allowance 350 lbs. per Adult.

CHILDREN'S FARES—**Intercoastal.** Twelve years of age and over, full fare. Two and under twelve years, half-fare. One child under two years, free. Additional children under two years, quarter-fare each.

Trans-Pacific. Ten years of age and over, full fare. Two and under ten years, half fare. Under two years, ten per cent of adult fare.

Orient-European. Twelve years of age and over, full fare. Three and under twelve years, half-fare. One child under three years, free. Additional children under three years, quarter-fare each.

Trans-Atlantic. Ten years of age and over, full fare. One and under ten years, half-fare. Under one year, $16.50.

Children's fares must be compiled by taking into consideration the age as applying to each section of the journey.

TICKET LIMITS—One Way—12 months.
Round the World—24 months.

HUGH MACKENZIE,
General Passenger Agent.

K.C.CO., 3M-2-11-24

SEE GRADES OF ACCOMMODATION AND ROOM NUMBERS—OVER

Author's collection

utation for being more important for what they did not say than for what
they did.

A week of parties, congratulations, festive receptions, toasts and exchanges of good wishes brought the excitement of the maiden sailing on the
new line to a fevered pitch. To a gala send off the PRESIDENT HARRISON
departed to Presidential orders transmitted by special radio hook up. Brain-
storm of Stanley Dollar and Shipping Board publicity men, a special radio
transmitter was set up on President Calvin Coolidge's desk where he was
surrounded by a few aides, a couple of technicians and a photographer on
the evening of Saturday, January 5, 1924. Pierside at San Francisco were
thousands of onlookers waiting for the ship to move. Seated at his desk,
President Coolidge touched a key on his desk. That transmitted the signal
to a receiver installed on the liner's bridge. Once her Master heard the signal
he gave the order to cast off. A brass band played as the ship inched away
from her pier and backed out into the Bay. She turned her bows towards the
Golden Gate and was on her way. Before she would return to San Francisco
again her journey would take her across the Pacific, the Indian Ocean, the
Mediterranean Sea, the Atlantic Ocean and the Caribbean Sea before her
Panama Canal transit brought her back into the Pacific. She would have
made 24 port calls in 14 countries. That inaugural voyage was not quite the
unmitigated triumph it seemed to be for before departure there had been a
hasty scramble to obtain navigational charts for much of her itinerary. No
store in America could supply them and only through the sympathetic help
of the British Consul at San Francisco could they be obtained in time. Worse,
there was not even a single American deck officer who had made a circumnavigation of the globe available to the ship as she started this new service.
So rare were American flag passenger ships that French authorities at Marseilles refused to accept her tonnage certificate. On her maiden round the
world voyage she lost a lot of money. For one thing, even with passage rates
set between a minimum per person fare of $1,250.00 for the trip all the way
around the world to a maximum of $1,890.00, the ship couldn't carry enough
passengers to offset any limited voyage revenues low freight bookings occasioned.

To a quiet send off on February 2, 1924 the PRESIDENT HAYES cast off
from San Francisco for ports around the world. As the remaining vessels
were also formerly "New York boats", their dates of entry into Dollar service
are always counted from the dates of their first New York sailings in Dollar
colors. Just four days after the PRESIDENT HAYES sailed from San Francisco, the PRESIDENT ADAMS, first of the former transatlantic "502"'s, came
into Dollar service with a February 6th sailing from New York. The PRESI-
DENT GARFIELD sailed next on February 21, followed on March 6th by the
PRESIDENT POLK. The first two "502"'s to enter Atlantic service were the
last two delivered to Dollar Line. The PRESIDENT MONROE began her
Dollar Line career with her March 20th departure from New York. Running
aground on her way to Havana put her considerably behind schedule but

GRADES OF ACCOMMODATIONS

The different grades of accommodations are shown below in separate groups, each group being prefixed by a key number. In selling tickets first locate the group and key number opposite which the room to be sold is shown. Fares for the different grades of accommodations as designated by the key numbers are shown on reverse side hereof.

Key Number	STEAMER	ROOM NUMBERS	ACCOMMODATIONS—ALL OUTSIDE ROOMS
A1 Private Tub Bath and Toilet	President Adams..... President Garfield.... President Monroe.... President Polk....... President Van Buren..	SALOON DECK 1, 2, 5, 6, 14, 15, 18, 19	PRIVATE TUB BATH AND TOILET—Rooms contain one single bed "A" and one lower berth "C." ———— When required these rooms provide also one upper berth "B" and one upper berth "D."
	President Harrison... President Hayes......	SALOON DECK 1, 2, 5, 6, 14, 15, 18, 19	PRIVATE TUB BATH AND TOILET—Rooms contain one single bed "A" and one single bed "B."
A2 Private Shower Bath and Toilet	President Adams..... President Garfield.... President Monroe.... President Polk....... President Van Buren..	SALOON DECK 9, 10, 11, 12	PRIVATE SHOWER BATH AND TOILET—Rooms contain one single bed "A" and one lower berth "C." ———— When required these rooms provide also one upper berth "B" and one upper berth "D."
	President Harrison... President Hayes......	SALOON DECK 9, 10, 11, 12	PRIVATE SHOWER BATH AND TOILET—Rooms contain one single bed "A" and one single bed "B."
A3 Private Shower Bath and Toilet	President Adams..... President Garfield.... President Monroe.... President Polk....... President Van Buren..	PROMENADE DECK 101, 102, 103, 104, 107, 108 ———— UPPER PROMENADE DECK 201, 204	PRIVATE SHOWER BATH AND TOILET—Rooms contain one single bed "A" and one lower berth "C." When required these rooms provide also one upper berth "B."
	President Harrison.... President Hayes......	PROMENADE DECK 101, 102, 103, 104, 107, 108 UPPER PROMENADE DECK 201, 204	PRIVATE SHOWER BATH AND TOILET—Rooms contain one single bed "A" and one single bed "B."
B1 Public Bath	President Adams..... President Garfield.... President Monroe.... President Polk....... President Van Buren..	SALOON DECK 3, 4, 7, 8, 16, 17, 20, 21	PUBLIC BATH—Rooms contain one single bed "A" and one lower berth "C." ———— When required these rooms provide also one upper berth "B" and one upper berth "D."
	President Harrison.... President Hayes......	SALOON DECK 3, 4, 7, 8, 16, 17, 20, 21	PUBLIC BATH—Rooms contain one single bed "A" and one single bed "B."
	BACHELOR ROOM President Polk.......	PROMENADE DECK 304	PUBLIC BATH—Contains one single bed "A."
B2 Public Bath	President Adams..... President Garfield.... President Monroe.... President Polk....... President Van Buren..	PROMENADE DECK 105, 106, 109, 110 ———— UPPER PROMENADE DECK 205, 206, 207, 208, 209	PUBLIC BATH—Rooms contain one single bed "A" and one lower berth "C." ———— When required these rooms provide also one upper berth "B."
	President Harrison.... President Hayes.....	PROMENADE DECK 105, 106, 109, 110 UPPER PROMENADE DECK 205, 206, 207, 208, 209	PUBLIC BATH—Rooms contain one single bed "A" and one single bed "B."
B3 Public Bath	President Adams..... President Garfield.... President Monroe.... President Polk....... President Van Buren..	UPPER PROMENADE DECK 202, 203	PUBLIC BATH—Rooms contain one single bed "A" and one upper berth "B."
	President Harrison... President Hayes......	UPPER PROMENADE DECK 202, 203	PUBLIC BATH—Room 202 contains one single bed "A" and one upper berth "C." Room 203 contains one single bed "D" and one upper berth "C."
B3 Public Bath	BACHELOR ROOMS President Adams.....	PROMENADE DECK 301, 303 305 307	PUBLIC BATH Rooms contain one lower berth "E" and one upper berth "F." Room contains one lower berth "C" and one upper berth "D." Room contains one single bed "A" and one upper berth "B."
	BACHELOR ROOMS President Garfield....	PROMENADE DECK 300, 301, 302, 303 304 305, 307	PUBLIC BATH Rooms contain one lower berth "E" and one upper berth "F." Room contains one single bed "A" and one lower berth "C." Rooms contain one single bed "A" and one upper berth "B."
	BACHELOR ROOMS President Polk.......	PROMENADE DECK 300, 301, 302, 303, 305, 306, 308 307	PUBLIC BATH Rooms contain one single bed "A," one lower berth "C" and one upper berth "B." Room contains one single bed "A" and one upper berth "B."

SEE FARES - OVER

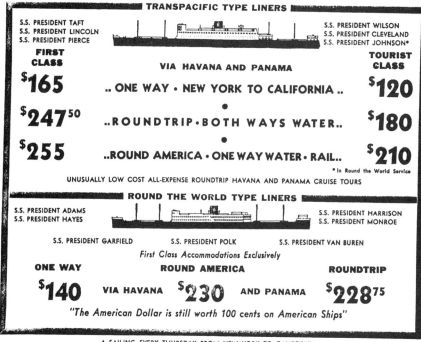

DOLLAR STEAMSHIP LINES
NEW YORK - CALIFORNIA
HAVANA • PANAMA • ROUND THE WORLD • HAWAII • ORIENT

NEW LOW FARES
BETWEEN
NEW YORK and CALIFORNIA
EFFECTIVE APRIL 17, 1934

TRANSPACIFIC TYPE LINERS

S.S. PRESIDENT TAFT
S.S. PRESIDENT LINCOLN
S.S. PRESIDENT PIERCE

S.S. PRESIDENT WILSON
S.S. PRESIDENT CLEVELAND
S.S. PRESIDENT JOHNSON*

FIRST CLASS

TOURIST CLASS

VIA HAVANA AND PANAMA

$165 .. ONE WAY • NEW YORK TO CALIFORNIA .. $120

$247⁵⁰ ..ROUNDTRIP•BOTH WAYS WATER.. $180

$255 ..ROUND AMERICA • ONE WAY WATER • RAIL.. $210

* In Round the World Service

UNUSUALLY LOW COST ALL-EXPENSE ROUNDTRIP HAVANA AND PANAMA CRUISE TOURS

ROUND THE WORLD TYPE LINERS

S.S. PRESIDENT ADAMS
S.S. PRESIDENT HAYES

S.S. PRESIDENT HARRISON
S.S. PRESIDENT MONROE

S.S. PRESIDENT GARFIELD   S.S. PRESIDENT POLK   S.S. PRESIDENT VAN BUREN

First Class Accommodations Exclusively

ONE WAY   **ROUND AMERICA**   **ROUNDTRIP**

$140   VIA HAVANA $230   AND PANAMA $228⁷⁵

"The American Dollar is still worth 100 cents on American Ships"

A SAILING EVERY THURSDAY FROM NEW YORK TO CALIFORNIA.
FORTNIGHTLY FROM LOS ANGELES AND SAN FRANCISCO TO NEW YORK.

CONSULT YOUR LOCAL AGENT

(OVER)

Author's collection

in a world moving so much slower than ours, it was not that big a deal. Finally, the PRESIDENT van BUREN joined the round the world line with her April 17, 1924 sailing from New York. A few months after the inauguration of this fortnightly service around the world via the Far East, the Shipping Board stepped in and ordered co-ordination of sailings between the Pacific Mail Steamship Company and the Dollar Line. Responding to the Government's mandate these rivals on the Pacific devised an interlocking schedule of sailings from San Francisco. Moving their Tuesday departures from San Francisco to Saturdays, Pacific Mail's "535"s then alternated sailings with the Dollar Line's "502"s.

Some foreign steamship companies were openly hostile to the new American-flag service and their animosity to the Dollar Line was considered the cause of several anonymous harassments suffered by Dollar Liners ranging from false distress reports publicized to make intending travelers reconsider their bookings to a curious number of minor mishaps and fires that stopped as suddenly as they started. But without pointing an accusatory finger, the Dollars looked for favorable publicity and notices. That's why the Line participated in the story of "Hobo", a straw hat left during the autumn of 1922 with an onward ticket to New York City on a Delaware & Hudson train by P.J. Fagan of Wilkes-Barre, Pa. It didn't take "Hobo" very long to achieve celebrity and before long the straw hat had made it all the way to California before winding up in the Far East. When the PRESIDENT HAYES reached Hong Kong on her first Dollar Line trip around the world, Captain Dollar found "Hobo" aboard his ship. The idea to use the hat for publicity was not a long stretch for a man like him.

With a good deal of fanfare and a passage ticket signed by himself and San Francisco Mayor Rolph, "Hobo" the straw hat was ensconced in a cabin aboard the PRESIDENT GARFIELD. To the attendance of publicists and news men, ship and hat sailed from San Francisco on February 14, 1925. During the Honolulu call a week later Hawaii's Senate paused from its business to greet "Hobo". Important officials welcomed the hat to Kobe but perhaps it was New York's own fabled Chauncey Depew who went all out to welcome "Hobo" with "the honor befitting a great traveler."[8]

Propaganda gimmicks were one thing but it was the high degree of personal contact with his customers, shippers around the world, upon which Captain Dollar relied for continued financial success. He had long been accustomed to securing cargo for his ships through personal contact with shippers at home and abroad, so Captain Robert Dollar often travelled overseas. He was on one of his many goodwill for business trips, determined to promote cargo for the newly acquired ships, when the round the world passenger and cargo service was inaugurated by the PRESIDENT HARRISON. In one aspect of the entire program Captain Dollar was a total neophyte. That was the passenger trade and his strict teetotalling, fervent Protestant faith

---

[8] *The New York Times* May 8, 1925, page 8.

and upright mien hardly seemed to suggest a genial host. He probably looked upon the prospect of passenger trade with a jaundiced, narrowed eye, unwilling to cater to certain expected demands of an increasingly cosmopolitan and sophisticated traveling public. Nor could he look favorably upon the fabled gluttony of the steamship traveler. A strict Calvinist who worked his way up from nothing, Captain Dollar was unlikely to brook the waste associated with the sumptuous table a successful passenger liner must set. Against his religious beliefs were ledger sheets suggesting revenues to be gained from serving the traveler. His own managers reasoned that a successful passenger trade would bring in tremendous sums of monies, so Dollar set his sights high, offering his passengers a very high standard of hotel service and catering. His company then began doing everything possible to attract passengers and with the "502"'s the Dollar organization began a passenger department unrivalled, if only because of the eventual scope of their far-flung itineraries, in American maritime history. Captain Dollar soon proved himself up to the tasks of the passenger trade, putting as much into the various aspects of a passenger line as he did to attract cargo to his ships. Dollar Line regraded the ships' passenger accommodations as "First Class", initially limiting passenger capacity in the "502"'s to the ships' original 78 berths. Demand for space quickly outpaced availability and after a while both "Bachelor Quarters" and upper berths were available again. To make things easier for prospective passengers and steamship agents around the world, not to mention their own staff, cabins were grouped into seven types and graded type A1 through A3 for cabins with private bath and Type B1 through B3 for cabins without.

The Robert Dollar clan and their ships were always news. Whether it was for one of the venerable patriarch's round the world business trips or a festive sailing attended by important passengers, the press often carried items publicizing Dollar activities. Of limited interest in the general press, news of the leasing of a new pier in New York was worth a few column inches in the maritime trade press. Signing a lease with the Erie Terminal Company at the close of 1926, as of April 1, 1927 Dollar ships began using Erie Terminal's new Pier 9 at Jersey City. At 1,250 in length it was then the longest pier in the port of New York. Not only was it near the new Holland Tunnel, Erie Terminal's Pier 9 had excellent rail connections. Utilizing that new pier allowed Dollar Steamship Lines to avoid both the additional time spent lightering cargo as well as the extra expense working cargo into such additional craft entailed.

Dollar ships offered prospective passengers several "American vacations by sea" opportunities. The Dollar Line arranged and marketed a great many interesting itineraries and tours. Passage was offered aboard the "502"'s for the full round the world trip, the segment between New York and California, or between any two ports if space were available. Intercoastal passengers could go out to California in a "502" or "535" and return in a "535", inbound from the Orient. The full round the world trip was aggressively marketed.

Well aware that the majority of American ocean shipping was intercoastal, the Dollar firm reasoned that there should be plenty of intercoastal passenger business, too, even though at this point they could offer only one way passage by sea from East Coast to California. To compensate for this inherent one way sea traffic, the Dollar Line organized a variety of "See-America" tours" featuring passage westbound to California in a "502" and an enticing array of options for travel to points anywhere east of the Golden State. That there was still demand for sea passage between America's ocean coasts was amply proved by the I.M.M. and Grace Line, each of which then operated American passenger ships in the intercoastal trade. Despite losing money on the first few years of the round the world trade, other Dollar services earned tidy profits and allowed the company to pay the debts incurred by the expensive world service. Not once did the Dollar family nor the Dollar financial syndicate have to dip into their own personal accounts to make up any losses incurred by these "502"'s.

During the late 1920's both companies would prove their commitment to the run, ordering a total of seven fine liners between them, the CALIFORNIA, PENNSYLVANIA and VIRGINIA for I.M.M.'s Panama Pacific Line[9] and the SANTA ROSA, SANTA PAULA, SANTA LUCIA and SANTA ELENA for Grace Line. When the Dollars extended their transPacific passenger service to New York in 1929, they had enough passenger ships to carry travelers both ways through the Canal. Eventually a full 25% of the passenger business for the round the world ships came from the intercoastal trade between New York and California. Competition for the intercoastal traveler was fierce and on Dollar Line, anyone booking passage via one or more intermediate ports could have stopover privileges.

Interchangeable at face value among the ships of the fleet, passage tickets were valid for travel in any Dollar ships, and prospective passengers were advised that they could take good advantage of the company's fleet to complete their voyage. There were several travelers eager enough to try as many Dollar ships as possible. One couple left New York in the PRESIDENT COOLIDGE, left her in Havana, boarded the PRESIDENT LINCOLN to Panama, got on the PRESIDENT PIERCE at Balboa and got off at San Pedro, then took the PRESIDENT van BUREN up to San Francisco.

By the early 1930's, passage fares for the full round the world voyage, with tickets valid for up to two years, including travel in the same direction in any number of Dollar liners, ranged from a minimum fare of $1,250.00 to $3,500.00 per person for one of the charming new suites designed by Ferris for the improved "502"'s. Minimum rates aboard the unimproved vessels began at the same figure as that aboard the others but did not reach the latter figure. Dollar Line was careful to point out that all these ships operated liner, not cruise service, though the many passengers remaining aboard for a full

---

[9] If the Depression had not taken over, there would have been three more identical sisters built for the Panama Pacific Line.

round the world voyage in effect made a world cruise. With business slump-ing precipitously in the first two years after the October 1929 stock market crash, Dollar Steamship Lines joined the Panama Pacific Line in a drastic fare cut. Effective May 8, 1932 First Class rates were cut to a minimum of $175.00 per person in an outside room on a "502" class steamer. Extending a dis-counted fare for round trip bookings, Dollar Line brought the fare down to the equivalent of one and a half times the one way fare, the lowest inter-coastal round trip fare offered since the opening of the Panama Canal. Trav-elers booking a roundtrip with the Dollar Line could return to the East Coast by sea in a "535" or in one of the new flagships or in a Panama Pacific steamer. Also aggressively marketed was a round trip featuring an east-bound trip by rail.

The round the world itinerary rarely changed except by degree. A pier in a given port might fall out of use, the schedule might speed up or get slower, but the core ports always remained except in times of military action. A Bombay call was added to the itinerary in February 1932, but a "535" type ship then working the round the world run, the PRESIDENT PIERCE, beat the "502"'s to the first call there, making the inaugural call there with a February 1, 1932 arrival. The seven sisters began calling there with the Feb-ruary 11th call of the PRESIDENT MONROE. Following her in order were the PRESIDENT van BUREN, PRESIDENT GARFIELD, PRESIDENT POLK, PRESIDENT ADAMS,PRESIDENT HARRISON and PRESIDENT HAYES. The reason for the addition of that exotic port was simple. It was fifty-one days steaming from San Francisco and only about 30 days more to New York. Unfortunately for all concerned, it would be years before the line was supplied with enough ships fast enough to make the promise of such quick times a reality. Even if they had no cargo to work and had no laying in port time to consider, the "502"'s had a rough job trying to complete the round the world trip in 81 days steaming time.

The duration of the round the world voyage, originally 120 days, was reduced to 105 days in 1929 when the Dollar Lines shuffled their fleet around. When the three "502" class ships PRESIDENT ADAMS, PRESIDENT GAR-FIELD and PRESIDENT HARRISON were withdrawn from the round the world service and sent to Newport News, Virginia for rebuilding, Dollar Line had replacements ready to take their places. Those were the recently purchased PRESIDENT FILLMORE and PRESIDENT JOHNSON, Pacific Mail veterans that had spent more than a decade under IMM ownership as the MONGOLIA and MANCHURIA. A pair of "535"'s, the PRESIDENT WILSON and PRESIDENT PIERCE, were also assigned to the round the world line. The speed of the bigger ships and the improved accommodations of four rebuilt "502"'s seemed to suggest that the three unimproved sisters would be permanently reassigned. It certainly seemed that way once the Dollar Line sent the PRESIDENT HAYES and PRESIDENT MONROE onto an abbreviated line to Manila. That left only two "502"'s on the round the world line in midyear 1929, the PRESIDENT POLK and PRESIDENT van

BUREN. The former already had improved passenger accommodations and retention of the PRESIDENT van BUREN suggests that the Dollars had planned to make her the fourth of the ships to be refitted under the terms of the Jones-White Act, but it was soon apparent that in any configuration a "502" class ship had trouble keeping up on the faster schedule. It was just too tight for them and the cargo ships on that line. Only the big passenger ships easily managed it. To ensure proper adherence to the printed schedule, a 112 day round the world voyage was soon instituted. The PRESIDENT HAYES began the Manila run in August 1929 and the PRESIDENT MONROE joined her in late September. The Manila service was not viable and the two "502"'s were withdrawn in March and August of 1931, respectively, and reassigned to the round the world service.

Dollar Line ended the good years of the 1920's with a "triple play" - the reconstruction of three of the round the world "502"'s, the purchase of the MONGOLIA and MANCHURIA, which became the PRESIDENT FILLMORE and PRESIDENT JOHNSON respectively for the round the world service, and the crowning achievement of the Dollar fleets, the trendy PRESIDENT COOLIDGE and PRESIDENT HOOVER in 1931. With the exception of the amazing MARIPOSA, MONTEREY and LURLINE, they were the finest American liners ever seen on the Pacific. Mail contracts had provided extra operating capital since 1925, but the Line took little notice of world conditions, and committed itself to major expenditures just as the world's economy went into apoplexy after October 1929. It would take some years for the Dollar enterprises to feel the full effects of that and associated events.

Throughout their Dollar Line days a constant adversarial relationship between militantly union crew and virulently anti-union management plagued the entire operation. Some years went by with hardly a skirmish but others, whether or not the wider maritime industry were effected as they were during major strikes in 1934 and 1936, were fraught with frequent discord and occasional violence.

Bad luck of another nature sometimes came into the lives of the "502"'s during their years on the round the world service. After the grounding episode of the PRESIDENT MONROE on her first Dollar Line sailing, the next "502" to suffer misfortune was the PRESIDENT POLK. At her New York pier she suffered a serious fire which burned out most of her superstructure on October 11, 1924. Surveying the damage, Dollar Line awarded Newport News Shipbuilding & Drydock Company the repair contract. Making the best of a bad situation, Dollar Line took the opportunity to substantially alter the vessel, using Theodore Ferris' plans for extensive alterations to the ship's accommodations. With his plans and under his supervision, the POLK's passenger accommodations were increased by about fifty percent. About half a million dollars later, the PRESIDENT POLK was redelivered to Dollar Line on April 10, 1925. Not immune to stranding, the PRESIDENT HARRISON exhibited a family trait by grounding on Bonham Island in the mouth of the

Yangtze River on November 6, 1926. Her bottom was pretty badly damaged and it was several weeks before she was on her way again.

January 1929 was proved to be an agonizing time for the Dollar Line. Two of the "502"'s ran aground that month. Grounding off Panama on January 12th the PRESIDENT ADAMS so badly damaged herself she had to be withdrawn for the duration of an entire voyage while repairs and an eventual rebuilding were effected. The Admiral Liner RUTH ALEXANDER was chartered to replace her while Newport News Shipbuilding and Drydock Company's workforce transformed the badly damaged ship into a handsome passenger liner. Just over a week later the PRESIDENT GARFIELD also went aground, going ashore in the Bahamas on the 20th. News of the second incident in 8 days made headlines all over the United States. Worse publicity followed when on June 1st of that year in Massachussetts waters the PRESIDENT GARFIELD collided with and sank the veteran Merchants & Miners coastal freighter KERSHAW.

That year saw important rebuildings of three of the "502"'s. An ambitious mid-1928 Dollar Line plan to build five superfast 630 foot long passenger and cargo motor ships for the round the world service was going nowhere and still laughing were shipping men, scoffing at Stanley Dollar's announcement that the new liners would even carry passenger aircraft to offer shore excursions to their passengers. To come from yards on both Atlantic and Pacific coasts, they were to take only two years to build. Of course they never were built . . . and still in shock were financiers and Dollar Line shareholders who could not justify the minimum $35 million dollar price tag the ambitious scheme carried. Instead of his grand fleet of innovative new liners, Stanley Dollar had to content himself with updated versions of his existing round the world liners. He never did get to buy the PRESIDENT HARDING or PRESIDENT ROOSEVELT, both of which were retained for sale in 1929 with the rest of United States Lines. The Shipping Board didn't feel a need to take advantage of Stanley Dollar's offer to buy them for his company's round the world service. Taking advantage of the ship improvement provisions of the Jones-White Act of 1928, Dollar Line applied for loans for betterments to several "502"'s. Ultimately, on May 29, 1929 the Shipping Board authorized loans for the reconditioning of four sisters, providing loans of $257,000 for the PRESIDENT HARRISON, $250,000 for the PRESIDENT GARFIELD, $425,829 for the PRESIDENT ADAMS (both for improvements and to repair the damages suffered in her recent grounding) plus another $250,000 to refurbish one more sister, at Dollar Line's choice. Repayment terms included a minimum interest rate with the loan to be repaid over a period of 15 years at three percent interest. As late as December 8, 1930 plans to upgrade the accommodation spaces of a fourth sister (most likely the PRESIDENT van BUREN, depending on the ship's location at the time a refit could be scheduled) were under discussion, but with the PRESIDENT POLK already rebuilt in 1925 after her serious fire, Dollar Line opted to limit the project to the three sisters for which loans had already been made, leaving the remaining three in nearly original condition.

Using the plans of the PRESIDENT POLK as a guide, the PRESIDENT HARRISON was refurbished between early February and May 1929 at the yards of the Newport News Shipbuilding and Drydock Company at Newport News, Virginia. Also rebuilt there that season were the "grounded" sisters, PRESIDENT ADAMS and PRESIDENT GARFIELD. They emerged as handsome 12,000 gross ton passenger liners (though the finances of the day led the owners to register them at only 10,553 gross tons). Fewer suites were fitted in these three sisters than had been installed four years earlier in the PRESIDENT POLK, but otherwise these three were now almost internally identical to that ship which had proved to be the most popular among intending passengers. Worldwide, prospective passengers tried to book her in preference to any of the others because of her better passenger facilities.

The 1930's saw the beginning of a precipitous decline in the fortunes of the Dollar shipping enterprises. In borrowing heavily for the reconstruction of the three "502"'s, the building of the twin flagships, and the purchase of other units, the Dollars overextended their reach. Mortgages were not being met. The 1933 freak accident of the PRESIDENT MADISON in a Seattle drydock turned out to be a lucky break for the Dollars since they were able to apply the insurance settlement towards mortgages overdue on their Admiral Line's "535"'s. But it was hardly enough. The Shipping Board and the Dollars began having troubles with each other, particularly after the inauguration of a Democratic administration under President Roosevelt.

Had the Depression been less depressing, the older "502"'s would likely have been rebuilt like their sisters. Authorization to convert one more of them, as well as a promise of funding from the Construction Loan Fund, had already been granted by the Shipping Board. The new safety regulations prescribed by Congress in the Bland Act, as a direct result of the tragedy of the MORRO CASTLE fire, came into effect. The four refitted ships were close to standards eventually required by Congress for a passenger certificate, requiring little more than the installation of a fire sprinkler system and a loudspeaker system. The unimproved "502"'s were eventually denied passenger certificates. As the thirties progressed, in spite of mounting operating losses, the Dollar management continued earning outrageous salaries. Had these sums been used to pay their company's bills on time, settle mortgages, keep the ships in good repair, the Dollar Line might well have held on long enough to reap tremendous earnings before the war. Conventional wisdom judges the owners greedy, and evidence suggests that they were more interested in short term personal profit than in the long term health of their steamship company. Mismanagement is blamed for a heavy toll on the Dollar Steamship Lines and its associated companies.

The Depression was a great negative factor for the Dollar Line, but so too were West Coast dock strikes, escalating to violence in the 83 day long Big Strike of 1934, and a less bloody but even more devastating nationwide

maritime strike of 1936–1937. Serving on a committee of San Francisco business leaders which was formed to insure maintenance of law and order,
American Hawaiian Steamship Company president Roger D. Lapham was
in frequent touch with all factions and aware of all aspects of the walkout.
Commenting on the 1934 strike just after its conclusion, Lapham said:

> No strike as far-reaching as this one (Pacific Coast longshoreman's strike),
> culminating in a general strike, could have lasted 83 days without the pres-
> ence of a strong radical element, whose announced objective is the over-
> throw of our present form of government . . . Ours was no mere longshore
> or maritime strike: it was a deliberate attempt to overthrow established au-
> thority.
>
> I would find it difficult, myself, to believe what took place were it not
> for the fact that I lived through it. From the day the strike commenced on
> May 9, it became increasingly apparent that there was a strong minority of
> strikers who did not wish to see any settlement made. This minority was
> strengthened as time went on by an active group of Communists, who
> flocked here from all directions, and who did everything possible to prevent
> a reasonable and fair settlement.[10]

Blame the Communists! Think of it! Today we have to rely on little more
than ad hominem attacks!

Relations between labor and management healed not at all after the October 1934 decision awarding the unions control of hiring. An even longer
strike was ahead. The ninety-nine day long 1936–37 seamen's strike, anathe-
matic at very best to conservative shipping men like R. Stanley Dollar, was
another of those major blows, like the Depression itself, that helped put the
company into bankruptcy by the summer of 1938. It had been a long spiral
to financial debacle and came as no surprise. Indeed, as early as 1932 there
were indications that the Dollars would be in trouble when they missed a
number of mortgage payments. By January 1936 the Dollar companies had
overdue principal payments on mortgaged ships totalling $2,820,101.00 on
outstanding obligations, and the aggregate debt was $15 million! Absolutely
devastating to the Dollar Steamship Lines, Inc., Ltd. was a the clause in the
1936 Merchant Marine Act that abolished mail contracts in favor of direct
operational subsidies on a limited number of essential services.

The end of the Dollar Steamship Lines had been a long time in the making and when it came it did not happen all at once. Indications of hard times
should have been at the fore in the wake of the Big Strike of 1934, but if the
Dollar management had any inkling of the future, they kept it to themselves.
That year saw them advertise the Round the World service at the very attractive minimum fare of $833.50 per person in outside rooms without fa-
cilities. For a room with a private bathroom in that nadir year of economic
Depression the minimum per person rate was $923.90. A suite in one of the
unimproved "502"'s went for $1,231.55 and for anyone preferring to splurge,

---

[10] Quoted in the August 8, 1934 edition of *The New York Maritime Register*.

a suite in one of the four improved sisters cost $1,849.75 per person. Results for 1935 didn't lift any holiday spirits either. Then came 1936, perhaps the most seminal year in American shipping since 1916 and the establishment of the Shipping Board. Following in the footsteps of Senator Wesley Jones and 1914 era Congressman Joshua T. Alexander, Virginia Congressman Schuyler Otis Bland took up the tattered cause of the American Merchant Marine. Authoring the Merchant Marine Act of 1936, Bland gave the industry a document and conditions later called the "Magna Carta of the American Merchant Marine." Riven by politics and nearly moribund since incoming President Franklin Roosevelt demoted it to the status of a Bureau in 1934, the new law abolished the United States Shipping Board. Handing its prerogatives and powers to the new Federal Maritime Commission, Representative Bland perhaps inadvertently, perhaps not, put major nails into the coffins of some mighty impressive American steamship operations. Those of the Dollars, the Munsons and the syndicate behind American Export Lines leap to mind. Heavy-hitting contributors to Republican political causes and favorites, those firms did VERY well during the Republican led 1920's. Not one of those three enterprises survived the Democrats and the New Deal. Coincidence or not, and in the highly politicized world of American merchant shipping, little happened by coincidence, and the Dollars could have seen it coming. Bland's laws gave more than one hint. Not only would the Dollar Steamship Lines lose their mail contracts, new safety standards meant that major capital investment in the company's aging fleet was just around the corner. But for many reasons, shortages of cash reported among them, no one put aside the money to do more than piecemeal improvements of the most important ships when that became necessary. Worse was the situation in Seattle, where the struggles of the last few years to prop up Dollar's subsidiaries American Mail Line and the Pacific Steamship Company (trading as the Admiral Line) were for naught. Nothing could stop those companies from hemhorraging cash. October 1935 brought the announcement of the end of the Admiral Line's coastal services. What was left of the American Mail Line had long been integrated into the Dollar Steamship Line's transPacific services.

Then came another Big Strike in late October 1936. Within a month as many as 150 ships were strikebound at ports on the West Coast while across the country along both Atlantic and Gulf Coasts crews in sympathy with the strikers tied up another 213 vessels.[11] At year's end, 1936, the entire Dollar Line fleet was out of service as a result of the nationwide maritime strike. Dollar Line had long been known for nepotism, favoritism and general harsh treatment of labor. Wages were low, advancement rarely possible, and every ship seemed to sail with up to 50% of the crew replaced at the start of every voyage. Sympathy for the Dollars was quite limited. Here's the situation of

---

[11] Figures provided by the American Shipowners Association.

the passenger fleet of the Dollar Steamship Line as well as subsidiary American Mail Line as of December 30, 1936:

PRESIDENT ADAMS: (502) Sailed from Kobe, October 17, 1936. Continued scheduled round the world voyage. Arrived at New York on December 16th, scheduled for Boston . . . idle at New York on account of strike.

PRESIDENT CLEVELAND (535)—Sailed from New York October 22, 1936. Arrived Los Angeles on November 6th. Held there because of strike.

PRESIDENT COOLIDGE (luxury liner)—Sailed from Manila on October 28th. Hong Kong Oct 30/sailed 31 Shanghai Nov 2/sailed 3 Kobe Nov 5 Yokohama Nov 6 Honolulu Nov 13 Arrived at San Francisco on November 18th. Held there because of strike.

PRESIDENT FILLMORE (ex MONGOLIA)—Laid up at New York because of Depression.

PRESIDENT GARFIELD (502)—Sailed from Marseilles on November 6. Arrived at New York on November 20, 1936. Held there because of strike.

PRESIDENT GRANT (535)—Sailed from Manila on October 7, 1936. Arrived at Seattle October 28, 1936. Held there because of strike.

PRESIDENT HARRISON (502)—Sailed from Kobe, October 31, 1936. Continued scheduled round the world voyage. Sailed from Marseilles on December 18, 1936. At sea Dec. 30th due to arrive at New York on December 31st, scheduled for Boston..then held idle at New York on account of strike.

PRESIDENT HAYES (502)—Sailed from New York on October 2, 1936. Arrived San Francisco on October 21, and sailed on round the world voyage on October 23, 1936. Got to Honolulu and idled there.

PRESIDENT HOOVER (luxury liner)—Sailed from Manila on October 3, 1936. Ports as PRESIDENT COOLIDGE. Arrived San Francisco on October 24th. Idle there.

PRESIDENT JACKSON (535)—Sailed from Manila on November 4, 1936. Arrived Seattle on November 25, 1936, held there on account of strike.

PRESIDENT JEFFERSON (535)—Sailed from Manila on October 21, 1936. Arrived Seattle on November 11, 1936, held there on account of strike.

PRESIDENT JOHNSON (ex MANCHURIA)—Laid up at San Francisco because of Depression.

PRESIDENT LINCOLN (535)—Sailed from Manila on November 18th. Hong Kong Nov 20/sailed 21 Shanghai Nov 24/sailed 25 Kobe Nov 27 Yokohama Nov 28 Arrived Honolulu Dec 10, 1936 for San Francisco. Held there because of strike.

PRESIDENT MADISON (535)—Wrecked and laid up at Seattle.

PRESIDENT McKINLEY (535)- Sailed from Manila on November 25th. Hong Kong Nov 27/sailed 28 Shanghai Dec 2 Kobe Dec 4 Yokohama Dec 6 Arrived San Francisco on December 10, 1936. Held there because of strike.

PRESIDENT MONROE (502)—Sailed from Boston on October 26th and from New York on October 28, 1936 for another round the world voyage. Arrived at Los Angeles on November 15, 1936. Held there because of strike.

PRESIDENT POLK (502)—Sailed ex Kobe, October 2, 1936. Continued scheduled round the world voyage. Arrived at New York on December 2th, scheduled for Boston. Idle at New York.

PRESIDENT TAFT (535)—Idle at New York because of strike.

PRESIDENT van BUREN (502)—Idle at New York because of strike.

PRESIDENT WILSON (535)—Sailed from New York October 21, 1936. Arrived Los Angeles November 1, 1936. Held there because of strike.

That ninety-nine day strike went on to take an enormous toll on West Coast steamship companies and was partly responsible for the demise of a number of old, established shipping firms like Swayne & Hoyt, McCormick Steamship Company, the Nelson Steamship Company, Admiral Line and of course, the Dollar Line, too. It was a sad, painful death struggle for them all. With the end of the strike, the fleet began sailing again. First of the big fleet to return to sea was the PRESIDENT ADAMS, which sailed on February 5, 1937, leaving her fleetmates PRESIDENT GARFIELD, PRESIDENT HARRISON, PRESIDENT POLK, PRESIDENT TAFT and PRESIDENT van BUREN to follow her out past the Statue of Liberty. From Honolulu the PRESIDENT HAYES sailed on February 6th, a day after the PRESIDENT ADAMS. Before long most of the fleet was back at sea and only the PRESIDENT FILLMORE and PRESIDENT JOHNSON were left behind to sit idle.

All of these ships steamed into borrowed time. The wreck of the Dollar Line was in the offing. By law Dollar Line mail contracts ceased with their June 30, 1937 cancellation. That meant that mail payments which had effectively been the operating subsidy under which the Dollar ships were able to trade during the troubled years of the 1930's were no more and as of July 1, 1937 the company was on its own. Permissible under the provisions of the Bland Act were fair settlement of claims for cancelled mail contracts and operating differential subsidies, but both items were payable at the discretion of the new Maritime Commission. After the Maritime Commission cancelled Dollar Line's Mail Contracts, most Dollar ships stopped sailing and the company sued the Maritime Commission. Soon only the PRESIDENT COOLIDGE was able to continue in service as before, while Maritime Commission officials in Washington and Dollar Line executives in San Francisco worked out an emergency agreement and most of the fleet was underway again to steam into a highly uncertain future. All the Maritime Commission allowed the Dollar Steamship Line was a six month emergency extension of the old mail contract. That allowed the services of the company to be maintained until the end of the year.

Reorganizing the nation's ocean shipping under the provisions of the Bland Act of 1936, the new Maritime Commission did not consider the Dollar firms in suitable financial condition to take part in the new order. Wily as ever, Stanley Dollar knew his company's future was on the line by early 1937. Late that year he knew that 90% of the stockholders in Dollar Steamship Lines had approved refinancing plans which would render the company's finances palatable to the Maritime Commission which had further insisted in major but unpublicized changes in the corporate structure.

Dollar Line died a slow death in 1938. By the end of January of that year the company and Maritime Commission had agreed on a temporary operating differential subsidy agreement. In exchange for that new funding the Dollars dropped their suit against the Commission. Disposition of the case was entered "with prejudice" by the Clerk in the United States Court of Claims, thus foreclosing the possibility of reinstatement of the same case. Hard to follow through machinations of government and corporation, ships in service and ships laid up, sailing schedules printed and sailings suspended, ships into lay up and ships back to service, the story of the last 12 months of the Dollar Line is probably a book in itself. There isn't room for more than a few highlights here. At January 1, 1938 the PRESIDENT ADAMS was at New York along with the perennially idle PRESIDENT FILLMORE. Idle at San Francisco were the PRESIDENT CLEVELAND, PRESIDENT LINCOLN and PRESIDENT WILSON and the long indolent PRESIDENT JOHNSON. Out of work at Seattle was the damaged PRESIDENT MADISON. Still working as the year began, the other members of the fleet were sailing through the courtesy of emergency operating subsidies, but as each of the ships in service returned to either New York or San Francisco, she would be laid up. Guaranteed to remain in operation by virtue of public funding was the important PRESIDENT COOLIDGE. That winter Dollar Line was able to announce a new sailing schedule for its various services. That new schedule called for an average of three monthly departures from San Francisco, two on the transPacific line, one on the round the world run. Under new thinking the intercoastal service would be limited to westbound sailings from New York in conjunction with the round the world ships. Planned to handle the transPacific service, which was renamed Line A, were the PRESIDENT COOLIDGE, PRESIDENT CLEVELAND, PRESIDENT WILSON and PRESIDENT TAFT. The new plan had room for only four "502"'s—the PRESIDENT ADAMS, PRESIDENT GARFIELD, PRESIDENT HARRISON and PRESIDENT POLK. The new Maritime Commission was willing to allow a six month operating subsidy only in order to get the ships back to sea. That was not a gift, and the Dollars and their shareholders were required to put up cash before any public money hit their corporate account. Sad to say, though, the Dollar Line's financial picture was scandalous. With a debt load of some $11 million, monthly interest payments amounted to more than $300,000.00. Because of their astounding liabilities, the Maritime Commission lacked any confidence in the Line's ability to put its financial house in order. Defending the public trust, so they said, the Maritime Commission rejected Dollar Steamship Line's proposals for continued subsidies. More frustrating to all concerned were union gripes and expensive refits the aging Dollar fleet needed. Some of the trouble would abate once crew quarters in the improved "502"'s were rebuilt and crew in the other three moved into passenger cabins. February 1938 brought a repair contract for the PRESI-

DENT HARRISON, and April brought a similar pact for the reconditioning of the PRESIDENT POLK.

Services were again suspended in early March, though in a couple of weeks a few of the ships began moving again. Two repair contracts had also been let to New York yards. In late February United Dry Docks won an order to repair the PRESIDENT HARRISON. Late March brought the Robins yard a contract to get the PRESIDENT MONROE ready for sea. That season also brought news of the return to sea of a "502". That was the PRESIDENT ADAMS and on March 18, 1938 *The Los Angeles Times* noted the resumption of Dollar Line's suspended round the world service as well as a million dollar refit for the four improved "502"s. But it did not last and most of the ships laid up.

The six month emergency subsidy would soon be used up, and expiration was set for June 24, 1938. Emergency infusions of cash got some of the ships to work during 1938. Mid June brought news of a five year subsidy of some $3 million per year for operations by a fleet of 12 ships authorized by the Maritime Commission for the Dollar Line. Eligible for subsidy would be the PRESIDENT ADAMS, PRESIDENT CLEVELAND, PRESIDENT COOL-IDGE, PRESIDENT GARFIELD, PRESIDENT HARRISON, PRESIDENT HAYES, PRESIDENT LINCOLN, PRESIDENT MONROE, PRESIDENT PIERCE, PRESIDENT TAFT, PRESIDENT van BUREN and PRESIDENT WILSON. Unstated in most press reports was that the Dollars would not be at the helm of the line for much longer. The days of the Dollar Line were at an end but before the end of the Dollar Line came, much of the fleet whiled away their time in lay up, some at New York, some at San Francisco, others at Seattle.

As part of the first year's subsidy was an advance of a million and a half dollars given by the government to the line to get idle ships back to sea. Nothing published in trade papers carried any indication that a new firm was in the making. The only clue was mention of reorganization of debt and the date, ten days from the date of authorization by which Dollar had to agree to the terms of subsidy agreement. Here is where the ships of the Dollar and their subsidiary American Mail Line fleet were at mid year:

PRESIDENT ADAMS	— Laid up at Boston.
PRESIDENT CLEVELAND	— In service, arrived Los Angeles from Manila on June 12th.
PRESIDENT COOLIDGE	— In service, sailed San Francisco for Japan on June 3rd.
PRESIDENT FILLMORE	— Laid up at New York.
PRESIDENT GARFIELD	— Laid up at New York.
PRESIDENT GRANT	— Laid up at Seattle.
PRESIDENT HARRISON	— In service, sailed June 2 from Suez for Mediterranean and New York.
PRESIDENT HAYES	— Laid up at San Francisco.
PRESIDENT JACKSON	— In service. Sailed June 8 from Seattle for Far East.

PRESIDENT JEFFERSON	— In service. Sailed May 24 from Manila for Seattle.
PRESIDENT JOHNSON	— Laid up at San Francisco.
PRESIDENT LINCOLN	— Laid up at San Francisco.
PRESIDENT MADISON	— Laid up at Seattle.
PRESIDENT McKINLEY	— In service. Sailed May 11 from Seattle for the Far East.
PRESIDENT MONROE	— Laid up at San Francisco.
PRESIDENT PIERCE	— In service. Sailed May 10 from San Francisco for Far East.
PRESIDENT POLK	— In service, round the world line.
PRESIDENT TAFT	— Laid up at San Francisco.
PRESIDENT van BUREN	— Laid up at New York.
PRESIDENT WILSON	— Laid up at San Francisco.

Every report about the demise of the Dollar Liner refers to a total suspension of the fleet and at least the hint that the entire fleet was long laid up but that was not the case, as the movements of seven passenger liners indicates. In fact, four Dollar Line ships worked well into the summer of 1938 but only the PRESIDENT COOLIDGE still carried passengers. Leaving lay up to make a round the world trip as a freighter under emergency financing that summer was the PRESIDENT ADAMS. Also working as a freighter was the larger PRESIDENT PIERCE. Last of the four active Dollar Line ships was the small ADMIRAL HALSTEAD. One of 150 sister "Sub Boats" fabricated at Port Newark, New Jersey for the Emergency Fleet Corporation, the ADMIRAL HALSTEAD was one of 32 of them finished for the account of the builder. After a less than spectacular career under the builder's own steamship company as the SUWORDENCO, she was sold to the Pacific Steamship Company and put to work on their Admiral Line's Pacific Coastal freight service. The only one of Admiral Lines fleet of eleven sister freighters to keep on working into 1938, she was on a slow service between California and the Philippines. Before going on to gallantry at war the ADMIRAL HALSTEAD actually turned out to be the last active Dollar Liner.

By the end of the summer, every Dollar ship was reported to be out of service. Meanwhile Dollar Line officials continued to do whatever they could to evade disaster. Whatever it was willing to do or to be, the Maritime Commission was hardly willing to be conned and publicly stated that their view of the Dollar Line's financial condition provided no ground for confidence. But they were willing to work with Dollar management to get the ships back in service. Some steps taken, including those by the Maritime Commission. were either ultimately destructive or immaterial. One long standing agreement with the Matson Navigation Company was brought into question. Late August brought disallowal of them by the Maritime Commission. One in particular could have brought some relief, were Dollar's finances not so rotted. Since 1930 the Dollars had been paying Matson 50% of Dollar's gross receipts on the West Coast—Hawaii traffic. In exchange, Matson had greatly increased Dollar Line's business on other Pacific segments such as Manila to Honolulu. Accepted by the old Shipping Board on April 30, 1930, one day after the two companies filed it with them, the Maritime Commission objected on the grounds of finding this agreements detrimental to the commerce of the United States. Discussions with the Maritime Commission allowed the Dollar Line to publish blurbs that they were soon to resume service. Referring shippers to their schedule #26, they announced impending resumption of regular weekly sailings from Los Angeles and San Francisco to the Far East and fortnightly service from those West Coast ports to New York via Panama and Havana. First of the ships to work under this schedule was to be the PRESIDENT ADAMS, set to sail as a freighter on August 3rd from San Francisco. On that date she was already at Kobe, Japan. How she could sail from both California and Kobe at the same time is quite a mystery, especially to believers in popular maritime history whose orthodoxy says the whole Dollar fleet was out of business by the summer of 1938. Obviously a reporter gave his paper erroneous information and other writers drew from similar erroneous conclusions. Meanwhile another Dollar liner was about to depart. That was the big PRESIDENT COOLIDGE, which sailed from Los Angeles for San Francisco on that same day and for Japan on August 6th.

According to R. Stanley Dollar, the Maritime Commission was the real villain in the story, structuring everything since its inception that the Dollars could never keep control. Everything Stanley Dollar ever said or wrote in connection to the end of his family's control supports his suspicion that the men of the Maritime Commission wanted to take over the Dollar fleets all along. Not only did they cancel mail contracts only to later agree to grant emergency subsidy . . . they withheld all payments they agreed to make . . . ensuring the demise of the Dollar Line. Stanley Dollar further claimed in a pamphlet he commissioned in 1952 "During that time the Dollar Line was forced to maintain its services without allowances of any kind by the Government, doing so at weekly losses of between $60,000 and $70,000."[12] The Commission also refused to grant an operating differential subsidy. Stanley Dollar felt singled out for punishment and did his best to publicize his points of view. But his contention that his was the only company refused such public sums was an exaggeration at best, for other financially shaky steamship companies were also kept at arms length when their principals came to Washington trying to root out some cash. According to Stanley Dollar, for more than six months the Maritime Commission refused to advance the Dol-

---

[12] "Highlights of the Dollar Case" December 6, 1952 pamphlet apparently authored by R. Stanley Dollar. Privately printed for the Robert Dollar Company.

lars as much as one thin dime. Yet someone was advancing money because there were quite a number of Dollar sailings that year.

Separated from the San Francisco operations was the American Mail Line which won a 90 day extension of a September 1937 temporary operating subsidy in late March 1938. But there was a warning in the largesse, a Maritime Commission admonishment that further extensions would not be forthcoming if the firm's financial picture did not improve. The Dollars were able to get their Seattle subsidiary nightmares calmed down when the local chamber of commerce formed a new company by late June. Under the Chairmanship of P.E. Harris and new directors, American Mail Line gave way to the Pacific-Northwest-Oriental Line. In typical fashion there would be no quick transition from financially wounded American Mail service to sailings of the new outfit.

Warm weather had arrived in the Northeastern part of the United States and the Dollar Liners PRESIDENT GARFIELD, PRESIDENT HARRISON, PRESIDENT POLK and PRESIDENT van BUREN were all in lay up at New York. Then idle at San Francisco were more Dollar Line "Presidents", the PRESIDENT CLEVELAND, PRESIDENT HAYES, PRESIDENT LINCOLN, PRESIDENT MONROE and PRESIDENT WILSON. Laid up at Seattle were the PRESIDENT MADISON and PRESIDENT GRANT. Completing their late spring voyages, the PRESIDENT JACKSON and PRESIDENT JEFFERSON joined their sisters in lay up at Seattle. Temporary operating subsidies hardly mattered any more and when one such shot in the arm expired on July 25th, so much of the fleet was idled, hardly anyone noticed. Nor was a late August 30 day extension much of a balm. The same four Dollar ships remained in service, their operation fueled by emergency federal largesse. They were the flagship PRESIDENT COOLIDGE holding up the vital transPacific run and the PRESIDENT PIERCE, PRESIDENT ADAMS, the last of the "502"'s to sail for Dollar Line and ADMIRAL HALSTEAD.

Even when the six month emergency subsidy extension was granted, it was obvious that the government would have to take over the ailing Dollar enterprises. The big question was "When?" Government involvement presented the only viable option to the financial nightmare that was Dollar Steamship Lines. Deemed guilty by innuendo ever since, Dollar Line management actually stood a chance of criminal charges and under today's less permissive attitudes, it is certain that much of the upper management of Dollar Line would have been indicted on a number of criminal charges stemming from their alleged plunder of the line. According to some, this included lining their pockets with cash. Questionable practices were noted as beginning as early as 1923 with the completion of the purchase of the sale of the "502"'s, when Captain Dollar paid a "finders fee" to his son Stanley Dollar. That, in effect, was the Government's claim.

Stanley Dollar offered a theory of conspiracy, believing the loss of his company was part of a plot to relieve him and his family of control of his shipping company. Under Maritime Commission control, his line could provide jobs free of civil service requirements for Commission favorites and cronies. Seems like quite a fantastic idea, to take a major steamship company to pay off political favors. And had William McAdoo, son-in-law of the late President Woodrow Wilson and former Senator from California not taken the position of Chairman of the successor company, few might have given Dollar's contention any weight at all.

On June 6th, Admiral Land, Chairman of the Maritime Commission, announced the decision to grant Dollar Steamship Lines, Inc. a five year, $3,000,000.00 operating subsidy. But behind the scenes, the company could no longer have the Dollars or their associates at the helm. A solution to the more pressing problem of repayment and corporate stock was needed. Here is what happened. On August 15, 1938, to secure a debt of $7,500,000 and to provide some $4,500,000 additional working capital, R. Stanley Dollar assented to an agreement exchanging his personal and corporate liability for the release to the government through the Maritime Commission of 92% of Dollar company stock. An August 19th agreement between the Commission and the Dollars included the grant of up to $1,500,000.00 for repair and rehabilitation of 12 Dollar ships. September 27, 1938 brought an announcement of final approval from the Maritime Commission of the August adjustment plan to get the Dollar ships sailing again. With a loan from the Reconstruction Finance Corporation of up to $2,500,000 for working capital, advances to repair ships took care of shipyard repair bills. The Commission also approved a $3 million subsidy plan. All it cost the Dollars was this: surrender of 90% of their stock to the Maritime Commission and retirement of present management. By this plan former U.S. Senator William McAdoo, son-in-law of President Wilson, became Chairman of the Board, Joseph R. Sheehan took over as President. The rest of the reorganization did not come with lightning speed and there was a window of over two months before a new company replaced the old. Not until October 26, 1938 did R. Stanley Dollar resign as president of Dollar Steamship Lines, taking his executives with him. On that day they jointly turned over to the Maritime Commission 2,200,145 shares of Dollar Steamship Line stock. Thus did control of what had once been the largest American steamship company pass over to the Maritime Commission which gave quick birth to the successor company.

Agreeing to the surrender of 90% of its stock, the Dollar Steamship Lines Inc., Ltd. permitted the Maritime Commission to use the Dollar Line name for six months. That gave all concerned plenty of time to name the new firm. When a name was finally chosen it was a good one, an obvious choice considering the system of nomenclature of the fleet inherited but American President Lines, seemingly such a natural choice, was a last minute decision. As late as October 26th when maritime trade papers reported an impending change of the Dollar Line name, two other names were mentioned. Harking back to real Shipping Board styles, American Oriental Line and Pacific Oriental Line were the leading contenders but somehow gave way to American President Lines.

Read the words of R. Stanley Dollar, as reported by Professor John Niven in his fascinating corporate history, "The American President Lines and its Forebears, 1848–1984": "Under our agreement with the Maritime Commission, we surrendered our stock, and in return were relieved of our obligations under the mortgages. The outcome is that the Maritime Commission now owns approximately 90% of the stock in the new Company and thus are in a position to control the Directorate."[13] Dollar subsidiary American Mail also came under federal control, for much the same reasons. Aware of several years of mismanagement, lessened prestige and general neglect, the Maritime Commission readily agreed to R. Stanley Dollar's request that the successor company not use the Dollar family name. On November 1, 1938, the corporate name of Dollar Steamship Lines was changed to American President Lines, Ltd., Inc. Beginning on that day crews removed the "$" from former Dollar liner funnels. In their stead went up white eagles framed by four white stars.

With the failure of Dollar and American Mail Lines, the ships were laid up. Some, badly maintained in the past, were in deplorable condition. When a new corporation to take up the interrupted Dollar Line services was established, the "President" names of the Dollar ships gave the Maritime Commission the easily derived name of "American President Lines". First priority of the new American President Lines was to get the ships back to sea and start earning money. It was a long road back to sea. A special loan for repairs was arranged, and ships not in condition for sea were sent for repairs if they could be restored to a condition acceptable for subsidy payments. For the "535"'s PRESIDENT LINCOLN and PRESIDENT WILSON, it was too late. They were too far gone to justify the expenditure required. Both ended up under the Spanish flag, sold in a seller's market in 1940. Later that year, they became the twin flagships of the Ybarra Line, the CABO DE BUENA ESPERANZA and CABO DE HORNOS respectively and continued in passenger service through 1958. Also ready for disposal were the veterans PRESIDENT FILLMORE and PRESIDENT JOHNSON, but there were no buyers for them as yet. For the remainder, each saw quite a bit of work before sailing again. Each former Dollar liner was drydocked where her underwater body was thoroughly cleaned of all accumulated marine growths and then carefully "examined for any damage including defects in structural plating, propellor blading, examination of propellor shafts and outboard bearings, and check of rudders and appendages. Any defect had to be repaired to the satisfaction of the U.S. Bureau of Marine Inspection and American Bureau of Shipping. Then bottoms were painted with Germicide Anti-fouling paint, sides painted with Super Tropical Germicide Anti-fouling paint, both manufactured by the American Marine paint company."[14] Super Tropical Ger-

---

[13] Page 121 . . . Niven, "The American President Lines and its Forbears"

micide was then the best paint available for ships working tropical waters and was touted for its ability to kill any grasses ships steaming or sitting in such waters might grow. Once the underbody work was completed, the ship left the drydock for the fitting out pier where new equipment was installed and machinery repaired. "New regulations for safety at sea and crew comforts were responsible for most of this class of work."[15] In all cases American President Lines showed favoritism for local yards, and awarded Bay area concerns the lion's share of all work. Only because they were laid up at New York did several former Dollar Liners undergo such work there, but much of the work done on the East Coast utilized as much material and equipment from San Francisco firms as possible.

Now a white eagle, that familiar American symbol, sat on the red band of the vessels' funnels, now painted dark blue instead of black. A priority for the new American President Lines company was to restore the round the world service, though no longer could the seven ships offer a fortnightly passenger sailing on the round the world line. For that matter, at the very beginning it was tough to provide ANY passenger service on that traditional "route of the Presidents". The three unimproved ships were not allowed to carry more than twelve passengers. American President advertising material says of them: "These ships do not carry passengers."

A new sailing schedule was quickly set up. Yokohama was added to the itinerary while Shanghai was still omitted for so many reasons. Now instead of Thursdays at 4:00PM, "President" liners would sail from New York at 6:00PM on Fridays. The Boston side trip was also retained. Four days after a "502" made her Tuesday return to New York from her world voyage, the "502" sailed for Boston and a Sunday arrival. Departing there on Tuesdays to return to New York on Wednesdays gave these ships two more days to prepare to sail out for her ports around the world. A new table of rates was published. Even lower than mid 1930's rates which began at $1,087.00 per person, new fares ranged from a minimum rate of $970.00 per person, double occupancy in a cabin without facilities, to a maximum of $1,980.00 per person, double occupancy in one of the best suites aboard. Single rates then ranged from a minimum of $1,455.00 to $3,767.00.

First of the "502"'s to return to service was the PRESIDENT ADAMS. From New York for Boston on October 30, 1938 she made her first APL sailing as a freighter without passengers. She sailed out from New York on her voyage 48 on November 4, 1938. On the following day, November 5, 1938, with the colors of the new American President Lines flying at her masthead, the PRESIDENT MONROE sailed from San Francisco. Having been the most ne-

---

[14] December 1938 article "Full Steam Ahead for The American President Lines Round the World by APL Publicity Director Gene Hoffmann. Printed in December 1938 issue of *Pacific Marine Review*.

[15] ibid.

glected, the PRESIDENT HAYES did not make her expected November sailing for she still needed substantial repairs. She returned to service sailing from Los Angeles as a freighter on January 3, 1939. Carrying freight only, the next of the class to resume service was the PRESIDENT van BUREN, which sailed from Boston for New York on November 11, 1938 for New York. She sailed from there on November 18th.

First of the sisters to return to passenger service was the PRESIDENT HARRISON, which cast off from New York on voyage 46 on December 2, 1938. Next out was the PRESIDENT POLK which sailed at the end of the month on December 30, 1938. Her first American President Lines voyage, it was listed in company literature as voyage 45. Last of the sisters to resume service was the PRESIDENT GARFIELD, which sailed on January 27, 1939. The round the world passenger service was back, but now on a monthly basis. Taking her first American President Lines sailing with passengers, the PRESIDENT ADAMS left New York on February 24, 1939. New to the resurrected round the world service was a 103 day schedule. Dropped from the itinerary was Shanghai. Otherwise the itinerary remained as it had been operated when the Dollars ran the show. From New York a "502" still sailed out to Havana, Panama and California, arriving at San Francisco on the 20th day of the trip from New York. Thirty days from New York brought the traveler to Honolulu and another 12 days brought him to Japan. On the 49th and 50th day the "502" was scheduled to be at Hong Kong. Two days later the ship would be at Manila and on the 58th day of the voyage the round the world "President" liner reached Singapore. Four days later saw her dock at Penang and on the 67th day out of New York the ship was at Colombo. An undisputed highlight of the trip was always the Bombay call. Fifty days from San Francisco and seventy from New York, "502" passengers brought them to the "gateway to India". To reach the Suez Canal took eighty one days steaming and calling at various ports. Then it was on to Naples, Genoa and on the 90th day the last port of call, Marseilles, from whence the transAtlantic crossing began.

After the war in Europe began on September 3rd of that year, the unimproved trio were also pressed into service to help repatriate Americans. Under emergency certificates granted by American Consuls General in the ports where passengers would embark, the PRESIDENT van BUREN, PRESIDENT MONROE, and the PRESIDENT ADAMS began carrying American "refugees" home to the United States from Europe after war broke out in Europe on September 3, 1939. With war tensions mounting, these old ships were earning previously undreamed of sums of money. Between the summer of 1939 and late 1941, the "502"'s were able to earn gross revenues of between $500,000 and $750,000 per voyage. At the time of Italy's declaration of War against France on June 10, 1940, the PRESIDENT HARRISON was bound for home with as many as 187 passengers.

New times, new rules and new requirements for operating subsidies meant that American President Lines had to replace the aging "502"s on the round the world line if they wanted to be able to collect public monies. They did and thought that six fast ships could do the job of seven. Since the seven marvelous "502"s had carved a fine reputation for themselves in ports around the world, American President Lines wanted their successors to carry their familiar names. To allow the newbuilds their names, five of the ships would take new names. Once it became apparent that they needed seven new ships, a sixth "502" would lose her name, too.

Within days of the autumn 1940 requisition by the Navy of the five CITY OF BALTIMORE class combination passenger cargo vessels thus far operating on a combined Baltimore Mail/American President combined service to Manila, rumors about the next American passenger carriers the Navy would grab began to fly. Soon proved correct was what the trade called "number one rumor" - that the Navy was going to requisition ships building at Moore DryDock in Oakland for Moore McCormack Lines. Second among the words on the street was the expectation that "some" APL ships, likely the older, smaller round the world liners of the "502" class would go to the Navy as the new C3 P ships could replace them. That rumor was countered by the suggestion that the Navy would NOT take over the "502"s because the defense effort required the cargo lift these ships had and that as displaced by new ships on the round the world line, the "502"s would in turn replace the CITY OF BALTIMORE ships on the Manila run. The Navy did take the Moore McCormack ships but left the "502" alone for many more months. But as American defence efforts expanded and fewer passenger cargo ships remained to serve private operators, the "502"s increasingly undertook off-subsidy voyages on other routes. On February 13, 1941, by which time six of the seven sisters had new names, the Maritime Commission granted authorization to American President Lines to divert four of the sisters from the round the world line and make four unsubsidized trips elsewhere that spring. To sail from New York on April 11, 1941 for Penang and Singapore on American President Lines' Line A, the transpacific service via Panama, Los Angeles, San Francisco, Manila and Hong Kong would be the PRESIDENT TAYLOR (ex PRESIDENT POLK). The next unsubsidized "502" to sail for a roundtrip voyage to Malaya for rubber was the PRESIDENT MADISON (ex PRESIDENT GARFIELD), scheduled to sail on May 2nd. Next was the PRESIDENT BUCHANAN (ex PRESIDENT MONROE), with a scheduled sailing for Penang on May 16th and then there was a June 20th departure listed for the PRESIDENT HARRISON. At that the schedule was subject to further action for things changed quickly and often in those uncertain times. About a month after the scheduled sailing of the PRESIDENT BUCHANAN the Maritime Commission met on June 19th and rescinded permission for that ship to effect her Line A voyage and granted authorization for a trip she was already on, one to the Red Sea.

The shipping situation was serious enough to draw the attention of President Roosevelt who issued a directive on the matter on May 26, 1941. Six American President Lines' ships had passed to the control of the military (both Navy and War Departments) and company services on both Lines A (the transPacific and B (round the world) were disrupted. Here's what Maritime Commission Operations and Traffic Director G.H. Helmbold said:

> To provide for a resumption of sailings at regular intervals the Commission on July 29, 1941 approved our recommendation that, effective with the sailings from California after July 1, 1941 and continuing through the calendar year of 1941, the subsidized operation of the following eight vessels be permitted on either Line "A" or "B" on outbound schedules approved by the Division of Operations and Traffic and reported monthly to the Commission.

LINE "A"	*LINE "B"*
PRESIDENT HARRISON	PRESIDENT GRANT
PRESIDENT TAYLOR	PRESIDENT MONROE *(new)*
PRESIDENT MADISON	PRESIDENT van BUREN *(new)*
PRESIDENT POLK *(new)*	PRESIDENT GARFIELD *(new)*[16]

The first of the class to go into service on the round the world line, the PRESIDENT HARRISON was something of a sentimental favorite, or her name was. So for that reason she wasn't renamed by American President Lines. Still manned by her own civilian crew, late autumn 1941 saw her under military control. Ordered from Manila to Hong Kong to be hastily equipped to evacuate American troops, she shipped temporary bunks for about 800 men and sailed for Shanghai to evacuate American marines. She landed them in the Philippines on December 4, 1941. With no regard for the future of any merchant ship that would transport them, American military men leaving China had latterly been very concerned with the transport of their own baggage and souvenirs. Had they been less materialistic, more men might have been shipped out and the PRESIDENT HARRISON might not have been ordered to sail immediately that December 4, 1941 for Tsingtao, in northern China to evacuate more uniformed American personnel. On the bridge, the vessel's Master, Captain Orel Pierson, was well aware of the danger that lie ahead. He expected war would soon erupt between the United States and the Empire of Japan. He believed he had but two options in the event war should break out while he had his passenger steamer in a potential war zone. He could either try to make for Australia or attempt to break past Japan and, by the northerly route, head for home. Neither option was viable. For one thing, the Navy had not permitted him much fuel. The

---

[16] August 18, 1941 memo from Helmbold. Copy in 901 file for the ssPRESIDENT HARRISON in RG 178 at Maritime Administration.

NEW YORK - CALIFORNIA
ONE WAY FIRST CLASS PER CAPITA FARES
(502 TYPE STEAMERS)
S. S. PRESIDENT MADISON, S.S. PRESIDENT HARRISON

First Class Fares	ROOMS	From New York to Los Angeles and San Francisco — Minimum One Way $185		From New York to Havana — Minimum One Way $70		From New York to Cristobal and Balboa — Minimum One Way $115		From Havana to Cristobal and Balboa — Minimum One Way $70		From Havana to Los Angeles and San Francisco — Minimum One Way $165		From Cristobal and Balboa to Los Angeles and San Francisco — Minimum One Way $140	
		With Bath	Without Bath	With Bath	Without Bath	With Bath	Without Bath	With Bath	Without Bath	With Bath	Without Bath	With Bath	Without Bath
		$	$	$	$	$	$	$	$	$	$	$	$
UPPER PROMENADE Suites, bedroom, sitting room, trunk room, shower and toilet.	C, D..........	325	......	150	......	225	......	150	......	300	......	250	......
Rooms with tub bath and toilet.	E, F..........	250	......	95	......	155	......	95	......	210	......	180	......
Rooms with shower and toilet.	202, 203, 204, 205	220	200	85	75	135	125	85	75	190	175	165	150
	210, 211, 212, 215	205	185	80	70	125	115	80	70	180	165	155	140
Rooms without bath or toilet.	206, 207, 208, 209	......	200	......	75	......	125	......	75	......	175	......	150
	200, 201, 214, 216, 217, 218, 219....	......	185	......	70	......	115	......	70	......	165	......	140
LOWER PROMENADE Rooms with tub bath and toilet.	100, 101........	220	......	85	......	135	......	85	......	190	......	165	......
	102, 103........	230	205	90	75	145	130	90	75	200	180	175	155
	104, 105.......	205	185	80	70	125	115	80	70	180	165	155	140
Rooms with shower and toilet.	110, 111, 112, 115	220	200	85	75	135	125	85	75	190	175	165	150
	114, 116, 117, 118, 119, 120, 121, 122, 123, 124, 125, 127	205	185	80	70	125	115	80	70	180	165	155	140
Rooms without bath.	108, 109........	......	185	......	70	......	115	......	70	......	165	......	140
SALOON DECK Rooms with shower and toilet. *Pres. Harrison has two beds only.	9*, 10*, 11, 12..	225	......	90	......	140	......	90	......	195	......	170	......
Rooms with tub bath and toilet. *Pres. Harrison has two beds only.	4*, 5*, 6*, 7*, 8*, 14, 15, 16, 17, 19, 20, 21, 23......	215	190	85	75	130	120	85	75	185	170	160	145
	22, 24..........	215	190	85	75	130	120	85	75	185	170	160	145

Fares from Boston $10.00 higher than from New York.
Local fares between Balboa and Cristobal $5.00.

These fares were valid on the intercoastal portion of the round the world trip. From APL's April 15, 1941 rate booklet. Author's collection.

PRESIDENT HARRISON steamed off with only 10% more than enough fuel to take her from Manila to Shanghai and back. Off the Chinese coast, quite near the mouth of the Yangtze River when he heard on the radio of the attack on Pearl Harbor, he knew that his ship was in danger. Once escape became impossible, Captain Pierson decided to try to wreck his ship rather than let the Japanese capture her intact. He aimed the ship toward land at full speed, hoping to destroy her on the rocks. His efforts were good and the ship was severely damaged, but after some six months of work, the Japanese were able to reclaim the vessel and put her into transport service as the KAKKO MARU. Later renamed KACHIDOKI MARU, the former PRESIDENT HAR-

RISON was torpedoed on September 14, 1944 by the American submarine U.S.S. PAMPANITO. Tragically, most of her "Passengers" were Allied prisoners of war. Hundreds of British and American lives were lost in the sinking. Ashore, no less than sixteen of the PRESIDENT HARRISON's crew died in internment in Japanese prison camps.

The PRESIDENT POLK was renamed PRESIDENT TAYLOR and took her first sailing under that name on December 13,1940. Almost one year later, on December 7, 1941, she was given to the War Shipping Administration on a Voluntary charter. She was allocated back to American President Lines under the July 1941 service agreement (WSA 224). Accommodating up to 1,742 troops, the PRESIDENT TAYLOR had one of the briefest trooping careers of any American troopships. Her first voyage, American President Lines voyage number 55 began on December 7, when she left for San Francisco for Honolulu. She arrived in Hawaii on January 7, 1942 and thereafter made her way back to San Francisco, returning on January 24, 1942. She departed from San Francisco on her second wartime voyage sailing for Canton Island on January 31, 1942. Arriving at her destination, she stranded on Canton Island on February 14, 1942 and was later abandoned. While all aboard were safely removed from the stricken vessel, and some of her cargo was salvaged, the ship was eventually destroyed by Japanese air attacks.

After the war American President Lines resumed the round the world service with two C3 P passenger cargo ships and five C 3 freighters. None of the other C3 P ships was ever returned to the company nor would seven American passenger cargo ships ever again stock this important American trade route. Plans for a new series, initially a group of three to be followed by four more sisters at a later date came to naught when the Navy commandeered three ultra-modern sisters building for the route at Camden in the early 1950s. No, the story of American passenger ships on the round the world service is really that of the seven ungainly "502"'s, the seven ships that brought America to a 26,000 mile route around the world through their regular appearances in ports on four continents, showing the flag in ports where American passenger carriers had never been seen. They worked long and hard for many operators during long, productive lives, transporting people of dozens of nationalities and cargo of nearly every conceivable type. Even during the Dollar Line's slow decline and quick death, the "502"'s remained popular with their passengers. As ugly as ships could be, the seven "502"'s turned in fascinating commercial careers. In 16 years of commercial service on the round the world line they carried 110,000 passengers and 5,500,000 tons of revenue cargo. In that span of time the fleet of round the world liners, not just the seven "502"'s, but the old PRESIDENT FILLMORE and PRESIDENT JOHNSON and the several "535"'s detached from trans-Pacific service to run the round the world service with the "502"'s earned and distributed some $66,000,000.00 in freight and $22,000,000.00 in passenger revenue, much of it distributed to American suppliers, shipyards and personnel. Their fuel bill alone came to some $14,000,000.00! They served well in peace and war, serving as both troopships and, in several instances, hospital ships. Despite Atlantic service for two companies, the United States Mail Steamship Company and United States Lines, transpacific service for Pacific Mail Line, the work of two of them between the Pacific Northwest and the East Coast of South America on Pacific Brazil Argentine Line service, their few years under the white eagle of American President Lines and military service after that phase of their careers, they are surely best remembered as the "President Liners", the Dollar Line's "502"s.

And what of the aftermath of the transfer of stock from Stanley Dollar to the Maritime Commission? That is also a part of the story of the "502"s. In 1945, R. Stanley Dollar, the man who had bought the ships twenty years earlier, brought suit against the United States Government, demanding restitution of his and his family's stock. It was no easy matter to settle, for prominent Democrats ranging all the way up to President Truman were arranged against him and there were compelling, cogent arguments on both sides of the dispute. There is much to support the Dollar family side of the dispute and perhaps the saga of Stanley Dollar and his fourteen year struggle to regain control of his company should be required reading for all Americans and serve as a cautionary tale of Government hubris and avarice. Keep in mind that by September 6, 1943 the Dollars had repaid the debt of $7,500,000.00. With the end of the Second World War the Maritime Commission offered American President Lines for sale. Unable to buy back his family firm, Stanley Dollar felt constrained to sue for return of the stock. For seven years in a number of cases he persevered. Finally, in 1952 the Dollars and the Government agreed to sell the line and split the proceeds. On November 12, 1952 the matter was settled when the Treasurer of the United States received Dollar's check in the amount of $9,128,557.53, representing half the proceeds of the sale.

Deck Plans Showing Arrangement of Accommodations

President Monroe
President Van Buren

KEY TO ABREVIATIONS

A—BED
B—UPPER FOLDING BERTH
C—SETTEE BERTH, LOWER
D—SETTEE BERTH, UPPER
E—PERMANENT LOWER BERTH
F—PERMANENT UPPER BERTH
W—WARDROBE
D T—DRESSING TABLE
W T—WRITING TABLE
T—TABLE
D R—CHEST OF DRAWERS

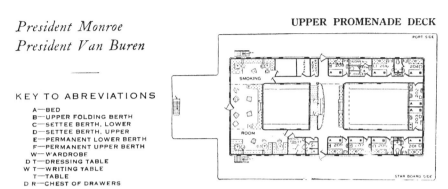

UPPER PROMENADE DECK

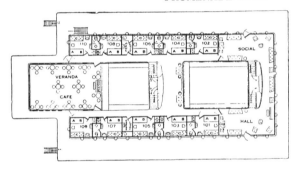

PROMENADE DECK

SALOON DECK

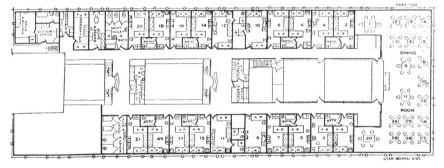

This plan for the PRESIDENT MONROE and PRESIDENT van BUREN was issued by United States Lines. Almost identical was the PRESIDENT HAYES, then on the Pacific. Author's collection.

Deck Plans Showing Arrangement of Accommodations

President Adams
President Garfield
President Polk

KEY TO ABREVIATIONS

A — BED
B — UPPER FOLDING BERTH
C — SETTEE BERTH, LOWER
D — SETTEE BERTH, UPPER
E — PERMANENT LOWER BERTH
F — PERMANENT UPPER BERTH
W — WARDROBE
D T — DRESSING TABLE
W T — WRITING TABLE
T — TABLE
D R — CHEST OF DRAWERS

UPPER PROMENADE DECK

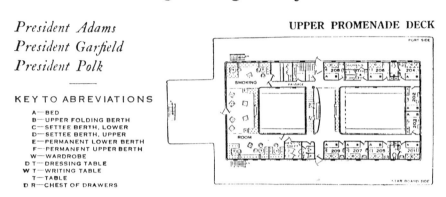

PROMENADE DECK

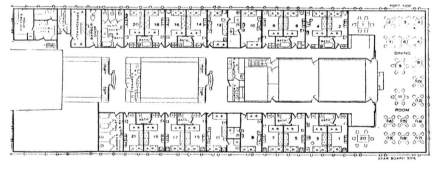

SALOON DECK

For the minor differences in their passenger accommodations, United States Lines issued a separate plan for the other three sisters then on the London line. Author's collection.

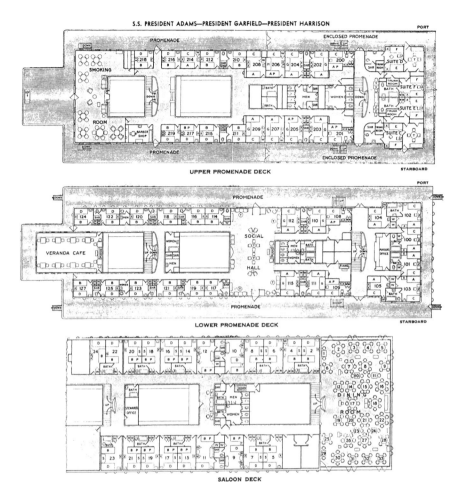

Compare this plan of the passenger quarters in the PRESIDENT ADAMS, PRESIDENT GARFIELD and PRESIDENT HARRISON with that of their original spaces. Author's collection.

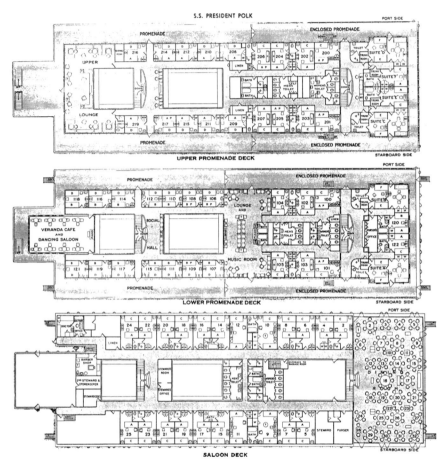

Because she had two extra suites and her cabins were numbered differently, a separate plan was issued for the PRESIDENT POLK. Author's collection.

The Panhandle State/ President Monroe: President Buchanan, Iris, Emily H. Weder

◇

She was the PANHANDLE STATE, the first commercial passenger and cargo ship delivered to the Emergency Fleet Corporation by any yard in the United States and frankly, she was as ugly a ship as the world had ever seen. Yet despite her sorry appearance and unprepossessing size, she was a ship of quite a few "firsts". Years in the planning and too many months in construction, she was the first of two classes of twenty-three passenger and cargo ships delivered to the United States Shipping Board Emergency Fleet Corporation, the first passenger carrying ship solely owned by the United States government. The PANHANDLE STATE was also the first ship in a class of seven identical passenger and cargo vessels. Since other intended passenger ships built during the war years had been completed for the Shipping Board and delivered as troop transports, the PANHANDLE STATE was the first passenger vessel delivered by the Camden yard of the New York Shipbuilding Company in at least five years.

By no means was she supposed to be the first of the class delivered. She wasn't even the first of a pair of them begun on the same day. As hull number 247, she was really intended as the fourth unit of the series but under the emergency shipbuilding program keels went onto the stocks when the slipways earmarked for them were ready, rather than get their keels laid down in sequential hull number order. Second of two members of the eventual "502" class laid down on May 13, 1919 at the Camden, New Jersey yards of the New York Shipbuilding Corporation, when the first keel plates went onto the stocks on slipway J her intended name was ICARIA. The Emergency Fleet Corporation carried her on the books as hull number 2588, and despite her place of "primogeniture", the Shipping Board long carried the eventual PANHANDLE STATE on their statistical lists as the second of her class of seven ships.

By November 1919 the Shipping Board opted for a new system of nomenclature for the "535"'s and "502"'s then either building or planned. Each of the twenty six ships still under contract would carry a nickname of a state of the Union. A name for this ship could wait if it had to, but the Board had already chosen one for her. In honor of the landlocked state of West Virginia this pioneering vessel would be called PANHANDLE STATE. An actual name for her was not yet urgent for on December 4th she was deemed but

145

50% complete, and that statistic was truly more of a projection than an a reality. Getting her into the water was quite another matter for the winter of 1920 was a severe one in the Northeastern part of the United States and early March brought fierce storms and snows to the whole Philadelphia area. Windy weather had already forced a delay in the planned February 28th launching of sister "502" OLD NORTH STATE and that ship was out over a full day late. The weather worsened and a blizzard on March 5th was so bad it forced the "Sub Boat" steamer MARSODAK ashore on Cape Henlopen, Delaware. Across the river from Philadelphia, Camden was badly affected by the weather and the planned Sunday, March 7, 1920 launching of the PANHANDLE STATE didn't go off as scheduled either. After the noon hour winds increased considerably, growing so fiercely that at low tide the level of water in the Delaware River was so low that yard officials felt it unwise to let the ship run down the ways after Miss Louise Hughes, daughter of Rear Admiral C.F. Hughes, Commandant of the League Island Navy Yard, pronounced the magic words giving the ship a name at 3:30PM. After such a long time in the planning and building stages, after so many design changes, this was but another disappointment along the way and elicited very little comment either in the press or among Shipping Board offices. The weather cleared a bit on Monday and to no particular ceremony the ship was launched on Tuesday, March 9th. In short order the pace of work at the fitting out pier pointed to a July delivery. The following weeks saw her outfitting progress, but activity was too slow to allow the builders to meet the anticipated July completion date.

Meanwhile, her future became the subject of a great deal of speculation both within the halls of the Shipping Board and in steamship offices in major American port cities. On July 10, 1920 Shipping Board Traffic Manager Fred L. Murphy presented then Shipping Board Chairman Admiral Benson with a memo on the possible assignment for this first Government passenger ship. As a measure of thinking in the shipping business of that era, it's worth a look:

> ... On account of the small passenger capacity of this type, known as the "502" which carried but 84 passengers and has a deadweight capacity of 12,000 tons, I believe it would be best to consider the intercoastal services and the transAtlantic services on their own merits.

As to the Intercoastal Services:

> While it is true that the former policy of the Board has been to encourage private initiative and to withhold whenever possible the assignment of Shipping Board tonnage in competition, I feel that the present unfortunate state of the rail lines does not permit the movement of our own domestic products from one extreme of the country to the other with the freedom necessary to serve the interests of the people; and that the function of the Shipping Board is to meet such a situation with the investment of the people by such assignments as the Board will find appropriate. The present freight rates in

Intercoastal service average about $33.00 per ton. With the speed of this vessel at 14 knots it is safe to estimate on a turnaround from New York and return of 50 days.

As to transAtlantic Services:

Account of the combination passenger and cargo features, it would appear that the vessel should be placed on one of our largest berths, and after a careful analysis of this situation the Antwerp berth which continues most active would no doubt be the proper service. The going rates are $23.00 per ton from North Atlantic to Antwerp/Rotterdam range and should show a turnaround of 60 days.

The demand for passenger space at the present time in the transAtlantic work is far above normal; reports indicate that it is almost impossible to secure space until early winter.

If it is decided to place the SS PANHANDLE STATE in Intercoastal work, it appears that the Luckenbach Steamship Company have evidenced their ability and intentions in our permanent marine by extensive investments by their own funds would be the appropriate operator. If it is decided to put the vessel in transAtlantic, Antwerp berth, the qualifications of the Black Diamond Steamship Company or the Cosmopolitan Shipping Company may be examined for a choice. The Black Diamond Steamship Company has purchased for cash one of our Shipping Board Steamers, the SS NEW BRITAIN.

Apart from the above, the vessel may be considered a splendid advertisement, both for the Board and for the Merchant Marine, and may be exploited with this in view. Probably a larger reflection may be expected if this is considered in the transAtlantic work than in the Intercoastal work.[1]

But two ex-German vessels chartered on May 28, 1920 by the United States Mail Steamship Company were not yet available for service and US Mail's chief Colonel (or Judge) Mayer, who for a few brief months during 1920 and 1921 shined as the Shipping Board's "Golden Boy" of passenger liner operations on the Atlantic, asked for allocation of not only the PANHANDLE STATE but the next one scheduled for delivery, the identical OLD NORTH STATE. Had Colonel F. Mayer not been so actively pursuing ex-German and other Government tonnage at about that time, the PANHANDLE STATE might instead have gone under allocation to one of the companies named above but with Mayer's United States Mail Steamship Company concentrating so heavily on the development of American flag passenger services, the Shipping Board decided to facilitate the expansion of that company's fleet and once asked for tonnage of the "502" type, saw its way clear to assigning such ships to them.

Though the ship was not yet finished late that July, the Shipping Board

---

[1] July 10, 1920 memo from Fred. Murphy to Shipping Board Chairman Admiral Benson. Copy in the ship's 1091 file in RG 32 at National Archives.

heeded Traffic Manager Fred Murphy's July 19th call for a quick and definite assignment of the PANHANDLE STATE and her sister OLD NORTH STATE. Commissioners and Trustees evidently agreed and the Shipping Board soon informed the United States Mail Steamship Company of the impending allocation of the PANHANDLE STATE and OLD NORTH STATE. Admiral Benson's assitant Richard Bailey took a few minutes on July 24th to let Murphy know, writing " . . . O wish to advise that this action has already been taken."[2] Except for some Steward's department fittings and most of her furniture, purchased from the New York firm of W. & J. Sloane for delivery and installation at New York prior to the ship's entry into service, the PANHANDLE STATE was nearly ready to sail on her trials when the Shipping Board made definite the allocation of the ship to U.S. Mail was July 26, 1920.

Over the first two weeks of August the thousand and one items a passenger ship needs were brought aboard. As the noise and activity of workmen's tools died down aboard the brand new liner, the yard notified the Shipping Board that the ship was ready for visitors. Open for guests' inspection at her fitting out berth during the evening of August 18, 1920, the ship was ready to perform her trials on August 19, 1920. Specially invited by New York Shipbuilding's Senior Vice President H. Magoon, Chairman Benson could not make it and had sent his regrets. The trials went on without him. At 6:00 a.m. on August 19, 1920 the PANHANDLE STATE departed her Camden fitting out pier, turned into the Delaware River and headed south for Cape Henlopen, Delaware to run her sea and speed trials. Successfully passing all her tests, she surprised participants by making a top speed of 16 knots, two more than her contract speed. Back at the Camden shipyard after her fine performance, workers applied finishing touches to the PANHANDLE STATE. A week after the ship's trials, on August 26th, paperwork regarding her delivery was completed and though still property oft he yard, the new ship was officially delivered to the Division of Operations. Four days later, on August 30, 1920, delivery to the United States Shipping Board and it was a simple rite. It was a procedure that had been performed so many times in American shipyards over the last three years, one which would be repeated many times over the next two years.

The simple transaction took place aboard the ship. On the bridge of the PANHANDLE STATE, New York Shipbuilding Company Vice-president H. Magoon handed over the ship's papers to E.A. Opplet, chief resident inspector of the Shipping Board at Camden. In return, Opplet gave Magoon a receipt on behalf of the Emergency Fleet Corp. The flag of her builder came down and the flag of the Shipping Board went up. The first of the class finished, she was completed at a cost of $4,085,516.44, a figure publicized (and at times, criticized) for two years. That figure didn't include the costs

---

[2] July 24, 1920 memo from Richard Baily to Fred Murphy. Copy in the ship's 1091 file in RG 32 at National Archives.

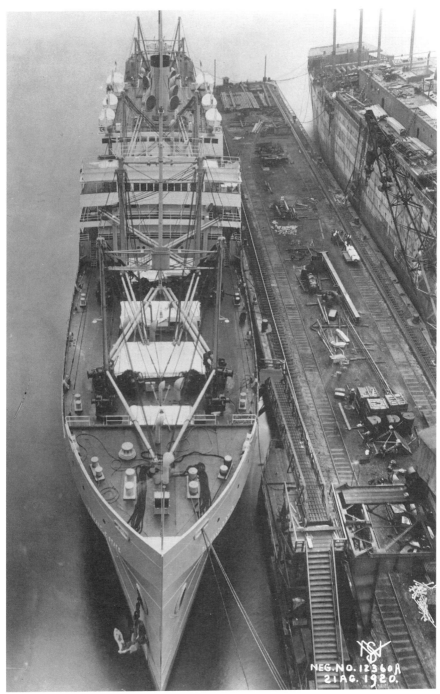

Two days after running her trials the PANHANDLE STATE was photographed on
August 21, 1920. Taken from a crane towering above the fitting out pier, this shot
provides a very rare bird's eye view of a "502". Across the pier is a "535" type
steamer, probably the AMERICAN LEGION. New York Shipbuilding Collection.
Courtesy of the Independence Seaport Museum Library.

It's September 6, 1920 and workmen at the yard are applying finishing touches to the PANHANDLE STATE before the ship sailed for New York and the beginning of her career on the London line. To starboard were the "535"'s SOUTHERN CROSS and AMERICAN LEGION. New York Shipbuilding Collection. Courtesy of the Independence Seaport Museum Library.

of furnishing her passenger accommodations. Factored into the ship's building costs, her "final" pricetag was a hefty $4,117,495.00. Under the command of Captain Clarence M. Stone and his crew of 116 officers and men, the new ship was registered at Philadelphia under the ownership of the United States Shipping Board Emergency Fleet Corporation. According to Shipping Board figures the PANHANDLE STATE was of 10,533 gross register tons, 6,195 net tons and 13,100 summer deadweight tons. Her cargo capacity was listed as 465,940 cubic feet (bale) plus some 52,300 cubic feet of insulated space.

Within hours of the August 18th arrival at the shipyard of the first guest invited to spend the night aboard ship and attend her trials, the Shipping Board's Division of Operations formally granted a managing operator's order. On a standard MO-2 form to the United States Mail Steamship Company, the Shipping Board formalized assignment of both the PANHANDLE STATE and her twin OLD NORTH STATE, then nearing completion at the same yard. An MO-2 form designated a managing agreement through which a private company acted as manager of a Government vessel on behalf of the Division of Operations of the United States Shipping Board. Terms of such agreements guaranteed the operating Line a commission of 10% on passage monies received plus a minimum of $250.00 for discharging inward freight. Firms thus operating important Government tonnage such as passenger liners and big, fast new freighters were soon switched over to another operating agreement, an MO-4 form. When so asked, the United States Mail Steamship Company duly signed the amended standard managing operators agreement, but the actual document was never delivered to the Board. Seemingly a minor technicality, the forces of the Shipping Board and Federal Court would one day use the failure of U.S. Mail Line to present the signed document became big news. Shipping Board Chairman Admiral Benson may well have signed it and maybe he didn't, for the Board later took the position that they never executed that agreement. Nonetheless, when a seaman's strike broke out in mid May, 1921, the Board had been treating with the U.S. Mail Line as if such an agreement were in hand. For the time being, it was of no matter. In the event, the document only became important once Colonel Mayer's star came crashing down in the summer of 1921 when his United States Mail Steamship Company suddenly failed. Without that important piece of paper, when U.S. Mail Line tried to claim certain monetary compensation for their operation of the ship, the Shipping Board claimed no authority to act upon invoices tendered to them in conjunction with the Line. Quite a number of people spent much of the late summer and autumn quarrelling, all because no one at United States Mail Steamship Company could produce a copy of an MO-4 agreement bearing both corporate and Shipping Board signatures.

Getting a jump on their colleagues in other cities, the men of Philadelphia's press saw her first, introducing the new ship to their readers as a ship of many firsts. Running both interior and exterior photographs of the new liner to accompany their stories, theirs was a fine impression of what American designers and shipbuilders could do. The first passenger liner owned solely by the United States government, the PANHANDLE STATE was the first commercial passenger ship in the world flying flags denoting government ownership. The first passenger liner delivered to the United States Shipping Board by any yard in the country, she was the first of a group of seven sisterships from the Camden plant, the ship was the first passenger ship completed by New York Ship in five years, not counting the ORIZABA, SIBONEY, SANTA ELISA, SANTA LEONOR and SANTA TERESA, ordered as passenger ships but completed as troop transports.

Rhapsodizing in print, the *Philadelphia Inquirer* reported:

> It was not the bright and spotless American flag at her stern which identified her nationality. The conspicuous legend on her bow—"PANHANDLE STATE" - was unmistakable. Such colloquial native flavor is inimitable and may be significantly contrasted with clumsy German flattery as expressed in such craft as the GEORGE WASHINGTON or PRESIDENT LINCOLN.
>
> The PANHANDLE STATE is not only a boat of another origin, but she is a ship, which, in a sense, marks the beginning of a new epoch. For this handsome vessel, constructed in Camden and launched on the Delaware last March is the first passenger vessel ever built for the United States Government. The Shipping Board is her owner, although she will be allocated to private interests and operated in competition with foreign steamship lines which heretofore have all but monopolized the transAtlantic service . . .[3]

And still, the ship had yet to earn a dime. All she had done thus far was cost a lot of money. And costs were mounting quickly. Between August 30th and September 17th 1920, expenses for the preparation of the new PANHANDLE STATE for commercial service totalled $43,406.21, a good bit of that for furnishing and equipping her passenger spaces. Under a temporary managing operating agreement, the PANHANDLE STATE was allocated to the United States Mail Steamship Company with the proviso that when other vessels came abailable to them, the PANHANDLE STATE would be withdrawn should the Shipping Board deem that advisable. Before the ship sailed there was sufficient time for the usual press inspections and U.S. Mail Line was able to get the media to introduce this new American ship to the public but there really wasn't enough time for them to advertise the inaugural sailing of the new London service. Consequently few people booked passage in the new ship. On the other hand, the "high" season was over and demand for eastbound passage less than it would have been had the ship been delivered in May, for instance. In terms of precentage of space booked, the ship would sail with almost a third of her beds occupied, a figure not out of line with other ships sailing from New York that week. Her passenger cabins booked or not, the ship had to sail. The PANHANDLE STATE took on the last of her eastbound cargo and mails, embarked 25 passengers and began her maiden voyage, sailing from New York at Noon on Saturday, September

---

[3] *Philadelphia Inquirer,*August 31, 1920.

Painted in the livery of the United States Mail Steamship Company, the PANHANDLE STATE was photographed at New York. Frank O. Braynard collection.

18, 1920. Scheduled to make an eastbound call at Queenstown, Ireland en route to London and Boulogne, the tense political situation on the Emerald Isle had prompted British authorities to close Irish ports to most ships. Despite such an embargo, United States Mail Line affirmed their intention to have the new ship show the flag and introduce herself with a call at Queenstown. They were no match for the British Home Office, who asked the Foreign Office to intercede and prevent the American liner from calling at an Irish port on her maiden voyage. In the face of British pressure on the State Department, the United States Shipping Board ordered the ship to bypass Queenstown. United States Mail backed off, too, and instructed Captain Stone to bypass Ireland, and head directly to Boulogne.

Averaging 14.5 knots on her first foray into the Atlnatic, the ship reached European waters on schedule. After her short Boulogne call, the PANHANDLE STATE crossed the Channel for the Thames and her first visit to London, her main eastern terminal. Tying up at London on September 28th, many aboard expected at least a hint of a reception, but no one expected the range of reports their vessel occasioned. A newly built American passenger and cargo liner, she was by her very origin and nature a rare bird in that British port. A real curiosity, she attracted the jaundiced eye of the whole of Britain's influential shipping press. Potshots at her began well before she tied up at London. Waiting for her arrival so they could criticize her in the harshest terms, British shipping writers awaited her with undisguised glee. Alas, the gawky-looking Yankee liner didn't fail them. Because of her unevolved external appearance, consensus held her an "Ugly Duckling". Other were less kind. The subject of a good deal of commentary in both the general and shipping press, everyone seemed to have an opinion about this American liner. One observer flat-out called her "one of the ugliest ships afloat." Maybe she was, but what an interesting ship she was and would continue to be! In spite of themselves, and despite fault found with her awkward appearance, all commentators seemed favorably impressed with her high grade of one class passenger accomodation, cargo capacity, and sea worthiness. Unusual in a goverment project, many remarked, was that little expense had been spared in furnishing the new ship. The high standard of her passenger spaces and the quality of furnishings was not expected in a government owned ship, as British observers condidly remarked. The well known New York firm of W. & J. Sloan had decorated and furnished the ship's passenger and officer spaces and would do the smae for the PANHANDLE STATE's six sisters. The famous New York department store, Gimbel's, supplied bedding, linens and a host of sundry items for the "502"s. The well furnished, handsomely decorated First Class won favorable comment from many quarters.

Commenting on her on September 11, 1920, the *Manchester Guardian* took a broad shot at the United States and its Merchant Marine in general and the PANHANDLE STATE in particular: "One of the unhappy legacies of war has been the stimulus given it to the doctrine if "nationalism" in politics,

Decorated with a fine hand the Dining Room aboard the
PANHANDLE STATE found great favor with passengers and
visitors alike. Frank O. Braynard collection.

trade, finance and everything else. The disease of "nationalism" is comparatively new in the world's history; one experiences little of its virulence till
about the eighties of the last century. Certain symptoms such as a movement
towards trade protection within geographic boundaries were evident before
the eighties, but they were due to vague prejudices rather than to definite
doctrines. There have always been lines of mental divisions between races,
between languages, and between religions. But the special feature about "nationalism" in its latest manifestations is that it pays small regard to race of
language or religion. It is concerned almost exclusively with political boundaries, and its essential principal is that those who dwell within a specific
political system should make themselves as far as possible commercially self
sufficient. If the "foreigner" desires to buy of the "national" products, no
obstacles as a rule are put in his way, but if the "foreigner" wishes to sell to
the "nation", or to discharge commercial or financial services for the benefit
of the nation, then he is an enemy to be kept out by tariffs, or prohibitions,
or esclusive legislation.

The Merchant Marine Act

At the end of the war the United States found themselves with a large merchant marine in the water and on the stocks. The submarine campaign had
forced the Americans to become shipbuiilders, regardless of expense, and
after the Armistice suggested a halt, yet so vast had been this programme
that the United States have afloat some thirteen million tons of shipping

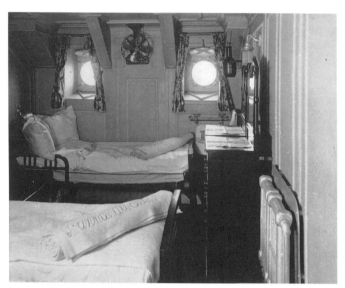

One of the big comfortable outside double cabins on Saloon
Deck. Frank O. Braynard collection.

instead of two million tons, mostly on the lakes, before the war. They have
become, by and with the advice and assistance of Great Gritain during the
war, a maritime nation second only to Great Britain after the war. If there
were no disease of "nationalism" to blind men's eyes to their real interests,
the British and American people would work together hand in hand to
reduce the costs of sea transportation and to facilitate the exchange of products between the countries divieded and connected by the seas. But unhap-
pily, the Americans, during an attact of "nationalsim", have, through their
Congress, decided to run their new merchant marine as the wexclusive possession of the United States, and, as a privileged competitor with Great
Britain's ships in so far as the trade of the United States is concerned. It is
long since Britain gave up the parochial "national" policy if the Navigation
Laws, but America has enacted them in all their short-sighted exclusiveness.
The Americans had an opportunity to share with Great Britain in the sea
carriage of the world; they have elected instead to become by privilege the
sea carriers of America and America's dependecies. If Great Britain proceeded on the same principle, we should reserve to British ships the whole
of sea communications of the British Empire and its dependencies.

Whining on for many more paragraphs, the Manchester paper conveniently omitted salient items like the American contribution to the recent victory as well as America's right to sail its ships where it wished. Unquestionably, fear of American ability prompted such a chauvinistic tirade on the eve
of the arrival of a new American passenger liner.

Pessimism rang from the page of the *Syren and Shipping,* which felt "no
great expectations of the long life and prosperity of the great merchant ma-

A view of the Smoking Room in the PRESIDENT MONROE. Author's collection.

Another view of the Smoking Room in the PRESIDENT MONROE. Author's collection.

rine which has been erected during the war by the United States Shipping Board. Also scaring British observers was a perceived unwritten alliance between American and German shipping operators, one which could bode no good for British shipping interests.

Fairplay rang in on September 16th with a short article about the inauguration of U.S. Mail Line's London passenger and cargo service. Of the ship they said: "Inasmuch as the PANHANDLE STATE is a well deck steamer, with a great many cargo booms stopped by ten king posts, she is an ungainly craft. Admiration has been expressed for her passenger accomodations, as the cabins are fitted out handsomely and there are decidedly attractive public rooms. While the ship lacks a bar, she has a spacious dining saloon, and a particularly inviting smoking room ... There has been considerable comment in shipping circles on the inauguration of the service because it competes directly with the Atlantic Transport Line of I.M.M. It seems that the Shipping Board is especially antagonistic towards the International Mercantile Marine Company, and there are ample ground for this belief." Sympathy for the Shipping Board in London was running low.

But perhaps it was London's *Daily Mail* which ran the most antagonistic copy. An undated extract (likely printed on September 11th) held in the the general files of the Shipping Board at the National Archives reads:

> A new transAtlantic passenger, mail and cargo service is shortly to be established between New York, Queenstown, Boulogne and London. The first steamer, the PANHANDLE STATE, will leave New york on Saturday week. The PANHANDLE STATE (so called after an unorganized tract of land in Texas) has not yet been to sea. a 10,000 ton vessel of about fourteen knots, she was laid down as an army transport, but after the Armistice her plans were changed to those of a passenger liner. With her sister, she is among the ugliest boats afloat, having five "stunt" masts and enormous funnel. She is built on absolutely straight lines from stem to stern. Against the popularity of the new service are the facts that the new ships which will fly the American flag are "Dry". Also, to crowd greater numbers of passengers on board, the majority of the berths are "across" the ship instead of fore and aft, with the result that the rolling of the vessel produces a most unhappy motion for the traveler who takes to his bunk to avoid sea-sickness. Instead of rolling from side to side, the passenger's head is flung up and down with every wave. British designers abandoned this system 50 years ago. The American Government built 17 of this class of boat and most of them are to be on the Pacific trade.

Rife with errors and calculated inaccuracy, this vicious piece was certainly concocted to cast a pall over prospective British bookings.

Experience gained in operation of the ship on a single Atlantic crossing prompted United States Mail Steamship Company's Vice President in charge of Construction and Repairs O. W. Koester to ask the Shipping Board for some alterations, further asking them to effect the same changes to the OLD NORTH STATE before turning her over to them. Once in the hands of the Division of Construction and Repairs, US Mail's "want list" was annotated by Commander Gatewood who considered each request. US Mail wanted accommodations for five additional waiters. Gatewood thought it could be done but noted "have 10 waiters now for 84 passengers." To US Mail's wish to fit the Doctor's waiting room as a bedroom for the Second Steward, Gatewood gave his "O.K", adding "previously suggested by Farrell." The Commander differed on the Line's third request. US Mail wanted a butcher shop installed in place of the present steward's mess-room, a room the company felt expendable. Commenting that the cold storage room was too cold for men to work in there, the Line concluded that they needed a place where meats could be cut up and cared for until use. Gatewood didn't think much of that idea but granted their request "if they want it." His associate Thayer was more succinct on Koester's request for the butcher shop: "NO." Both Gatewood and Thayer authorized a ventilator for the Chief Steward's room as they did the last item, provision to open Galley deadlights.

By the time she had sailed from London on October 7th for the homeward leg of her maiden voyage, enough people had visited the ship and they made up their own minds. Consensus held that as ugly as she was externally, she was quite evolved internally, with beautiful accommodations offering extraordinary comfort at reasonable prices. After the ship returned to New York on October 17, 1920 at the end of her maiden westbound Atlantic crossing, her Purser turned in the voyage report. While expectations for good news were heady when the PANHANDLE STATE left New York with $100,260.19 in freight revenues, a figure which grew to $105,183.19 once passenger fares were added, the report dripped red ink. Shipping Board accountants had a chance to examine the voyage report for her thirty three day (twenty two days steaming, eleven day in port) maiden outing. Besides outward freight and mail revenue of $74,270.05 on 2,760 tons of cargo there was an income of $4,923.00 in passenger fares. Voyage expenses amounted to $92,413.12, yeilding a profit on the eastbound crossing of $12,770.07. But homeward figures were less positive since the ship's holds were filled to only 21% of capacity. Except for some sacks of mail, her holds were mostly empty. The final result of the ship's maiden voyage was a loss of $30,511.90. Before the ship docked at New York, there had already been time for some consignees of an eastbound shipment of fruit to file damage claims against the ship. A shipment of pears had to be written off and its £5,900 value was paid by the Shipping Board, but a claim for a shipment of apples, damaged by the high temperatures that had ruined the pears went unresolved for sometime. Apparently the juice of the pears ran over and soaked into the barrels holding the apples, adding to the damage. Since the jobbers were able to sell more than half of them at a good price, the Shipping Board offered no more than 20 per cent of the £540/12/10 claim. A check for $1,937.13, representing nearly 2 per cent of the revenue of her outbound voyage, was cut on December 15, 1922. It was, by the way, the last claim paid against the PANHANDLE STATE for her United States Mail days.

Once the ship sailed on her maiden voyage, America's shipping press retained enough interest in the new ship to comment on her again. Under the headline "Starts New U.S. Line to Europe", "*Marine Review*", *Pacific Marine Review* and "*Shipping Review*" all ran another story about the ship, this one focusing on her role as a passenger carrier. Here, in part, is what they said:

. . . Although these ships will probably make their largest return from freight, the passenger accommodations are made most attractive. It is understood to be the intention of the operators to have these ships known as "bridge-table" vessels, inasmuch as their limited capacity and their more leisurely passage of the Atlantic will offer a inducement to small parties desiring a crossing in comfort and exclusive company.

It is in the interior decoration and modern improvements that the new liners have their charm. The decorative features are from the designs of American architects and follow closely the colonial period. Mahogany and white comprise the main color scheme in the dining saloon, library, lounge and other public saloons, while the smoking room is finished in fumed oak.

The chief interest of the voyager is in the stateroom. While some are larger than others, none is small and all are identical in design and furnishing. There are no berths in any of the rooms. In their place beds of steel, finished mahogany color, have been substituted. The appointments of all the staterooms are unsurpassed on any ship afloat or any hotel ashore. Many of the rooms have private baths and all have hot and cold running water. Cunard is building some so-called "intermediate" vessels. Many foreign shipping authorities have prophesied that the "intermediate" vessels will be the carriers of the future. Their plans, however, are all in the future. The Shipping Board is the first agency actually to make a start with this kind of vessel and attempt a service on a new run. Shipping men therefore, are watching the outcome of this experiment with considerable interest. . .[4]

A few days after the ship's return, Voyage 2 began. To no particular press notices she sailed on that trip on October 23rd. While the ship's crew concerned themselves with Voyage two, the press were amused by the 40 giant Costa Rican turtles, each weighing between 200 and 300 pounds, which were on their way to grace the tables of Americans in London for Thanksgiving. During the week ending October 22, 1920 the Shipping Board had granted the United States Mail Steamship Company a managing operating agreement (known as an "MO-4" agreement) covering the PANHANDLE STATE, meaning that that company could contemplate getting many months of uninterrupted service out of her even though no contract between the Board and the Company was ever really finalized. Later it became clear that the Chairman could be faulted for believing that an agreement calling for U.S. Mail to pay the same figure—$3.50 per register ton that month—that they were paying for their chartered ex-German ships. For the record, after discharging passengers and mail outside the breakwater at Boulogne on November 2nd the ship arrived at London a few hours later on her second voyage. A week was now allotted there and on November 9th she sailed for home via Boulogne and Queenstown. Sailing from Ireland on November 12th the PANHANDLE STATE reached New York on November 22nd. A few days later Captain Stone disembarked to be replaced by Captain Harold Cunningham, a man eventually to become one of the most celebrated ship-

---

[4]"Marine Review" "Starts New U.S. Line to Europe" December 1920 article.

masters in American maritime history. Besides this "502" he commanded the glamorous GEORGE WASHINGTON and glorious LEVIATHAN before going on to command America's fabulous "Cabin Liners" MANHATTAN and WASHINGTON.

Sailing from her home port on November 27, 1920 the ship was ready to meet the winter North Atlantic and though the ship would win every time, the sea managed on several occasions to get a few licks in. At very least the unorthodox design of the "502"s often saw them wet fore and aft. At least the pitching stopped by the time the ship reached London on December 8th. Just what the ship was like from a passenger viewpoint can be gleaned from the comments of W.F. Dunning, Assistant to the Special Commissioner, who imparted his feelings to Admiral Benson in a December 11, 1920 letter.

> As I know of your interest in the operation of American passenger vessels I want to tell you of the very pleasant trip which I enjoyed from London to New York in the PANHANDLE STATE.
>
> We sailed from Tilbury Dock November 10th (Voyage 2 Westbound), calling at Boulogne and Queenstown. There were forty-five (45) passengers aboard and a little over a thousand tons of cargo. In addition they had about twenty-seven tons of water ballast. This of course means that the vessel was in a somewhat light condition. You are no doubt familiar with the very comfortable and attractive staterooms and I can only add that the luxury of such spacious accommodations and a private shower makes one feel that they were stopping at a first class New York hotel rather than on the high seas. There was practically no vibration. The meals were excellent and the service could not be improved upon.
>
> After leaving Queenstown we encountered very severe weather, having a series of almost full gales from then on until we reached Newfoundland banks. Owing to the light condition of the ship this resulted in the propellors being out of the water a great deal of the time, with a consequent slowing down to 6.5 knots at times. However as the winds were straight ahead, there was very little side rolling but of course considerable pitching and tossing. I believe that if the vessel had had an additional two thousand tons of ballast, we would have made our schedule without difficulty.
>
> After reaching the banks we made an average of 16.5 knots, whereas the contract speed is only 14 knots, and the last day to New York we made a record run of 393 miles in 24 hours and 35 minutes.
>
> You are to be congratulated upon the splendid master, Captain Cunningham, at present in charge of this vessel. He was formerly navigating officer in the ss LEVIATHAN and is a man of broad practical experience, as well as possessing a charming personality. As a result of such a capable master, the splendid conduct and discipline of the other officers and crew is easily explained.
>
> The present operation of the vessel is certainly a credit to the American Merchant Marine and I only hope that it will not be a great while before both the passenger and freight business will result in profitable operation.[5]

---

[5] Letter from Dunning to Admiral Benson in 1091 file for ss PANHANDLE STATE in RG 32 in National Archives.

But perhaps he had felt an obligation to be pleased. Certainly U.S. Senator William Kenyon had no reason to curry favor with Admiral Benson. Member of that august body that had quite a lot to say in the matter of appropriations for the Shipping Board, the Senator could well have looked upon the operation of the PANHANDLE STATE with a jaundiced eye. Government ships were losing money, lots of money, in fact. An undated abstract from a letter of his in the files tells a different story.

> I am certainly a strong booster for the PANHANDLE STATE. The officers on the boat were especially courteous and kind and the whole trip was the most restful and pleasant I have ever taken.
> I am going to get up a little interview for the press on the duty of Americans to help in the creation of an American (Merchant) Marine by riding on American boats.
> I was not the only one on the boat delighted with the trip. Every one on the way over was pleased, and the same on the way back.[6]

A nice accolade to be sure, but passenger totals for the ship suggest that the Senator never did get to spread the word to the American people. The ship was just back from her December trip when the question of fitting her and the OLD NORTH STATE with steerage was again addressed in a December 31, 1920 memorandum to the Chairman. At the Board's January 19, 1921 meeting, the Commissioners agreed with the recommendation of the Committee on Operations which felt that the question of fitting steerage accommodations in the two ships and sending them to work on another line "should only be done after careful consideration and more time to consult with the Director of the Division of Operations and other interested parties."[7]

Of the passengers who crossed in the PANHANDLE STATE in her early days, none was more famous than ballet dancer Anna Pavlova, who, accompanied by her Russian ballet company, chose the ship en route to her 1921 American tour. They were aboard for Voyage 3 Westbound and sailed from London on December 14, 1920. Ship, passengers and crew were at New York on December 24th, just in time for Christmas.

During 1921, that benighted year of depression in the freight markets and in shipping in general, the PANHANDLE STATE made eleven complete voyages, carrying a total of 594 passengers, 294 eastbound and 300 westbound. Even before the ship departed New York on January 1, 1921, the United States Mail Steamship Company was already in trouble. Still in highest Shipping Board favor, Trustees of the Board and Emergency Fleet Corporation refused to notice. In fact, records suggest that the Shipping Board paid no attention to the company's actual condition, ignoring the heavy operating losses Shipping Board steamers posted on US Mail Line routes and

---

[6] From a letter from Senator Kenyon in the 1091 file of the ss PANHANDLE STATE. RG 32 National Archives.

[7] Jan. 20, 1920 memo to the Director of Operations from Secretary Flaherty. In 1091 file for the ss PANHANDLE STATE in RG 32 National Archives.

actively assisting the firm with advances of sizable chunks of operating capital. The ship arrived at London on January 9th and sailed on the 14th, just around the time in mid January 1921 when the Board's Committee on Operations recommended that the Shipping Board grant the company an advance of $200,000.00 for use in connection with the operation of the PANHANDLE STATE and OLD NORTH STATE. Onto the shaky financial state of thè operator and the possibility of their allocation to another operator, that committee was savvy enough to suggest the deferment of any possible installation of steerage quarters in the two ships. Committee, Shipping Board and US Mail were all still talking of the eventual bright future on the London line when the ship sailed back into New York on January 29th.

Despite the occasional kudo received by the Board, even paeans of praise by some near and dear to the heart of the Shipping Board, it was a fact that not only were the PANHANDLE STATE and her sister OLD NORTH STATE hemhorraging money on the London line, so was the United States Mail Steamship Company on every service then operated. By January 15, 1921, operation of the two "502"s, exclusive of the costs of fuel oil, had racked up deficits of $260,000.00. Two days later the Shipping Board put all the financial figures concerning the two ships before a committee on operations chaired by Commissioner John Donald. Curiously, neither the PANHANDLE STATE nor OLD NORTH STATE had run full load trials. Considering the performance of the next two ships, CREOLE STATE and WOLVERINE STATE, a pair of ships that HAD run such trials, Manager of Construction Thomas Pitts came to the conclusion that the Shipping Board would be best served by waiving the requirement for full load trials for the first pair and issuing final acceptance receipts for them. The question of withdrawing both ships from the operation of the U. S. Mail Line naturally arose, and the committee agreed to consider alternative operators. But not only did Judge Mayer still have friends at the Board which meant that for the meantime he could continue to advertise regular fortnightly sailings on the London line, his stature was great enough for the Board to consider his January 19th request for the immediate appropriation of $200,000.00 to cover the operations of the PANHANDLE STATE and OLD NORTH STATE. There is no doubt that sound business practices would have demanded he be thrown out on his ear and his entire operation immediately investigated. But the Shipping Board played by its own arcane rules mired under layers of bureaucracy and procedure, so Mayer remained safe for the moment and the Board paid up.

Indicative of the amount of business she attracted that year is Voyage 5. Her London call that time was scheduled to last a scant four days. Out from New York on February 9th, she carried 34 passengers, 1,834 tons of general cargo and 4,069 sacks of mail, providing a total revenue of $84,860.14. Such revenues would have made her a profitable ship but westbound cargo and mail loads for the ship's February 24th sailing from London hardly approached such gratifying numbers. One source of revenue was technically "off-limits" to the ship. That was the transport of "Irish political agitators" whose passage from Queenstown was specifically forbidden by the Shipping Board. But whether the U.S. Mail Line had been conscious of their identity or not, such passengers were reportedly carried, eliciting complaints by the British to President Harding, who referred the matter to the Shipping Board. Indeed, Operations Director Foley had previously cautioned Judge Mayer "that under no circumstances was he to book westbound passage for any political agitators, including Mrs. McSwiney, or to do anything of that character that might in any way lay the Board open to the very charges which have already been made.[8] More than that, only the dollar figures on that trip occupied US Mail and Shipping Board before the ship's March 6th return to Pier 7, North River, New York. Over the course of her first five round trips, the PANHANDLE STATE had averaged a daily consumption of 634.6 barrels of oil while steaming at an average of 13.2 knots. That was higher than her sisters, but easy to explain. She had operated all winter when, her engineers said, she had to work harder and burn more fuel to keep her speed than she would have in pleasant weather and calm seas.

Sailing again on March 15th, the ship was on Voyage 6, a trip that brought her to London on time ten days later. For home she cleared both London and Boulogne on March 31st and arrived back at New York on April 10th.

As with so many other American ships, labor troubles plagued the PANHANDLE STATE during the winter and spring of 1921. Smarting over a new wage scale that cut wages by some 15 per cent as of May 1st, union organizers delayed the ship's April 16th departure for London on Voyage 7. She got away two days late, sailing on April 19th[9] for Britain. On the day she was originally to have reached London that time she was again the subject of more Shipping Board discussion. Construction & Repair Division's R.D. Gatewood mentioned the subject of steerage in the PANHANDLE STATE and OLD NORTH STATE in an April 26, 1921 memo to R.H. Bailey, Special Assistant to the Chairman, advising him that it had been decided to install steerage accommodations in the CENTENNIAL STATE and BLUE HEN STATE, then building and slated for allocation to the United States Mail Line to replace the PANHANDLE STATE and OLD NORTH STATE, which were to be assigned to the Ward Line, the New York & Cuba Mail Steamship Company. But a combination of American labor troubles and a dwindling demand for passage on the Spanish service kept all four ships assigned to the U.S. Mail Line. That same week, it seems, Ward Line announced their intention to abandon the Spanish trade, obviating the need for tonnage of the "502" type. No one yet answered the question of fitting steerage accommodations in the first two "502"s. Nor did many pay attention to the ship's

---

[8] From a memo from Director of Operations Foley to Chairman Benson. Held in the 1091 file for the ss PANHANDLE STATE in RG 32 National Archives.

[9] Some sources say she sailed from New York on April 18th.

movements and only those concerned with her paid attention to her April 29th arrival at London. On May 5th, five days after the new Shipping Board wage scale kicked in, Captain Harold Cunningham ordered all lines ashore and took his ship down the Thames towards Boulogne, Plymouth, Queenstown and home.

Once the ship returned to New York on May 16th, union men including engineers, firemen, stewards and seamen gave 24 hour notice and then quit the ship. Unable to risk the tie up of their fleet of Government steamers, the United States Mail Steamship Company contracted with the Industrial Service Bureau on that same day. Strikebreakers were recruited to man the ship but no one but a watchman and a few non-striking crewmembers were aboard while the PANHANDLE STATE was tied up at Pier 7 on lower Manhattan on May 19, 1921. Preparations to load her for Voyage 8, a trip that would prove to be her last U.S. Mail Line round voyage, had already begun for the ship's scheduled sailing on May 26th. But things went awry after 6:50 PM when a cigarette carelessly tossed away rolled onto oil waste under # 4 boiler in the forward fire room. The smoldering butt burned on before igniting its bed of flammable waste, resulting in a ferocious fire, a blaze that very likely could have destroyed the nearly unmanned liner. The few crewmen then aboard ship quickly responded. From the pier the Fire Department was called. Lest the weight of water cause the ship to sink, the New York City Fire Department made every gallon pumped into the ship count. New York's "bravest" fought valiantly to save the ship, pouring streams of water into the engine room both by fireboat and by land based crews. They worked for nearly two hours and had almost brought the fire under control when Fire Chief Martin noticed that oil leaking from several seams in one of the ship's oil tanks was flowing into the bilges. Floating on water, that oil immediately blazed up. This new blaze almost could have destroyed the still new liner for the extreme heat in the burning engine room made it very difficult for fire fighters to get near enough to the new fire to effectively fight it.

To prevent a possible pier fire or a worse catastrophe, officials then decided to tow the ship away from the pier. Calling for the salvage firm of Merritt Chapman to send a lighter and prepare salvage, five tugs dragged the burning liner from her berth. As the ship was towed out into the Bay the fireboats NEW YORKER and WILLETT continued their work. With the lighter behind her, the PANHANDLE STATE was beached on Bedloe Island flats. Still blazing at 8:00 AM on the following morning, authorities felt she was in danger of sinking. Luck was really with the PANHANDLE STATE for her sturdy construction ensured her survival. By 10:30 AM it was apparent that the situation was in hand. The fire was out and salvage craft refloated the big ship and towed her to Pier 74 where repairs were immediately begun. In spite of the length of the duration of the blaze, it had been contained to a relatively small area of the ship. Damage was limited and at a cost of about $10,000.00 was repaired in two days' time. Not missing the chance to smack organized labor and "Reds" over the head, officialdom and common wisdom quickly blamed striking workers suggesting at first that disgruntled labor elements deliberately "torched" the ship. As it was a moment of maritime strikes and other labor unrest, such a charge resounded far and wide, giving a shot in the arm to management and Shipping Board attempts to reduce seamen's wages and roll back benefits and powers won during the First World War. Others voices suggested that the fire was caused by new crewmembers unfamiliar with the engine spaces. Any "egg" on anyone's face was soon forgotten when the truth that a cigarette had caused the fire was broadcast. Apart from any controversy about unions, quick reaction of the ship's Master and his skeleton crew were praised for prevention of a more serious fire.

Exacerbating labor tensions in the American Merchant Marine in that year of significant labor unrest and at least one major seaman's strike was the matter of alien nationals working in American ships. On her Voyage 5, which she had operated during February, the PANHANDLE STATE counted 126 men among her officers and crew. Composed of a 36 man Deck Department, 42 man Engine Department and 48 man Steward's staff, only 46 men were American citizens. By department, there were 12 American citizens in the Deck Department, 20 in the Engine Department and 14 in the Steward's Department. It looked like the voices in favor of American labor had a point, and it appears that some one listened for by the time the ship sailed on Voyage 9 in July, the situation was quite different. Manned by a 105 man crew, the 33 men in the Deck Department, 38 in the Engine Department and 34 in the Steward's Department were all United States citizens and the Shipping Board could proudly boast that this American built, American owned, American operated ship was manned by a crew that was 100% American.

Already foiled in its attempt to acquire for its fleet the *crème de la crème* of former German tonnage like the LEVIATHAN and the two four-stackers AGAMEMNON and MT. VERNON, United States Mail Steamship Company attempted to win a mail contract from the British. The possibility that they might actually get one that May seemed to suggest continued operation of both the PANHANDLE STATE and OLD NORTH STATE on the London line. Even at that late date the Shipping Board still planned to allocate two "502"s to the New York & Cuba Mail Steamship Company, more familiarly and simply referred to as the Ward Line, for that company's service just abandoned triangular service from New York to Cuba, Mexico and Spain. Maybe the Commissioners of the Shipping Board and the Division of Operations thought the delivery of a pair of spanking new ships might convince New York & Cuba Mail Line to reconsider their position on that trade so heavily patronized by Spanish emigrants. Already in the works for quite some time, initial reports on the subject of "502"s for Ward Line suggested that the last two "502"s, the CENTENNIAL STATE and the BLUE HEN STATE, would be finished for the Spanish immigrant trades. These two ships were to run from New York across the Atlantic to the northern Spanish ports of La Coruña, Vigo and Bilbao and then return across the Atlantic, but in a more southerly direction, and make their first landfall in the Americas at Havana, Cuba. There was, even in ordinary times, a great deal of seasonal movement of Spanish workers to and from Cuba, where they worked cutting and harvesting sugar cane. The Shipping Board planned to capitalize on the transportation of these seasonal workers. From Havana the ships were to go on to Veracruz, Mexico, and then return to New York. Ward Line was involved in this trade competing with both the Compañía Trasátlantica—then known as the Spanish Royal Mail Line in English speaking countries (and called Spanish Line after the overthrow of the Spanish monarchy in 1931.) and the Compañía Trasmediterranea, a newer company formed in 1917 by the merger of several small firms operating primarily in Spanish domestic trades. For passenger service on this run, Ward Line operated their twin flagships ORIZABA and SIBONEY, the chartered Mallory Line combiship HENRY R. MALLORY and the Shipping Board's BLACK ARROW, the confiscated Hapag steamer RHAETIA of 1905. Additionally, the New York & Cuba Mail Steamship Company dispatched quite a few standard emergency built American freighters allocated by the Shipping Board, some "Sub Boats", the subject of the preceding volume in this series, among them. The "draw" of a new ship was realized, and before 1920 had given way to 1921, Ward Line had applied for allocation of two ships of this type. After deliberating for a while the Shipping Board approved Ward Line's request, allocating a pair of "502"s. Neither was ever delivered to New York and Cuba Mail. Spain's wartime economic boom, as much a product of wartime neutrality as the increased maritime links between Spain and the United States, suddenly went bust in the winter of 1921, taking the demand for passage with it. Even though passenger and freight carryings dropped suddenly and precipitously, prognostications for its revival remained strong. The Shipping Board then did what it did so well . . . it hesitated . . . it vacillated . . . and waited for the situation to force its hand. The situation on the Spanish route really never returned to its World War I glory days. Beyond the precipitous drop in passenger demand on the run were other factors eliciting Ward Line's withdrawal from the Spanish trade. Not least of them were complicated Spanish tax laws, new American immigration quotas, a corresponding decline in freight offerings on the run and the competition from Spain's old Cía. Trasátlantica and new Cía. Trasmediterranea. So poor did the financial returns on the run become, that Trasmediterranea gave up as well and thereafter limited itself to waters closer to home, going no further than Spain's colonies in West Africa.

As late as the March—May 1921 period the Board intended to withdraw allocation of the PANHANDLE STATE and OLD NORTH STATE from the United States Mail Steamship Company and turn the pair over to the Division of Operations as caretaker, sending the ships themselves to the Brooklyn yards of the Morse Drydock Company where Third Class accommodations for up to 650 passengers would be installed. For months both a figure of 450 in a "closed" (cabins instead of the large open dormitories of "open" steerage) steerage, or 650 berths in an "open steerage" were mentioned in a number of reports published in both the shipping and general press. Expected to receive allocation of these ships as late as May 1921 was the New York & Cuba Mail Steamship Company for the triangular transAtlantic trade. Finally, the mouthpieces for the Shipping Board announced that the last two "502"s would not enter service in the Spanish trade after all and accommodation plans for the last two were changed again as the Board. With no other really viable operator for the PANHANDLE STATE and OLD NORTH STATE then in sight, both ships remained on the London line. None of the "502"s ever sailed on the Spanish route nor was any ever allocated to the Ward Line, which gave up all activities beyond the waters of the Caribbean by 1922.

All thoughts of "502" class service to Spain were dropped after May 1921 and the rare light that shined upon these ships resumed its usual focus on labor woes. Just having escaped disaster, the ship was only a few days behind schedule when she departed from New York on Voyage 8 on May 29th to arrive at London on June 10th. Perhaps there was a further connection to unsatisfied labor during that voyage, but none was proved after the PANHANDLE STATE suffered engine trouble when the starboard dynamo turbine became totally disabled once the connection rod with the forward blower broke and a crank shaft bent while the ship lay at her berth at London on June 12, 1921. Worse, the port dynamo turbine burst, killing Chief Engineer Ritchie and Junior Assistant Engineer Green. Two days later repairs had been completed and the liner sailed for home on June 14th and arrived at New York on June 24th.

The PANHANDLE STATE should have sailed again from New York on July 1st. On that date she was on Voyage 9, but instead of working her way to London, she was withdrawn from service and temporary laid up at New York. While awaiting repairs to her machinery the Shipping Board tried to pull off their equivalent of a "magic trick" or sleight of hand. Trying to mollify the harsh criticism appearing daily in newspapers all across America, the Shipping Board made the allocation of the last two "502"s appear to presage replacement of the first two. Late June 1921 brought the suggestion from the Acting Director or Operations that the farce be dropped. His June 28th suggestion to fit the PANHANDLE STATE with "closed" steerage accommodations and retain her on the London line was accepted and authorized by the Shipping Board at its July 5th meeting. Everyone on the Shipping Board knew that there was really no hope just then of finding gainful alternative employment for the "502"s. The slump in shipping was fast becoming a Depression. Things would soon get worse, especially for the United States Mail Steamship Company.

Well aware of his company's shaky finances and precarious position, U.S. Mail Steamship Company president Colonel F.J. Mayer attempted a preemptive strike to forestall expected trouble with the Shipping Board. Trying to protect his name if not anything else, Colonel F.J. Mayer wrote to Shipping Board Chairman Admiral Benson on July 6, 1921. "Begging to acknowledge receipt of the Admiral's June 14th letter", Mayer discussed his company's operation of the PANHANDLE STATE and OLD NORTH STATE. No student of maritime history should ignore his words for they really tell a long story:

> While it is true that the figures taken by themselves without knowledge or explanation of all the facts and conditions governing the operation of the two services might seem to justify an inference that would seriously reflect on the good faith of the Company, it is felt that full acquaintance with the controlling factors with effectively prove that such an inference is unwarranted in fact.[10]
>
> The S.S. PANHANDLE STATE and S.S. OLD NORTH STATE were placed in the New York London Boulogne service at a time when American passenger service on the North Atlantic had practically ceased to exist and at a time when freights, whether eastbound or westbound, had nearly disappeared.
>
> Your Board and the Division of Operations were frequently informed that in view of the unsatisfactory conditions of the freight market and the fierce foreign competition that these vessels would encounter that the vessels would be compelled to rely upon the mails and the refrigerating space for the major part of their voyage revenues. The Company stated that the limited passenger accommodation of these vessels made it difficult to secure additional revenues from passenger tariffs, and that consequently it was highly desirable to install accommodations for upwards of 500 steerage passengers which would allow of a substantial increase in passenger revenue with practically no increase in overhead and a comparatively small increase in operating cost.
>
> In face of opposition and delays on every hand, the Company with the active assistance of your Board finally, after a number of voyages had been completed, did succeed in obtaining a satisfactory share of westbound mail for the vessels, and had it been possible to have secured this result at an earlier date the operating expense would have been largely decreased. The refrigerator boxes have been practically filled westbound on every voyage. The first-class passenger accommodations are now full each voyage westbound, and approximately 68% eastbound.
>
> This result again has only been secured in spite of great difficulties and in face of an active propaganda, whatever the source, that has been and is now being carried against this service. This propaganda included statements as to the possibility of enforcing discipline and of maintaining a high standard of service under the American flag and under the privileges which passengers are accustomed to enjoy in the high seas, insinuations as to the faulty construction, slow speed, and the seaworthy character of the vessels and of magnifying every slight mishap of which fortunately there have been very few, whether this mishap was the result of strike conditions not making

---

[10] July 6, 1921 letter from Colonel Mayer to Chairman Benson. Copy in 1091 file for PANHANDLE STATE. RG 32 National Archives.

for 100% perfection over 3,000 miles of water at all seasons and under all conditions of weather. There is one way to counterattack propaganda and that is by demonstrating through the factual experience of the passenger that it is false. This has been done and the Company feels that in the consideration shown for the welfare of those travelling by the S.S. PANHANDLE STATE and S.S. OLD NORTH STATE and the precautions taken for the protection of life, it need not fear comparison with any line on the Atlantic whatever the flag.

The Company is in receipt of many letters in which voluntary expression of appreciation of the service shown and of gratification that such a service is possible on an American ship, is given.

The S.S. CENTENNIAL STATE has been fitted by your Board with steerage accommodation and it is our understanding that similar accommodation will be placed in the S.S. PANHANDLE STATE. As it is now believed that both of these vessels are earning their operating costs even under present unsatisfactory conditions, grounds are afforded for the confident hope that an added accommodation will enable the Company to secure a fair proportion of the Irish third class passenger trade and to show a satisfactory margin of profit over operating costs.

Your attention is called to the fact that the S.S. PANHANDLE STATE and S.S. OLD NORTH STATE have not been operated in competition with vessels chartered by this Company from your Board. Neither of these vessels could have been placed in the Boulogne-Danzig service owing to their absence of steerage accommodation as well as by reason of the fact that had they been placed in this service they could not have secured the advantage of the Mail revenue. On the other hand neither the S.S. SUSQUEHANNA, S.S. POTOMAC, S.S. PRINCESS MATOIKA, nor S.S. POCAHANTAS would have been run in the London service on account of their age, speed, and inferior accommodations.

Your attention is further called to the fact at the time when the oil freights were at a high level the Division of Operations refused to allow us to carry oil at the market rate and requested us to carry oil for your Board at an arbitrary rate which was less than 50% of the market rate at that time.

This action while materially affecting the earnings of the vessels for several voyages, though as an inter-departmental transaction, the difference in the net result to your Board was comparatively small."[11]

Mayer continued his letter offering Admiral Benson an explanation of the facts surrounding the egregious operating losses of his Company's ex-German liners before concluding:

This Company has never made any distinction between vessels operated under MO-4 agreement and those operated under Charter from your Board, and has made every possible effort to secure for the vessels the maximum amount of revenues without consideration as to whether these efforts might adversely affect the revenues of the vessels in which the Company had a more direct financial interest. In fact, I have no recollection that our foreign

---

[11] ibid.

agents have ever been informed by this office that our direct financial interest in the successful operation of the S.S. HUDSON is not as great as in the
other vessels constituting the line.

The above facts, which we are ready and anxious at all times to support
and extend by the records of the Company, it is believed will sufficiently
prove that any inference that there has been or is now in existence any
discrimination on the part of the Company between ships operated and
ships chartered is unwarranted.[12]

Considering the enormous operating losses the PANHANDLE STATE
and OLD NORTH STATE posted on voyage after voyage, the Shipping
Board never directly answered United States Mail's request to fit substantial
numbers of steerage berths in these ships. The United States Mail Line had
but a short time left for it went bankrupt that summer. Over the course of
eight roundtrips for the line, the PANHANDLE STATE had rung up a
healthy chunk of United States Mail Line's losses. At the time her operators
went belly up, this ship alone had completed eight voyages and was on her
ninth, turning in so far, depending upon accounting methods, operating
losses in the amount of $544,792.84.

In spite of several previous Shipping Board authorizations for such work
to be done, steerage quarters had not yet been fitted in the PANHANDLE
STATE during the spring of 1921. A further authorization, this one to install
"closed" steerage, was made in the closing days of June, as the ship was at
New York completing Voyage 8. Curiously, just as they took her out of
service, the Shipping Board approved her continued service on the London
line, opting to pair her with the newly delivered and steerage equipped
CENTENNIAL STATE. That would leave the brand new BLUE HEN STATE
and the OLD NORTH STATE available to other operators, should anyone
be able to successfully again con the Shipping Board. Finally, with steerage
berths enabling the CENTENNIAL STATE to take a share of the Irish emigrant trade on westbound calls at Queenstown (Cobh), Ireland, the Shipping
Board went ahead and asked for bids from parties interested in fitting the
ship with Third Class berths for 122 passengers.

Making the hunt for documentary evidence about Third Class in the
PANHANDLE STATE and OLD NORTH STATE more frustrating are several Shipping Board authorizations for the installation of steerage quarters
for up to 140 passengers in the PANHANDLE STATE. To be installed by the
Morse Dry Dock Company at Brooklyn during a spring 1921 refit, no further
word remains nor does further correspondence refer to any dispersement of
authorized payment for installation of such accommodation. The question
about Third Class in the PANHANDLE STATE and OLD NORTH STATE
remains to be answered but the memo to Mr. Love, the only available reference to an extant Third Class must not be overlooked. Complicating the
story of Third Class in these first two ships was a late June 1921 plan to

---

[12] ibid.

reverse the employment of the BLUE HEN STATE and PANHANDLE STATE. Expecting to replace the older sister with the newest "502" on the London line, the Shipping Board reversed itself after the delivery of the BLUE HEN STATE to the US Mail Line. Ordering retention of the PANHANDLE STATE on that service under allocation to that company, on July 5, 1921 they authorized installation of "closed" steerage in the first of the "502"s.

Since it was always a footnote in the minds of Shipping Board personnel who reckoned steerage passengers as nothing more than live cargo, they paid Third Class such little attention that extensive Shipping Board paperwork and comment on such quarters in the PANHANDLE STATE and OLD NORTH STATE are almost as much an exercise in self flagellation as the hunt for confirmation of the existence of such spaces. One item in the September 1921 issue of *The Marine News* tantalizes the interested observer: "Sun Yard Low Bidder on PANHANDLE STATE Job" ran the headline on a page 114 item reporting that the Chester, Pennsylvania shipyard had tendered the lowest bid to fit that ship with steerage accommodations for 602 passengers. "While the contract was not awarded, the tender was lower than that of any other yard . . . " The Sun bid of $139,554.00 included voyage repairs and some structural changes. Under the headline "PANHANDLE STATE TO BE RECONDITIONED" the September issue of *Marine Engineering* reported:

Bids for reconditioning the Shipping Board steamer PANHANDLE STATE, the specifications calling, among other things, for the installation of 596 third class passengers and 84 first class passengers, were opened at 45 Broadway, New York City on Wednesday, August 10, 1921, with the following results:

Sun Shipbuilding Company $139,544.00
Bethlehem Shipbuilding Corporation 153,500.00
Robins Dry Dock & Repair Company 159,000.00
New York Harbor Dry Dock Company 159,668.00
W. & A. Fletcher Company 169,000.00
Morse Dry Dock Company 179,000.00
Standard Shipbuilding Corporation 196,000.00
Merchant Shipbuilding Corporation 219,000.00
Baltimore Dry Docks & Shipbuilding Corp. 236,336.00

Nothing in the Shipping Board's General files including the files for these ships nor in the Construction Files states anything concrete on this subject except one item, a December 20, 1921 memorandum for Vice President Love of the Emergency Fleet Corporation from Acting Secretary J.P. James. No record of a contract traceable to those bids can be found and if the ship had been fitted with almost 600 Third Class berths, it would certainly have been money poorly spent. Only one Shipping Board document surfaced to confirm Third Class in the PANHANDLE STATE and here's what it says:

The United States Shipping Board at a meeting on December 20, 1921, deferred action on your recommendations, approved by the Trustees, E.F. C., on December 19, 1921, that the steamers BLUE HEN STATE or OLD NORTH STATE be immediately assigned to the United States Lines for operation in their London—New York service and that authority be granted to make such changes in the third cabin accommodation of the steamers CENTENNIAL STATE, PANHANDLE STATE and either BLUE HEN STATE or OLD NORTH STATE as may be necessary to meet the requirements of the said trade, pending discussion with General Manager Rossbottom of said United States Lines on Wednesday, December 28, 1921 at 9:00 o'clock AM.[13]

Other than obscure Shipping Board references to a Third Class of 140 berths, nothing suggests that either the PANHANDLE STATE or the OLD NORTH STATE ever had such quarters. There simply is no available record of any authorized Third Class accommodations actually being fitted to either ship. Maybe they were so fitted, maybe they weren't.

The ship was so fitting on September 9, 1921 when the Traffic Department of the Shipping Board took up the subject of the fleet of the former United States Mail Steamship Company in a memo detailing the August 27th operating agreement under which Moore & McCormack, the Roosevelt Steamship Company and the United American Lines accepted management of the new United States Lines. According to the Traffic Department, for "unknown reasons" but perhaps because of her presence in the yards, reconditioning at Government expense, the PANHANDLE STATE had been dropped from the roster of ships listed in the agreement. But for whatever reason she had been omitted, the oversight was soon corrected and papers redrawn to show her a unit operated by the new line and once released by the shipyards, the refitted vessel joined the fleet of United States Lines. Maybe the new concern should have tried to refuse to take her for by the time she finished her second round trip for the new outfit, she had racked up a further operating deficit of $69,619.51.

Since June 24th the ship was at New York. Repaired and modified, the time had finally come for her to return to service. Flying the colors of the new United States Lines the PANHANDLE STATE sailed from New York on Voyage 9 on October 25, 1921. Via Plymouth on November 4th, the ship stopped at Boulogne before she reached London on November 5th. Only five days were spent at London before the ship began her westbound trip on November 10th for her first westbound crossing in US Lines colors. That was Captain Cunningham's last trip with the vessel. A promotion to Commodore had come in for him and after the PANHANDLE STATE arrived at New York on November 20th, he left the ship to take command of the big GEORGE WASHINGTON.

Winter, traditionally a slack time on the North Atlantic, approached and

---

[13] December 20, 1921 memorandum to VP Love from J.P. James, copy in the ship's 1091 file in RG 32 at National Archives.

with Voyage 10 the ship got a new Master, Captain Ferguson[14]. He took her out from New York on November 26th. The ship was eastbound on the Atlantic on that voyage when a small fire broke out. Once more luck was hers and the crew quickly extinguished the blaze before any more than slight damage was wrought. Any damage was repaired while the ship was at London between December 4th and December 10th.

As the ship started that Voyage 10 in late November, the Maintenance & Repair Department of the Shipping Board requested performance information about the five "502"'s already in operation from the Operating Department. Culled from engineer's passage reports, fuel consumption by the PANHANDLE STATE had so far outstripped that of her sisters. Averaging a speed of 13.2 knots over the course of five round voyages on the London line, the first of the clan had an average daily fuel oil consumption of 634.6 barrels. That was quite a contrast to the 469.1 barrel average consumption of the identical CREOLE STATE which posted an average speed of 13.6 knots over one round voyage from Baltimore, Maryland to Colombo, Ceylon via Panama, San Francisco, Honolulu, Manila and Singapore. Surely certain variables like North Atlantic weather could account for some of the difference reported by the two sisters, but knowing of the rampant corruption wherever the Shipping Board shield stood, it seems easy to point to one of the oldest engine room scams in the steamship business. That's the one where the chief engineer signs for, say, 1,000 tons when the bunkers in fact required perhaps 800 tons. Billed for the full amount would be the owner and receiving a hefty chunk of cash for the phantom two hundred tons would be the chief engineer, and any others involved in the safeguarding of the scheme. One of the few ways shipowners were able to learn of this practice was precisely comparative performance reports. Officials of the Shipping Board finally did notice how badly these ships did financially. While it's clear that some of the Commissioners of the Shipping Board were clearly troubled by the staggering and ever mounting operating losses racked up by these sisters, other voices in the bureaucracy of the Shipping Board pointed to improving passenger figures turned in by these liners under United States Lines management. Don't attribute that success simply to the change of management for other factors really accounted for the better figures. And there is no reason to suspect that dollar figures for the ship's return passage on Voyage 10 that saw her dock at New York on December 20th were any cause for cheer. Once again the ship was in port at Christmas.

As the year came to a close, Voyage 11 started and the PANHANDLE STATE sailed for London on December 27, 1921. Across the Atlantic on January 7, 1922, the ship made the last of her usual stops outside the Boulogne breakwater to land passengers. Then she once again crossed the Channel to

---

[14] He may well have been in command for a few months earlier, but *The New York Maritime Register* lists Captain Cunningham as her master through the end of Voyage 13. The dates of the ship's arrivals and departures in those months, though, are believed to be correct.

dock later that day at London. At home, the Shipping Board was getting ready to act on a United States Lines' suggestion intended to make the "502"s on the London line more profitable. It came down to a matter of grading the ships' accommodations. No matter how good the ships' cabins were, and many of them were indeed quite good, the "502"s were by no means First Class ships. Not express or even mail liners, they were simple plodders with damn good passenger spaces. It was not enough to fill their cabins very often. Confident that lower rates charged for Cabin Class would attract more passengers to these homely sisters, United States Lines soon petitioned the Shipping Board for permission to downgrade the passenger accommodation in the "502"s from First to Cabin Class. Allowing management to charge significantly lower rates at a time when shipping was very slowly beginning to recover from the general postwar slump, such a change should make the "502" class liners on the London line more attractive to a growing number of budget minded travelers. Both the Shipping Board and United States Lines agreed on those points and First Class was discontinued in January 1922 with the Board's approval of the proposed installation of additional berths in existing cabins that could take them, and generally downgrading service and food standards to Cabin Class. With that move, fares were lowered by as much as 50 percent of those charged for passage in a major liner. For the year, she carried a total of 1,348 passengers, 646 of them eastbound, and 704 westbound to New York.

Meanwhile the PANHANDLE STATE had sailed from London for New York on January 12th. Aboard were her last First Class passengers on the London line, 18 travelers who chose to brave the winter North Atlantic in this sturdy ship. And they were patient souls, too, for the ship had a terrible crossing. Heavy seas, high winds and engine trouble plagued the ship all the way across. On January 22nd, when she should have arrived at New York, she was off Nova Scotia. Making a speed of 3 knots, her fuel was hard to burn. Captain Ferguson called for assistance. Tugs came out from Halifax and brought her into port. Two days later on the 25th she was at New York ready to begin her next trip.

Now a cabin liner, she had more passengers than might otherwise be expected for a midwinter eastbound crossing. Her cabins had yet to be fitted with extra berths. No refit to the ship's passenger spaces was made until the Shipping Board opened the purse that spring and took out the hefty chunk of cash needed to allow the installation of Third Class accommodations for 400 more passengers as well as the installation of 24 extra beds for Cabin passengers. Plans for the renovations included installation of a Ladies Lounge, Smoke Room and Dining Room as well as small cabins for 2,3, 4 and 6 passengers in Third Class. Once again the PANHANDLE STATE was refitted at the yards of the Morse Dry Dock Company. Extra berths were added over existing beds in Cabin Class but it seems that no Third Class beyond the 122 beds fitted earlier was installed, nor, it seems, did Morse Dry Dock's bill approach anything like the sum of $150,000.00 allocated for the refit. Downgrading the ship to Cabin liner seems to have helped her on the North Atlantic.

Sailing on Voyage 12, the ship departed New York on January 31st. No longer did she stop outside the Boulogne breakwater to land passengers for the continent. Instead, a Cherbourg call was added to the itinerary for this ship and a couple of her sisters then operating for United States Lines. Homeward from London on February 17th, the ship called Cherbourg in the early hours of the 18th for passengers and mail. Ten days later the liner reached New York to dock at her usual pier on February 28th.

Typical of her work that season was Voyage 13 and it was her last trip as PANHANDLE STATE. She sailed from New York on that trip on April 4, 1922 for Plymouth, Cherbourg and London. Aboard were 45 Cabin Class passengers. Booked for passage to Plymouth were four adults who paid a total of $290.00 for their one way passage. To Cherbourg were traveling 23 adults and 2 children whose tickets brought in $3,797.50. Disembarking at London were 15 adults and one child whose passage fares amounted to $2,047.50. All told the ship earned a total of $6,135.00 in passenger revenue. Put into another perspective, ten years earlier a big suite with private deck on the brand new TITANIC had a tariff rate of $4,500.00. Other factors provided the ship with additional revenue. On that spring sailing the ship had 711 tons of freight which brought in $11,221.30. One thousand sixteen sacks of mail brought $3,251.00, on-board sales of souvenirs, gifts, soft drinks (beers, wines and spirits were a "no-no" on this dry American ship), haircuts, shaves, hair styling, etc amounted to $400.00 while rug and chair hire brought $45.00 for a total outbound revenue of $21,052.50. Even before the ship made London on April 15th, it was clear that the operation of the PAN-HANDLE STATE once again lost money.

During that same month of April, 1922 the Shipping Board decided to rename most Government owned passenger ships. Besides some of the ex-German ships like the LEVIATHAN, which was slated to be renamed PRESIDENT HARDING (the Chief Executive demurred and declined the honor of using his name for the nation's largest ship), all but four of the 23 ships of the "535" and "502" classes were given "President" names.

From both London and Cherbourg on April 21, 1922 the PANHANDLE STATE sailed for New York and a May 1st arrival. On the following day, May 2, 1922, she was renamed PRESIDENT MONROE and besides a new name and a new port, she got a new Master, Captain Pittman. Voyage 14 was her first trip under her new name and she sailed for the first time as PRESIDENT MONROE from New York on May 6, 1922. There was also a new port to service that time, Hamburg. A call there had been scheduled between London and New York and after loading at London, she crossed the North Sea and make a maiden call there. Tragicomedic human drama played out on her first outing as a "President" liner and it began when the ship was six days out from New York. Mrs. Gertrude MacGregor, a cabin passenger, seemed to have developed "acute mania (in the parlance of the time)" on the evening of the 12th and was confined to her cabin under guard. She was under guard when the ship stopped at Queenstown and Plymouth on May 15th and was not permitted to land at Cherbourg on May 16th so she was retained aboard for the passage to London where arrangements were made for her to be kept while the ship made her short Hamburg trip. The ship was back at London by May 20th and among those boarding was Mrs. MacGregor, who was repatriated to the United States without sojourning at liberty in any European port. By all accounts she was an unhappy passenger bound for the United States aboard the PRESIDENT MONROE when the ship sailed for the first time under her new name on May 23rd from Tilbury Docks. Just how unhappy a camper was Mrs. MacGregor remained to be seen but before the ship arrived at New York on June 2nd, she was deemed "violently insane". Unfortunately she gave plenty of supporting evidence of that diagnosis, and managed to badly damage her cabin, breaking all its furniture, destroying its fixtures and defacing the paint and varnish. Taking up the matter of this errant soul with its attorneys, the Shipping Board itemized the expenses of Mrs. MacGregor's passage. For the eastbound crossing, Mrs. MacGregor had had a ticket at the prevailing fare of $130.00. For wages and subsistence of nurse Pope, who was employed looking after the deranged woman from May 16th through June 18th, the Board claimed $53.34 (Miss Pope's monthly wage was $50.00). For damage to the cap, uniform and watch of nurse Amy Gildersleeve, the sum of $21.00; for subsistence at New York, $7.00; for damages to Cabin 1, the sum of $230.00; making its case crystal clear, the Shipping Board sued the MacGregors for damages.[15]

Far less dramatic were the passengers aboard the ship on Voyage 15. The ship sailed from New York on June 7th and arrived at London on June 18th for a six day call. Calling at Cherbourg on June 26th westbound, on July 2nd the PRESIDENT MONROE reported herself 743 miles east of Ambrose Light. She arrived at her home port in the evening of July 3rd. During the next week there was time to effect several voyage repairs and attend to all kind of ship's business before the ship got underway again, sailing from New York on Voyage 16 on July 12th. Four days later she reported herself 1,248 miles east of Ambrose Light. Eastbound into Britain on July 22, 1922, the PRESIDENT MONROE called at Plymouth, reporting steering trouble. There, all passengers, regardless of destination were landed, and the trouble repaired. Quickly repaired the ship made London on July 24th. Her work completed she sailed for home on August 2nd. After a Cherbourg call on the early hours of the 3rd, the ship arrived at New York on August 12th.

On the following trip, Voyage 17, no such drama traumatized ship, Mas-

---

[15] September 10, 1923 and other dates. Correspondence on the subject from and among Shipping Board and United States Lines personnel. Copies in the ship's 1091 file in RG 32 at National Archives.

ter or crew. A largely uneventful voyage, the ship sailed from New York on August 16th, stopped at Queenstown and Plymouth on August 26th and arrived at London on August 27th. September 2nd was sailing day for Cherbourg and a September 12th arrival at New York. Equally restful was Voyage 18 and that trip saw the liner leave New York on September 20th for her usual ports across the Atlantic. After a week in port, Captain Pittman took his ship out of London on October 7th and brought his ship home to New York where he gave orders to tie up on October 17th. In port between October 18th and 25, 1922, various workmen sent by a number of contractors effected $4,558.00 worth of repairs to the PRESIDENT MONROE. From the W.A. Fletcher yard came a bill for $400.00 for an October 22nd job of extending 6 inches of fuel oil escape pipes from bridge deck to navigating bridge. Morse Drydock men spent six working days doing various repairs in the engine room, to steward's equipment and the hull, further expending attention towards vessel operations. Their work cost $1,232.00. Other men from the Morse yard worked on engine maintenance. They submitted an invoice of $600.00. From their labor force Atlantic Basin Iron Works sent men to fit jack rods for weather cloths on the Promenade Deck. That took five days and cost $750.00. As many days were spent by employees of the B.S.E. Marine Company who worked on boiler C. Their bill was $345.00. T.G. Egan sent workmen to repair firebricks in the boilers. That cost $720.00. Then there was a bill for $50.00 for maintenance work Tietjen & Lang did for the steward's department. By no means was the ship idle . . . She sailed for London again on Voyage 19 on October 26th. On the 30th her radio reported her 1,576 miles east of Ambrose Light. Crossing a bit slower that time the ship stopped at Queenstown late in the evening of November 3rd, Plymouth on November 4th and after a Cherbourg call, London on November 5th. The November 11th sailing from there was Captain Pittman's last with this ship and after the November 21st arrival, he was relieved by Captain Kreibohm.

Under a new Master the ship operated a typical off-season sailing, departing from New York on Voyage 20 on November 29, 1922 sailing. Heading across the Atlantic were only 14 passengers, one for Plymouth, five for Cherbourg and eight for London. Their combines passage fares were an unimpressive $1,705.00. Light was her mail room. Only 20 sacks of first class mail were aboard. At five dollars each, the Post Office paid $100.00 to the ship's voyage revenue. But there was a fairly heavy cargo that time, 1,598 tons of general cargo and 3,576 tons of grain, some 5,174 tons of freight in all. That earned the ship a total of $29,800.00. But onboard revenues were rather sorry. Each passenger hired a chair and steamer rug, but for their entire crossing they spent an average of 50 cents per person. Canteen revenues totalled $7.00. The ship's outbound income of $31,626.00 was still not enough to offset inbound losses or make much of a dent against past deficits. Worse was noted in her books that time for the homeward passage was tough. Everything looked all right when the ship sailed from London on December 16th. Touching both Cherbourg and Plymouth on December 17th, the PRESIDENT MONROE headed into a very stormy Atlantic Ocean. At noon on Christmas Eve she reported herself in a position some 1,516 miles east of Ambrose Light. It was tough going for the homebound liner but her Europe bound sister PRESIDENT ADAMS had it worse, for on December 28th when the PRESIDENT MONROE reached New York, the other ship was nearing Ireland, much the worse for wear, with broken windows, smashed portholes and damaged life boats.

Before taking her first sailing of 1923 the PRESIDENT MONROE had some off for a quick overhaul. That year showed her carrying even more impressive passenger totals but ever mounting financial losses. No matter that a total of 1,707 passengers chose to sail in her that year, the operation of the PRESIDENT MONROE on the one-class service on the London line was a very expensive proposition and it didn't get any better. Here's a brief rundown of her trips that winter and spring:

On Voyage 21 from New York on January 17th, the PANHANDLE STATE bucked winter North Atlantic weather but once again maintained her schedule and arrived at London on January 27th. She sailed for home on February 3rd. Across the Atlantic she arrived at New York on February 16th. Next was Voyage 22 and on that trip she sailed from New York on February 21st, arrived London March 4th and sailed March 10th to arrive back at New York on March 10th.

More uneventful voyages followed. On Voyage 23 sailing day from New York was March 29th, and after her ten day passage the ship stopped in turn at Queenstown, Plymouth and Cherbourg before arrival at London on April 9th. She sailed from there on April 14th to arrive New York on April 25th. When she sailed on Voyage 24 from New York on May 2th, high season was almost at hand. With a fair number of passengers the ship arrived at London on May 13th. After a six day stay the American liner sailed for home on May 19th to arrive New York on May 29th.

Voyage 25 from New York on June 6th proved a tad more eventful than those preceding it. After Queenstown and Plymouth the ship arrived at London on June 17th. While docking there she hit the British steamer CATER-SIDE, then moored at the Tilbury Coal Jetty. Slightly damaging the stationary vessel, the American ship did herself no apparent damage and continued maneuvering. Right on schedule the PRESIDENT MONROE sailed on June 23rd for New York where she arrived via her usual ports on July 3rd.

Before departing from New York on July 11th on Voyage 26 the PRES-IDENT MONROE got another new Master. He was Captain J. Pendlebury, the usual Master of the sistership PRESIDENT ADAMS. Captain Pendlebury took the ship across to arrive at London on July 22nd. The PRESIDENT MONROE sailed from Tilbury for Cherbourg on July 28th and reached New York on August 8th.

Not any more typical of the ship's North Atlantic service was Voyage 27 and the ship sailed from New York on that one on August 15th. She called at Queenstown late in the evening of August 24th and after sailing after midnight headed for Plymouth and a call later that day. After calling at Cherbourg that evening, the ship made for London and an arrival on August 26th. Coming into port, though, things went a bit awry when the ship damaged her windlass after taking on the pilot. She had to slip her port anchor and about 15 fathoms of chain before proceeding into London. While she worked cargo before sailing from there on September 1st, anchor and chain were recovered. Uneventful was the westbound passage and the ship arrived back at New York on September 11th.

From New York the PRESIDENT MONROE sailed on the first leg of Voyage 28 on September 19, 1923. She was more than halfway across the Atlantic on her way to Britain six days later when she was sold along with her six sister ships to the Dollar Steamship Line. Inc., Ltd. on September 25, 1923. Content not to begin service with their new passenger cargo vessels until after the first of the year, the Dollar Line accepted deferred delivery of the five sisters working on the Atlantic until suitable vessels could replace them. The PRESIDENT MONROE would remain on the Atlantic long enough to complete two 1924 round trips on the London line. The ship reached London that time on September 29th. Sailing for home on October 6th the ship arrived at New York on October 16th.

Though under contract of sale the ship still had work to do for United States Lines. Voyage 29 was next and the ship departed New York on that trip on October 24th to reach London on November 4th. She sailed from London on November 10, 1923 for New York. After calling the following day at Cherbourg the ship headed west and arrived at New York on November 20th.

Instructive is the detailed information in her late Atlantic voyage reports. Results for the outbound leg of Voyage 30, her November 28, 1923 sailing from New York to London via Cherbourg show how each factor, passenger fares, cargo and mail income and incidentals can affect voyage revenue. Though she had 50 passengers (quite a good number for a late November sailing for a ship of her size) and 6,301 tons of cargo, she had but 17 bags of mail. Her income was about $42,000.00. Heavy as her cargo was, it brought in just $35,700.00 even though rates had held steady, volume offerings had declined. Fruit, a high revenue earner, and a staple in most of her earlier cargo manifests was not aboard that time as the markets in Britain were both well supplied and competition from South Africa and South America cut into American fruit exports to that country. Had the PRESIDENT MONROE taken a hefty mail shipment, she would have taken in enough money to make a decent profit on the outbound leg. From London on December 15th the PRESIDENT MONROE sailed for Cherbourg and New York. On December 22nd she reported herself 971 miles east of Ambrose Light. She arrived off New York late on Christmas Day and docked on December 26th.

Lifting the first parcels of her outbound cargo at her New York pier at 11:45 AM on the morning of December 27, 1923 the PRESIDENT MONROE technically began Voyage 31 and it was a voyage well patronized by passengers and shippers. She also had a new Master, Captain Lock. Her cargo loaded and stowed, she embarked 78 Cabin Class passengers and sailed from New York at 12:15 PM on January 2, 1924. Let's look at some of the figures from her voyage report. Beyond some $9,513.73 paid by her passengers for ocean transportation, shippers booked 6,454 tons of cargo including produce and grain. In addition the ship took on a lot of mail, no less than 2,272 sacks of mail. That brought in about $50,000 more. Incidental revenue including canteen income, chair and rug hire and a paltry $2.13 in excess baggage charges amounted to a total income of $60,199.77. Eastbound expenses totalled $42,381.79. Calling at Queenstown, Plymouth and Cherbourg all within the twenty-four hours of January 12th, the PRESIDENT MONROE arrived at London on the following day. After discharging cargo from New York she loaded a mere 567 tons of westbound freight including 158 tons of straw hats and 33 tons of jute. Sailing with 73 Cabin Class passengers but no mail on January 19th, she had a total westbound income of only $14,712.46. Unfortunately her operating expenses on the homeward segment totalled $26,149.00, yielding another impressive deficit. After her homeward call at Cherbourg, the ship crossed the Atlantic and arrived at New York at 10:30 AM on February 1st. On that 36 day trip she had spent 13 days in port and 23 days at sea, steaming at an average of 12.30 knots. For the round trip, against $74,912.23 in income, expenses totalled $81,599.03 including $11,067.69 for maintenance and repairs. In just over two years the Shipping Board spent $257,792.31. The bottom line on that voyage report read simply: Losses to date: $881,526.66.

One more round trip on the London line remained to her. That was Voyage 32, her 24th for United States Lines. Aboard the ship when she sailed from New York on February 6, 1924 were 30 passengers, of whom 14 were bound for Boulogne. Their combined fares were $3,742.00. Again she carried a heavy outbound cargo, some 6,290 tons, for which $40,400.00 in ocean freight had been paid. But she had only 14 mail bags aboard her, and that contributed only $70.00 more to her voyage income. And now, despite the enormous losses charged thus far against her operation, her total outbound income of $44,212.00 suggested that cargo passenger ships could pay their way on the run, provided enough mail and westbound freight were directed their way. But that would have to wait for another type of ship, for this class was already beginning to serve new masters.

The PRESIDENT MONROE returned from her final London voyage to New York on March 1, 1924 with only 19 passengers. Hers had not been a spectacular career on the North Atlantic and the Shipping Board was no doubt relieved to soon deliver the liner to her purchasers. As soon as the ship had arrived at New York, the ship's documents were delivered to the Collector of Customs who then wired his counterpart in San Francisco that the ship's papers were en route to him by mail. Two days later, on March 3, 1924, the PRESIDENT MONROE was delivered to the Dollar Steamship Line. Her San Franciscan buyers had allotted nearly three weeks to perform the tasks required to prepare the vessel for a career under private ownership. Once more the ship entered the facilities of the Morse Dry Dock Company in Brooklyn. This time her funnel was repainted in Dollar Line colors—black with a wide red band highlighted by a big white dollar sign. As per the sales contract, the ship underwent a thorough survey, as had her sisters prior to joining Dollar Line for results of such inspections delineated what repairs would be made at Shipping Board expense. Needing attention were eleven items in the engine department, all considered usual and ordinary repairs, renewals and replacement incident to maintenance and operation so the Board placed them under Purchaser's Account and refused to pay for any of them. Two hull items, however, proved a matter of contention as did the matter of deciding who would pay for renewal of some 180 feet of cargo batons and a broken grab iron in number 8 tween deck hatch. Never logged, it was thought that this item was broken while the ship had worked cargo and was listed under the Shipping Board's account. More serious were other things including a leak in panelling adjacent to Cabin # 10. Believed the result of heavy weather encountered between February 10 and 12, 1924 as the ship steamed through the Atlantic, obligation to pay for its repair rested with the Shipping Board. Also revealed during the ship's survey at the Morse yard were fifteen further items listed under "Marine Losses". Twelve of these items related to bottom damage and most, if not all were covered by usual marine risk insurance. Incidental were items 12, 13 and 14. All items in this section were placed on the list for the Purchaser's Account. Beyond the technical items and requisite repairs the ship needed, the PRESIDENT MONROE was turned into a Dollar Liner at the Morse yard where all manner of Dollar Line equipment was put aboard and stored in cabins, pantries, dining saloon, public rooms and deck lockers.

Back at her pier, the ship signed on a Dollar Line crew and longshoremen stowed a westbound cargo for the sixth of the "502"'s to enter the round the world service. Under the command of Captain H.W. Dowling the PRESIDENT MONROE sailed for the first time under the Dollar Line houseflag on March 20, 1924 from New York bound for Havana and San Francisco. Running southward off Florida four days later on March 24th the PRESIDENT MONROE embarrassed herself, running ashore four miles south of Ferry Rock Lighthouse on Pacific Reef off Miami. Quickly speeding to the scene was the Coast Guard cutter SAND KEY which offered moral support but little horsepower to pull the stranded liner free. Despite the best efforts of his engines, Captain Dowling was unable to refloat his ship from her perch. On the night of the 24th the ship moved twenty feet and at high tide on March 25th Captain Dowling tried again to free his ship. On March 26th he decided to lighten the ship and asked for removal of his passengers and their baggage. Steaming up to the ship from Key West came the Coast Guard cutter SAUKEE which brought the ship's travellers and their bags to Key West where they waited for their ship. Luckily the PRESIDENT MONROE refloated on the 27th and made Key West at 11:30PM that same day. That accident of course delayed her scheduled Havana arrival but luckily the ship was little damaged and sailed again on March 29th to continue her delivery trip, hopefully without further untoward incident other than frazzled nerves in the California Street headquarters of the Dollar family in San Francisco. March 31st brought Shipping Board Chairman T.V. O'Connor a frenzied telegram from R. Stanley Dollar: "PRESIDENT MONROE is five days behind schedule and we have issued instructions to vessel to make all possible speed during passage to San Francisco so that we may dispatch her hence on scheduled date. Have radio report vessel arriving Cristobal four PM Tuesday afternoon. Have cabled agents endeavor arrange transit immediately upon arrival. It would be greatly appreciated if you could do anything to assist me in arranging so that this vessel may be able to transit the canal the night of arrival as otherwise she will be further delayed and you know how anxious I am to keep these vessels on their schedule. Shall appreciate a wire advising if you can help out in this situation. With kindest regards." At 8:10AM on April 1st the PRESIDENT MONROE arrived at Colon but because of her tardy arrival was unable to make an immediate passage through the canal. A day later at 6:18AM the liner entered the canal en route to her new homeport of San Francisco. At 3:16PM she was through and with her passengers and 1,205 tons of general cargo, cleared for sea that afternoon at 4:20PM. Once cleared for sea Captain Dowling had to try to make up for some of the time lost as a result of the grounding. Ten days were allotted on the schedule to reach San Pedro, but this time the ship did it in nine to reach the port of Los Angeles on April 11th where she remained overnight. She was dressed all over on the morning of April 12th when she steamed past the Golden Gate to make her maiden entrance into San Francisco harbor. Then came two hectic days as Dollar Line worked hurriedly to get her away on her first sailing from San Francisco. Amid little of the hoopla that sent the PRESIDENT HARRISON off on the company's first round the world sailing in January, the PRESIDENT MONROE cast off from Pier 42 and sailed out on April 14, 1924 only one day later than planned. It was the first of an eventual fifty five peacetime voyages around the world she would make from San Francisco. Honolulu was her first stop and the ship was still behind schedule. Her first call there was on a Sunday. Incurring extra overtime to crew and shoreside labor, it lasted twenty hours. Late in the evening of April 21st the ship sailed on her way to Kobe, where she docked on May 4th, two days behind schedule but when she arrived at Shanghai on May 7th she had picked up a day of her delay. With her sailing from Hong Kong on the 13th the ship was back on her printed schedule, a very important item in the Dollar scheme of things. Next was Manila where she arrived on time at 6:00AM on Thursday, May 15, 1924. At the appointed hour of 5:00PM on the following afternoon, the liner sailed for Singapore where she arrived on time on Wednesday, May 21st for a two day call. Penang, Malaya was next and she made her maiden call there on Sunday, May 25th. From there it was four days' steaming through uncertain weather including a fierce hurricane the

American ship managed to evade en route to Colombo, Ceylon, where the liner made her first appearance with her 11:00AM arrival on Thursday, May 29th. There, she loaded tea and rubber for the United States before sailing at 10:00AM on Friday, May 30th for Suez. To reach that port was a ten day passage through some very warm weather. After steaming through the Suez Canal on June 10th the PRESIDENT MONROE steamed to Alexandria where she spent June 11th working cargo while her passengers who had made an excursion to Cairo rejoined the ship before her 11:00PM departure. Naples was next and the call there was a short one, only 8 hours long. Arriving at 6:00AM on a Sunday, the Naples call was really made to allow passengers to or from Rome easy access to the Dollar Liner, for not much work is ever done in Italy on a Sunday morning. The ship made her maiden arrival at Naples on June 15th. The ship sailed for Genoa at 2:00PM and after a 26 hour passage arrived at the fascinating city of Genoa at 4:00PM on Monday. The PRESIDENT MONROE first sailed past Genoa's famous "Lanterna" on June 16th. She sailed at 6:00PM the following day for Marseilles, the last foreign port on Dollar Line's round the world itinerary. The ship made her first visit to that ancient port city on Wednesday, June 18th. When the ship cast off from that port at 7:00PM she was bound for home. Boston was her first American port of call and after her 12 day crossing, she arrived there to dock at Army Base at 2:00PM on Monday, June 30th. Thirty-one hours were allotted there for a "502" and at 11:00PM on Tuesday, July 1st, the ship sailed for New York where she arrived after her first 112 day Dollar Line voyage on July 3, 1924.

This time operating per her printed schedule, the PRESIDENT MONROE headed out again from New York on Voyage 2 on July 10th. Calling the same ports in their set order, the ship worked her way around the world again. On that second trip she called at Havana on July 14th and made her transit of the Panama Canal on the 18th to arrive at San Pedro on July 28th. From San Francisco on August 2nd, the PRESIDENT MONROE steamed on on her ever westward journey around the world. By October most of the journey was behind her and she was in the Mediterranean. She saw Naples on October 4th and after her overnight Genoa call sailed on October 8th from Marseilles for Boston. Upon her arrival there on October 20th United States Immigration inspectors performing routine examination of passengers and crew discovered sixteen Chinese stowaways. Forbidden to land there, they were consigned to Ellis Island in New York harbor and after the ship arrived at New York to completed her second round the world trip after her October 23 arrival, the hapless Chinese travelers were taken under guard to the immigration station to await deportation to Shanghai at Dollar Line's expense. Voyage 3 saw the PRESIDENT MONROE sail again from New York on October 30th and after making her way to California, the ship continued from San Francisco on November 22nd. As 1924 drew to a close the PRESIDENT MONROE was in the Far East. Passengers and crew celebrated Christmas at Manila and greeted the New Year at Singapore. She sailed from there on her

Off New York in the mid 1920's the PRESIDENT MONROE had her picture taken. Eric Johnson collection.

way west January 12th. In the Mediterranean, the ship left Marseilles on January 27th for a February 9, 1925 arrival at Boston. Sailing from Massachussetts the next day the PRESIDENT MONROE reached New York on February 12th. After a week in port she sailed from New York on Voyage 4 on February 19th. From San Francisco on March 14th, by April 3rd she was at Kobe. When she sailed from Penang on April 25, 1925 the liner was en route via Colombo to Suez and her May 11th transit to the Mediterranean. Six days later the ship sailed from Naples for Genoa, Marseilles, Boston and New York. From that last port the ship sailed on Voyage 5 on June 11th. That time her sailing from San Francisco was scheduled for July 4th and with flags proudly flying this American liner steamed out of her home port on America's 149th Independence Day. After a July 11th call at Honolulu where the weather is never oppressive, the ship steamed on through warm weather to Japan for a July 28th arrival at Kobe. Working her way through her Asian ports during the height of the summer the PRESIDENT MONROE reached Suez on a warm September 8th. At Boston on September 28th the ship reached New York on the 24th. On round the world Voyage 6 the PRESIDENT MONROE departed New York on schedule on October 1st and from San Francisco on October 24th. Let Kobe on November 14th, Shanghai between December 17th and 20th, Hong Kong on November 23rd and 24th, Manila on November 27th, Singapore between December 1st and 3rd, Genoa on December 28th serve as milemarkers for the ship's sixth trip around the world on which she began her homeward leg at Marseilles on December 30, 1925.

Taking her first outbound sailing of 1926 from New York on January 21th, the ship began Voyage 7. In order to perform some maintenance work on the ship, her San Francisco call was a long one that time. She steamed into her home port on February 9th, and did not steam out until February 13th. Across the Pacific, there was a March 9, 1926 grounding at Shanghai, but no repairs were urgent and the ship was given waivers and permission to defer attention to minor leaks and the vibration resulting from a damaged propellor that the grounding caused until her next scheduled drydock. The ship ended Voyage 7 back at New York after her May 6, 1926 arrival. She sailed a week later on Voyage 8 from New York. That springtime voyage brought her to San Francisco on June 2nd. She sailed out again on June 5th. From Kobe the PRESIDENT MONROE sailed on June 19th. From Manila she sailed on July 9th and reached Suez on August 2nd. From Marseilles on August 11th the ship headed for Boston and an August 24th arrival. After arriving at New York on August 26th Voyage 8 was completed. Continuing to circle the world the ship sailed on Voyage 9 from New York on September 2nd. That trip continued from San Francisco on September 25th and from Kobe on October 19th. Sailing through the Suez Canal on November 22nd, the ship sailed from Marseilles on December 1st for Boston. Voyage 9 ended after the ship's December 16th arrival at New York.

After the ship sailed from New York on Voyage 10 on December 23rd, the round the world service started posting profits and within a few months had much reduced the mountain of red ink the first few years of operation had produced. The ship was in Panamanian waters as 1927 began, having cleared Balboa for sea in the evening of December 31st. She arrived at Los Angeles on January 11, 1927. After her January 13th San Francisco arrival the ship was sent to a local yard where four plates were renewed, one removed, faired and returned, two plates faired in place and a spare propellor fitted in place of one that had been damaged in the Shanghai grounding. Repaired and no longer vibrating, she left San Francisco on January 15th for Honolulu and her usual ports. That time the ship sailed from Kobe on February 5th. February 28th was sailing day from Penang and on March 14th the ship made her way through the Suez Canal. Completing that trip at New York on April 7th, the PRESIDENT MONROE tied up at Dollar Line's new Jersey City pier. First of the round the world liners to use Erie Terminal's Pier 9, she was followed by her fleetmates to become familiar sights on the Jersey side of the Hudson River. The ship sailed out again on Voyage 11 on April 14th.

Off on her final sailing of that year the ship was on Voyage 13 and she departed New York on October 25th under the command of Captain A. Ahman. The liner called Havana on the 29th en route to her November 2nd Panama Canal transit. After her customary three day call at her home port, she departed San Francisco on November 16, 1927. The trip remained typical enough until January 8, 1928. With 300 people aboard, she had left Kobe earlier and was working her way through the Sea of Japan bound for Shanghai on a hazy Saturday night when she neared Moji. One of the rockiest and most dangerous parts of the Inland Sea, there seemed no extraordinary danger. It was then that the liner grounded on Hiroshima Island just off Moji. A distress call was sent out and heard at both Moji and Shimonoseki. An attempt to refloat the PRESIDENT MONROE was made at high tide. This failed. Then the sea picked up but tugs and a wrecking barge came out anyway and stood by to take off the liner's passengers should they need to evacuate the ship. With her cargo ready to be jettisoned in an effort to lighten the ship should that be considered necessary to get her off, the ship came clear. Incredibly she was undamaged and was able to continue on her way under her own power to Shanghai for repairs. In usual sequence the steamer called at Shanghai, Hong Kong, Manila, Singapore, Penang, Colombo and Suez on her way into the Mediterranean. Her brief grounding delayed her scheduled March 15th sailing from New York not at all. Her next outbound sailing from New York was on August 16th. That was the beginning of her Voyage 14.

The late autumn of 1928 found the ship once more in the Far East. She sailed on December 7th from Kobe on her way to her usual range of ports. At New Year's the ship was on her way into Colombo, Ceylon, where she arrived on January 2, 1929. Three weeks later the ship sailed from Marseilles on her way to New York.

The PRESIDENT MONROE sailed from New York on another world voyage on February 14, 1929. She called her scheduled ports in their usual order, continuing her trip from San Francisco on March 9th.

After she called at Panama on June 14th of that year the ship reported suffering minor damage when a fresh water pipe burst in No. 4 hold, soaking quite a bit of the cargo stowed there.

When Dollar assigned several "535"'s and the newly purchased old timers PRESIDENT JOHNSON and PRESIDENT FILLMORE were assigned to the round the world service in September 1929, they announced the withdrawal of the PRESIDENT MONROE from that trade and gave her a slot on their new run between New York and Manila via Panama. According to everything written since, the ship's autumn trip on the round the world line seemed to be her last for a while. From Kobe she sailed on November 8, 1929 for her usual ports of Shanghai, Hong Kong, Manila, Singapore, Penang, Colombo, Port Said, Alexandria, Naples, Genoa and Marseilles. The PRESIDENT MONROE returned to New York on January 7, 1930. From there, the newly reconditioned Dollar Liner PRESIDENT FILLMORE took her scheduled January 15, 1930 round the world sailing and the PRESIDENT MONROE sailed from New York on January 13, 1930 for California. *The New York Maritime Register* listed her for a round the world voyage, but since that was her customary run, the paper may have overlooked her new role.

While on that new transPacific service that year she carried Third Class passengers suggesting that Dollar Line had retained such quarters in her and that she could have carried at least some steerage travelers all along. She also made the news a couple of times. First was her January 30th arrival at Panama. There the Dollar Line could allow a delay to repair a few defective rivets to put an end to a slight leak or they could permit the ship to go on to San Francisco and fix her there after her February 9th arrival. The owners opted for an undelayed transit and ordered the ship to proceed to San Francisco. Once she arrived there, further damage to the ship was revealed. So was the cause. Somewhere along the way from New York the PRESIDENT MONROE had struck a submerged object, damaging more than a dozen of her own plates. It took over a week to repair all the damage and get the ship underway on her first trip on the Manila run. With a new certificate of seaworthiness granted before departure, the ship sailed from San Francisco on February 19th for a February 25th arrival at Honolulu and the beginning of her long non-stop journey to the Manila where she arrived on March 13th for an overnight call. She turned around there that time and on her way home called at Honolulu on April 8th. A week later the PRESIDENT MONROE was back at San Francisco, the first time she had come into her home port directly from ports across the Pacific. In a move of the loop up to Boston from New York on the Atlantic, the schedule for this experimental Philippines service called for the "502" to steam south to work cargo San Pedro between voyages. This ship made called there on April 18th and 19th. Then it was once more back to San Francisco Bay where after her April 21st arrival she continued loading at Dollar Line's piers before sailing away again on April 22nd. Again Honolulu was on the itinerary and after her April 29th call there she continued on her voyage. This time she had a new port to visit, Guam, where she made her maiden call on May 11th on her way to her May 16th arrival at Manila. By then the itinerary had been extended to include a call at Singapore where she loaded rubber and tropical oils during her May 23rd call. On her eastbound return to San Francisco, the PRESIDENT MONROE again called at Manila and Honolulu. Steaming past the Golden Gate on June 20th, the ship had four days to work cargo before sailing on June 24th for San Pedro and an overnight visit. Outbound from San Francisco again on June 28th the third of these transPacific trips, the PRESIDENT MONROE called at Honolulu on July 8th, Guam on July 19th and arrived Manila on July 24th. The ship worked cargo at Singapore again on August 1st. Of course there was a Manila call on the homeward itinerary and after her call there the steamer made her way to Honolulu and an August 22nd call. A week later on August 29, 1930 the ship steamed into San Francisco Bay to tie up at Pier 42. She docked to a chorus of an embarrassing spate of newspaper reports about her inbound sailing. As the liner docked at San Francisco, word was broadcast that six male Filipino steerage passengers had died aboard the vessel during her run in from Manila. Buried at sea were five dead from complications of pneumonia while the sixth was said to have crawled out a porthole and leaped into the sea. According to contemporary reports, the ship was one week out of Manila when pneumonia broke out among her steerage passengers. Eventually 73 of them were so

A port quarter view of the PRESIDENT MONROE taken on February 13, 1933. Eric Johnson collection.

afflicted while aboard the liner, twenty were treated in the ship's hospital and made full recoveries. All of the deaths of her unfortunate passengers occurred at sea between Manila and Honolulu. After the usual four days in port, the PRESIDENT MONROE sailed on September 3rd for San Pedro and the start of her fourth voyage on the Philippines service. She sailed again from San Francisco on September 9th. As usual it took her a week to reach Honolulu from whence it was another ten days' steaming to Guam, where she worked cargo on September 26th. October 1st was arrival day at Manila where she stayed to work cargo until sailing on October 3rd for Singapore. From the Straits Settlements port the Dollar Line steamer sailed on October 10th for Honolulu and a November 7th arrival at San Francisco.

By the winter of 1931 the PRESIDENT MONROE had been reassigned to the round the world trade and on May 7th she departed San Francisco for Japan via Honolulu. After an absence of more than a year, she arrived at Kobe on June 4th. Sailing from there on the tide on June 5th the PRESIDENT MONROE called at all the usual ports on the round the world itinerary. Here are some of her sailing dates for that voyage: From Shanghai on June 9th, Hong Kong on June 14th, Manila on June 17th, Singapore on June 23rd, Penang on June 25th, Colombo on June 29th, Suez on July 13th, Naples on June 19th, Genoa on June 21st and Marseilles from whence the ship sailed on June 22nd for New York and an August 3rd arrival. Next was another round the world trip from New York and she sailed out on August 15th. That voyage continued from San Francisco with a September 4th sailing. From the East Coast of the United States the ship began one more round the world voyage that year, sailing from New York on December 3, 1931. The PRESIDENT MONROE was half a world away from her sister PRESIDENT HARRISON whose December 4th sailing from Kobe was actually within hours of the New York departure. After a Havana call, a Canal transit and a visit to Los Angeles, the unimproved "502" type steamer PRESIDENT MONROE cleared San Francisco on Christmas Day, December 25, 1931 on her way around the world.

The ship greeted the new year with her January 1, 1932 call at Honolulu. Little of note occurred during her 1932 voyages and she kept her name out of casualty lists that year. She did get a new port to add to her itinerary. That was Bombay. First of the Dollar Liners to call there was a "535", the PRESIDENT PIERCE, which called there on Monday, February 1st. Beginning an almost fortnightly parade of "502"s into that port the PRESIDENT MONROE arrived there on February 11th. From Marseilles on March 2, 1932 the PRESIDENT MONROE headed out for the Atlantic on her way to New York and a March 15th arrival. On her next outbound sailing of the year the ship left her Jersey City pier on March 24th on her way around the world. Sailing day from Kobe that time was May 7th. The ship continued her voyage, sailing from Singapore on May 24th and from Bombay on June 3rd. Next came her midyear voyage and it began at New York on a hot, humid July day. The ship sailed out on July 14th. From New York on November 3,

1932 she began another routine round the world voyage, sailing from San Francisco on November 25th. From Kobe the ship sailed on December 16th for Shanghai. Fans of the holiday season might like to know that on Christmas Day the PRESIDENT MONROE sailed from Hong Kong for Manila.

Her schedule often called for her to take late spring sailings from the East Coast of the United States. Sailing for foreign ports she cleared New York on Voyage 31 on June 15, 1933. With sailings from San Francisco on July 7th, Kobe on July 28th, Hong Kong on August 5, Manila on August 7th, Singapore on August 15th, Bombay on August 25th, a transit of the Suez Canal on September 4th and a sailing from Marseilles on September 13th, that trip ended back at New York after her 10 AM arrival on Thursday, September 26th. About to sail from there at Noon on Saturday, September 28, 1933 on her way to Boston before the start of Voyage 32, the ship was delayed when it was discovered that one of her propellor shafts was fractured. Quickly taken into drydock, repairs were made and the ship arrived at Boston on October 2nd, a couple of days behind schedule. Getting back on Dollar's all-important timetable, the PRESIDENT MONROE sailed from New York on Voyage 32 at 4:00 PM on Thursday, October 5th and was able to arrive at Havana on time on October 9th. Continuing on, the ship made her way through the Panama Canal on October 13th for an October 22nd arrival at Los Angeles. Her next port was of course San Francisco and after her customary three day stay the PRESIDENT MONROE cast off from Dollar's Pier 42/44 complex at 4:00PM on Friday, October 27 to steam out across the Pacific once again. After another uneventful crossing, the American ship was working cargo at Kobe on November 17, 1933 when one of the lighters alongside her caught fire. Luckily it was confined to that vessel and did not spread to the PRESIDENT MONROE though it did bring the "502"'s name into the casualty lists. Later that day the Dollar Liner sailed for Shanghai. Other sailing dates from Voyage 32 were December 7th from Penang, December 24th from Suez, December 25th from Port Said and January 4, 1934 from Marseilles. Through the Mediterranean the ship headed out into the stormy North Atlantic on her way back to New York where she arrived at 10:00AM on Tuesday, January 16th.

Back from Boston at 8:00AM on Monday, January 22, 1934, the ship took on her last outward freight before embarking passengers on afternoon of January 25th. Now on Voyage 33, the PRESIDENT MONROE sailed past the Statue of Liberty just before 5:00PM. Adhering as well as possible to Dollar Line's published schedule, the ship cleared the Golden Gate on her February 16th sailing from San Francisco. From Kobe on March 9th, the ship continued her customary westabout course, sailing at Singapore that time on March 27th. From Colombo on April 2nd and from Bombay on April 5th, every turn of the ship's screws brought her nearer American waters. Through the Suez Canal on April 16th, the ship called at Naples on April 21st and sailed from Marseilles on April 25th. Across the Atlantic once more, the PRESIDENT MONROE pulled into New York on Tuesday, May 8, 1934. She was at her Jersey City pier the next day, May 9, 1934 when members of almost every union employed in the maritime industry in San Francisco walked off their jobs. Followed in short order by their union brethren in other major port cities along the West Coast, their action nearly paralyzed the maritime industry in California, Oregon and Washington. Except for strong-armed anti-union Panama Pacific Line and undauntable Grace Line, many ships were unable to get cargo in or out of San Francisco. Quite a few were idled there, strikebound for the duration. Dollar Line had further luck that time and was able to keep the "502"s sailing. Though hers was mostly a San Francisco based crew, the men of the PRESIDENT MONROE voted to keep working. At a time when so many other West Coast registered ships were going nowhere when their crews struck in sympathy and solidarity, the crew of this "502" took their ship out from New York at the start of Voyage 34 at the appointed hour of 4:00PM on Thursday, May 17th.

Dollar Line officials knew that they would be taking quite a chance should they try to bring the ship into San Francisco during that voyage, for no one knew if her crew would remain loyal or defect to the strikers. There was no chance that should they bring the ship into San Francisco that any shoreside labor would cross picket lines to work cargo nor was there any chance that if the ship came into San Francisco she would be able to resume her voyage before the end of the strike. Nor were the union men out on the picket lines up and down the West Coast getting any more pliable. In fact, the reverse was quite true, for as the strike passed into its third and fourth weeks it turned deadly violent, taking the lives of a number of men in street battles in San Francisco. But the story of maritime labor in the 1930's is only peripherally the story of these "502"s, and here we divert our attention from union grievances—justified and not—and return to the movements of the ship. With passengers and 2,598 tons of general cargo the ship steamed through the "Big Ditch" on May 25th to make a June 3rd arrival at San Pedro. Because of the power of headbreaking opponents of labor in Los Angeles, unionists never managed to completely shut down either San Pedro or Wilmington, so all cargo that might have been handled at San Francisco was worked at San Pedro where a customary overnight call stretched into five days. Keeping Los Angeles open relieved some of the pressure on major West Coast operators like Dollar Line and Matson. Both companies ordered their captains to skip San Francisco and use Los Angeles instead. Any passengers booked from San Francisco joined the ship at San Pedro and on June 8th the ship cast off for Honolulu. The rest of the Asian portion of the itinerary was operated as usual. Luck was still hers at Singapore on July 14th when off the main wharf she collided with the Blue Funnel Liner ANTENOR. The "President" liner suffered hardly a scratch, but the ANTENOR's bow was somewhat damaged but not enough to trouble either ship with undue delay. The PRESIDENT MONROE was between Bombay and Suez on July 31st when the strike on the West Coast was settled after 83 acrimonious and occasionally bloody days. On the face of things management seemed to win

again but an arbitrated decision that came through in October actually fa-
vored the unions and gave them the right to control hiring. But removed
from such important decisions, this "502" made her transit of the Suez Canal
on August 7th and after working cargo on the 8th at Port Said, made once
again for Italy. Printed schedules listed an August 15th call at Marseilles
from whence she sailed for home. Once across the Atlantic she pulled into
New York on August 31st. That was a few days later than expected and as
a result the Boston trip was delayed. The PRESIDENT MONROE sailed on
the following trip, Voyage 35, from Pier 9, Jersey City, on September 6th.
From San Francisco on September 28th the voyage continued with the ship's
sailing for Honolulu. October 19th was sailing day from Kobe that time and
on November 6th the ship steamed out of Singapore on her way to Penang
and points west. From Bombay on November 15th the PRESIDENT MON-
ROE began her ten day run to the Suez Canal and a December 1st arrival at
Naples. After the usual overnight Genoa call the ship moved over to Marseilles and a December 5th sailing from Marseilles. After a thirteen day crossing the ship arrived back at New York on December 19th where she worked
cargo until sailing for Boston on the 21st. Returning to Pier 9, Jersey City on
December 24th, the officers and men of the PRESIDENT MONROE had that
rarest of treats for seamen . . . Christmas in New York.

Sailing on another globe-girdling voyage from New York on Voyage 36
at 4:00PM on December 27, 1934, the ship was at sea from Havana on December 31st when 1935 began. That year didn't see much heady American
shipping news nor were there many bright notes to brighten that bad year
of the Depression. Those hard times were taking a toll on everyone, and not
spared were ships and shipping companies. The Dollars managed to keep
the fleet underway, though it is true that whenever they had to make a choice
between paying their own salaries or investing in ship maintenance, their
own pockets came first. The Shipping Board already knew the company's
financial condition was terrible. As the months passed, the ships, except
perhaps the new twin flagships PRESIDENT COOLIDGE and PRESIDENT
HOOVER grew shabby. The PRESIDENT MONROE was NO flagship—with
her limited passenger capacity she came in for a bit of neglect. Among her
movements that year were her January 4 canal transit and her January 11th
departure from San Francisco. During her second voyage of 1935 the ship
suffered the embarrassment of losing her radio. En route to Honolulu from
San Francisco, the ship's wireless equipment burned out, leaving her Hawaii
agents to scramble to replace her radio during her May 16th call. With her
new wireless equipment the ship continued on her way across the Pacific for
a May 30th arrival at Kobe. On that trip the PRESIDENT MONROE called
at Manila on June 10th en route to Singapore and points west. From Singapore on June 18th she made for Penang, Colombo and Bombay on her way
to the Mediterranean and the homeward leg of the trip. After that she pretty
much kept her name out of the papers as she continued to work her way
around the world as more uneventful voyages followed.

Under the command of Captain William Weaver the ship returned to New York on October 20th from her July 9, 1936 sailing. Maritime industry workers on the West Coast were once again out on strike and no one knew how long the tie up would last. While at New York, inspectors performed a condition survey on October 22nd and 23, 1936. Their inspection complete, they found her in better condition than other units of the "502" class and pronounced everything "clean" though her boilers needed some attention. Pronounced fit after that statutory condition survey, she was ready to go back to sea. Now on her bridge as Master was Captain P. Jokstad, the man who had spent years the last years of the 1920's and three years of the 1930's in command of this ship. Under him were a crew of 143 officers and men including a Deck Department of 34, and Engine Department of 38, and a Steward's Department of 27 white and 44 Chinese. On the 24th they sailed the ship to Boston from whence the next outbound sailing began. The usual New York call to load more cargo and embark passengers went smoothly enough and the ship sailed away on October 29th, 1936 with 2,740 tons of general cargo for Havana and Panama where she made a November 6th transit. Then she steamed up to San Pedro, California and that was it as far as her crew was concerned. Once the ship tied up on November 15th, the ship went no further. The great maritime strike of 1936 caught up with her and labor now held the ship in its thrall. Not until February 11, 1937 could she resume her voyage when she cleared Los Angeles for San Francisco. Her interrupted voyage continued from her home port on February 15th with her sailing for Honolulu. April 4th saw her arrive at Bombay and in early May she was back on the East Coast of the United States, sailing out from New York again on May 13th.

After that came her last sailing as a passenger cargo ship for the Bland Act of 1936 with its host of goodies for the American Merchant Marine came into full force. To the detriment of the further careers of a number of well-known passenger carriers were stringent safety requirements for American passenger ships. These new rules the PRESIDENT MONROE was simply unable to meet so she was reclassified a freighter from the summer of 1937 and restricted to the carriage of but 12 passengers. When she sailed from Boston on May 10th she was still permitted to carry a full complement of passengers but when she sailed from San Francisco on June 5, 1937, she did not carry more than 12. Dollar Steamship Line fully intended to upgrade the PRESIDENT MONROE to bring her into compliance with the latest safety rules but the Line simply didn't have the money necessary to do the job. But a lack of cash did not prompt the line to follow the lead of United Fruit which cut down several of their "5,000 tonners" once those ships were also unable to retain their passenger certificates. Dollar retained all extant passenger accommodations in the PRESIDENT MONROE, fully expecting to be effect a sufficient financial recovery to refit this ship and her two similarly effected sisters, PRESIDENT HAYES and PRESIDENT van BUREN.

That day never came for the fortunes of the Dollars continued to decline.

Maritime Commission cancellation of mail contracts and their refusal to advance any federal money to the line only served to hasten the end. But the PRESIDENT MONROE still had miles to travel. She sailed from Kobe on June 26, 1937. Four days later, on June 30th mail subsidy participation ended when Maritime Commission cancellation of the Dollar Line's mail contracts came into effect. As of July 1st, all operations would have to be funded by the line's own earnings. That would be a very tough road for the Dollar Line to travel. It was soon apparent that they could not. And still the ship's screws beat their path around the world. From Shanghai the PRESIDENT MONROE continued on June 30th and from Hong Kong on July 4th. Like clockwork she arrived and departed her remaining ports, sailing from Singapore on July 13th, at the end of a normal two day call. From Penang on the 15th the "502" continued her beaten path to Colombo to load tea and rubber on July 20th. Bombay on July 20th was next. Then it was on to Suez for an August 2nd canal transit and then after visits to Port Said and Alexandria, it was once more on to Naples, Genoa and Marseilles. Then the PRESIDENT MONROE headed for home, sailing from France on August 12th. Across the Atlantic she steamed up the Hudson on August 25nd.

With Dollar Line's back literally to the wall, the PRESIDENT MONROE sailed out for another trip. First she steamed up to Boston with her August 29th departure. Back at New York she took on her last consignments of freight and sailed on September 3rd for Havana and the Panama Canal. Hardware and cotton figured prominently among the 4,343 tons of freight she took through the Panama Canal on September 11, 1937. After a typical two day call at Los Angeles the ship steamed north along the California coast to pull into San Francisco on September 23rd. Four days later, on the 27th, the voyage continued when the ship departed for Honolulu. Most of the way around the world, the PRESIDENT MONROE sailed from Marseilles on December 3rd for New York.

The PRESIDENT MONROE arrived at New York on December 16th. After her Boston side trip, the ship sailed again from New York on December 31, 1937. There remained only one more trip to her as a Dollar Liner. The ship had just returned to New York when the crew acted up again. Like colleagues aboard other Dollar Liners, crews now decried the poor condition of their living quarters, grousing loudly about "their present unfitness for human occupancy". The present engine room crew pledged not to sail beyond San Francisco unless their accommodations were improved, imploring the Maritime Commission to compel the Dollar Line to improve crew quarters. But because there were all those unoccupied passenger cabins, the Line was able to deflect late those union threats. It really would not matter for very long. With the Maritime Commission cancellation of their mail contracts, the Dollars really didn't have the money to continue full operations. Almost every Dollar Line was withdrawn. In fact, the PRESIDENT MONROE was not going to sail further than San Francisco anyway, though it is likely that none of her crew yet knew. For its part, no matter what its wishes in this case, replied the Maritime Commission, the ship was not then under subsidy thus the Government's power to compel the Dollar Line to reconstruct anything was limited.[16]

After her Havana call she arrived at Cristobal for a January 12, 1938 transit of the Panama Canal with 3,475 tons of general cargo and a January 22nd arrival at San Pedro. The end of the line was just ahead. Arriving at San Francisco with 12 passengers on January 24, 1938 from Marseilles, Boston, New York, Havana, Panama and Los Angeles, the PRESIDENT MONROE was withdrawn from service and laid up with four other Dollar Liners. Curiously, the ship became eligible for subsidy participation on January 26, 1938.

Money had been pretty scarce for most of the world during that decade. After making sure that their own salaries and bonuses were paid them Dollar executives felt that whatever monies the Dollar companies could spare for the maintenance of their ships should go first to the twin flagships PRESIDENT COOLIDGE and PRESIDENT HOOVER and next to a few of the "535"'s. The unmodified "502"'s PRESIDENT MONROE, PRESIDENT HAYES and PRESIDENT van BUREN were the last of the passenger fleet to feel the effects of a dime of preventive maintenance. Despite emergency advances and promised extension of Maritime Commission aid, nothing improved the position of the Dollar Line. By summer 1938 Stanley Dollar had to trade 90% of his family's stock in the company to the Maritime Commission in exchange for the assistance needed to get the fleet sailing again. Finally arranging a rescue package that included an advance of over $1.5 million to get the ships reconditioned for sea, the subject of crew quarters proved once more to be a sticking point. As in the cases of the nearly identical PRESIDENT HAYES and PRESIDENT van BUREN, crew was moved into unused passenger spaces. Even before Dollar Steamship Lines became American President Lines on November 1, 1938, planned refits of crew quarters remained on the table, but there were more pressing items on the agenda and since plans for the immediate future of the PRESIDENT MONROE called for her to carry freight only, the need to improve crew quarters along the lines of those in the four improved sisters was shelved and crew in this ship were moved into now unoccupied passenger cabins. With resuscitation of the round the world service in the offing, the Maritime Commission had agreed to advance monies to get the idle "Presidents" in running condition. Second Dollar liner drydocked for surveys prior to returning to service, the PRESIDENT MONROE went for inspection at Bethlehem Shipbuilding's Hunter's Point yards at San Francisco. She needed quite a lot of attention and repairs before returning to the sailing schedule. In the wake of the collapse of the Dollars, the PRESIDENT MONROE was the second of the fleet to go for drydocking for survey in anticipation of her overhaul before returning to service. She was still in Dollar livery and still listed under their

---

[16]Several documents in the ship's 901 file at Maritime Administration concern this dispute.

ownership on all her official documents like her registry papers and marine document when bids by interested San Francisco yards were opened on October 13, 1938. Despite coming in at a total $33,447.00 and a 12 working day estimate, a bid higher than three other firms, Bethlehem got the job. On that day she shifted across to Pier 44, Hunters Point plant of the Bethlehem Steel Corporation from Pier 42, San Francisco. As the ship entered the shipyard, she was expected to sail for her round the world ports between November 5th and 11th, an expectation the pace of work at the shipyard allowed her to eventually meet.

It would take a crew of the shipyard's labor force twenty working days to complete exterior work and as many days to complete overhaul of her interior. Hunters Point Drydock crews got down to the business of getting the tired PRESIDENT MONROE ready for sea on October 28th. when they put the ship into drydock. There they worked on her exposed underbody through November 4th. There was much to do, for as the job continued, the ship was definitely scheduled to sail for the Far East on November 5th.

Neglect and disinterest by her owners took a certain toll. Here's an October 24, 1938 description of the situation on board the idled liner:

> All equipment and supplies were more or less in disorder, and it was necessary to use seamen to place storerooms in order, before contents could be counted and examined. . . .
>
> All storerooms were more or less dirty, disarranged and untidy, due to vessel being laid up for considerable time and shore gang getting vessel ready for sea.
>
> . . . there was no fresh water in the ship, and only a small amount of fuel oil—half of it unusable, due to the presence of water and muck."[17]

The Maritime Commission was finally able to begin to dispose of the matter of crew quarters. In an October 25, 1938 telegram to all concerned parties they said: "Plan SF 324 changes to crew quarters MONROE HAYES van BUREN not approved. We propose arrangement which will be forwarded as soon as possible." On the next morning came the logical conclusion of this tempest in a teapot when the Commission authorized the berthing of crew in unutilized passenger cabins in the three unimproved "502" sisters. Here's what the next telegram to San Francisco said: "Conference Frick today crew quarters PRESIDENT MONROE class agreed permit crew utilize existing passenger space this voyage making extensive changes to existing crew spaces due to lack of time and expense. Corrected plan referred to in our telegram will be forwarded for future replacement at owners convenience. Advise Dollar Line this also applicable van BUREN and HAYES"[18] Before redelivery by Bethlehem, her funnel was painted in the colors of the new American President Lines. Now a blue band circled her red funnel di-

---

[17] from inventory reports, November 1938. 901 file/RG 178 Maritime Administration.
[18] Copy in the ship's 901 file. In custody of Maritime Administration.

viding it into two red stripes of unequal height. A white eagle perching on the blue where the dollar sign used to be, she returned to service on the round the world line. Added to the ship were new chilled spaces and new radio equipment. With none of the passenger safety requirements completed the ship's passenger certificate was withdrawn and one for her allowing her to operate as a freighter issued in its place. Plans to rebuild her crew quarters were now held in abeyance and crew members moved into former passenger rooms. She sailed for San Pedro and Hong Kong on November 5, 1938. Left behind on the dock at San Francisco was much of her passenger ship equipment. On November 18, 1938 the ship was officially registered to American President Lines who two days later on November 20, 1938 sent much of the ship's passenger equipment into storage ashore. Sent by the Stewards Department into storage were 10 steerage class benches, 270 berth frames, 140 berth stanchions, 9 steerage tables, 11 electric fans, 2 bassinets, 72 deck chairs (18 of them broken), 61 dining room chairs, 32 stateroom upholstered chairs, 5 small stateroom chairs, 5 Social Hall chairs, 1 desk chair (in poor condition), 3 Queen Anne chairs, 8 leather upholstered Smoking Room chairs, 7 upholstered Chesterfield sofas, 2 child's high chairs, 5 child's beds, 2 stateroom beds, 2 day beds, 2 bolsters, 88 cabin pillows, 99 steerage pillows, 1 piano bench, 36 carpets (6 good, 18 fair, 12 old), 1 vacuum cleaner, 3 dressers, 14 mattresses of 4 different sizes, 42 framed pictures, 9 settees, 2 barber chairs, 5 Smoking Room tables, 4 writing desks, 14 Dining Room tables and 5 serving tables, 5 tray stands, 3 broken and condemned plant stands, 3 lamp stands, 25 framed mirrors, 1 GE refrigerator, 2 DeVry 35 mm projectors, 1 amplifier, 1 power supply, 1 change over device, 1 screen while the Deck Department sent ashore for storage on Pier 44 six lifeboats, 5 life rafts, 299 adult and 39 child sized life preservers. Everyone knew that should the ship ever be upgraded again to passenger ship status, everything removed would have to be returned.

Her first American President Lines voyage from San Francisco was recorded as Voyage 46 and it began with her Saturday, November 5, 1938 departure at noon for Los Angeles where she arrived on schedule at 9:00AM. After working cargo at San Pedro the PRESIDENT MONROE sailed from Los Angeles at 3:00PM on Monday, November 7th. First port of call was of course Honolulu. Dropping Shanghai from the route, American President Lines was adding Yokohama to the round the world itinerary but on the ship's first trip for APL, there would be no call there so the ship made her usual course for Kobe where she arrived at 7:00AM on November 25th for a nineteen hour call. From Kobe the ship took her first APL sailing at 2:00AM on Saturday, November 26th. Since there was no longer a Shanghai call on the schedule the ship made her way straight to Hong Kong to work cargo during a two day call before sailing at noon on December 2nd for Manila. She sailed from there on December 5th and from Singapore at noon on Tuesday, December 13th. From Penang this time on December 15th and Colombo on December 19th, the PRESIDENT MONROE made her Bombay call, arriving there as scheduled at noon on Thursday, December 22nd. She sailed from India at 10:00AM on Saturday, December 24th for Suez and her passage into the Mediterranean. In the New Year the ship called at Suez on January 2, 1939 and Port Said on January 3rd. Alexandria was next on the 4th and then the liner crossed the Mediterranean to Naples for a one day call on Saturday, January 7th. She spent Monday night at Genoa before heading on January 10th to Marseilles and a January 11th sailing for New York. Not quite two weeks later at 10:00AM on Tuesday, January 24, 1939, the PRESIDENT MONROE entered New York harbor, there to complete her voyage. On that first APL trip she made no sidetrip up to Boston and worked all cargo for the outbound trip at New York.

On the conclusion of that first APL voyage, she sailed from New York on Voyage 47 at 6:00PM on Friday, February 10, 1939. San Francisco saw her again on March 1st and she sailed from there again on her second voyage for them at noon on Saturday, March 4th. There was a typical Honolulu call on March 11th and then the PRESIDENT MONROE detoured from her scheduled itinerary. She omitted her Kobe call and steamed directly to Manila where she arrived on March 26th. Hong Kong was next and then Singapore. With permission from the Maritime Commission to call at Rangoon, the PRESIDENT MONROE called there on her way to Colombo and Bombay. While between Penang and Colombo on that trip American President Lines on April 13, 1939 telegraphed the Maritime Commission about the ship's next outbound voyage: "PRESIDENT MONROE V-48 sailing Boston May 30th, freighter basis, New York June 2nd, San Francisco June 24th, account favorable cargo offerings, desire route Honolulu, direct Manila, omitting Japan ports thence Hong Kong, Singapore, will remain Singapore 3 extra days, sailing on schedule and will proceed regular ports of call to New York. Extra time Singapore should substantially increase our revenue from that port. Would appreciate prompt approval by wire."[19]

Because very little cargo for Japan was then being offered to American ships (Japanese ships long since having won the lion's share) and other APL ships including the PRESIDENT ADAMS from New York on June 16th and the PRESIDENT COOLIDGE from San Francisco were due there in mid July, the Maritime Commission saw no reason to oppose the Lines' request. In fact, except low paying freight like pig lead and cotton from the West Coast, so little freight to or from Japan was available to the round the world ships that the Maritime Commission seriously considered rerouting the three unimproved "Presidents" MONROE, van BUREN and HAYES from Honolulu directly to Manila. On April 21, 1939 the Maritime Commission approved the Lines' request for the ship's next outbound sailing, Voyage 48, from New York be taken on Line A, the transPacific service. American President asked for permission to omit calls at Japanese ports, sail directly from Honolulu to

---

[19] April 15, 1939 telegram quoted in entirety in Maritime Commission Examining Division paper on the request. Copy in ship's 901 file in RG 178 at Maritime Administration.

Manila and thence to Hong Kong and Singapore where after her 3 extra days' stay, would resume her usual place on Line B, the round the world line. Five days passed before the Commission notified the Line in an official recommendation authorizing the PRESIDENT MONROE to sail on that amended itinerary from New York on June 2nd.

Here is her actual schedule for the outbound trip—From Boston at noon on Tuesday, May 30, she arrived New York at 5:00PM on May 31st. After loading her last outward cargo she sailed on Voyage 48 at 6:00PM on June 2nd for Cristobal for a June 9th Canal transit. After overnighting at Los Angeles on June 19th, she steamed into San Francisco on June 21 for a three day call before sailing on June 24th on the transPacific portion of the voyage. July 1, 1939 saw her at Honolulu. Then it was 17 days steaming to Singapore for a two day call. The PRESIDENT MONROE was at Hong Kong on July 21st and back at Singapore again on the 26th. She sailed from there for India on August 1st. Far less cargo than usual was booked from Bombay for her August 12th sailing and American President Lines wanted a full ship so they asked the Maritime Commission for permission to allow the ship to deviate from her schedule for a few hours and make an unscheduled stop to load more freight at Aden. July 26th brought a Maritime Commission Examining Division recommendation that not only should the PRESIDENT MONROE be permitted to make such an Aden call, but that American President Lines lose none of its scheduled subsidy payment any deviation could otherwise entail. Since no ship of either the American Pioneer Line or the Isthmian Line, the American lines usually serving that port, was scheduled for Aden for the period the PRESIDENT MONROE could be there, the Commission deemed American President's request reasonable. The nineteen year old PRESIDENT MONROE made her maiden call at Aden with her August 18th

In American President Lines' colors the PRESIDENT MONROE steamed out from Boston on May 30, 1939. Richard Hildebrand photo. Eric Johnson collection.

arrival. She spent but one day there before steaming up through the Red Sea for an August 22nd arrival at Suez and an August 23th arrival at Port Said. After a stop the following day at Alexandria the PRESIDENT MONROE continued on to Italy. She sailed from Genoa on August 31st for Marseilles. Few in the shipping business doubted that the Europeans were going back to war. Decades after the end of World War II it's easy to forget how little surprise its outbreak occasioned. Knowing the value of merchant ships of this size and capabilities, the Maritime Commission was ready for any exigency. Aware that the PRESIDENT MONROE would be the first APL ship in what would be considered a "danger zone" the Maritime Commission was ready. Witness this August 31, 1939 telegram from the Maritime Commission to American President Lines' President Joseph Sheehan, Jr.:

> RE PRESIDENT MONROE sailing through existing danger zones, and which American President Lines, Ltd. (herein called operator) proposes to return direct to United States unless adequate protection is assured. In view of vital necessity of vessels calling at Genoa and other Mediterranean ports before returning in order that American citizens at said ports may be evacuated Commission has determined that its interest in said vessel equals $1,240,000, which includes mortgage lien of the Government on said vessel and value of interest of Government in performance of obligation of the vessel to complete such voyage and to call at said ports, and has insured in its insurance fund against war risks, under policy dated August 30, 1939, and in effect 3:00 PM, E.S.T. August 30, 1939, its interest in the vessel in such amount, under section 10 of Merchant Marine Act, 1920. In order to induce operator to complete said voyage and to call at said ports as here before set forth, Maritime Commission consents to deviation of said vessel from Route (Line B—Round the World) specified in Subsidy Agreement dated October 6, 1938.[20]

Minutes later, it seemed, the Maritime Commission's General Counsel weighed in with his own telegram to Sheehan saying:

> Extent Necessary and will agree that in case of damage or loss to vessel by reason of any risks against which Commission has insured its interest in vessel, as aforesaid, Commission will (A) in case of actual or constructive total loss, either replace said vessel with another vessel determined by the Commission to be of similar type, size, capacity, age and condition and of equal value (as near as may be) (author's note—I can't imagine what ship might fit this bill), but with said vessel, but not in any event of a value greater than the value of the interest of the United States in said vessel, as here before specified, said vessel to be subject to the same liens and other obligations in favor of the United States as the vessel so replaced would have been if not lost, or at the Commission's option, pay to operator an amount equal to amount of the Government's interest in the vessel, less the amount of any lien which the Commission may hold against such vessel, such

---

[20] August 31, 1939 telegram from Maritime Commission to APL president J. Sheehan. Copy in ship's 901 file in RG 178 at Maritime Administration.

amount to be used for replacement of said vessel, and (B) in case of partial loss, pay to operator an amount sufficient to indemnify it against the loss or damage resulting from such risks. Foregoing us subject to proviso that if operator can obtain insurance at reasonable rate covering all or any of the aforesaid risks, obligation of Commission will be reduced so that in case of loss due to risk so covered Commission will bear only a proportionate share in case of partial loss, and, in case of actual or constructive total loss, will not be obligated to pay any amount in excess of the difference between amount of such insurance and actual value of the vessel (without added increment by reason of existing emergency) as determined by Commission. It is intended that the agreement herein expressed is immediately binding upon the Commission. A final agreement which will embody the exact terms of the Commission's commitment will be executed, however, which may include such changes and further conditions as Commission shall deem desirable to effectuate the intent hereof. In any event, subsidy payments shall be subject to adjustment in such amount as Commission may determine to be reasonable in view of added benefits to operator as result of this commitment.[21]

War risk insurance for virtually all American merchant ships was not long in coming. Coverage for the PRESIDENT MONROE on her one way trip from the Mediterranean to New York would cost an extra $3,100.

News of shooting between Germans and Poles reached San Francisco very quickly and American President Lines swung into immediate action, instructed their Genoa agent that morning to prepare the ship to carry 250 passengers should Americans want a ride home. Cabling Washington a bit later they informed the Maritime Commission that with Consular permission and his certificate authorizing passengers, they stood ready to help bring Americans home and that arrangements were underway to provide the ship with requisite life saving gear and other equipment for such a number of travelers[22]. People did want westbound space—in fact there was a veritable horde of Americans travelers anxious for immediate passage home—so in this emergency she began carrying passengers again, eventually bringing hundreds of them to safety in neutral America. At Marseilles on September 1st when the Germans went into Poland, the sailing of the PRESIDENT MONROE was delayed to allow a decision regarding the emergency carriage of Americans fleeing Europe. Back in the states, people who could make the decision did so quickly, transmitting their orders to the proper offices in Europe. With the biggest load of passengers she ever carried, all aboard the American freighter felt great relief when the ship cast off for home. At that moment deemed critical, her extemporaneous re-entry into passenger service was neither publicized nor did American President Lines have to invest time

---

[21] August 31, 1939 telegram from Maritime Commission General Counsel Carl F. Farbach to Joseph Sheehan, Jr. President, American President Lines. Copy in ship's 901 file in RG 178 at Maritime Administration.

[22] Copies of September 3, 1939 cables in this regard are in then ship's 901 file in RG 178 in the custody of the Maritime Administration.

or money normal circumstances would have demanded for restoration of her passenger certificate. Nor was it permanent, for immediately upon completion of her voyage, the PRESIDENT MONROE resumed the role of freighter with consideration of the war emergency, temporary passenger certificates could be had at any American consulate abroad. Predicated on the number of spaces in her lifeboats and liferafts, the PRESIDENT MONROE was allowed to carry 113 passengers in "permanent" beds but additional berths were allowed in those special circumstances. For the record, the PRESIDENT MONROE dropped off her emergency guests at New York towards the tail end of Voyage 48 on September 14, 1939.

Just how American President Lines was able to carry dozens of passengers in a statutory freighter and not face stiff fines and penalties was simple and refers back to the laws that had led to the loss of the ship's passenger ticket in the first place. Among its provisions, the Merchant Marine Law of 1936 provided American consular officials with the power to grant American vessels temporary passenger certificates in times of emergency and the outbreak of the European war certainly qualified as such a time. With Maritime Commission approval, the business of taking Americans home from Europe in a statutory freighter was left in the hands of the Department of State. Maritime Commission Chairman Land wrote to Secretary of State Cordell Hull and suggested he instruct the American Consular in Genoa to use his discretion should American citizens need a ride home. Under such authority could the unimproved "502" be provided with a temporary passenger certificate every time she needed one. And it surprised no one that a crew returned to original spaces would gripe, prompting further talk of effecting the changes to crew spaces postponed just over a year earlier. Alterations would be made to crew spaces, but just when those were effected remains unclear.

Talk of the young war was everywhere when the PRESIDENT MONROE sailed on Voyage 49 from New York on September 22, 1939. With 5,398 tons of cargo she made her Canal transit on September 29th. Unfortunate as the war in Europe was, for American President Lines it was actually very good for business. Business boomed all along the round the world route and there was little empty cargo space from then on. During that first season of Europe's war the American liner made a winter North Atlantic crossing, sailing from Marseilles on December 20th for New York.

Still in command of the ship when she sailed from New York on Voyage 50 on January 15, 1940 was Captain Kenneth Graham. This time his ship had an even heavier cargo than last time. With 6,135 tons of machinery and general cargo stowed in her many holds the vessel transited the Panama Canal during the night of January 21–22, 1940. The voyage continued from San Francisco on February 7th. Now omitting calls at ports in both Japan and China, the PRESIDENT MONROE arrived at Singapore on March 10, 1940. Next was Penang on the 13th followed by a Bombay call on March 21st. From there she did not follow her old course through the Indian Ocean to make a turn to starboard off Aden and steam into the Red Sea. Instead she was routed south to South Africa. Now she would need no special permission to carry more than 12 passengers from consular officers in the Mediterranean, for Egypt and Italy were no longer on the itinerary by the time the ship reached Bombay and with the enactment of the Pittman (Neutrality) Act of November 1939, all three "502"'s working as freighters began working the new itinerary westbound from Bombay to New York via Cape Town and Trinidad. About five days longer overall than the original route, the trip between Bombay and Cape Town was scheduled for fifteen days with twenty-two days allowed between Cape Town and New York. Other events came to influence normal operations of American President Lines' now vital services. From India the PRESIDENT MONROE made her way to Cape Town, where she arrived on April 7th.

There was still time for the PRESIDENT MONROE to make a few more commercial round the world voyages before the increasing demands of the European war would call her away from her regular work. Neutrality markings still bright on her sides, she left New York on May 7, 1940 on Voyage 51 with 6,428 tons of general cargo. Captain Graham was still in command of the ship and her crew. Under him were his 4 Deck and 8 Engine officers, 3 Pursers, 1 Radio Operator, 2 Deck Cadets, 3 Engine Cadets, a deck crew of 18, an engine room crew of 28, and 20 in the Steward's Department. The ship made her way through the Canal on the night of May 13–14 and made her way north. Omitting a Los Angeles call, she arrived at San Francisco on May 25. She sailed four days later on her way to the Far East, the Straits, Bombay, South Africa, Trinidad and New York. Of all the cargo carried home to the United States in her since the outbreak of the war in Europe, perhaps nothing was more vital than rubber. Synthetic rubber had yet to be developed so every pound that could be brought home was a prize. Modern warfare proved just how important it was, for without it, airplanes could have no tires. Most of the world's rubber came from the Dutch East Indies and Malaya and American President Liners loaded hefty rubber cargoes at both Singapore and Penang. Sale during the summer 1940 to the Navy of the six Baltimore Mail Line combiships that had been lately serving on a New York/ Penang line in a joint service with American President Lines left APL short of tonnage to handle the vital shipments of rubber as well as sisal being shipped from the area. Everything loaded at Manila during her June 21st call and her calls at both Singapore and Penang days later was of vital interest to America's defense industry. All were anxious for the ship's safe return and relieved once she steamed up the Hudson in late August.

At this time of war in Europe and emergency at home, steamship sailings were subject to immediate revocation. Ships were liable to be requisitioned at any time by the military and special voyages seemed to be the norm rather than the exception. From New York the ship sailed again on September 3rd and it would be the last time she would begin a voyage from there as the PRESIDENT MONROE for the ship would be renamed before she could make any special voyage. But a new name was some months in the future and there were more important exigencies for Maritime Commission and American President Lines to consider now. To help cover a temporary shortage of ships, while the PRESIDENT MONROE was underway on Voyage 52 on her way from Balboa to California, APL applied to the Maritime Commission on September 13, 1940 for permission to send the PRESIDENT MONROE out to Singapore and Penang on one round trip voyage on that unsubsidized line. The Commission took its time before acted on the line's request.

In addition to her usual ports of call was a November 4—5th stop at Rangoon, made with appropriate Maritime Commission consent. From Bombay on November 16th the ship made for Cape Town where she made a call on November 28th. Sailing from Cape Town on December 1st for Trinidad and New York the PRESIDENT MONROE would be at New York in time for Christmas.

The time for a new name was at hand. Changing the name of an American ship was still not a matter of simply painting out the old and affixing the new. It required paperwork, extensive paperwork and several agencies. By late October 1940 the paper chase pursuant to the name changes were well in the works. The Loan agency of the Reconstruction Finance Corporation, with the United States Maritime Commission one of the holders of October 24, 1938 Blanket Preferred mortgages on the "502"s gave its consent on October 29, 1940. From Washington the Maritime Commission approved the name change in a Resolution dated November 5, 1940, and Order C -767 issued that same day approved surrender of her marine documents. The PRESIDENT MONROE was scheduled to arrive at New York again on December 22nd, after which date her marine documents in that name could be surrendered and papers issued in her new name. Providing them with the certificates of ownership for the six ships to be renamed on November 7th, American President Lines' attorneys informed the Line that should proceedings required to effect the name changes not be completed before the scheduled November 22nd sailing from New York of the PRESIDENT HAYES, marine documents could be surrendered at San Francisco and new ones issued there.

Inbound from Trinidad and Cape Town, the PRESIDENT MONROE arrived Boston on December 21st. Sailing on the following day, December 22, 1940 for New York, she was technically renamed PRESIDENT BUCHANAN, but the change was not official until new marine documents were issued for her, and those were not completed until 2:12 PM on December 27th. Expected to arrive at New York on December 23rd, rough weather delayed her a few hours and she came in on the 24th.

The Maritime Commission had finally acted on American President Lines' request to send the PRESIDENT MONROE to Singapore and Penang, giving its authorization for the trip on December 20, 1940. Permitting withdrawal of the ship from the Operating Subsidy Differential Agreement with

American President Lines, the liner could legally make one unsubsidized voyage in the New York/Penang service.

Still under the command of Captain K.M. Graham the ship began Voyage 53, sailing from New York for Penang on January 7, 1941. Adding to the confusion for record keepers, for subsidy purposes, it was Voyage 8. Her first sailing as PRESIDENT BUCHANAN, she was unsubsidized on departure, but demand for rubber in the United States was such that she was still expected to earn a profit for her that single voyage on the New York/Penang route. First port of call was Boston, and from there she returned once again to New York and sailed for the Panama Canal from there at 7:00 PM on Friday, January 17th. Omitting her usual Havana call, she made her Canal transit on January 24th with 5,408 tons of general cargo and arrived Los Angeles at 8:00 AM on a foggy February 2nd. After her call there she made her way up the coast and made her first arrival at San Francisco as PRESIDENT BUCHANAN on Wednesday, February 5, 1941. After tying his ship up once more at Pier 46, Captain Graham signed off to be relieved by Captain F.W. Dutton. At 6:14 PM on Saturday, February 8th the ship departed for Manila. There was no Honolulu call westbound on that trip, but there was some heavy weather. Seas ran high enough to toss the ship around severely enough during the night of February 14th that several drums of her deck cargo of airplane fuel and gasoline were washed overboard. More fierce weather impeded her passage on February 20th, when more drums of fuel went over the side while the ship reported herself rolling heavily in a whole gale. Once she reached Manila on March 4, 1941, investigation of the extent of heavy weather damage was made and added more pages to both voyage reports and the ship's files both at APL's San Francisco headquarters and the Maritime Commission's Washington, DC bailiwick. Through calmer weather she worked her way to Hong Kong and Singapore, where she arrived on March 15th. Now calling in quick succession at Penang between March 17th and 19th and once again at Singapore on the 21st and Manila again, the PRESIDENT BUCHANAN returned to Hong Kong on March 30th. She departed on April 1st for San Francisco. After a three week passage the ship steamed under the Golden Gate on April 21, 1941. She remained in port for less than twenty four hours before heading out again. A one day, 22 hour and 8 minute trip brought her to Los Angeles and then Balboa was next. On May 5th the ship made one of her rare Atlantic bound transits and six days later was off New York. There, at 7:16 PM the first line was ashore. An hour later she was all fast but the long unsubsidized voyage was not yet over. The PRESIDENT BUCHANAN sailed from New York at 6:52 PM on May 17, 1941 for Boston, where she once more worked cargo, and then returned to New York on the 18th.

Then the needs of an old friend in trouble took precedence over usual American Maritime policy and the PRESIDENT BUCHANAN was taken for service under Lend-Lease and assigned to the Red Sea berth. Her schedule brought her to the Suez Canal just in time for a 21 day German aerial bombardment of the region. In harm's way for the first time, the ship was damaged while in the Canal area.

Well known is Lend-Lend and the transfer of fifty old "four-pipe" destroyers to them, but little known are charters of American ships to the British in the spring of 1941 when America's old ally Britain was very hard pressed in her fight against the Nazis. Official American neutrality notwithstanding, there were things American steamship men could do to help. One area where American help could make a difference but still manage not to openly contravene neutrality laws was the Middle East and American steamships made the difference. April 1941 brought talk of a diversion to the Red sea service on the next outbound sailing of the PRESIDENT BUCHANAN. Allocated for service to the Red Sea for the month of May 1941 were 17 American vessels, nine under the agency if not ownership of Isthmian Lines, the remainder to be handled by American Export. But more ships and more British control was needed and Section 9 of the Shipping Act of 1916 provided for just such an exigency The British Ministry of War Transport asked to charter the PRESIDENT BUCHANAN for one voyage from New York to Suez. Finding no legal objection, and in conjunction with the Division of Emergency Shipping, the Operations and Traffic Department of the Maritime Commission approved the charter of the "502" as well as the American steamers ANTINOUS and VERMONT to the British for one voyage each from a United States North Atlantic port or ports to Suez or to ports in the Cape Town/Karachi range.

Legal technicalities and requisite paperwork almost delayed these vital charter sailings. The PRESIDENT BUCHANAN was still on Voyage 53, outbound from New York for Boston on May 17th when Maritime Commission Director of Operations and Traffic G.H. Helmbold addressed American President Lines' Washington, D.C. General Agent D.F. Brennan on the subject of the ship's upcoming sailing to the Red Sea.

> Confirming our conversation of today, I regret that I cannot give you definite information as to the arrangements to be made for the voyage of the PRESIDENT BUCHANAN in the Red Sea service. I can only suggest, therefore, that the vessel be placed on berth, loaded and be permitted to proceed on her voyage and leave the details to be worked out later.[23]

After Voyage 53 ended at New York on May 20, 1941, inward freight was quickly discharged and the ship shifted to Staten Island where loading for the Red Sea trip began under the aegis of Isthmian Lines as agents for the charterer. With a heavy cargo of 520,870 cubic feet of invaluable material, she sailed from New York on May 25, 1941 for Cape Town and Mombasa. At prevailing freight rates, American President Lines billed $449,721.30. Order CH-564 covered this hire, and authorized the ship to sail on the trip on

---

[23] May 17th letter from Helbold to Brennan. Copy in the ship's 901 file in RG 178 at Maritime Administration.

or about May 24th. Charter to aliens was officially authorized per Certificate C-3 of May 29th and Certificate No. 80, also issued on May 29, 1941, officially allowed a second charter and alien involvement. It was not until June 2nd that the Maritime Commission sent letters with copies of the charter agreements the Commission wanted signed to the ten American steamship companies which had just chartered ships to the British. American President Lines signed the charter agreement on June 10th. Technical Maritime Commission approval was only granted on June 19th, weeks after the ship was chosen to run in this service.

Under this charter the ship's officers had no control of how cargo was stowed. All Chief Officer Frank Wood was permitted to do by the British was to tell them where, based on weight, it might go. Sacked flour was stowed between boxed automobiles, machinery went in with cased goods, cartons and rolls of barbed wire was stored on top. It would be a real mess to unload once the ship got to Egypt, where she would discharge cargo for the Royal Air Force, Tank Corp, and Army in addition to general commercial cargo. The PRESIDENT BUCHANAN reached her final destination, Suez, at 12:53 PM on July 8, 1941.

On June 29th American President Lines asked the Maritime Commission to permit them to schedule the ship's return via Panama, proposing that from Suez the PRESIDENT BUCHANAN go to Colombo, Penang, Singapore, Manila, Hong Kong, San Francisco and Los Angeles before going through the Canal on her way to New York. On July 8th, the day the ship arrived at Suez, A.E. King, then Assitant Director of the Emergency Shipping Section of the Maritime Commission cabled further instructions to American President Lines regarding the PRESIDENT BUCHANAN. Once she completed discharge of cargo at Suez she was to proceed to Colombo, Ceylon, there to load a full cargo of 1,000—1,500 tons of graphite, 500 tons of rubber and fill the rest of her cargo holds with tea for U.S. North Atlantic ports.

It didn't take the ship's Master, Captain Elijah A. Cooper, much time to figure out that this would not be a run of the mill call. Almost three hours passed before any official came aboard. Only at 4:00 PM did a British Boarding Officer representing Port Control get there. With him were two others, one of them was Captain Woodward, a representative of the U.S. Maritime Commission. Minutes later a Mr. Woodhead of the British Coaling Company, the local Isthmian Line agency, and a representative of Worms & Company come aboard. Nearly surprised to see the ship, these gents clamored for any information Captain Cooper could provide, as other than a copy of the charter and written orders given to Captain Cooper, they knew nothing. To Mr. Woodhead Captain Cooper gave a letter to the English Coaling Company advising them that the ship was ready to begin discharging immediately. Because the Port Control people had decided that the PRESIDENT BUCHANAN would be shifted the following day and discharge into lighters, their man vetoed that idea.

English Coaling wanted a favor from the Captain. In a local mental ward was an American seaman Eugene Donovan, late of the Matson steamer

EWA. English Coaling wanted the PRESIDENT BUCHANAN to take him home to the United States. Here, Captain Cooper smelled a rat and further remarks seemed to bear him out!

Around noon on the 9th the ship was shifted to an anchorage at Attica, Suez Bay. Because neither Worms & Co. or English Coaling had orders of any kind to handle either the PRESIDENT BUCHANAN or her freight, nor to give any crew advances, everyone was relieved when English Coaling volunteered to take over such matters until discharge were completed. But nobody ever did get any further written notices besides the charter party and the Captain's written orders, and nature abhors a vacuum, so the British Port Control Office seemed to take over. That led to some indecision regarding priority of cargo to be discharged and resulted in continued shifting of freight from hold to hold during which, Captain Cooper reported, commercial cargo took quite a beating.

Some days later Benjamin Riggs, the American Consul at Port Said (there was no such official at Suez), came to visit. Over beverages he raised the subject of seaman Donovan, still retained in a mental ward, and, considered violent and troublesome, under constant guard. Captain Cooper was hesitant to ship the disturbed man home in the PRESIDENT BUCHANAN, firmly telling the Consul that his crew would have nothing to do with the man but if the Consul could get the man and his guards to the ship, he'd get them all home. Now Riggs was ready with another offer of unneeded manpower, and suggested that since ships' papers allowed additional crew to be signed on, Captain Cooper might sign on three destitute Americans, one of them a physician who had lately been practicing in Syria and let them serve as the patient's guards. Captain Cooper consented to this and with the three destitute men signed on as guards at a rate of $0.25 per month, and with their signatures before the Consul on a document absolving the ship of any responsibility for their safety in war zones, they were that much closer to home.

With sixty some-odd "camel driving farmers" working aboard as stevedores as Captain Cooper told it, on the night of July 14th, the ship was blacked out when a German air raid on Suez Bay began. Reporting to the Steamboat Inspection Service on the same day, Captain Cooper informed American authorities:

> At about 0300 hours in the morning of July 14 this vessel was subjected to an hour's bombing by German planes. Three bombs were dropped in at different intervals during this time, jarring the vessel considerably each time.
>
> The first bomb dropped very close up under the starboard quarter and the others dropped on each side of the ship, close to. Bilge soundings were taken but the vessel did not make any water. Although lights were extinguished at the first "alert" signal from shore, we could see very easily around the docks because of the bright moonlight. Men were at their fire stations, laying down, waiting. Pressure was kept on the fire lines at all times.
>
> We had no trouble with the crew at any time during the raid. In fact,

after it was all over, I believe some of them enjoyed having had the experience.

Survey of the vessel revealed considerable minor damage; Leaky water tanks, broken lamps, windows and pipes; bulkheads sprung and paint cracked. Number One Lifeboat had been used the day before for drilling the crew in sail and rowing and had been left secured under the stern. It was badly shook up; thwarts adrift, etc.[24]

Frightened out of their wits by the German air raid, the Egyptians scattered and found hiding places all over the ship. They would be of no further use for quite some time. It took forty eight hours to round up another gang to do the required work. This time the Port Control office sent some soldiers with some experience in steamship offices or around docks to act as hatch bosses. Now "guests" of the PRESIDENT BUCHANAN, the ship had to feed and house them. And though they tried hard enough, none knew anything about the ship's cargo nor it's gear so it was slow going from then on. Worse yet in Captain Cooper's eyes was the new crop of local stevedores, "camel driving farmers" rounded up from all over the country, being paid much more than they had ever received before, who could not be disciplined, were naturally lazy and dirty, afraid of being bombed and afraid of being marooned on a ship a mile from shore, in fact, men who did not want to work."[25] This inefficient crew seemed to delight in yelling, handling cargo badly and damaging the ship herself. There were not even enough barges to handle the ship's valuable cargo.

On July 22nd the ship was permitted to dock. Ordered to a come alongside at Port Tewfik at the mouth of the Canal, the ship moored and then began discharging whatever general cargo and army cargo onto an open dirt quay. Need it be said that rough handling and poor piling damaged quite a lot of that freight, too. One particularly appealing commercial consignment that spewed forth from the vessel's hold was a shipment of 5,000 cases of American beer in cans. Ripe for pilferage, it was a powerful magnet for sheisters. English coaling finally hired Army trucks at $50.00 per day and carted the beer to an uptown warehouse.

Captain Cooper had a few important things to say about the port of Suez:

> This port is badly handicapped for handling any amount of cargo, especially heavy lifts that ship's gear doesn't handle—anything over five or six tons. If a vessel laying outside and discharging into lighters, it is almost impossible to get ashore or get in touch with the office. It would actually pay a ship to have her own motorboat to speed up the paperwork and allow better contact with the office.
>
> Water and supplies is another thing. Although the water is good and

---

[24] Captain Cooper's report to Steamboat Inspection Service. Copy in 901 file in RG 178 at Maritime Administration.

[25] From Captain Elijah A. Cooper's September 26, 1941 report to APL Vice President and Operating Manager H.E. Frick. Copy in the ship's 901 file in RG 178 at Maritime Administration.

plentiful, it sometimes takes four days to get a water barge alongside when big transports are in port. They keep barges overly busy. Prices for food-stuffs are exorbitant as well as for laundry work. It is practically impossible to get bacon or ham or eggs in the open market. Green stuff is not so hard to get but it is of inferior quality.[26]

At the Port Tewfik dock, unloading continued for another week. At 8:00 AM on July 29th the PRESIDENT BUCHANAN returned to the open road-stead to wait for the water barge, ordered four days prior. By 1700 hours, 250 tons of water had been pumped aboard. The ship required more water, but Naval Control told Captain Cooper that the moon was brightening again and the Germans would probably be back again. It seemed safer to make for Aden and pick up more water there. A notation in the ship's log reports: "departed Suez—1748 hours June 29, 1941. Lay time at Suez 21 days 3 hours, 55 minutes." Captain Cooper noted in his report to the home office that New York had loaded his ship in about a third as much time. Closing his com-mentary about his three weeks at Suez: "All during this time we had fine, dry weather with light winds. It had been disagreeably hot and the ship infested with flies. Some of the men were down with dysentery and the entire crew was about ready to blow up. If it hadn't been for the Chief Steward watching the food carefully and keeping the crew satisfied, we might have had more discontent. As it was, we had very little actual trouble with the crew outside of the usual run of complaining from certain members. Very little drinking went on aboard the ship. It was too hot to do much of it ashore.[27]

Even after the ship's August 4th arrival at Aden there was a delay, and it took three days for her to top off her fresh water tanks. A plan to send the ship to Colombo was realized and the ship reached Ceylon on August 17th. From there she made her way to South Africa, arriving Cape Town on Sep-tember 3rd, she was again delayed trying to replenish fuel and water sup-plies, and didn't get away until September 5th. With permission of the Mar-itime Commission and with no objection from either American South African Line or the Seas Shipping Company (operating the Robin Line), the PRESI-DENT BUCHANAN and the new C3 P ships PRESIDENT van BUREN and PRESIDENT GARFIELD were permitted to carry American citizens as pas-sengers from Cape Town and were further authorized to make a Port Eliz-abeth call, if desired. There was no need for the additional port and with relieved Americans in both her passenger and crew berths, the PRESIDENT BUCHANAN sailed back into New York to dock at Castle Pt. Pier, Hoboken on September 29th.

Just over a week earlier, on September 21, 1941, word was passed down that the ship's next outbound voyage would be operating under a space charter to the Ministry of War Transport and once again return to the Red

---

[26] From Captain Cooper's report to Frick. *op.cit.*
[27] Closing paragraph of Captain Cooper's report to Frick. *op. cit.*

Sea. Assuming arrangements and certificates issued in May covered this trip and thus absolved of the need to submit requisite paperwork in conjunction with this unsubsidized voyage, American President Lines made no application for permission to operate this voyage. They would hear about this later—in October 1945, for the Maritime Commission had a long memory where open files were concerned. Only then, years after the fact was the October 1941 voyage approved.

Begun in peace, the next voyage was completed during war and the July 1941 charter agreement between American President Lines and the War Shipping Administration had come into force. All of that generated scads of paperwork relating to the machinations of the ship's war service. She sailed under charter from New York as expected on October 11th and reached Cape Town on November 6th. Overnighting at Aden on November 21st, the ship was blacked out, lest she make her presence widely known. She left Port Sudan on November 28 for Suez, where she arrived with some 6,600 tons of cargo on December 1st. No one was sure when she would sail again, for on her last call there it took local workers 21 days to discharge 4,288 tons. This time it took two weeks to offload a rather bigger cargo. Halfway through the job, America was attacked and entered the war. Because American President Lines had been able to garner commitments for her to lift 6,000 tons of rubber at Singapore, they attempted to persuade the Maritime Commission to order the ship to head for that port once she had finished discharging at Suez. Because of the defence nature of that freight, the authorities had agreed and ordered the ship to steam out to Malaya to pick up that rubber. Homewards to New York the ship was expected to head home via India and the Far East. Taking a moment to look at the movements of American merchant vessels at this stage of the new war the Navy took an immediate dim view of permitting the PRESIDENT BUCHANAN to sail to the Malayan peninsula, Dutch East Indies and the Philippines. On December 12, 1941 the U.S. Navy ordered the ship to keep to safer waters. Other ships already in the danger zone of the Malaya—Philippines area might try to pick up the rubber intended for the PRESIDENT BUCHANAN. American President Lines's Washington, D.C. office informed the ship on December 20th: "Penang is dangerous therefore present Colombo and Bombay for loading. Take all fuel necessary Colombo. Proceed from Bombay via Durban to New York."[28] There was rubber to be loaded at Colombo and the ship would load that cargo there. From Suez on December 14th, the PRESIDENT BUCHANAN made for Colombo and Bombay where she would turn around for New York via Mombasa, Durban, Cape Town and Trinidad. Now painted grey all over she made her way to Bombay where she was reported on January 6, 1942. There she worked cargo for the next five days, and departed from there at 4:42 PM on January 11th for Mombasa. Since omission of the Durban call could help speed the ship on her way home, messages were sent to both the

---

[28] Copy in the ship's 901 file at Maritime Administration.

British Ministry of War Transport and to the ship's agents in southern Africa asking that her available spaces be topped off at Cape Town with sisal and wool. That was done and the ship skipped Durban. After her Cape Town call, the ship steamed north to Trinidad for fuel and water. As on her first Red Sea voyage, there was no subsidy for the ship this time either. By late January of 1942 American President Lines was able to report to the Maritime Commission that after her late February return to New York they could deliver the ship to them on a charter basis as per their long-standing agreement, WSA-224. There was technically a separate agreement for every liner in the American President Line's fleet, and for this ship that was WSA-105. With her holds filled with strategic materials the grey liner steamed into New York on Wednesday, February 25, 1942. At 1:25 PM the PRESIDENT BUCHANAN passed Ambrose Light ship at the entrance to New York harbor. At 3:02 PM she anchored off quarantine to complete formalities of entry and a few hours later was tied up at Pier 9, her usual Jersey City pier where a few days later her commercial career ended forever. A nation at war needed her now and once that conflict ended the first of the "502"'s was too worn out to appeal to any further to any private operator.

Covering all bases, the Maritime Commission sent this superfluous standard form telegram to American President Lines 29 Broadway, New York, NY office on February 28th:

> The War Shipping Administration requires use of your vessel ss *PRESIDENT BUCHANAN* and offers to charter same for about one year with the option in either party to cancel at termination of any voyage on fifteen days prior written notice. Charter hire to be determined in accordance with Maritime Commission General Order Number 49 and in reliance on vessel data information supplied by you. Trading limits to be worldwide but marine insurance within institute warranties limits. However have your marine policies provide automatically held covered for worldwide trading. Premiums for trading beyond institute warranties limits for account administrator. Insurance values to be in accordance with Maritime Commission General Order Number 53 plus actual value consumable stores and supplies. Delivery *As early as possible where free of cargo* and redelivery at *U.S. north of Hatteras port*. Charter terms to be in accordance with standard form published in Administrators General Order Number One. Formal Charter agreement covering foregoing will be made shortly. Advise Approximate date delivery. Acknowledge.[29]

After one night at her pier during that first wartime visit to New York, the PRESIDENT BUCHANAN was shifted on February 26th into Bethlehem Steel's Hoboken yard where defense features were installed. The starboard side of the Smoke Room was converted into a dormitory and fitted with 20 standee bunks for gunners. Other spaces were also utilized for multiple

---

[29] Feb. 28, 1942 telegram from Ralph Keating, Director of Allocations, WSA to American President Lines. Copy in ship's 901 file in RG 178 at Maritime Administration.

berths, all to enable the ship to carry 133 passengers without going to the extent of joining the two houses of the superstructure. Over the course of the next three weeks workers prepared the ship for wartime, but for some reason no degaussing equipment was provided. Meanwhile the Charter Hire Committee of the United States Maritime Commission prepared the paperwork under which the Government had already taken over the PRESIDENT BUCHANAN and her sisters PRESIDENT FILLMORE and PRESIDENT TYLER. Originally time charters, those were changed to bareboat charters and each ship was hired at a daily rate of $1,011.91. That allowed a depreciation value of $108.00, an overhead allowance of $403.91 and a profit to the owner of $500.00. That arrangement soon gave way to an amended fee schedule, and for use of the PRESIDENT BUCHANAN, American President Lines was paid a daily rate of $608.00 and a daily overhead allowance of $403.91. It was actually a lot less than the ship's $689.09 daily rate of earnings in 1940 which were reckoned at $1,093 before overhead.

Once again the ship was assigned to the Red Sea berth under the agency of American Export Lines and scheduled to be ready to begin loading towards the middle of the month.

Most of the initial conversion for war complete, the PRESIDENT BUCH-ANAN was officially delivered to the War Shipping Administration at New York at Noon on March 12, 1942. Aboard were 13,770 barrels of oil and 105 tons of fresh water. A great deal of paperwork followed this transfer. First were papers referring to the official time charter of that date of the ship by the WSA. Next came a convolution of receipts and standard forms, all of them dated March 12, 1942. There was a receipt of delivery from American President Lines by the War Shipping Administration and a nearly identical one back to American President Lines from the WSA. Under backdated WSA Agreement #244, a General Agency Agreement immediately took force. Under its terms, the PRESIDENT BUCHANAN was to be allocated by the WSA for operation by American President Lines on a voluntary bareboat charter basis. A maddening paper chase, it had no noticeable impact on the daily operation of the ship, which continued handling Lend-Lease cargo, operating pretty much as she had been while on charter to the British.

With all that paper flying around, few noticed that the voyage number clicked up a notch. The many paper transfers done owner's Voyage 56, which also became WSA Voyage 1 began at New York on March 12, 1942. There was still plenty to do to get the ship really ready for war. The shipyard sent a workforce to Pier 9, Jersey City to continue work on the ship on Saturday, March 14th. Because delivering vital war cargoes to Suez for the Allied defense efforts in the Middle East was as urgent at that moment than the immediate need for this ship to carry soldiers, no further passenger accommodations were fitted at that time and the early March allocation of the ship for the Red Sea berth under the agency of American Export Lines remained in force for that voyage, the first of four voyages she would make for the WSA under the arrangements signed that day. Now there was a whole new set of standard forms to complete. Let's look at the ship's first "Loading Report—Vessels Handling Lease-Lend Cargoes".

Just a standard form, it gave no clue to the real treasure trove of cargo aboard but the cargo manifest did. In the ship's copious holds were cases of auto parts, 450 trucks, 4 boxed airplanes, 3 boxed bombers, cases of ammunition, 63,000 .30 caliber cartridges, 3,000,736 .303 caliber cartridges, 22 .303 caliber machine guns, 20 .50 caliber machine guns, 66,000 cartridge links, assorted quantities of tires and tubes, gas pipe, steel bars and sheets, steel beams, steel bars (this was among her commercial cargo as was some of the lubricating oil she had onboard), tinplate, ferro-silica, copper wire, wirebound boxes and crushers. There was also other commercial cargo—6.8 tons of electrical equipment, 36.5 tons of miscellaneous cargo for Pan American World Airways and 4.1 tons of general cargo. There was more—food. Bound for the Persian Gulf and Red Sea were 640.8 tons of canned potatoes, 71.6 tons of canned fish, 356.6 tons of evaporated milk and 1,638.4 tons of wheat plus 52.4 tons of provisions for Massaua, a port in the former Italian colony of Eritrea, recently wrested by the British.

The ship's Log for Saturday 21 March, 1942 recorded the following:

13:30—engines turned over.
14:15—Pilot A.C. Howell aboard.
14:28—Standby—DALZELLEA and DALZELLMORE alongside
15:20—Cast off.
15:21—Slow astern, let go forward and aft.
15:28—All clear of dock.
15:36—Ship swung.
15:58—Ship off Battery.

In grey war paint she was now but the excitement of the moment of sailing was no less. Indeed the potential for danger could well enhance the feeling of those first few minutes as the liner began her was to the Delaware Bay, Trinidad, Cape Town, Port Sudan, Suez, Bombay and Colombo. In her split superstructure, her passenger cabins were full. Taking advantage of those rooms, the Traffic Department of the War Shipping Administration had made arrangements with the Army Transport Service for the PRESIDENT BUCHANAN to carry civilian passengers on her outbound sailing. Bound for a project in Aden were over 100 of them, employees of the engineering firm of Johnson, Drake & Piper, while 27 passengers originally scheduled to travel in the freighter ALCOA POLARIS were transferred to the "502"s. And those were not the only outbound passengers. On the Red Sea route, Egypt for the *umpteenth* time was on the itinerary again, and so was the Persian Gulf once more but now the PRESIDENT BUCHANAN was going to make her first call in the East African port of Massaua, Eritrea. Beside some 2,500 cubic feet of perishable cargo for that port were 62 passengers, contractors's employees destined to the North African Mission Base. It was a call that had quite an effect on officials in both the United States

Loading Report—Vessels Handling Lease-Lend Cargoes

Name of
Vessel __PRESIDENT BUCHANAN__   Port of Loading __NEW YORK__

Deadweight tons __13050__   Owners __AMERICAN PRESIDENT LINES__

Bale Cubic __473670__   Chartered Owners __U.S.M.C.__

Aver. Speed (loaded) __13__   Agents __AMERICAN EXPORT__

Port Activities

Pier No. __9 Erie, Jersey City__

Reported Ready _____   Date _____   Hour _____

Docked _____   Date __3–12–42__   Hour __12 noon__

Commenced loading _____   Date __3–12–42__   Hour __2 PM__

Completed loading _____   Date __3–20–42__   Hour __12 midn.__

Shifted to Pier No. _____   Shifted to anchorage _____

Docked or anchored _____   Date _____   Hour _____

Resumed Loading _____   Date _____   Hour _____

Finished Lashing Deck Cargo ___3–21–42 8:00AM___

Date sailed __3–21–42 3:16PM__   Date due ____Red Sea____

Summary of Cargo

	Cubic Feet	Weight Tons
Underdeck Cargo	383.131	7532
On Deck Cargo	78.477	430
Total Cargo	481,808	8012
Broken Stowage	90,539	Percent 19
Lend-Lease cargo	146,911	3077
U.S. Govt.	2,984	52
British Military Purchases	263,797	3926
Commercial Cargo	47,916	987
Total	481,608	8012

Commercial Cargo
Revenue ____$33,379.60____   Estimated Stevedoring Expense _____

Comments on Stowage of Cargo, Delays in Loading, Etc.

No operations Sunday Mar. 25 account repairs to be made

and Britain since no provisions were yet in effect for a call there by an American vessel. WSA Traffic Director A.E. King wrote Captain Conway of the WSA New York office on May 12: "Whenever vessels are required to proceed to Massaua to land personnel and/or cargo, please advise earliest possible. This information is essential in order to instruct Aden to call ships forward. Have been advised PRESIDENT BUCHANAN, SANTA RITA and BUCHANAN[30] will proceed Massaua first port."[31] It seems that only the PRESIDENT BUCHANAN made that call, as she alone had both cargo and enough passengers to warrant such a stop. For Massaua, the SANTA RITA only had 2 disembarking passengers so she was instructed not to call there.

During the time the ship was on that voyage the matter of alleged preferential treatment for British ships by the British Purchasing Commission arose. At least one American firm, the Scolan Trading Company of New York was interested enough to demand an explanation, and complained directly to the War Shipping Administration. A.E. King handled the matter and his March 25, 1942 letter to A.A. Alexander of the WSA's New York based Office of Supervision of Cargo Clearance tells some of the story:

> We are quoting below telegram received late today from the Scolan Trading Corporation, 40 Wall Street, New York City.
>
> Reliably informed American steamers such as MORMACSWAN PRESIDENT BUCHANAN and others destined Suez and Alexandria sailing regularly with considerable unutilized cargo space because British Purchasing Commission, refused authorize American Steamship companies accept much needed cargo. Consequently thousands of American shipments are, left stranded on the docks and railroad yards of New York, Philadelphia and Baltimore causing heavy losses to American firms, some of which face actual ruin. We protest energetically such arbitrary and bureaucratic action penalizing American Firm who accepted in good faith orders authorized by the Egyptian Government. We American shippers are patriotic and agree to the principle that war material should have precedence over commercial shipments but protest the absurdity and criminality of permitting American ships to sail partially loaded when the American steamship companies glad and anxious accept additional cargo. We ask your prompt and energetic intervention in this matter as understand several steamers now in port will sail partially loaded.

Suggesting he knew the complaint was not without merit, King told Alexander:

> It is our understanding that you have been watching very closely the situation concerning these vessels proceeding to the Middle East and that you have insisted upon small cargo being provided for each vessel to insure the maximum utilization of all available space. We would like to have your

---

[30] that's right, BUCHANAN, no confusion here, there was the PRESIDENT BUCHANAN and this other one, a ship operated by American Export Lines.

[31] May 12, 1942 letter from King to Conway. Copy in 901 file in RG 178 at Maritime Administration.

advice by return mail as to the exact situation relating to the steamers mentioned in the message quoted above, namely the MORMACSWAN and the PRESIDENT BUCHANAN. Meantime we have telegraphed the Scolan Trading Corporation as per copy attached. It may be desirable that you also talk to these people.[32]

At Bombay in early July passengers paying American President Line's prewar fares from that port to New York were embarked, and the ship sailed from there on July 5, 1942 for East and Southern Africa. An inbound PRESIDENT BUCHANAN was one day from Cape Town on August 6, 1942 when the U.S. Navy commented further on her in a memo to the War Shipping Administration:"Do not use this ship for certain cargo. Her speed is only 13.5 knots."[33] Certainly permitted was anything requiring refrigeration and South Africa is justly famous for her agricultural produce. The ship still retained 30,047 cubic feet of reefer space and that was topped off with South African fruit and sea food. That Cape Town call proved a tad embarrassing to the Americans. Anchoring in Table Bay at 2:27 PM on August 7th, the ship was ordered to a berth at 4:30. The windlass started at 4:46 PM and just as the anchor was seated, it let go, taking quite a bit of chain with it. Without further incident the ship tied up. Making a total of 63 fare paying New York bound passengers, more passengers embarked on August 8th. Leaving an anchor in the waters of Table Bay, the ship sailed out into the South Atlantic on her way to Trinidad and New York.

That first WSA voyage lasted just a week less than seven months. Returning to New York on September 12, 1942, the voyage was completed on September 19th once the last bit of inbound cargo was ashore. On the day before that the War Shipping Administration signed SM-1 Warrant #911 for the PRESIDENT BUCHANAN, a piece of bureaucratic paper that allowed the WSA fuller operational control. Like other such warrants, it was to remain valid through the end of hostilities. Now through October 14th came a period during which the ship was carried on the books as "idle". Before owner's Voyage 57, WSA Voyage 2, began on October 15th workers assigned to her overhauled her machinery, effected voyage repairs and cleaned her up. Now under the subagency of Isthmian Lines, her next outbound cargo was load while the ship was still "idle" in order for the ship to get underway as soon as possible after the beginning of Voyage 57.

Just what cargo would go into her had caused a flurry of activity in many quarters. About a month before that first trip under WSA control ended back at New York on September 19, 1942, War Shipping Administration's Ralph Keating informed Colonel Franklin (he of United States Lines fame) that the U.S. Army intended to use the ship for a single voyage on her next outbound trip to transport cargo for the account of the U.S. Army Iranian Mission. For

---

[32] March 25, 1942 letter from A.E. King to A.A. Alexander. Copy in the ship's 901 file in RG 178 at Maritime Administration.
[33] Copy in the ship's 901 file at Maritime Administration.

With defensive armament fore and aft, liferafts on skids in all her well decks, the PRESIDENT BUCHANAN is pictured at New York in this September 12, 1942 Coast Guard photo. Eric Johnson collection.

that reason no plan had been made to retain the ship on the Red Sea berth. But when another ship assigned that run, the steamer MATTHEW P. DEADY, was assigned elsewhere in, the Division of Traffic decided in mid August to have the PRESIDENT BUCHANAN take that ship's scheduled place on the Red Sea line. Some indecision regarding her next cargo remained while she lay at her Brooklyn, New York pier. Overseas, America's allies needed so much material assistance. This time help was sent to the Soviets and the ship's roomy holds were utilized for Russian Lend-Lease cargo. Supplies could reach the Soviets through the Persian Gulf so the PRESIDENT BUCHANAN was assigned to work to both the Red Sea and to ports on the Gulf. Last to board the ship before her October 15th sailing were 101 civilian passengers. Travelling with the co-operation of the Army Transport Service were 95 Civilian Technicians—77 employees of the firm of Johnson, Drake & Piper bound for Aden, the remainder remaining aboard to Bombay; 5 War Department and 1 Navy Department personnel. Passage fare collected per civilian was $450.00, with a provision that a charge of $7.00 per person per day be collected for every day over 60 days occupied by making the voyage. Ahead lay a voyage of over eight months, a trip that did not go flawlessly. As early as her call at Trinidad the ship encountered delay, and was further detained awaiting orders at Cape Town. It took 69 days to complete the outbound voyage to the Red Sea. That made the ship's schedule something of a joke and by the time she got to India, American President Lines' accounting department officials were just short of apoplexy. The long duration of that outbound sailing cost a lot more money than expected and the owners, unwilling to cover the expense of housing and boarding the ship's passengers for a period so much longer than originally intended protested to the War Shipping Administration. A reluctant WSA authorized American President Lines to accept that $450.00 as the full first class fare from New York to Bombay, and allowed them to drop any idea of pursuing any attempt to collect additional passage monies. After Bombay she called at Basra, Iraq on March 11. For the homeward trip, American South African Line served as ship's agent and it was they who ordered her to make a call at Beira, Mozambique where she docked at 10:05 AM on March 28, 1943. With sabotage watches standing by, loading commenced at 6:30 AM the next morning. Under orders from local Pilots, the PRESIDENT BUCHANAN shifted into the stream on April 3rd and secured with a flying moor but bad weather set in before loading resumed. Twenty hours were lost while waiting for the weather to clear. It took until 6:00 AM on April 6th to finish loading and before the ship got away to sea, she had lost her starboard anchor and 90 fathoms of chain. Captain Elisha Cooper tells what happened next:

In heaving short to sight the chains preparatory to leaving, found one turn in the chains. Tried to take it out at slack water with the engines but found that the tide does not slack much; it just changes directions, swinging clockwise at about two knots speed. Sent signals ashore at 1330 hours for a tug but got no response until about 1750 hours.

The tugs swung us twice during the night on the so-called slack tides getting one full turn out of the chain. We sighted the chains the next morning, 7th April, and found the starboard anchor had lifted the port anchor clear of the ground along with the bight of its chain and some turns. At the rate the tugs were helping us, we could not have made the tide at 1700 hours that day (which was the last available highwater for us for the next ten days.) Called the repair barge (tug) "ALMADA" to lay under our starboard bow to cut the starboard chain and assist in taking out the turns. A strong tide (5 to 6 knots) was running, making it difficult and we had to assist with the engines. When we hove the port anchor home, another full turn was found. The "ALMADA" came in under our port bow and helped to clear that. Then, instead of going back onto the starboard bow to connect the broken starboard chain, allowing me to drop the port anchor to hold the ship, they insisted on staying where they were (trying to save time and make the tide). My log entry reads "1610 port anchor clear and hove home. ALMADA crew proceeding to repair the starboard anchor shackle. 1647 windlass on the ALMADA collapsed allowing her to swing clear of the ship taking the starboard anchor and chain with her. Vessel ordered to proceed to sea by Mr. Raymond Maddock (local agent) to make last available tide; the starboard anchor and chain to be sent on to us. 1700 hours proceeding to sea.

I was holding the ship on position with the engines. When the ALMADA's windlass collapsed, she swung clear of us, held in position by our starboard anchor, about forty feet off our port bow. This left us with only the starboard bow. This left us with only the starboard chain hanging in the water. The ALMADA had refused to go back onto the starboard bow, trying to save time, most of the weight coming on her mooring wire made fast to the windlass. Under the circumstances to go ahead with retrieving the anchor, we would have missed this last tide; so Mr. Maddock ordered me to proceed to sea which was the only thing to do, the anchor and chain had to be sent on to the next port.[34]

Owners of the ALMADA blamed the PRESIDENT BUCHANAN for damage to their vessel, but Captain Cooper "emphatically repudiated any liability" referring all concerned to his report mentioning his suggestion to the AL-MADA that she come around to the other side, and the Portuguese crew refused.[35]

At Beira, the ship loaded as much of 5,000 tons of chrome, 1,500 tons of copper and 2,000 tons of sisal as she could. But with but 265 tons of boiler water aboard (Captain Cooper tried but couldn't get any more), the PRESI-DENT BUCHANAN sailed down the East African coast for Durban. Cape Town was next and while she loaded frozen lobster tails for New York, ten Canadian nurses embarked for the trip north. The ship was steaming north-bound on May 22nd when American President Lines received cancellation of the allocation from the War Shipping Administration to load cargo for the next outbound voyage at New York for the Red Sea. After a call at Trinidad the steamer arrived at New York on June 6, 1943. Once discharge was com-pleted, the voyage ended on June 23rd.

On the 24th of June, at the start if owner's Voyage 58, WSA Voyage 3, the War Shipping Administration requisitioned the ship under a bareboat charter basis pursuant to Section 902 of the Merchant Marine Act of 1936, as amended. That legal technicality had no perceptible effect on the ship's daily operations. Before steaming out of New York harbor, voyage repairs, loading and a thousand and one other details had been effected. On the last day of that month her civilian crew signed articles for the next voyage, a trip ex-pected to last nine months. Lines ashore, she backed out into the Hudson River and pointed her bows towards the Narrows. Passing Ambrose she set a course for Britain. That trip ended on August 26th. Again earning but a single night's rest between sailings, she began owner's Voyage 59 on August 27th and soon again cleared New York on her way back to Britain.

That Britain trip kept her busy through the end of October. The last of her cargo discharged at Pier 9 Jersey City, New Jersey on October 28, 1943, owner's Voyage 59, WSA Voyage #4, ended and Captain E. A. Cooper and his crew of 27 Deck, 43 Engine and 34 Steward's personnel signed off ship's articles. That day Ralph Keating sent G.H. Helmbold a short note: "The subject vessel has been assigned to the Army for conversion to a hospital ship. Vessel is to be requisitioned for title which will be transferred to the Army."[36] Over the next two days inspectors conducted a condition survey

---

[34] April 7, 1943 report from Captain E. Cooper to H.E. Frick. Copy in the ship's 901 file in RG 178 at Maritime Administration.

[35] April 22, 1943 letter from Captain Cooper to Sturrock (Cape) Ltd., the ship's Cape Town agent. Copy in ship's 901 file in RG 178 at Maritime Administration.

[36] Oct. 28, 1943 letter from Keating to Helmbold. Copy in the ship's 901 file in RG 178 at Maritime Administration.

of the ship. Still in a seaworthy condition as a passenger and cargo vessel, the ship had worked very hard in the year since her last survey. Keep in mind that the PRESIDENT MONROE was a ship and ships are by their very nature great metal monsters. The inspection report goes on for pages but here are some things the inspectors marked "Unsatisfactory":

DECK DEPARTMENT

Engine, fire room and shaft alley tank tops showed considerable accumulations, with some sediment, of oil.

No. 6 port and starboard tank tops showed evidence of leaks in seams and rivets.

No. 7 port and starboard tank tops showed evidence of leaks in seams and rivets.

There was evidence of leaks along the bulkhead connecting angle rivets in the forepeak tank top and lower cross drain well in No. 1 cargo hold.

No 1 lower fuel tank top leaked between frames Nos/ 1 to 31.

Evidence of leaks from the open areas of Boat Deck into quarters below.

"B" Deck platings B-C and D, between transverse frames Nos. 109 to 112 port side in way of bake shop and entrance to adjacent athwartship passage aft were heavily buckled and deck tilings in bake shop were humped and heavily cracked.

These damaged deck platings and structural members were all in way of the port fireroom settling tank.

Composition covering of upper promenade deck starboard side was worn, gouged and cracked as was the deck covering in the crew's mess room.

Bulwark rail, portside weather deck aft, set in and chain rails supporting posts were bent, chain buckles frozen over major portion of equipment.

Evidence of oil leaks in way of port and starboard settling tanks on Engine and fireroom bulkhead.

Bilges were almost uniformly fouled and dirty, some clogged.

Sheathing of aft bulkhead in No. 4 hold was splintered and fractured; about 30% of the sheathing was entirely missing.

Watertight doors in fore and aft bulkheads in No. 2 upper tweendeck had been welded shut.

12 bent dogs on the watertight doors to port and starboard of the reefer hatch.

Four bent and defective securing dogs on No. 5 cargo space.

More defects of that sort were noted for the No. 4 upper tween deck watertight door leading to No. 5, two watertight doors at Bulkhead frame No. 136.

Door frames for watertight doors for the poop deck shelter space were rusty, gaskets were hard and unserviceable.

Many cargo holds were rusty as were several hatchways. Bilge ceilings were missing in No. 1 hold. Much of the ceiling planking in No. 2 hold was checked and rotted.

In Nos. 3 and 4, much of the ceiling planking was gouged and rotted. Cargo battens for about four hundred feet in these holds were missing. Pipe casings in No. 3 were broken.

Similar were the ceilings in No. 5, 6, 7 and 8. In contrast Nos. 9 and 10 were in pretty fair shape.

About 25% of hatch boards were broken and missing in way of Nos. 1,2,3,4,5,6,7,8 and 9 upper tween decks and Nos. 1,2,3,4,7,8 and 9 lower tween decks were checked, splintered and gouged. Hatch coamings stiffener channels supporting wedge cleats on Nos. 2, 3 and 7 port and forward end of No. 7 port side reefer hatch were heavily wasted.

Strongback sockets were heavily rusted and bent on both reefer hatches.

In poor condition over all were the steam winches, some of which had broken frames, worn cylinders and valves, while some had broken cranks. Missing in almost their entirety over all units was the insulation over steam cylinders and steam lines to the winches. No. 3 starboard outboard winch had bent crank and guards while the inboard winch was condemned as unfit. Cracked was the steam valve on the No. 4 port inboard winch and its frame cracked.

Over fifty light fixtures on lower promenade and saloon decks were missing or broken, the electric circuit cable box for cargo lights and fixtures on No. 3 port kingpost was wasted and unsound for about 30 feet. Similarly in poor shape were light fixtures and/or cable boxes at Nos. 5 and 6 king posts. Cargo light cables and switches on all kingposts both forward and aft were generally weather worn and in unsound condition.

Two smoking room and three gun crew quarters windows on upper promenade deck aft had broken panels. About 12 weather doors in various sections of the deck housings had worn, defective locks and thus were subject to insecure latching.

Rails on both approach ladders from well deck to forecastle head had bent hand rails as did the starboard ladder from well deck to lower promenade deck. Six feet of railing was missing from the approach ladder from the forward well to the lower promenade deck. The rest of the railing was bent.

Similar distortions were noted in many other cases and ten of the ship's funnel guys were rust bound and wasted, with turn buckles frozen.

Of special interest were boats, equipment and handling gear because war time brought an added chance these would be needed. All six lifeboats were inspected and their capacities noted. Three could seat 37, the remaining three could each take 50 people. Only boat No. 3, a 37 seat "Welin" type showed any sign of indentation, and that was limited to the port sheer strake plating. Mounted on skids on the forward deck were two life rafts as were two on the after deck. All were apparently in sound condition.

Navigating and radio equipment was also checked and found to be well maintained and in good order though evidence of leaks in several areas of the deck head of the radio room and over the power panel was noted as a possible source of danger.

ENGINE DEPARTMENT

Packing of port high pressure valve was scored and worn.

Leaking copper by pass line on starboard main engine to low pressure cylinder.

Renewal of furnaces in all boilers was required by Coast Guard order. Tube sheets on both ends were badly corroded and metal brittle. Old stay tubes were badly corroded. Front and back heads of main boilers grooved and showed evidence of corrosion and cracking.

Shells around feed and water column mountings were corroded and metal was brittle.

All wrapper sheets were badly buckled and where riveted were deeply corroded around rivets. All metal parts were very brittle.

All stay bolts holding stay red yokes were badly corroded.

All furnace sheets at "Horse collar" landings had excessive amounts of fire cracks and showed evidence of brittle metal.

Hammer tests and internal inspection of fire and water side of all six boilers showed evidence that they were all unfit for use at former pressure and allowable steam pressure could then be governed by the thinnest section of the shell of each boiler. Under Coast Guard order, all of these items had to be corrected before the ship could again put to sea. There were more unsatisfactory items noted in the ship's boiler room, things like evidence of salt around boiler mountings, insufficient packing on main stops, water column and blow valves and rust—rust in too many places, even in uptakes. And so the report went on for many more pages with tens of items noted as missing, defective, worn or in need of replacement. Leaks were also noted in several oil tanks and the shaft alleys.

Steward's Department items began on page 37 of the inspection report. Plates of the oil fired galley range were found to be worn and unserviceable. Three sections of the steam pressure cooker were rusted. Packed with standee bunks the former Social Hall on Lower Promenade Deck was dirty and needed paint. Many door handles, locks, little items throughout accommodation spaces needed renewal or replacement. The condition survey report concludes with a reproof for the Steward's Department:

> Department is generally lacking in an ordinarily clean and well maintained condition throughout as sighted at this period with due consideration given to the lack and laxity of department personnel during the port period."[37]

Appended to the survey report was a table of estimated repair and/or replacement costs. To correct all items in the Deck Department, surveyors estimated a cost of $43,320.00; for the Engine Department, $33,325.00 and for the Steward's Department, $3,315.00 for a grand total of $79,960.00.

Under the terms of the existing requisition bareboat charter, the General Agency Agreement with American President Lines terminated at 12:50 PM on November 1st, when the WSA redelivered the ship to the Line. But at the same moment the War Shipping Administration redelivered the ship to her owners, they requisitioned the ship for title and took immediate possession and simultaneously turned her over to the Army.

---

[37] From the Oct. 29, 30 condition survey report, a 42 page document listing hundreds of items and their condition. Copy in the ship's 901 file in RG 178 at Maritime Administration.

As these formalities were transacted, lines were cast off and the PRESI-DENT BUCHANAN began a short passage across the harbor and into the Brooklyn yards of the Atlantic Iron Work where she docked at their Pier 45 at 2:15 PM. With her arrival there the WSA transferred title to the old liner to the War Department.

Here's the text of the War Department's receipt given at New York that afternoon:

> The Secretary of War hereby accepts, as Purchaser, delivery and title of S/S "PRESIDENT BUCHANAN" including all consumable stores, equipment, spare parts and appurtenances, whether on board or ashore, from War Shipping Administration, Owners, at 2:15 P.M., Eastern War Time, on the 1st day of November 1943, at Pier 45, Atlantic Basin Iron Works, Brooklyn, New York, pursuant to and in accordance with the provisions of a form of agreement, to be executed, as arranged in Washington between the War Shipping Administration and the War Department."[38]

A minute later another paper was signed and the PRESIDENT BUCH-ANAN was back in the hands of American President Lines under a new General Agency Allocation agreement.

At Atlantic Iron Works the PRESIDENT BUCHANAN was converted into a hospital ship. This work began immediately on November 1st and lasted just over seven months. This time the two separate houses of super-structure were joined much in the manner of the four "502"s improved in the 1920's. Early during her stay in the yards the ship was renamed IRIS. Addressing the Secretary of State by letter on February 26, 1944 Secretary of War Henry L. Stimson informed his colleague:

> The War Department hereby designates the IRIS (ex PRESIDENT BUCH-ANAN) as a hospital ship be operated in accordance with international prac-tice under the terms of the Hague Convention. The U.S. ARMY HOSPITAL SHIP IRIS has a length of 502.1 ft., has 4 masts, 1 funnel, the length of the foredeck is 44 ft., and the length of the poop deck is 44 ft. The distance from bow to foremast is 135 ft., funnel to mizzenmast is 93 ft., mizzenmast to jiggermast is 74 ft., and jiggermast to stern is 72 ft. The midship structure is 254 ft. long with two deckhouses above, one is 200 ft. long and one is 172 ft. long. Wheelhouse and quarters above are 59.ft long.
>
>   The vessel will be illuminated continuously from sunset to sunrise and will bear the following marks of identification.:
>
> a. Hull and superstructure painted white.
> b. Horizontal green band about a metre and a half in breadth the whole length of the ship, on both sides.
> c. Red Cross painted in the middle of the starboard and port sides, illumi-nated electrically at night.
> d. Red Cross painted on deck and illuminated electrically at night.

---

[38] Copy of this receipt in the ship's 901 file at Maritime Administration.

e. Red Cross painted on each side of funnel and illuminated electrically at night.

f. The name painted on the port and starboard side of the bow and on the center line of the stern as follows:

U.S. ARMY HOSPITAL SHIP
IRIS.

g. The life boats will be distinguished by similar painting.

It is requested that notification of the foregoing designated characteristics and markings be made through the appropriate channels to all the enemy governments and that the War Department be informed of the date of delivery of the notification to each of the governments concerned and the date of their respective acknowledgements thereof.

Since the conversion of this vessel is expected to be completed by the first of April it is requested that this matter be handled as expeditiously as possible.[39]

Getting the ship ready for hospital service took longer than expected. In the interim the name IRIS was discarded and on July 5, 1944, fitted with beds for 743 patients, the ship emerged from the yards as the 11,029 gross ton U.S.A.H.S. EMILY H. WEDER, named for a recently deceased nurse who had served with the American Expeditionary Forces in Vladivostok during World War I and who served three years in the Philippines as well as "stateside" military hospitals. The vessel began her first trip as a hospital ship in the middle of that month. From New York in mid July the ship steamed to Naples, from whence she performed mercy work throughout the central Mediterranean for two months before heading back to the United States. That October she made her first call at Charleston, South Carolina, home port for Army Hospital ships, where it was expected she would remain for some time. But she was needed elsewhere and was quickly dispatched to the Pacific. Before the end of the year the ship had showed her red crosses to Finnschafen, Hollandia and Biak, her last call before steaming to the Philippines in January 1945. Then through June of that year the ship worked in the Southwest Pacific region, revisiting ports she called in late 1944 and adding Leyte, Lingayen Gulf, Subic and Manila to her roster of places visited. The EMILY H. WEDER next returned to an American port on July 31, 1945, when she steamed into Los Angeles harbor. The war in Europe was over and the Pacific war seemed to be winding down, so the Army sent the ship for extensive and much needed repairs. By the time those were completed in late September, World War II was over, a subject for occupation forces and historians and the authorities decided to invest more money in this old ship, converting her now into a dependent and troop transport.

---

[39] February 26, 1944 letter from Secretary of War Stimson to Secretary of State Hull. Copy in the ship's 901 file in RG 178 at Maritime Administration.

Now with a single superstructure, red crosses on her funnel and on her white hull identify the vessel as a hospital ship. She was called EMILY H.M. WEDER when this photo was taken. U.S. Government photo.

In November 1945 she was sent to the yards of the Consolidated Steel Corporation at Los Angeles for general repairs and extensive conversion for postwar service. In early December she was decommissioned as a hospital ship and those hospital markings that once guaranteed her unmolested passage were removed. Now the ship was renamed once more, Taking back her second "President" name, the 25 year old ship was renamed once more. She was again the PRESIDENT BUCHANAN. Consolidated's workforce did their jobs with great dispatch to complete the major overhaul on this ship toward's the beginning of the new year. Some attention towards economies were made, for the ship's cruising radius was extended to 11,850 miles, up almost a thousand miles from previous figures. They redelivered her to the War Shipping Administration in January 1946. Now measuring 11,992 gross tons, the PRESIDENT BUCHANAN could berth 1,241 troops and "civilian" passengers, particularly military dependents like war brides and their children but also any dependent or civilian government employee offered transportation in her. Naturally most of that berthing space came at the expense of cargo capacity. Only 19,660 cubic feet remained. The renewed ship's first assignment was a Pacific crossing after which she was scheduled to participate in repatriation work. Once again the ship was passed over for trooping duty because even refitted, the Army didn't consider her a first rate carrier. Cabling the WSA Shanghai office to inform them on January 22, 1946: "PRESIDENT BUCHANAN leaving San Francisco for Shanghai via Pearl. War Department here advises Army will not need vessel homeward therefore ask C.G. (Commanding General) your theatre to release passengers space to

With liferafts slung against her superstructure, the PRESIDENT BUCHANAN
wears the colors of the Army Transportation Service. U.S. Government photo.

WSA and you can book American Repatriated families to San Francisco as
per Traffic Regulation No. Six, Revised.[40]
    The ship did nothing to prove them wrong. On her first post refit out-
bound trip her boilers were damaged by salt water forcing her to put into
Honolulu for repairs. She sailed no further for quite a while and was lying
at her berth there on April 1st when a "tidal" wave hit Kaena Point. After
being given only enough attention to allow her to get home she sailed for
San Francisco on May 1st, and arrived there on May 7th. There was another
Hawaii sailing, but the date is uncertain. Sailing on that last trip from Hawaii
on August 3, 1946, she carried but 86 Army personnel. She made at least one
further trip before going into "mothballs". Details of her itinerary that time
are sketchy but it is fairly certain that she sailed from Fort Mason, San Francisco at 7:00 PM on August 26th for the Central Pacific with 58 War Department employees and 149 Army dependents. The ship turned around at Sai-
pan in the Central Pacific on September 17th when she picked up the last of
her westbound passengers and headed home. With 725 troops and 205 civilians, the ship sailed under the Golden Gate Bridge on October 26, 1946.
It was her final arrival at that port that for over twenty years had seen her
movements.
    From the Maritime Commission's Washington D.C. Traffic Division of-
fice on November 8, 1946, Mr. Short sent a message to the Commission's San
Francisco office by teletype: "Understand Army returning PRESIDENT

---

[40] Jan. 22, 1946 cable from F.M. Barr, War Shipping Administration to WSA Shanghai office.
Copy in ship's 901 file in RG 178 at Maritime Administration.

BUCHANAN which has been operating in Dependents program. In view of age presume ship not fit for service our program but would like you to develop and confirm."[41] Considered obsolete, and no doubt she truly was, the PRESIDENT BUCHANAN had reached the end of the road. A tug maneuvered the old "502" into Anchorage 26 at the reserve fleet in Suisun Bay at 11:15 AM P.S.T. on the morning of December 3, 1946. At that same time the War Department simultaneously released the PRESIDENT BUCHANAN from service and redelivered her to the U.S. Maritime Commission Reserve Fleet Division. A sum of just over one million dollars was suggested as compensation to American President Lines for the ship, but of course the company got less. Rusting and collecting dust and bird droppings at Suisun Bay, the PRESIDENT BUCHANAN remained idle for about a decade. Offered for sale in early 1957, scrap was her only fate. The Maritime Administration opened all bids received for her on March 21st. The winning tender came from the Learner Company of Oakland which offered $276,480.00 for her. A short while later a tug went to get her and towed the ship around to Oakland where she was scrapped.

---

[41] Nov. 8, 1946 telex. Copy in the ship's 901 file in RG 178 at Maritime Commission.

Old North State/
President Van Buren:
President Fillmore/Marigold

◇

If order of keel laying had anything to do with things, Emergency Fleet Corporation hull number 2585 would have been the first of the "502"s. This pioneering unit of the "502" class of intended Army transports was provisionally named WOODBURY when New York Shipbuilding Corporation set her keel onto the stocks on slipway U on March 20, 1919. The yard knew her as hull number 244. November brought new names for the Shipping Board's passenger steamers and this ship was given the name OLD NORTH STATE in honor of North Carolina. When the Statistical Department took a look at the progress of her construction on December 4, 1919, they estimated she would be 55% complete by January 1, 1920. In fact she was a bit further ahead than that and would be far enough along for the yard to get ready to launch her in late February. Severe winter weather triumphed over the timetables of man and his governments and the yard's plans to launch the first of these "502" class passenger and cargo steamers were scotched on February 28, 1920 when high winds and low tide forced the yard to postpone the ship's launching. But with so many people gathered around to witness the spectacle of putting over this important vessel, the christening ceremony went off as planned. Sponsor of the important new ship was Miss Ruth Neal Magoun, daughter of New York Shipbuilding Corporation's Executive Vice President H.H. Magoun, who named the ship OLD NORTH STATE. When the winds died down on the following day, the ship slid down the ways. Once in the water tugs towed the hull to the fitting out basin, where less than two weeks later she was joined by her recently launched sister PANHANDLE STATE. Over the next few months the OLD NORTH STATE was joined by more sisters. Tied up port side in at the fitting out pier at one point as she approached completion, the OLD NORTH STATE had the company of sister ships in varying stages of construction. Next to her was the CREOLE STATE and then the GRANITE STATE, which sat next to the WOLVERINE STATE, starboard side in to her fitting out pier.

The OLD NORTH STATE lost pride of place to the PANHANDLE STATE when work on her lagged, and rather than lead the pack out of the shipyard, the OLD NORTH STATE followed her sister into service. Identical to the PANHANDLE STATE in all particulars, the OLD NORTH STATE differed from that ship only by nuance and building costs. Second ship of the "502" class to be completed, the OLD NORTH STATE cost $4,078,153.38. Measuring 10,533 gross, 6,195 net and 13,075 displacement tons, the new liner departed for her trials at daybreak on October 19, 1920. With a number of well known shipping men including the president and two vice presidents of the builder's yard as well as Philadelphia and New York financiers among the 40 passengers aboard, the ship steamed down the Delaware River and out to sea. Guests included reporters representing more than ten important newspapers. In charge of the trials was C.B. Edwards, assistant to New York Shipbuilding's vice president H.H. Magoun. Under the command of Captain Marshall was a crew of 118 officers and men, all anxious to outperform the PANHANDLE STATE. Their hopes were dashed when their ship turned in a top speed well below the 16+knots of the PANHANDLE STATE. Commenting on the trials of this second "502", maritime trade papers noted that the OLD NORTH STATE attained a top speed of 14.75 knots but little information about the ship's actual performance ever made it into the general press. Nor were there any words comparing the performance on trials of the twin liners. All that came through from the Shipping Board on the day of the October 19th trials was an authorization of release of the news that the ship had been officially allocated for service. Two days later on October 21st, America's newest liner was delivered to the United States Shipping Board and handed over to the U.S. Mail Line for operation on the London line. Philadelphia saw her on the 22nd and on the 23rd the new ship sailed on her delivery run to New York where she arrived on October 24th. Before sailing on her maiden voyage the OLD NORTH STATE was opened for visitors. Trying to assuage resentment of continuing financial losses and ceaseless criticism from many quarters, the Shipping Board thought it a good idea to introduce the public to "their" ship and made some effort to make the general public both aware of and proud of this new American ship. During that introductory period, an estimated 20,000 visitors trooped aboard for a look around. They were among the lucky strangers who got a good look at the Captain's suite. His bedroom and combined office/sitting room were panelled in birds eye maple with Honduras mahogany trim. Red plush upholstery and a large four poster bed gave the apartment the air of a suite in one of the country's finest hotels. Over the coming years the more social men among her Masters would host occasional gatherings there, but invitations to those prized soirees were rare indeed.

By the time the OLD NORTH STATE embarked her first passengers for London, the PANHANDLE STATE had already completed her first two round trips. Adding another 78 First Class/One Class berths to the U.S. Mail Line's service, the OLD NORTH STATE departed on her maiden sailing from New York for Queenstown, Boulogne and London on November 6, 1920. Aboard were passengers, 2,045 tons of general cargo and mail. A generally uneventful voyage, the new "502" delivered her passengers and cargo to their destinations and arrived at London on November 16th without the glare of publicity the first ship of a new type garners. The OLD NORTH STATE called attention to herself for other reasons. Westbound for New York on the homewards leg of her maiden trip, she had sailed from London on November 23rd and from Boulogne on the 24th. In her roomy holds were a mere 6 tons of freight. Passing Ireland on November 25th the new ship steamed into some of that heavy weather that makes the sailor so respect the winter North Atlantic. A day out of New York on December 3rd, she met a gale so fierce it caused the ship some internal damage. As a result of violent rolling and pitching, the cement ceiling and cork flooring of the refrigerated cargo spaces were broken up and strainers choked with bits of cork, making it impossible to pump the bilges. When an engineer made an inspection, he learned that a few inches above the tank top, a 3/4 inch rivet was missing on the portside bulkhead between the reefer chamber and the engine room. But the ship was neither in danger nor did the storms much slow her passage. Completing her maiden voyage, the OLD NORTH STATE arrived at New York on December 4, 1920 where after the 40 day maiden voyage damage was repaired. Apparently no one thought to test the bulkhead though someone in authority should have known better and ordered it done. That failure soon enough proved an unwise attempt to save money. After sailing the ship ran into further heavy weather and missing rivets again allowed water to get through. Back on land, the Shipping Board's accounting department didn't get much of a smile from the ship's voyage report for her maiden outing. Her financial results were not at all encouraging. Against a voyage income of a total of $65,528.71, including $10,498.05 for passage fares, revenues fell below expenses. Fuel cost $31,218.00; wages amounted to $15,056.80; subsistence for passengers and crew cost $7,810.75; agents' commissions amounted to another $4,042.12 while voyage expenses totalled $40,542.75. The terribly small westbound cargo brought in almost no money at all. On her first trip the ship made a $34,140.09 operating loss.

Like the PANHANDLE STATE, the OLD NORTH STATE was scheduled for a monthly sailing from either end of the Atlantic. Easily settling down into her role as a passenger cargo ship, the OLD NORTH STATE began Voyage 2 and sailed with 2,139 tons of cargo in addition to passengers and mail on December 14, 1920. She arrived in Britain just in time for her crew to spend Christmas in London. Now Colonel Mayer's experience in transporting livestock across the Atlantic paid off for the OLD NORTH STATE. Before departing London for Boulogne and New York on December 30th, the ship loaded a cargo of polo ponies and 18 grooms hired to look after them. Accommodations for them were a bit of a problem. No one would buy them First Class passage tickets, and as the ship then carried no other class of passenger, they were slated to be berthed in steward's accommodations. Because the grooms proved to be poor sailors after the ship's January 1, 1921 sailing from Boulogne, the head groom made an arrangement with the Captain to berth them in minimum cabin accommodation, and that the American Polo Association would pay the extra $1,092.00 in ocean fares. But the head groom hadn't the authority to make such a transaction and though the Shipping Board tried to collect over the next four years, the money was never paid and the matter eventually dropped. Their addition to the passenger list brought the total of First Class passengers to 44 and

The Shipping Board shield on red, white and blue funnel mark the brand new OLD NORTH STATE a unit of the new United States Mail Steamship Company. The builder's official photographer recorded her on film as the ship left the yard on her delivery voyage to New York. New York Shipbuilding Collection. Courtesy of the Independence Seaport Museum Library.

Second "502" on the London line, the OLD NORTH STATE was photographed at New York. Author's collection.

they were to have a rough, slow crossing highlighted, perhaps, by an un-expected chance to tour Halifax in winter. Heavy weather would plague the OLD NORTH STATE and her sisters over the course of their entire lives and the ship's second westbound Atlantic crossing was a further reminder of what nature could do. Ceaseless storms caused the ship trouble with her fuel feed pumps and the new liner broke down and stopped at sea three times. So slow was her passage that the ship was forced to put into Halifax on January 13th for fuel. Once again, missing rivets were blamed when oil and water came in through three holes in the bulkhead between engine room and reefer compartment. Water leaked into a compartment where meat was stored and before anyone could do anything about it some 2,000 pig car-casses were ruined by sea water. The damage occasioned by that water set off a trail of paper work that went on for years. Before sailing from Halifax on January 14th she filled her bunkers with more than enough oil to get her home. She arrived at New York on January 15th. Financial results of the ship's second voyage were even worse than those for her maiden voyage. Over the course of that 41 day trip the ship racked up $42,144.27 in losses.

Dockworkers and crew worked hard to turn the ship around and within four days the ship was ready to sail again. When she pulled away from her Manhattan pier on Voyage 3 on January 19th, she had only 19 hardy souls in her spacious passenger cabins. In her holds were 3,238 tons of freight, almost all of it for discharge at London after her January 29th arrival there. Maybe the reason for her poor outbound passenger bookings was the timing of her eastbound departures but the OLD NORTH STATE seemed to attract greater custom on westbound winter crossings. On schedule the "502" sailed from London on February 2nd for New York where she arrived on February 14th with 36 passengers. Once more she came home with almost NO cargo. All she had were about five tons of inward freight. But for a change, dollar figures were written in black. Results from the 31 day Voyage 3 show a $19,383.66 profit.

After an eight day turnaround the ship sailed from New York on Voyage 4 on February 22th. Passenger figures gave no room for optimism. This time she took out only 12 First Class passengers, all booked to land at London following the ship's March 6th arrival. Sailing westbound on that trip, she departed London on March 10th and landed 36 passengers at New York on March 21. Winter was technically over when she sailed out again on Voyage 5 on March 29th. She had 32 passengers that time. Spring was in the air when sixty-five travellers chose her for her April 14th westbound sailing and an April 24th New York arrival.

The OLD NORTH STATE had been advertised to sail on Voyage 6 on April 28th but she did not get away on schedule. Labor trouble was the reason for the Shipping Board had come into further confrontation with organizing maritime labor. American shipowners stood foursquare behind the Shipping Board, egging them on to diminish crew wages and generally obstructing any path to improved living and working conditions for seafarers. Never mind that 79 passengers were booked to sail, 49 to London and 30 on to Boulogne. Unimportant it was to disgruntled crew that 3,091 tons of cargo and 2,101 sacks of mail were loaded. They did not care a whit about the $75,516.36 in revenue for that trip. What mattered to them (and who can really blame them?) was that their wages had been reduced. With a new wage scale in force as of May 1st, wages were cut by 15 per cent. Many crews of Shipping Board steamers went on strike and this labor unrest nearly interrupted the ship's planned departure. In solidarity with striking crew, engineers seemed likely to refuse to sail. With the support of the Commandant of the Third Naval District, United States Shipping Board Chairman Admiral Benson was able to convince them, Naval Reservists all, to be at their stations for the sailing of a government ship carrying the U.S. Mail. With a capacity passenger list the OLD NORTH STATE sailed on May 4th for London. Addressing the matter of labor grievances with the United States Mail Steamship Company several days after the ship's delayed departure, Admiral Benson informed the Line that the Shipping Board would permit them to pay their men according to the old wage scale, since under no other circumstances would the crew have sailed, but future sailings would be under the new terms.

The ship reached London on May 15th. Homeward on Voyage 6, the OLD NORTH STATE sailed from London on May 21st and the westbound leg of that trip raised eyebrows of some officials within the State Department after Captain Marshall refused to embark six "consular passengers" - destitute

American seamen during the ship's May 22nd call at Le Havre. Boarding instead were revenue passengers and a cargo of horses. Under current rules, Shipping Board masters were obliged to transport such men should space permit. Many ship captains refused as a matter of course, prompting investigations and occasional reprimands. In today's vernacular, Captain Marshall got a bad rap in this case, for he had indeed been willing to take the men and bring them home, but content to stay at the local YMCA and receive a daily stipend of 10 francs, the sailors preferred to remain behind. Further action on the matter revealed that with postwar deflation, thousands of seamen were thrown out of work and Shipping Board cargo steamers were capable of repatriating stranded sailors. The State Department was then instructed not to insist on free transportation on government passenger vessels. The Master of the OLD NORTH STATE was no longer under the threat of prosecution by vindictive bureaucrats.

After her June 2nd arrival at New York with 46 passengers, it seemed that the "handwriting was on the wall" for the United States Mail Steamship Company. For the PANHANDLE STATE and OLD NORTH STATE, anyway, it looked as if their days on the London line were definitely coming to an end. As April came to a close, the Shipping Board had seen fit to demand installation of steerage quarters in the still incomplete CENTENNIAL STATE and BLUE HEN STATE and assign them to U.S. Mail in place of the PANHANDLE STATE and OLD NORTH STATE which could then be assigned, as long planned, to Ward Line. A decision about installation of steerage berths in the older pair was deferred even when months of speculation about eventual Spanish service by the PANHANDLE STATE and OLD NORTH STATE came to a close with the news that the first two sisters would go on the triangular transAtlantic route after all. They never did, for a financially troubled Ward Line dropped a bombshell of their own when they precipitously gave up their Spanish services. They would have no need of these sister ships nor would they require any tonnage like the "502"s. A shocked Shipping Board greeted New York & Cuba Mail Steamship Company's abandonment of the Spanish trade with silence. Making no comment for public consumption, the Board was left with the need to figure out a place to employ so many seemingly redundant "502"s. Now the Division of Operations considered how to employ even more ships on the London line, a route that lost so much money. Meanwhile the OLD NORTH STATE sailed on Voyage 7 on June 8th. Once again she had 79 passengers. Shortly after leaving New York the forward fan engine became totally disabled when the piston rod bent and a connecting rod broke. Suspected work of unhappy crew, for four days the ship had to steam on three boilers under natural draught and once temporary repairs were made, the ship continued her voyage at a speed of about 12 knots. Fully repaired at London, the OLD NORTH STATE sailed for New York on schedule on June 23rd. She came home on July 4th with 50 passengers, a decent number for her.

Meanwhile, the Shipping Board once more addressed the question of steerage accommodations in the "502"s. In a June 28, 1921 memorandum, the Board authorized and directed the installation of such quarters in the PANHANDLE STATE. In an action that confuses today's observer, the Shipping Board then authorized retention of the PANHANDLE STATE on the London line in place of the OLD NORTH STATE. However, and likely pursuant to damage the PANHANDLE STATE had recently suffered at London, that ship was withdrawn after her June 24th return to New York. In her place the OLD NORTH STATE partnered the new CENTENNIAL STATE. That August the Shipping Board accepted bids to fit the PANHANDLE STATE with accommodations for 122 Third Class passengers. The directive authorizing the PANHANDLE STATE to go for repairs and installation of steerage confirmed continued assignment of that ship to the U.S. Mail S.S. Co. for their London/Boulogne service, but left the future of the OLD NORTH STATE up in the air, making her available for other work once withdrawn from US Mail. Paired with the BLUE HEN STATE for uncertainty to come, the Shipping Board entertained requests for their eventual allocation. The OLD NORTH STATE remained on the London service all summer but instead of getting steerage berths like the PANHANDLE STATE did, all the OLD NORTH STATE got now was some quick attention from the W. & A. Fletcher Company which won a $7,320.00 contract to perform voyage repairs on this liner.

With 61 passengers aboard for Britain and France the OLD NORTH STATE sailed out again on the 12th of July on Voyage 8. The usual summer "high" season eastbound was ending and the homewards movement of Americans was about to begin so she was well patronized when she sailed from London on July 28th. The OLD NORTH STATE arrived back at New York on August 8th, landed 75 passengers and sailed out again on Voyage 9 on August 16, 1921 with 45 passengers on what turned out to be the final sailing of the United States Mail Steamship Company. Aboard the ship might well have been Admiral N.C. Twilling of the Office of Intelligence of the United States Navy. If he and his wife were aboard, they would have paid $195.00 each for their passage, for in response to his request for a "free pass", on the advice of Admiral Benson, Judge Mayer responded firmly: "We would like very much to be of assistance to Government officials in a matter of this kind were it possible for us to do so. However the U.S. Shipping Board is charged with the proper handling of Government funds and if it is to carry out this trust, we will be unable to furnish free transportation to you. The steamship passenger business is very good and the various steamship companies operating passenger vessels on the North Atlantic are having all sorts of demands made upon them for passenger space. In view of that fact, U.S. Mail Steamship Company, the operators of the OLD NORTH STATE, could use the cabin which it would be necessary to give you free and obtain the prices referred to in Mr. Roys' letter to you for the Government."[1] Before arriving at London on August 27th, the OLD NORTH STATE made a customary stop at Plymouth on August 25th but before her Cherbourg visit called at Southampton as well, the first time she showed her self at that port.

That summer, of course, the United States Mail Steamship Company crashed to a halt but not before the OLD NORTH STATE had completed another Atlantic crossing for them. Over the course of her voyages for the United States Mail Line the OLD NORTH STATE usually operated at a loss but through the conjuring of clever bookkeeping, turned in the occasional profit. As of August 27th, the appointment of Moore & McCormack, Roosevelt Steamship Company and United American Lines to manage United States Lines became official and the OLD NORTH STATE had a new "boss".

After eight and a half voyages under the houseflag of the United States Mail Steamship Company, the OLD NORTH STATE was turned over to the United States Lines. She began her career for them at London, first sailing in their colors with her August 31, 1921 departure with 74 passengers for New York. After the ship's September 9th arrival crew and stevedores worked fast to get her turned around quickly. Voyage 10 began with cargo loading on September 10th and when the ship sailed two days later on September 12th, "high" season over, so although owners and operators had cause for lament, they were not surprised that the ship sailed with only 12 passengers. That was the ship's last departure for Britain and France for 1921. Before beginning her westbound passage at London on October 6th she embarked 36 passengers. Later that day 14 more travelers boarded the ship at Boulogne for the leisurely crossing to New York. While the ship was only one day out of New York on October 15th, the Shipping Board took decisive action regarding the ship's immediate future. She was going to be withdrawn and spend time in lay up. After her October 16th arrival at New York the OLD NORTH STATE was prepared for redelivery to the Shipping Board which authorized her transfer to the Division of Operations as of midnight on the 15th. One reason for the recall: the Shipping Board had ordered and the Courts confirmed redelivery of the ex-German liners PRESIDENT GRANT, MOUNT VERNON, AGAMEMNON and SUSQUEHANNA. The OLD NORTH STATE was included in the package. Now equipped with Third Class accommodations, the PANHANDLE STATE replaced her.

Passengers ashore and cargo discharged, the ship was withdrawn from the London service to spend the next few weeks idle at New York. With Shipping Board clerks tallying her figures for her 1921 operations, passenger carryings were easy to figure out. Under both United States Mail Steamship Company and United States Lines operation, the government-owned OLD NORTH STATE carried a total of 806 passengers, some 328 eastbound, and

---

[1] July 27, 1921 letter from Judge Mayer to Admiral Twining held in 1091 file for the ss OLD NORTH STATE in RG 32 at the National Archives.

478 westbound[2]. Now came preparations for a winter lay up at New York. On November 17th United States Lines redelivered the ship to the Division of Operations of the United States Shipping Board. Until that transaction, United States Lines and its managers remained liable for any and all expenses incurred or charged against the vessel.

So the OLD NORTH STATE joined her youngest sister BLUE HEN STATE in indolence. No one had a clue about the duration of their inactivity but everyone felt that winter was a bad time to put the two idle sisters back to work; there would be little hope of finding many passengers and little chance of booking much cargo for them. As an economy measure the Shipping Board decided to move them out of New York and send them to lay up at New London, Connecticut, where they could moor alongside a pier at a reasonable cost and not remain subject to the vagaries of winter weather as did ships at anchor. Departure from New York for the two idle sisters was November 30, 1921 and the OLD NORTH STATE headed for New London under the command of her usual Master, Captain Marshall. While discussions about their next employment were held in various Shipping Board offices, the OLD NORTH STATE remained idle at New London for about six weeks but the BLUE HEN STATE remained there for several months. On December 20th, Acting Shipping Board Secretary J.P. James informed Emergency Fleet Corporation Vice President Love that the Shipping Board had deferred until the 28th his recommendation that the OLD NORTH STATE and BLUE HEN STATE be immediately assigned to United States Lines for operation on the London line and that permission be granted U.S. Lines to alter Third Class spaces in any or all of the four "502"s then on the Atlantic, the PANHANDLE STATE, OLD NORTH STATE, CENTENNIAL STATE and BLUE HEN STATE.

In a move calculated to make the "502"s more competitive by virtue of charging the lower Cabin Class rates then accepted by the North Atlantic passenger conference, her accommodations were downgraded to Cabin Class after her January 23rd return in tow to New York. As was done aboard her sisters, upper berths were fitted in existing passenger cabins. It was also at about that time that the funnels of the first few "502" ships were raised. A peculiarity of the American shipbuilder to fit a ship with a very short funnel, many instances of vessels whose funnels needed to be raised can be found in American shipbuilding. Not only the "502"s but many of the "535"s as well as the magnificent MANHATTAN of 1932 and AMERICA of 1940 entered service with incongruously short funnels and were later given an extra stage or two. With her refit behind her the OLD NORTH STATE shifted from shipyard to United States Lines' Manhattan piers. Under the command of Captain Ferguson on her first outing as a Cabin liner, the ship sailed from New York for London on March 18, 1922. From London the return trip began

---

[2] According to figures in accepted works like annual "Passenger Arrivals in the Port of New York".

with her March 29th sailing and the OLD NORTH STATE concluded her first round trip of the year after her April 8th arrival at New York.

Because of her late start that year, she would carry only 656 cabin passengers eastbound from New York, and 782 westbound, for a total of 1,438—still, that was 90 more than carried by the PANHANDLE STATE. But by early May 1922, just before she was renamed, this ship proved herself a steady money-loser, turning in an operating deficit of $24,131.46 over the course of her last three round trips. And none of those losses factored in construction and related charges such as voyage repairs. Her next trip would be her last as OLD NORTH STATE and on that one she sailed outbound from New York on April 13th for Queenstown. Via Plymouth and Cherbourg the ship reached London on April 23 for a six day stay. Arriving at New York on May 10, 1922 the ship was involved in a collision off Hoboken with the Shipping Board freighter WEST ELDARA, sustaining the minor damage of an indentation about 1″ to 2″ deep covering an area of about a square foot on the third plate below the sheer on portside.[3] After thirteen round voyages, on May 12, 1922, the OLD NORTH STATE became the PRESIDENT van BUREN and her registry transferred from Philadelphia to New York. She began her first voyage under her new name with a new Master, Captain Schofield, with her sailing from New York on May 17th, arriving at London ten days later on May 27th. The homeward sailing began on June 3rd and on June 13th the ship reached New York.

Another man ascended her bridge before sailing time on June 21st. He was Captain George Miles and his tenure aboard the ship was short and troubled enough for New York newspapers to cover the ship's July 18, 1922 return to New York. Trouble had begun aboard during her eastbound voyage. After all, with the ship's ten day crossings, there was plenty of time for things to go wrong and by the time the ship reached London on July 3rd, crew resentment was smoldering. According to preliminary reports, two days after leaving New York, H.G. Baxter, a pantryman, began running through the ship brandishing a razor. Thus reported deranged, Captain George H. Miles ordered him arrested and placed in irons in one of the holds. About 48 hours later Baxter was considered calm enough to be moved and was brought to the isolation hospital aft where he was detained under guard. On the morning of the 26th he seemed ill but not much was done for him. That evening he died. Once the ship docked at London, several of Baxter's shipmates made their way into town, there to seek out the American Consul, Robert B. Skinner. They wanted him to begin an investigation into the cause of their friend's death. Instructing them to return to the ship, Mr. Skinner promised to forward all pertinent information to the proper authorities in New York. Captain Miles' troubles really began on the homeward voyage.

---

[3] Mariners, naval architects and I might not care for that description but the Shipping Board's Division of Construction and Ship Repair did. That's how they described the location of the damage.

Six days out of New York, on July 12th, fuel in the tank below number 5 hold caught fire. With the fire limited to that area and little chance of spreading, the New York office of United States Lines instructed Captain Miles to steam clean the hold three times before entering New York. Donning a smoke helmet, Captain Miles went into the hold to supervise. According to contemporary reports, he inhaled fumes of burning oil and when the ship docked, was removed in a stretcher and taken to St. Mary's Hospital in Hoboken, New Jersey. Curiously, reports filed after the ship's arrival mentioned that Captain Miles was stricken when he went into the hold to check on men cleaning flues, but made no mention of a fire. August 17th brought further news of the curious case of the van BUREN's June voyage. Captain Miles was arrested on a charge of murder on August 15 by the Deputy U.S. Marshall for the Southern District of New York and was arraigned on the 16th.

Let "The New York Times" tell the story:

> Charged with murder on the high seas, Captain George H. Miles, former commander of the United States Shipping Board steamer PRESIDENT van BUREN, was arraigned yesterday before United States Commissioner Samuel M. Hitchcock and committed to the Tombs. He was arrested on a complaint made "on information and belief" by Assistant United States Attorney G. Tarleton Goldthwaite, who has been examining witnesses for weeks.
>
> On the voyage of the van BUREN to London it is alleged that Captain Miles, making his first voyage as commander of the vessel, so cruelly beat H.G. Baxter, a pantryman, that he died next day, June 5, from his injuries. This is denied by the captain, who said that Baxter died following collapse from taking drugs. He said that he had a record of twenty-eight years following the sea and that for sixteen years he had commanded American vessels. During the war he commanded the United States transport SANTA OLIVIA.
>
> The PRESIDENT van BUREN left New York on June 21. When the vessel reached London a committee of the crew called upon the American Consul and made charges against the skipper. With the return of the PRESIDENT van BUREN an investigation was started by the Shipping Board and the matter was finally turned over to federal authorities here.
>
> In his complaint Mr. Goldthwaite alleged that at the time of the alleged beating Baxter was manacled and chained to a stanchion in the hold of the ship. It is alleged that the Captain kicked and beat the helpless Baxter and left him so badly injured that he died the next day.
>
> It is probable that the case will turn on the testimony of Dr. G. P. Farquhar, the ship's surgeon who attended the injured pantryman. From the testimony of the doctor and other members of the crew it appeared that on the morning of the day he was taken to the hold, the pantryman's pulse was normal. Later in the day it was found that Baxter was in such serious condition that instant medical attention was required. In the meantime, the Captain had visited the hold.
>
> When questioned regarding his visit to the pantryman in the vessel's hold, Captain Miles said that he had been attacked by Baxter, and that he

had defended himself. The Captain is 6 feet tall, about 42 years old and powerful.

From 4 PM Friday, June 23, until 8:30 PM the next day Baxter remained in the hold, according to testimony, and during that time he either refused food or was unable to eat it. The testimony showed that a few hours after death the body was weighted and dropped into the sea.

In a statement made out at sea, while under the direct command of Captain Miles, Dr. Farquhar gave it as his opinion that Baxter's death was the result of acute mania. Mr. Goldthwaite said yesterday that when examined on shore he had modified his statement. He said that Baxter's body showed signs of maltreatment.

When the van BUREN returned to this port in July it was reported that the pantryman had become deranged and had run around the deck with a razor. For this the Captain had him placed in irons.

Captain Miles was removed from the van BUREN on her arrival on a stretcher suffering from gastric poisoning through having inhaled the fumes of fuel oil when the Captain went below shortly after the vessel arrived where the men were cleaning the flues. Captain Miles was in St. Mary's Hospital, Hoboken, a few days, after which he went to his home in Brooklyn. Shortly after he got home, the Captain, in denying that he had beaten Baxter, was quoted as having said: "All I am able to say for publication is that there does not exist the shadow of foundation for these charges. They are due to an attempt to get somebody more important in the service than I am through me. I do not think the plan will succeed."[4]

A passenger on that sailing, a James Smith of Brooklyn, wrote to P.A. Shanor of the Order of the Moose on July 18, 1922:

I was a passenger on ss PRES. van BUREN on last trip, and it is now in port in Hoboken. I want to call your attention to a case of extreme cruelty ending in death, caused by Capt. Miles, to a man named Baxter, a pantry man, who wore a Moose button and ring. This poor fellow at times was demented, but perfectly harmless, and well-liked. One day, while in one of these absent minded spells, the Captain noticed that he was not working as well as was expected, he called this man before him and had him thrown in the hold of the vessel, shackled and without food for 36 hours, and no one was near. After the 36 hours had elapsed, the Capt. had this poor fellow called before him and he fell at the Captain's feet; the Captain called the ship's doctor and asked if the man was able to work and just stalling. This doctor (?) took the man's temperature, which was 105, and said yes, he was able to work. Capt. Miles then kicked this poor fellow, which caused his death, and he was buried at sea. This Capt. Miles was drunk a part of each day on this trip. I understand from the crew there is no use to report anything of this nature to N.Y. (office of the) Shipping Board, as no attention will be given it, as these officers are all placed by politicians and never removed. But I thought as he was a member of the Order of the Moose someone might take this up with the proper authorities and justice would be meted to such an

---

[4] Quoted in *The New York Times*.

officer. You can verify this by interviewing any member of the crew of the ss PRESIDENT van BUREN.[5]

But the Shipping Board had acted, going so far as to place Mr. Smith's letter in evidence against Captain Miles after an indictment was handed down against him on a charge of First Degree Murder on September 5th. He was convicted that year on a lesser charge of mistreating and responsibility for the death of a member of his crew. February 20, 1923 brought him a three year prison sentence. There is no hint that he ever again commanded a Shipping Board vessel.

There was no problem replacing him on the bridge of the PRESIDENT van BUREN. After all, the World War I rush to train officers and men for jobs at sea had produced a pool of 14,000 licensed personnel. Next to command the ship was Captain Moore and he took her out from New York on July 26th. From London on August 12th the ship took her usual leisurely course across the Atlantic to reach New York on August 22nd. He was still in command when the ship sailed from New York again on August 30th. After a September 12th arrival at London the ship worked cargo for the next few days and then sailed for New York on September 16th. She reached New York after another usual ten day crossing on September 25th. With time out for some quick repairs, the PRESIDENT van BUREN got underway on her next voyage from New York on October 4th for London. Across the Atlantic again the ship arrived at Cobh (Queenstown) on October 11th, crossed to Plymouth for a brief stop the following morning and arrived at London via Cherbourg on October 15th. She had six days at London that time and sailed for home on October 21st. She came into New York on Halloween, October 31st. Next outbound sailing was scheduled for November 8th and as usual, she sailed on time and arrived at London ten days later on November 18th. With winter coming the London call was extended and that time the ship remained a full week before sailing for New York on November 25th. The liner steamed up the Hudson on December 5th. A week later on December 12th the PRESIDENT van BUREN sailed from New York on her final round-trip voyage of the year. She arrived at London ten days later for a seven days' stay. Calling at Cherbourg on December 30th on her way home to New York, the ship greeted the new year at sea.

During 1923, the PRESIDENT van BUREN's passenger totals improved. Over the course of the year she carried a total of 1,752—919 passengers westbound and 833 eastbound. The Shipping Board's decision to increase the Cabin Class berths of these ships in the spring of 1922 seemed correct though the actual dollar figures turned in by the "502"s on the North Atlantic continue to appall.

Reporting herself 657 miles east of Ambrose on January 8, 1923 the PRESIDENT van BUREN steamed on towards New York and a January 10th ar-

---

[5] op. cit.

rival. So began her last year as a Shipping Board steamer. Her first outbound that year was another routine winter voyage to London. She sailed from New York on January 24th. That brought her into the Thames to dock at her London pier on February 4th. Six days later on February 10th Captain Moore ordered all lines ashore. Hours later the ship made her customary stop off Cherbourg en route to Plymouth and Queenstown. Due to arrive at New York she reported herself some 677 miles east of Ambrose Light on February 19th. Two days later she docked at her New York pier. On her following trip the ship sailed on February 28th for London where she arrived on March 10th. Her call there lasted a full week and after sailing from London on March 17th the ship once again anchored off Cherbourg in the early hours of the 18th to take on passengers and mail. Via Plymouth and Queenstown the ship made her way to New York and a March 28th arrival. Sailing out again on April 4th, Captain Moore reported the ship in a position 1,623 miles east of Ambrose Light on April 9th. After calling the usual ports the ship reached London on April 15th for a six day call. Departing for New York on April 21st, the ship sailed for a reasonably uneventful voyage and returned to New York on May 1st. May 9th was sailing day on the subsequent voyage. She reached London on that trip on May 19th for a seven day call. Completing another westbound Atlantic crossing the PRESIDENT van BUREN arrived back at New York on June 5th. Quite the fixture on United States Lines' weekly London Cabin service, the ship next sailed for Britain on June 13th. Once more things were pretty routine with the eastbound trip taking ten days to complete. Then the ship spent six days in London before sailing on June 30th for Cherbourg, Plymouth, Queenstown and New York where she arrived on July 10th. There the steamer spent another full week before sailing away again on her outbound voyage to London on July 17th. On the day before the ship reached her first ports of Queenstown and Plymouth, Captain Moore quietly celebrated the first anniversary of his first sailing from New York in his ship. On the 28th the ship reached London for another seven day call before heading out on the homeward journey on August 4th. The westbound crossing once again occupied ten days and on August 14th the second of the "502s" returned to New York harbor. Another call of a week lay ahead of the ship before it was again time to sail again for London on August 22nd. She sailed into the Thames and tied up at London on September 2nd. Six days later on September 8th she cast off for New York, which she reached after ten days' steaming.

While at her New York pier on September 25, 1923 the PRESIDENT van BUREN was sold to the Dollars, a purchase that had no immediate effect on her next outbound sailing, scheduled for the following afternoon. Aboard the PRESIDENT van BUREN were 88 cabin passengers, 3,252 tons of freight and 34 sacks of mail when she sailed for London at 1:00 PM on September 26, 1923. Against an income of $11,362.50 for passenger fares, $20,598.00 for cargo, $170.00 for carrying mail and $204.00 for miscellaneous onboard sales, estimated expenses were expected to amount to $68,000.00, meaning another operating loss to add to the red ink racked up thus far. Losing money or not she had a schedule to keep and on October 4th the ship called both Queenstown and Plymouth before stopping off Cherbourg on the following day on her way into London on October 5th. She sailed for home on the 13th, reaching New York on October 23rd. During her stay there Captain Moore signed off for a much deserved vacation. In his stead came Captain Cummings, who took the PRESIDENT van BUREN out from New York on Voyage 28 on November 7, 1923. That time the ship had 91 cabin passengers and a hefty cargo of 6,247 tons of freight and 269 bags of mail. On November 16th she arrived at Queenstown for a short call to deliver passengers, mail and a bit of freight before moving on to Plymouth where she called on the following day. Next, of course, was the stop off Cherbourg. After that call the ship sailed up the Thames to dock at London on November 19th. On her return voyage she sailed on November 24th for New York and was back there on December 4th.

Next was Voyage 29, her last outbound trip of 1923 and as usual it began at New York. Sailing for London on December 12th her numbers looked pretty good. She had 79 passengers and a lot of freight, nearly filling her many holds with 6,895 tons of general cargo. Maybe it was a question of saving the best for (almost) last, for it was "the best freight list that we have ever had on one of the London steamers".[6] Passenger fares and cargo tariffs brought in $51,300.00. Queenstown was on her itinerary again and after dropping off Christmas mail, some cargo and a few passengers, the ship steamed on to Plymouth to repeat the process. The ship reached London on December 23rd. Her call there lasted the usual six days and on December 29th the PRESIDENT van BUREN sailed for home via ports, arriving at New York on January 9, 1924, four days after her sistership PRESIDENT HARRISON steamed out of San Francisco to inaugurate the round the world passenger service.

Remaining to the PRESIDENT van BUREN before she steamed off to begin her career under Dollar Line ownership in 1924 were two more round trip trans-Atlantic trips and Captain Cummings continued to command the ship during both of them. It was quite cold in New York when she sailed down the Hudson River towards open sea on voyage 30 on January 16, 1924 on her way to London. After a call at Plymouth the ship reached London on January 27th. Returning from the United Kingdom on her first trip that year she sailed from London on February 2nd. On the eighth her radio reported her 1,482 miles east of Ambrose Light and she finally arrived at New York on February 13th. Then came voyage 31, her final sailing for United States Lines and her last as a government steamer and on that trip the PRESIDENT van BUREN sailed from New York on February 20, 1924. Aboard were 67

---

[6] From the December 12, 1923 confidential notification of the ship's departure from US Lines' Managing Director to the Commissioners of the Shipping Board. Copy in the ship's 1091 file in RG 32 at National Archives.

cabin passengers but even better was the heavy cargo of 6,267 tons of general merchandise in her holds. She also took out 2,090 sacks of mail. Figures from her voyage report show outbound revenues on those items of $53,744.37. On those two 1924 trips the ship carried a total of 288 passengers, 135 eastbound, and 153 westbound. For the record, on March 2nd the PRESIDENT van BUREN called at Queenstown and Plymouth inbound to London where she docked on March 3rd. Sailing for New York on March 8th from London were 90 passengers who landed at New York after the ship's March 19th arrival.

The time to deliver the ship to her buyers was at hand and with all the paperwork in hand, the PRESIDENT van BUREN began the three week process that made her into a Dollar liner. After all arriving passengers had landed, inward freight discharged and crew paid off, Captain Cummings relinquished command, disembarked the ship and remained with United States Lines. Dollar Line gave command of the ship to Captain John Lane and with his Dollar crew took over when the PRESIDENT van BUREN was delivered to the Dollar Line at New York on March 20, 1924, the last of the seven ships to hoist the flag of Robert Dollar's clan. The ship lay at her New York pier that same day when the Commissioner of Navigation telegraphed news to the Collector of Customs at San Francisco that the marine document of the ship was on the way there, adding instructions to prepare a new one indicating the name of her new owners. It was a good thing that Dollar Line had allotted three weeks to get the ship ready for the round the world service. There was plenty to do to bring the ship into tip-top condition. In a

On her way out of New York, the Dollar Liner PRESIDENT van BUREN will soon set a course for Havana. Eric Johnson collection.

New York area shipyard workmen corrected numerous items, among them the following, all attributed to collision, none of it covered by entries in any of the ship's log:

> Second strake of shell plating below main sheer, port side, was removed and faired.
> Third shell plate below main sheer, port side, removed and faired.
> Adjacent plate partly removed and faired in place.
> Nine badly indented frames removed, cropped or faired in place as necessary.
> All brackets in connection with buckled plating to be removed and faired.
> Incidental work like replacement of cargo battens, scupper lines was done and then shell plating was tested with hoses.[7]

Because that minor damage antedated the ship's September 1923 sale, the Shipping Board and arbitrators felt that repairs were for the account of Dollar Line and their repair costs were duly charged to the Dollars. It was no major job, costing only about $3,500.00. Divided into three groups, "For Shipping Board Account", "For the Account of Purchaser (Dollar)" and "For Arbitration", the list of items for repair went on for pages. Some bear repeating here: items like fixing a leak over a berth in Cabin 10, which developed after September 25th was eventually charged to the Shipping Board. Four items covering hull repairs were listed in the "debatable" column, meaning that it was not patently clear without close inspection of the ship's log, if heavy weather, whose damages were covered by marine insurance, were the cause of the work. None of the repairs was substantial, and ranged from cleaning of scuppers to repairs to manhole plates above tanks in #8 hold. Work was also carried out in the Engine room where ordinary wear and tear was held responsible for minor problems in the panoply of the ship's machinery equipment. All accommodation spaces for both passengers and crew were cleaned and the PRESIDENT van BUREN sparkled like a newbuild when she made ready to receive cargo and passengers for her first outbound sailing on the round the world line.

With the big white dollar sign on the red band of her black funnel, the PRESIDENT van BUREN sailed from New York on April 17, 1924 to join her San Francisco based sisters. After calling at Havana where her passengers enjoyed a night ashore the van BUREN sailed on April 22nd to Panama. Arriving at Cristobal at 5:30PM on April 25th the ship remained in port overnight before beginning her transit of the Canal at 6:20AM on April 26th. In the Pacific after completing her canal passage at 1:03PM, the ship cleared for sea at 2:46PM. Aboard were 940 tons of general cargo, the smallest amount any of the sisters took through on her first Panama passage and one of the lightest loads ever noted for a member of the "502" class by Canal officials, by whose rules the PRESIDENT van BUREN measured 12,023 gross

---

[7] Evidentiary lists of damage to the "502"ts listed by party responsible to pay for repairs in each ship's 901 file in RG 32 at National Archives.

and 8,495 net tons. Overnighting at San Pedro on May 5, the PRESIDENT van BUREN arrived at San Francisco on May 8th to take her place in the round the world service from there. She left San Francisco on May 10, 1924, this time to ports in 14 countries "around the world", the last of the class to begin sailing on the Dollar Line's Round the World service. Once again her passenger accommodation was graded First Class. After a week at sea the ship reached Honolulu on May 17th. Next was Kobe where she overnighted after her May 30th arrival. From there the latest ship to follow the "route of the Presidents" steamed to Shanghai where she arrived for the first time on June 3rd. Hong Kong and Manila were next and on June 14th she sailed from the Philippine capital for Singapore. She continued her passage westabout on June 21st with her sailing for Penang. On June 27th the seventh sister running on the round the world line called at Colombo, Ceylon and then headed off towards the Red Sea and the Suez canal, a ten day passage. July 9th saw the ship at Alexandria, her crew attending to cargo operations, her sightseeing passengers returning from excursions to Cairo. Further sightseeing beckoned passengers while the ship was at Naples on July 13th and at Genoa on July 14th and 15th. After spending July 16th at Marseilles, the PRESIDENT van BUREN sailed at 7:00PM for Boston. All seven sisters had completed their first visits to the foreign ports on the itinerary. All that was left of the maiden round the world voyage of the PRESIDENT van BUREN was the homeward leg and she came into Boston on time on July 28th. Sailing the following evening at 11:00PM the ship made her leisurely passage to New York to arrive at 6:00AM on Thursday, July 31st. She tied up in Brooklyn, last of the Dollar sisters to go there for some time. Several weeks earlier, Dollar Line had leased Pier 7, North River and were to move in on August 1st. That pier was but one of several they used in New York before finding a more permanent home at Pier 9, Jersey City during 1927.

As scheduled, Voyage 2 began at New York and at 2:00PM on Thursday, August 7th the ship sailed from her Brooklyn pier. After a 16 hour Havana call on August 11th the ship steamed on to Colon, Panama Canal Zone where she arrived at 6:00AM on August 15th. A few hours later the ship made her second transit of the Panama Canal and after her Master completed technicalities, was cleared for sea by 11:00PM. Ten days later the ship reached San Pedro and after an overnight call of 40 hours, the "502" sailed further north to San Francisco where she arrived at 6:00AM on Thursday, August 28th. After a 59 hour call there the voyage continued with her 5:00PM sailing on Saturday, August 30th. The following Saturday saw her at Honolulu. Sailing at 10:00PM that evening the ship headed for Kobe and arrival at 7:00AM on Friday, September 19th. She sailed the following day on the tide. Shanghai, Hong Kong and Manila were next, and after her overnight call at that Philippines port, her voyage continued with her 5:00PM sailing on Friday, October 3rd. Next was a two day call at Singapore and the PRESIDENT van BUREN arrived on time at 6:00AM on Wednesday, October 8th. She sailed on Friday for Penang where she arrived at 11:00AM on Saturday. She sailed that evening at 6:00PM for Colombo where she arrived at 4:00PM on Wednesday, October 15th. Sailing from there at Noon on Thursday, October 16th, the ship steamed ever westwards to arrive at Suez eleven days later on October 27th. After calls at Port Said, Alexandria, Naples and Genoa the ship shifted to Marseilles where she arrived at 8:00AM on Wednesday, November 5th. At 6:00PM that evening the PRESIDENT van BUREN sailed for Boston and New York on her second Dollar Line voyage. After a twelve day passage the ship arrived at Boston at 2:00PM in the afternoon of Monday, November 17th. Boston sailings were then scheduled for 11:00PM on Tuesdays and at that hour on November 18th the ship cast off for New York and a leisurely 32 hour passage to conclude her second round the world voyage at New York after her 7:00AM arrival there on Thursday, November 20th. A week later on November 27th, Captain Lane still in command, the ship headed out again on her third Dollar Line sailing. Steaming out of San Francisco on December 20th, the ship was at sea on Christmas, her first as a privately owned liner. The ship greeted the new year at sea and arrived at Kobe on January 9, 1925. Continuing her way westabout the world she sailed from Manila on January 23rd, Colombo on February 4th. From Marseilles on February 25th the PRESIDENT van BUREN began the Atlantic that would bring her to American waters. Arriving at Boston on March 9th she tied up at Army Base, South Boston to work cargo before sailing on the 10th, for New York where she returned once more on March 12th.

Dollar Line Voyage 4 was the ship's first outbound sailing from a United States port in 1925 and she sailed on that one from New York on March 19th. After Havana, Panama and Los Angeles the ship continued her voyage from San Francisco on April 11th. Across the Pacific she grounded on May 1st off Kobe, Japan. Not badly damaged she refloated at high tide around noon on May 2nd and was soon able to continue on her way. That time the ship sailed from Shanghai on May 8th, from Hong Kong on May 12th, from Penang on May 23rd and arrived at Suez on June 8th. That fourth trip around the world ended at New York on July 2, 1925. By then round the world service was routine for the ship and her crew. It would be a while, though, before she started earning profits. A week later on July 9, 1925, the ship sailed from New York on her next trip, Voyage 5. That kept the ship busy through October 22nd. Voyage 6 was the ship's last round the world trip of 1925 and that time the PRESIDENT van BUREN sailed from New York on October 29th. Transiting the Panama Canal a week later on November 2nd, the ship continued her voyage from San Francisco on November 21st. Via Honolulu a week later the ship reached Kobe on December 12th. Passengers and crew alike enjoyed a Christmas treat at Manila, for the ship arrived there at 8:00AM on Christmas Eve and sailed at 2:00PM on Christmas Day. At the tip of the Malayan peninsula at year's end the PRESIDENT van BUREN called at Penang on January 2, 1926. Through the Suez Canal on January 19th the ship entered the Mediterranean on her way to her last foreign ports of that voyage. Her Atlantic voyage began with her sailing from Marseilles

Whiling away an afternoon at cards in the Veranda Cafe of the PRESIDENT van BUREN. Author's collection.

on Wednesday, January 27, 1926. Twelve days later the ship reached Boston and on February 6th arrived at New York.

Voyage 7 took her out of New York on February 18th. That time she sailed from San Francisco on March 13th, from Kobe on April 6th, from Singapore on April 22nd and from Colombo on April 28th. May 19th was sailing day from Marseilles and on June 3rd the PRESIDENT van BUREN arrived at New York at the end of Voyage 7.

As usual the ship was allowed a week at New York and on June 10th the ship sailed on Voyage 8. From San Francisco the ship continued her voyage on July 10th. She made a September 4th call at Naples that time and began her Atlantic crossing from Marseilles as scheduled with her September 8th

Always popular at sea are deck sports. Author's collection.

sailing. The ship reached Boston on September 21st and New York on September 23, 1926.

On September 30, 1926 the PRESIDENT van BUREN sailed from New York on Voyage 9, another globe-girdling voyages. October 19th saw her pull into San Pedro and on October 23rd she sailed from San Francisco.

Another popular venue for relaxation was the glass enclosed promenade. Author's collection.

Across the Pacific the ship sailed from Kobe on November 13th, from Manila on November 26th and from Singapore on December 2nd on her way westabout the world.

From Boston on January 13, 1927 the PRESIDENT van BUREN sailed south to New York. Twenty-four hours later she tied up at Dollar Line's Brooklyn pier. Less than three weeks earlier Dollar Line had signed a lease with Erie Terminals to use their new piers in Jersey City. But with a few months to go on their lease on their current Brooklyn complex at Pier 22 and Pier 23, the PRESIDENT van BUREN worked cargo for this trip at Brooklyn. Six days later on January 20th the ship took her last departure from a Dollar

Line Brooklyn pier. Through the Panama Canal on January 29th the ship reached San Pedro on February 7th. After her customary three day call, she sailed from San Francisco on February 12th. By March 1927 she was approaching Asian waters, and on March 4th arrived at Kobe for an overnight stay. She sailed from Singapore on March 24th and from Colombo on March 30th. On April 11th the ship sailed through the Suez Canal on her way into the Mediterranean. From Marseilles the PRESIDENT van BUREN sailed for home on April 20th. After April 1, 1927 Dollar ships at New York began using Dollar Line's new facilities at Erie Terminal's Pier 9 at the foot of 12th Street, Jersey City so when the ship arrived at New York on May 3rd, she made her first appearance at the new pier.

Leaving her Boston pier for New York on August 24, 1927, one of her screws was fouled by one of her own hawsers. It took two hours for a diver to clear the line from the propellor and the ship was able to go on her way. From New York on December 22, 1927 the PRESIDENT van BUREN began again another circuit around the world calling at Havana on December 26th and Balboa on the 30th. Spending New Year's Day, January 1, 1928, off the coast of Central America, the liner arrived at San Pedro on January 9th and San Francisco on the 11th. She sailed for Honolulu on January 14th. Next port as usual was Kobe and when she sailed from there on February 4th her Captain set a course for Shanghai. She left there on the 8th for Hong Kong where there was always a lot of cargo for her to work. Departing on February 12th for Manila the liner steamed south into the torrid zone and her crew and passengers prepared for sultry weather. Some, no doubt, took advantage of the swimming pool fitted into a hatchway. From Manila on February 15th the "502" steamed her way on to Singapore, Penang and Colombo. March 13th saw her at Port Said. A day later she was at Alexandria on her way to Italy where she arrived at Naples on March 17th and Genoa on the 17th. She had three days there before moving on to Marseilles to pick up her last European freight before heading back to the United States. There were three more round the world sailings from New York for her that year. Next was her April 12, 1928 sailing. That port next saw her sail out on a hot, steamy August 2nd. Calling at her usual round of world ports she departed Kobe on September 14 and Marseilles on November 1st on her way back to New York and her November 22nd sailing beginning her final trip of the year. Sailing from San Francisco on December 14th the PRESIDENT van BUREN was at sea in mid Pacific between Honolulu and Kobe when 1929 began. After landing passengers and cargo, loading more freight and welcoming a few new faces aboard, the ship steamed forth from Kobe on January 4, 1929. By the end of the month she had serviced all her Asian ports, sailing from Colombo on January 30th for the Suez Canal. From Marseilles on February 20th the ship made her way to New York and a March 5th arrival. Her next round the world trip took her from New York on March 13th.

By December 1929 the PRESIDENT van BUREN was back in Asian waters and she sailed from Kobe on the 6th. More serious an incident than her last mention in casualty lists was a fire that broke out when boiler No. 2 backfired and set fire to the ship's bilges while she lay working cargo at Singapore on Boxing Day, December 26, 1929. Officers had the presence of mind to evacuate the passengers and despite the best efforts of crew fighting the blaze, flames burned through Numbers 4 and 5 holds before spreading to Number 6 hold and some accommodation spaces. Though the fire itself never reached passenger spaces and was soon out, smoke and water damaged them nonetheless. Some parts of the ship fared poorly and suffered extensive damage, as did 150 of the 700 tons of rubber and 100 tons of general cargo stowed in the path of the fire. All three holds were damaged by both fire and water. Temporarily repaired locally, the ship resumed her voyage on December 28th and she called at Penang on December 30th. Her bad luck continued once she reached the Mediterranean. At Alexandria, Egypt on January 15, 1930, her stern hit a mud bank. That cracked her rudder frame and rudder plate. The PRESIDENT van BUREN steamed on to Naples to be drydocked on January 21th. Surveyors insisted the ship drydock at Naples. She did so and before the ship was able to continue her voyage to the United States, some $86,104.61 worth of damage to rudder, steering gear and bottom plating was repaired.

Arriving at Honolulu on October 23, 1930 the PRESIDENT van BUREN was again in the news. Under the headline "Stowaways on Liner Clipped"[8] the subtitle "Pair aboard van BUREN lose hair and are kicked off" pretty well summed up the attempt by two young men to hitch a free ride to Hawaii. Discovered before the ship cleared the Golden Gate, the men were brought before the ship's Master, Capt. H.S. Bauer. Wearing satisfied smiles and giving a "what are you going to do about it" attitude, they were not prepared for what Captain Bauer was about to do. Before sending them off in the pilot boat, he called for the ship's barber who ran his electric shears through their flowing, wavy hair. That treatment instantly wiped smug smiles off their faces.

Onto the casualty lists once more went the name of this ship when a fire that broke out aboard the PRESIDENT van BUREN at Singapore on December 26, 1930. Breaking out in the ship's cargo the fire spread into passenger spaces damaging both ship and cargo.

As 1931 began the ship was on voyage 23 and Captain H.S. Bauer was still in command. On the whole the ship had a quiet year, making her usual three and a half runs around the world without getting her name into the casualty lists. The PRESIDENT van BUREN remained behind the PRESIDENT MONROE and on her final outbound voyage of the year sailed from New York on December 17, 1931, two weeks after her immediately older sister sailed on another round the world trip. On Christmas Day 1931 the PRESIDENT van BUREN made her Panama Canal transit. She continued her voyage from San Francisco sailing on January 5, 1932. On that trip she made

---

[8] "*Honolulu Advertiser*" October 24, 1930.

her first call at Bombay, arriving there at 1:00PM on February 25th for a twenty-four hour call.

The cherry trees had long before bloomed when the PRESIDENT van BUREN departed Kobe on schedule on May 20, 1932. The usual ports remained on her route and she called them in the usual order. In July she was in European waters and from there on July 7th the transAtlantic crossing began with the ship's sailing from Marseilles. Her passage swift for a "502", she made New York on the 11th day after sailing from France and after an uneventful voyage, the ship reached her Jersey City pier on July 18th. Resuming her usual timetable, she remained in port until July 23rd when she departed for Boston. Like clockwork she cast off from her Massachussets pier just after midnight on July 25th and quickly proved that she was no less likely than any other ship to stay completely out of harm's way. Sailing into a foggy night, the PRESIDENT van BUREN was steaming slowly, groping her way through thick fog when the Clyde Mallory Line freighter ONEIDA sideswiped her while both ships were steaming through Pollock Rip Slue at 1:05AM. Both ships were slightly damaged, that on the PRESIDENT van BUREN limited to the liner's port bow, bent stanchions and a few dented bow plates. Well able to continue her voyage despite such minor damage, the "President" liner was soon on her way and back at New York to top off her holds and embark passengers before her next round the world sailing.

That trip saw her sail from Kobe on September 4th for Shanghai. From Bombay on October 2nd the ship reached Suez on October 11th and sailed through the Canal. Departing from Marseilles on October 21st the PRESIDENT van BUREN headed for New York. On her last voyage of that year the ship sailed from New York on November 17th and from San Francisco on December 9, 1932. She pulled into Kobe on schedule on December 29th and while she worked cargo her passengers enjoyed a variety of options for touring Japan. As always, some passengers finally disembarked there. After their stay in that country, quite a few of those picked up another Dollar Liner to continue their voyage. After a New Year's Eve at sea the PRESIDENT van BUREN arrived at Shanghai on January 2, 1933. Rounding Garden Bend in the Whangpoo River after sailing from that Chinese port on January 3th for Hong Kong, the American liner collided with the Chinese steamer KIANG WAH. Holing the smaller vessel forward, the PRESIDENT van BUREN suffered minor damage and tied up at Buoys 11 and 12 where divers looked for any underwater damage. Temporary repairs to the collision damage were effected on the spot after which a certificate of seaworthiness was granted. At 8:00 PM the ship left the buoys for Woosung to wait for high tide. A while later an additional item of damage was revealed when raising anchor before proceeding to sea. Due to a fracture suffered in the collision, the port anchor shackle parted and the anchor dropped into the water. Leaving her property for later retrieval by others, the PRESIDENT van BUREN proceeded on her way. By late April she was back in Japanese waters, to sail again from Kobe on April 27th. May 9th was sailing day from Singapore and on May 19th the ship sailed from Bombay on her way to the Suez Canal. In the Mediterranean on May 29th the ship worked cargo at Port Said, Alexandria, Naples and Genoa in turn before tying up at Marseilles at 8:00AM on June 7th. Back in American waters this "502" arrived at New York on June 19th. She landed passengers, delivered mail and worked cargo before sailing on the 21st to Boston. Back at her Jersey City pier on June 27th, the ship received additional cargo, supplies, mail and passengers before heading out to sea again.

Taking a summer sailing from New York on June 29th the PRESIDENT van BUREN was on voyage 31. With pleasant weather and a loose schedule she had no trouble making her appointed arrival and departure times and arrived at San Francisco on July 18th for a three day call. Off again towards Asia on July 21st the ship reached Japan on August 10th when she docked at Kobe. From Bombay on September 8th the ship made her transit of the Suez Canal on September 18th. She called at Naples on September 23rd then Genoa on the 24th. Last was Marseilles and she called there between 8:00AM and 5:00PM on September 27th. After her 13 day passage from Marseilles, the ship came into New York on October 10, 1933 towards the end of Voyage 31. Out for Boston two days later, she was back at her Jersey City pier at 8:00AM on Monday morning, October 16th.

Thursday, October 19th was sailing day from New York on Voyage 32. Havana saw the ship on October 20th and on the seventh day since leaving New York the ship made her transit of the Panama Canal. As always the run up the Pacific coast of Central America and Mexico took her nine days and she arrived at Los Angeles on November 5th. The voyage continued with her sailing from San Francisco at 5:00PM on Friday, November 10th. Via Honolulu a week later, once more the liner adhered to her printed schedule and tied up at Kobe on November 30th. From there she sailed on December 1st. Departing from Singapore on December 19th, the PRESIDENT van BUREN spent Christmas day at Colombo, Ceylon. The ship sailed from Bombay on December 29th and after New Year's Eve at sea continued her passage to Suez and a January 8, 1934 transit into the Mediterranean. From Marseilles on January 17th the ship began her passage home. After a winter crossing of the North Atlantic the ship steamed into New York harbor on the morning of January 30th. By February 5th the ship was back at her Jersey City pier to complete loading for her next round the world voyage.

Sailing from New York on Thursday, February 8, 1934 the PRESIDENT van BUREN was on voyage 33. That time she sailed from San Francisco on March 2nd. Across the Pacific she sailed from Kobe on March 23rd. Long a fixture of her itinerary by then, she worked cargo at Bombay during her two day call there on April 19th and 20th. Nine days later the ship reached the Suez Canal and on May 5th called at Naples. Overnighting at Genoa as usual, the PRESIDENT van BUREN crossed over to Marseilles on May 9th. Some 9 hours ahead of Pacific Standard Time, the ship had sailed from France before word of the Big Strike that began at San Francisco quickly stopping almost all of the Pacific Coast maritime industry. Word of the militant action soon enough found its way to the ship's crew but in midocean when they learned of the strike at home, were literally in no position to walk off the job just then. Anyone who did was liable to a charge of mutiny. After the ship's May 22nd arrival at New York crew members voted to stay on the job and on May 31st the ship steamed out of New York on Voyage 34. After her June 8th transit of the Panama Canal Dollar Line officials kept an ever closer watch on labor conditions at San Francisco. By the time the PRESIDENT van BUREN reached San Pedro on June 17th it was clear that there was no point in even trying to bring the ship to San Francisco to meet her scheduled June 19th arrival, so the ship's Los Angeles call was lengthened to allow the ship to work as much San Francisco cargo there as possible. Omitting San Francisco the ship made for Honolulu and a June 29th call. From Kobe the "502" continued her voyage with her July 13, 1934 sailing for Shanghai. Out from Singapore on the 31st the ship worked her way towards Bombay. After her overnight at that most exotic port the ship sailed on August 10th. The next ten days were spent in the exhausting heat of summer in one of the hottest regions of the world. The heat hardly diminished by the time the ship completed her transit of the Suez Canal on August 25th and continued while the ship sailed the Mediterranean. Sailing from Marseilles on August 29th the PRESIDENT van BUREN arrived back at New York on September 11th. The weather cooled down after that but no matter who was aboard, "502" crews always complained about the heat in their quarters. By all indications they had plenty of cause for their gripes, for as built, there were plenty of "hot zones" aboard the ships. In some of those spaces temperatures averaged as much as 100 degrees.

On Voyage 35 the PRESIDENT van BUREN departed from New York on September 20, 1934. After making her Panama Canal passage eight days later on the 28th the ship continued on to California and an October 7th arrival at Los Angeles. Two days later she was back at San Francisco. Fifth "502" class ship to reach San Francisco since the July 31st end of the Big Strike, she sailed from there on October 12th on her way around the world. Call her November 5th Kobe sailing, her November 20th Singapore sailing and her November 30th Bombay sailing as mile markers of her thirty-fifth passage around the world. From the Mediterranean port of Marseilles the ship began her homeward trip with her December 19, 1934 sailing. The North Atlantic lived up to its reputation that time and offered the PRESIDENT van BUREN plenty of heavy weather. Though Christmas came and went on time heavy seas and high winds slowed the ship down and she did not make her scheduled arrival at New York on New Year's Day, January 1, 1935. From Jersey City's Pier 9 at the Erie Terminal the ship began her side trip to Boston on January 7th. Her sortie to work cargo at New England's largest port done, the PRESIDENT van BUREN returned to New York on Thursday, January 10th. Now Dollar Line was able to reduce the ship's delay. Instead of the usual three day stay at Pier 9, the ship remained overnight and sailed out on Voyage 36 on January 11, 1935. A generally quiet year in the steamship business, the PRESIDENT van BUREN made her usual tours of the world, sailing from her ports in turn. Midyear saw her in Japanese waters and her June 11th sailing from Kobe. On that trip the ship called her usual ports again, so call her June 22nd departure from Hong Kong and June 24th sailing from Manila milemarkers for her on that voyage.

January 10, 1936 saw the PRESIDENT van BUREN sailing again for Havana and Cristobal. Concluding the intercoastal portion of the trip with her January 29th arrival at San Francisco, her world voyage continued with her sailing on February 1st. She had enough time that year to complete two full round the world trips before labor woes brought her engines to a stop. Her summer 1936 sailing from New York on July 23rd would be her last outbound sailing for quite a while. The outbound leg from San Francisco began on August 13th. On that trip she departed Kobe on September 4th and sailed

Very well fitted and furnished in the best of taste were passenger cabins aboard the "502"s. Here's one aboard the PRESIDENT van BUREN. Author's collection.

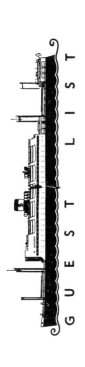

GUEST LIST

S. S. PRESIDENT VAN BUREN

Voyage Twenty-two

Sailing from SAN FRANCISCO, October 17, 1930

H. S. BAUER, COMMANDER

H. J. Ehman	*Chief Officer*
F. C. Simonds	*Chief Engineer*
F. Spengler	*Purser*
V. H. Vogel	*. Surgeon*
T. Williams	*Chief Steward*

HONOLULU

Mrs. Andrew Amacher	Medford, Ore.
Mr. Benjamin F. Baker	Lancaster, Pa.
Mrs. Benjamin F. Baker	Lancaster, Pa.
Miss D. M. Barrett	Bloomfield, N. J.
Mr. J. W. Conklin	Vancouver, B. C.
Mrs. J. W. Conklin	Vancouver, B. C.
Mr. J. B. Corstorphine	Lihue, T. H.
Mrs. J. B. Corstorphine	Lihue, T. H.
Mr. Ran Court	Honolulu, T. H
Mr. A. A. Crofts	San Francisco, Calif.
Mr. R. L. Dancy	Honolulu, T. H
Mr. B. R. Elliott	San Francisco, Calif.
Mr. J. M. Grant	Honolulu, T. H.
Mrs. Innis Kinney	Winchendon, Mass.
Rev. St. John O'Sullivan	San Juan Capistrano Mission, Calif.
Mrs. Kenneth B. White	Winchendon, Mass.

KOBE

Dr. Roger Hannon	Seattle, Wash.

SHANGHAI

Mr. Leon A. Fritchman	Summit, N. J.
Mrs. Leon A. Fritchman	Summit, N. J.
Mr. Herbert Henderson	Shanghai, China
Miss Jennie D. Jones	Futsing, China
Rev. Thomas Murphy	Chicago, Ill.

MANILA

Mrs. Clara H. Palmer	West Chester, Pa.
Rev. Frederick J. Zwierlein	Rochester, N. Y.

SINGAPORE

Miss Rose Bush	San Francisco, Calif.
Mr. Carleton Clough	Pleasantville, N. Y.
Mrs. Carleton Clough	Pleasantville, N. Y.
Mr. Tao Labanukrom	Bangkok, Siam
Miss Pearl Hughes	Antioch, Ill.
Miss M. Little	Rangoon, Burma, India
Mr. William T. McIntyre	Rangoon, Burma, India
Mrs. William T. McIntyre	Rangoon, Burma, India
Miss Mary Ellis McIntyre	Rangoon, Burma, India
Master William T. McIntyre, Jr.	Rangoon, Burma, India
Miss Beulah Swan	Des Moines, Iowa

PENANG

Mr. Harry B. Goldstein	Washington, D. C.
Hon. David E. Kaufman	Washington, D. C.
Mrs. N. McHutchinson	Penang, S. S.

COLOMBO

Miss Jessie Mae Cronk	Salem, Va.
Dr. Sigrid Eabern	Los Angeles, Calif.
Miss Blanche Morrow	Los Angeles, Calif.
Rev. A. F. Schmitthenner	Englewood, N. J.
Mrs. A. F. Schmitthenner	Englewood, N. J.
Master A. F. Schmitthenner, Jr.	Englewood, N. J.
Master J. E. Schmitthenner	Englewood, N. J.
Master S. W. Schmitthenner	Englewood, N. J.
Miss Christie E. Zimmerman	Selln's Grove, Pa.

ROUND THE WORLD

Dr. L. S. Eastlake	Hollywood, Calif.
Mrs. L. S. Eastlake	Hollywood, Calif.
Mr. George Flehman	San Jose, Calif.
Miss Erma Flehman	San Jose, Calif.
Mrs. R. Wilson	Toronto, Ontario, Can.

FROM HONOLULU

Mr. H. W. Gildemeister	Mrs. E. P. Miller
Mr. H. S. La Motte	

Author's collection.

from Marseilles on October 23 for New York. At the conclusion of that voyage around the world the ship steamed into New York on November 3, 1936. A few days later she went up to Boston to work cargo and then returned to her usual Jersey City pier, there to remain while West Coast maritime unions virtually paralyzed Pacific shipping for more than three months. While held at New York the PRESIDENT van BUREN had the company of several fleetmates ranging from the perennially (so it seemed) idle PRESIDENT FILLMORE to the other "502"'s PRESIDENT ADAMS, PRESIDENT GARFIELD, PRESIDENT HARRISON and PRESIDENT POLK and the bigger "535" type PRESIDENT TAFT. Among other things the strike delayed the end of the ship's Voyage 41. After the walkout was settled the PRESIDENT van BUREN was sent into the yards of the Robins Dry Dock Company where after her 7:30AM arrival there on March 25, 1937, she was given routine voyage repairs and prepared to return to sea.

The PRESIDENT van BUREN did not sail again until April 1, 1937 when she cast off from New York under the command of Captain John Murphy. His crew numbered 145 officers and men. With 4,447 tons of general freight in her holds the PRESIDENT van BUREN cut through the "Big Ditch" at the Isthmus of Panama on April 7th. Outbound from San Francisco she continued her voyage on April 23rd. May 15th saw her at Kobe from whence once again she continued her routine port calls on the way around the world. On that first voyage since the strike the ship called at Shanghai overnight on May 18th, spent the night of May 22nd at Hong Kong and the 25th at Manila. She called Singapore on May 30th and sailed on June 1st for Penang and an overnight call there before sailing on June 3rd. On the 8th the PRESIDENT van BUREN called at Colombo and on June 11th steamed into Bombay for a two night call. She departed on the 13th for Suez and a June 23rd transit of the Canal. A week later the ship was heading into the final leg of the trip and sailed from Marseilles on July 1st. Subsidy through payments for carriage of the mail ended for the PRESIDENT van BUREN on June 30th and Dollar Line was on its own to sink or swim financially when the PRESIDENT van BUREN sailed out from New York on another round the world voyage on July 22, 1937. That time the ship sailed from Kobe on September 4th. But never mind Dollar Line's problems with finances and with the Maritime Commission, for crew problems continued to plague the American Merchant Marine and Dollar Line's "502"'s were not spared. Nor were seamen's complaints restricted to management. Chinese crew often came under written attack by white American colleagues and October 1937 brought this complaint penned by Ship's Delegate R. Adams to the Chairman of the Maritime Commission, the Marine Cooks and Stewards Association of the Pacific and to O.H. Smith, Dollar Line's Port Steward at San Francisco:

> On behalf of the members of the Steward's Department of the steamer PRESIDENT VAN BUREN the following protest is made to all ultimately concerned with the welfare of the American Merchant Marine.

That it is the practice of the Chinese members if the crew on vessels of the Dollar Line to bootleg beer and liquor to white members of the ships crew with demoralizing results. That it is practically impossible to keep certain members of the said personnel sober at sea, to the dissatisfaction of the sober members of the crew and at the same time interfering with the comfort of the passengers.

In view of these circumstances we are of the opinion that some drastic action be taken to do away with this evil.[9]

Because the ship was not then subsidized, the Maritime Commission directed Adams to deal directly with Dollar Line.

The new safety regulations became effective that fall and the PRESIDENT van BUREN could not comply with the requirements for passenger ships. Since Dollar Line needed whatever money passage tickets brought in, they wanted her to continue carrying passengers, so they made arrangements for the ship to be upgraded to meet new standards and retain her passenger certificate. It didn't work out that way and while waiting for requisite items to bring her up to compliance with the new standards, the ship began working as a freighter so she did not need to have insulation fitted in port and starboard alleyways in crew quarters; she did not have to alter her schedule to allow time for shoreside labor to make improvements to her ventilation; her petty officers' wash room was not retiled, nor did the firemen get the fresh water shower requested; nor were handles fixed in locker rooms. Maybe the awning requested for # 7 hatch was delivered before sailing but at least as a freighter, the owners did not have to invest heavily in refitted crew quarters. They simply moved crew into unoccupied passenger cabins. Without the desired betterments the PRESIDENT van BUREN sailed as a freighter from Boston on November 9 and New York on November 13th. The ship made her Canal transit on November 20 carrying a few passengers and 4,788 tons of general cargo into the Pacific. Now, in order for the ship to continue to meet her schedule, she was certified as a freighter when she sailed from San Francisco on Saturday, December 4, 1937. She could now legally carry only twelve passengers but when she sailed from San Francisco, all twelve passenger berths were occupied.

Meanwhile, Dollar Line announced their decision to upgrade the ship to comply with new safety standards and return her to passenger ship status upon the conclusion of that voyage. They either overlooked their promise or knew that their finances could not allow them to install improved fire safety equipment in this ship. They just could not afford it so Dollar Line retained the PRESIDENT van BUREN in service on the Round the World line as a freighter until an emergency subsidy ran out. At least they would avoid the expense of constructing new crew quarters for as a freighter, crew could be housed in otherwise empty passenger cabins. Machinations shore-

---

[9] Text is adjunct to Oct. 27, 1937 letter to Adams from Daniel S. Ring, Director, Division of Marine Personnel. Copies of both in ship's 901 file in RG 178 at Maritime Administration.

side had little tangible effect on the ship's schedule and on December 26th the PRESIDENT van BUREN sailed from Kobe for Hong Kong where she closed out 1937. On January 2, 1938 this "502" sailed for her customary ports of Manila, Singapore, Penang, Colombo and Bombay where she arrived on January 21st. Some writers report that the ship was at Bombay when the Dollars ran out of money for her to continue her voyage and there she remained, but that is not quite what happened. She WAS at Bombay when the till ran dry but the Maritime Commission granted Dollar Line a temporary operating stipend at the end of that month and the ship kept on going, sailing from Bombay on January 26th for a February 4th arrival at Suez. After her February 5th call at Alexandria she crossed the Mediterranean for Naples and Genoa and then from Marseilles on February 10th the PRESIDENT van BUREN sailed for New York on her final leg of that trip. She sailed past the Statue of Liberty on February 26th. There her screws stopped beating and would not turn again for many months. Now, months before Dollar Steamship Lines collapsed, the PRESIDENT van BUREN was again idled as was the entire fleet except the big PRESIDENT COOLIDGE on the transPacific run. That autumn extensive paperwork filed with several Government departments brought the ship under a new corporate ownership.

When R. Stanley Dollar resigned from the presidency of Dollar Steamship Lines on October 30, 1938, the PRESIDENT van BUREN was still laid up at New York. She was there on November 1, 1938, the following day, when she passed under the ownership of newly formed American President Lines. On November 4th the PRESIDENT ADAMS inaugurated American President Lines' round the world service from New York. Next out and second of the former Dollar ships to leave New York, the PRESIDENT van BUREN resumed service when she sailed from New York on November 11, 1938. Carrying freight only she first set her course for Boston and then after returning to New York, she sailed on Voyage 45 on November 17, 1938 for Havana and Balboa. With 2,088 tons of general cargo in her holds she made her way through the Canal on her way to California on November 25, 1938. December 5th and 6th saw the ship at Los Angeles and on December 7th she showed the white eagle on her funnel to San Francisco as she steamed under the Golden Gate for the first time as an American President Liner. During her three day stay there much of her passenger equipment and furniture was offloaded and trucked from the pier to storage in a San Francisco warehouse. Also put ashore were lifeboats not needed for a ship limited to 12 passengers. At this point in her career the PRESIDENT van BUREN as well as her two unimproved sisters PRESIDENT MONROE and PRESIDENT HAYES did not even take that many. A footnote in the company's sailing schedule Number 1 read: "These steamers do not carry passengers." Everything removed was carefully logged for eventual return to the ship before she sailed at Noon on Saturday the 10th on her first APL sailing from San Francisco. Honolulu and Yokohama were next.

The PRESIDENT van BUREN was at Kobe when 1939 began and sailed on January 2nd for Hong Kong. There for a one day call on January 7th, she resumed her earlier itinerary with her sailing for Manila, Singapore, Penang, Colombo, Bombay and the Mediterranean, making her Suez Canal transit on February 6th. From Marseilles the homewards voyage began when the PRESIDENT van BUREN sailed at 7:00PM on Wednesday, February 15th. Across the Atlantic at the end of her first APL voyage, the ship reached New York on Tuesday, February 28th. Remaining at Pier 9 through Noon on Saturday came the usual hectic job of unloading inward freight and loading some of the outbound cargo before the ship sailed for Boston. The schedule generously allowed 24 hours to reach that Massachussetts port. There the round the world "502" remained through 5:00PM on Tuesday when she sailed for New York to complete loading for the world voyage. By now an APL veteran, this ship returned to dock at New York at 5:00PM on Wednesday, March 8th. Two nights in port were allowed an outbound round the world liner and at 6:00PM on Friday, March 10th the PRESIDENT van BUREN sailed from Pier 9 on Voyage 46.

Following her well trodden path the ship made San Francisco on March 29th for an April 1st sailing. On her second voyage as an American President Lines' freighter, the PRESIDENT van BUREN was at Hong Kong and sailed on from there on April 28th. Following her usual route she visited her customary ports in turn. From Singapore on May 6th and Bombay on May 18th the ship entered the Mediterranean on May 30th and sailed from Marseilles on June 7th for New York and Boston. From that New England port where she once more worked cargo the PRESIDENT van BUREN sailed on June 28th for New York and Voyage 47. Outbound past the Statue of Liberty again on July 1, 1939 the ship set her usual course for Havana. On July 7th with 3,989 tons of general cargo in her holds the steamer made her Panama Canal transit. As always Los Angeles was next and then San Francisco where she spent three days before sailing on July 22nd for an outbound crossing on American President Lines' transPacific service, Line A. Omitting calls at Japanese and Chinese ports that time, the PRESIDENT van BUREN steamed nonstop to Manila and an August 12th arrival. Sailing from there she went up to Hong Kong where she called overnight on August 16th and 17th. Then the ship made her way to Singapore from whence after a five day call between August 22nd and 29th she resumed her usual service on APL's round the world service, Line B. Next, of course, was Penang and a two day call before heading to Colombo with an August 31st departure.

The ship was en route to Bombay on September 1, 1939 when German troops invaded Poland. When the ship arrived at Bombay on Monday, September 4th, her crew was anxious for whatever news they could learn of the war declared by Britain and France against Germany the day before. The ship resumed her voyage with her sailing on the 6th for Suez. By the time the ship reached Egypt for her September 15th transit of the Canal both sides of her hull were marked with her name, nationality and an American flag. The ship headed into Naples on the 18th and by the time she reached Genoa on September 20th, the PRESIDENT van BUREN was temporarily restored to passenger ship status, so operating under emergency passenger certificates issued by American consuls in ports where Americans anxious for a ride home embarked. Also taking part in the evacuation of Americans from Europe were the other "502"s, which also required emergency waivers to exceed their certified passenger capacities in the current emergency. By the time she sailed from Marseilles on September 22nd, the PRESIDENT van BUREN had a big load of passengers happy to be aboard the safety of an American liner on her way home. At least a few felt like kissing the ground after they walked down the gangway upon the ship's October 5th arrival.

By the time the ship sailed from New York on Voyage 48 on October 13th, she was back on schedule. Right on time on November 2nd she sailed from San Francisco. Now it was more vital than ever that she remain in service and fill her holds with all kinds of cargo useful to the nation's embryonic defense efforts. When the PRESIDENT van BUREN sailed from Genoa, Italy on January 16, 1940, it marked the last time she would make her way through the Mediterranean on the homeward leg of the round the world service. When Italy went to war that spring, the neutral American merchant fleet was diverted from Mediterranean routes. Among the treasures in her hold for her February 8, 1940 New York arrival were 518 tons of rubber for the Boston Army Terminal.

When she sailed from New York on Voyage 49 on February 11th, she followed her sisters out to San Francisco. While the ship was there the subject of crew food arose. Union man V.J. Malone, Secretary of the Pacific Coast Marine Firemen, Oilers, Watertenders & Wipers Assn. wrote to Admiral Land on March 7th. Proving nothing was too petty or specious to bring to the attention of the busy Maritime Commission Chairman, Malone declared:

This week there were three vessels in the Port of San Francisco subsidized by the U.S. Maritime Commission—the S.S. PRESIDENT VAN BUREN, S.S. PRESIDENT TAFT, and S.S. PRESIDENT CLEVELAND.

On all three ships the crews were in an uproar due to the fact that the feedings of the crews was away below the proper standards. On investigation we found the crew complaints were justified. In all cases moreover, we found the quality and quantity of the provisions placed aboard the vessels by the company were very creditable.

In the case of the PRESIDENT VAN BUREN, the steward was replaced by a new steward. In the case of the PRESIDENT TAFT and the PRESIDENT CLEVELAND the steward and chief cooks were likewise replaced.

On closely analyzing the facts of the case, we believe that the Maritime Commission should set forward a policy to insure that the stewards and cooks hired on American flag vessels should be fully qualified men.

In this connection we wish to point out that in the case of members of our Association, firemen have to pass comparatively strict examinations in order to pass on up the line to oilers, watertenders, machinists, refrigerating engineers and electricians. Very strict examinations are given to insure that no unqualified men shall be issued certificates. The same thing applies to mates licenses and engineers licenses.

In the case of many of the cooks and many of the stewards supplied, the men are fully qualified. However in many cases that have come to our attention we find that men not qualified to handle the diversified duties of a ship's cook or ship's steward are shipped out.

How these men are shipped out is simple. In the first place, there are in the United States thousands of hamburger, hot dog, sandwich or waffle shops. A young fellow would start as bus boy or waiter at one of these outfits, and within a week or so is promoted to the job of cook, That is, he would make up an order of ham and eggs, pour in a bit of waffle batter, or flip up a few hot cakes.

There is no examination or test for this man, when he is sent out as a cook on a ship, that is comparable to that given to firemen, oilers, electricians, etc.

That is when the trouble starts, because on voyages ranging from two to five months the menus must not only be well diversified, but in many cases the chief cook or steward must be something of a dietician, particularly on tropical voyages.

On the case of the VAN BUREN it was clearly proven beyond any shadow of doubt that the steward was incompetent. His ice boxes were full of provisions that should have been issued to the crew; and it was found that several crates of fruits and vegetables had to be thrown overboard on the voyage as they had rotted and thus were not fit for the crew's consumption.

Moreover, in no instance was a proper diet put out suitable for a tropical voyage.

In less degree the same complaints were true on the PRESIDENT TAFT and PRESIDENT CLEVELAND.

We trust that the Commission will give serious thought to this matter.[10]

Following her usual outbound course, Honolulu was next before the ship crossed the Pacific to Asia. Then from Colombo, Ceylon on April 19th, the van BUREN made her way for the first time to Cape Town, South Africa where she tied up on May 10th. Some crew still found reason to gripe. Here's one of their more spurious complaints addressed to Maritime Commission Chairman Admiral Emory Land on May 29, 1940:

In view of the much valued and excellent work you have done for us of the United States Merchant Marine, we would like to take this opportunity of thanking you for all you have done for us.

Also, we would like to call to your attention a slight difficulty which has arisen on this ship, and ask your assistance in straightening it out.

Our Steward's Department, of which I am the delegate, is composed of twenty (20) members, of which many have no regular place in which to eat.

---

[10] March 7, 1940 letter from V.J. Malone to Admiral Land. Copy in the ship's 901 file in RG 178 at Maritime Administration.

These men must stand while eating, chiefly in the Saloon Pantry, which is at best a busy place, thus adding to the general turmoil.

There are two places on the ship which could be adapted to thus use with ease, and with very little expense. One is the port corner aft of the Dining Saloon, which is never used at present, and which could be partitioned off very readily. This is also directly opposite the Pantry. The second place is a vacant room aft of the Petty Officer's Messroom, in which tables and benches could be arranged with little difficulty.

The Chief Mate informs us that such changes may not be made without authorization of the Maritime Commission, therefore it would be greatly appreciated, not only by ourselves, but by all Steward's Departments sailing on this ship after us, if you can find the opportunity to assist us in straightening this matter out."[11]

They were lying, of course, about having to eat standing in the Saloon Pantry as Maritime Commission's Pacific Coast District Director June 29, 1940 letter to the Maritime Personnel office in Washington proves:

On all of the American President Lines ships the Steward Department crews are permitted to eat in the main dining saloon, just prior to the serving of the passenger meals. As the PRESIDENT van BUREN is (a) 502 Freighter status and, as only the Engineers and Mates are eating in the main dining saloon, I found no one on board who had objected to members of the Steward's Department taking their meals as is the custom, either before or after the ship's officer hours. As far as the Steward Department's delegate's proposal to partition the main dining salon, the company officials have received similar requests from members of the Deck and Engine Departments on board the steamers PRESIDENT HAYES and PRESIDENT MONROE. This request has always been rejected.

One other factor in the request is that accommodations are being made for twelve passengers this voyage of the PRESIDENT van BUREN from the Far East to New York; with the carrying of these passengers the Engineers will have to move back into their old quarters just aft of the present P.O. messroom. And it will not be possible to partition the main dining saloon. Mr. Seeley has been notified.[12]

She made no less than two more circumnavigations of the globe via South Africa. After the PRESIDENT van BUREN arrived at San Francisco on June 27, 1940, her Master, Captain D.C. Austin, authorized Maritime Commission Representative B.J. O'Sullivan to conduct a condition survey of his ship. For the record, the ship was on Voyage 50 and had a complement of 4 licensed Deck and 8 Engine Officers, 4 deck cadets, 2 engine cadets, 1 radio officer, 16 deck, 28 engine and 20 steward's personnel making a total crew of 85.

---

[11] May 29, 1940 letter from union delegate Joseph Siswick to Chairman Land. Copy in ship's 901 file in RG 178 at Maritime Administration.

[12] June 29, 1940 letter from Maritime Commission Pacific Coast District Manager E. C. Mausshardt to Philip King, Chief of Field Section, Maritime Personnel—Maritime Commission, Wash., D.C. Copy in 901 file for PRESIDENT van BUREN in RG 178 at Maritime Administration.

It seemed there was always some crew problem. This time it was a radio officer who managed to delay the ship's departure. Unless American President Lines paid him for 500 hours of overtime, he would not sign on. A claim disputed by other radio men, another member of the Commercial Telegrapher's Union was signed on in his place and the ship finally sailed at 1:30 AM on June 30, 1940.

On the homeward leg of that round the world voyage, the PRESIDENT van BUREN was on her way into Trinidad when she grounded on Drew Bank on the Caribbean island of Tobago on September 23, 1940. Very quickly refloated, she proceeded into Port of Spain, Trinidad for repairs. Quickly patched up, she continued on her way without further undue delay. Previously damaged by heavy weather she would be fully repaired once she had arrived at New York. Repairing the ship was a big job requiring three plates to be renewed, 5 removed and 17 faired, 60 floors and a number of frames straightened and some renewed, 21,000 shell internal rivets renewed, seams caulked, all hold ceilings lifted and repaired where needed, bilge keels and rudder repaired, 40 fuel tanks steam cleaned, tested and retested, one bronze blade replaced and others renewed and both propellor shafts inspected and repaired where needed. During this round of repairs, one betterment was made, a concession to crew. Acting on a request for better ventilation in their messrooms from both Deck and Engine Departments, the inboard bulkhead was removed and replaced with steel screening. By the time the ship left dry dock, nearly $95,000 had been spent to put the ship back into "tip-top" shape. That did not include an additional $8,852.00 for drydocking but did take into account a charge of $15,400 for steaming and cleaning.

That autumn saw the delivery of the first of APL's new round the world liners. With the PRESIDENT JACKSON in service and the six ships to come to take "502" names, the time had come to rename the "502"s. Paperwork for this ship continued to fly in many directions. Maritime Commission Order C—770 of November 5, 1940 authorized the issuance of a registry certificate for the ship as PRESIDENT FILLMORE though her name would not be changed for several weeks. The ship was half a world away on Voyage 51.

Though calls at Japan had been largely dropped as unprofitable by American President Lines, there was a Kobe call on that trip. It would be her last visit to a Japanese port, she was there on December 9, 1940.

Reports of her location after 1940 are confusing but it is known that the PRESIDENT van BUREN began the fateful year of 1941 at Singapore, sailing from there for San Francisco on January 2nd. By then she was one of four American President Lines' steamers working on Route A, the old Dollar Line transPacific service, a route which American President Lines came to name the Atlantic-Straits service. Each such voyage required Maritime Commission permission for authority to operate the ship on another such unsubsidized voyage and the planned February 28, 1941 trip from New York to Penang and Singapore via Los Angeles, San Francisco, Manila, Hong Kong and Singapore and return via the same ports needed official sanction. The

Line telegraphed their request for approval on January 8th. Taking its time to respond, the Maritime Commission approved the request on the 28th and on January 29th wrote American President Lines a letter of approval covering both the upcoming sailing of the PRESIDENT van BUREN but also that of the newly renamed PRESIDENT BUCHANAN, the old PRESIDENT MONROE which sailed on January 17th on a similar trip. Permission to operate the voyage was contingent upon a few things: no subsidy money for operating differentials, results of these voyages would be factored into net earnings, value of the ships factored into figures for calculating operating differentials and that the voyages not be included in figuring American President Lines' compliance with minimum and maximum sailing requirements under existing subsidy agreements.

Now came the time to rename the PRESIDENT van BUREN. She was the last of the six sisters to take a new name. On February 24, 1941 she was renamed PRESIDENT FILLMORE, taking the name of the old MONGOLIA, which, after a long lay up following a few years of trading under her "President" name, had been sold in February 1940. The "502" had hardly carried her new name for twenty-four hours when an incident of labor unrest found its way into the log book. It happened as the PRESIDENT FILLMORE was on her way into Boston on February 25, 1941. Barley soup was on the lunch menu in both Officer's and Petty Officers' messrooms that day. The Chief Officer ordered a bowl. In his bowl was a cube of what seemed to be a piece of carrot, but it was not, it was piece of a bar of Life Buoy soap. Similar cubes dotted the soup bowls of both Captain Austin, the ship's Master, and the 2nd Officer. On the Chief Mate's discovery of the nature of the cubes, all three officers rose and made for the pantry where they found further pieces of soap cut to resemble carrots. Asking which crew member was the joker brought the Captain and his Officers no names. One of the two messmen assigned to the Petty Officers' mess, Abraham Diaz, was known aboard as a troublemaker. Diaz had a reputation for caring little for personal hygiene or his own appearance. On several occasions during the voyage round the world, fellow crewmembers told him to clean himself up. Declaring the soap in the soup an accident, his colleague, John Boyce, who said that Diaz did not get along well with anyone on the ship, admitted that he saw something fall out of Diaz' pocket. Both men paid off at New York and the case of soap in the soup was forgiven as an accident though on the way to New York on February 28th, something like soap was found in a milk pitcher in the Petty Officer's messroom.

On her first voyage as PRESIDENT FILLMORE, this "502" sailed from New York at 2:20 AM on March 5th for the West Coast on her unsubsidized voyage to the Straits/Settlements. Though she seems to have omitted her usual Havana call, she arrived at Panama on schedule on March 11th with 7,960 long tons of cargo. She made no stop there this time and after transit quickly cleared for sea. When she sailed from San Francisco on March 27th, she steered a course for Singapore via Manila. Departing Hong Kong on the homeward trip on May 22nd, the ship made her first eastbound transPacific crossing. She steamed into San Francisco on June 12th. Bound for ports on the Atlantic the PRESIDENT FILLMORE cleared the Golden Gate two days later on June 14, 1941. Next on her itinerary was New York, where she arrived on July 3rd. Authorized by Maritime Certificate C-39, the PRESIDENT FILLMORE was Lend-Leased to Britain for one trip on the Red Sea berth. A charter agreement covering the ship and that voyage was signed on July 1st. Like her sister PRESIDENT BUCHANAN, the PRESIDENT FILLMORE was technically chartered to the British Ministry of War Transport and was to be handled by both American Export Lines and Nacirema Line but the outbound voyage was actually operated by the Isthmian Line. The PRESIDENT FILLMORE departed New York on July 22, 1941 on her way south to Cape Town before steaming up the coast of East Africa and the Red Sea to Suez.

A second voyage to Suez was arranged and this time she would carry passengers—a lot of them. Berths for 800 were arranged along with everything a ship needs to handle that number of passengers. One item of cargo to be lifted from Suez would require special permission from several Government departments. Getting the ball rolling to facilitate shipment of 434 cases of opium for use in manufacture of pharmaceutical products was the State Department which cabled the Treasury Department for import licenses in late September. Per a November 27th directive from the Navy, once the ship reached Boston after December 26th, the ship would be fitted with defensive armament. She neither went to Boston for armament, that was fitted at New York, nor did she sail as planned. Almost at the last minute, the PRESIDENT FILLMORE was withdrawn from the Red Sea service and kept idle at New York. A.E. King confirmed this decision in a January 9, 1942 memo to the Director of Operations and Traffic. Taken over by the War Shipping Administration under time charter from February 9, 1942, the PRESIDENT FILLMORE was delivered that day at 12:01 AM at New York and simultaneously redelivered to American President Lines as General Agent under then terms of Service Agreement WSA#224. Aboard were 8,616 barrels of fuel oil and 338 tons of water. Before starting out on her wartime career the ship was to be refitted to carry 171 officers and 1,790 troops at Bethlehem Shipbuilding Company's 56th Street yard at Brooklyn. To that end, 514 new life preservers were put aboard on March 3rd and the Navy agreed to supply 645 more.

The first of eight voyages she made for the War Shipping Administration began on March 9, 1942. Owner's voyage 54, it took her from New York to Tocopilla, Chile, where she arrived on April 16, 1942 and thence to San Francisco for a May 2nd arrival. WSA Voyage 1 ended there five days later when the last of her passengers and cargo were landed. Then came a brief overhaul at a local yard before beginning WSA Voyage 2, owners #55, on May 8th. Lifting her first parcels of cargo that morning, the PRESIDENT FILLMORE filled her holds with vital war cargo and her berths with both civilians and military personnel and cast off from her usual San Francisco pier on May

20th. Now when the ship cleared the Golden Gate the ship didn't follow her usual course out towards Honolulu. Instead she turned to starboard and made her way north to Alaska to deliver both fighting men to defend the territory and supplies and war materieles to see them through the fight. That trip ended at Seattle on June 20th. For the next few months this "502" worked on the Alaska shuttle, beginning and ending her trips at Seattle. Her next trip was numbered WSA Voyage 3 and it occupied her between June 21st and July 27th. That round trip to Alaska was followed by another one as WSA Voyage 4 which she operated between July 28th and September 7th. Respite from the rigors of transport service came next. Before WSA Voyage 5 began on September 26, 1942 the PRESIDENT FILLMORE enjoyed a general overhaul and voyage repairs at Seattle yards. Both Alaska and Hawaii were on the ship's schedule during WSA Voyage 5 and she ended that trip back at San Francisco on December 30th.

Whatever this aging "502" was by then or wherever she was, she was not ideal for trooping in Alaskan waters and a serious December 10, 1942 fire aboard led the Army to bring charges against her civilian Master, Captain Murphy. The last of her troops and military cargo were discharged at Adak and the ship put back to sea. Off the Aleutians in position 53°N 176°W at 3:40 AM on December 10th, fire broke out in the midships cabin section on Promenade Deck. Before being extinguished at 5:20 AM, it had spread and consumed much of the cabin accommodation on that and Boat Deck. By no means affecting the ship's seaworthiness, the results of the fire were far from pretty—five men had burned to death and one Navy officer seriously injured.

In a December 21, 1942 memo to Ralph Keating, WSA Assistant Deputy Administrator J.E. Cushing put it concisely:

> It is unnecessary that you read the rather voluminous file attached unless you want to do it as a matter of interest. The substance is that the Army authorities in Alaska have preferred charges against Captain Murphy of the FILLMORE, claiming that he is overcautious. I know Captain Murphy and his record and share Mr. Lintner's view that the charges are unjust.
>
> The vessel is really too big and too clumsy for her present service and it would be a god send if the Army could be persuaded to switch her to transPacific and put some smaller transport in her place as sooner or later we are almost certain to have a serious casualty and, as you know, we are none too long on good troop ships.[13]

Inexplicably, the ship was idled for the next ten weeks so it must be presumed that a massive overhaul and perhaps substantial structural work was done on the ship. Whatever she did, a change in her status was in the works and at San Francisco Bay at 12:00 noon on February 9, 1943 the ship's charter was backdated into a bareboat charter and then converted into a

---

[13] copy in ship's 901 file in RG 178 at Maritime Administration.

requisition bareboat charter. Once ready to resume service, WSA Voyage 6, Owner's Voyage 59, began on March 11, 1943. A 27 day voyage that lasted until April 6th, that trip took her back to Hawaii as did WSA Voyage 7 which she began at San Francisco on April 7th. The ship returned to her home port on June 18th where the ship technically completed the trip there on June 20th, 1943, but it was a voyage her crew would long remember. For much of the time covered by the articles of that voyage, the ship was at Attu where liable to Japanese air attacks, the ship's crew received war risk bonuses in their pay packets. At Dutch Harbor on June 3, 1942 while on a regular trooping voyages to Alaska, the PRESIDENT FILLMORE came under enemy attack twice. From his San Francisco office of the Marine Firemen, Oilers, Watertenders & Wipers Assn. on June 29th, V.J. Malone sang the praises of everyone on board. Here's his letter to Captain Edward Macauley of the Maritime War Emergency Board:

> I would like you to know the authentic details regarding the part played by the SS PRESIDENT FILLMORE and its crew during the recent Japanese raid on Dutch Harbor, Alaska on June 3rd.
>
> This vessel, on the night of June 2nd, discharged fifteen hundred troops. At 5:50 AM the next day, a flight of five Japanese bombers came over Dutch Harbor dropping bombs right and left, accompanied by two fighters.
>
> This ship had its regular armament and Navy gun crew, assisted by the merchant marine crew. She carried one four-inch gun forward, one four inch gun aft, and 2 50-caliber machine guns amidships. As luck would have it, she was also carrying eight 37mm. anti-aircraft guns on deck as deck cargo to be discharged ashore in Alaska. She also had on board the Army gun crew to man these anti-aircraft guns, described by our crew as very very wicked and very very effective.
>
> When the first flight came over, the Navy gun crew immediately manned the heavy and light armaments; the Army anti-aircraft crew manned the eight 37mm guns. The merchant marine crew—engine room, deck and stewards departments—hopped in to help them.
>
> The ammunition for the eight 37mm. anti-aircraft guns was in No. 6 hold. These guns certainly spurt out a mass of metal, and in very short order they were out of shells. The crew formed a continuous line to No. 6 hold to bring up this ammunition. In very short order, also, the four-inch guns cleaned out the ammunition lockers fore and aft, and ammunition for these guns was also in No. 6 hold and was brought up by the crew.
>
> Some of the anti-aircraft men had rifles which other members of the crew secured together with the Army ammunition and fired at some of the Japanese low diving bombers.
>
> The crew claimed that in the first flight over Dutch Harbor they knocked down two of the assaulting aircraft.
>
> Evidently the Japanese took photographs of the ship laying alongside the dock, for in the afternoon at 6 o'clock a second flight of about twenty planes came in. The ship, however, had moved out into the stream, but the Japanese bombers concentrated on the docks and sent one bomb right through the old NORTHWESTERN—an Alaska Steamship vessel which had been con-

demned for merchant service but which had been pressed into service as a floating hotel. One plane dived so close to the PRESIDENT FILLMORE that the men with rifles had a very clear shot.

In this latter raid, the crew claimed that three or four Japanese bombers were shot down or so badly damaged that their return to base was very unlikely.

It is our belief that the entire crew, without exception, showed very high gallantry under fire.[14]

Few other former American passenger and cargo ships could claim to have shot down two Japanese fighter planes and one torpedo bomber, but as a result of the good shooting of her gunners at Dutch Harbor, the PRESIDENT FILLMORE could. Next came the ship's 110 day Voyage 61. Beginning on June 21, 1943 it lasted until the ship's charter expired on October 8, 1943. Because officialdom concerned with this ship were more interested in matters other than itinerary, details of the ship's movements on that trip are lacking. All that is documentable is her June 27th departure from San Francisco. Considering the length of the trip, the likely destination was Australia though some writers credit the ship's gunners' kills during a summer 1943 call at Dutch Harbor.

By their very nature passenger ships are well suited to conversion to hospital ships, and a combination passenger cargo ship like an unimproved "502" was considered just dandy for such purposes by the Army. Though chosen for conversion to hospital ship in the summer, the PRESIDENT FILLMORE was not sent for alterations just yet. Only after October 8, 1943 when the requisition charter expired and title to the ship passed to the War Shipping Administration, did the authorities make a move towards refitting this "502" for mercy work. After title to the ship passed to the Government, the next step was her simultaneous delivery to the Army Transport Service at the Seattle Port of Embarkation. Responsible for the projected conversion was Lt. Col. John Barthrup of the Seattle Port of Embarkation, Water Division, whose staff included the man directly in charge of the conversion project. That was Major Rowe of the Maintenance and Repair Department and he was ably seconded by Lt. Murray. They didn't have any time to spare so they were lucky that the needed plans for the conversion of unimproved "502"s into floating medical centers were already extant. All they had to do was to get the ship into a local yard and get the project moving. Local shipyard giant Todd Shipyards won the contract for the ship's conversion into an Army Hospital Ship and the job began at their Seattle yard.

It seemed that the first order of business was to remove all remnants of the ship's earlier finery. Thought contrary in a fireproof ship was the ship's beautiful woodwork. Out came wood panelling and ornamental work of all kinds. Fire resistant materials were installed in their stead. Removed were a

---

[14]June 29, 1942 letter from V.J. Malone to Capt. E. Macauley. Copy in ship's 901 file in RG 178 at Maritime Administration.

good many cabin bulkheads in order to make room for hospital wards. Within less than two months the interiors of the PRESIDENT FILLMORE had been stripped to bare metal. By then it was obvious to officials at the yard that the scope of the conversion was so momentous that they would only be able to meet the contracted June 1st delivery date if they assigned 1,000 men to work on the ship. Problem was, they could spare only 500. There was too much other work to do. Then Todd devised the bright plan to finish the job at their yard at Tacoma, Washington where in the yards of the Seattle-Tacoma Shipbuilding Company at Tacoma some "2,000 men, designers, fitters, welders, plumbers, electricians, machinists, engineers, painters—all the crafts working around the clock ... under Al McNeil, superintendent"[15] worked for ten weeks to bring the ship to completion. Following the concept of joining the two main houses of the superstructure as had been done in 1925 in the case of the PRESIDENT POLK and in 1929 in the reconstruction of the PRESIDENT ADAMS, PRESIDENT GARFIELD and PRESIDENT HARRISON, workmen at the Tacoma yard joined together the two houses of the PRESIDENT FILLMORE to give her a 225 foot long midships structure. Before the yard deemed their work complete, they decided to pour 2,000 tons of iron ore and concrete ballast into her lower holds, forward, to lessen the ship's movement and give her a slower roll. Despite expected wartime delays in the arrival of materials and equipment ordered, all was in order by May 31, 1944. The ship's hospital was ready to care for 763 patients.

Inherent in the concept of hospital ship is safety and in connection with safety in a ship, lifesaving gear is naturally the first item to come to mind. To that end a "502" converted to hospital ship was fitted with plenty of lifeboats. In the case of this one, twenty two boats including two motor boats had a capacity of 1,152, more than enough room for everyone aboard. Beyond the boats were twelve life rafts and twenty two floats with a combined capacity of 670 persons. But it was perhaps the sense of added security from enemy attack provided by painting and lighting plans as outlined by the rules of the Geneva-Hague Conventions that allowed a modicum of confidence to all who sailed in the hospital ships and the five red crosses, wide green band and white hull and superstructure marked this "502" steamer as a hospital ship. Other than "diplomat" exchange ships like the GRIPSHOLM and DROTTNINGHOLM and a few neutral passenger liners like Portugal's SERPA PINTO, JOÃO BELO and COLONIAL, only the hospital ships steamed through the nights of the war years with their lights on. In fact, the rules called for the red crosses to be spotlighted by floodlights and those in the MARIGOLD were. Her livery and lighting were her only protection, for the rules forbade hospital ships from carrying even the lightest defensive armament.

Also rated noncombatant was the crew from Master to ship's boys.

---

[15] ibid. p.57.

Wearing the ship's wheel insignia on their Army Transport Service uniforms were the ship's regular officers and crew. Every man assigned to the MARIGOLD was from the Seattle Port of Embarkation and as a mercy ship, the vessel needed plenty of them—a crew of nearly 400 included the expected group of deck and engine officers and a Chief Steward and a deck, stewards and engine crew of 144 Army Transportation Service crewmen, 4 ATS Pursers (accountants), 4 signal corpsmen, radio operators, while the hospital required a staff of 232. There were 18 doctors, 37 graduate nurses, two dentists, a veterinarian (food inspection), 1 dietician, a Red Cross supervisor, 6 Medical Corps administrators, 166 medical attendants and two chaplains. Unlike the home-grown ship's crew, the medical department counted men and women from all over the country, members of the Army 212th Hospital Ship Complement. The doctors came from private practices in eight different states, the nurses from eighteen, while as many as forty states were represented in the make-up of the medical attendants. All of them wore the caduceus of the Medical Corps on their Army uniforms.

Colonel Raymond Hicks, Assistant Chief of the Army Transport Service, Water Division came aboard for a look around just before the ship sailed from Seattle and succinct were the words he spoke to Captain Skalley: "The ship is yours, take good care of her, she's very valuable." The Captain never forgot those words. Below, the engine department was in the charge of Chief Engineer Harry Johnson, late of the DAVID W. BRANCH, formerly the Grace-owned Panama Mail liner ECUADOR. Chief Steward was Army Transport Service veteran Bert Williams who had transferred from San Francisco to Seattle. Under him were more than fifty men, most from the Philippines.[16]

The Office of the Surgeon General renamed the ship MARIGOLD. The ship's outfitting was supported by large donations of money from patriotic, civic minded women of the Seattle area who would come to regard the ship as "theirs". Especially hard working to get this ship in service were no less than 22 different women's groups like the Bank's Women's Organization and the Women's Clubs of the Women's Division of the King County War Finance Committee. To prove more devotion to the project than their sale of some $4 million worth of war bonds, they commemorated their work to the ship with a plaque that read: THIS HOSPITAL SHIP WAS SPONSORED AND MADE POSSIBLE BY THE WAR BONDS SOLD BY THE WOMEN OF SEATTLE, WASHINGTON."[17] It was affixed to a bulkhead aboard ship for all to see.

Her commissioning ceremony at the Tacoma yard on June 10th was one of those gatherings that seemed to have attracted "anybody who is anybody" and it's true, the guest list was impressive. Beside Major General Robert H. Lewis, Commanding Officer of the Pacific Northwest Sector was a lot more Army brass while British and Chinese Consuls headed the roster of foreign

---

[16] Skalley, Michael quoted Hicks in "A Medal for Marigold", p. 4. Used here by permission.
[17] ibid. p. 81.

dignitaries. City councilmen and mayors, representatives of the many wom-en's clubs and Seattle financiers were there and so, too was the MARIGOLD and her proud crew. The hospital staff stood at attention on the after decks for the reading of the ship's Certificate of Commissioning. Then, with orders for him to bring the ship to Pier A, Seattle Port of Embarkation for finishing touches, Port Commander, General Ely Denson handed the ship over to Cap-tain Robert Skalley. "The Red Cross flag now waved in the breeze from the main mast; the MARIGOLD was in commission."[18]

Her run to Pier A was the extent of her trials so the Army ordered a couple of big new tugs to keep her company . . . "just in case". The Army allowed newspapermen and photographers to hitch a ride in the tugs to Seattle and even allowed them to photograph the "new" hospital ship un-derway. They got some dandy shots of her before the steering gear pooped out some five miles from Tacoma. Until air could be forced out of the hy-draulic system between bridge and steering engine room, the ship was out of control. Captain Skalley stopped his ship and in the intervening two hours, crew were able to check off about half of all items as satisfactory. At 5:00PM the MARIGOLD was fast alongside Pier A. Open house was held two nights later and a host of vistors trooped aboard. Many of the women who had worked so hard to sell the bonds to get the ship converted came aboard. They were all shown the plaque. Every visitor seemed to come loaded with questions . . .

1. Was a hospital ship ever attacked? Answer: In the First World War, yes. In this one, no . . . though two British ships were accidentally damaged but that's not QUITE the end of it . . . the Italian hospital ship CALIFOR-NIA was bombed and destroyed while blacked out in a Sicilian port.
2. How do you get wounded aboard? Answer: Ambulatory patients or litter bearers came them through side ports or up the accommodation ladders. Sometimes ship's gear could hoist litters from craft pulled up alongside.
3. What about seasickness? Answer: It's a cause for real concern and avoid-ing rough weather or putting the ship in the most favorable position to the sea were the only practical alternatives.
4. Charge nurses were asked: Wouldn't you prefer shore duty? Answer: No, we applied for shipboard duty . . . friendships were much closer and there was more unity of purpose.[19]

Of great interest were the operating rooms and dentist's office but visitors also wanted to have a look at the chapel, store rooms, pharmacy, laundry, galley and bakery. Two decks down from the main wards were the psychi-atric wards and visitors took interest in facilities for men deranged through acts of war. Over a hundred visitors looked over the locked rooms, the pad-ded rooms, the regular rooms. Ten percent of the casualties were expected to be mental cases and for them the facilities even included shock treatment

---

[18] ibid. p. 9.
[19] ibid. p. 10–113.

machinery. Some 140 visitors trooped up to the bridge and asked about 1,400 questions.[20]

On June 17th, with all the last minute things done, the MARIGOLD slipped from her Seattle pier and made for the degaussing range, some ten miles up Puget Sound. Once tests showed the degaussing system in order, the ship headed over to Point Wells oil dock for bunkers. On June 18th, all lines were cast off and Captain Skalley set a course for the Panama Canal, sixteen days' sailing to the south. While the ship was tied up at Balboa it seemed everyone ran ashore to do some shopping . . . or in some cases, a LOT of shopping, for some came back thoroughly encumbered by duty free purchases. Then it was on to a July 11th arrival at Charleston, South Carolina, home port for Army Hospital Ships. There she would get her further orders before sailing on July 21st for Naples and other places in the Mediterranean. At Naples the MARIGOLD was joined by a number of Army hospital ships, her exact sister EMILY H. WEDER, originally the PANHANDLE STATE and formerly PRESIDENT MONROE and lately PRESIDENT BUCHANAN, among them. While at Naples several units of the 7th Army were assigned to the ship for transportation to beachheads on August 16, 1944. At long last the MARIGOLD was heading into the war zone, on her way to the beaches off St. Maxime, France. She would head north through the Straits of Bonifacio and steam on to the Gulf of St. Tropez. That night there was no moon and the illuminated hospital ship ran in the dark, avoiding blacked out ships as she headed north. Her stay in the war zone was over pretty soon. On August 21st she steamed back into Naples where it took six hours to land a full complement of patients. Three days later came sailing orders. This time it was to St. Tropez. Once there a navy lieutenant told Captain Skalley that because there had been a severe air raid by the Germans the night before, the ship's arrival was a blessing. In ten hours the MARIGOLD had taken aboard 776 patients, a full load of wounded. Back at Naples the ship was given a thorough cleaning before sailing for Charleston on September 5th with a full load of patients, mostly wounded veterans of African and Italian campaigns, for the United States.

Her first westbound Atlantic crossing with a full load of passengers put all areas of the ship to every kind of test. The most basic question of all was whether or not the ship's evaporators were up to the job of providing the tremendous amount of water necessary for a hospital ship carrying over 1,100 people. And a lot of water she needed indeed—about 24,000 gallons a day. Roughly working out to some twenty gallons per man per day, a year's time saw the ship's laundry wash about 100,000 sheets and about 120,000 towels, all of it in fresh water.

Nightfall brought extra diligence and sharp lookouts for no matter the ship's Red Cross markings, Captain Skalley would take no chances with the safety of his ship or charges. When the MARIGOLD was about halfway across the Atlantic, the call of "Man overboard" shattered the ship's peaceful

---

[20] ibid. p. 12.

A photograph by now familiar to many, this is still the most evocative shot of the PRESIDENT van BUREN as the hospital ship MARIGOLD. Frank O. Braynard collection.

routine. Swinging the ship hard left away from a man in the sea, someone aboard threw a life ring. Captain Skalley ordered one engine astern in an attempt to stop the ship and help rescue the man. Before the MARIGOLD had a boat in the water the man had disappeared from sight, never to be found again. All that would be known was that he was one of a group of mental patients brought up to one of the after decks for some fresh air. Looking after these disturbed veterans were six attendants who could do little more than sound an alarm when the man suddenly and quietly climbed a rail and jumped over the side. Of course that man's tragic antic had the effect of reducing the amount of time mental patients were permitted to spend on deck . . . as well as impinged somewhat on their freedom of move-ment . . . they were required to remain seated when topsides. On the bridge Captain Skalley ordered orange smoke canisters to be available for launch into the sea should another jump into the water. The next man jumped over the side the next day. Within minutes another man jumped. Both engines went full astern, smoke floats went over the side and the Chief Officer took command of the boat that went into the water to retrieve the jumper. The second man overboard turned out to be a battle fatigued infantry captain who saw the first man dive off the ship. He jumped in to try to save the first one. The ship's boat pulled the captain from the sea but an hour's search failed to turn up any trace of the first man and the MARIGOLD's boat gave up. After that men were posted at the rails to stop anyone from jumping and no one else decided to try to swim for home. The 22nd of September brought the MARIGOLD into Charleston.

Quite a reception committee awaited ship and her complement. On the pier was a long line of ambulances. Shortly after the ship was tied up, two gangways were put down. First off were ambulatory patients. By 2:00PM the last of the ship's patients were ashore and the time to clean up and prepare for the following voyage was at hand. Some of the staff had shore leave, others did not. Visiting the ship was General Kirk, Surgeon General of the Army who brought his staff for a look at the Army's newest floating hospital. Port Commander General Duke also came over for a first hand look at the MARIGOLD. Both ranking generals liked what they saw and both were quite liberal with their words of praise.

Raising the specter of the civilian past, quite a few of the Seattle based crew grumbled about serving in a Charleston based crew. Amazingly enough, Captain Skalley was able to do something about it and in five days time got authorization for his Seattle men to go home. Getting out while the going was good were the Chief Officer Fosse who left for a refresher course at Navigational School and two Deck Officers, Chief Engineer, engine offi-cers and almost the entire engine crew including the entire black gang, Chief Steward, a few petty officers and most of the ship's seamen. Remaining were Second Officer Roy Robeck, two junior officers, many petty officers, some of the deck crew and most of the Filipino crew. Where promotions failed to fill vacancies, new men signed on and in no time crew was back up to strength.

The few days at Charleston were highlighted by some repairs. Then, with the Captain's assent, the MARIGOLD was ordered to the Los Angeles Port of Embarkation for a tour of duty in the South Pacific, a job guaranteed to keep her busy for many months at time and would keep her men away from home for at least a year.

Sailing day was October 9, 1944 and the destination was Finnschafen, New Guinea, five weeks and 12,000 miles away from South Carolina. A week later on October 16th the MARIGOLD made her transit of the Canal and returned to the waters of the Pacific. Shortly after leaving Balboa, the ship passed the first set of buoys. She gave everyone a scare when. The quartermaster discovered that he could not swing the ship to starboard even with the wheel hard over. A quick thinking Captain Skalley grabbed the engine room telegraph and pulled port handles to FULL ASTERN. Luck was with him. The ship responded and the bow began swinging left. Now the Captain rang FULL AHEAD on port and FULL ASTERN on starboard. The ship's stern cleared the buoy by ten feet. Luck had been with the MARIGOLD that night. Had there been any traffic the ship would have had been in a nasty collision. With a great sense of relief the men on the bridge set the ship on a course under a Navy routing for the South Pacific. The next stop was about 11,000 miles and 29 days away. The next sixteen days brought nothing to look at other than ocean and sky. When about 5,500 miles west of Panama the ship made her first landfall when she passed Malden Island. Many more islands were sighted during the next thirteen days of the ship's trip to New Guinea where she arrived at 9:00AM on November 14, 1944.

The next weeks brought the MARIGOLD into a number of New Guinea harbors but Christmastime brought the doughty hospital ship into the war zone again. Leyte was the location and with bombs and firing going on all around her, she was truly an oasis, as long as she was not a target of enemy or friendly fire. Five days later on December 30th the MARIGOLD, all of her beds taken by wounded soldiers, sailed for Hollandia, New Guinea, some 1,200 miles away. By January 7, 1945 sailing day was again at hand and the MARIGOLD began another voyage to Leyte where another 765 casualties waited for a ride to hospital in the comparative safety of New Guinea. On that northbound voyage, the weather turned rough. Giving the MARIGOLD a real test of her mettle, the ballast forward did what was wanted, and limited her roll to an alarming 20 degrees. A freak wave hit alongside and smashed into a couple of boats, knocking them off their chocks, but luckily neither was lost over the side . . . the water in them kept them anchored to the spot. At Leyte the MARIGOLD was ordered to anchor near Tacloban but a good look at the area suggested that it was not the place to be during air attack. Captain Skalley agreed to remain during daylight hours but with nightfall, his ship would move. No sooner did the ship anchor than a pair of LSTs brought the first of some 300 patients out to the big ship. While embarking these casualties, Captain Skalley was peeved to see five cargo ships come in and lock the MARIGOLD into position. Despite assurances that three of them would soon move on, the MARIGOLD was forced to remain at her Tacloban anchorage until 3:00AM. Right on schedule the Japanese bombers showed up that evening but once more the luck of the MAR-IGOLD held, even though she was really in the wrong place for a hospital ship with a load of wounded. By January 22, 1945 with 300 ambulatory and 465 bed patients the ship was full and ready to sail for Hollandia, five days' away.

February 6th brought the MARIGOLD another departure for Leyte and embarkation of more wounded. While there the Navy was able to spare enough oil to refill her tanks and give her another 40 days steaming time. In exchange the MARIGOLD gave the Navy oiler some beef. During her night at that time no Japanese air raiders disturbed the starry night and on February 11th the ship was ready to take her full complement of casualties to Hollandia.

The memory of the MARIGOLD's beef was strong and when the ship returned to Leyte, the commander of the oiler asked Captain Skalley if he wanted to top off his tanks. Of course he did. On February 25th the MARI-GOLD sailed from Hollandia, this time for Surigao in the Philippines where American forces engaged Japanese in fierce fighting. March 1st brought the white mercy ship into Lingayen Gulf and into anchorage off Dagupan where the port medical officer told the MARIGOLD to take fifty patients and on the 3rd continued on towards Manila. The liberation of the Philippines was but days away. Since Dagupan had no need of the medical facilities a ship like the MARIGOLD had, the vessel moved on and reported to the Navy Base at Olangapo in Subic Bay, one of the places her former sister PRESI-DENT HARRISON had visited before sailing back to Shanghai and capture. There at Olangapo the MARIGOLD had a freak accident of her own. Calling for more water pressure to clean mud off the anchor chain, it was apparent that something was not right. On the Captain's orders, a junior officer went down to main deck to open a hydrant. Once water splashed over the deck, those in charge knew that the pump was working. By then quite a few by-standers had gathered around to watch when:

> Suddenly shrieks did get through to the bridge from the crowd below. Drops and pellets of black goo hit the onlookers on hair, face and shirts. They ducked below the rail but too late, the damage had been done. Gallons of heavy black fuel oil in wind-blown globules splattered the whole super-structure and onlookers before the bridge could call the engine room to stop the fire pump. Fuel oil could be still be seen dribbling out of the deck over-flow pipe connected to the forepeak fuel tank. The rain of oil happened because someone at sometime closed the fire line valve to the hydrant and opened the seldom-used saltwater ballasting valve to the tank-both valves opened off the fire line. Water pumped into the tank forced the oil to over-flow out of the gooseneck-shaped vent on the forecastle head. A padlock and chain eliminated the possibility of this recurring.
>
> The oil-shower victims' hands and faces cleaned up with mechanic's soap but four shampoos were necessary before the oil and smell disappeared from their hair. Regrettably, since there was no alternative, the oil-spotted

blouses and shirts had to be thrown over the side. The nurses asked the Captain if there was any chance the shower-bath lines might spout oil!

Kerosene, cleaners and brushes failed to remove all the superstructure stains and even repainting was not wholly successful. The cleaning went on for two weeks but for months small pockets of bunker-C fuel oil were discovered. Captain and crew were most unhappy with the defacing of their clean white glossy ship received but they decided there was no use crying over spilled oil.[21]

Next on the ship's itinerary was Olangapo where the MARIGOLD stood by for nine days. During most of that time deck crew worked to clean up traces of oil. On March 13th the MARIGOLD sailed, this time for Manila. Her passage up Corregidor was a marvel to anyone on deck and the sights and sounds of those eleven miles lived on in anyone who was there as every one of twenty US Navy units passing the MARIGOLD sounded her whistle in salute and the Army hospital ship returned every one of them. It took until March 15th to get in close enough to take on wounded for Hollandia. And so it went for the next few weeks that the MARIGOLD was always there to take wounded fighting men, look after them and carry them back to safety. Then came orders for the ship to head for home. She departed Hollandia on April 19th and by early May she was about 2,000 miles from Los Angeles and she arrived on May 13th.

The local Bethlehem yard saw her soon after she disembarked the last of her patients. It had been almost a year since she had sailed from the Tacoma yard and since then the MARIGOLD had worked long and hard, steaming tens of thousands of miles without much maintenance. Captain Skalley had time to go to Seattle, While he was away, former Chief Officer Ray Fosse returned to the ship. By June 1st the repairs were almost done, the crew assembled and ready for sea again. Recognizing the excellence of the MARIGOLD's crew, the Army chose her to transport some 700 nurses across the Pacific, 150 of them to Honolulu, the rest of them to the Philippines. After a fifty-four day hiatus spent in the port of Los Angeles, the MARIGOLD was ready to sail on July 5th but her passengers were not able to board until the following afternoon. At 3:00PM on the 6th a number of railway cars showed up at the MARIGOLD's pier and disgorged the nurses. Forming two columns after a goodbye cup of coffee, they boarded the MARIGOLD for the transPacific trip. The ship sailed at 6:00PM and within days the ship wanted for water. Once at Honolulu technicians checked and discovered hard packed salt choking the tubes. Quickly put right, the evaporators gave further trouble after the ship's July 17th departure. They were adding only about ten tons of water every day. Water would have to be limited before the ship reached Manila so everyone was asked to shower with salt water and rinse with fresh and to be careful with water use in wash basins. That simple precaution saved thousands of gallons of fresh water. By August the ship was in Philippine waters. Then the Chief Engineer had

---

[21] ibid. p. 900.

some bad news for the Captain: "One of the two fire pumps was out of order and his crew couldn't repair it. It had gone out during a fire and boat drill that afternoon. The evaporators and now the fire pump!"[22] On the following day the Leyte nurses disembarked. Only the Manila bound contingent remained and they wanted to give a hand so Chief Officer Fosse took ten of them and put them to work soogeying the decks. He told them he would give them seaman's discharge papers marked V.G. for both ability and character . . . and they could use those papers should they decide to become seamen! One day out of Leyte brought more water woes when during the morning deck washdown the hoses went limp. Now the ship had NO working fire hose. Four uneventful but edgy days brought the MARIGOLD into Manila where authorities asked her Master to house the nurses for another five days. From the station tanker the hospital ship took 250,000 gallons of fresh water. Coming round to the tanker's starboard side, the MARIGOLD's port engine stopped working. Only the starboard engine responded because a throttle on the port engine was now inoperative. Hours later Captain Skalley went ashore and arranged for a new Chief Engineer and First Asst. Engineer to replace the ones he had. They joined the MARIGOLD the following day and within a week had the throttle, evaporators and pumps back in order.

Sailing orders came. The MARIGOLD was to depart Manila on August 20th for a location as yet undisclosed. There were thirteen days to kill and not much to do while waiting. Manila was mostly a wreck and there was little to see or do. Five days before sailing, hostilities came to an end. The day everyone wanted so dearly brought forth spontaneous celebrations, fireworks, joy, laughter, whistles and all manner of merrymaking. On the 18th came news that the MARIGOLD would sail on another passenger voyage. The 42nd General Hospital with all their equipment, possessions and personnel came aboard for a ride to Okinawa where they landed on the 25th. A day later the ship sailed for Tokyo Bay. She actually went to Nojima, Saki, Japan, some forty miles at the end of Tokyo Bay where she arrived on August 30, 1945. After the surrender of Japan the MARIGOLD docked at Pier 7 at Yokohama where her medical facilities were put to good use by hordes of newly liberated POWS and a host of dignitaries. Among those coming aboard who required no medical attention was New York's Cardinal Francis Spellman and he offered a mass on the pier.

The MARIGOLD remained in Japan through November 10th when she sailed for Manila with a shipload of ambulatory patients. Three hundred of them were to remain aboard all the way to the United States. Manila was reached on the 17th and on the 20th the MARIGOLD sailed for California. On her homeward voyage the ship's newspaper ran a variety of interesting features detailing her successes. Service awards approved for MARIGOLD personnel included:

---

[22] ibid. p. 1161.

The American Theater Campaign Medal
The Europe-Africa-Middle East Campaign Medal
Battlestar for the Rome-Arno Campaign
Battlestar for the Invasion of Southern France
The Asiatic-Pacific Campaign Medal
Battlestar for the Luzon Campaign
Battlestar for the Leyte Campaign
Battlestar for the New Guinea Campaign
Battlestar for the Western Pacific Campaign
The Philippine Liberation Medal
The Good Conduct Medal
The Medal for Service in World War II
The Meritorious Service Unit Award
The Bronze Star[23]

There was more . . . the MARIGOLD had sailed over 75,000 accident free miles, crossed the equator fourteen times, burned 217,000 barrels of fuel. The ship had treated 10,000 hospital patients and cared for 2,000 former POWs. On December 15, 1945 with the ship safely tied up at Los Angeles, Captain Asa Harris boarded to relieve Captain Skalley who, with his Chief Officer Ray Fosse and Third Officer Richard Richings left by car on the following afternoon for Seattle and a well deserved rest.

To the tune of *"Home on the Range"*, a ditty reputed to be quite a favorite of President Franklin Roosevelt, a now anonymous nurse of the 7th Army who worked aboard the MARIGOLD in August 1944 was moved to write *"A Ballad for MARIGOLD"*. Mike Skalley used it as something of a frontispiece in his book and agreed it should be further reproduced here:

O Lord bless the trips of our hospital ship
A Red Cross marks her snowy white sides
For mercy to all is the MARIGOLD's call
As she sails on the waters worldwide . . .

Sail . . . sail on the waves
Where the whales and porpoises play
Where never is heard a disparaging word
And the skies light up MARIGOLD's way . . .

Where giving a hand by a devoted band
Of good doctors and nurses and crew
Make our MARIGOLD fair an island of care
Midst the flotsam and jetsam of war . . .

Sail . . . sail on the waves
Where the whales and porpoises play
Where never is heard a disparaging word
And the stars light up MARIGOLD's way . . .

---

[23] ibid. p. 1424.

O ship sail back then with our heroic men
And their valor to heaven do send
As a hard won peace is by sacrifice made
For the land of the free and the home of the brave . . .

Sail . . . sail on the waves
Where the whales and porpoises play
Where never is heard a disparaging word
And the sun light up MARIGOLD's way![24]

There was some more hospital ship work in store for her but without the urgency of war, it remains largely undocumented. The ship's career was almost over anyway for on June 8, 1946, she was decommissioned at San Francisco and turned over to the Maritime Commission. They restored the name PRESIDENT FILLMORE to the twenty six year old ship on June 16th. A place in the Reserve Fleet at Suisun Bay was her next stop. At 9:45 AM on June 28, 1946 the ship arrived at Anchorage 26 under tow. At that moment the War Department redelivered the vessel to the Maritime Commission. Paperwork was a tad more involved, because there was the old bareboat charter to deal with as well as the fact that the War Shipping Administration was still legally extant. So papers were simultaneously signed transferring the ship out of charter and back to the WSA and thence to the Commission. It really didn't matter because this obsolete liner was going nowhere for a while. She remained laid up at Suisun Bay for about two years. When the Maritime Commission listed a number of ships including the JOSEPH DICK-MAN, ex PRESIDENT ROOSEVELT, and the SAMARITAN for sale for breaking in the autumn of 1947, the PRESIDENT FILLMORE was on that list. Highest bid for all three ships came from Kaiser Metals and in one of the quickest of all sales of Government property, the United States Maritime Commission accepted their bid on December 30, 1947. Accepting Kaiser's offer under the terms and conditions of Invitation for bids # DD-X-35, the Maritime Commission passed title to the buyer on December 31, 1947. No grass grew under either party when it came time to transfer the ship. At 11:30 AM PST on January 14, 1948 a tug came by and picked the ship up in the channel in Suisun Bay. Once her towrope was connected to the old "502" the delivery was complete. Towed to Richmond, California she was scrapped during the same month.

---

[24] For the longer version we have to thank the memories and collection of Captain Robert Skalley and the pages of his son, Michael Skalley, author of the fine book *"A Medal for Marigold"*. And when I say thank I know what I am talking about, for Mr. Skalley was kind enough to help my book by giving me permission to quote from his and to reproduce certain items like *"A Ballad for MARIGOLD"* and part of the crew list.

CREOLE STATE/PRESIDENT HAYES: PRESIDENT TYLER/ HOWARD A. MCCURDY

◇

New York Shipbuilding Corporation gave this ship hull number 245. Bearing Emergency Fleet Corporation hull number 2586, the Shipping Board planned to call this ship IASSUS. She should have been the second of the "502"s but in fact she was the third completed and delivered. One of two keels laid at the Camden yard on May 22, 1919, the keel of this ship was set onto slipway T. The other keel went onto ways U and grew to become her sister GRANITE STATE. Losing her intended name in November 1919, a December 4th memo from the Statistical Section estimated the ship 36% complete by January 1, 1920. From that time on workmen concentrated their efforts on this project and got ready to put her over by late April. Mrs. Mary Benson Craft, daughter of Shipping Board Chairman Admiral Benson, named the ship CREOLE STATE at the christening ceremony just prior to the ship's launch on April 27, 1920. This was the third "502" class ship to go into the water. To the cheers of the gathered throng, seconds after Mrs. Craft snipped the cord, the new ship slid down the greased ways and into the waters of the Delaware River. Her name honored Louisiana. After months fitting out the ship was completed and steamed out of the yards to run her trials. Meanwhile, Shipping Board accounting personnel compiled a report of her construction expenses and derived a building cost of $4,085,573.61, a figure which rose to $4,110,857.10 when certain accommodation fittings were included. Only her displacement tonnage of 13,005 tons differed at all from the particulars given for her two sisters. Registered under the ownership of the United States Shipping Board Emergency Fleet Corporation at the port of San Francisco, California, the CREOLE STATE was delivered to the Shipping Board on December 6, 1920 at her builders' Camden yards. Captain G. Dockstader was first to command her.

Originally expected to run on United States Mail Line's London service with her sisters PANHANDLE STATE and OLD NORTH STATE, the earliest days of the career of the CREOLE STATE have confused some maritime historians and writers. Perhaps they relied too heavily on single sources like the newspaper advertisements announcing the CREOLE STATE's planned November 27, 1920 sailing for London. The CREOLE STATE never sailed for US Mail nor did she make that scheduled sailing nor was that sailing cancelled. Here is what happened before the CENTENNIAL STATE took the CREOLE STATE's promised slot in the United States Mail fleet a few months later. The scheduled departure was taken, not by the CREOLE STATE but

Painted in Shipping Board/EFC colors, the new CREOLE STATE prepares to run her trials. *New York Shipbuilding Collection.* Courtesy of the Independence Seaport Museum Library.

by the PANHANDLE STATE, which had been idle in New York for some time. The decision to substitute one ship for another was made on the spur of the moment for the CREOLE STATE's planned November 27th sailing for London was being advertised in newspapers as late as November 10th. A couple of days later the papers ran a new US Mail advert. It showed the PANHANDLE STATE, at first scheduled to sail on December 4th, would sail on November 27th. The United States Mail Steamship Company still held out hope that they would win allocation of this third "502" and advertised a December 11, 1920 departure for London for the CREOLE STATE. A second sailing from New York was announced for January 15, 1921. These sailings for U.S. Mail Line never happened. Instead, heeding the pleas of the resurgent Pacific Mail Steamship Company for tonnage for the Calcutta service, a freight line established in 1917, the Shipping Board assigned the brand new steamer to the San Francisco firm. The first mention of the ship's impending sailings from San Francisco appeared in that city's newspapers on November 27th, the date the ship would otherwise have sailed from New York for London.

To defray the expenses of the ship's delivery voyage to San Francisco, the Shipping Board allowed Pacific Mail to carry passengers. A large advertisement sponsored by the firm of American Express appearing on November 27th told the story: a "19 Day Cruise" to San Francisco from Baltimore aboard the "palatial new CREOLE STATE". Quoting a rate of $300.00 to San Francisco, and $145.00 to Cristobal, it was further announced that the new ship would leave Baltimore on December 27, 1920. An article in *The New York Times* on November 28, 1920 repeated the official word, announcing allocation of the CREOLE STATE to the Pacific Mail Steamship Company for operation on the Calcutta service.

Convinced that the run was viable in the postwar world, Pacific Mail was already awaiting allocation of two more new "502"s, feeling sure that the Calcutta service could make good use of the fine cabin accommodation in these ships.

Within hours of her December 6th delivery, the ship was on her way to begin her career. From Philadelphia/Camden she steamed down the Delaware River bound for a transit of the C & O Canal and Baltimore where she was delivered to Pacific Mail. Like the other "502"s, the CREOLE STATE was delivered with only 78 First Class beds. Both Pacific Mail and the Shipping Board agreed that the Calcutta line would earn increased revenues by the carriage of Steerage passengers. Only the timing was uncertain. Everyone wanted to put such berths in before the ship began her Pacific Mail career but there wasn't enough time. Steerage would have to wait. The ship left Baltimore as advertised on December 27, 1920 for her home port with 40 passengers and 5,000 tons of general cargo and steel. After a couple of day's steaming through wintry weather, the ship entered warmer climes, reaching Cristobal in the tropical Canal Zone at 6:45 AM on January 3, 1921. At 12:06 PM she entered the Canal for her first transit, and passed through at 6:54 PM to tie up at Balboa where she delivered the bulk of her cargo. While there her booms lifted aboard for passengers' use a collapsible swimming pool, ten feet long, fifteen feet wide and seven feet deep, that had been specially built at local shops for the ship. Local papers commented favorably on her interiors, noting the mahogany woodwork and ivory colored bulkheads of her accommodation spaces.

After she sailed from Balboa at 1:20 PM on January 4th, it took the CREOLE STATE ten days to reach Los Angeles. The first of the Shipping Board's new passenger ships assigned to serve from the West Coast, residents of her California ports paid her arrival great attention. San Pedro greeted the new liner at her arrival on January 14th. Even more festive was the send off locals gave the new ship when she cast off for San Francisco at 10:00 AM the next day. After leisurely steaming up the coast, the CREOLE STATE passed through the Golden Gate on the 16th to begin more than two decades of service from the port of San Francisco. Fabled shipping center of the West Coast, San Francisco went wild for her. She was the largest commercial vessel under the American flag[1] seen there since Pacific Mail had sold off the KOREA, SIBERIA, MANCHURIA and MONGOLIA during 1915. Save the gigantic four stacker AGAMEMNON, which had called at California ports in the wake of World War I, the West Coast had not seen an American passenger ship of this size since 1915. Over 10,000 visitors trooped up the gangways to see for themselves what their tax dollars had wrought. By all accounts, the new CREOLE STATE impressed nearly all of those attracted to her during the few days of her first San Francisco visit though only shipping men would have cared about her cargo spaces including the deep tanks in which she could bring home about 1,000 tons of coconut oil on every trip.

Scheduled to begin her maiden voyage on January 28, 1921 for Honolulu, Manila, Saigon, Singapore, and Calcutta, the new CREOLE STATE actually sailed at 1:00 PM on February 3rd under the command of Captain J.E. Miller. Before the maiden departure of the vessel, Pacific Mail quietly sacked most of the Americans in the steward's department and replaced them with Chinese. That move brought a telegram of protest from the Secretary of the Marine Cooks and Stewards Association entreating the Board to: "Please take immediate action as ship sails February 3rd at 1:00PM" nor did reminding the Shipping Board that "the Seaman's Act was passed in order to encourage Americans to go to sea and not Orientals . . ."[2] do any good.

First of the newly built Emergency Fleet Corporation passenger carriers to operate on the Pacific, the new CREOLE STATE replaced the smaller, less well equipped COLUSA on the Calcutta line. Pacific shipping men felt that the operation of these new American ships, providing Manila with the finest passenger and mail link with the United States, would silence all protests from Philippine shipping interests who, by all accounts, still smarted over

---

[1] Some of the larger "ex-German" troopships had called there in the meantime, but of course they were not on commercial service.
[2] Feb. 3, 1921 telegram. Copy in the ship's 1091 file in RG32 at National Archives.

It's sailing time for the CREOLE STATE and the new ship has just cast off from San Francisco for her long voyage to Calcutta. Mike McGarvey photo.

Dressed fore and aft the CREOLE STATE docks at Honolulu on her maiden voyage. Mike McGarvey photo.

the Shipping (Jones) Act of 1920 and its prohibitions of foreign vessels to engage in many American trades. The schedule allowed the new "502" class ship six days to reach Honolulu, 22 days to Manila, 28 to Singapore and 39 days to Calcutta. On that maiden voyage the ship experienced minor engine trouble. A high pressure turbine cylinder rod was out of order and it could not be repaired until after arrival at Honolulu. After her Hawaii call it took the ship another 15 to 16 days to get to Manila and she made her first arrival there on February 28th. From there it took three days to reach Saigon, where the March 4th arrival of an American passenger liner was treated as a curious and extraordinary event. Americans, at least in French colonies, were still remembered and regarded affectionately as heroes of the late war. French Indochina was happy to welcome some! Describing in flowery terms the ship, the service and the welcome reception held aboard, local newspapers seemed most impressed by the ship's green hull and the music played by her orchestra as the ship tied up. Indeed, no less a personage than the Governor of "Cochinchina", accompanied by a number of prominent members of French colonial Saigon society were among the 300 people who attended a champagne reception and luncheon aboard the ship. After sailing from Saigon, it took the CREOLE STATE another three days to reach Singapore, where once again the arrival of a new American liner was heralded. The liner's March 7th arrival elicited favorable comments, much of it in praise of the ship's appointments. Again local dignitaries were feted and treated to a festive meal, pronounced "excellent" by the diners. As "THE STRAITS TIMES" told it; "The accommodation for passengers on these three new steamers compares favorably with that on the finest steamers afloat.[3] Further impressing the Singapore observers were the ship's extensive laundry installation and her chilled storage spaces to keep California fruit and vegetables fresh. Five more days steaming brought the CREOLE STATE into Calcutta on March 12th. A call at Colombo, Ceylon not scheduled for inclusion on the regular itinerary until the third of the "502"'s entered the Calcutta service, was made on the first homewards sailing. The CREOLE STATE was there on March 29, 1921.

Otherwise the new ship called at the same ports on the eastbound leg of her maiden voyage. Her midnight sailing from Honolulu on April 25th was especially poignant. Now was fulfilled the promise of service to the mainland with yet another ship with top-drawer accommodations. Concluding her maiden voyage, the CREOLE STATE arrived at San Francisco on May 2nd, pleasing both Pacific Mail and the Shipping Board with a $42,470.21 profit on the inaugural trip. Records from that trip showed a gross revenue of $267,045.21 against (estimated) operating expenses of $224,575.00. Hopes for continued profitability were high. Three weeks would pass between the time the ship returned from Calcutta and her next sailing for the Bay of

---

[3] March 9, 1921 issue of *The Straits Times* (Singapore). Copy in the ship's 1091 file in RG 32 in National Archives.

Bengal. During that time steerage, subject of so many memoranda among Shipping Board officials and operators of the "502"s, US Mail and Pacific Mail, was installed in the ship.

During the ship's three weeks stay at San Francisco "Oriental Steerage" for 246 passengers was fitted into No. 6 tweendecks at a cost of some $29,000.00. Those Third Class quarters were not much noticed by First Class passengers and only the presence of extra lifeboats indicated the carriage of additional passengers for no one in positions of authority wanted to call attention to the ship's steerage capabilities. Steerage in the Pacific Mail "502" was less an exigency for the Calcutta market than an attempt to siphon off trade from foreign ships coming in to California from Manila. Certain American industries like West Coast agribusiness and Pacific Northwest salmon interests were actively hiring Filippino workers and Pacific Mail wanted to carry them to the United States.

The "502"s were ultimately unsuccessful on the East India service and none of the steerage accommodations fitted in them ever pulled voyage revenues into the black. Dollar losses may have been as simple as the timing of the ships' entry into service but it may as well just have been that there was not enough business on the run to make the service pay. There may have been other factors at play as well but the facts speak loudly. The Calcutta line was not the place for the "502"s, especially at a time when the shipping business the world over was going into a deep slump. The "State" sisters attracted little cargo and few passengers. Results were so discouraging that even had they debuted together, the three "502"s could likely not have been operated on the line simultaneously. In fact, they only operated on that run for about a year. The original pair of ships running on the service, the 5,000 tonners SANTA CRUZ and COLUSA, with their much smaller passenger capacities, turned out to be more suitable than the "502"s on this rather unprofitable line.

At San Francisco on May 21, 1921 the ship's registry was officially transferred from Philadelphia to the local register. The scant freight bookings and few filled passenger cabins for the CREOLE STATE's second departure on May 23rd pointed to disappointing prospects. For other reasons, that outbound trip lived on in the memory of many men associated with the ship, the Shipping Board and those concerned with the status of American labor. In the midst of the general shipping depression came a pay cut for sailors prompting a number of seamen's strikes. Rancor ran rampant that season in all sectors of America's merchant marine. One CREOLE STATE crewman had already been separated from the ship, charged with theft, and convicted. One year in the penitentiary was his punishment. While the ship steamed placidly westwards on the Pacific Ocean on her second Calcutta trip, William O. Dunleavy, the ship's 2nd Assistant Engineer, Joseph Wing, an oiler and fellow oiler Joaquin Barranchina were arrested, charged with attempting to sabotage the ship's engine and machinery by placing emery powder in the bearings. Captain Miller arrested them, charging them with committing crime on American territory by virtue of the ship's registry. As the ship tied up at Manila, the prisoners were brought before the American consul at the request of the General Agent of the United States Shipping Board and taken before the Insular Collector of Customs before being remanded to the custody of Philippine authorities. Meanwhile the CREOLE STATE continued on her way. Again at Manila on July 15th, at the request of the ship's Master, Captain Miller, the men were returned to the ship for return to the United States as Federal prisoners in the charge of Special Customs Agents William K. Kennedy and William A. Brown. Held under armed guard, the accused were turned over to the United States Marshal of the San Francisco district upon the ship's August 6th arrival. Wing seems to have been the ringleader and the Board turned much of its attention in the case to prosecuting him, using him as an object lesson to others. There may well have been grounds to convict all three. Discovering what he called "fatal flaws" in the original indictment, District Counsel J.J. Dwyer brought three new indictments in mid January 1922. The trial of the accused began on January 23, 1922. In spite of new indictments, Engineer Dunleavy and oiler Barrachina were acquitted of all charges but Joseph Wing was convicted of sabotage and sentenced to imprisonment for seven years at McNeil Island.

After the ship returned to San Francisco on August 5, 1921, pursers turned in figures for Shipping Board accountants to dissect. Included were charges for ocean transportation for the two Customs Agents who served as armed guards from Manila in charge of the trio who went out to bring back the CREOLE STATE prisoners. The matter of their passage fares was a matter that took on a life of its own. Both Pacific Mail and the Shipping Board looked to the War Department for payment of the Agents' outbound passage in the CREOLE STATE and homeward travel in the GOLDEN STATE. On the grounds that the War Department was not concerned in this matter, they refused to pay the bill for ocean fares. Turning to the Attorney General, the Shipping Board learned on September 30, 1922 that these expenses could not be paid from judiciary appropriations but that the Board could use some of its own monies to pay a part of this cost. Eventual acquittal of two of the three accused men occasioned a further paper chase when the matter of their entitlement to their wages cropped up. Who will be surprised to learn that the Shipping Board stood opposed to paying either man any money for either the period through the end of the voyage or for that period plus the duration of the voyage?

While the various departments worked to solve the matter of payment of ocean fares and defense attorneys prepared their cases, the CREOLE STATE continued her career. Captain Miller was replaced by Captain Dockstader who by late 1921 turned command of the CREOLE STATE over to Captain T. Fleming. Captain Dockstader moved on to another Pacific Mail passenger liner. On September 14th the first of the "502"'s on the Pacific was off to Calcutta again, not to return to San Francisco until December 14th. There was no Saigon call on that trip, the ship's third to Calcutta.

With a number of passengers booked no further than Honolulu, the CRE-OLE STATE sailed on her fourth voyage from San Francisco on December 22, 1921. After Christmas at sea, the ship reached Hawaii on the 29th. Once more across the Pacific, the CREOLE STATE made her way via Manila and Singapore, from whence she proceeded on January 21, 1922 to Calcutta where records report she arrived on January 26th.

Facing the dreariest financial results on that long-haul line, the Shipping Board had already decided to withdraw one of the big new ships and rear-range the service on which Government-owned tonnage would then run. Excerpted from the minutes of the meeting of the Shipping Board is this item: "It is also recommended that the S.S. CREOLE STATE, expected to sail from San Francisco March 25th and the S.S. WOLVERINE STATE, expected to sail from San Francisco April 22nd, limit their voyages to not further to Manila."[4] Allocation of the sistership GRANITE STATE was withdrawn from Pacific Mail and the ship was assigned to the New York—London Cabin service then managed by United States Lines.

Homeward on Voyage 4 the CREOLE STATE sailed from Calcutta on February 2nd. The eastbound passage was longer than the earlier ones be-cause the ship was ordered into Shanghai where, after her February 23rd arrival, loaded cargo for California. She reached San Francisco on March 15, 1922. The question of future employment of the CREOLE STATE and the WOLVERINE STATE was quickly answered. The Commissioners of the United States Shipping Board followed recommendations and in February issued orders that ports beyond Manila be dropped from the itineraries op-erated by the pair. Even Saigon became an inducement port, to be called only if the inducement of sufficient freight offered. That line was now billed the "San Francisco—Manila Direct Service (via Honolulu)." Advertisements for this new line first appeared in San Francisco newspapers on March 14th. Listed for departure from the Bay on April 21 was the CREOLE STATE. Below her name was the notation that there were to be sailings every 28 days thereafter.

The CREOLE STATE did not sail on time nor did the original trade name of the new service see long life. Weeks later local sailing lists called the line "San Francisco—Manila—Hong Kong Service (via Honolulu)". Instead of sailings every 28 days, a sailing every 35 days was now promised. Noting calls would be made at Pearl Harbor and IloIlo if inducement were sufficient, the CREOLE STATE was listed for departure to Honolulu on May 4, 1922. Shippers were advised that the ship would begin receiving cargo on April 26th and continue taking freight until 5:00 PM on May 3rd. In Washington, D.C. on April 29th, authorization was granted to change the ship's name to conform to the new "President" style of nomenclature for Shipping Board passenger ships. Word of that impending name change appeared in San

---

[4]January 31, 1922 memorandum to Chairman Albert Lasker by Secretary Clifford W. Smith. Copy in the ship's 1091 file in RG 32 at National Archives.

Francisco papers on May 1st, when both the *"Chronicle"* and *"Shipping"* listed her in sailing lists, slightly before the fact, as PRESIDENT HAYES. In parenthesis for better identification was her previous name. On May 3rd, while receiving the last of her outbound cargo, the San Francisco registered CREOLE STATE was renamed PRESIDENT HAYES. Her sister was listed in local shipping papers as WOLVERINE STATE until May 6th when she was first listed as PRESIDENT HARRISON. That ship's first sailing as PRESI-DENT HARRISON was scheduled for June 1st.

Under the command of Captain T. Fleming the PRESIDENT HAYES de-parted on her fifth trip from San Francisco with her scheduled May 4th sailing for Honolulu, Hong Kong and Manila. For the record, she called at Honolulu on May 11th, Manila on May 27th and Hong Kong on May 31st. From that Crown Colony the American ship sailed for Honolulu on June 2nd. Half a world away in Washington, D.C. the Shipping Board finally acted on concerns about the extensive operating losses turned in by the "502"'s on the Pacific. At a meeting on June 9, 1922 the Shipping Board withdrew Pacific Mail's allocation of the PRESIDENT HAYES, effective at the end of her cur-rent voyage. Completing her transPacific passage she steamed into San Fran-cisco Bay on June 27th. After landing passengers and discharging inbound cargo at the end of her only trip as a Pacific Mail "President" liner, she was redelivered to the Shipping Board. Results for that voyage had once more been as distressing as earlier forays and impending unemployment turned into the real thing. In fairness, monetary losses were not the only reason behind her withdrawal. Once Matson Line turned the "535" type sisters BUCKEYE STATE and HAWKEYE STATE back to the Shipping Board, Pa-cific Mail was granted the pleasure of operating those prestigious ships in the service between San Francisco and the Far East, a run they soon named the California Orient Line. With five big "535" type ships in their transPacific fleet, Pacific Mail didn't need the smaller "502"'s anymore, so once the Ship-ping Board began making noises about having managing operators share in operating losses as they did in profits (if any), it was not long before the Pacific Mail looked to dump the "502"'s. The Shipping Board had certainly not been pleased with the results these ships turned in on Pacific service and there are plenty of letters and memos to prove their frustration. Under their arrangements with W.R. Grace and Company, then principal owners of the Pacific Mail Steamship Company, the Shipping Board was paid only an amount equal to 5% of the gross revenues earned by a particular ship in return for a vessel's allocation. Withdrawal of the smaller "502's was hardly speculative, as they had lost oodles of money prompting Pacific Mail to instigate their withdrawal and return to the Government. Now unemployed, the PRESIDENT HAYES lay up at San Francisco to await the Shipping Board's decision about her future work.

Removal of Pacific Mail as managing operators brought quite a bit relief to several voices in Washington. No sooner had word of W.R. Grace & Com-pany's suggestion to their Pacific Mail subsidiary to get rid of the "502"'s leaked out, that a number of other shipping men willing to try their hand in the operation of these prestigious sister ships applied for allocation for their operation. Most interested were several West Coast firms who loudly proclaimed their interest in acquiring these two units, lobbying both locally and in Washington, but to no avail. Among them was an Oregon syndicate, the Columbia Pacific Steam Ship Company which eventually became the States Steamship Company.

The many insistent applications for the allocation of these ships would have to wait. The Shipping Board had learned a great deal about business in the past two years. Many independent operators had been granted favorable terms to operate Shipping Board tonnage. Very few were successful, and the returns of many of these were disgraceful. Wizened by the experience of multiple lawsuits brought to repossess their ships from bankrupt, fly-by-night companies, the Shipping Board was finally growing careful with its tonnage, exercising a new caution when time came to allocate ships. In 1921 about 100 operators ran Shipping Board tonnage. Mid 1921 brought the news that 903 Shipping Board vessels were idle and by 1922 just 39 companies still merited allocation of government-owned vessels. There was no longer any hurry to allocate these important passenger cargo vessels. Oft burned, the Shipping Board was now shy. They refused to be hurried by supplicants chanting applications for publicly owned tonnage and refused to reallocate either ship yet. Months of considerable lobbying for allocation of these capable steamers brought an operator for them in October 1922. There was no one standing around to applaud when the Shipping Board made its decision to allocate for later delivery both the PRESIDENT HAYES and the PRESIDENT HARRISON to the West Coast firm of Swayne & Hoyt. Clarification of the purpose was soon forthcoming from the Division of Operations which reported that the two ships were going to go to work on a line then referred to as the Pacific West India and East Coast of South America Line, a trade name soon mercifully shortened to Pacific-Argentine-Brazil Line. Too long at that, the service was usually referred to by its initials, "P-A-B-L". Shipping men hooted their private derision, suggesting a decision even more foolish than the idea to use them to Calcutta. The choice of operator and service was in great measure a political move, bringing additional prestige as an international trading center to the still young city of Seattle. Successor to the sporadic sailing ships and occasional steamers carrying local products to Argentina and Brasil, the Pacific-Argentine-Brazil line gave the area an alternative to the old routine of sending South America bound cargo by rail to the East Coast where it was loaded into southbound freighters. Expecting big passenger loads on the long haul line it had been managing for the past three years, Swayne & Hoyt convinced the Shipping Board to allocate a third passenger steamer to the service. That brought the addition of the Shipping Board steamer SUSQUEHANNA, a reconditioned ex-German vessel. Originally the North German Lloyd's migrant and cargo steamer

RHEIN, her postwar refit left her with a fine Cabin Class for about 150 passengers, a large Steerage capacity and roomy holds for plenty of cargo.

A leading firm in the Pacific Coast lumber trade, Swayne & Hoyt thus far enjoyed Shipping Board favor and was operating other Shipping Board services besides the Government's line linking the Pacific Northwest and California with the major ports along the East Coast of South America. New to them was the passenger trade. So far all they knew about carrying passengers was what they knew from carrying passengers along the Pacific Coast in steam schooners, small vessels whose *raison d'etre* was the carriage of lumber. Opportunity to make both a name for itself and a profit, entering the passenger trade was not without its own pitfalls. Opposition to the allocation of the sisters came from expected sources, the big established passenger carriers on the Pacific Coast. Neither the Pacific Steamship Company's Admiral Line gave any inkling of tolerating the newcomers to the Pacific passenger trade nor did Pacific Mail offer Swayne & Hoyt much support. Not yet in the passenger trade, the Dollars pretty much kept out of the squabble ensuing upon the December 10, 1922 assignment of the PRESIDENT HARRISON and the December 15th assignment of the PRESIDENT HAYES to Swayne & Hoyt. Intent on keeping the newcomers out of the passenger trade, both Admiral Line and the Pacific Mail Steamship Company dispatched their fiercest remonstrations against this perceived interruption to their business. Their complaints eventually wrought a partial victory but for the moment the Shipping Board kept mum.

At first expecting the ship to take her inaugural sailing from Seattle on January 25, 1923, Swayne & Hoyt was able to get her away a week earlier. Assigned command of the PRESIDENT HAYES was veteran Swayne & Hoyt skipper Captain K. A. Ahlin who was on the bridge when the big "502" moved from lay up. Leaving San Francisco Bay for Bellingham, Washington on January 6, 1923, the PRESIDENT HAYES arrived there and loaded lumber on the 9th. Then she shifted to Port Townsend for similar lading. Tacoma warmly welcomed her on the 11th. Already accustomed to watching the comings and goings of the bigger "535" class ships, Seattle residents may have been a bit blase when they first saw this ungainly ship steam into their harbor to dock at Connecticut Street terminal on her maiden arrival on Saturday, January 13th. While the ship loaded cargo including some 15,000 boxes of Washington State apples there, no visitors were allowed aboard nor did the ship host any receptions. Even though local residents could not get aboard to see her, the reason for her presence in port was enough to whip up local enthusiasm for the ship. Nothing proved young Seattle's growing importance in the scope of things than assignment of passenger ships to the P-A-B-L and many of her citizens were determined to show their interest. Sensing quite an opportunity in this service, several members of the local Chamber of Commerce booked passage. So did members of the Commercial Club and members of business organizations from Tacoma, Bellingham, Yakima and Everett, all of them determined to do their part to drum up enough business for their home towns and to make the service profitable. Those staying home reckoned that sailing day was as good a time as any to show their support and they did. They agreed with the Seattle *Post-Intelligencer*'s note of optimistic confidence that "the PRESIDENT HAYES will depart on an epoch making voyage in Pacific Coast shipping"[5].

Dawning cold and wet, sailing day, Wednesday, January 17, 1923, was as nasty a day as the wet Pacific Northwest can muster. Against uncertain weather punctuated by heavy rain showers and high winds, quite a big crowd gathered at the dock to give the ship an affectionate send-off when she cast off at 11:00AM with passengers and 3,000 tons of products of Washington State. First port of call for the southbound PRESIDENT HAYES was Astoria, Oregon and then San Francisco and San Pedro where she picked up more passengers and cargo. Arriving at Balboa at 10:30PM on February 6th for her first transit to the Atlantic, the liner entered the Panama Canal with 4,262 tons of general cargo on the following morning at 11:47AM. Once through the Canal at 8:45PM, her agents had her cleared an hour later on February 7th. Then the PRESIDENT HAYES set a course for Curaçao where she called on the 9th. From that Dutch island the ship diverted northward to Puerto Rico where her calls at both Ponce and San Juan, Puerto Rico provided the traveler and shipper alike a rare, first class link with both the Pacific Northwest and the River Plate. Sailing from San Juan on February 14th, it was almost a two week passage in her to Rio de Janeiro. The PRESIDENT HAYES was but a couple of days out of Rio when her sistership PRESIDENT HARRISON sailed from Seattle on February 25th on HER first trip to Argentina. In Rio on February 27th and 28th, as in ports further south, Shipping Board steamers were no longer a novelty; "535" type steamers operated by Munson Line had already made quite a good name for themselves. Nonetheless, a passenger liner coming from the West Coast of the United States was unheard of and the ship was received accordingly. Montevideo was next for the PRESIDENT HAYES on March 4th and then, finally, nearly seven weeks since leaving Seattle, the PRESIDENT HAYES made her maiden arrival at Buenos Aires on March 5, 1923. Typically, a call there was at least a week long. This one was no exception, but it lasted nearly two weeks. From Buenos Aires on the 15th, the PRESIDENT HAYES had plenty of room and time to load cargo at intermediate ports. Homewards, the itinerary included South American calls at Montevideo, Santos (for coffee) and Rio. While on that first trip, a scheduled homeward call at Bahia was abandoned on account of an outbreak of yellow fever ashore. In the Caribbean, the liner called at San Juan on her way to the Panama Canal. With 6,700 tons of cargo including refrigerated produce, linseed, coffee and fertilizer, the ship arrived at Cristobal at 11:10PM on April 11th. She worked cargo there during the next day and at 6:13AM on the 12th began her trip through the

---

[5] From the column *"Along the Waterfront"* in the January 13, 1923 issue of the *Seattle Post-Intelligencer*.

canal, emerging at the Pacific side at 3:16PM. At 1:40AM on April 14th the PRESIDENT HAYES cleared for sea on her way to the major West Coast ports of San Pedro, San Francisco, Astoria and Seattle. April 24th saw her in the port for Los Angeles for an overnight call. For points north, sailing time was 4:00PM on the 25th. San Francisco was next and the ship was there between April 28th and May 5th. There Captain Ahlin disembarked for vacation. In command of the liner when she sailed for Astoria was Captain A. Ahman. Out into the Pacific the ship rode to deliver northbound freight and mail. Inbound to Seattle from Oregon the ship arrived late in the evening of Thursday, May 10th and at 11:00PM docked at the Connecticut Street dock where her long voyage had begun four months earlier. On the following morning stevedores began off-loading the ship's inbound cargo, a load of freight notable for consignments of some 10,000 bags of coffee from Brasil, hundreds of tons of general merchandise, shipments of South American hardwood and tons of fertilizer. Notable and gratifying was a refrigerated shipment of 500 pounds of pork tenderloins shipped as an experiment at Buenos Aires. Under the watchful eye of Chief Engineer Jack Ehle, the meat arrived at Seattle in perfect condition.

While the PRESIDENT HAYES was homeward bound on her inaugural trip on the Pacific-Argentine-Brazil Line, the aged SUSQUEHANNA had sailed on April 5, 1923 from Seattle for San Francisco, Los Angeles, Panama, Rio de Janeiro, Montevideo and Buenos Aires, and a number of intermediate ports as well. That ship made only one voyage on this route and then went into lay up and was eventually scrapped in Japan after her 1928 sale to scrappers in that country.

Though their Steerage accommodations were considered a likely asset on that trade, as incomes in Latin America were quite low, such space was only marginally successful. Figures do not suggest that Third Class rendered this passenger and cargo service attractive to low income passengers and such berths in all three ships went largely unoccupied. The passenger business on this line was hardly profitable, especially since the major American passenger lines on the Pacific so vehemently opposed Swayne & Hoyt's passenger service. Indeed, considering themselves vulnerable to the newcomer's possible success, Pacific Mail took steps to make sure that Swayne & Hoyt would not draw passengers from the traditional Pacific Mail run between California and Panama while Admiral Line worked to keep Swayne & Hoyt from using the three passenger carriers from attracting custom from their magnificent fleet of coastal liners. The established players had a point, of course, and Pacific Mail's strong opposition remained steeped in a certain irony. Having been unable to make the two "502"s turn a profit on their own transPacific run, Pacific Mail was not about to permit those same ships to pull passenger traffic away from Pacific Mail's Panama route. In a Solomonic moment, the Commissioners of the Shipping Board acted in this matter during the time the PRESIDENT HAYES was on that first trip. Their solution was Solomonic in its simplicity . . . Swayne & Hoyt could carry passengers no further north

With a black funnel the PRESIDENT HAYES worked for Swayne & Hoyt on the long haul between the Pacific Northwest to Buenos Aires. Mike McGarvey photo.

than San Francisco. As things turned out it was a pretty good idea, for not only did the two "Presidents" and the SUSQUEHANNA turn in about half a dozen voyages among them, the coastal traveler could reach his destination much quicker by taking another ship on that leg. Just for comparison's sake, the fastest of the coastal liners, the H.F. ALEXANDER, easily made a speed of 25 knots, a full 10 knots more than a "502". "Galloping Ghost of the Pacific Coast", the H.F. ALEXANDER usually made the run between Seattle and San Francisco faster than the crack express train. The Swayne & Hoyt ship took several days and made at least one stop.

Homeward on her first Argentina trip, the PRESIDENT HAYES fueled rumors of the impending suspension of the Pacific-Argentine-Brazil Line service to Northeast Brasil when she omitted a northbound Bahia call. Causing concern in many quarters, the State Department got into the act to reassure all parties. Acting on advice from the United States Consul at Bahia, the Secretary of State wrote to Chairman Lasker on April 30, 1923 who answered him several days later. Noting no impending suspension of the trade, Lasker informed the Secretary that "introduction of passenger steamers resulted in a temporary dislocation of previous arrangements to handle requirements from minor ports of Brazil to our Pacific Coast. While it was not economically sound to send a passenger steamer to Bahia, the ss PRESIDENT HAYES, the first of the passenger steamers to make the voyage from the Pacific Coast to the East Coast of South America was authorized to call at Bahia, northbound, on account of the prevalence of yellow fever, however, the call was not made." Continuing, Lasker wrote:

> It has not been planned to entirely withdraw large steamers from the trade, and until it is definitely determined by experience what cargo steamers will be required, two of those which have heretofore been employed in the trade will be retained in the service. The requirements of space in the steamers southbound for minor ports in Brazil are negligible, and for a while at least the cargo steamers will proceed to the East Coast of South America via the Straits of Magellan, making calls northbound on the homeward voyage via the Panama Canal. There is no reason for shippers to be disturbed, and we shall be glad if the Consul of the United States at Bahia will be good enough to let it be known to the shippers at that port that our service of cargo steamers has not been abandoned.[6]

After discharging her first inbound cargo, the PRESIDENT HAYES shifted to the nearby port of Everett to take on a big shipment of lumber and a hefty load of canned salmon. Then it was back to Seattle to load additional freight like apples before sailing from the East Waterway Terminal. Before sailing for her second South America trip refrigerating engineers assisted by local workmen made extensive repairs to the ship's refrigeration equipment.

---

[6]May 4, 1923 from Shipping Board Chairman Albert Lasker to Sec'y of State. A copy in the ship's 1091 file in RG 32, National Archives.

Captain Ahlin returned from vacation and resumed command of the ship[7]. After loading the rest of an outbound freight including one million board feet of lumber, a heavy shipment of canned salmon and 2,000 tons of general cargo including both light and heavy American machinery consigned to both Brasil and Argentina, the PRESIDENT HAYES shifted to Tacoma on Saturday May 13th. She sailed out on the following day. Southbound, the ship's port calls included a five day stay at Astoria and three days at San Francisco before she sailed on May 25th with cargo and passengers for the East Coast of South America. Uneventful and little chronicled was her passage out. With a July 20th call, the PRESIDENT HAYES was one of the first and only, American passenger carriers to appear at the Argentine port of Bahía Blanca. Entering Buenos Aires to load for the homeward trip, the PRESIDENT HAYES seriously damaged a propellor forcing her to put back to Bahía Blanca. Not sailing from there until July 24th, she missed her planned July 28th sailing from Buenos Aires and she got away on August 1st. Northbound, the ship called once again at Montevideo, Santos and Rio de Janeiro from whence she sailed on August 9th. After a direct sailing for Panama, the ship arrived at Cristobal on August 23rd. Northbound she put into Manzanillo, Mexico on August 28th and on September 4th steamed into San Francisco Bay. After the ship tied up and the ship was cleared by local authorities, all remaining passengers disembarked. Then the ship continued on to Astoria and Seattle where September 12th saw her tied up at East Waterway Dock.

The PRESIDENT HAYES was soon ready to began her third and last trip on the South America line from the usual Pacific Coast ports. With her sale to private interests not yet closed, the PRESIDENT HAYES began her last voyage on the Pacific-Argentine-Brazil Line, sailing from Seattle under the command of Captain Ahman at 6:00PM on Tuesday, September 18, 1923. Astoria and Portland were next, the former on the 19th, Portland on the 21st. The PRESIDENT HAYES sailed into San Francisco on the 25th, the actual day of her sale to Dollar Line. Indicative of the high cost of doing business on the line, and effective with that sailing, Swayne & Hoyt had raised passage fares between San Francisco and Buenos Aires by $15.00. Two days later, on September 27, 1923, cargo was loaded at San Pedro and then she began her passage to the Panama Canal. Bound for Balboa, Cristobal, Ponce, San Juan, Rio de Janeiro, Montevideo and Buenos Aires were 40 Cabin and 7 Third Class passengers and 5,109 long tons of cargo including 1,492,045 board feet of lumber, but no mail. Against revenues of $50,304.77, estimated outward expenses of some $80,000.00 assured a heavy loss. October 10th saw her making a regular call at Ponce, Puerto Rico and then it was on to San Juan from whence she sailed on the 16th. After a twelve day passage, the

---

[7] Here primary sources run into conflict because Captain Ahlin was also listed as Master of the PRESIDENT HARRISON at about the same time, suggesting he did not take the PRESIDENT HAYES all the way to South America on that voyage, transferring at some point to the other ship.

PRESIDENT HAYES was at Rio on her way to Buenos Aires where the outbound voyage ended on November 2nd. After discharging lumber and general cargo there, she loaded hides and assorted Argentine goods before taking on a few passengers for her final sailing from Buenos Aires on November 11, 1923. Calling northbound at Montevideo, Santos, Rio and San Juan, the PRESIDENT HAYES once again crossed the Caribbean for the Panama Canal and the trip north to the United States. Calling at San Pedro on December 14th and San Francisco on the 16th, she ended her career of three roundtrips on the Pacific-Argentine-Brazil Line.

Sale of the "502"s to the Dollar Line came at a good time for the financially strapped passenger ships on the Pacific Northwest—East Coast of South America passenger service. Other than the few passenger voyages made by these three ships, under their operation, Swayne & Hoyt remained wisely disinterested in the development of the passenger trade. In fact, they retained management of the Pacific-Argentine-Brazil Line only until 1926 when the United States Shipping Board sold the Line to McCormick & Company of San Francisco. When McCormick liquidated its assets in 1938 the line passed under the control of Pope & Talbot Lines. Moore-McCormack Lines bought the line in 1939 and renamed it Pacific Republics Line. Swayne & Hoyt concentrated for the most part on the development of its lumber trade and its intercoastal routes linking the West Coast and the Gulf of Mexico.

With her January 15th delivery to private owners in the offing, now was a busy time. In exchange for a $1,000.00 fee, the Bill of Sale was completed on December 27, 1923. Relieved of her valuable scrap metal ballast after her

Open at its after end the Veranda Cafe was very popular both night and day. Author's collection.

Slightly lighter in its execution was the Smoking Room
aboard the PRESIDENT HAYES. Author's collection.

delivery to Dollar Line, the ship was prepared to take her place on the new
round the world line. Making a quick run to San Pedro to load cargo the
PRESIDENT HAYES sailed south on January 27, 1924. After a two night call
the ship returned to her home port, arriving at San Francisco on January 31st
and remaining long enough to embark passengers and load the last of her
cargo. On the bridge again was Captain Ahman. With the ship's February
2, 1924 departure from San Francisco, the PRESIDENT HAYES began her
work on the round the world service. For the first time since the end of her
Pacific Mail days she returned to Hawaii, calling at Honolulu on February
9th. The small teething troubles experienced by the PRESIDENT HARRISON
on her historic inaugural voyage were apparently not visited upon the PRES-
IDENT HAYES but of course, she met little of the fanfare which greeted the
calls of the first ship. Making her first circuit around the world, the PRESI-
DENT HAYES arrived at Kobe for an overnight call on February 21st, Shanghai on February 26th, Hong Kong on March 4th, Manila on March 6th and
Singapore on March 12th. Next was Penang, which she called on March 16th.
Then it was on to Colombo for a March 21st call. Suez on March 31st saw
the "502" make her first appearance in the Mediterranean and an April 7th
sailing from Genoa for Marseilles and an April 9th departure for home. Completing her first Atlantic crossing, the PRESIDENT HAYES made Boston on
April 22nd before arriving at New York on April 25, 1924.

About a week later on May 1st the PRESIDENT HAYES sailed for Havana. Outbound from New York she was on voyage 2, but because of the
nature of her whereabouts when she entered service her first voyage from
San Francisco had yet to be completed. After arriving at Cristobal at 3:10AM

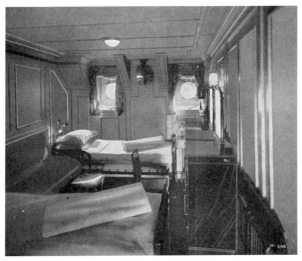

One of the large, comfortable Saloon Deck cabins.
Author's collection.

on May 9th she entered the canal at 8:33AM. Not quite seven hours later at 3:24PM the ship completed her first transit of the Canal as a privately owned ship. With 1,790 tons of general cargo the 12,023 gross and 8,443 net ton (by Panama Canal rules) vessel cleared for sea at 8:34PM and sailed that evening for California. It took ten days for the ship to reach San Pedro where she arrived on May 18th. Completing her first circumnavigation of the globe, the somewhat overlooked second round the world liner returned to San Francisco on May 22nd. There Voyage 1 was officially completed and voyage 2 from there began.

May 24th was sailing day. A generally uneventful voyage, the ship reached her accustomed ports in usual sequence, making Kobe on June 13th, Singapore on July 2nd and New York on August 15th.

There was enough left of 1924 for another complete circuit of the globe. The liner sailed from New York on voyage 3 on August 21st and from San Francisco on September 13th. A notation on San Francisco Marine Exchange card number 5 for her shows the names of three men who commanded her that year. Scratched out was the name of Captain Ahman who was relieved by Captain Blain. Another notation on that card records a 6:10 AM and a 10:00PM September 20th call at Honolulu. Voyage highlights were calls at Kobe in early October, at Manila in the middle of that month and at Alexandria, Egypt on November 11th and at Genoa for New York on the 17th. When the PRESIDENT HAYES left New York again to begin voyage 4 on December 11th, Captain P.E. Anderson was her Master. On the last day of the year the ship sailed from San Pedro for San Francisco.

Dollar Line's second "502" steamed into San Francisco on New Year's

Day 1925. She sailed from there on voyage 4 on January 3rd. That time there was a January 23rd arrival at Kobe, a January 27th arrival at Shanghai, a Penang call on February 14th, an Alexandria visit on March 4th and a crossing beginning at Marseilles on March 10th. Two weeks later on March 24th the PRESIDENT HAYES sailed into Boston and on the 26th of March the ship reached New York and docked once more at her Brooklyn pier.

The ship sailed from New York on April 2, 1925 on voyage 5. Outbound from San Francisco that time the ship sailed on April 25th. Out from Kobe on May 16th the ship's propellors beat the water pushing the ship along on her appointed route. On the 26th of that month the PRESIDENT HAYES sailed from Hong Kong for Manila. She sailed from Colombo on June 11th for Suez. From Marseilles the homeward crossing began with the ship's July 1st sailing. After a Boston call the ship steamed into New York to complete her voyage from there after her July 16th arrival.

Sailing for her sixth trip around the world the PRESIDENT HAYES cast off from Brooklyn on July 23rd and from Pier 42 at San Francisco on August 15th. September 8th was sailing day from Shanghai and on October 1st the ship sailed out of Colombo on her way to the Mediterranean. Through the Suez Canal on October 14th the ship made once again for Italy. She sailed from Genoa on October 20th and on the next day cleared Marseilles for Boston and New York, where she arrived on November 6th.

Voyage 7 took her out on a November 12th sailing for Havana and a December 5th departure from San Francisco to Honolulu. At New Year's Day 1926 Captain Anderson greeted his passengers and crew, spreading his best wishes for the new year for all onboard. They sailed from Hong Kong on January 5, 1926. Further movements of the PRESIDENT HAYES that season included her March 4, 1926 departure from New York on voyage 8.

Protected from the tropical sun by covered deck passengers aboard the PRESIDENT HAYES spent many enjoyable hours outdoors. Author's collection.

"The food's good" was the consensus of Dollar Line passengers. Author's collection.

Before sailing again from San Francisco, Captain J.J. Cadogan relieved Captain Anderson and the ship sailed out past the Golden Gate on March 27th and Hong Kong on April 25th. It was another generally uneventful trip until she reached Italian waters. Leaving Genoa for Marseilles on June 2, 1926 the PRESIDENT HAYES collided with the Italian passenger liner PRINCIPESSA MAFALDA. It was but one of many appearances the American liner made in casualty lists over the years but the PRINCIPESSA MAFALDA, sister of the PRINCIPESSA JOLANDA which earned eternal fame for capsizing on launching, went to her doom just over a year later after crashing on Abrolhos Rock off Bahia, Brasil on October 25, 1927. With a horrifying death toll of over 300, she remains a favorite of "disaster ship" buffs. But in her accident with the PRESIDENT HAYES she suffered no damage as did the American ship which arrived back at New York on June 17th. Captain Cadogan retained command and the esteem of his employers. The ship sailed out from New York on voyage 9 on June 24th and from San Francisco on July 17, 1926. Voyage 10 took her out on an October 14th sailing from New York and a November 6th departure from San Francisco.

Her American flag did not always protect either herself or her passengers. Now on voyage 11, the PRESIDENT HAYES took her last departure from Dollar Line's Brooklyn piers, sailing from New York on February 3, 1927. From San Francisco on February 26th the ship had an uneventful Pacific crossing. After her Kobe call the liner was docking at Shanghai on March 24, 1927 when bullets believed shot from the Chinese quarter but fired from hands unknown riddled her with bullets. Though none of her 58 passengers nor any of her crew was hurt, who can deny that all returned with stories to excite the imagination of countless grandchildren? Without further incident the ship worked her way west to her usual ports, calling at Hong Kong on March 29th, Manila on an overnight call on March 31st, Singapore on

S. S. "PRESIDENT HAYES"

J. J. CADOGAN, COMMANDER.

BREAKFAST

California Grapefruit   Sliced Oranges
Sliced Banans   Iced Papia   Stewed Apricots

Corn Flakes   Wheat Hearts   Grape Nuts
All Bran   Force   Shredded Wheat
Puffed Rice   Boiled Rice

Fried Pan Fish Maitre d' Hotel
Cod Fish Tongues & Sounds en Cream
Southern Beef Hash Family Style
(TO ORDER.—FROM THE GRILL—TEN MINUTES)
Grilled Pork Chops Straw Potatoes
(EGGS TO ORDER)
Boiled, Shirred, Scrambled, Poached, Turned, & Fried.
OMELETTES:— Plain Minced Chicken Cheese Brains

Broiled Ham   Grilled Breakfast Bacon

POTATOES:— French Fried   Boiled

COLD MEATS
Roast Beef   Head Cheese   Smoked Salmon

Wheat Cakes with Honey or Maple Syrup

Dry and Buttered Toast   Napkin Rolls

Asst Jams   Marmalade   Jelly

Tea   Postum   Coffee   Cocoa

F. C. Rood, Chief Steward.   Monday, Sept. 1st, 1930.

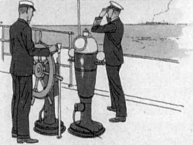

A STEAMER passes on the horizon, and you wonder how far away she is. Visibility at sea varies according to atmospheric conditions, but on clear days a passing steamer is visible for about ten miles from the promenade deck. From the flying bridge, due to its height, the vessel can be seen eighteen miles away.

No matter where in the world a "502" went, a hearty American breakfast awaited her passengers. Author's collection.

April 7th, Penang on the 8th and Colombo on April 13th. Two weeks later the American liner reached the Suez Canal on her way to the Mediterranean. Otherwise it was a routine trip and the liner departed New York again to start voyage 12 on May 19th. She was not back until September. Heavy weather during the voyage westward once more took a toll on the ship, carrying away sections of her railings, breaking several ports, but worse, damaging the liner's steam steering gear. Passengers were slightly inconvenienced when water streaming in through broken port holes seeped into the Dining Saloon. Undaunted the ship steamed on, sailing on voyage 13 from New York on September 15th, making other appearances in casualty lists that autumn. First was a small fire that broke out in refrigerated cargo space while the ship was off the Pacific coast of Mexico on September 29th. The blaze was enough to force her to put into nearby Manzanillo where the fire was extinguished. Damage was slight and the ship continued on her way to Los Angeles and an October 3rd arrival. Continuing her outbound voyage, the steamer sailed from San Francisco on October 8th. At Woosung during a Shanghai call on November 1, the liner went aground. The ship was quickly refloated and divers were sent down to have a look at her below the waterline. They discovered that the impact of the grounding had broken off about a quarter of a blade of the starboard propellor and badly distorted and bent a blade on her port prop. Authorities issued her a certificate of seaworthiness and she proceeded to Hong Kong for repairs. More bad news was in store. The Atlantic was very rough and on her homeward crossing the PRESIDENT HAYES suffered heavy weather damage as well as damages to her steam powered steering gear. After the ship reached New York on December 29, 1927 workmen got busy putting it all right, replacing rails swept into the sea, fixing broken ports and replacing broken glass while others steam cleaned water damaged rugs.

If the results of the ship's trials over the past year was deemed of little, if any, interest to a general public both used to ship news of that nature, or thoroughly disinterested in shipping news, New Years' Day 1928 brought the ship's name before the public again. Dollar Line was still digesting the costs to put right further damage the ship had suffered on her crossing to New York. All was in tip top shape when the PRESIDENT HAYES departed New York without passengers for Boston on December 31, 1927. She had hardly been underway for an hour when she collided in Ambrose Channel with the British freighter TARANTIA, damaging herself. At first things looked bad enough to force the liner to require a tow back to her Jersey City pier. Actually, the "502" simply anchored off Robbins Point to await the results of a survey of the damage. January 1st was of course a holiday, so no inspection was done that day. Dollar Line waited for the next morning for experts to survey the extent of the damage suffered. Inspection revealed nothing worse than some dented plates on starboard. Unconcerned by those dents, inspectors declared the vessel seaworthy enough to proceed on her way. Now two days behind schedule the PRESIDENT HAYES steamed out of New York on January 2, 1928 for Boston. There the last of her inward cargo was offloaded after her January 3rd arrival.

Again uneventful was the following voyage. From New York again on January 5th the PRESIDENT HAYES sailed for her ports around the world. She made a Havana call on the 9th and went through the Canal on January 15th on her way to California, where her outbound sailing from San Francisco was on January 27th. On her next voyage that year the PRESIDENT HAYES had some unusual guests among her passengers. Sailing with her from San Francisco on May 18th was a student group. Accompanying them on their world cruise were instructors who offered extensive courses of study highlighting history, art and cultures of the countries visited. Two other student parties went out that year in Dollar Line "502"s, one group went in the PRESIDENT ADAMS, the other in the PRESIDENT POLK. The PRESIDENT HAYES began her next trip, her 16th sailing from New York, with her April 26th departure. Uncertain is the date when Captain Orel Pierson replaced Captain Cadogan on the bridge of the PRESIDENT HAYES, but he did so that year. Cadogan came back to the ship in 1930. After circling the globe and doing her quick Boston side trip, the PRESIDENT HAYES began another voyage from New York with her August 16th sailing from New York. Completing that trip in December, the liner found herself at her home port, San Francisco on Christmas Day, 1928. There, many members of her crew had a day off and were able for a change to spend the holiday with family, a rare treat for a seaman.

Shortly after sailing from New York for Boston on November 29, 1928 a mishap to her steering gear delayed her until December 1st. After she docked she discharged the 1,000 some-odd tons consigned there and sailed back to New York to load for her next outbound sailing.

While the PRESIDENT HAYES and her sisters steamed their way around the world that year, and without any specific thoughts of the hard-working "502"s, Congress passed a new merchant marine law in 1928. Known for its authors and always referred to as the Jones-White Act, it gave American steamship companies the opportunity to win mail contracts and to renew their fleets through construction loans. When Dollar Line took advantage of new financing possibilities to order sumptuous new flagships, they also took out loans to improve some of the "502"s. The PRESIDENT van BUREN might have been one of four sisters to be so treated, but when the time to improve the ships came around, financial circumstances couldn't permit so ambitious a plan and only three were rebuilt. Because the PRESIDENT HAYES and PRESIDENT MONROE were to work on a new service, there was no plan to upgrade the accommodations in these ships. Partly to upgrade the round the world line during the absence of three sister "502"s, the company bought the MANCHURIA and MONGOLIA, prepared them for and attached them to the line. The company also extended the transPacific service to New York and assigned a couple of the bigger "502"s to it. A couple of "535"s were also assigned to the round the world service that year.

Those ships gave the Dollars the chance to send a pair of unimproved "502"s to try their luck on a new line to Manila.

As 1928 gave way to 1929 the PRESIDENT HAYES was plodding on her usual world service, crossing the Pacific on her way to Kobe, from whence she sailed after working cargo and handling passengers on January 18th. February 4th saw her at Singapore and she sailed away on the 7th. Into the Mediterranean on the 26th, she departed Marseilles on March 5th for New York and Boston. That voyage completed, she sailed from New York on March 20, 1929 for San Francisco on yet another round the world trip. The ship sailed from San Francisco on April 19, 1929 for Kobe, Shanghai, Hong Kong, Manila, Singapore, Penang, Colombo, Suez, Alexandria, Naples, Genoa and Marseilles, from whence she sailed in late June for New York and a July 18th arrival.

Withdrawn from the round the world service in August 1929, the PRESIDENT HAYES left the East Coast with an August 12th sailing for Havana. In from the last of her round the world sailings, the ship arrived at San Francisco on August 23, 1929. She began her new job when she sailed for Manila on September 4th. Via Honolulu on September 11th, the ship reached her destination on September 27th. The PRESIDENT MONROE joined the new run from San Francisco in late September. Hong Kong was on the eastbound itinerary and from there the PRESIDENT HAYES sailed on October 2nd for Honolulu. After her October 16th call there the liner set her course for the West Coast. Docking on October 23, 1929 at Pier 44 at San Francisco at the end of that first Manila trip, the PRESIDENT HAYES struck the pierhead, damaging the shed, and scratching her own bow. Damage was too slight to much delay the ship's October 24th sailing for San Pedro. Overnighting there, the "502" sailed on the 25th on her way back to San Francisco and an October 29th sailing on her second Manila voyage. After the ship's November 21st sailing from Manila, the ship made for Singapore where she loaded rubber. Then it was back to Manila for a December 5th sailing for San Francisco where she arrived on December 28th. Another quick Los Angeles trip followed with the ship's December 31st southbound sailing.

The ship sailed on her third Manila trip with her January 7, 1930 departure from San Francisco. Ports that time included Honolulu, Manila and Singapore. As usual there was a homeward Honolulu call and on March 8, 1930 the PRESIDENT HAYES steamed back into San Francisco. The Los Angeles side trip completed with the ship's March 15th return to her home port, the ship was ready to top off her holds and sail on her fourth Manila trip on March 18th. Across the Pacific the ship arrived at Manila on April 10th and at Singapore on the 18th to begin a three day call. Sailing for home the ship left Manila on April 24th. Via Honolulu as always, that time the ship reached San Francisco on May 16th. So she continued without diverging from that routine itinerary until her seventh Manila voyage. With her August 5, 1930 sailing the PRESIDENT HAYES made for Honolulu and Guam, where she called August 22nd on her way to Manila to arrive on August 28th. After her allotted stay there the ship steamed on to Singapore before heading back across the Pacific on her way to California and an October 3rd arrival at San Francisco. A Guam call was again a feature of her eighth trip on this Manila run. That time the PRESIDENT HAYES departed San Francisco on October 14, 1930, making her Honolulu call on October 21st, Guam on November 1st and arriving at Manila on November 6th. Singapore was next with another three day call there through November 13th. Outbound from Manila on November 20th the ship called Honolulu on December 5th to arrive at San Francisco on December 12th. That was the end of her career on the Manila line. During that year three men had commanded the ship. Captain Pierson was still aboard as the year began. Relieved for a while by Captain Cadogan, Captain Makepiece Ridley took command of the PRESIDENT HAYES sometime later that year.

Captain Ridley took the ship out on a round the world itinerary with the ship's December 26, 1930 departure from San Francisco. The ship made news about a month later. That time this "502" stopped at Honolulu on January 2, 1931, Kobe on January 15th and arrived at Shanghai on January 19th. Passing Amoy island while outbound from Shanghai to Hong Kong during the early morning hours of January 24, 1931, the PRESIDENT HAYES found herself steaming in fog. Besides her crew, about a hundred passengers were aboard. Visibility low, she grazed the portside of the 3,341 net ton British flag steamer KUMSANG. Both ships came away slightly damaged. Into Amoy steamed the KUMSANG as the PRESIDENT HAYES worked her way to Hong Kong harbor. Damage to the "President" included a dented forecastle, damage to Promenade Deck and Upper Promenade Deck midships. None of this at all affected her performance at sea, so surveyors allowed her to proceed, giving the Dollar Line permission to arrange repairs at their convenience. The American ship continued on her way to Manila, Singapore, Penang, Colombo and Suez. February 23rd saw her at Alexandria and on March 17, 1931 the PRESIDENT HAYES arrived at New York. After a two day call she left for a side trip to Boston.

The PRESIDENT HAYES had not taken a round the world sailing from New York since August 10, 1929. With the coming of spring the PRESIDENT HAYES sailed from Boston for a round the world sailing on March 21, 1931. That trip continued with her April 17, 1931 sailing from San Francisco.

On her next visit to the East Coast there were none but her crew of 165 aboard when the PRESIDENT HAYES sailed from New York on July 10th for Boston on her customary "side trip" to handle cargo. That evening found her steaming through dense fog on her way into Boston. In one of three accidents suffered by a "502" in Massachussetts waters, the PRESIDENT HAYES stranded on Monomoy Point at Shovelfull Shoals near the entrance of Nantucket Sound. Resting easily on sand, the ship was not considered to be in danger and her Master, Captain A. Orel Pierson, declined offers of assistance, believing the ship would be able to free herself in the evening tide. She wasn't and on the following morning, she tried to free herself on high tide, with thoughts of discharging cargo into lighters an option. Not until 9:30 PM on the 12th, with the help of salvage tugs RELIEF and COURAGE supplied by the famed salvage firm of Merrit Chapman was there any positive movement. Divers took to the water to inspect the hull. Luckily, damage was not significant enough to delay the ship further. She was not leaking nor were any plates broken. That evening the PRESIDENT HAYES floated free. She put back into Boston for survey but repairs were deferred until after the ship's San Francisco arrival. To expedite departure of the liner's passengers, Dollar Line bought train tickets from New York to Boston for some hundred passengers and procured and paid for hotel rooms for them in Boston where they awaited the departure of the repaired steamer. From New England waters the PRESIDENT HAYES came into New York to work cargo on July 17th. A few days later she was ready to sail southwards again and cast off for Havana on July 20th. After arriving at San Francisco on August 6th the ship was drydocked for repairs at a cost of $5,336.00. The liner continued her voyage with her August 7th sailing from San Francisco for Honolulu. That voyage took her through late October when she steamed into New York from the Mediterranean.

Sailing from New York again on November 5th and from San Francisco on November 27th, the PRESIDENT HAYES closed out the year of 1931 in East Asian waters, sailing from Kobe on December 19th for Shanghai, Hong Kong, Manila, Singapore, Penang and her other ports. As the calendar turned, the ship was at sea between Manila and Singapore where she arrived on January 2, 1932. After her two night call the ship sailed for Penang on time on January 4, 1932.

There was a new port for the ship that time. That was Bombay and the PRESIDENT HAYES reached port on May 5th after a three night run from Colombo. From now on, after departure from Ceylon the ship would sail north to Bombay for a twenty-four hour call before heading for Suez, ten days away at 14 knots.

Still under the command of Captain Orel Pierson, another routine voyage was to follow her June 16, 1932 sailing from New York. She went through the Panama Canal on the 24th and arrived at Los Angeles on July 3rd. The voyage continued with her July 8th sailing from San Francisco. Across the ocean the PRESIDENT HAYES sailed on July 29th from Kobe and on August 17th from Singapore on her way to Penang and Colombo.

On her final voyage of 1932 the PRESIDENT HAYES sailed from Kobe on November 18, Shanghai on November 23, Hong Kong on November 27th, Manila on November 30th, Singapore on December 6th, Penang on December 8th, Colombo on December 12th, Bombay on December 16th and made her passage through the Suez Canal on December 26th. At Naples on New Year's Eve, she sailed on January 1, 1933 for Genoa and Marseilles, arriving at New York twelve days later.

It's July 13, 1929 and the PRESIDENT HAYES has her picture taken. William B.
Taylor photo. Eric Johnson collection.

Mid spring of that year saw the PRESIDENT HAYES begin voyage 34[8]
at New York. In command was a new man, Captain D.D. Waldron, who
came aboard to relieve a vacationing Captain Pierson. The "502" sailed out
on May 18th for her usual ports. On May 26th the ship took her passengers
and the 3,218 tons of general cargo stowed in her many holds through the
Panama Canal. After a sunny run up the Pacific Coast of Central America
and Mexico, the PRESIDENT HAYES reached Los Angeles on June 4th. After
an overnight call at her San Pedro berth the ship steamed north to her San
Francisco home port. On the way to Hawaii and Japan, the ship sailed on
June 9th. Across the Pacific the ship arrived at Kobe on June 29th. After an
overnight call she departed Shanghai on a festive July 4th and arrived Suez
on schedule on August 7th. Summer in the Mediterranean is always popular
and she was at Genoa on August 14th in time to take part in the annual
homeward migration of Americans whose European journeys had to end
around Labor Day. She sailed from there on the 15th and from Marseilles
on August 16th to arrive at New York on August 29th. Two days later came
the Boston sidetrip where Voyage 35[9] technically began. After returning to

---

[8] That's how Dollar Line numbered the trip . . . don't ask ME how the PRESIDENT HAYES
could be on Voyage 34 and her sister, which had entered the round the world service a few
weeks earlier could be several voyages behind her. Think Manila run!

[9] Somewhere along the line Dollar Steamship Lines decided to number round the world voyages
from Boston. Adding a delicious confusion to these ships forever, most company and all government paperwork in connection with the ships continued to note voyage beginnings and
endings from both New York and San Francisco.

K.L. Speer thought the PRESIDENT HAYES worth a shot in this 1932 view. Eric Johnson collection.

the Hudson on September 4th there were three more days before the voyage continued.

The ship sailed from New York on September 7th for Havana and Panama. She took the shortcut between the seas on September 15th with 3,121 tons of cargo in her holds. On the 26th she arrived at San Francisco where she remained until it was time to sail out again at 5:00PM on Saturday, September 29th. Like clockwork the PRESIDENT HAYES sailed on October 20th from Kobe. Departures from principal ports that time included her October 30th sailing from Manila, her November 17th sailing from Bombay, and her November 28th transit of the Suez Canal. By December 2nd the ship was in Italy and from the French Mediterranean port of Marseilles began her Atlantic crossing on December 6th. The trip was routine enough for a winter North Atlantic crossing but the ship suffered engine trouble severe enough to delay her by a few hours and to bring the ship's name into the casualty lists. After her December 19, 1933 arrival at New York she was quickly repaired because she had a schedule so tight that nothing as serious as a Depression could keep her from her appointments. The ship was able to keep it and was at Boston to unload a meager cargo on December 26th as well as begin Voyage 36, another regular round the world trip from New York on December 29th 1933.

The worst year of the Depression was at hand, though with 3,610 tons of cargo aboard during the January 5, 1934 Panama Canal transit things didn't look too bad just then for this ship. The PRESIDENT HAYES sailed from San Pedro on January 15, 1934 for San Francisco and her January 19th outbound sailing. She sailed from Kobe on February 9th, from Singapore on February 27th and from Bombay on March 9th. The Atlantic portion of that voyage began with her March 28th sailing from Marseilles for an April 10, 1934 New York arrival. On her following sailing, she cleared New York at the beginning of Voyage 37 on April 19th. It may have been coincidence or it may have been the continuing economic slump, but when the ship transited the Panama Canal on that trip she had only 2,536 tons of cargo. After the customary Los Angeles call overnight between May 6 and 7th, the ship sailed up to San Francisco. Arriving there on May 8th, she was at Pier 42 on May 9th when workmen through out the maritime industry walked off their jobs. Scheduled to sail from San Francisco on May 11th, the PRESIDENT HAYES was delayed by a hesitant crew. Luckily the ship got away on May 12th before the strike paralyzed shipping up and down the West Coast for 83 days between May and the end of July.. Across the Pacific she sailed on June 1, 1934 from Kobe. On the 29th of that month she was at Bombay and was able to bring Voyage 37 to an uneventful end at New York a few days behind schedule on August 3rd, a few days after the strike was settled. So far from the scene of hottest conflict, the ship managed to work her way around the world, little effected by the hostility that brought death to the San Francisco waterfront. The only thing that gave outsiders a hint of trouble was that the ship arrived at New York on a Friday instead of Tuesday. To get the ship back on schedule the Boston/New York loop was shortened. When the ship transited the Panama Canal with 3,090 tons of general cargo in her holds on Voyage 38 on August 13th she was again on schedule. Her voyage continued on schedule and by September 21st she was ready to sail on the tide from Kobe. From Singapore on October 9th and from Bombay on October 19th the ship worked her usual itinerary to reach Marseilles on November 7th.

Even though that strike was long settled, when the PRESIDENT HAYES arrived back at New York on November 21st from Marseilles after that following trip, there was some question of whether or not her crew would walk out. They didn't and the ship worked her inbound cargo, steamed up to Boston to work cargo for and from that port, and was back at New York again on November 29th. Sailing from New York on Voyage 39 on December 2, 1934, she arrived at San Francisco on December 18th and sailed on December 21st for Honolulu where she made a December 28, 1934 call. Not even the tropic Hawaiian sun could have served to let the crew know that the PRESIDENT HAYES left the worst year of the Depression behind. Into a new year the ship sailed from Kobe on January 11, 1935. Shanghai, Hong Kong and Manila were on the way to Singapore where the PRESIDENT HAYES arrived on January 26th. After her three day call the ship steamed on to Penang on her way to Colombo and Bombay.

Money tight, rules, regulations and safety laws impelled the Dollar Line to continue maintenance programs and regular drydockings. Out of the water in a San Francisco drydock in mid April 1935, inspectors found the ship's hull very heavily encrusted with marine growth. Assorted ocean biota removed, some 10,000 square feet of the hull on both sides abaft of midships was scaled and painted before the ship was redelivered to her owners.

From Kobe on May 3, 1935, the PRESIDENT HAYES steamed on, her propellers beating their path through Asia to the Suez Canal. After passing Port Said on June 10th, her crew could finally feel like they were on their way home. Naples was on the 15th, Genoa on the 17th and then overnight at Marseilles before sailing for New York on June 19th. From San Francisco the voyage continued with her outbound sailing on August 2nd. Last of her round the world trips for 1935 saw her sail from New York again on November 1st. Between December 13th and 28th, 1935 the PRESIDENT HAYES worked her way from Kobe, Shanghai, Hong Kong, Manila, Singapore and Penang on her long trip around the world.

The PRESIDENT HAYES greeted 1936 with a Penang arrival on January 1st. Sailing the next day, it took her four days to reach her next port, Colombo. Bombay was next and after her January 10th sailing, she set her course for Suez. Across the Atlantic the ship reached New York on a cold February 13th. After a night in port, it was time to head back to Boston and then on February 14th the ship sailed from New York again on another trip around the world.

The PRESIDENT HAYES took the line's June 1, 1936 sailing from New York, reaching Los Angeles on June 28th after calling at her usual intercoastal ports. It was a voyage that gave her the notoriety only American labor unions of the 1930's seemed able to bring. Between Honolulu and Kobe, from whence the ship continued her voyage on July 24th, dissent broke out. Worse was to come before the ship reached Singapore when a minor incident between two relatively unimportant players in the engine department brought the ship to a near standstill. Consular documents tell the story of how self injurious American union men could be in the volatile 1930's.

American Consulate General,
Singapore, S.S., August 15, 1936.

Memorandum: Dispute Between Master and Crew of S.S. PRESIDENT HAYES.

On August 10, 1936, at about 9:15 a.m. Patrick J. Doyle and Andrew Richelsen, seamen of the S.S. PRESIDENT HAYES, appeared at the Consulate General and reported that as a result of a dispute with the officers, the entire engine room section, deck section, and steward's section of the crew, exclusive of the Chinese members, had stopped work. During the interview there appeared Captain O. A. Pierson of the S.S. PRESIDENT HAYES and B. R. Bates, local manager of the Dollar Steamship Lines, who confirmed the statement of Doyle and Richelsen. In the circumstances a hearing was set for 11 a.m., the earliest hour at which it was considered feasible to produce the witnesses.

The facts of the dispute according to the oral statements of the appearing witnesses were substantially as follows: During the 12 o'clock watch on August 7, 1936, while the S.S. PRESIDENT HAYES was at sea, a dispute,arose in the engine room between Carl West, an oiler, and T. B. Frink, a junior engineer. West had come on watch without an oil can. After sharing one with the other oiler on watch for some time, he asked Frink to get him a can or send him a relief in order that he might get the can himself. Frink said he would not get a can and told West to get it himself, allegedly making use of an obscene expression in giving the order. West thereupon refused to leave the engine room unless a man was sent to relieve him. During the ensuing argument West replied to Frink in the same sort of language, saying that if he did not receive an oil can or a relief by 1:30 p.m. he would quit work. At 1:30 p.m. he left the engine room and went on deck. Frink reported the matter to H. Norman, the first assistant engineer, who asked West for an explanation. West said that he objected to the language and manner in which he had been addressed by Frink, and refused to obey the order of Richard Pedersen, the Chief Engineer, to return to duty. As a consequence West was disrated to fireman, and an oiler on another watch volunteered to finish West's watch. John D'Antone, a fireman, was subsequently promoted to oiler and assigned to West's former Position.

Later in the day a delegation from the crew interviewed the Master, stating that in the opinion of the crew West was in the right, that it would be dangerous for D'Antone, who was not an experienced oiler, to try to do West's work, and that West should be reinstated. The Master refused, stating that in the interests of maintaining discipline aboard his ship he concurred in the action taken against a man who had flatly refused to perform duty and that, in the opinion of the Chief Engineer, D'Antone was quite capable of performing the duties of oiler without endangering any person or machinery. The delegates said the subject would be reopened in Singapore.

The S.S. PRESIDENT HAYES arrived at Singapore on August 8, 1936, at 7:00 a.m. and was scheduled to sail at noon on August 11. The members of the crew performed their duties as usual until after breakfast on the morning of August 10, when the delegates renewed their discussion with the Master, again demanding that West be reinstated as oiler. The Master refused once more, and the delegation thereupon stated that the engine room section, the deck section, and the steward's action would quit work until West should be reinstated, and at about 8:30 a.m. these three sections, comprising 68 members of the crew, stopped work.

As a counter measure the Master then ordered that no meals should be served to the crew until they returned to duty. Native labor was hired to proceed with the loading of cargo and meals were served to passengers by the Chinese room stewards. As a precautionary measure the Master acting in conjunction with the local representative of the Dollar Steamship Lines requested police protection, and about six native Harbor Board policemen were accordingly placed aboard the ship.

The hearing held in accordance with Section 312 of the Consular Regulations was conducted by Vice Consul Patrick Mallon, who called as witnesses, the Master, O. A. Pierson, the Chief Engineer Richard Pedersen, the first assistant engineer, H. Norman, the oiler who had been disrated, Carl

West, the fireman who had been promoted to oiler, John D'Antone, and delegates appearing on behalf of the remainder of the crew, Patrick J. Doyle, Andrew Richelsen, and about ten others who did not testify. T. B. Frink, the junior engineer, could not be found. The statements of O. A. Pierson, H. Norman, John D'Antone, Carl West, and Patrick J. Doyle were taken and the hearing was then adjourned until three o'clock in order that the junior engineer, T. B. Frink, might be present to make a statement. These statements were duly subscribed and sworn to before Vice Consul Patrick Mallon. The originals and copies accompany this report.

An opportunity was given both sides to make statements and cross question witnesses, but no new information in addition to that set forth in the sworn statements was brought forth.

After the evidence had been reviewed by Consul General Davis, it was found that the complaint concerned,(l) a disciplinary act on the part of the Master, viz: the disrating of a member of the crew for refusal to perform duty, (2) that the crew had not been subjected to unusual or cruel treatment such as to entitle them to discharge, (3) that food had only been refused such seamen as willfully and without sufficient cause refused to perform their duty, (4) that the members of the crew were not justified in failing to obey orders, of the Master and other officers of the ship. It was therefore recommended that the men return to work forthwith and defer anything in the nature of a labor dispute until the arrival of the vessel in the United States.

Vice Consul Mallon then proceeded to the vessel and in the presence of the Master and officers repeated the finding to the entire crew. After discussing the matter among themselves however the man sent word to the Master through their delegates that they would not return to work until their demand that West be reinstated as oiler should be met. The Master on his part said that his action had been taken in the interest of maintaining discipline and that he would not accept dictation in such a matter from the crew, but vouchsafed that if the men returned to duty there would he no discrimination against any of them on account of this incident prior to the arrival of the vessel in the United States, when the matter would be out of his hands in any event, and that he would submit the dispute to arbitration. This was communicated to the crew at about 5:30 p.m., but they continued to refuse to return to duty except upon their terms, viz: the reinstatement of the oiler.

Since the ship was not due to sail until noon the it was hoped that a solution to the difficulty would be found before the time of departure, but was informed by telegram dated August 11, 10 a.m. of the possibility that the ship might be delayed. The same morning (August 11) a telegram was received by the crew from their union in San Francisco telling them to return to duty and postpone all further action in the matter until their arrival in the United States. They continued obdurate, however, expressing the opinion that the union was not fully informed in the premises and had telegraphed these instructions while under the impression that the crew's action was the result of previous trouble which had transpired between Honolulu and Kobe, Japan, and which had been reported to the union. The delegates also expressed doubt at first as to the authenticity of the telegram.

The delegates then requested the Consulate General to send a telegram of over fifty words to their union setting forth the cause of the dispute and subsequent happenings. They were told that the Consulate General had no funds for such a purpose. The local representative of the Dollar Line and the Master also refused to advance funds for the telegram.

Since the ship was due to sail at noon (August 11), the Master called the crew at about 11:50 a.m. informing them that the vessel would leave the dock at sailing time and anchor in the loads and that if they refused duty he would come ashore and request the Consulate General to discharge then. It was pointed out that if they left the ship, they would be in the Colony in violation of the local immigration laws and would be dealt with accordingly by the local authorities. The 68 members of the crew left the vessel at 11:50 a.m. and remained on the dock. The vessel actually left at about 12:30 p.m. and anchored in the bay. The Master came ashore at about 2:30 p.m. and made an official protest in affidavit form, the original and copies of which accompany this report.

The members of the crew repaired to the Boustead Institute, a seamen's home in Tanjong Pagar Road, Singapore, where they were advised by the police to await orders from the local authorities. Shortly after the vessel left delegates of the crew appeared at the Consulate General seeking relief as destitute seamen, but they were informed by Consul General Davis that they were not destitute seamen within the meaning of the act, 4577, Revised Statutes (46 U.S.C. section 678), since their vessel was still in port and they could obtain food and lodging by returning to duty as they had been directed to do. Moreover, they were warned that if they persisted in their refusal to perform duty, thus preventing the Master from working the ship, they would lay themselves open to serious charges. They asked whether transportation to the vessel was available and intimated that they would put the matter up to their fellows and recommend a return to duty. The Dollar Line office gave assurance that launches could be procured, and the head of the immigration service said the question of their status would again be brought to the attention of the men. In the meantime, however, the extreme element again prevailed away and the seamen voted to remain ashore, and at about 5 p.m. (August 11) the Consulate General was informed by the Chief Police Officer, Singapore, that acting in conjunction with the immigration authorities, his representatives had given the seamen until 8:00 a.m. before any action would be taken against them locally.

At 6:00 a.m. on August 12 Vice Consul Mallon received a telephone call from one of the delegates of the crew, who stated that another telegram had been received from the union instructing the man to return to duty as their action was jeopardizing the September negotiations. Shortly thereafter Vice Consul Mallon was informed over the telephone by R. Bates, local manager of the Dollar Line, that he had received a telegram from his home office authorizing the Master to sign on an alien crew. The message also stated that the Department of State had telegraphed the Consulate General to the same affect. At 8:00 a.m. the members of the crew decided to hold a secret ballot to determine whether or not they would return to duty. Present at the Boustead Institute were two police officers, the Immigration Officer and Vice Consul Mallon, who informed the men that such of their number as refused to obey the Master's orders would be discharged by the Consulate General and if necessary aliens would be signed on the ship to replace them. The man then voted 37 to 29 for return to duty, two men apparently not voting.

Accompanied by officials mentioned the entire 68 men proceeded to East Wharf, where police launches were waiting to transport them to the ship, but at the last minute twenty-five refused to leave the jetty, and were taken first to the nearby immigration depot, where they were charged with violating the alien's ordinance (Straits Settlements Ordinance No. 18 of 1932, sections 10 and 18), and were then taken to the Central Police Station.

Here it was intended to question the men individually and to order each man separately to return to duty. In the meantime one of the delegates who had gone out to the ship returned with word from the Master that if the remaining twenty-five returned to duty at once, there would be no fines or discrimination except the deduction of 4 days' pay for 2 days' absence from duty. Several of the man still refused to go back unless the Master would give this guarantee in writing. One of the police officers at this point stated that if the men returned to the ship and the Master refused to make his statement in writing he, the police officer, would issue a written statement setting forth what he had heard the Master say in regard to fines and discrimination. At this all the men agreed to return to the ship and last man arrived on board at 12:30 p.m.

Upon arrival on board three delegates of the crew were summoned to the Master's cabin. The Master repeated his statement regarding fines and discrimination but refused to put it in writing. Thereupon Mr. Hope-Falkner, Assistant Superintendent of the Singapore police, issued a signed statement, a copy of which is an enclosure to this report, setting forth what he had heard the Master say. The original was given to the delegates of the crew and signed copies to the Master and the Consulate General. The men returned to duty at once and the police officers with Vice Consul Mallon left the ship, which weighed anchor and sailed out of the harbor at about 4:00 p.m. on August 12, 1936."[10]

Mulling over local press reports on the recent labor dispute on the PRESIDENT HAYES, Consul General Davis summarized such commentary for the Secretary of State three days later. In quintuplicate (!), under the heading "Press Comment on the Delay of the S.S. PRESIDENT HAYES at Singapore due to Labor Trouble", Consul General Davis began:

> I have the honor to refer to my despatch No. 29 of August 15, 1936 regarding the delay to the S.S. PRESIDENT HAYES at Singapore occasioned by a dispute between the Master and the crew, and to submit a brief report on the publicity given this occurrence.

Quite understandably the local press seized upon the strike as a first rate sensation with potential international news value. On the whole accounts of the trouble and comment thereon were moderate in tone and fair to Amer-

---

[10] August 15, 1936 despatch No. 29 of Consul General Monett B. Davis to the Secretary of State. Written by Vice Consul Patrick Mallon. Copy in the ship's 901 file in RG 178 at Maritime Administration.

ican interests. The first despatches included a statement by the Company to the effect that their ships had been calling at this port for twelve years and that this was the first instance of trouble here, and due prominence was given throughout to the fact that the men were orderly and subjected the passengers to comparatively little inconvenience.

A tendency to emphasize the radical nature of the dispute was noted in certain quarters. The *STRAITS TIMES* (daily) of August 12 said for example that "the power of the Seamen's Union in America is indicated by statements by several of the crew that they would definitely "walk off" the PRESIDENT HAYES when they returned to San Francisco as a protest against their "starvation" in Singapore; and again the *Singapore Free Press* (daily) of August 12 stated that one of the strikers "admitted that the majority of the crew belonged to one of the most "militant" sections of the Union", that all the members of the crew of the PRESIDENT HAYES were union men, and that over half of them were involved in the big San Francisco waterfront strike two years ago.

The leading article of the *Singapore Free Press* of August 14, 1936, was inclined to be critical in tone: starting with the rather Pharisaical sentiment that the occurrence served to emphasize how fortunate the local population was in its comparative immunity from strikes, it continued that all will be pleased to know that this affair was purely an internal affair of discipline and had nothing to do with dissatisfaction over wages, conditions on board or any other matter that might affect the passengers more intimately. It expressed the hope, however, 'that American shipping and labor troubles will not in future extend half across the globe'. The *Malaya Tribune* (daily) of August 13, on the other hand, was definitely sympathetic and congratulated officials of the American Consulate General, the Dollar Steamship Line, and the police and immigration authorities on the solution of what it termed 'an almost unique' problem. It said that a situation that might have been ugly was handled successfully through diplomacy and that 'tact was used instead of a show of force and tact won the day.' It commended the men for their orderly conduct but remarked pertinently that 'if every case of disciplinary action . . . resulted in a man's comrades going on strike, then there would be an end to activity altogether.'[11]

With paperwork flying in so many directions the PRESIDENT HAYES sailed into New York on September 23, 1936. That was the last round the world trip the ship could complete for quite some time. All was routine when she departed from New York on her following outbound trip from New York on October 2, 1936. With 2,960 tons of general cargo aboard, the PRESIDENT HAYES sailed under the command of Captain L.M. Graham. After her usual Havana call and November 9/10th Panama Canal transit, the ship arrived at San Francisco on October 21 but this time she was allowed only

---

[11] August 18, 1936 analysis of local press reports by Consul General M. Davis to Secretary of State. Copy in the ship's 901 file in RG 178 at Maritime Administration.

two days at her home port before sailing for her round the world voyage again on October 23, 1936. She got as far as Honolulu where she arrived on November 30th before labor troubles caught up with her and idled her there for the duration of the ninety-nine day strike. When the West Coast walk out ended on February 5, 1937, the PRESIDENT HAYES was ready. Her engine department had steam up and the ship finally left Hawaii on February 6th, both following and preceding (depending upon how you look at the comings and goings of a round the world liner) her sister PRESIDENT ADAMS which had sailed from New York the previous day. Sometime that year Captain H.S. Bauer took command of the PRESIDENT HAYES. On that first trip after the conclusion of the strike, the ship sailed from Kobe on February 21st, Shanghai on February 25th, Hong Kong on March 2nd, Manila on March 5th, Singapore on March 12th, Penang on March 16th, Colombo on March 19th, Bombay on March 24th and Suez on April 2nd. Next were the usual Mediterranean calls at the ports of Alexandria, Naples, Genoa and Marseilles. From there this "502" sailed on April 11th for New York where she arrived eleven days later on April 22, 1937.

The provisions of the 1936 Merchant Marine Act that would take away her passenger certificate were not yet in effect. Still permitted to carry her usual complement of passengers, the PRESIDENT HAYES attracted pretty fair numbers, sailing full on most segments of the following trip. Still months behind schedule because of the strike, the ship sailed from New York on May 3rd and from San Francisco on May 21st. All indications suggest that when the ship sailed on that round the world voyage, but she may well have been able to hang on for one more trip. Documentation on this score is curiously vague. The ship was on that voyage when Maritime Commission cancellation of Dollar Line's ocean mail contracts came into effect on June 30th. Effective July 1, 1937, no further mail subsidy would be paid, and the Dollar ships were on their own to earn their keep or face withdrawal. A few rounds of wrangling brought an emergency extension of federal payments to the company but it was not enough to keep the fleet trading for long. Following on the heels of the cancellation of mail contracts, the safety provisions of the Merchant Marine Act of 1936 kicked in, and the ship definitively lost her passenger certificate. Now she could legally carry no more than 12 passengers. For the accounting department, this effectively cut off another source of voyage revenue for the PRESIDENT HAYES, which fell somewhat short of newly mandated standards.

By the time the ship headed into the Atlantic, emergency financing allowed the ship to keep sailing. From Boston she sailed on August 17th for New York where she arrived on schedule the next day. The outbound sailing was taken on August 19th when the PRESIDENT HAYES cast off for Havana and Balboa. With 3,861 tons of general cargo the ship made her way between the seas on her way to a September 5th arrival at San Pedro. She sailed from her Los Angeles pier on the following day to arrive at San Francisco on September 7th. After working cargo there the ship continued her voyage, sailing from her home port on September 12th for Honolulu. Kobe was next and the ship was there on October 2nd and 3rd. Because of Japanese military action in China, the ship made no Shanghai call that time, steaming instead directly from Kobe for Hong Kong where she arrived on October 8th. She sailed on the 11th for Manila, Singapore and Penang, Colombo and Bombay where she arrived on October 31st. The voyage continued on November 2nd with the ship's departure for Egypt, Italy, France and the United States. With her early December New York arrival came the effective end of the Dollar Line career of the PRESIDENT HAYES. She never again made another complete round the world trip under the Dollar sign.

Idleness was again in the cards for her when she sailed from New York on December 7th for Boston. Overnight there on December 8th, she sailed on the 9th and made her way into New York on the 10th. Following her usual schedule, the PRESIDENT HAYES sailed from New York on December 11, 1937. With 2,243 tons of cargo for the West Coast, the liner made her Panama Canal transit on December 18th. California was the ship's final destination that time and after a San Pedro call between December 27th and the early hours of the morning of the 29th, this ship steamed up the coast on her way into her San Francisco home port where she arrived on December 30, 1937. That's as far as she got for quite some time.

With the Maritime Commission's cautious refusal to prop up the failing Dollar Line, the ship's owners had decided their precarious financial condition could not permit them to send the ship out on the remainder of that scheduled voyage. While the Maritime Commission sorted out the Dollar Line's dwindling fortune, inactivity awaited the PRESIDENT HAYES during most of 1938. By June maritime journals carried her name in lay up lists. She remained inactive through late December while the Dollars and the Maritime Commission worked out arrangements to get the ships back to work.

While Dollar Line's finances had worsened, the ship was libelled by the Zenobia Company, Inc. of California which claimed $4,804.13 damages to cargo shipped just before the PRESIDENT HAYES went into lay up. It was the Maritime Commission which arranged bond to free the idle ship from arrest in late May 1938. Just prior to Dollar Line's collapse, all seven "502"'s were subjects of extensive reconditioning and the rebuilding of much of their crew quarters. While at anchor in San Francisco Bay the PRESIDENT HAYES had her survey prior to her refit. Years of minimum maintenance had taken a toll, revealed in the $40,000.00 estimate for hull repairs alone. Planned by Dollar Steamship Line, the reconstruction of the ship's aft crew quarters would be done under American President Lines', and thus the Maritime Commission's aegis. Late September 1938 brought instructions regarding such work to be performed in the PRESIDENT HAYES and PRESIDENT MONROE. Bidders were instructed to use the specifications and plans drawn for the renovations effected in the PRESIDENT ADAMS as their guideline. Money for this refit proved a stumbling block. It would also bring the attention of Maritime Commission General Counsel Bon Geaslin. On December

17, 1938 he informed the Collector of Customs at San Francisco: "Regarding telegram 12th owing delay obtaining consent Reconstruction Finance Corporation, Commission unable approve surrender documents PRESIDENT steamers CLEVELAND, HAYES, LINCOLN, WILSON and PIERCE in time for CLEVELAND sailing today."[12] In time the cost to recondition the PRESIDENT HAYES for commercial service as a 12 passenger freighter would rise to $189,101.00, a sum the Dollar firms could not consider paying. After the Maritime Commission takeover, the ship's bills were paid in large measure by money from the public purse.

Since the ship could not legally carry more than 12 passengers, and no one had any interest in spending the scarce dollars to upgrade her to qualify for a new certificate, it was finally time for the ship to divest herself of much of her passenger fittings. Instead of having her crew quarters substantially rebuilt, as were such spaces in her four improved sisters and a number of other American passenger cargo ships, once the ship returned to service her crew could move into unused passenger cabins. At least her freighter status would save her operators some money because there was no longer any need to rebuild crew spaces in this ship. Anything not needed for the accommodation of her crew was off loaded and sent into storage ashore on March 13, 1938. To further lighten the ship to reduce fuel consumption, redundant lifeboats and liferafts went ashore.

Like her sisters the PRESIDENT HAYES passed into the fleet of the new American President Lines in November 1938. Reconditioned for her return to sea the ship was ready to begin her first voyage as an American President Liner, sailing from San Francisco on December 30th. Instead of setting a course for Honolulu, her Master ordered a course set for Southern California and the ship steamed south to Los Angeles where she arrived the following day. There she greeted 1939, sailing for San Francisco on January 1st. For some reason American President Lines allowed the ship five days to work cargo at her home port and not until January 7, 1939 did she steam out again, once more bound for ports around the world. After her Honolulu call on January 14th she set her course for Yokohama and a January 26th arrival. On the following day she steamed south to Kobe where she once again remained in port overnight. Because of the military situation vis a vis Japanese occupation, there was no Shanghai call so after departing Japan the ship made her way to Hong Kong once where she arrived on February 2nd. She sailed the following day for Manila and her usual rubber ports of Singapore and Penang before heading to Colombo for more rubber and tea.

With Maritime Commission consent, American President Lines scheduled a Rangoon, Burma call for the PRESIDENT HAYES, but when "expected business did not materialize", that call was cancelled and the ship made no detour between Penang/Singapore and Colombo. On April 7, 1939

---

[12] December 17, 1938 telegram from Bon Geaslin. Copy in the ship's 901 file in RG 178 at Maritime Administration.

the ship sailed from New York on that trip on which she had approval to visit Burma. Permission to omit that planned call was granted on April 18th. Nothing further about Rangoon was mentioned in connection with her again and the vessel was reported in transit through the Canal on April 14th on her way to Hong Kong with 3,587 tons of general cargo. She sailed from San Francisco on April 29th.

In from Boston, the PRESIDENT HAYES arrived to load the last of her outward freight at New York on July 28th. The next outbound trip from New York was Voyage 51 and it got off to a poor start. Sunday, July 30, 1939 was sailing day but before getting underway there was still plenty of cargo to come aboard and most of it was loaded after midnight. Damning the enormous costs of weekend/night overtime, APL had nine shore gangs start work, loading the last of the ship's outbound cargo into all nine hatches at 1:00 AM that morning. By four o'clock the first gang finished but others still had hours to go before the last parcel of freight was off the dock. Any of the ship's crew not detailed to cargo loading could sleep that night and they awoke to the typical sailing day routine. There was something for most everyone to do. All bridge equipment was tested and main engine dock trial began at 8:30 AM. Two tugs came alongside the "President" liner at 8:45. And stevedores were still loading freight into the ship. Not until 9:00 AM, sailing time, was the last gang finished and all cargo aboard. Hatches were covered, the last stevedores trooped ashore. Then, ever so slowly, the gnawing toothache of labor unrest began again when deck department union delegate T. Kelleher, able bodied seaman, claiming the ship was unready for sea, refused to obey Captain H.S. Bauer's and his officer's orders to let go fore and aft. A hasty talk with the remaining deck crew brought agreement with remaining deck personnel to turn to and take the ship out to sea without Kelleher's help. Lines were cast off at 9:15 AM and five minutes later the liner was clear of the dock. At 9:25 as the ship swung around to head downriver the docking pilot scampered off and boarded his tug while Pilot Capt. Mahlman guided the "502" south towards Ambrose Light. Captain Bauer ordered "stop engines" at 11:09 and four minutes later the pilot boat came alongside to take off the pilot. Full ahead rang out at 11:14, and that was the official hour given in the ship's log as the time of departure from New York for Cristobal. Stewing since his showdown with the Captain a few hours earlier, Kelleher wasted no time at all before taking revenge. Venting his vexations with shipmate W. Crouch, Kelleher's venality tripped them both up. Corralling another deck crewmember to their side, they refused to turn to at 1:20 when called to secure deck gear, opting instead to demonstrate their power. All they really accomplished was a further demonstration that American vessels so often shipped the worst of the worst in their crews. Heading down to Engineer Officers' quarters, the two malicious hotheads violently assaulted Chief Engineer J.D. Fay and Second Assistant Engineer Gardiner, claiming the two men were "Finks". Captain Bauer, long experienced in dealing with the militant vermin who won places in the crews of

Dollar Line and then American President Lines' vessels, now had to deal with a felony.

Captain Bauer lost no time in alerting both New York and San Francisco offices of American President Lines of this latest outrage. Now following instinct and instructions, little by little, and very quietly, Captain Bauer and his officers aboard the PRESIDENT HAYES and American President Lines executives in New York, Washington and San Francisco built an airtight case for the prosecution of the two union thugs. Neatly bundled together and wielded as the prosecution's best weapon, Captain Bauer's own telegrams to shoreside offices, cables to him aboard ship and the collection of statements from various officers and crew, both victims and bystanders, were enough to convict both accused men, not quite the outcome the two thugs smugly contemplated before beginning their vicious attacks.

Captain Bauer's paper trail began with several July 31st cables to American President Lines offices. Only the slightest hint of Captain Bauer's disgust with the thugs and the apparent sympathy they had from the ship's apathetic deck crew seeps through log entries and paperwork on that subject. Even more informative than his first cable informing shore staff of the latest outrage was a second message he penned to American President Lines' Marine Superintendent Captain Foshee during the night of July 31st. It was the first of a round of eleven telegraphed messages between the ship's Master and her owners. Sending this message at 12:15 EDT on August 1st to the PRESIDENT POLK for relay to shore, Captain Bauer's message lacks any hint of the horror, anguish and frustration engendered by the inevitable militant laborites who lived only to destroy:

From Captain H.S. Bauer, Master of the PRESIDENT HAYES:

DELIVER TO CAPTAIN FOSHEE ON ARRIVAL URGENT ASSAULTED MEN J FAY CHIEF ENGINEER AND C GARDNER SECOND ENGINEER JULY 30 AT 1:20 PM STOP DECK CREW SECURING GEAR STOP THREE MEMBERS OF DECK CREW DID NOT TURN TO STOP TWO MEN KELLEHER AND CROUCH WENT DOWN TO ENGINEERS OFFICERS QUARTERS LOOKING FOR THE FINK DOLLAR ENGINEERS STOP THE CHIEF ENGINEER FIRST ENGINEER SECOND ENGINEER JUNIOR ENGINEER WERE RESTING IN THEIR ROOMS STOP THE TWO SAILORS ENTERED THE JUNIOR ENGINEERS ROOM BUT HE RAN FROM HIS ROOM AS THEY THREATENED HIM STOP NEXT THEY WENT TO THE SECOND ENGINEERS ROOM WHO WAS ASLEEP STOP THEY PULLED HIM OUT OF HIS BED AND KNOCKED HIM DOWN STOP HE RAN OUT OF HIS ROOM TO THE ENGINE ROOM STOP HIS EAR WAS CUT AND THE BACK OF HIS HEAD STOP THE TWO SAILORS NEXT WENT TO THE CHIEF ENGINEERS ROOM AND WOKE HIM UP AS THEY ENTERED HIS ROOM STOP HE GOT UP AT ONCE AND ONE OF THE MEN SWUNG TO HIT HIM BUT HE EVADED THE BLOW STOP THEY SAID THEY WERE AFTER THE FINK SECOND ENGINEER AND WERE ON THIS SHIP TO CLEAN IT OF DOLLAR FINKS AND SCABS

STOP THE CHIEF ENGINEER SHOWED THE SAILORS HIS STRIKE CLEARANCE CARD OF 1934 AND TRIED TO QUIET THEM DOWN AND TOLD THEM TO LEAVE HIS OFFICE AND GO TO THEIR OWN QUARTERS STOP

THEY STARTED FIGHTING AND STRIKING THE CHIEF ENGINEER IN HIS OFFICE AND MOVED OUT TO THE PASSAGEWAY IN THE ENGINE OFFICERS QUARTERS WHERE ONE MAN JUMPED THE CHIEF ENGINEER AND HELD HIM ON THE DECK CHOKING HIM WHILE THE OTHER KICKED HIM IN THE FACE AND EYES AND BACK OF THE HEAD AND KIDNEYS AS MANY TIMES AS HE COULD BEFORE THE CHIEF ENGINEER COULD BREAK THE OTHER SAILORS HOLD ON HIS NECK STOP NO ONE WAS AT THAT TIME AROUND TO LEND ASSISTANCE TO THE CHIEF ENGINEER STOP BOTH EYES OF THE CHIEF ENGINEER WERE CLOSED FROM THE KICKS AND A LARGE CUT UNDER ONE EYE AS WELL AS WELTS ON BACK OF HEAD AND BRUISES ON BODY FROM THE SAILORS KICKING WHEN HE WAS HELD DOWN ON THE DECK STOP.

BOTH ENGINEERS NOW CONFINED TO THEIR ROOMS FROM INJURIES STOP CH OFFICER AND FIRST ENGINEER REPORTED TO BRIDGE THAT TWO SEAMEN WERE AMOK BELOW AND ASSAULTED TWO ENGINEERS STOP I ORDERED THE CHIEF OFFICER TO GET THE DECK CREW AND BRIG THE TWO SAILORS STOP THE DECK CREW WERE SECURING NUMBER FIVE HATCH GEAR STOP I WATCHED THE CHIEF OFFICER FROM THE BRIDGE GIVE ORDERS TO THE BOSUN AND A LOT OF UNNECESSARY TALK SEEMED TO BE GOING ON SO I RUSHED TO THE BRIDGE AND RELIEVED THE SECOND OFFICER WHO WAS ON WATCH AND TOLD HIM TO GET ALL OFFICERS AT ONCE AND RUSH TO THE FIGHT AND BRIG THE MEN THEMSELVES STOP DURING MY STAY ON THE BRIDGE WATCH I NOTICED THAT THE DECK CREW DID NOT RESPOND TO THE CHIEF OFFICERS ORDER AND DID NOT GO BELOW AT ALL STOP THE MEN IN THIS GANG WERE BOSUN F RENO ABLE SEAMAN S SEARS N DEREVAN J WESTERMAN S CASTLE 0 STANLEY J HOPKINS R SEAMAN AND ORDINARY SEAMEN J HARRIS J JENNINGS STOP

ON RETURNING FROM BRIGING THE MEN THE CHIEF OFFICER ASKED THE BOSUN WHO WAS BY NOW WORKING ON NUMBER EIGHT HATCH GEAR WHY HE DID NOT COME TO THE SCENE OF THE FIGHT WHEN ORDERED STOP THE BOSUN SAID THAT THERE WAS ENOUGH DECK AND ENGINE OFFICERS AND THAT HE WAS NOT A POLICEMAN STOP MEN NOW LOCKED IN SEPARATE BRIGS ON FULL RATIONS STOP KELLEHER HAS CALMED DOWN BUT CROUCH STILL TROUBLESOME STOP DECK CREW WARNED THAT ANY ASSISTANCE RENDERED TO THESE MEN IN THE BRIG WOULD BE DEALT WITH ACCORDINGLY STOP CREW HOLDING MEETING TONIGHT TO ELECT A NEW DELEGATE AS KELLEHER WAS THE DECK DELEGATE STOP ON DEPARTURE FROM DOCK NEW YORK CREW REFUSED MASTER AND OFFICERS ORDERS TO LET GO LINES STATING THAT THE SHIP WAS NOT YET SECURED FOR SEA STOP AFTER CONFERENCE WITH MASTER DECK CREW TURNED TO ON

HIS COMMAND STOP WILL HAVE COMPLETE REPORT ON THIS SUB-JECT FOR OFFICIALS BOARDING COLON AND WILL AIRMAIL YOU COPY OF SAME STOP ALSO ALL ENTRIES IN THE OFFICIAL LOG BOOK STOP ENGINEERS INTEND TO PROSECUTE STOP CREW TODAY VERY QUIET STOP BELIEVE SAFE TO PROCEED TO SAN FRANCISCO.[13]

The batch of telegrams joined the written statements of officers and crew. Here is what 2nd Assistant Engineer C. Gardiner, had to say on the day of his beating:

> About 1:30 pm this afternoon, a sailor entered my room while I was asleep in my bunk and pulled me out on the floor and asked me who I was, and I told him I was the 2nd asst. Engineer, and he said wait here awhile, and went out the door and called another to come on down, I have one in this room.
>
> The two of them entered my room and demanded to know where I was in the 1934 strike, and demanded to see my clearance card. I asked them who they were and they answered they were sailors, and were going to clean off all the Dollar Line Finks off of the ship and they were going to tie the ship up in San Pedro.
>
> I told them I was not a Fink, and that I was on the PRESIDENT ADAMS in 1934—a clear ship—and then one of the sailors hit me and knocked me down. I got up and passed them and ran into the passage down to the 1st asst. Engineers office with them after me. The 1st Asst. Engineer was not there and they hit me several times in the back of the head and over the left ear and knocked me down and kicked me several times; and one of them said let's dump him over the side of the ship.
>
> I broke away from them and ran to the Chief engineers room and called to him. He was asleep and got up and asked the sailors what the matter was, and they said I was a Fink. He told them I was no such thing, and kind of quieted them down, and got them out in the Office. I went over to the 1st Asst. Engineers Office and started to wash the blood off my face when Mr. Huber, a Jr. Engineer came running in and said they were beating the Chief Engineer up.
>
> I told him to run up to the bridge and notify the Officer on watch. I rushed out in the alley yelling for help. The sailors had kicked the Chief on the deck near the Pursers Office and one of them kicked him in the face. The 1st Asst. appeared on the scene and got them aside. The Officers from the bridge arrived then and took charge and placed both of the sailors in the brig.[14]

Chief Engineer J.D. Fay weighed in the following day with his own account to Captain Bauer:

> Yesterday (July 30th) around the hour of 1:30 p.m., I was sleeping in my room. I heard some noise and my door open, and as I came to the door I

---

[13] August 1, 1939 telegram from Captain Bauer to Captain Foshee. Copy in the ship's 901 file in RG 178 at Maritime Administration.

[14] July 30, 1939 letter from 2nd Asst. Engineer C. Gardiner to Captain Bauer. Copy in the ship's 901 file in RG 178 at Maritime Administration.

was surprised to see two deck sailors. As I came to the door, one of the sailors tried to hit me with his fists, in my eye. I ducked and evaded the blow. They said they were after my "FINK" 2nd asst. Engineer, and that they were on the ship to clean it up.

I tried to talk with them and quiet them down, and showed them my own clearance picket card from the 1934 strike. They claimed that there was a lot of "FINKS" on this ship. my 2nd asst. was one of them. I got them out of my room and into the Office where they kept talking about the 2nd asst. I told them to leave my Office and go back to their own quarters, and they started fighting with me.

The both of them started throwing whatever blows they could at me, and centered them at my face, most of which I warded off. I backed out of my office, and they kept fighting; and we went to it in the Engine Officers passageway. This went on for about ten minutes, until I lost my balance and fell to the deck.

At this point the blond sailor got a hold around my neck, and tried to cut off my windpipe and my air. While I was breaking his hold, the other black haired sailor started kicking me in the face and head, and wherever he could. He managed to get a lot of kicks at my face and head before I could break the other sailors hold on my neck. He kept kicking me in and around the head and the kidneys.

The 1st asst. Engineer must have heard the noise and the banging around the deck, and came rushing out of his room. As soon as he showed up they stopped fighting, as I think they thought he had a gun. At this time the Chief Officer came, and I was asked to go to my room, which I did.[15]

Junior Engineer Richard F. Huber told what he knew:

About 1:30 PM two sailors came into my room while O was asleep and woke me up and demanded to know where the 2nd asst. Engineer was. I told them I didn't know and to get out of my room. They then wanted to know who I was. I told them I was a Junior Engineer, and they said they didn't like Junior Engineers, and I told them to get out again.

They started to get tough then I ducked out of my room and went down to the 4th asst. Engineers room and talked to him for a while, A little later I went through the Chief Engineers Office and found the 2nd Asst. Engineer in the 1st Asst. Engineers room bleeding from a cut in back of the ear. He told me to go up and get the Mate, so I went up and got Mr. Wank, and he got the 2nd and 3rd Mates. We then went down below and found the 1st asst., the Purser, the Steward, the 4th asst. Engineer, and the Chief Engineer and the two sailors.

The Chief was bleeding badly for he had been cut about the face. The two sailors were calling him a dirty Fink and etc. There was a lot of arguing there and finally we took the smaller sailor back to the brig, and came back and took the other one back to the brig also.[16]

---

[15] July 31, 1939 letter from Chief Engineer J.D. Fay to Captain Bauer. Copy in the ship's 901 file in RG 178 at Maritime Administration.

[16] July 30, 1939 statement of Junior Engineer Richard F. Huber in the ship's 901 file in RG 178 at Maritime Administration.

First into the brig was Kelleher, who protested his planned incarceration. Slimy to the last, Crouch at first objected to the idea of being locked up in the brig, demanding that the Chief Engineer be isolated as well. He was huffy, too, insisting that no one could PROVE that he had assaulted the two Engineers and went into the ship's jail screaming for ANOTHER union meeting!

Days later Huber added more information to Captain Bauer's growing file, affirming: "On my way to the Bridge to call the Chief Officer, I passed the Bos'n and a number of his men, who were working on number five and six hatches. As I passed I told him that two of his men were fighting with the Chief Engineer, and to go below and stop them. His reply was that he didn't give a damn what they were doing. I did not stop to argue, but went on up to the Mates room."[17]

Marine Superintendent Captain Foshee was quick to respond, cabling instructions to Captain Bauer at 2:34 PM on July 31st:

TAKE ALL PRECAUTIONS YOU CONSIDER NECESSARY TO PROTECT YOUR SHIP OFFICERS AND LAW ABIDING MEMBERS OF CREW WILL ADVISE LATER AS TO DISPOSITION OF KELLEHER AND CROUCH AT CANAL.[18]

That afternoon Captain Bauer sent off another message, once more having it relayed by the radio operators aboard the PRESIDENT POLK.

DLNYK MR FOSHEE R VETTERLING OILER FAILED TO JOIN AT NEW YORK STOP SEARS ABLE SEAMAN IS TO BE OMITTED FROM DISOBEDIENCE OF ORDERS ON DECK AS HE WAS DRUNK AND BELOW STOP MEN IN BRIG PEACEFUL TODAY BUT DEMAND TO HAVE THEIR CHARGES READ TO THEM WHICH WILL BE DONE TODAY STOP ALSO DEMAND TO SEE COMMISSIONER IN THE CANAL ZONE STOP ALL QUIET ON BOARD STOP CHARGES OF MISDEMEANOR AND USURPATION OF AUTHORITY LEGALLY INVESTED ON OFFICERS OF THE PRESIDENT HAYES NAMELY MR R WANK CHIEF OFFICER AND H S BAUER MASTER BY WILFUL BREACH OF DUTY IN NOT RESPONDING TO ORDERS WHEN LIFE AND LIMB OF THE ENGINEER OFFICERS WERE IN IMMEDIATE DANGER TO ASSIST THE CHIEF OFFICER IN PLACING THE MEN TO KELLEHER ABLE SEAMAN AND W CROUCH ABLE SEAMAN IN THE BRIG STOP THIS CHARGE WILL BE READ TO THE MEN THE DAY BEFORE ARRIVAL IN THE CANAL AND COPIES GIVEN TO EACH OFFENDING MAN STOP T KELLEHER ABLE SEAMAN AND W CROUCH ABLE SEAMAN IS HEREBY CHARGED WITH ASSAULT ON MR J D FAY CHIEF ENGINEER AND MR C GARDNER SECOND ASST ENGINEER WHILE THEY WERE IN THEIR ROOMS

---

[17] ibid.

[18] July 31, 1939 telegram from Captain Foshee to Captain bauer. Copy in ship's 901 files in RG 178 at Maritime Administration.

ASLEEP DOING BODILY HARM TO THEM STOP THIS CHARGE WILL
BE READ TO THESE MEN TODAY.[19]

Who cannot see Captain Bauer sputter with rage that same afternoon
when he read this note brought to him from Kelleher and Crouch:

Sir:
We, the two men you are keeping confined would like you to define our
status as this confinement is uncalled as we believe we are confined unjustly
as we have not been found guilty, and the other two men are allowed the
run of the ship. So please clarify our status and we would like to have the
U.S. Commissioner of the Canal Zone see us as soon as we arrive there.[20]

Their separate brig accommodations were carefully considered by Captain Bauer and his men. From the moment of incarceration, each man had
been provided with drinking water and a bucket for evacuation of bodily
wastes. Full meals were served to each man twice a day and fresh water
replenished. A toilet contraption was placed in each cell during the 8:00 AM
to noon watch on August 1st, during which time each man was allowed out
of his cell for one hour to take fresh air. Each man was taken out of his cell
a couple of times every day for between half an hour and an hour, each
"airing" noted in the log. The men even got fresh linens on the 3rd.

Not ignored were the disobedient men of the deck gang. Various notations of the ship's log detailed their actions or inactions:

_____ is hereby charged with misdemeanors by Usurpation of authority legally vested in officers of the S/S PRESIDENT HAYES. Namely—
Mr. R. Wank, Chief Officer, and H.S. Bauer, Master, by willfull breach of
duty in not responding to orders when life and limb of engineers Mr. J.D.
Fay, Chief Engineer, and C. Gardner, 2nd Asst. Engineer, were in immediate
danger, to assist the Chief Engineer in placing the men, Wm. Crouch, A.B.,
and T. Kelleher, A.B. in the brig.

Nine times that statement appears in the ship's log that day, in each instance
a charge against a different man—Jack Westerman, A.B., Stanley Castle, A.B.,
Joseph Hopkins, A.B., Russel Seaman, A.B., O. Stanley, A.B., Frank Reno, #1
Maintenance Man A.B., N. Derevan, Deck Maintenance, John Harris, O.S.,
Joe Jennings, O.S.. All men answered the charges against them in a similarly
indifferent vein: "I heard no orders.", "I had no orders." "That's all". "I
have nothing to say."[21]

Sensing a chance to take a wide swing at the atrocious seamen and their
unyielding militant union, shoreside offices of American President Lines
sprang into action. One thing was certain. The Line was going to do what it
could to nail these guys! From the New York office went out the first of ten

_____

[19] ibid.
[20] August 1, 1939 note from Kelleher and Crouch to Captain bauer. Copy in the ship's 901 file
in RG 178 at Maritime Administration.
[21] These charges are quoted verbatim from the logbook of the S/S PRESIDENT HAYES.

telegrams in this matter. Only too willing to pounce upon the miscreants, Vice President Frick cabled his colleague T.E. Cuffe of the New York office on July 31st:

> Please relay in code following message Master PRESIDENT HAYES Quote Understand Department Justice will take action against Kelleher Crouch at Canal. Make complete log entry naming all parties disobeying your instructions to place seamen in brig. Make up detailed report also full detailed statements of witnesses. Have ready arrival Los Angeles as San Francisco considering court action against men refusing obey orders therefore impose no penalties meantime unquote.[22]

Making the next move, T.E. Cuffe cabled Captain Bauer on the evening of August 2nd:

> San Francisco approves of your action present difficulties but suggests in meantime no penalty imposed leave this Department of Justice otherwise likely to affect case.[23]

APL wired Captain Bauer again on August 3rd advising him this time that the authorities at the Canal Zone were definitely removing Kelleher and Crouch and might even arrest and take off any other crewmembers who had disobeyed orders. From American President Lines' head office in San Francisco, his colleague, Vice President Frick advised Cuffe that should Captain Bauer take ANY disciplinary action against the others, the crew members might then claim they had been punished, thereby stilting any possible criminal case American President Lines could bring against them. On the 4th Frick sent this message to the ship as she approached Panama on August 4th:

> What time is HAYES due? While anxious see proper punitive action taken against crew members charged disobedience orders Consult United States Attorney how this may be done without delaying vessel and without losing jurisdiction under Section 41 of Jurisdictional Code. Nothing herein refers to two men charged with assault who should be dealt with by Canal Zone United States Attorney who will be assured of full cooperation this company. Request Master keep San Francisco fully advised all developments not hesitating telephone if needs instructions. In any event tell him phone eleven o'clock your time Saturday and give verbal report developments up to then. Can reach me Sutter 7200 up to eleven your time after that at my office.[24]

---

[22] July 3, 1939 cable from H.E. Frick to T.E. Cuffe. Copy in the ship's 901 file in RG 178 at Maritime Administration.

[23] August 3, 1939 (according to GMT, but the evening prior in New York) telegram from T.E. Cuffe to Captain bauer. Copy in the ship's 901 file in RG 178 at Maritime Administration.

[24] August 4, 1939 telegram from APL VicePresident Frick to the ship. Copy in ship's 901 file in RG 178 at Maritime Administration.

Not a man of many words, Captain Bauer cabled the Line's Cristobal agent on August 4th: "Anchor 6:00 AM Notify District Attorney to board vessel on arrival."[25]

The ship got in a little later than that. Taking on the pilot and under the assistance of a tug, the PRESIDENT HAYES arrived at Cristobal at 8:50 A.M. on Saturday, August 4th. Representing Canal Zone District Attorney's office, Lieutenant S. Rowe and Sgt.R. W. Griffith boarded the ship along with Boarding Personnel of the Line's local agent, the Panama Agencies Company. In his office, Captain Bauer gave Lt. Rowe his stack of paperwork including every signed statement regarding the assault case and photographs of the men's wounds, as well as an impressive amount of paperwork impugning the bos'n and deck crew for disobedience in their unwillingness to come to the rescue of the Engineers. Then Lt. Rowe explained to Captain Bauer just how the District Attorney's intended to proceed and the nature of legal action to be taken in regard to his charges against the several men.

On the Port Agent's suggestion, Captain Bauer went ashore at Cristobal accompanied by the Chief Engineer and Second Ass't. Engineer Gardner. In the Port Agent's offices the ship's officers discussed the matter by phone with the District Attorney's office at Balboa. Because only the assault charge could be given immediate hearing by the Canal Zone court, the District Attorney's office prompted the Chief Engineer and Second Assistant Engineers to swear out a warrant for the arrest of Crouch and Kelleher. This was something both men were happy to do.

The charge of disobedience was another matter entirely, the Canal Zone District Attorney pointed out. To try the men in the Canal Zone District Court on such a charge would engender a terrific delay to the ship and exceptional losses of money as such a trial would require the presence ashore and in Court of the entire deck-gang. Then, if cause were found, all parties involved, other than officers, would have to be held at the Zone until the ship came back some four months later. Since the available pool of Able Seaman at the Canal Zone was insufficient to replace all the ABs, and the PRESIDENT HAYES could not make her voyage from the Canal to California without such men, Captain Bauer agreed to allow local authorities to press only the assault charge at that time.

Requisite arrest warrants were quickly issued for Crouch and Kelleher, and both men were brought from the ship's Brig to Cristobal jail by Cristobal Police. Then, when the Assistant District Attorney agreed to come from Balboa on the 1:00 p.m. train to Cristobal, the case was set for hearing at 2:30 P.M.

Meanwhile, there was a relatively large steamer waiting to transit the Canal. Since both Captain and Chief Engineer were likely to remain ashore for some hours more, Captain Bauer asked the Port Captain to accept his ship for Canal transit under the command of Chief Officer R. Wank and First

---

[25] August 4, 1939 cable from Captain Bauer in ship's 901 file in RG 178 at Maritime Administration.

Assistant Engineer J. C. Kilbride. The PRESIDENT HAYES entered the Canal for her northbound transit at 12:30 p.m.

Now really prisoners, Crouch and Kelleher appeared before Judge E.I.P. Tatelman in Cristobal's Magistrate Court at 2:30 P.M. Typical of those who so willingly trample the rights of others but so vigilant of their own, both men demanded Counsel. In accordance with Canal Zone law, a Public Defender, C.P. Fairman, was appointed to represent them at public expense. To no one's surprise, both defendants asked the Court to permit them to produce their witnesses, naming almost the entire deck crew of the PRESIDENT HAYES as well as the Chief Officer and First Engineer. Of course, none of those men had been eye witnesses to the assault. Naturally Judge Tatelman had to grant their request. For a few minutes it looked as though the ship would be seriously delayed, unless the defense could be satisfied by the presence of the Chief Officer and First Assistant Engineer alone. Both men were aboard the ship and could not be removed from the vessel until she anchored at Balboa.

Not only were both Judge Tatelman, himself a Master Mariner, and Assistant District Attorney Ramirez conversant with shipping, they understood its contemporary difficulties. Instead of delaying the PRESIDENT HAYES further, they agreed to go through a change in venue in order to try the case at Balboa that same night. Easily sizing up his adversaries, Assistant District Attorney Ramirez quickly concocted a way to let the defendants' rights work against them, adding further incarceration to whatever punishment the two malcreants might eventually get. At that point, Mr. Ramirez informed the defendants' attorney that the Canal Zone had the right to hold Crouch and Kelleher without trial for a period not exceeding 120 days, and rather than run the risk of delaying the vessel's sailing from the Pacific Terminal, he, Mr. Ramirez would avail himself of his rights. Knowing that both men would have to remain in jail locally until the ship returned to Panama some 110 to 120 days hence, Mr. Ramirez thought it would be dandy for Crouch and Kelleher to press their request for the testimony of the stipulated witnesses. Ramirez then told them that if the desired witnesses were not aboard on the vessel's return they would have prolonged their jail term by at least 110 days for nothing.

Knowing their game was up at that point, Crouch and Kelleher agreed with their attorney to plead guilty to the charges. Judge Tatelman then bound them over to the Canal Zone District Court and fixed bond at $500.00 each, a sum neither man had a prayer of scraping together.

Defendants Crouch and Kelleher were then signed off ship's Articles as Captain Bauer, Chief Engineer Fay, Second Assistant Engineer Gardner, Junior Engineer Huber and Purser Havens gathered their papers together and made ready to make their way to the station for the 5:00 p.m. train to Balboa.

Meanwhile the PRESIDENT HAYES steamed through the canal. She passed the inner harbor at Balboa at 6:55 P.M. and anchored in the bay that same evening. Leaving their erstwhile shipmates behind as guests of the

Canal Zone's penal system, Captain Bauer and party boarded a launch to take them back to their ship. Once they were back aboard, Captain Bauer had time to sit down at his typewriter to write Mr. Frick a letter for the Pilot to take off. Recapping the day's events, the Captain informed Frick: "if any change in present pleadings develops then men will be held over until vessel's return, and will be tried before Judge Bunk Gardner, Judge of the Canal Zone District Court. Might state that William Crouch and William Tassin, A.B., now onboard my vessel, both have long troublesome records with the American Hawaiian Line and it might be advisable to look into this with them. N. Deveran. A.B., now delegate joined at New York, is daily making demands and complaints, none of which I am heeding. Pilot about ready to leave ship, and with fine weather, should arrive schedule."[26] The letter written, Captain Bauer took his place on the bridge. Then the PRESIDENT HAYES hoisted anchor and at 9:33 P.M. the ship cleared the Pacific Sea Buoy. In light of the circumstances, she had been but very slightly delayed.

Always economical with his telegraphed words, Captain Bauer signalled San Francisco on the early morning of August 6th: "Departed 9:37 PM August 5th." Without further comment, he added: "Kelleher Crouch ashore Airmailed full detail report."[27]

No strangers to agitation, both Kelleher and Crouch were well known by reputation to American shipping men. Scourge of the American Hawaiian Steamship Company, Crouch had managed to thoroughly alienate the master of the ss CANADIAN on which he had shipped to Chile the previous year. That ship's Master, Captain J. Thompson had cause to complain bitterly about this man's conduct to the United States Consul at Chañaral, Chile on April 23, 1938. Here is what Captain Thompson said:

> The following information has been furnished by the officers and members of the crew who witnessed or were involved in the riot aboard the S.S. "CANADIAN" on April 22, at Antofagasta.
>
> That the two men William Crouch and Edward Tassin, who were turned over to the police at Antofagasta, were solely responsible for starting the riot is very apparent from the following.
>
> Crouch and Tassin stood around the gangway from about 12:30 till 2:00 A.M. waiting for certain members of the crew. While waiting at the gangway they were overheard planning what they were going to do to certain men when they returned on board. During the time they were waiting they were drinking liquor from a bottle which was passed from one to the other. I made an attempt to take the bottle from Crouch but it was thrown over the side, struck the gangway and broke against the ship's hull.
>
> About 2:00 A.M. a motor launch with several members of the crew in it returned to the ship. Tassin and Crouch rushed down the gangway and as

---

[26] August 5, 1939 letter from Captain Bauer to H.E. Frick. Copy in 901 file in RG 178 at Maritime Administration.

[27] ibid.

the launch came alongside the ship, these two men jumped into the launch and the fighting started at once.

The fighting raged back and forth across three motor launches (two men went overboard) up the gangway and about the ship. Everything at hand was used in the fight, cups, dishes, bottles, etc., even to a fire axe which Tassin had in his hands (He used a fire axe in another fight aboard this vessel) and was rushing back into the fight just as the police arrived. By this time the crew was in such a state of mind that the police had some difficulty protecting Crouch and Tassin, and I feel that they would surely have been killed if they remained aboard the vessel.

The past conduct of these men has been very unsatisfactory. On three former occasions they have been the leaders in drunken fights. In these past fights they have always managed to work out on the smaller members of the crew. This time they took on men who were not afraid of them and who were fed up with the general conditions on board. The result was that all the past sufferers joined in to help and the fight turned into a riot.

There were several men injured in the riot and one of these may be very serious, a possible concussion of the brain.

I have logged these-man for starting a riot (R.S. 5359 U.S.C. 18–483) and in addition have classed them as deserters because by reason of an unlawful and willful act of their own doing they were not on board when sailing from a foreign port.

If you refuse to accept this classification, I request that they be paid off as allowed by Executive Order of Oct. 16, 1937, 202-I.

In view of the above information and facts if there is any attempt to place these men back on board the "CANADIAN" it mould be against my advice and any person, officer or agent, who orders these men returned to the "CANADIAN" assumes full responsibility for their safety.

Under the present conditions and feelings their very safety would be endangered by being allowed to return to this vessel.[28]

Panama Agencies Company manager E.J. Brown was well acquainted with the episode. Tassin, in fact, had been present at the hearing that Saturday, and true to his bad form, was unruly. Here are Brown's words to H.E. on the CANADIAN's troubles:

> Our records indicate that Crouch and Tassin were removed from the CANADIAN in Chile and repatriated to the Canal on outside vessels as steerage passengers, and thence to California by vessels of the American Hawaiian Line.
>
> No doubt Messrs. American Hawaiian Line have their Master's full report on the case, and would be glad to furnish you with the details in the event that you are interested. We attach hereto copy of report of the Master of the CANADIAN to the American Consul at Antofagasta in this regard.[29]

---

[28] April 23, 1938 letter from Captain J. Thompson, Master ssCANADIAN, to U.S. Consul at Chañaral, Chile. Copy in the 901 file for the ssPRESIDENT HAYES in RG 178 at Maritime Administration.

[29] August 7, 1939 report from Panama Agencies Company to APL VicePresident H.E. Frick. Copy in the ship's 901 file in RG 178 at Maritime Administration.

Neither Kelleher or Crouch had predicted the furious reaction of steamship line and civil authorities. Nor, it seems, did they wit one inkling of the proceedings of a special U.S. Senate Committee then investigating conditions aboard American merchant ships. Chairman of that Committee, Senator Josiah W. Bailey of North Carolina asked APL president Joseph Sheehan for information about the incident on August 5th. Sheehan provided details by letter to Senator Bailey on August 10th:

It seems to me that the best way to give you a graphic report concerning the incident referred to in your letter to me of August 5 is to send you copies of the correspondence which was exchanged between the Master of the President Hayes, our New York office and our San Francisco office. These copies are herewith enclosed and will give you a running story of developments as they took place chronologically.

You will see that the two men who assaulted the two Engineers were finally taken off the ship in the Canal Zone, brought before the Magistrate's Court there, where they pleaded guilty and were held over for the District Court. The case will come up for hearing about August 15th.

In addition to the correspondence above referred to, I am also enclosing the complete report which was received on Tuesday, August 8, from the Master of the vessel. It is not possible for us to conclude from these reports how many men may have been guilty of disobedience of orders, although it seems as though at least one may be so charged. With a view to taking prompt and proper action with regard to these men our attorney in leaving San Francisco tonight for Los Angeles. He will most the President Hayes outside the breakwater at Los Angeles before the ship is docked next Monday morning, August 14, and will immediately take testimony from the officers to ascertain to what extent disobedience actually took place, the number of men involved and the nature of the charges to be brought against them. It is expected that our attorney will be accompanied by a representative of the United States Attorney from Los Angeles and that the action of the United States Attorney with regard to these son will be predicated upon the nature of the testimony given by the ship's officers.

As you will see by the cablegram which were exchanged between our home office and the vessel, we were distinctly anxious that no complications arise which might make it technically impossible for the two men who committed the assault to receive the full punishment which might be applicable under the law, and it is our intention to prosecute to the fullest extent those men who may be charged with disobedience of orders.

Although your letter referred solely to the incident on the President Hayes, I know that as Chairman of the Special Committee to Investigate Conditions In the American Merchant Marine you will be interested to learn of two other incidents which have occurred on ships of our Company. On July 25 the Master of the President Coolidge advised that one of the men on his ship had been assaulted by another with a meat hook on July 15, when the vessel was on the high seas, and had been seriously injured. Immediately upon receipt of this information our Counsel communicated with the United States Attorney and the result of their conference was that we intend, upon the arrival of the President Coolidge in San Francisco, to bring charges against the man involved for assault with intent to commit murder. The Master of the ship has been instructed to keep the man in the brig, to impose no other penalty and to deliver him into the hands of the authorities when the ship arrives in San Francisco. The Special Agent in Charge of the Federal Bureau of Investigation at San Francisco has been given full information regarding this matter and has advised that the Bureau will make an appropriate investigation upon the arrival of the Coolidge in San Francisco.

The other affair occurred on the last voyage of the President Garfield which terminated New York on May 17. On this voyage the night pantryman was assaulted by an oiler. When the ship arrived in New York charges against the oiler were preferred before the Bureau of Marine Investigation. On May 10 this Bureau held a hearing and it has been reported to me that the oiler appeared at the hearing drunk and insulted practically everybody in the room. The Bureau charged the oiler with misconduct and intemperance and set his trial for May 18th. However, on May 16 the Bureau advised that the case was 'postponed until further notice'. No further notice has ever been given and it is not to be expected that when the ship again arrives in New York after its voyage round-the-world all the essential witnesses and the oiler will be available or that the postponed hearing will then be held. It appears therefore that the oiler will escape all penalty. This man had been logged and penalized while on board ship and about the only thing left for us in this particular case was to bring charges against him before the BMI and ask that his certificate be taken away from him. It was the experience that we had in this particular case which has made it necessary for us to advise our Masters that in the case of serious trouble they should not impose superficial penalties at sea but merely enter the incident in the log and thus make it possible for us to bring action when the ship returns to port.

Tuesday, while in conversation with the Counsel of the Matson Navigation Company, he told me that he had a case on his hands which happened on the last voyage of the SS Mariposa. This was also a case of assault, and I suggested to Mr. Harrison, the Counsel referred to, that he write you and give you the whole story. This, Mr. Harrison said he would do, and you will undoubtedly hear from him in the near future.

In sending you this rather formidable list of unusually bad cases involving ships sailing under the American flag, I hope I may be permitted to express the opinion that Conditions generally on the ships of this Company are far from being as bad as these cases might make them appear to be. On the other hand, these are outstanding and very exceptional and we have begun to feel that passengers and shippers may now expect at least as good service on our ships as they can got on ships of any other nation. This feeling seems to be borne out by the fairly large number of letters which we have received from passengers who have commended our service and who have in some cases gone to great lengths to assure us of the excellence of the food and attitude of the crews. For several months now we have enjoyed splendid patronage and our revenues have been excellent. I have been very much pleased to note that these incidents which I have outlined have been kept out of the press as publication of them would do us a great deal of harm.

If there is any other information or data which you should want I shall, of course, be most happy to supply it at once.[30]

Joseph Sheehan was in touch with Senator Bailey once more during the month of August 1939. Informing the Senator further, the shipping executive wrote:

I have received your letters of August 16 and 17, and I am sure that you are completely correct in your attitude toward incidents like that which took place on our ship, the PRESIDENT HAYES. Such occurrences are unusual and I am very happy to report that since the services of this company were re-established they have been noticeable by their absence. I have endeavored to develop a better understanding and good relations with the various maritime labor unions and I feel that much has been accomplished along these lines. Certainly the numerous letters which we have received from passengers have indicated that the crews on our vessels have been trying to do a reasonably good job.

When the PRESIDENT HAYES reached Los Angeles on August 14 she was met by representatives of the Department of Justice, of the Bureau of Marine Investigation, and our Counsel. After a preliminary hearing held on board ship the representatives of the Department of Justice decided that there was no basis for action on their part. When the ship arrived at San Francisco, however, the Bureau of Marine Investigation held a hearing to decide what action, if any, should be taken with regard to the men who were alleged to have been guilty of disobedience of orders. We do not know what report the representatives of the B.M.I. will render so that at this moment I am unable to advise you what the final outcome of the whole matter will be.

In my previous correspondence I referred to an assault case which took place on the President Coolidge. This ship arrived in port last Friday and the alleged assailant is now in the hands of the United States Marshal pending further notion.

I do not know whether or not you desire to be kept informed with regard, to the developments in these various matters. I shall be very glad to send you the details if you desire, but do not wish to burden you with a lot of correspondence if you prefer not to have me do so.[31]

Languishing in jail under the hot Panamanian summer sun, Crouch and Kelleher were convicted of mutiny by virtue of their own plea. The PRESIDENT HAYES was long gone from Panama when both men were sentenced on August 26, 1939 to five months at hard labor at Gamboa Penitentiary. From his Washington office at the Maritime Commission commented Ralph King to a colleague: "this was a break for the men. Lundberg (a Maritime Commission attorney) himself expected two years . . ."[32]

---

[30] August 10, 1939 letter from Joseph Sheehan to Senator Josiah Bailey. Copy in the ship's 901 file in RG 178 at Maritime Administration.
[31] August 24th letter from Joseph Sheehan to Senator Bailey. ibid.
[32] Memo in the 901 file for the PRESIDENT HAYES in RG 178 in the custody of the Maritime Administration.

Such stories help explain the lack of esteem for maritime unions held by so many people over the years.

The voyage continued from San Francisco with her August 20th sailing. When war broke out in Europe on September 3rd, the PRESIDENT HAYES was in the Pacific, arriving at Singapore in the middle of that month. Further aggravation awaited Captain Bauer at Port Said on October 17th. This time it wasn't his crew but local officials who frustrated him. Since war had broken out between Britain and Germany, British officials detained the PRESIDENT HAYES on October 22nd and took their time effecting a leisurely search for contraband. When they found nothing they released the ship on the following day and allowed her to continue on her way to Italy and France. With the provisions of America's Pittman Act taking effect in November, the ship's October 25, 1939 call at Marseilles was her last there in order not to contravene American neutrality. By the time American ships were allowed into French ports in 1941, the PRESIDENT HAYES was no longer routed homeward through the Mediterranean. The homeward voyage was slow and with a large number of passengers the ship arrived at Boston on November 12th.

The PRESIDENT HAYES closed out 1939 on the West Coast. Looping down from San Francisco to work cargo, the HAYES greeted the New Year at Los Angeles. Then the PRESIDENT HAYES steamed up the coast to her home port for a brief appearance before setting out on another globe-girdling trip. By January 31, 1940 she was on her way out of Bombay. There was no Suez Canal transit nor any Mediterranean ports on that trip. Conforming to the spirit of American neutrality laws, American President Lines routed the round the world liners away from any immediate harm they might suffer in the Mediterranean and when the PRESIDENT HAYES departed Bombay, she set a course for South Africa and her February 15th maiden call at Cape Town. From there she returned to North America and a March 8, 1940 arrival at New York.

Scheduled to sail from New York on March 8th, her departure was delayed and her second trip that year began on March 17th. Two days earlier she had come in from Boston where she had unloaded the last of her inbound cargo from the previous voyage.

Tension reigned on the deck of every neutral vessel steaming through the waters of a world heading towards total war. Many American ships carried cargo for the nation's young defense effort. Aboard the PRESIDENT HAYES was such a cargo when the Maritime Commission advised the War Department by wire on February 7th: "HAYES due New York 3/7/40 with 1,337 tons of rubber for New York. They ask arrangements be made shift ship to Brooklyn Army Base to make direct delivery and avoid lighterage expense."[33] Happy to comply, the Army invited the liner to unload rubber at their Brooklyn terminal. After discharging her cargo there, on March 11th

---

[33] Copy in the ship's 901 file. RG 178 Maritime Administration.

she shifted to Robins Drydock for inspection and voyage repair. Eight days later she returned to her Jersey City pier to resume loading for her next sailing around the world.

Crew tensions, so disruptive in the past, settled down a little. One unlicensed engine room man was out on report, but over the course of the trip, the most notable item in crew relations with the Line was a letter from Union Delegate Andy Anderson. Representing Local #1733, he sounded like an enthused passenger in his March 31st note:

> A word of appreciation is in order this time in re: the Chief Steward Louis Kurtz.
> The food this time has been excellent both in quality and quantity, and variety, as well as the service the entire voyage around the world.
> This man as Chief Steward is a credit to any ship, and is most worthy of these few words of our esteem.[34]

The PRESIDENT HAYES sailed once more under the command of Captain H.S. Bauer from San Francisco on April 13th. Aboard was a rather large crew (for a freighter) numbering four deck and eight engine officers assisted by one deck and three engine cadets; 16 men in the deck department, 28 men in the engine department, 1 radio operator, 21 stewards. Occupied were all 12 of her passenger beds and it was obvious that the ship would once again be carrying more than that number. The ship was in the Indian Ocean in June when serious talk about refitting her passenger beds was heard. The American Consul at Cape Town wanted to use the PRESIDENT HAYES to carry home a number of Americans clamoring for northbound passage. Asked if they had any objection to the carriage of passengers from South Africa to the United States by American President Liners, both the American South African Line and the Seas Shipping Company, America's two subsidized lines to the region, expressed their approval. Permission to allow this freighter to resume her earlier status as a passenger and cargo liner and carry over 100 passengers northbound on that trip was sought. A telegram from Admiral Land, Chairman of the Maritime Commission to American President Lines on the matter was blunt. If the Line wanted to increase the number of passengers the ship could carry, she would need a temporary certificate, implying the need to follow the rules even in the "present emergency". However, he further noted, the Consul had the authority to grant such a paper and left the matter in his hands. In a separate communication to Secretary of State Cordell Hull on June 6th, Chairman Land indicated that the State Department would have to affix the number of passengers and grant a temporary certificate on a voyage by voyage basis.

Inbound from her second Cape Town and Trinidad calls the PRESIDENT HAYES arrived at New York on July 6, 1940. It must have been about that

---

[34] March 31, 1940 letter by Union delegate Anderson to American President Lines' Port Steward Robinson in the ship's 901 files in RG 178 in Maritime Administration.

time that Captain Bauer was relieved by Captain Valdemar Nielsen. With no hope of an early end to Europe's war, it was evident that the ship would be carrying more than 12 passengers for the foreseeable future. To handle added paperwork, three pursers were added to the ship's complement. In time, another ten men would be added to the ship's steward's department to look after her passengers.

Her last trip as PRESIDENT HAYES began at New York on July 19, 1940 and from San Francisco on August 14th. From Manila on September 8th and Hong Kong on the 11th, the ship visited Singapore, Penang, Colombo, Bombay plus the "new" ports of Cape Town and Trinidad. An October 29, 1940 message from the Maritime Commission advised American President Lines to prepare all bills of lading for the ship's next sailing, then scheduled for November 22nd, with the ship's new name PRESIDENT TYLER. One of the C3 P combination passenger and cargo liners then building at Newport News was ready for a name. American President Lines wanted to continue the names of six of the "502"s on the round the world service and assigned her the name PRESIDENT HAYES. On the November 5th authorization to surrender her marine documents, Order C-766, was issued. The old ship arrived at New York on November 10, 1940. On the evening of November 14th the "502" sailed from New York for Boston, still named PRESIDENT HAYES. She would be renamed shortly after her return to New York. On November 20th, her marine documents as PRESIDENT HAYES were turned in at the Customs House, where at 3:30 PM new documents for her in the name PRESIDENT TYLER were handed to representatives of American President Lines. She was the first of the "502"s to get her "President" name changed.

A short commercial career as PRESIDENT TYLER awaited her. Sailing from New York with a crew of 80 officers and men under the command of Captain Bauer on November 22, 1940 for the first time under her third name, the ship called at ports familiar. There was a Canal transit on November 29th and a San Francisco arrival on December 11th. That trip kept her busy until her March 16, 1941 New York arrival and was her last subsidized sailing. While the ship was underway, the Maritime Commission had acted on an American President Lines' request to allow the ship to operate an unsubsidized voyage from New York on American President Lines' Line A—to Singapore and Penang that summer.

Pursuant to a grounding and some earlier problems there were repairs to be made. These included renewal of lower stem, renewal of ten plates forward as well as repair and straightening of floors, frames and tank tops as well as partial renewal of machinery. The main engine was opened and overhauled where needed as were condensers and auxiliary circulators. Fuel tanks were steam cleaned and other sundry damage made good.

On this special voyage the ship sailed from New York on March 26, 1941. With a heavy cargo she went through the Canal on April 2nd, and arrived Los Angeles on April 11th. She sailed for ports across the Pacific from San

Francisco on April 18th. Calls this time were few. No outbound stop was made at Honolulu and the ship reached Manila on May 10th, Singapore on May 21st and Penang on May 26th. Next was Colombo, and from there to Bombay, Cape Town and Trinidad. By the time the PRESIDENT TYLER arrived at New York on July 21st, the Maritime Commission had authorized another trip on the same run. Dock workers quickly landed some cargo and the ship steamed up to Boston for more freight and was back in time to depart from New York for the Straits on July 31st. This time there was no San Francisco call and she sailed from San Pedro on August 20th for Malaya. This time she called at Shanghai, stopping there for a two day call between September 11th and 13th on her way into Hong Kong where she made a September 15th arrival. Manila was next and the ship pulled in to that American run port on September 23rd. Homeward the PRESIDENT TYLER made another Shanghai call, stopping there on October 2nd. On that rare crossing east across the Pacific, this "502" called at Honolulu on November 16th bound for San Francisco where she arrived on November 23rd. Two days later she slipped out of port on her way south to Los Angeles. By then few in the military or shipping business maintained much of an illusion that America would much longer remain neutral in the war. That's one reason why the Maritime Commission had permitted the Line to operate the ship on that unsubsidized voyage. Towards the middle of that month the Navy ordered the ship to be fitted with degaussing equipment, defensive armament and an armed guard. That work was scheduled to be performed during the ship's December 19th call at Boston but things did not happen quite that way. As the ship arrived at San Pedro on November 27, 1941 orders were issued for the ship to receive some light defensive equipment and degaussing cable at New York after her December 15th arrival at Pier J, Erie Basin, Brooklyn. From Los Angeles the PRESIDENT HAYES sailed for New York on November 28th. She was off Panama on her way to the Panama Canal on December 7, 1941 when America was attacked by military forces of the Empire of Japan.

An approaching war didn't do much to quell fractious activities of some of the PRESIDENT TYLER's crewmembers. Their unruly conduct occupied men in the Maritime Commission once more. Frustrated after a decade or so of intense labor unrest in the maritime industry on the Pacific Coast, more and more executives and officials were determined to quell problematic crew men. On November 28, San Francisco Field Representative addressed the topic in a letter to Ralph King, then Chief of the Commission's Maritime Personnel Division, Field Section in Washington:

> I am enclosing a copy of the disciplinary action on board the S.S. PRESIDENT TYLER for this vessel's past voyage.
> From reports of the Engineers and Mates onboard this ship, the crew ran wild in all ports. I was also told that unless the Government makes some attempt to properly discipline these men, that it will soon be impossible to retain the capable Engineers and Mates who are now manning these ships.

They feel that logging and fining these men is not the answer and that some other procedure will have to be worked out.

In the case of the PRESIDENT TYLER in port, no one would turn to, and as for making the average repairs to the main engine, it was a case of the Engineers and one or two of the sober men doing all the work.

It was reported that in some ports men that were assigned to donkey watches would be required to work from twelve to twenty hours without being relieved. It was so bad that men who ordinarily remain sober and on the jobs after being forced to stand some drunkard's watch, would go ashore and get drunk in self-defense.

These drunks are driving the good men off the ships and it will eventually leave only the "gas hounds" to sail them. All attempts by the Unions to discipline their members meet with little, if any, success, as the usual procedure is to fine them. The fine is paid and then they sail out on some other ship.

Some way should be created to take up the certificates of the chronic drunks from thirty days to six months, and longer for the habitual drunkard.

With the wages, bonus and overtime now being paid onboard the ship's, the mere paying of fines ceases to be a factor of control over the men, and it is the opinion of the majority of the interested parties who have been consulted on this matter that the only effective procedure will have to be the removal of the certificates for certain specific charges of drunkenness.

Would it be possible for the Department of Commerce, the U.S. Attorney General and division to collaborate in drawing up certain penalties for drunkenness onboard ship; and after the penalties have been made into laws, allow the U.S. Shipping Commissioner the power to enforce the law and make it mandatory that prior to paying off, all such disciplinary action shall take place with the crew assembled. Such logbook entries could be read off and the disciplinary action take place immediately.

Placards could be printed showing the various penalties for drunkenness and other infractions of the ships discipline and when these characters get drunk, miss watches, etc., they know what the penalty will be and that *it will be enforced.*

Some of the fines that were paid for missing watches, drunkenness, etc. on the last voyage of the PRESIDENT TYLER are—

Strand	(Oiler)	$74.69
Fleming	''	64.02
Leonard	''	42.68
Butrica	''	21.34
Sotomayor	(Fireman)	35.00

Your cooperation in this matter will be appreciated.[35]

When war broke out while the ship was in Central American waters, orders came for her to proceed in blacked out conditions for New York where she arrived unheralded a few days later. Now painted grey all over, five

---

[35] November 28, 1941 letter from B.J. Sullivan to Philip King. Copy in the ship's 901 file in RG 178 at Maritime Administration.

days into the new year, on January 5, 1942, the PRESIDENT TYLER shifted into the yards of the Robins Drydock Company where $161,000.00 was invested in modifications to render the ship suitable for war purposes. That sum wasn't the extent invested in her this time, for the Maritime Commission authorized the expenditure of another $85,000.00 to cover repairs to the ship for heavy weather damage on her previous trip. Actually, nature caught her twice and once more pounded her severely. The liner suffered weather damage during a storm between September 5th and 6th, 1941 while steaming between Los Angeles and Shanghai and the ship was again damaged while between Shanghai and Hong Kong between September 15th and 16th, 1941.

On January 8, 1942, one month and one day after Japan's attack on Pearl Harbor, Hong Kong and the Philippines, the United States Maritime Commission officially chartered the PRESIDENT TYLER and her twin PRESIDENT FILLMORE. They announced a quick allocation of both vessels to the United States Navy. At the Robins yard at 10:00 AM on January 9th the PRESIDENT TYLER was delivered to the Maritime Commission under time charter at a rate of $1,011.91 per day. She was simultaneously turned over under a sub-charter to the Navy. Aboard were 2,767 barrels of oil fuel and 90 tons of water, which the Maritime Commission paid for in its first monthly charter payment to American President Lines. For recording purposes the ship began Owner's voyage 58 and WSA voyage 1 at the moment of delivery to the Government. Damage repairs were completed by January 15th, and modifications to suit the ship to the needs of a nation of war took two days longer. Remaining with the ship for the time being were Captain H.S. Bauer and his civilian crew of 95 officers and men. All had signed articles for a voyage to Suez but the Navy had another destination in mind for the ship. At 1:55 PM on January 18, 1942 the PRESIDENT TYLER sailed from New York on her first War Shipping Administration voyage. Her first port of call: Charleston, South Carolina. Then it was on to the Panama Canal and the South Pacific and Australia. February 26th brought her assignment to the management of the Oceanic Steamship Company for her northbound voyage to San Francisco. A Papeete call was scheduled so she could load 4,500 tons of copra, a highly fragrant commodity, but not a very sweet one. She arrived at San Francisco with that pungent cargo on March 13, 1942. Through April 7th the ship remained at San Francisco, technically idle. Actually there was quite a bit going on aboard her at the time.

Legalities, technicalities and paperwork covering the PRESIDENT TYLER, as it did her surviving sisterships, occupied the authorities from time to time. While she served the War Shipping Administration as an allocated troopship, she was covered by service agreement WSA 224, a blanket agreement backdated to cover the first days of any of the APL ships taken for war national service even before the outbreak of war. As for the paperwork covering the delivery of the PRESIDENT TYLER to the War Shipping Administration and the military, the Maritime Commission authorized rewritten paperwork on March 26, 1942. On the following day the original time charter was amended to read "bareboat" charter and papers altered accordingly. Ready for signatures some time later was a new version of WSA-111, the document specifically written to cover the PRESIDENT TYLER. The ship spent three years under this arrangement, but American President Lines was equally interested in prompt payment of charter hire. The original Time Charter was duly cancelled by the Government on March 27th and the ship came under bareboat charter, backdated to the moment of her January 9th delivery. At the end of March 1942 the company noted receipt of the Maritime Commission's check to them in the amount of $82,554.97, to cover the ship's charter hire to date plus the fuel and water on board upon delivery.

Fulfilling the concept of her origin in the emergency shipbuilding program of World War I, the PRESIDENT TYLER was now fitted to transport soldiers. At a cost of $104,761.48, the unimproved "502" passenger and cargo liner was converted into a troop transport with sleeping space for about 2,000 troops, officers, and anyone else who managed to procure travel orders beyond the requisite facilities to permit sustenance, basic sanitation and ventilation. Modifications to the vessel extended topsides. In the style of four sisters modified before the war, her superstructure was enlarged by connecting forward and aft houses. Her funnel was modified as well, topped by a strange cap that made it look like a mushroom. It must have achieved the expected results, for she carried that funnel cap until the end of her days.

Her outbound wartime voyages, 58 through 75 were all under the management of American President Lines, though whenever coming inbound from the Antipodes, the ship was handled by sub-agents, usually the Oceanic Steamship Company, a subsidiary of Matson Navigation Company. There was a bit more to the complex array of her control. Though from the beginning of Voyage 58 on January 9, 1942 she was nominally in Navy hands, the ship was actually under charter to the War Shipping Administration, and later passed under Army control. No matter which branch of the service was actually paying the sub-charter, she spent most of the war years carrying primarily Army personnel.

Working mostly in the Pacific, she made five voyages between San Francisco and Honolulu in 1942, and six in 1943. After her brief refit at San Francisco the PRESIDENT TYLER began Voyage 59 on April 8th and sailed on her next outbound voyage from there on April 12th. That early wartime cruise brought official investigation into the conduct of some of her crew while ashore on May 17th at Suva, Fiji. Raising eyebrows all over, it brought the ire of military officials upon a carousing crew:

> Conduct of Merchant Marine personnel while ashore in Suva, Fiji Islands of such nature as to bring disgrace upon our Government. At Royal Theatre, Suva, during the playing of the British National Anthem, members of Merchant Marine Crew, executed Nazi salute, while pictures of His Majesty, George VI, flashed on screen. Riots at public dance hall, resulting in bad feeling against Americans. District Commissioner, Lavuka, Fiji Islands, very worried relative to report Police Commissioner, Suva, to effect that Ameri-

348 ◇ CREOLE STATE/ PRESIDENT HAYES

cans on board PRESIDENT TYLER, very bad crew, carrying knives and pistols ashore, as well as molesting women during the blackouts. Results of drunken and boisterous conduct of Merchant Marine personnel, were very damaging to prestige of American. I believe this problem very serious one, and am convinced that it could be remedied by extension of Naval Authority over Merchant Marine personnel, ashore in foreign ports, where no direct control may be exercised by Merchant Marine Officers.[36]

That report worked it's way up the chain of command until Lieutenant H.A. Burch, an officer in the Office of the Chief of Naval Operations sent it on in confidence to the Maritime Commission on July 6th.

After her trip to Australia she arrived back at San Francisco on June 16, 1942 to end that second wartime voyage there on June 21st. Next was Owner's Voyage 60, WSA Voyage 3 and after it began on June 22nd, the ship took on cargo and men for the Antipodes. On June 30, 1942, by addendum 9 to Contract WSA-111, the ship's charter rate was increased to $1,045.33 per day as of June 30th. Further clarification of how the technicalities of the ship's operation came forth on September 17th. Included in the message was not just the PRESIDENT TYLER but a number of other ships as well. From then on until the end of hostilities, the PRESIDENT TYLER and her sisterships PRESIDENT FILLMORE and PRESIDENT GRANT, the new C3 P ships PRESIDENT POLK and PRESIDENT MONROE, the aged PRESIDENT JOHNSON and a number of freighters including the "Liberty" ship John C. Fremont served under Navy orders but under American President Lines' operation under SW-1 warrants. Aboard the PRESIDENT TYLER on July 21st, her Master and Oceanic Steamship wired the War Shipping Administration for permission to load a homeward cargo in her and in the accompanying "Hog Islander" NIRA LUCKENBACH, rather than sail the ships back to San Francisco in ballast. Also dated September 17th was a form letter to the Line from the San Francisco War Shipping Administrator that assigned her to the United States Army Transport Service, the ship was allocated to American President Lines for operation under a General Agency agreement and was ready to go on berth. Luckily, someone scribbled the word "Hawaii" in big letters, suggesting that's where the ship next went when she finally sailed on Voyage 60 on July 8th. She may have gone further into the Pacific because she only returned to her home port on September 20th. There was not much to unload, for the voyage ended on the following day. Beginning Voyage 61, WSA Voyage 4, on September 22nd the PRESIDENT TYLER sailed again on the 26th, this time on a shuttle trip to Hawaii that ended back at San Francisco on October 19th, a day after her arrival.

Further word of her status came from Ralph Keating of the Washington, D.C. office of the War Shipping Administration who advised the San Francisco office of the WSA that the PRESIDENT TYLER was one of 24 merchant

---

[36] July 6, 1942 confidential memo from Lieutenant Burch to Huntington Morse of the Maritime Commission. Copy in the ship's 901 file in RG 178 at the Maritime Administration.

ships on Navy Special Service through October 31st of that year. Unfortunately, wartime constraints limited his message to those few words and details of just what that special service was are lacking.

Indications of her movements, including limited expenditures for consumable stores and expendable equipment, suggest that the ship made at least two round voyages to Hawaii during the fall and early winter of 1942. Voyage 62, WSA Voyage 5, was a 25 day trip occupying her between October 20 and November 13th. She sailed on that trip on October 23rd. From November 14th began a period of idleness, probably a euphemististic description for the time period during which the ship had a brief overhaul at a San Francisco area yard. In any event it lasted util December 2nd. Then came Voyage 63, WSA Voyage 6, and it lasted from December 3rd through the 29th. As the year came to a close the War Shipping Administration asked the Navy for permission to add an extra Purser to the PRESIDENT TYLER as "she is in service with lots of troops and passengers." Such leave was granted and an extra man signed on in time for Voyage 64, WSA Voyage 7, which began on December 30, 1942. She sailed from San Francisco with a capacity load of troops and friends on January 11, 1943. Back again on February 2nd, that voyage would end two days later on February 4, 1943. While she was on that trip a tremendous amount of paperwork handled a change in her official status. With three fleetmates the PRESIDENT TYLER was then requisitioned for title, effective upon the completion of the ship's current voyage. Though the decision to that effect came through on January 1, 1943, the War Shipping Administration took its time getting word of the transaction to the ship's owners who received the Government's January 12th telegram on the following morning. Here are the words the Large Vessels Procurement Section of the War Shipping Administration used to inform Captain Granville Conway, Atlantic Coast Director of the WSA of what was in the works:

> Administrator signed and sent following telegram to American President Lines Inc. Quote 'War Shipping Administrator desires to requisition possession and use of your SSs PRESIDENT TYLER, PRESIDENT JOHNSON, PRESIDENT MONROE and PRESIDENT POLK on bareboat basis, pursuant to section 902 of Merchant Marine Act, 1936, as amended. Administrator agrees requisition charter to be substantially similar to existing charter covering vessels except for minor modifications effective from date of taking under this requisition. New requisition charter to include provision as to indemnification and provide for redelivery of vessels in same condition on redelivery as required by existing charters. Furthermore, administrator willing to waive condition surveys of vessels and inventories and agrees to adopt inventories and surveys taken when vessels were originally delivered under previous form of charter. Just compensation for use of such vessels and valuation in event of loss to be determined by administrator after consultation with your representatives, in accordance with above mentioned provision of law. Administrator desires that this requisition shall be effective as of expiration of previous charters. Kindly advise immediately if this is

acceptable. Otherwise this requisition shall be effective as of noon January 14, 1943. Captain Conway, Atlantic Coast Director, has been instructed to take possession of the vessels and he or his representative will give you appropriate receipts therefor. Please confirm with him.' You will be advised as soon as possible as to the effective date of this requisition so that proper receipts may be issued.[37]

The line of course had to accept the requisition but APL president Henry Grady still thought a few points uncovered. He cabled Washington on January 13th stating:

Requisitions of PRESIDENTS TYLER, JOHNSON, MONROE and POLK per terms of your telegram this date acceptable, subject to understanding first. References your telegram that requisition effective as of expiration of previous charters refers to dates of completion pending voyages and not to extensions of such dates to permit restoration to condition at time of delivery, and second, if determination regarding compensation for use and valuation in event of loss, when made, should be unacceptable within acceptance shall in no way prejudice or impair legal rights otherwise available.[38]

In response to continuing complaints about the shoreside conduct of many American merchant crews, Congress opened an investigation of slack discipline aboard American ships, particularly the PRESIDENT TYLER during March and the PRESIDENT POLK during January 1942, hearing the first witnesses on February 8th, 1943.

Considering the emergency conditions of the time and the dangers to which her soldiers, officers and passengers could face from enemy action, the Maritime Commission issued a waiver of navigation laws for the PRESIDENT TYLER on January 20, 1943. Under that waiver the ship was exempt from all rules then extant for passenger carrying vessels. Under that waiver the War Shipping Administration, the Navy and or the Army could send the ship to sea with more "souls" aboard than permitted by any normal certificate, let the ship proceed to sea in an overloaded condition, and carry less than the requisite amount of life saving apparatus. In short, that document permitted the Government to supersede any and all conditions of the rules established by various conferences and conventions regarding the safety of life at sea.

American President Lines again acted as General Agent when Articles for owner's voyage 65, WSA Voyage 8, were signed at San Francisco on February 4, 1943, the day before the official beginning of the voyage. Her first trip under War Shipping Administration ownership, she sailed on February 8th and made her way once more to the South Pacific. Fan Tan was

---

[37] January 12, 1943 telegram from War Shipping Administrator William Radner to Captain Granville Conway. Copy in the ship's 901 file in RG 178 in custody of Maritime Administration.
[38] January 13, 1943 telegram from American President Lines' president Henry Grady to Admiral E.S. Land, Administrator, War Shipping Administration. Copy in ship's 901 file in RG 178 in the custody of Maritime Administration.

the wartime code name for Suva, Fiji, which she departed on April 3rd. Then she went on to Australia before beginning her return to the USA with her April 16th sailing from Brisbane, reported to Washington by telegram: "PRESIDENT TYLER sailed for FAN TAN 117 bags mail 3 US personnel. ADOBE 16th for San Francisco"[39] Articles were to terminate on April 19th and though the ship had reached port on that date, the voyage was not over, so they were extended.

On April 5th the War Shipping Administration heard from the Navy about this ship again, but this time the subject was armament. The Navy wanted to remove the ship's forward 4" gun and in its place install two 3"/ 50mm double purpose guns if the gun foundation aboard the ship could take them. Otherwise they would equip the ship with one 3"/50mm gun on the centerline. Nothing more on the subject appears in Maritime Commission records for the ship, but undoubtedly the Navy got its way in the matter.

In 1943 her APL Master, Captain Valdemar Nielsen, was relieved by Captain J.H. Barnhart. Though at San Francisco since April 19th, the ship's eighty-seven day long Voyage 65 only officially ended on May 2, 1943. Among the paperwork was the summary statement of consumable stores, expendable equipment and dunnage for the voyage. Filling in the allotted blanks to account for requisite expenses, such items including rope and oils came to a total of $9,450.19. Pursuant to Section 902 of the Merchant Marine Act of 1936, delivery of the PRESIDENT TYLER under requisition for title finally occurred at San Francisco at 12:01 AM, Pacific War Time on May 3, 1943. Paperwork handled in early May called the arrangements between the War Shipping Administration and American President Lines a "requisition bareboat charter" but it would be months before details of this transaction were finally sorted out. Two days later all crew members signed articles valid for the next 12 months.

Her first four voyages made under requisition charter seem to have taken her to Hawaii, relatively short haul runs made under allocation to the Navy. The ship got off to a slow start on the first of these, Voyage 66, WSA Voyage 9, colliding immediately after sailing on May 8th with LCT (5) No. 392 at Pier 44, damaging herself enough to require repairs. On her return voyage to San Francisco the authorities named Matson Navigation Company to act as sub-agent. Shared agency of the ship by American President Lines for outbound sailings and by Matson Lines inbound continued for some time, albeit on a voyage by voyage basis. That voyage ended on June 1, 1943. A day after the June 2nd start of owner's Voyage 67, WSA Voyage 10, crew signed articles valid through the 29th and on June 5th the ship was again assigned for her next outward voyage to the United States Navy. She sailed from California again on June 8th and was able to complete that voyage on June 30th. On the following day she began Voyage 68, WSA Voyage 11. July

---

[39] April 3, 1943 telegram from San Francisco office of WSA to Washington headquarters. Copy in ship's 901 file in RG 178 at Maritime Administration.

1, 1943 brought the usual form letter to American President Lines from the authorities who informed them "that the ship will soon be here (San Francisco) and has been assigned to the Navy for her next outward voyage."[40] In turn, the Navy allocated her operation to American President Lines. As usual American President Lines was informed by form letter that the ship was at San Francisco and would be under allocation to them. This letter differed a bit. Assigned to the Navy for her next outbound voyage, with her July 8th sailing to Hawaii from San Francisco, there would no longer be a general agency. Rather, American President Lines would handle the vessel under a Service Agreement Form TCA. Her destination that time is also undocumented, but she could not have gone further than Hawaii, for she returned to San Francisco on July 26th from Honolulu and the ship was under the sub-agency of the Matson Navigation Company. That voyage ended on August 3rd, several days after agreements were made for American President Lines to once again handle the ship.

Beginning on August 4th, owner's Voyage 69, WSA Voyage 12 would be a long one. On the same day the Navy asked for further allocation of the PRESIDENT TYLER for a trip from Hawaii to the South Pacific. That was approved days later as H.N. Middleton, Chief of Allocations and Assignments in San Francisco informed Captain M.S. Davis, Port Director of the Naval Transportation Service: "We have now cleared this with Washington and as usual in such cases will charge these assignments against your South Pacific requirements from this coast."[41] The ship sailed from San Francisco again on August 8th and three days later on August 11th came word from the military that the PRESIDENT TYLER would be assigned for a trip to the South Pacific. How far south the ship went on that trip is now a matter of some conjecture and what followed next is unclear. Under Matson's aegis, the PRESIDENT HAYES was supposed to sail from Honolulu on August 25th for the South Pacific. The ship sailed but apparently not on any southerly course as a memo from Jay J. Murphy, Hawaii regional director of the WSA, informed H.N. Middleton:

> Further to our letter August 6 to Mr. E.J. Bradley, copy to you, and your telegram received August 13 approving assignment of above vessel to the Navy, please be advised that she left here this morning.[42]

And though the usual form letters suggested she sailed "for South Pacific", she actually made a quick crossing to San Francisco where she arrived on October 4th. Crew articles terminated there on October 5th, and the sixty-five day voyage concluded two days later on October 7th. Next followed

---

[40] Memo to American President Lines from U.S. Navy. Copy in ship's 901 file in RG 178 at Maritime Administration.

[41] Aug. 11, 1943 letter from H.N.Middleton to Capt. Davis. Copy in the ship's 901 file in RG 178 at Maritime Administration.

[42] August 25, 1943 letter from J.J. Murphy to H.N. Middleton. Copy in ship's 901 file in RG 178 at Maritime Administration.

Voyage 70, WSA Voyage 13, a seventy-one day outing that began on October 8th and lasted through December 17th, two days after her return to San Francisco. Sailing on October 13th, it is fairly certain that the PRESIDENT TYLER made her way to Australia. This time notification of the ship's arrival from the South Pacific came to American President Lines from Washington D.C., from whence WSA Division of Traffic manager T.J. White informed the Line by letter on November 15, 1943 that any inbound cargo coming with the ship into San Francisco would be handled by sub-agent Matson Navigation Company.

The subject of valuations for the four APL ships requisitioned by the Government was addressed on paper on November 19th when the Chief of the Appraisal Section gave the heavy word. Basing his appraisal on the 1940 sale of the PRESIDENT HARDING, PRESIDENT LINCOLN, PRESIDENT MADISON and PRESIDENT WILSON, the market value of a "502" was then $655,000.00. Since the PRESIDENT FILLMORE brought $360,000.00 when sold in 1940 he allowed a figure of $360,000.00 for the nearly identical PRESIDENT JOHNSON. He allowed, however "consideration . . . to a rise in the market value although no vessels of the type were sold after 1940, the rise in market value between 1940 and 1941 being assumed to be the same as that of cargo vessels during the same period . . ."[43]

About a month later the Assistant Deputy Administrator for Maintenance and Repair prepared a statement of general repairs, defense installations and military requirement expenditures for the PRESIDENT TYLER for the period April 19—May 8, 1943, the time when the ship was requisitioned for charter by the War Shipping Administration. General repairs including repairs to main and auxiliary steam lines, main engine and feed pump, bilge suction line, blowing of valves, brine line, repair of starboard engine, port condenser, repair of seven winches, repair of ventilators, cargo booms and galley equipment and adjustment of bearings of steering engine plus replacement of chain rail and ventilator cowl, ladders and anchor light cost $38,744.39. Defense installations including removal of four 50 caliber and two 3 inch/23 guns and the installation in their place of eight 20mm and three 3"/50 ready service boxes, two battery boxes, four additional 20 mm and two 3"/50 caliber guns plus four 20 mm gun tubs, life rafts and additional gun crew quarters as well as various blackout and convoy measures cost $32,983.59. Provision of necessary requirements for military purposes, an unexplained item, cost a further $30,906.54. The total of these items was $102,634.52 to which the authorities had to add a further $2,127.46 for purchase of berthing equipment, latrine fittings and sundry stewards' department items making a grand total of $104,761.98.

December 17, 1943 brought another form letter to American President

---

[43] November 19, 1943 Valuation from Geo. W. Sturm, Chief of Appraisal Section to Director of Foreign Repairs and Salvage Operations. Copy in ship's 901 file in RG 178 in custody of Maritime Administration.

Lines informing them, that the PRESIDENT TYLER, assigned once more to the Navy for her upcoming outbound voyage, (she was actually IN San Francisco, but this was wartime and most communications regarding ship's movements and locations were either coded or couched in ambiguous terms) was at that moment about to dock at San Francisco inbound from the Central Pacific with cargo to be handled by Matson Navigation Company as sub-agent. Once again the ship would be assigned to American President Lines for the outbound voyage under a Service Agreement Form of General Agency. In fact the ship spent the period between December 18, 1943 and January 17th at San Francisco were she was given a much needed overhaul. APL handled the ship during that period of time, too.

Fresh from the yards, the PRESIDENT TYLER began owner's Voyage 71, WSA Voyage 14, on January 18, 1944. Her first trip that year, it began with the ship's January 20th departure. The ship was still eight days away inbound to San Francisco when a teletype message on March 7, 1944 to the San Francisco office of the War Shipping Administration confirmed round trip allocation extensions through April of five of the district's vessels. One of them was the PRESIDENT TYLER. Also mentioned were the American liners LURLINE and MATSONIA, the Dutch BLOEMFONTEIN and the Grace Line freighter SANTA MONICA. The usual preprinted form letter with blanks filled in on March 11, 1944 told American President Lines to expect the ship inbound from the South Pacific. After coming into her home port a few days later the voyage ended on March 20th. From March 21st the ship was on owner's Voyage 72, WSA Voyage 15. That turned out to be a short run for the Navy to Hawaii and back which took her out of San Francisco on March 25th and brought her back on April 11th, the day the voyage ended, so it is obvious she came in very light if not empty.

The next two weeks were spent idle at San Francisco. In all probability the WSA had local yards perform some work and sundry voyage repairs on her at that time. Someone must have been asleep at the switch for on April 14, 1944 the Navy sent the usual form letter to American President Lines to inform them that the PRESIDENT TYLER would soon arrive from the Central Pacific. The ship was already there.

For owner's Voyage 73, WSA Voyage 16, the PRESIDENT TYLER was once again allocated to the Navy for her subsequent outbound trip. American President Lines once more was to handle everything in connection with her departure. The ship would sail again on May 8th but let what happened to Junior Assistant Purser Stanley Russell who was rushing to get ashore at noon on May 6, 1944 as a gangway was being removed stand as a warning to all that derring-do sometimes doesn't do at all! To the scene came Captain William J. Ball, Marine Casualty Investigating Officer. An excerpt from his report about the accident that befell the Junior Purser as the PRESIDENT TYLER prepared to shift from San Francisco's Pier 41 to Pier 37 to load government cargo sheds light:

The gangway abreast of No. 9 hatch was being removed, all of the lashings having been let go, the inshore end being on a fork lift truck which was accomplishing the removal of the gangway. Despite three warnings from the Military Policeman at the end of the gangway aboard the ship and of the Pier Officer on the apron of the wharf, Russell jumped onto the gangway in an endeavor to get ashore. This caused the gangway to slip from the ship's side and fall approximately fifteen feet to the stringer, and Russell to fall to the apron of the wharf and sustain direct injuries, which consist of a broken rib, contused chest, and lacerations over his right eye. Russell was taken to the Fort Mason dispensary, where he was treated and ordered confined to sick quarters for thirty days.[44]

Considerably eased since their furious days in the 1930's, crew trouble showed up aboard the PRESIDENT TYLER in yet another form, perhaps one of the oldest known to man. On July 21, 1944 two crew members, a waiter and a room steward, accused of theft from a shipmate, were removed from the ship. Returned to the United States aboard the CAPE BRETON, John Perry and Harold Cleminson were tried for theft on the high seas. Convicted, Perry went to jail for six months while Cleminson won probation. From each man's wages, the Navy asked American President Lines to deduct the sum of $172.00 to cover the cost of his passage home. Not asked to perform any duty other than keep their quarters on the CAPE BRETON clean while en route to the United States, in light of their conviction, the Navy felt no need to reduce the passage cost to the usual $2.00 per day per man subsistence charge.

It was not long before the ship was once more the subject of a flurry of paperwork. Leaving Tarakina on June 26, 1944 the PRESIDENT TYLER grounded, damaging her hull between frames #10 and 11 and some fresh water tanks. When steel ruptured, salt water contaminated those fresh water tanks. After her mid August return to San Francisco, the voyage ended on the 25th. Then began her fifth period of idleness since coming under WSA and navy control in January 1942. Now the ship went to one of the Bethlehem Steel Company yards in the Bay area for repairs and general overhaul in a refit lasting over two months. At an initial estimated cost of $126,000.00, voyage repairs included drydocking; underwater examination; routine repairs; cleaning, painting and scraping of her hull; removal of ceiling in No. 2 hold; repair of leaking doublebottom tanks; caulking of wooden decks throughout the ship; renewal of deteriorated stack stays; installation of random doublers' repair of insulation in cargo reefer space; repair of cylinders and valve chests if main engines; renewal of deck coverings throughout the vessel; repair of lifeboat skids; repair of port and starboard main condenser; repair and realignment of port main circulator; overhaul of the main feed pump; renewal and repair of leaking settling tanks; repairing and cleaning

---

[44] May 12, 1944 report from Captain Ball to Pacific Coast Regional Counsel of the War Shipping Administration—case #232.Copy in the ship's 901 file in RG 178 held by the Maritime Administration.

of fire and water end of main boilers; repair and realignment of generators; installation of fathometer and installation of permanent ballast. While at dry-dock, defense features were repaired and modified at a cost of $5,000.00. Finally, troop berthing areas, mess areas and sanitary facilities were cleaned and painted. The troop bake shop was relocated and a new butcher shop installed. Mechanical equipment in living spaces in the ship were repaired. As a final touch, the yard modified existing mental wards. That work was estimated to cost $29,000.00. It looked like that trip to the shipyard would cost the Government $160,00.00. It actually cost a bit more, but final figures would take many months for cost overruns to appear. In the long run the Government was willing to expend enormous sums of money on this old ship, probably because she was extant and the money spent on her would prove so easy to ignore when contrasted against the much larger picture of World War II shipbuilding and ship repair.

At that, paperwork to justify earlier actions could wait and in this case did. The final recommendations pursuant to expenditures to repair the ship in the autumn of 1944 came out about a year later. Here is a copy of the expense recommendation in connection with the PRESIDENT TYLER:

The Administrator, War Shipping Administration September 27, 1945
The Assistant Deputy Administrator for Maintenance and Repair

S.S.PRESIDENT TYLER

The S.S. PRESIDENT TYLER, a passenger vessel, built in 1920 by the New York Shipbuilding Company, and owned by the American President Lines, was requisitioned by the War Shipping Administration on January 9, 1942 under Bareboat Charter, and simultaneously delivered to the American President Lines under

General Agency Agreement. This General Agency agreement terminated as of February 8, 1945 and the vessel was simultaneously delivered to the War Department under Bareboat Charter. On March 30, 1945, title to this vessel was taken by the War Shipping Administration.

Your approval for the expenditure of $160,000.00 on subject vessel was recommended on September 29, 1944 and approved October 6, 1944. It now develops that an additional expenditure of $320,000.00, making a total estimated expenditure of $480,000.00, is required for additional work, segregated as follows:

Maintenance Repairs

Renew both tail shafts and repairs to stern tubes and bearings; additional expense involved in making double bottom tank tops water tight; additional doublers as directed by the American Bureau of Shipping; additional work discovered on both main engine cylinders, valves and bearings, discovered after complete examination; additional expense installing new water boxes, retubing condensers, repairing settling tanks and boilers as directed by the American Bureau of Shipping. $170,380.00

Defense

Major alterations to gun crew quarters, vessel's armament and defense systems. $ 14,520.00

Coast Guard Requirements

Alterations and repairs to wartime life saving equipment as directed by the Coast Guard representative during annual inspection. $ 3,805.00

Conversion

Additional expense installing new butcher shop and bake shop; major alterations to ventilation system and its mechanical equipment; items as would be expected on trooper of this size for this extended period.
$ 73,400.00

Alterations and Additions

Installing permanent ballast. $ 8,240.00

Damage Repairs

(Damage claimed to have been caused by grounding at Torinkana Bay, Bouganville, about June 20, 1944)—Damage is in a general area from keel and D strake port side between frame 160 and 194. Renew, crop and fair in place punctured, dented, fractured and/or distorted shell plating and internal structure in way of damage and other area as may be affected in general damage area. $ 23.445.00

Other Costs

Clean ship after repairs; furnish tugs to assist going to dry dock, temporary lights and power; gas free certificates. $ 3,500.00

Miscellaneous Expenses

Clean and chlorinate all fresh water tanks; paint hull from water line to rail; clean and paint quarters; assistance during annual inspection; garbage disposal; fresh water $ 22,700.00

Work on this vessel was performed at San Francisco, California, by the Bethlehem Steel Company starting August 26, 1944 and completing November 5, 1944.

RECOMMENDATION

It is recommended that an additional expenditure of $320,000.00, making a total estimated expenditure of $480,000.00, be authorized to cover the work outlined herein on the S.S. PRESIDENT TYLER, with the understanding work was performed in accordance with the provisions of the Warship ping Administration and that the Maintenance and Repair Organization will make the necessary apportion-ment of the cost involved.

This recommendation is submitted for your ratification and approval; however, the repairs described herein were awarded and performed before my appointment to office and the issuance of Administration Order No. 54 (2nd revised).

C.A. Dunn
Assistant Deputy Administrator
for Maintenance and Repair[45]

---

[45] Copy of same from the ship's 901 file. RG 178 at Maritime Administration.

That recommendation would not come for many months. Meanwhile, there were still several weeks of 1944 left. After that latest round of work the ship was able to transport about 2,400 troops. Owner's Voyage 74, WSA Voyage 17 began on November 1, 1944, and with her redelivery to the WSA by the Bethlehem yard on November 5th, she was ready for another outbound voyage. The authorities had already assigned the PRESIDENT TYLER for another South Pacific trip. November 4th brought American President Lines the usual form letter informing them that the ship was on her way to San Francisco from the Southwest Pacific and should be available soon for an outbound trip under allocation to the Navy. She sailed on another Hawaii trip on November 6th. The ship returned to San Francisco on December 4, 1944 and the voyage ended on December 14th. Then began her last WSA voyage, Number 18. It was owner's Voyage 75. That was her last wartime trip, and, as before, it began at San Francisco. Crew once again signed articles for 12 months on December 12, 1944. She was shorthanded and her Master had to sign a Coast Guard crew deficiency report in order to win clearance to sail. Missing from the crew that time were a First Assistant Engineer, one A.B., four oilers and two firemen. Taking the places of those men were the 2nd Asst. Engineer, an ordinary seamen and six wipers. On the 15th the voyage technically began and five days later, on December 20, 1944, she sailed. Hawaii was on her itinerary once more, but not until the voyage was weeks old would her last port be known. When word came of her final destination, it was quite a surprise to everyone.

While the ship was underway on that voyage, her possible utilization in the Army's hospital ship program was taken under serious consideration. After making a close inspection of the ship and totalling up the various expected conversion costs, the Army took a long look at the proverbial bottom line. To transform the twenty-four year old transport into a modern hospital ship would be expensive and thus the military felt that they should acquire effective ownership of the vessel before investing hefty sums of money in her conversion. From the Quartermaster's Department of the Army went a memo to the War Shipping Administration instructing them to prepare the paperwork required to take title to the ship, by requisition, if necessary.

A memorandum from the Director of Allocations on December 22, 1944 told the story:

> The Joint Chiefs of Staff have approved an additional Hospital ship program. Included in this program is the conversion of the PRESIDENT TYLER which we understand is still owned by the American President Lines and is under bareboat charter to the WSA. It is understood that the cost of converting this vessel will be at least two million dollars. It is presumed therefore that requisition of title will be necessary.[46]

---

[46]Quoted by W. Gheradi in a Dec. 27, 1944 letter to Percy Chubb. Copy in the ship's 901 file in RG 178 at Maritime Administration.

The ship, then under requisition charter, was in the Hawaiian Islands when definitive approval for her conversion came through. She was ordered to proceed to Mobile, Alabama, where a local yard would convert her to care for wounded men. Once commissioned as a hospital ship, she would return to Honolulu via New Orleans.

As late as December 28, 1944 the War Shipping Administration remained unsure of just who would pay the conversion costs. In a letter that day to R. T. Lemon, General Manager of the WSA's Maintenance & Repair Division, WSA Ship Operations Executive Assistant W.C. Hipkins wrote:

> . . . The vessel is expected to be ready at San Francisco between January 10 and 15, 1945, and more than likely the question as to whether the conversion work is to be done by WSA or the Army will have been clarified by the time the vessel is available for conversion. Decision as to whether or not vessel is to be requisitioned for title will, no doubt, be made within the next several days.[47]

Actually, the decision to requisition the vessel for title had already been made. Only the location of the transfer was unclear as a letter that same day written by Division of Allocations Director D.B. Donald to Walter R. Gherardi, Division of Large Vessel Procurement indicated:

> Referring my memorandum of December 22nd regarding the PRESIDENT TYLER, this vessel will be converted to a Hospital ship at Mobile, Alabama and has been ordered to proceed directly from the Hawaiian Islands to Mobile via New Orleans.
> It is presumed therefore that requisition of title will be effective at either New Orleans or Mobile.[48]

That was by no means the last word on the subject of the requisition for title of the ssPRESIDENT TYLER. Everything had to be justified for posterity. To the Director, Large Vessels Procurement and the Director, Large Vessels Disposal on January 31, 1945 came this three page memorandum:

> Recommendation as to taking title to the PRESIDENT TYLER
>
> The PRESIDENT TYLER is a twin screw cargo and passenger vessel, 502' × 62' × 42', gross 10533, net tonnage 6195, DWT 13240.
> Requisitioned on bareboat basis May 3, 1942 at a daily rate of $608.00. It had previously been under bareboat charter since January 9, 1942 on voluntary basis at a rate adjusted to $1045.33.

---

[47] Dec. 28, 1944 letter from W.C. Hipkin to R.T. Lemon. Copy in ship's 901 file in RG 178 at Maritime Administration.
[48] Dec. 28, 1944 letter from D.B. Donald to W. Gherardi. Copy in ship's 901 file in RG 178 at Maritime Administration.

After requisitioning, it was converted to troop ship at a cost of $104,761.48.

In December 1944, pursuant to the requirements of the Joint Chiefs of Staff, it was selected for conversion to a hospital ship. The estimated cost of such conversion has been stated to be more than $2,000,000.00.

In view of the extensive conversion required for a hospital vessel and the probable cost of reconversion, the question arises as to whether title should be taken baby War Shipping Administration at this time.

The following is a statement of policy with respect to the question as to whether title should be taken in case of vessels converted to troop ships, as approved by Maritime Commission November 25, 1943.

(a) As a general policy that we requisition for title when the private owner agreed to contract for new construction.

(b) That when vessel is to be "blown up" we requisition for use, i.e., bareboat charter. When, however, it is converted to more than a mere "blow up", we follow other recommendations herein.[49]

(c) That we consider charter hire on the basis of time, up to January 1, 1946; that will mean 2 years now and less than that after January 1, 1944.

(d) That, assuming paragraph (a) above is not fulfilled, each vessel be settled on the merits of the case, i.e., estimate the cost of (1) conversion, (2) reconversion, and (3) charter hire. Where these costs are major and preponderant, the vessel should be requisitioned for title.

(e) In negotiating with the owner and doubt arises as to the economics of a particular vessel, a limit on reconversion costs should be set up.

(f) Where we are required to transfer title to the Army or Navy, we requisition for title.

(g) Where owners do not comply with (a) above, yet attempt to insist on our taking title, we should, if we take title, require them to agree to our delivering to them a comparatively newly constructed vessel similar in characteristics, subject to adjustments for variations in age and any other essential characteristics of which the Commission shall be the final judge.

In analyzing the case of the PRESIDENT TYLER against the above policy, the following is pertinent:

(a) The owner has not agreed to contract for new construction to replace the TYLER in authorized service. He has, however, applied for ten new C-3's to be used in extension of present authorized service of his company. This application has not yet been acted upon by the Chief Examiner because present conditions are not such to permit a complete view of the post-war shipping situation in the Pacific.[50]

---

[49] "blow up" refers here to the practice of fitting berths/sleeping quarters for vast numbers of passengers, in this case, of course, troops.

[50] The reason there could have been no contract for a vessel to replace the PRESIDENT TYLER is because they already HAD replaced her on the round the world service. The three first C3 P ships, the PRESIDENT JACKSON, PRESIDENT MONROE and PRESIDENT HAYES were the direct replacements for the unimproved "502"s. Their availability to work on the round the world service permitted American President Lines the flexibility to charter two ships to the British for the Red Sea berth.

(b) Conversion to a hospital ship involves much more than a mere "blowing up" and, therefore, under (d) of the policy statement, maintenance of the charter agreement should depend upon cost of conversion, cost of reconversion, and charter hire.

(c) Although about a year has elapsed since the 2-year basis of charter hire was adopted, considering the present war situation, it seems that two years would still be a reasonable basis for estimating duration of charter hire.

(d) Although the vessel has been allocated for use of the Army after conversion, the Army will not require title. This eliminates point (f) of the policy stated above.

There remains for consideration the factor of the cost of conversion, cost of reconversion, and charter hire as related to the cost of acquiring title to the vessel, mentioned in point (d) of the policy.

The value of the PRESIDENT TYLER under GO 37 is about $954,000.00. Settlement with the owner in the case of the four sister ships lost in the war has recently been made on the value of $951,000.00 for each ship , excluding deduction for deferred repairs. In a telegram to the Administration dated January 26, 1945, the owner indicates a willingness to transfer title of the TYLER to the Government on the same basis. This, of course, may have been done with the view not only to disposing of the vessel at a good price, but also as a prod to the Commission to act on his application for extension of service and the allocation of ten new C-3's to operate therein.

No detailed estimate of cost of conversion of the TYLER to a hospital ship is available. However, Colonel Hicks of the War Department has stated that the cost is expected to be several millions of dollars. The PRESIDENT MADISON was converted to a hospital ship by the Navy at a cost of $3,246,879.00. In the case of three other vessels so converted by the Navy the cost ranged from $2,947,000.00 to $4,627,000.00 for conversion of the TYLER, therefore, would appear to be a conservative guess. As to the cost of reconversion, it is difficult to obtain any estimates that are consistent. In early 1944, the Maintenance and Repair Division estimated reconversion cost on a number of vessels that have been converted to troop ships at an average of about 50% of the conversion cost. On this basis, the cost of reconverting the TYLER would be at least $1,000,000.00. However, experience following the last war showed that actual reconversion costs ran far beyond the estimates. We have recent evidence that owners will be very exacting regarding the reconditioning of their ships. For instance, in the case of the MATSONIA, converted to a troop ship, the conversion cost was about $800,000.00. The owner has recently sent in an itemized list of items which he feels should be accomplished in the reconversion of the vessel. He estimates that it will cost $2,587,000.00, based on two 8-hour shifts. A review of the requirements listed by the owner shows them not to be extreme, although no opportunity has been had to check the cost as stated by him. Assuming his estimate to be extravagant, discharge of the Government's obligation under Section 902[51] undoubtedly will run far above the cost of conversion.

---

[51] Section 902 refers to that section of the 1936 Merchant Marine Act that granted the Government the authority to take the ships for war service.

The present charter arrangement of the TYLER carries no limitation of the cost of reconditioning, and it is not likely that any such limitation would be accepted by the owner, particularly after extensive conversion to a hospital ship.

The cost of charter for the TYLER is $221,920.00 per year; for two years it would be $443,840.00.

The PRESIDENT TYLER is 25 years old and is powered with obsolete reciprocating engines. It is consequently not eligible for an operating subsidy. This, together with the future availability of better ships, makes it unlikely that the vessel will ever again be placed in commercial operation under the U.S. flag. Nevertheless, the owner is entitled under Section 902, Merchant Marine Act 1936, to restoration to former condition, less ordinary wear and tear, or a lump sum in lieu thereof.

A rough analysis of the tax aspects of the case indicates that there would be no financial advantage to the Government in keeping the vessel for the present under charter, eventually taking title.[52]

And that is what happened. The Government did eventually take title to the ship. As expected, the liner never resumed commercial trading under the American flag. BUT, there were several years of service left to her and the plan to convert her into a hospital ship went forward.

Between January 10th and 15th the ship called at San Francisco on her way to Alabama. There she was allocated for conversion. Eight days later, on January 23rd, word came down from the brass that rather than convert at Mobile, the PRESIDENT TYLER would be altered at Boston. Orders were wired to the ship diverting her from her planned course to Mobile and she made her way to Boston where she docked on February 1, 1945. Pursuant to the new work awaiting her, the War Shipping Administration then withdrew allocation of the PRESIDENT TYLER from American President Lines. After discharging men and materiele, the ship shifted to the Simpson plant of the Bethlehem Steel Company in East Boston where Voyage 75 ended at midnight on the night of February 7th. At 12:01 on February 8, 1945, American President Lines General Agency terminated when they redelivered the ship to the War Shipping Administration. Accomplished within perhaps five minutes, upon taking delivery of the PRESIDENT TYLER, the WSA delivered the vessel under sub-bareboat charter to the United States Army at a daily rate of $608.00.

Mentioned nowhere in Maritime Commission records was the War Department's Bureau of Public Relations' January 15th announcement of impending stripping of armament and conversion of vessels into Army hospital ships. That would bring the total of such vessels to 29 and the five ships in question, the SATURNIA, PRESIDENT TYLER, COLOMBIA and WILLARD A. HOLBROOK (lastly the "535" type steamer PRESIDENT TAFT), had been chosen not only because they would add 5,355 new patient beds but had sufficient speed to allow them to be "ambulance" hospital ships. Once con-

---

[52] Copy of that recommendation is in the ship's 901 file in RG 178 at Maritime Administration.

As the United States Army Transport PRESIDENT TYLER, the former CREOLE STATE is shown in her final aspect. Her superstructure has been joined and a cap has been fitted to her funnel. U.S. Government photo.

verted to their new roles, all would be manned and operated by the Army Transportation Service Forces. In her role as a hospital ship the PRESIDENT TYLER was to be able to transport 650 litter and 158 ambulatory patients.

Conversion of the PRESIDENT TYLER took just under eight weeks. At the same time, the hull was sandblasted and painted anew. While refitting on February 13th, the ship was renamed HOWARD A. McCURDY, thus honoring the first dental officer killed in action, who died on January 16, 1942. There is some uncertainty over her use of that name, and she never did sail as HOWARD A. McCURDY because before her conversion to mercy ship was complete, Japan surrendered. With diminishing need for hospital ships, the authorities changed their minds again and devised a new future for the old vessel. Now the War Shipping Administration ordered Bethlehem Steel's East Boston Simpson yard to fit the old "502" for the carriage of 2,175 troops. With such numbers aboard, she would have been a very uncomfortable, cramped, unpleasant ship. Few were grieved when the planned work was scaled back when plans for the ship's future changed again.

The PRESIDENT TYLER was still named HOWARD A. McCURDY on March 30, 1945, when at 12:00 noon, title to the ship passed to the War Shipping Administration at Boston. At that moment American President Lines redelivered to the WSA, who simultaneously handed her back to American President Lines for operation. Financial details were ironed out later. The Maritime Commission eventually paid American President Lines the sum of $675,000.00 plus an allowance for her wartime duty for the ship.

One man who remembers her being stripped down to the bare hull at that time is Eric Fischer. New holder of a Second Mate's License, he was assigned to the ship as Senior Third Officer under Captain Edward Murphy. He joined the ship at the yard in March. He remembers it as watching a house being built bit by bit. Even now he recalls the smell of welding and the noise of construction work. Before workmen had gotten very far towards their assigned end, transportation authorities changed their plans for the ship and decided that she was better suited for service as a dependent carrier than as a hospital ship. Thus she was ordered to be modified to carry 622 passengers, particularly military dependents, in addition to a number of troops. Quarters were renewed for the 223 officers and men in her crew. Toward December Fischer had been promoted to Second Officer but unfortunately came down with a case of pneumonia and signed off around the time accountants were digesting the reports of the $234,000.00 cost of the ship's refit.

Now with a quarter of a century of water in her wake, she ran trials off Boston between January 3rd and 5th, 1946 before beginning the last phase of an illustrious career. Still under the command of Captain Murphy, the PRESIDENT TYLER began her first voyage in her new role as a war bride, dependent and troop carrier from Boston to Southampton on January 21, 1946. The westbound crossing ended at New York, from whence she made more trips to Britain, the first ending at New York on April 1st, where her 642 passengers were predominantly war brides and children. Arrivals of war brides and children were still important enough that members of the press awaited their debarkation at Pier 84, North River. Not mentioned for public consumption was one precaution taken by Army Transport personnel to protect women passengers and the ship's female nurses. Army M.P.s stood guard outside their quarters around the clock. Handling the ship as agent that time were her previous owners, American President Lines. She next departed from Southampton on May 10, 1946 for a ten day crossing to New York. She steamed into port on May 20th. Her name disappeared from sailing lists from New York until August when she was noted as ready to begin another Atlantic voyage on August 5, 1946 with soldiers, war brides and children among her 275 military dependent passengers. Paying a visit to the ship that summer, Eric Fischer had a chance to hear about the ship from Captain Murphy. The "Old Man's" verdict on the ship was enthusiastic: "Excellent sea boat! Rides rough weather very well!" . . . quite an accolade for the old ship.

For "cabin passengers" a fare of $190.00 per person was reckoned and paid by the Army to the Maritime Commission. The TYLER steamed to Southampton and then continued on to Bremerhaven. Her first call there, her departure was scheduled for August 22nd. Her return to New York was scheduled for September 4th, but a massive dock strike and tie up of the port forced a change in her sailing schedule. The strike was bad enough to idle a total of 3,000 ships nationwide. Among those were 238 United States flag commercial vessels. Partly in fear of the strike, but also because no one had yet mapped out a plan of operation to handle incoming Army transport ships during such a strike, the ship remained at Bremerhaven from the time of her August 18th arrival until her appointed sailing hour on the 22nd, when she cleared for Southampton. There on August 30th she embarked the last of her 505 passengers including 262 war brides, 59 children and sundry government employees before heading westbound across the Atlantic. When the PRESIDENT TYLER arrived at New York on September 10th, the port was in the midst of a major maritime and dock strike. With no longshoremen willing to cross picket lines and handle the ship, soldiers manned the ropes and did the work of striking stevedores. Some think that the end of her active career coincided with the end of that particular voyage and upon discharging the last of her inbound cargo, the ship was withdrawn, but that is not so. The PRESIDENT TYLER still had some work left in her and sailed for Southampton with a load of dependents on September 17th. A group of 256 happy war brides trooped down her gangway upon the ship's October 18th New York arrival. There are records of one further trip, one from Bremerhaven to New York between December 8th and 22, 1946.

That was the end of the line for the third of the "502"s. Shortly after her return to New York the United States Army Transportation Service, Water Division redelivered the ship to the Maritime Commission which at that time planned to place her in the James River Reserve Fleet off Norfolk, Virginia. At New York the idle ship was prepared for lay up. On March 20th the order to have her lay up with the ships in the James River was cancelled and new orders written to send her up to lay up in the Hudson instead. Not really ready to let go of her, the Army advised the Maritime Commission on April 13th that they wanted to remove 12 of the ship's lifeboats and 12 pairs of davits for use aboard other transports. Five days later the Maritime Commission heard from the Army again. Now the service wanted the Commission to hand over to them some life rafts, refrigerating units and certain food service items such as slicing machines still aboard the idle "502". The Army was given the desired items before the ship was taken upriver. Finally, on April 24, 1947, the PRESIDENT TYLER, ex PRESIDENT HAYES, ex CREOLE STATE, listed at 5,618 net tons, was stricken from Military lists and turned over to the Maritime Commission. At 10 AM on the same day the ship was technically delivered to the Hudson River Reserve Fleet. Having seen service for the Pacific Mail, the Pacific Brazil Argentine Line, the Dollar Line and American President Lines, and done her part during a long war, she was a weary old ship ready for a rest.

The ship was now under the ownership of the United States of America (Dept. of Commerce). She was still registered at San Francisco and remained on that city's register until the end. In light of the great sums of money invested in her there was no rush to press for her destruction. Within months of her arrival at Jones Point, interest in her came from an unexpected, but logical, source. Acting for unnamed foreign interests, I.C. Felleman & Company of New York wrote to the Maritime Commission on July 16, 1947 asking if the ship could be bought for further trading under a foreign flag. Unwilling to consider disposal of the ship at the time, the Commission politely put off that company's request.

"So many ships, so little money!" must have been the reasoning behind Maritime Commission thinking on September 8, 1947 when they certified the ship for disposal. No one waving a certified check came forth just then but on April 5, 1948 the Maritime Commission informed a few discreet inquirers that the ship was not for sale "at this time" but a week later was opening bids for her and a few of her contemporaries. Less than two weeks later, on April 16th, the Grimaldi Brothers, an up and coming Italian firm, offered the Maritime Commission $426,260.00 for the ship, adding in their bid an alternative offer. After the Grimaldi's bid came the much lower bid of $156,000.00 from the China Industrial Corporation. The Italian offer prompted some interest from the Commission, as they included an offer for an alternate ship should the PRESIDENT TYLER not remain on the sale list. In that case the Grimaldi's would pay $326,260.00 to buy the smaller WILLIAM P. BIDDLE. Another ship of the emergency shipbuilding program of the First World War, the BIDDLE had spent the first twelve years of her life as the ECLIPSE, one of two "name" ships of a class of big freighters built at Bethlehem's Alameda, California yards in 1918. Also known as the INDEPENDENCE class, five of them were sold in 1930 to the new Baltimore Mail Line, a company formed by Kermit Roosevelt and P.A.S. Franklin to take advantage of mail contracts on a new run from Baltimore and Norfolk to northwestern Europe. Lengthened, re-engined and converted to plans drawn by William Francis Gibbs, the five freighters became the handsome 8,424 gross ton combination passenger cargo liners known as the CITY OF BALTIMORE class. Entering intercoastal service in September 1938 upon the demise of subsidies once the Baltimore Mail Line was declared a non-essential service by the Maritime Commission, the sisters spent the final months of peace under a joint service arrangement with American President Lines. Working from California to Manila, each could carry 81 First Class passengers and carry great amounts of cargo. Renamed GEORGE F. ELLIOTT, one sister, the CITY OF LOS ANGELES was a war loss. All the others survived but only this one came close to being sold to foreign owners for further trading.

Had the Army not intervened in early May, the Maritime Commission would have sold the PRESIDENT TYLER to the Grimaldi Brothers. Though they had no need of her at the moment, the Army would not relent. On May 4th they sent the Maritime Commission a letter strongly urging withdrawal of the ship from sales lists. On May 14th the Maritime Commission acceded to military considerations and removed the name of the ship from sales offerings. Nor did the Commission sell the WILLIAM P. BIDDLE for further trading at that time. Interested in the transportation of emigrants and displaced persons from Europe, the Grimaldis began their passenger services in 1948 sending the "Liberty" ship ORIONE, the former MARY WILKINS

FREEMAN, from Italy to South America with 800 passengers in cramped dormitories. For more serviceable passenger tonnage once the Maritime Commission denied their applications to buy obsolete American passenger vessels, the Grimaldis looked elsewhere and began passenger services that same year with some very interesting old tonnage. Instead of old American ships they bought British, taking the CASTALIA from the Anchor Line and the RUAHINE from the New Zealand Steamship Company. After beginning service as the MARENGO, the CASTALIA was renamed URANIA II. They followed up in 1951 with the purchase of the CITY of HONG KONG from Ellerman City Line. As CENTAURO, the old CITY of HONG KONG still had a few seasons left in her, but in February 1952 her classification was expunged from Lloyd's for non compliance. It was the AURIGA, the ex RU-AHINE, that had the biggest effect. She steamed on until 1957, helping Grimaldi develop a fine reputation for good food and service in exchange for modestly priced fares.

Therefore, at an unrestricted sale offered by the Maritime Commission for September 11th, the Italians were no longer interested and no sufficiently high bid came in for the PRESIDENT TYLER. All the while the onetime CREOLE STATE remained at anchor in the Hudson River. She was still named PRESIDENT TYLER when she passed into the fleet of the Maritime Administration in 1952. Still carrying official number 220.858 and signal letters KDLB, the ship was listed in the 1953 edition of the *RECORD* of the American Bureau of Shipping at 9,903 gross, 5,618 net and 21,100 displacement tons. In 1957 bids for the purchase of the ship for breaking up were invited. Despite a higher offer of $277,777.00 from the Boston Metals Company of Baltimore, the old ship was sold to the Sun Shipbuilding Company of Chester, Pennsylvania for $260,000.00. The Maritime Administration ruled that the Boston Metals bid had not been responsive to its invitation. The ship's short voyage to oblivion began on March 19, 1957 when under the supervision of Captain Frank Ferrell, the PRESIDENT TYLER left her Jones Point, New York anchorage under tow to the Chester yard.

The old liner arrived at the breaker's yard on March 20th. Because of the scope of the demolition project, yard workers would keep a log book detailling dates, weather conditions, operations performed and time involved, total days worked and an inventory of salvageable items. Arriving at the yard after a three days passage on March 22nd, the last "502" was warped into the north side of # 5 berth to await demolition. After yard workers took soundings of all tank spaces aboard the ship, including fore and after peak tanks, fuel oil settlers and double bottoms, all safes were opened to see whether or not anyone had inadvertently left any treasures behind. There was not so much as a note saying "Thank you for the cash". The prevailing quiet aboard the doomed liner was interrupted over the next few days by shipyard personnel making their rounds and checking over objects of special interest to them. On the 29th, yard Supt. A.A. Holbaur issued orders to begin scrapping the veteran vessel on Monday, April 1st.

Before scrapping began, water coolers were conveniently placed. Fire lines and temporary lighting were rigged throughout the dead ship. Similarly, special gas and oxygen manifolds were attached to the north side of the alloy shop to serve as outlets for the required burners lines. On a cloudy and mild Monday morning, Elmer, "Moo" Boulden put the first burner to the ship. With skill saws and jack hammers, the forward weather dock was stripped off. With its built in furniture, crew quarters in the forward section were destroyed wholesale. Chicken wire and plaster from the underside of the ship's decks and fiber glass insulation material was removed. All of this was considered junk and brought to a specially rigged dumpsite at the aft end of the pier.

Let's look at the major events of a typical day during the scrapping of this veteran liner. A month after demolition began, May 1st, the yard had three burners working aboard ship and eight on the pier as sections of Upper Promenade Deck including the after house were burned off. Then men began cutting up aft end of the engine room casing. Removing deck capstans, workers next turned their torches on the fan house on the poop deck. Next to go were the bulkheads of that house. On the pier, scrap was burned. A railroad car was ordered and cleaners set to work for two hours. That afternoon stagebuilders worked on the starboard side of bridge deck while shipfitters removed portholes.

On the last day of July, a Merritt-Chapman and Scott derrick barge stood by to take on the ship's boilers. As the weeks passed, torches and jackhammers led the parade of tools ripping pieces of ship from their source. Away went the forecastle head, booby hatches, fan houses and remaining A Deck superstructure opening B Deck and its three dining rooms, reefer boxes, butcher shop, main galley and forward staterooms to the sky. Once these were gone, the C Deck chapel and children's play area built during the ship's 1945 refit were taken. All the while, what was left of the PRESIDENT TYLER was kept pretty much on an even keel. As work progressed, it became evident that the forty ton rudder would have to be removed lest its weight cause the ship to sink aft section first. At the time the ship still drew 17 feet of water. Removing the main engines was expected to bring the propellors to the surface of the water allowing easy removal of the rudder. Not until ballast was removed could yard workers get to the rudder. Still aboard the remnant of the onetime CREOLE STATE were 500 tons of steel billets on the tank top in Number 2 hold, 500 tons of magnetite blocks on the tank top in Number 3, 600 tons of Belgian block (cobblestones) alongside the port and starboard shaft alleys and 160 tons of steel billets below the fresh water tanks. Magnets removed the steel billets to the delight of the yard's men who seemed happy to be able to hoist the magnetite out of the hulk in the same way. The cobblestones, though, had to be carried out manually, a long, unpleasant job. Now, remaining oil in Number 9 common tank was pumped out. Shortly after that, the starboard side of the shell below the water line cracked. Pumps were put to work to drain out whatever water had seeped in while a cement box covered the hole below.

The rudder proved uncooperative. After workers had removed the bottom section of the fantail, the only remaining steel above the rudder was the steadiment bearing, rudder stock and surrounding steel. Holes were drilled into the top of the rudder but it was not yet possible to access the lower gudgeon. To do so, all of the main engine foundations, main and auxiliary condensers, evaporator pipes and grating—some 200 tons of steel in all were hauled away. The lower gudgeon broke into the water and the rudder was lifted out and placed aboard a barge waiting alongside.

Now the PRESIDENT TYLER was but a hulk, but with half of her fuel tanks containing fuel, she was something of a dangerous one. Scrappers took care lest the oil catch fire or cause an explosion. As some sections of the double bottom were opened up, small fires did erupt. Maybe it was the last gasping protest of the dying liner. Though the fires were controlled and burned off unwanted fuel oil, they tended not to burn what the yard's men wanted burned. One other problem hampered this phase of the demolition of the old "502" - rain. Every time it rained, water entered the tank tops which meant that the pumps had to keep on working.

By March 19, 1958 the remnant of the hulk of the PRESIDENT TYLER was ready to be towed into drydock but the dock wasn't ready to take it. During the weeks until the hulk made its last pitiful trip, workers did all kinds of tasks associated with cleaning up and preparing scrap metals for resale. On March 30th the Dockmaster ordered lines cast off at 10:25 AM. Pulled into the drydock, the hulk was dry at noon. Now it was lifted away in 85 foot sections. The last piece of scrap of the PRESIDENT TYLER was burned on Number 5 Pier at 11:45 AM on September 10th. At 12:30 PM the bottom was opened up to allow water to drain off. Within three days all that was left on the pier were two sections of hulked metal which the Maritime Administration ordered to remain until their representative gave authority to remove it. Permission came at 1:30 PM on April 5th. Then at 3:15 PM Tony Mistecka made the final cut and the PRESIDENT TYLER was no more.[53]

---

[53] From an article in "*OUR YARD*" the house magazine of the Sun Shipbuilding Corporation.

THE WOLVERINE STATE/
PRESIDENT HARRISON: KAKKO
MARU/KACHIDOKI MARU

◇

At the busy Camden yards of New York Shipbuilding Company workers laid the first keelplates for two big transports on May 13, 1919. One was hull number 247, which grew into the first of the "502" class, the PANHANDLE STATE. The other was the project whose keel went onto the stocks on slipway O. Contract and hull number 248 at New York Shipbuilding Corporation, the Emergency Fleet Corporation carried her on their books as hull number 2589. They had an intended name for her, too. It was JAKIN. That name for hull number 248 would be changed by mid November. By January 1, 1920 when the PANHANDLE STATE was 50% complete, the yard had accomplished enough work on this one for the Shipping Board to deem her 25% complete. Clearly this ship was not the yard's first priority. When finally ready for launching on Thursday, September 16, 1920, two days before the maiden sailing of her twin PANHANDLE STATE, this one went into the water as the WOLVERINE STATE. Fourth of the "502" class and twentieth Shipping Board transport type launched, her name honored the State of Michigan. Since her construction had taken so long, the ship was actually well on her way towards completion when Mrs. Edith Tweedale, wife of Shipping Board Emergency Fleet Corporation General Comptroller Alonzo Tweedale, performed the traditional christening rite and sent the ship down the ways into the Delaware River. Finished by the end of the year she ran trials off Cape Henlopen, Delaware. At least her performance could assuage the ire of Shipping Board personnel, testy because the yard had taken so long to deliver her. Making a top speed of 16.5 knots, she had made a full knot and half more than her contract speed. After her trials the WOLVERINE STATE returned to her builders yard for finishing touches. Displacing 13,034 tons, the newest member of the class shared the particulars of her sisters, including a net tonnage figure of 6,195 tons. Her building cost was reckoned at $4,109,944.43 (a figure also reported as $4,085,889.93, a difference reflecting different accounting methods applied to charges for certain items in her accommodation spaces). Fourth of the class delivered to the Fleet Corp., the WOLVERINE STATE was delivered to representatives of the United States Shipping Board at Philadelphia on January 6, 1921. First to command the new liner was Captain Charles H. Porta. He brought the ship to San Francisco where Captain H.L. Jones relieved him.

In conjunction with the beginning of the ship's career and at the request

Built under cover from the elements, the WOLVERINE STATE nears the moment of her launch. New York Shipbuilding Collection. Courtesy of the Independence Seaport Museum Library.

This after view of the WOLVERINE STATE was taken on September 15, 1920. New York Shipbuilding Collection. Courtesy of the Independence Seaport Museum Library.

She had run almost to the end of the ways when the yard's photographer caught the final moments of the launch of the WOLVERINE STATE. New York Shipbuilding Collection. Courtesy of the Independence Seaport Museum Library.

of Pacific Mail, the Shipping Board authorized an additional expenditure of $44,900.00 in order to fit this ship with 246 steerage berths, a job to be performed once the ship arrived in San Francisco Bay. Handed over to officials of the Pacific Mail Steamship Company, the WOLVERINE STATE departed Philadelphia on January 9th for Baltimore where a local yard added finishing touches to the ship's accommodation spaces. At Baltimore, the new vessel also loaded cargo and took on a few passengers before shifting to Norfolk on January 22nd. There she loaded more cargo and mail and received some last minute shipments of provisions and supplies. The new ship continued her delivery voyage with her January 24 sailing from Norfolk.

Bound for her new home port of San Francisco, California, the WOLVERINE STATE arrived at Cristobal with 670 tons of cargo in transit to the West Coast at 4:47 PM on January 30, 1921. While in Canal Zone waters she shipped a collapsible swimming pool, an item expected to bring plenty of amusement to her passengers in the warm weather. Making her first canal transit, she entered the canal at 10:20 AM on January 31, 1921. Through to the Pacific at 5:38 PM she was soon tied up at Balboa. She sailed at 8:26 PM the following evening, February 1st, on her way up the coast of Central America, Mexico and California. After a February 11th call at Los Angeles she continued on to San Francisco, arriving there on February 13, 1921. Second of the big, new passenger and cargo ships to arrive at that port, her arrival occasioned several receptions and favorable comment among interested local citizenry. Before beginning her maiden sailing on the Calcutta line, the ship was shifted to the Oakland yards of the Moore Shipbuilding Company where Third Class accommodations for 246 passengers were installed. In truth it was less a real Third Class than an "Oriental steerage", the simplest form of open steerage known to the shipowner. Located aft, this accommodation was unlike the Third Class foreseen for the Atlantic "502"s, which was to be located forward and aft.

Fitting such accommodations entailed the installation of berthing spaces, water closets, wash rooms, pantry and dining facilities plus a hospital for that class within the spaces between Frames #152 and #184 on "A" and "B" Decks, in addition to the construction of a steel deck for a Third Class galley on "A" Deck between Hatches Nos. 8 and 9. Specified for "B" Deck was the installation of 232 Third Class berths (the remainder were in the hospital). To cater for the expected trade, these were but simple pipe-framed bunk beds equipped with canvas bottoms. Fastened with portable longitudinal supports, they were easily removable should a small passenger list and a heavy cargo load require use of any (or all) steerage berthing compartments for freight. With the sides of steerage accommodation spaces finished in painted cork, deckheads were sheathed. Naturally, sanitary and hygienic concerns were addressed by the provision of water closets and wash rooms on the port side of the after end of the ship. Four portholes were cut into the washroom to provide ventilation.

Six pipe berths provided with mattresses were fitted in the white-painted, wood-panelled steerage hospital. For adequate ventilation, three 12" port-holes and a 12" ventilator were fitted. Other items required for steerage included a furnished pantry and additional portholes. These new quarters were provided with 20 electric fans and steam heating but no more than 70 electric lights.

Because of her increased passenger capacity, the WOLVERINE STATE needed to carry three additional lifeboats. By strengthening existing davits, these were carried within existing lifeboats. Thus no new or additional space for boats was required. Long after the work was performed, the Shipping Board finally got around to granting Technical Authorization for all this work on April 26, 1922. A limit was placed on the expense of fitting the ship with steerage. Those quarters were to be fitted for no more than $44,900.00.

With the work completed, the ship returned to the San Francisco side of the Bay to prepare for her maiden voyage. With passengers, cargo (most of it for Calcutta) and mail she began her inaugural sailing on February 25, 1921, displacing the smaller, Pacific Mail steamer SANTA CRUZ, long-time running mate of the COLUSA, two combination passenger and cargo ships that were eventually returned to parent company Grace Line and put to work on traditional Grace routes to the West Coast of South America. Each of the Pacific Mail's "502"s was scheduled for a 39 day run out to Calcutta and a 39—40 day trip back. On her maiden voyage the WOLVERINE STATE called at Honolulu on March 4th, Manila on March 21st, Saigon on March 24th and 25th and Singapore on March 27th through 29th prior to steaming up the Hoogly into Calcutta on April 9th. Reading her voyage report, no one at the Shipping Board nor at the home office of Pacific Mail smiled. The ship had turned in an operating loss of about $70,000.00, and there was still another "502" to join Pacific Mail's Calcutta run, the GRANITE STATE.

Captain Jones was in command when the WOLVERINE STATE sailed from San Francisco on June 14th for her second voyage to Calcutta. After a week at sea the ship called at Honolulu and on July 8 the vessel reached Manila for a three day call. After a quick call at Colombo on July 24th, the WOLVERINE STATE arrived back in Calcutta on the 28th. The torpid heat through which the ship's cargo had to be worked can only be imagined, but for the few Americans in the area, the sight of a big ship flying the proud American flag, must have been a welcome sight. She sailed for home on August 3rd. There was a Singapore call on August 9th, and Manila on the 15th. Next was an August 29th call at Honolulu. Completing her long journey home, the ship reached San Francisco on September 5th. Then came a visit to local yards where besides voyage repairs, additional Oriental steerage was fitted. Inspiration for the extra berths aboard this ship and her two sisters running on the Pacific came on the heels of the recent debut of the CENTENNIAL STATE on the Atlantic where she offered the standard "502" class First Class but differed from the PANHANDLE STATE and OLD NORTH STATE with her several hundred Third Class berths. On the Pacific,

In drydock at San Francisco on June 6, 1921, the WOLVERINE STATE underwent voyage repairs and had her steerage passenger capacity increased. Mike McGarvey photo.

the three sisters had more steerage berths fitted into Nos. 8 and 9 Tween-decks at a cost of $29,000.00.

The weather must have been more pleasant when the WOLVERINE STATE departed on her third voyage west from San Francisco on October 15th. Westbound the ship reached Honolulu on October 22nd. Overnighting there, the ship sailed for Manila on the following day. After a sixteen day passage the ship arrived at Manila on November 8th. One consignment of freight loaded aboard the ship at San Francisco and carried to Manila caused consternation to all parties concerned. To ship 150 cases of California grown lemons to the Philippines, the Johnston Fruit Company paid the Pacific Mail Line $735.69 in ocean freight charges. Stowed in No. 1 tweendeck alongside other perishable cargo, once the fruit was landed at Manila after the ship's December 8th arrival, all the lemons in 107 cases had rotted. Pacific Mail declined the claim noting that the fruit must have been overripe when loaded so it was the Shipping Board that had to deal with the matter since the Johnston people claimed their cargo was not overripe when shipped. Rather, they countered, the poor ventilation in the WOLVERINE STATE's No. 1 tweendeck caused the fruit to overripen and rot. They had a point, as survey revealed that Hold No. 1 enjoyed only ventilation allowed by a single ventilator at the forward end and another one aft. No cargo stowed in the wing, or tweendecks, had any ventilation at all. This in mind, the insurers accepted the claim and paid half of the freight claim, leaving the Shipping Board to pay the rest.

After making an intermediate call at Singapore on November 15th, she made a November 21st arrival at Calcutta. Her turnaround lasted until December 3rd when she began the long trip home, the worst of the heat was over. The ship called at Colombo on December 7th. After a December 13th call at Singapore and a stop at Manila on December 19th, the WOLVERINE STATE sailed ever eastwards bound for San Francisco and her January 10, 1922 arrival there.

Low freight offerings and poor financial results on the Calcutta line troubled Shipping Board and Pacific Mail Steamship Company alike. Financially, the Calcutta service quickly proved itself a big loser. With the beginning of the winter 1921–1922 the Shipping Board discussed the losses incurred by the operation of the big "502"s on that long haul line. Quickly reaching the conclusion that three "502"s could not earn their keep on that run, the Trustees of the United States Shipping Board ordered an itinerary change. Banning their passenger cargo liners from further calls at Calcutta the Shipping Board ordered Pacific Mail to limit their outbound voyages to ports west of Manila. Two "502"s would suffice Pacific Mail on the newly abbreviated run. Detached from the Calcutta line, the Shipping Board cancelled allocation to Pacific Mail of the GRANITE STATE. Transferring her operation to United States Lines, that ship was ordered back to the Atlantic, leaving the CREOLE STATE and WOLVERINE STATE to handle whatever cargo and passengers they could find.

Even as the WOLVERINE STATE made ready to sail from San Francisco on January 19, 1922 on her fourth trip to Calcutta the end of the "502"s on the run was in sight. Three days later on January 22, 1922 the Trustees of the Shipping Board approved the recommendation of Shipping Board Vice President Barton Smull to remove the GRANITE STATE from the Calcutta run and send her to work on the Atlantic upon the conclusion of her present Pacific voyage. By the way, it seems to have been Smull's idea to limit the CREOLE STATE and WOLVERINE STATE to the area east of the Philippines. Backing him up, the Shipping Board ordered the two sister ships to proceed no further than Manila on subsequent voyages. Of course, with the Shipping Board, nothing was quite as simple as writing a directive and expecting everyone to fall into line. Paperwork about the termination of "502" service to Calcutta occupied many men over the following days. On January 31, 1922 Shipping Board Secretary Clifford Smith prepared this memorandum for Chairman Lasker and Commissioner Lissner:

> The Shipping Board at a meeting January 20, 1922 referred to the Chairman and Commissioner Lissner as a committee with power to act the following memorandum and recommendations of Vice President Smull, E.F.C. as approved by the Board of Trustees of the Emergency Fleet Corporation, on January 24, 1922.
>
> In order to lay out these passenger steamers to amply protect the projected routes in the Pacific and in the Atlantic, it will be necessary to return to the Atlantic side the S.S. GRANITE STATE after discharge of her cargo at San Francisco, where she is expected to arrive on February 10th.
>
> It is also recommended that the S.S. CREOLE STATE, expected to sail from San Francisco March 25th and the S.S. WOLVERINE STATE, expected to sail from San Francisco April 22nd, limit their voyages to not further than Manila.
>
> I am now asking the Board to recommend this action to the Shipping Board and I ask for their approval of the above.
>
> The Shipping Board also referred to the same committee with power to act the request of Vice President Smull for permission to assign the S.S. PENINSULA STATE to the United States Lines.
>
> Will you kindly inform this office of your action in the matter in order that the record may be completed.[1]

The WOLVERINE STATE still had miles to go before the new directives were her reality. Via Honolulu and Manila the ship made her fourth visit to Calcutta, arriving on February 24th. She sailed for home on March 3rd, calling as before at Colombo, Singapore, Manila and Honolulu before coming into San Francisco on April 13, 1922. That was the end of her career on the Calcutta line. It was also the end of her Pacific Mail career. Though ads to San Francisco shippers for her scheduled April 25, 1922 sailing were long since in circulation, Pacific Mail felt no pressure to operate the voyage since

---

[1]Jan. 31. 1922 memo from C. Smith to Chmn. Lasker and Cmssr. Lissner in the 1091 file for the ssWOLVERINE STATE in RG 32 National Archives.

the ship would be limited to ports east of Manila (depending upon where you are standing), and without any regrets declined to operate the ship further. Even before the ship reached California at the end of Voyage 4 operator and Shipping Board arranged to turn her back to the Division of Operations after the ship returned to San Francisco on April 13th. Once she completed discharging inbound freight her allocation was withdrawn by mutual consent and not a little relief on the part of Pacific Mail. Neither party had been pleased by the Calcutta line experience and letters between Board and Pacific Mail show a certain pique had somewhat cooled relations between the two. The Shipping Board felt that Pacific Mail should have paid them more for the use of the ship while the company had both operating losses and doubts about the suitability of that type of ship to contemplate. Curiously, it took some time before ads for the ship's next planned sailings were pulled.

Redelivered to the Shipping Board before the end of April, the WOLVERINE STATE was shifted into lay up at Alameda, California, just south of Oakland across the Bay from San Francisco. Withdrawal of her allocation to the Pacific Mail Steamship Company was not formalized until June 9, 1922, the day on which the still idle ship was renamed PRESIDENT HARRISON. Her San Francisco registry was unchanged. There was still no definite work in sight for her, but contingency plans were developed that she could be used to transport President Harding and his party during his scheduled 1923 West Coast and Alaska visit. Not publicized at the time was construction of a "Presidential Suite" for the use of President and Mrs. Warren Harding should they choose to use the liner during the summer of 1923. From Newport News Shipbuilding & Drydock Company came plans for the construction of several rooms aboard the ship for the Presidential couple. What seems lost to history is whether or not President Harding ever even saw that suite, for taking ill on that trip, he died suddenly and unexpectedly during cocktail time one evening as he lay in his sickbed in his suite at the Palace Hotel in San Francisco. But we are ahead of ourselves.

In September 1922 the PRESIDENT HARRISON was the object of some quick attention. The sum of $2,498.00 was spent for a movie projection booth and the recaulking of "A" Deck by the Crowley Shipyards of San Francisco. The ship's next movements came as a result of the unforeseen.

On her way from Los Angeles to Honolulu on charter to the Los Angeles Steamship Company (LASSCO), the Shipping Board's CITY OF HONOLULU caught fire and burned out during her maiden voyage to Hawaii on October 12, 1922. Aware that the Shipping Board's PRESIDENT HARRISON was at that time laid up at Alameda, the Los Angeles S.S. Co. wasted no time applying for her allocation as a temporary replacement for the burned-out CITY OF HONOLULU, asking for the "502" on the 13th. Though far from ideal as a replacement for the doomed prototype BARBAROSSA class steamer, the Shipping Board sprang into uncustomary action, instantly approving LASSCO's emergency request. Acting on the 14th, while the CITY OF HONOLULU was still a smoldering wreck, Chairman Lasker agreed to give the PRESIDENT HARRISON to LASSCO for one round voyage but insisted that the company's president, Harry Chandler, be told that the Board had already decided on another operator for the ship, and if Chandler planned to have the ship for a longer period, that he immediately disabuse himself of the notion. A further request that the Shipping Board assume the costs of insurance premiums was denied, especially in the wake of the recent disaster. Lasker justifiably asked LASSCO to assume any costs associated in returning the vessel to the Board in the same condition in which they had taken her, as well as to redeliver her free and clear from any maritime liens. On the 16th LASSCO officials including Fred Baker, Ralph Chandler and Captain Lester[2] headed to San Francisco to bring the PRESIDENT HARRISON to Los Angeles.

Insisting that LASSCO guarantees cover the ship from tie up to tie up, the Shipping Board allocated the PRESIDENT HARRISON to the Los Angeles Steamship Company on October 19th, two days after the hapless ex-German CITY OF HONOLULU was shelled and sunk by gunfire by the Coast Guard to prevent her becoming a menace to shipping. From lay up at Alameda, the HARRISON sailed that day under her own power to the Moore Drydock yards at Oakland to be prepared for service. When she sailed from San Francisco for San Pedro late that same night, it was not only the first time she had sailed commercially in six months, it was her first voyage as PRESIDENT HARRISON.

The ship arrived at the port of Los Angeles on October 20th, where, during a three day stay at their San Pedro pier, LASSCO introduced the ship to their clientele. But Hawaii called and on October 23rd, only ten days since the company called for a replacement for the burned-out liner, LASSCO sent another passenger carrier out to the islands. When the PRESIDENT HARRISON sailed that day, the company was only two days behind their printed schedule! Now under the command of Captain N.H. Anderson, the PRESIDENT HARRISON made ready for sea. Slipping her moorings, she nosed down the channel and out past the breakwater into the Pacific for Honolulu where she arrived at pilot station at 7:30 on October 30th. Handling passengers was easy. With her limited space, the HARRISON couldn't have carried more than 80 or so First Class passengers to the islands and likely carried no steerage travelers. But she had a big cargo lift and spent a full 5 days working cargo at her Honolulu pier before sailing for San Pedro on November 4, 1922. The eastbound passage took the "502" a week to complete. Concluding her maiden roundtrip Hawaii sailing, the PRESIDENT HARRISON docked at San Pedro on November 11, 1922.

Meanwhile the Shipping Board considered the time limits of the assignment and the ship's first trip was completed before the Board sent a telegram from Washington at 5:10 PM (local time) on November 15, 1922 asking LASSCO to execute the following agreement:

---

[2]Ship's 1091 file in R.G. 32

For and in consideration of the benefits to them severally accruing, the parties hereto agree that the agreement between United States of America represented by the United States Shipping Board Emergency Fleet Corporation and the Los Angeles Steamship Company, under date of October 19, 1922, covering one round trip voyage between Los Angeles Harbor and Honolulu (which trip has been completed) be and such agreement hereby extended to cover additional round voyages between the same ports, under all terms and conditions in said agreement set forth; and said agreement save as modified by the aforesaid extension shall be and remain in full force and effect.[3]

Happy to comply, LASSCO was able to operate the HARRISON through the end of January.

With that agreement in hand, LASSCO sent the HARRISON to Hawaii on Voyage 2 on November 18th. Arriving at pilot station Honolulu at 7:30 AM on the 25th after a leisurely one week crossing, she spent six days working cargo before departing for California on December 2nd. The ship arrived at San Pedro on the 9th. On the following day, December 10th, 1922, the Shipping Board granted the Seattle-based firm of Swayne & Hoyt allocation of the ship for a line eventually brought to a certain fame as the Pacific-Argentine-Brazil Line, but at the moment carrying the unwieldy moniker of the Pacific West India and East Coast of South America Line. An actual delivery date was not at first given. The Board stated simply: "future delivery". Getting an early start on the winter vacation season were the passengers aboard the PRESIDENT HARRISON on her December 15th sailing from Southern California. On that third trip, the HARRISON picked up her pilot at 6:00 PM on December 22nd. That gave her crew members a rare treat—Christmas in port—and by every indication the HARRISON's crew enjoyed that. Better yet was spending Christmas in Honolulu whose beaches are not far from the port. After a six day stay, the ship cast off all lines on December 30th and was at sea as 1922 slipped away and 1923 began.

Now with the Government's commitment to Swayne & Hoyt, the ship's LASSCO days drew to a close. Further allocation of the ship to LASSCO for a fourth and final Hawaii trip was made on December 28th. That began at San Pedro on January 13, 1923 with her sailing for Honolulu. Across the Pacific, she made an 11:30 AM arrival at pilot station on her January 20th arrival. With her departure for the West Coast on the 27th, her final LASSCO crossing was at hand. Back at San Francisco on February 4, 1923 at the end of her twelve week Hawaii career, the PRESIDENT HARRISON was redelivered to the Shipping Board.

The timing of the establishment of passenger service on the three year old Pacific-Argentine-Brazil Line had plenty to do with the impending Brasilian Exposition. As the Shipping Board so quaintly put it, putting "passenger boats" in service between the Pacific Northwest and the East Coast of South

---

[3]From allocation agreement between Shipping Board and LASSCO, copy in the ship's 1091 file in RG32 at National Archives.

America, Swayne & Hoyt reasoned, would undoubtedly attract tourists. The "502"s were selected for two other reasons. Swayne & Hoyt liked their refrigerated space and big cargo capacity. Then again, neither the PRESIDENT HARRISON nor the HAYES had any employment at the moment and Shipping Board policy regarding passenger vessels demanded an attempt be made to find work for them. Somehow Swayne & Hoyt's application for their allocation moved to the head of the pile and by October 1922 the pair was earmarked for later delivery to that well known West Coast operator. On December 10, 1922 the Shipping Board allocated the PRESIDENT HARRISON for service between Seattle and Buenos Aires. Five days later the Commissioners allocated the PRESIDENT HAYES to the same service. First of the pair to enter service on the Pacific-Argentine-Brazil Line was the PRESIDENT HAYES which took her first sailing from Seattle for Swayne & Hoyt on January 17, 1923. The PRESIDENT HARRISON remained about a month behind her slightly older sister. Prior to taking her first sailing to South America, the PRESIDENT HARRISON departed San Francisco on February 15th for Seattle under the command of Captain A. Ahman. Veteran mariner of the Great Northern Steamship Company, he had been the first Master of the marvelous American coastal racer GREAT NORTHERN. After the First World War that ship became the H.F. ALEXANDER. Arriving at Seattle on Sunday, February 18th, the ship had a week to load cargo before taking her inaugural sailing from Puget Sound. While there Captain Ahman had time to go over and visit his old command. Scheduled to depart from Seattle's Connecticut Street Terminal at 11:00AM on Sunday, February 25, 1923, the ship faced a delay when winter storms delayed delivery of her outbound cargo of lumber. To get the ship away as close to schedule as possible, she shifted to nearby Port Ludlow on Thursday the 22nd. Returned to her Seattle berth on Saturday evening, stevedores spent hours loading 3,000 boxes of apples and other cargo into her before Sunday morning and her departure for Oregon, California, Panama, Curaçao, Puerto Rico and South America. As far as Seattle's steamship line to the East Coast of South America line was concerned, there were indeed sufficient southbound fruit and lumber cargoes for the service that would soon come to be called the Pacific-Argentine-Brazil Line to make a successful showing, but northbound cargoes, generally limited to coffee and seasonal carriage of fruit and passenger totals were hardly gratifying. On her first sailing from Seattle the PRESIDENT HARRISON carried about a dozen passengers, mainly South American nationals. By the time she reached Argentina, opposition from more established passenger lines on the Pacific had prompted the Shipping Board to forbid Swayne & Hoyt to carry any passengers in these ships north of San Francisco.

Via Astoria on February 26th and Portland on the 28th, the PRESIDENT HARRISON returned to San Francisco on March 2nd. After working more cargo and embarking additional passengers, the "502" sailed from there on March 5th for Los Angeles. From there on March 6th the ship headed to Panama and her first Pacific to Atlantic transit of the Panama Canal, where officials charged her operators tolls based on their calculation of her gross tonnage at 12,031 and her net tonnage at 8,495 tons. Making Balboa at 6:15PM on March 17th, the ship took her 1,825 tons of general cargo through on March 18th, entering the canal at 6:50 AM and exiting the "ditch" at 2:13 PM that afternoon. Two hours later she cleared for sea and once in the Atlantic, the PRESIDENT HARRISON continued following the wake of the PRESIDENT HAYES making calls at both Ponce and San Juan, Puerto Rico before heading to Brasil. This ship reached Rio de Janeiro on April 8th and after a call at Montevideo on the 13th, finally arrived at Buenos Aires on April 14th. Homewards, while the ship called at Santos, Brasil between May 1st and 3rd, local dockworkers loaded a hefty shipment of coffee into her capacious holds. From Rio on May 5th the PRESIDENT HARRISON continued her long voyage home from Argentina, setting her course for the Caribbean and another call at Puerto Rico. She worked cargo at San Juan on May 18th before sailing for Cristobal and her night transit to the Pacific on May 22nd. At 6:50 AM on the 23rd the ship cleared Balboa for sea with 4,572 tons of cargo including hides, coffee and fertilizer in her holds. Steaming nonstop to California the ship called at San Pedro on June 4th for an overnight run to San Francisco. A four day call there was next before the ship sailed on to Astoria and Seattle, reaching her terminal on June 14th, nearly four months since she began the trip. Shifting to Tatoosh to load lumber that same day, she made ready for her second South America trip. In our frenzied world such a leisurely pace seems anathema, but this was no highly competitive service and the ship was hardly pressured.

While the ship was on her way homeward from South America the Shipping Board got busy with some planned alterations for some very special guests soon expected to embark in the PRESIDENT HARRISON. Because a sailing of this ship fit into the plans of President and Mrs. Harding, the Board ordered a reconstruction of several rooms in the PRESIDENT HARRISON. Plans for such alterations were ready by late May. The august couple never did get to the ship and no records remain suggesting either the scope or the actual realization of such work.

Captain Ahman was in command when the PRESIDENT HARRISON began Voyage 2 from Seattle on July 25th. On that trip the liner didn't arrive at Buenos Aires until September 9th. On the way south she called at Portland, Oregon, San Francisco and Los Angeles. The liner entered the Caribbean after an August 17th transit of the Panama Canal. San Juan, Puerto Rico was four days away. Then the "502" headed south for a call at Para, her first Brasilian port. Overnighting at Rio on September 2nd/3rd, those aboard the vessel could look forward to arrival in Argentina. After a ten day call at Buenos Aires, she began her return voyage on September 19th, calling first at Montevideo on September 20th, Santos on the 24th and Rio on September 26th. From there it was a long eleven days' steaming to San Juan, Puerto Rico where the ship called for water and supplies on October 7th. Four days later she went through the Canal and called at Manzanillo, Mexico on October 17th on her way to an October 22nd arrival at Los Angeles. Except for that call at Manzanillo, Mexico, this trip mirrored the first. But there was no third South America trip for this "502". Back at San Francisco on October 23rd, the ship went no further north and finished out her Swayne & Hoyt days in San Francisco Bay.

By the late summer of 1923, it was apparent that only a sale of the ship and her sisters could stanch the flow of red ink on their ledger pages. Even though the Dollar family offer for them represented but 12.5% of their building costs, the Shipping Board welcomed the Dollar purchase offer and in the September 25, 1923 sales contract agreed to deliver the ships in the condition in which they had been on that date, offering to absorb the costs to repair any damages, but not ordinary "wear and tear." Perhaps the Board was a bit hasty in its rush to sell the ships. First of the sisters scheduled for delivery to private hands was the PRESIDENT HARRISON. Before being turned over to her buyers, the ship went into drydock on December 19th, a few days in advance of her due date, and was further inspected and inventoried. Naturally, the Dollar Line found a number of defects and looked to the Shipping Board to put them to rights. Holding a local Steamboat Inspection Service inspection and classification survey then and there, Dollar awarded certain repair work to a local yard, the United Engineering Company. For $4,779.00, workers at United removed all pipe control rods, pads, etc. which had been in the way of #3 plate brackets in a corner of the fireroom in order to allow repairs. On Dollar's instructions, the work was billed to an unhappy Shipping Board.

Discharged from the United plant, the HARRISON shifted to the Dollar piers in San Francisco where she was made ready for her delivery in advance of her fifth "maiden" voyage! Not yet four years old this ship was preparing for her fifth inaugural trip—First was her Delivery Voyage—with passengers and cargo from the East Coast. Second was her "Maiden Voyage" to Calcutta. Third was her first LASSCO trip to Honolulu. Fourth was the inaugural sailing for Buenos Aires. Now, her fifth "maiden trip" was at hand; the first passenger sailing under the American flag on the Round the World service.

A major news item in its own right, the purpose of their acquisition was no less a story. Dollar Line's intended Round the World service looked like a corporate death wish to American shipping men, a highly conservative breed. Spotlighting the significance of the new service and making sure to score a publicity coup at the same time, Shipping Board Chairman Farley asked President Coolidge to demonstrate the advances of modern technology and participate in the ship's San Francisco departure without even leaving the Oval Office. Accepting the invitation, the President's secretary wrote Chairman Farley on December 19, 1923 noting that the President "will be glad to touch a button at the White House which will pull the whistle on the steamer PRESIDENT HARRISON, inaugurating the first round the world service from San Francisco, at eight o'clock, Washington time, on January 5,

1924."[4] In conjunction with this publicity stunt, expenses and provision of all wire arrangements were at the expense of the Dollar Line and the Shipping Board.

For all times the Shipping Board shields were removed from the PRESIDENT HARRISON. The funnel was painted black with a broad red band to which a big white "$" was affixed. Technically delivered on December 24, 1923, the ship was publicly delivered to the Company during a dedication ceremony held aboard the ship on Christmas Day. Hosted by Captain Robert Dollar and his second son, R. Stanley Dollar, San Francisco notables including Mayor Rolph eschewed a day at home with their families to attend. Fourteen young ladies wearing the folk costumes of each of the countries on the proposed round the world itinerary posed for publicity pictures on the liner's bridge. A festive meal was served, but with Prohibition in effect, no alcohol to offend the sensibilities of teetotalling Captain Dollar was in evidence anywhere on board. There was also a little publicized run down the coast to San Pedro which occupied the ship between December 29th and January 2nd, when she tied up again at Pier 42 at San Francisco.

With Dollar Line furnishings such as china, flatware, linens, blankets, post cards, stationery and the like already on board, the ship had hosted a round of parties, congratulations, festive receptions and exchanges of good wishes before embarking her first passengers on January 5, 1924. Literally at the last minute sufficient charts of the waters the ship was to travel were brought aboard. Dollar Line hadn't any, nor did the local office of the Shipping Board. The idea of an American ship ranging so far afield from a single American port on a single voyage was still quite a novelty. Legend has it that some charts were provided as a favor by the British Consul general who begged or borrowed them from British merchant ships then in port. Dockside, Mayor Rolph and the "March King" John Phillips Sousa awaited the moment of departure with Stanley Dollar. So great was the enthusiasm for the new San Francisco-based venture that thousands of residents came down to the waterfront to participate in the send-off. At 8:00 PM, Eastern Standard Time, or 5:00 PM San Francisco local time, President Calvin Coolidge issued the actual order to sail by touching a key on his desk in the White House. This radio signal to the PRESIDENT HARRISON blew the ship's whistle. Busy as ever with all manner of pressing business, passenger Robert Dollar missed the historic moment. On the bridge, Captain K.A. Ahlin, the ship's Master, ordered the crew to cast off all lines and the PRESIDENT HARRISON backed out of the slip. Soon she was clear of the Golden Gate on her journey across the Pacific bound for 24 ports in 14 far off lands.

First port of call was Honolulu. Already a familiar sight there thanks both to her Pacific Mail and LASSCO days, the new Dollar Liner called there on January 12th. Kobe, Japan was next and after her overnight call there she

---

[4]December 19, 1923 letter from C.B. Slemp to Shipping Board Chairman Farley. Copy in the ship's 1091 file in RG 32 at National Archives.

A swarm of well-wishers lined the dock on January 5, 1924 to give the PRESIDENT HARRISON a rousing send off as she prepared to sail on her maiden voyage around the world for Dollar Line. Mike McGarvey photo.

sailed from there as scheduled at 5:00PM on Saturday, January 26th. Steaming out into the South China Sea, Shanghai was next on January 28th. After sailing the following day, the PRESIDENT HARRISON found herself in collision with the tug ST. DOMINIC. Damaging a few of her own plates, the "President" liner was quickly repaired and soon on her way to Hong Kong where she called between February 3rd and 5th. Greeting the ship some hours after her arrival at Manila at 7:00AM on February 7, 1924, Governor Leonard Wood, heroic General of the First World War, hosted a reception for Captain Dollar. Fêted by a crowd of 250 leading residents invited by the Governor, Dollar mused: "It was probably the most enthusiastic of all the great receptions I have had. One would think I was some great warrior and not a humble citizen that had done nothing to warrant such honor."[5]

There Captain Dollar left the PRESIDENT HARRISON, taking the faster Cunarder FRANCONIA on a segment of her world cruise to Batavia, Malacca, Penang and Colombo (where he returned to the HARRISON) to lay further groundwork for the new round the world liners. With his mind always on his business, he carefully checked purser's figures learning that operating the PRESIDENT HARRISON cost about $2,000.00 per day. Luck-

---

[5]From an entry made in his diary by Captain Robert Dollar on January 11, 1924.

Clear of her pier, the PRESIDENT HARRISON is about to turn her nose towards the Golden Gate and the broad Pacific on her first Dollar Line voyage. Mike McGarvey photo.

ily, her income thus far yielded some $2,500.00 every day. Captain Dollar's personal touch added to voyage revenues on that very first trip. Calling on Egyptian produce merchant Rabib Hindi at Alexandria on March 6th, Dollar convinced him to ship 1,000 sacks of onions to Boston to see if the New England market would absorb such Egyptian produce.

His ship sailed on, departing from Manila at 7:00PM on Friday, February 8, 1924. Singapore, once a homeward call featured on the ship's itinerary while on the Calcutta run, would once more be a major port for her on the round the world service and as a Dollar Liner, the PRESIDENT HARRISON made her first call there between her 5:00AM arrival on Wednesday, February 13th and her departure at 10:00PM on Friday, February 15th, setting a leisurely pace she would follow in her many subsequent calls there over the next sixteen years. At Penang on Sunday, February 17th the ship loaded rubber. Next was Colombo, Ceylon, where tea figured prominently among local cargoes shipped there. After an overnight call the ship sailed on February 22rd. Then she followed a course to Suez and her maiden transit of the Suez Canal on March 4th.

At 10:00PM that evening she departed Port Said to tie up the following morning at 9:00AM at Alexandria. Naples was next and the stay there was but an eight hour Sunday call, so it was more an expedient for passengers and any urgent loading than a real cargo port for the Dollar liners. Most of her Italy cargo was worked at Genoa and the PRESIDENT HARRISON made her maiden call there with her Monday, March 10th arrival at 4:00PM. Scheduled to overnight there, she sailed on Tuesday at 6:00PM for nearby Marseilles where on March 13th, Captain Dollar said a temporary goodbye to the PRESIDENT HARRISON. At that port came proof of just how rare were visits by American flag passenger vessels when local port authorities refused to accept the ship's tonnage figures. Unwilling to risk an indefinite delay while agents and officers haggled, Dollar cabled the State Department for help. Only the intervention of that Department, which sent officials of the American Consulate to intercede with French authorities, brought the standoff to an end. Once the American Consular officials firmly explained American tonnage rules to the French, the matter was settled. More visible to all aboard the PRESIDENT HARRISON than the private tussle over tonnage figures was a mugging or a mutiny, depending upon your point of view. Drunk on the freedom of open consumption of alcoholic drink in Marseilles, two members of the engine room crew turned aggressively rowdy once back on board. Knifing the First Assistant Engineer, one of the rowdy pair hurled a knife at Captain Ahlin, nearly scalping him. Need it be said that neither man enjoyed a much longer career with the Dollar Line?

Marseilles was the ship's last foreign port. From there with her departure at 7:00PM on Wednesday, March 12th the ship began the homeward leg of the 120-day long voyage. Across the Atlantic, the PRESIDENT HARRISON ended her maiden Dollar Line voyage with her arrival at Boston at 2:00PM on Monday, March 24th. After a night at the Army Terminal in South Boston, she sailed at 11:00PM on Tuesday, March 25th to make a 6:00AM arrival at New York on Thursday March 27th. Ready for Voyage 2, the liner followed her printed schedule and sailed from New York on April 3rd on her way around the world. The first time she would go all the way around during the course of a single voyage, the ship arrived at Cristobal, Panama Canal Zone at 7:54AM on April 11, 1924 for her first transit of the canal as a privately owned vessel. She entered the canal at 8:50AM and was through at 4:21PM. With 2,256 tons of general cargo the 12,031 gross and 8,495 net ton (by Panama Canal rules) ship cleared for sea at 9:04PM that evening and sailed for California and an April 21 arrival at Los Angeles. On that trip the ship sailed from San Francisco at 5:00PM on Saturday, April 26th. From Europe the ship began her second transAtlantic sailing from Genoa on July 3rd. That brought her into New York on the 18th. July 24th saw the PRESIDENT HARRISON sail from New York on round the world Voyage 3. Following her published schedule brought her the favor of shippers and intending passengers alike and that first year of Dollar Line's round the world service, the PRESIDENT HARRISON had time to set out on her fourth globe-girdling trip, sailing from New York on November 13th.

The next few years passed in a comfortable routine with the ship working her way around the world like clock-work. The ship sailed from San Francisco on voyage 4 on December 2, 1924. Little out of the ordinary happened on that trip except a cryptic note that near Chios, Greece on February 8, 1925, she sent out an SOS call. It turns out that she did no such thing. Two messages sent by her Master were received at San Francisco but the reputed SOS call turned out to have been another incident of petty harassments sent Dollar's way. Three months earlier a Dollar ship was reported afire off Japan. Glad to tell the ship was not even close to the Japanese archipelago. More curious than that was her actual location at a Naples, Italy pier where she worked cargo. During 1925 Captain Ahlin was relieved by Captain Porta. That year the ship took departures from New York on February 26th, June 25th and October 15th while she sailed on voyages 5, 6 and 7 from San Francisco on March 28th, July 18th and November 7, 1925. During 1926 the PRESIDENT HARRISON took sailings from New York for California and the world on February 4, May 27th and September 16th and from her San Francisco home port on February 27th, June 19th and October 9th. Those, of course, were voyages 8, 9 and 10. Little trouble had come her way and when she sailed on voyage 10 on September 16, 1926 from New York, no one expected anything but a routine voyage. On schedule the PRESIDENT HARRISON called at Havana on September 20th, transited the Canal on the 24th and arrived at San Pedro for a short call on October 4. Sailing from San Francisco on October 9th, the liner made for Hawaii where she called at Honolulu on the 17th on her way to Kobe where she made an appearance on October 30th. From there Shanghai was next and after arriving on November 2nd, the liner worked cargo over the next three days before sailing on for Hong Kong on November 5th. On the following morning November 6, 1926, the PRESIDENT HARRISON ran into trouble, running ashore on Bonham Island in the mouth of the Yang Tze River. With four feet of water in No. 1 hold and eleven feet of water in No. 2, it was apparent that her bottom was seriously damaged but no one expected much of a delay. However, when she was refloated on the 7th surveyors found the liner damaged badly enough to need drydocking. The voyage interrupted, her passengers were landed on November 8th at Shanghai and supplied alternative transportation. On November 10th the ship dry docked there and over the next few days workmen got busy repairing the ship's damaged stem, renewing 29 shell-plates, fairing 10 others. Within the ship, floors in the forepeak were in need of renewal as were floors in Nos. 1,2 and 3 double bottom tanks starboard. In the grounding some frames had bent and during this time of repairs, these were renewed as well. Where damaged, Bulkheads Nos. 1 and 3 were inspected and renewed. Somewhat strained while trying to refloat the ship, machinery, both crank and thrust shafts, were lifted and re-lined. Further aft, the tail shafts were drawn and re-aligned. Before redelivery to

Dollar Line, several other minor machinery and hull repairs were done. Thus delayed for repairs, the PRESIDENT HARRISON finally sailed from Shanghai on January 28, 1927 for Hong Kong, where she arrived on January 31, 1927, several weeks behind schedule. Not until March 24, 1927 did she reach Boston and only on March 25th did she steam back into New York to tie up at Brooklyn's Pier 22 for the last time. Five days later Dollar Liners began using the Erie Terminal's new Pier 9 in Jersey City. After her six day stay at Brooklyn she sailed out past the Narrows on March 21st for another trip around the world. By then it seems that Captain Porta was ashore while on the ship's bridge was Captain James D. Guthrie.

On Voyage 11 the ship made a Havana call on April 4, 1927. Her Panama Canal transit was next on April 8th. Ten days later the liner tied up at San Pedro and on April 20th the PRESIDENT HARRISON came into San Francisco for the first time since her October 9, 1926 sailing. From her home port the liner continued her voyage with an April 23, 1927 sailing. Because her needed repairs took so long, the ship did not complete as many 1927 voyages as otherwise expected. She took further outbound sailings that year from New York on July 21st and November 4th. She took her San Francisco departures that year on August 13th and December 2nd.

That year's winter holidays found her in the Far East. She sailed from

A rare stern view of the PRESIDENT HARRISON shows how closely the after section of the "502" class steamers resembled the forepart. No wonder many still believe their construction was intended as a ruse to fool a sub's captain. Frank O. Braynard collection.

Marking her first voyage under private ownership, the PRESIDENT HARRISON was dressed fore and aft on January 12, 1924 when she arrived once again at Honolulu. Mike McGarvey photo.

Kobe on Christmas Eve, December 24th for Shanghai. Passing New Years' Eve at sea, the ship arrived Hong Kong on January 2, 1928. Just under a month later the PRESIDENT HARRISON was at Alexandria, Egypt on her way to Naples, Genoa, Marseilles, New York and Boston. Back on the East Coast of the United States that trip ended uneventfully and the next one began with the usual Boston side trip, bringing her back into New York on February 28th for a March 1, 1928 sailing for San Francisco.

That voyage continued from San Francisco on March 23rd. That year the ship continued her usual voyaging, taking further sailings from New York June 21st and October 11th and from San Francisco on July 13th and November 2nd.

One problem that seemed to take on an inordinate stature was smuggling. Under prohibition the temptation to bring in illicit narcotic and alcoholic substances was too big an invitation for everyone to ignore and those kind of items literally flooded into the country. More profitable than rum running was drug smuggling. United States Customs officials between January 1923 and September 1928 seized drugs, particularly opium from thirteen American ships which counted Chinese citizens among their crews. During that period drug smugglers had a decided preference for Dollar Line "535" type ships. In the period in question, narcotics were seized aboard all five of the San Francisco based sisters, though the PRESIDENT TAFT seemed by far the most popular with the smugglers. Aboard that ship Customs agents found "junk" five times, while next in popularity with the smugglers was the PRESIDENT LINCOLN where "T-men" confiscated contraband three times, while from the PRESIDENT CLEVELAND, PRESIDENT PIERCE and PRESIDENT WILSON drugs were caught only once each. Only four arrests were made and only three of those charged were convicted. Dollar

Here's the PRESIDENT HARRISON at Boston in this June 17, 1925 Richard Hildebrand photo. Eric Johnson collection.

Captains were heavily fined but the original levies totalling $608,210.00 were reduced to a total of $15,183.00. Except once, when the NYK Line paid a $100.00 fine for opium found aboard their KOREA MARU, Dollar ships suffered lesser monetary punishments. On her third charge the PRESIDENT LINCOLN had a $1,000.00 penalty assessed against her voyage report while on her fifth offense the PRESIDENT TAFT paid a $3,000.00 penalty. The very nature of the shipping business is of course an open invitation to secrete precious goods aboard a moving carrier for clandestine retrieval beyond the eyes and ears of delegated authority. Few incidents of narcotics and liquor smuggling matched the scope of that discovered aboard the PRESIDENT HARRISON in October 1928 when a cache of about a million dollars worth of opium secreted in 3,000 tins under about a hundred feet of anchor chain in the chain locker was discovered and seized by federal agents. Charged with smuggling were four of the ship's Chinese crewmembers but for permitting the transport of contraband aboard his ship, the Master was once again held culpable under the law and subject to an automatic fine. This time the amount demanded by the government was $399,250.00 from Captain J. B. Guthrie. It was lucky for the shipowner and Master that the law did not permit seizure of the vessel nor could the owner be charged as well unless his knowledge of the contraband could be established. With the help of Dollar Line's legal staff, Captain Guthrie appealed for remission of the fine. When the Department of the Treasury reduced the penalty to $7,500.00, the company settled and paid the Captain's fine. It was around the time of the case against him that year that Captain Guthrie took his leave and relinquished command of the PRESIDENT HARRISON to Captain L.S. Burgess.

In 1929, the Dollar Steamship Lines, Ltd., Inc. took advantage of newly available construction loans for refits, and borrowed $225,000.00 from the Construction Loan Fund to rebuild the PRESIDENT HARRISON's passenger accommodations. Repayment of the loan, which was rather less than the figure of $257,000.00 authorized for this ship, still represented 75% of the cost of the project, and of course was spread out over a period of fifteen years at a rate of interest of 3 per cent. This standard arrangement between the Shipping Board and certain American steamship operators had been recently codified into law by the passage of the Merchant Marine Act of 1928, the famed Jones-White Act.

The great rebuilding was scheduled to take place after the completion of the ship's last world trip of 1928, her sixteenth Dollar Line voyage. She departed Kobe on November 23rd, Shanghai on November 28th, Hong Kong on December 2nd, Manila on December 5th, Singapore on December 13th, Penang on December 15th, Colombo on December 19th, Port Said on January 1, 1929, Alexandria on January 2nd, Naples on January 6th, Genoa on January 8th, and Marseilles on January 9th before she headed home to United States waters. After pulling into New York on January 27th she sailed two days later for Boston. From there the PRESIDENT HARRISON sailed on February 1, 1929, setting her course directly for Newport News, Virginia where she arrived at the vast shipyards of the Newport News Shipbuilding & Drydock Company early on the morning of February 3rd. Rebuilding the PRESIDENT HARRISON as well as performing contract repairing in the running time of 85 days may not have been a record for such work but the yard deserved a healthy dollop of respect for accomplishing the job in only seventy-three working days. Discount the nine days lost to snow or heavy rain, and the job was done in sixty-four days of work.

Even though the planned reconstruction of the ship's passenger quarters were based on the plans Theodore Ferris drew in late 1924 to rebuild the burned out PRESIDENT POLK, the rebuilding of the PRESIDENT HARRISON was a big job. Because of careful planning and arrangements made before the ship arrived at the yard, Newport News was able to get the job done in about three weeks less time than a "502" needed to complete a single voyage. The reason for the tight schedule had everything to do with Dollar Line's own round the world sailing schedule. Should the PRESIDENT HARRISON be completed within ninety days, she could take the mid May sailing scheduled for the PRESIDENT GARFIELD which would be free to have her own refit at that time. Five important items overrode everything else in the organization of this rebuilding. First of all, the contract between the Dollar Steamship Lines and Newport News Shipbuilding and Dry Dock Company was signed far enough ahead of time to permit all preliminary work to be completed in advance of the ship's arrival at the yard. Second, every facet of the job was carefully mapped out and the expected elapsed times of each part of it was factored into the planning. That made it possible for the yard to have the required workforce in place and all requisite materials handy

Master schedule for the major refit and a safety sign greeted
all who boarded the PRESIDENT HARRISON while she sat
at her pier undergoing rebuilding at Newport News during
the spring of 1929. Author's collection.

once the ship showed up. Third, all preliminary drawings and everything
needed were at the yard before the ship got there. Fourth, as soon as the ship
arrived, workmen got busy. Before beginning the actual refit, the ship was
made weather tight. It was the fifth item on the planners' wish list that turned
out to weigh as heavily as the availability of men and material, and that was
the careful execution of following work schedules. When necessary, timetables were corrected and the morale of the workforce kept high.

When the PRESIDENT HARRISON tied up at a fitting out pier at Newport
News on February 3, 1929 almost all the steel, piping, ventilation and electrical drawings were out and about one half of the joiner drawings and
material covered by them was ordered. A good deal of it was in the yard.
All drawings not out were made to tie into or match existing work and even
on those, a lot of time was saved when draftsmen outlined drawings and
added all available information. Much of the steelwork was fabricated in the
yard's own shops. So, too, was much of the joiner work such as sills, plates,
furring, sheathing, ready for installation when the ship came in. Experience

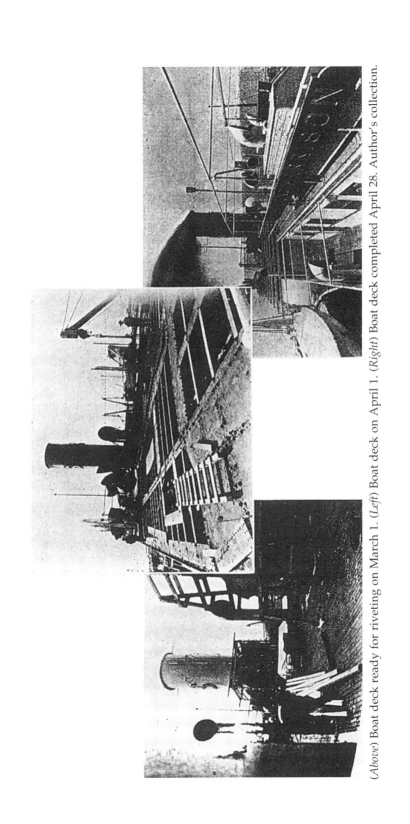

(*Above*) Boat deck ready for riveting on March 1. (*Left*) Boat deck on April 1. (*Right*) Boat deck completed April 28. Author's collection.

The new Main Lounge was something of a shambles on April 1st. Compare this with the Main Lounge aboard the refitted PRESIDENT GARFIELD. Author's collection.

It took three and a half weeks to join the two sections of the split superstructure. Author's collection.

gained in the refitting of the PRESIDENT HARRISON allowed the yard to have ready, assembled and riveted up where necessary toilet bulkheads, deck-house sides, bulwarks and light and air trunks for the next "502" to come in for rebuilding, the PRESIDENT GARFIELD. The work of subcontractors was also carefully choreographed. Among outside contract work were laying of quarry and ceramic tile, Asbestolith, rubber tile and carpets.

Within three and a half weeks of the inception of work, enough steelwork had been completed that the main thrust of the job, connecting the two separate deck houses of the superstructure, was almost done. Giving the ship a single midships superstructure, this work extended the Upper Promenade Deck and Lower Promenade Decks in way of Nos. 5 and 6 hatches, extended deck houses on both promenade decks so that once connected with extant houses on those decks, new passenger quarters could be installed in those new spaces. Also on the bill were rebuilding officer quarters on Boat Deck, relocating the swimming pool, fitting cargo ports on C Deck (to give access to Nos. 5 and 6), removal of the old laycock windows from the after end of Upper Promenade Deck and the installation of by new Kearfott windows at the forward end and across the front of Upper Promenade Deck. The work also had an aesthetic advantage. With the forward island of her superstructure connected to the main body of her upperworks and a new and large elliptical outer casing to her funnel, the external appearance of this ugly duckling was much improved.

Internal modifications gave the ship larger public rooms and a number of

One of the original cabins aboard the PRESIDENT HARRISON was every bit as comfortable after the refit. Author's collection.

new cabins and suites. While at the Virginia yard, thirty-six new passenger cabins were built, increasing the total number of passenger cabins to seventy-three. Best of the new cabins were two room suites fitted at the forward end of both promenade decks. Comprising a bedroom, sitting room, trunk room and bathroom, these were decorated with New York's Park Avenue in mind. Reflecting the standards of classic American hotels, decor in the new suites reflected the ambiance and glamour of urban luxury. Notable was the new Dining Room fitted during the ship's stay at the yards. Enclosed by ornamental iron balustrades with mahogany cap rails, a central staircase gave entrance into this most important space. Joiner work, fixtures and furniture were thoroughly renewed and some of it replaced. Adjunct to the Dining Room, the Pantry was enlarged and entirely re-equipped with the latest kitchen equipment available.

In this American ship, safety was an important concern and by no means neglected. When the new passenger quarters were fitted, workers extended and enlarged all piping, electrical, ventilating and fire alarm systems in order to bring the ship up to the standards of the best American hotels. Emerging at nearly 12,000 gross tons, the PRESIDENT HARRISON could now carry 158 First Class passengers in very comfortable accommodations. By early May the job was done and the Dollar Line had virtually a new passenger carrier.

With but little notice and even less fanfare she returned to New York. There, she took the place of the PRESIDENT GARFIELD on Dollar Line's round the world service, sailing from New York on May 11th. In command of the newly refitted liner was Captain J.H. Benson. Showing off her new look to her home port for the first time, she pulled into San Francisco on May 28th. On the 31st the voyage continued with her sailing for Honolulu and Kobe. The ship was still on that trip that August when her name appeared in casualty lists. On her way from Marseilles to New York she experienced engine trouble. That was not all the notices in the shipping press had to say about her just then. In the mid Atlantic on August 20th the PRESIDENT HARRISON picked up all 26 surviving members of the crew of the burned iron-hulled fruit boat QUIMISTAN, which was lost in the Atlantic in position 39'40° N latitude and 59'22° W longitude, after burning out on August 19, 1929. The ship's rescue of the survivors of the doomed fruit boat was overshadowed along the way by engine trouble on the PRESIDENT HARRISON. She would have to be repaired at New York. After arriving at New York on Friday August 23th, the QUIMISTAN's survivors landed with the PRESIDENT HARRISON's passengers. Any reporter who had come down to the dock to welcome the ship and interview Captain Benson and his men had long since departed when workmen got down to the business of repairing the liner's main engines. That work done, the ship got away on time on August 30th. Sailing from San Francisco for her second time since her rebuilding, she departed on September 22nd.

The PRESIDENT HARRISON departed Boston for New York on December 16, 1929. Travelling "light" and drawing but 17'6" forward and 26'6" aft, the PRESIDENT HARRISON wound up with "egg on her face" as she steamed in fog off Shinnecock Light near Block Island on December 17, 1929. There her path crossed that of the steamer PETER H. CROWELL and the ships collided just before 11:25 PM., rendering considerable damage to the starboard bow and midships of the smaller CROWELL. Not much more than scratched was the "502", which continued on her voyage without undue delay. The PRESIDENT HARRISON was making a speed of just 12 knots,

On April 6, 1930 Richard Hildebrand turned his camera on the refitted PRESIDENT HARRISON. Compare this with his earlier portrait of the ship. Eric Johnson collection.

the CROWELL only 9 knots, but the "502" was charged with speeding when the collision happened. A charge of reckless navigation against the PRESIDENT HARRISON's Master was dismissed in Federal Court at New Haven, Connecticut where blame was apportioned equally between the two vessels. The ship continued her career, sailing from New York on December 20, 1929 on another round the world trip. Through the Panama Canal on December 28th, a New Year's Party on December 31st was held off the coast of Central America and on January 10, 1930 the voyage continued from San Francisco. That trip saw her steam uneventfully around the world, calling at her usual ports. From Marseilles on March 19th the ship headed for an April 2nd arrival at New York. Her next outbound sailing was on April 10th and from San Francisco the liner continued her voyage with her May 2nd sailing for ports across the Pacific. That trip ended at New York after her July 21st arrival. There she worked cargo and ran up to Boston and back prior to taking her scheduled July 31st sailing for Cuba. But while the ship was at New York taking on her last bits of freight before sailing that evening, a fire broke out in No. 8 hold. Interrupting her scheduled departure for Havana and Balboa, the fire burned through the night. Overcome by smoke while fighting the fire were several of the ship's officers and crew. Coming to the ship's assistance were local firefighters. With their work the blaze was extinguished, but not before so much water had been pumped into the ship's after sections that when day broke the "502" had her stern resting in the mud.

Merritt & Chapman repair crews were busy pumping her out during the morning of August 1st. Luckily things looked a lot worse than they really were and authorities permitted the ship's crew to effect repairs while underway. With a newly granted certificate of seaworthiness, the PRESIDENT HARRISON sailed on August 2nd on her way around the world. By the time she sailed from San Francisco on August 21st, the scorched hold had been repainted and all tangible signs of the recent fire eradicated. By the time the ship returned to New York on November 11, 1930, the fire was a dim memory to all but underwriters and P & I men.

Now Captain Deneen took command of the PRESIDENT HARRISON as the liner made her way south from New York on November 20th. Sailing from San Francisco on December 12th, the liner was at sea for Christmas but she greeted 1931 with a January 1 arrival at Kobe, Japan. Little out of the ordinary happened to the ship that year. Let her New York sailings on March 10th, June 25th and October 20th and her San Francisco departures on April 3rd, July 24th and November 13th serve as milestone markers for her progress that year during which three more men served her as Master. First of them was Captain W.H. Weaver, followed in turn by Captains Burgess and Austin. The ship was in the Far East by December, sailing from Kobe on December 4th for her usual ports. As always, Shanghai, Hong Kong and Manila were next on the itinerary. On that trip the ship sailed from Singapore on Christmas Eve and worked cargo at Penang on Christmas Day, 1931.

She took all her scheduled sailings from New York and San Francisco. By 1932 authorities recorded her net tonnage at the slightly higher figure of 6,242 tons. Sometimes quite a minor inconvenience brought a ship's name to the casualty lists. So it was before the ship took her first sailing of 1932 from New York when a two hour delay in sailing from New York on February 11, 1932 was attributed to trouble with her steering engine. She sailed out again from New York on June 2nd and from San Francisco on June 24th. Her next sailing day from New York was September 22nd and from San Francisco on October 14th. From Kobe on November 4, 1932 the PRESIDENT HARRISON continued her way westabout the world, calling at her customary ports in their usual order. She closed out that year on the homeward stretch of her long voyage, sailing from Naples on December 18th, then from Genoa on December 20th. From Marseilles on December 23, 1932, the ship began the transAtlantic portion of Voyage 28 around the world trip and arrived at New York on January 3, 1933.

Sailing from New York on January 5th for her customary Boston weekend, the PRESIDENT HARRISON was back at New York on January 9th. Embarkation for passengers booked for Voyage 29 began around 1:00PM on Thursday, January 12, 1933. Indicative of how badly the slump in cargo bookings affected the "502"s, only 1,812 tons of general cargo were in her holds when she steamed through the Panama Canal on January 20th. From San Francisco the ship continued her voyage with a February 3rd departure. A typically uneventful voyage, it was mid April when the ship sailed on the

12th from Marseilles for New York. Up the Hudson River, the PRESIDENT HARRISON tied up at her Jersey City pier after completing her transAtlantic voyage on April 25th. Then it was on to Boston on April 30th before preparing to take on the last of her outbound cargo and sail again from New York on Voyage 30 on May 4th for Havana, Panama, California and the world. This time she had a larger cargo, carrying 3,421 tons of cargo through the Canal during her May 12th transit. From San Francisco the liner continued the outbound voyage with her May 26th sailing. It may have been at that time that Captain Austin was relieved by Captain W. Ehman. Her voyage continued from Kobe with a June 16th sailing for Shanghai. Uneventful as her trips were so far that year, they remained so for the rest of her 1933 passages. Other New York departures that year were taken on August 24th for Voyage 31 and December 14th for Voyage 32. In connection with those dates, the ship sailed from San Francisco on September 15th and January 5, 1934.

At least some of the officers and men of the PRESIDENT HARRISON had a rare chance to carouse on a New Year's Eve spent in port while the ship was tied up at San Pedro after her noon arrival there on December 31st. There was even time for anyone hung over to recover before the voyage continued with her noon sailing on January 1, 1934 for San Francisco. Maybe the hung over needn't have bothered to clear their heads for befogged might well have been the best way to have been during that year. A true "annus horribilis", it was the worst of the Depression and the most violent and strife prone in West Coast maritime history. On her first trip that year, the PRESIDENT HARRISON called at most of her scheduled ports in their usual sequence. Missing from the record that time was her customary Hong Kong call, "xxxed" over in San Francisco port records[6]. Here are her sailing dates from other harbors: January 24th from Kobe, January 29th from Shanghai, February 9th from Manila, February 19th from Colombo, March 7th from Port Said and Alexandria. After her customary calls at Naples, Genoa and Marseilles, the ship sailed for New York on March 14th. After the ship's March 27th arrival came the Boston side trip and an April 5th sailing on Voyage 33 from New York for Cuba, Panama Canal Zone and California. Sailing from San Francisco on April 24th, she was well away from her volatile home port when a massive strike broke out in the entire maritime industry on May 9th. Highlighted by bloodshed and acrimony, before it was settled after 83 days on July 31st, it turned out to be one of the seminal episodes of militant labor unionism. Throughout the entire 83 days strike while strikers in the West Coast industry maritime shut down virtually the entire West Coast of the United States except the port of Los Angeles, the PRESIDENT HARRISON continued in service, her crew co-operating with her owners to keep the ship's schedule until the ship returned to a United States port. From Kobe the ship sailed on May 17th, one week after the strike broke out at

---

[6]So it appears on card #7 (also known as #12) of the San Francisco Marine Exchange cards.

home. Her other ports called in order were augmented that time by an additional landfall, this one at Bombay, from whence the ship sailed on June 13th. Arriving at New York on July 24th, the crew decided to remain on the job and the vessel sailed for California on Voyage 34 without making her Boston detour. By the time the ship made her transit of the Panama Canal on August 3rd, the strike was over, but the hard feelings would long reverberate. The unions seemed beaten again which caused unionmen to become more passionate than ever. The atmosphere on board surely suffered when the ship continued on her way with her August 17th sailing. In the remaining months of that year the liner took another departure from New York, sailing on Voyage 35 on November 15th for her usual ports around the world. That trip was Dollar Line's 270th round the world sailing, a milestone that garnered very little publicity and only the merest mention in San Francisco shipping papers. Arriving at San Francisco on Tuesday, December 4th, the PRESIDENT HARRISON took her last sailing of 1934 on Friday December 7th. Another Master came aboard that year as well. He was Captain C.G. Hansen.

Closing out 1934 in Japanese waters the PRESIDENT HARRISON cleared Kobe on December 28th for Shanghai. During 1935 the PRESIDENT HARRISON welcomed yet another Master, Captain H. J. Ehman. He would remain with the ship for several years. Under his command the ship took departures from New York on March 7th, June 28th and October 18th. From Singapore on January 15, 1935 and from Bombay on January 25th, the liner spent the next ten days on her way to Suez and her February 4th transit to the Mediterranean. After calling at Port Said, Alexandria, Naples and Genoa, the ship entered Marseilles on February 13th. Sailing at 5:00 PM that afternoon for New York, thirteen days later saw the ship steam up the Hudson on February 26, 1935. She sailed two days later for Boston. Back at Pier 9 on Monday, March 4th, the PRESIDENT HARRISON cleared New York at the start of Voyage 36 on March 7th.

It never really mattered who was in command of the PRESIDENT HARRISON, for labor trouble was often on a Dollar Liner's bill of fare. Here is just one of many such stories:

> Board Settles Labor Dispute On Dollar Ship—Dispute over the Dollar liner President Harrison, which had been held up at San Pedro since Monday, was ironed out by the Seamen's Labor Relations Board yesterday, following arrival of the vessel here from the south. Seamen had struck in protest against the food served and had demanded dismissal of the chief Steward. Under an agreement reached yesterday the steward will be retained, but a supervising steward placed aboard. The President Harrison will sail for China tonight. She was permitted to come here under an agreement to submit the dispute to the seamen's board.[7]

Labor trouble hit the ship again when she reached San Pedro on November

---

[7]November 11, 1935 edition of the *San Francisco Chronicle*

4th. Demanding the ouster of the Chief Steward, crew struck in protest against the food served. It took a week before striking crew agreed to submit their dispute to the seaman's board. As for the Chief Steward, he kept his job but Dollar Line accepted the crew demand to put on a supervisory steward. From Los Angeles the ship sailed to San Francisco for an abbreviated call at her home port. Sailing from San Francisco on November 12th, a small fire broke out in one of her holds on the following day. Quickly extinguished, damage was minimal and the ship was able to continue on her way.

An even more difficult year for West Coast steamship operators was coming. It started out well enough and nothing out of the ordinary indicated the passions that led to a strike even longer than the Big Strike of 1934. As for the PRESIDENT HARRISON, she sailed from New York on her regular round the world voyages on February 4th and May 26th. Once more the ship found herself in Japan at midsummer, sailing from Kobe on July 10, 1936. August 19th saw the ship at Port Said and on the following day she worked freight at Alexandria while passengers took a tour to Cairo and the Pyramids. After Naples and Genoa, Marseilles was again her last foreign port of call and with her sailing on August 26th the PRESIDENT HARRISON was homeward bound. She steamed into New York on September 5th. With passengers, cargo and mail aboard, Dollar Line's sentimental favorite "502" sailed from New York for another voyage on September 17th. No one knew how fast the clock was ticking for West Coast shipping. On October 4th the ship arrived at San Pedro and two days later the liner steamed past the Golden Gate on her way into San Francisco. This time the ship remained at her home port for four days, not sailing until October 10th. At the end of the month the ship was at Kobe. She sailed from there on October 31st, the day the strike began at San Francisco. Once more Dollar Line was lucky and the ship's crew elected to keep working. Work, it seemed, even to the hottest heads aboard, was better than imprisonment in the brig on charges of mutiny. With the West Coast all but shut down, the ship continued on her way, making departures from Shanghai on November 5th, Hong Kong on November 8th, Manila on November 11th, Singapore on November 17th, Penang on November 18th, Colombo on November 23rd and Bombay on November 27. After calls at Suez, Port Said, Alexandria, Naples, Genoa and Marseilles, the PRESIDENT HARRISON made her way once more through the Mediterranean and Atlantic to New York where she arrived on December 30th. The strike on the West Coast was still on and though her holds still had cargo for Boston and California, the ship was held by the Dollar Line at New York. Another victim of the absurdity of grousing labor, the PRESIDENT HARRISON sat idle at New York for almost six weeks.

February 4th brought an end to the walk-out and the following day saw affected ships begin to move again. With the resolution of that destructive ninety-nine day West Coast maritime strike, the PRESIDENT HARRISON sailed from New York for Boston on February 13th. Then the liner returned to New York and sailed on February 20th for her usual ports around the world. When the steamer made her Panama Canal transit on February 28th

The curious small house in the ship's after welldeck, a structure seen in some shots of every one of the ships is evident in this classic broadside shot of the refitted PRESIDENT HARRISON. Eric Johnson collection.

Undeniably an attractive liner after her 1929 rebuilding, the PRESIDENT HARRISON awaits passengers at her San Francisco pier. Courtesy of National Maritime Museum, San Francisco.

she had 5,153 tons of general cargo in her holds. The reason she had such a heavy cargo for a "502" is easily explained. During the course of the strike thousands and thousands of tons of cargo backed up awaiting shipment. Once the strike was settled, it went into the holds and onto the decks of whatever ships that could take it. That first post strike voyage continued with the ship's March 15th sailing for the Far East. May 21st saw the PRESIDENT HARRISON slip her Marseilles' moorings on her way to New York where she arrived on June 10th. Maritime Commission cancellations of mail contracts were soon to take effect. Twenty days after the PRESIDENT HARRISON arrived at New York subsidy payments to Dollar Line under the terms of their mail contracts ceased. As of July 1, 1937 the Dollar fleet was on its own. During hard times for most American shipping companies, the Dollars shared with the Munsons the distinction of being in such fouled financial shape that the Maritime Commission had refused to accept their spring 1937 applications for operating subsidy until corporate entities could be restructured. At that time the PRESIDENT HARRISON was at San Francisco, having arrived on June 29th. Unsubsidized, the liner sailed out again on July 3rd. That first voyage without any formal government assistance ended after her September 22nd New York arrival. Nor was there a subsidy agreement in sight when the liner sailed again on October 1st at the start of another round the world voyage. With 2,353 tons of cargo aboard, the ship transited the Canal on October 9th. That month Dollar Line reduced the number of men in the ship's deck crew from 21 to 15, but aware of the company's shaky condition, the unions did not react as fiercely as they might have nor were their words as strident as expected. In fact they said that shipping 12 ABs and 3 OS would be about right for a ship this size operating as a freighter . . . "which the PRESIDENT HARRISON will be when she leaves this port" said E.C. Mausshardt, Pacific Coast Representative of the Maritime Commission on October 22nd[8]. Off from San Francisco, the PRESIDENT HARRISON sailed from Kobe on November 13th. There was no Shanghai call that time so Hong Kong was next. The ship then called at her usual ports in their customary order. She called at Alexandria on December 21st and after passing the holidays in Italy, the liner sailed from Marseilles for New York and a January 11, 1938 arrival.

While the ship was on that voyage, unionists had turned their energies to complaints about their living quarters. From Port Said, Egypt on December 21, 1937, E. Bellinger, an oiler, addressed engine room crew concerns to the Secretary of the Marine Firemen, Oilers and Wipers Union:

Dear Sir and Brothers:

The crew of the President Harrison (Unanimously) call your attention and most vigorously protest the quarters assigned to us. Our description follows:

---

[8]Copies of correspondence on this subject is found in the ship's 901 file in RG 178 at Maritime Administration.

We are lodged on B Deck amidships directly over the boilers for four rooms, each room designated for four men by the Dollar Line and certified by the U.S. Govt (and marked) as being adequate for three men. These rooms have their only door opening directly into the machine shop. This machine shop has the usual assortment of lathes, drill presses, anvils, et cetera.

The four rooms have a thin insulation on the deck, not thick enough by any means to permit the touch of the deck with bare or stockinged feet; they are much too hot for that.

The machine shop has an uncovered steel deck. A duck board is provided for the machinist to stand on while operating on the various machines consequently both quarters and machine shop are insufferably hot and noisy.

It is physically impossible for the watches to obtain any sleep or rest in the rooms during the day. Incidently the machine shop is not operated during the day alone. There is never a night passes that some repair job requiring hammering, grinding, or the operation of noisy machines is done.

The other four rooms are on the same deck just aft of those described. They are directly over the dynamo flat. They do not open into the machine shop, but do open into a passageway heading into the machine shop. It also has a steel door leading into the engine room.

We not only suffer from heat of the dynamo flat but are given a gust of tremendously hot air and an ear piercing noise every time the door to the engine room is opened.

This passageway has an uninsulated steel deck nicely suited for heavy pumps or other machinery going into the machine shop or to the next deck up being dragged across it usually to be taken ashore for repairs by shore workers.

On a schedule of this sort (round the world) with the exception of California, New York and Europe, the rest is entirely in the tropics, Singapore and Bombay being our longest stops, both red hot. It is physically impossible to continue on with such living conditions. We feel that they are detrimental to our health and must be changed.

This particular ship, PRES. HARRISON, sailed from San Francisco with twelve passengers. She can accommodate over one hundred and fifty. There are four decks above the deck on which we are attempting to live, having crew or passenger accommodations at least 75% vacant.

We demand of Headquarters that we be removed from our (present hog pen or Black Hole of Calcutta) surroundings to one of the decks above. It is our right as American workmen in general, and members of the M.F.O.W. in particular, to demand relief from the conditions described.

We feel that a relentless effort by Headquarters, by constantly hammering at the Port Committee, the Dollar Line and the U.S. Maritime Commission, this relief will be realized.

We herewith go on record as notifying Headquarters that another voyage cannot be started from San Francisco until the pathetic conditions aboard the Pres. Harrison have been straightened out.[9]

---

[9]Copy of Bellinger's letter in the ship's 901 file in RG178 at Maritime Administration.

Other PRESIDENT HARRISON crewmembers were also correct in another unkind assessment made that December that "crew quarters can be insufferably hot but also dangerously cold—no heating facilities and we are just above the water line and bare steel and no insulation separate us from seawater outside."[10] From the earliest days of both the "502"'s and their larger running mates, the "535"'s, crew and service areas of the ships had been subject to extremes of temperature and no one had yet devoted much energy or cash to curing the problem.

A committee of Maritime Commission and Dollar Line men inspected the PRESIDENT POLK for the purpose of judging the extent of improvements the "502"'s needed. Consider February 9, 1938 views of the Maritime Commission's Director of Marine Personnel:

> With reference to the S.S. PRESIDENT HARRISON, that vessel was not in port at the time of the Committee's visit to San Francisco and the actual survey was made on the S.S. PRESIDENT POLK. However, the type plan that was drawn up for the S.S. PRESIDENT HARRISON as being nearly representative of the group and the approval given by the Commission was limited to the S.S. PRESIDENT HARRISON.
>
> The gist of the complaint of the engine room crew on board the S.S. PRESIDENT HARRISON is covered by the demand that they be moved from their present location on "B" Deck to some deck above that deck which, or course, involves the use of existing passenger quarters with a consequent reduction in revenue. In view of the age of the vessels involved and the conditions of operation, great care has been taken not to recommend changes the cost of which cannot be justified, particularly when they involve a reduction in revenue-producing space.
>
> Referring to the location of these quarters on "B" Deck amidship, opposite the boiler and engine room casings, this location, as far as proximity to the engine and boiler rooms is concerned, does not differ from the quarters usually allocated on cargo vessels to the Chief Engineer and his assistants and is similar to the quarters now allocated to the engineer officers on the vessels of the Baltimore Mail Line. If the quarters are excessively hot, the remedy lies in adequate insulation and proper ventilation, not in putting the crew in passenger quarters.
>
> However, since the receipt of the complaint with reference to the crew's quarters on the S.S. PRESIDENT HARRISON and since approved plans for the rearrangement of crew's quarters on the various vessels of the Dollar Line were transmitted to San Francisco with instructions to proceed with the work, it has been found necessary in order to expedite the change on the S.S. PRESIDENT ADAMS, now at New York, to make a survey of that vessel. As a result of the survey, which was held in conjunction with the Port Engineer and the various officers of the S.S.PRESIDENT ADAMS, a new plan showing the arrangement of crew's quarters on this vessel has been prepared which it is believed eliminates almost entirely the conditions complained of on the S.S. PRESIDENT HARRISON. This plan supersedes

---

[10]ibid.

that previously approved for the S.S. PRESIDENT HARRISON and class and will be utilized in connection with the rearrangement of quarters on the S.S. PRESIDENT HARRISON, making only those modifications which may be necessary on that particular vessel.

The oilers and watertenders who are berthed on "B" Deck amidships in way of the engine casing have been moved aft to "A" Deck under the poop in quarters on the starboard side opposite the seamen's quarters on the port side, and such quarters should prove to be entirely satisfactory. The quarters should prove to be entirely satisfactory. The quarters thus released in way of the engine casing amidships have been utilized for the firemen and wipers and the quarters formerly occupied by these men have been eliminated entirely. The space thus released in way of the boiler casing will be utilized by the engine department for machine shops and storeroom purposes.

One room in the quarters now to be occupied by the firemen and wipers will be converted into a locker room for working clothes. New deck coverings will be fitted in all of these rooms and the underside of the deck over the dynamo flat will be thoroughly insulated. Likewise, the passageway between the rooms and the engine casing will have the deck insulated. The elimination of the rooms in way of the boiler casing will increase the supply of air to the rooms retained in way of the engine casing and this ventilating system will be thoroughly overhauled and placed in good operating condition. It is believed that with adequate insulation and ventilation these quarters will be thoroughly comfortable.

This change should eliminate entirely any discomfort from the use of the machine shop during the day as well as at night. The stock which is now stored on racks in the alleyway in way of the engine casing will be removed to a location in way of the boiler casing. It is not believed that the hot air and noise alleged to result every time the door to the engine room is opened will cause any great discomfort. Adequate heating facilities are to be installed in any quarters which do not now have such facilities.

This ship has been in operation now about nineteen or twenty years (Author's note -*WRONG!!!* and the Director's next statement is also incorrect—when new all of the "502"s and "535"s were criticized by shipyard officials, Shipping Board personnel, officers and crews alike) and it is rather remarkable that these quarters have suddenly become so unbearable. This idea appears to have originated, to a large extent at least, on the trip in question due to the fact that on a particular trip a vessel is carrying far less than her normal passenger list for which accommodations are provided does not justify moving the crew into passenger accommodations.

We cannot state definitely just when the rearrangement of quarters will be made on the S.S. PRESIDENT HARRISON as these arrangements must be made by the owners in order to suit sailing schedules, but in all cases the owners have been instructed to make such changes as soon as practicable.[11]

With the substantial investments in further capital improvements to the "502"s now necessary in order to prevent the loss of the ships' passenger certificates and maybe even their more important certificates of seaworthi-

---

[11]Copy of the original in the ship's 901 file in RG 178 at Maritime Administration.

ness, the time to work on them was now. Strapped for cash, the Dollar Line concentrated their energies and money on the four improved "502"s, promising to bring the other three up to code in the nearest future. Improvement to crew quarters was the biggest ticket item in the needed renovations. Bids from interested repair yards were invited.

The ship's January 11, 1938 arrival at New York signalled a temporary withdrawal from service. Bids to refit the ship's crew quarters came in from five yards. From the Maryland Drydock Company came the highest bid of $74,475.00, a price the Dollars quickly rejected. Bethlehem Shipbuilding bid a price of $52,950.00 and Atlantic Basin Iron Works wanted $50,490.00. Robins Dry Dock came in with a $44,823.00 offer but the winner was the newly formed United Dry Dock & Repair Company which came in with a bid of $35,839.00. That winter the PRESIDENT HARRISON went into United's Morse Drydock Company yards at Brooklyn where she was given an extensive overhaul. She would be the second of the improved "502"s to have her crew spaces substantially bettered. While at Morse, the Troy Marine Company effected $9,500.00 of voyage repairs. Two items related directly to retention of her passenger certificate and they were not cheap. Installation of a fire alarm system at a cost of $7,050.00 and of a public address system that cost $7,000.00 allowed her to keep on carrying large numbers of paying guests. For the crew "Item Number One" was a $36,829.00 rebuilding of their quarters. Plans used in the reconfiguration of crew spaces in the PRESIDENT ADAMS were to be used in renovations on this ship, but complaints by the crew of that ship, corroborated by Maritime Commission investigators, led to some changes approved by no less a personage than the Chairman of the Maritime Commission. Most of the desired alterations concerned cabin size and by moving a few bulkheads more space was given to occupants of the cabins concerned.

Maritime Commission Chairman Admiral Emory Land addressed North Atlantic District Representative Captain Granville Conway on February 24th. Here's what he had to say on the subject of the refit of the PRESIDENT HARRISON's crew quarters:

The receipt is acknowledged of your letter of February 18th, attaching blue print and specifications showing the proposed rearrangement of crew quarters on the S.S. PRESIDENT HARRISON.

It is noted here that there has been some complaint from the seamen that the rearrangement of their quarters as provided on the S.S. PRESIDENT ADAMS is not satisfactory and that Captain Holt and yourself, after inspection of the rearrangement now under way on this vessel, are of the same opinion. Confirming telephone conversation between Mr. Sanford and yourself on February 21st, you are advised that the suggestion made to the owners' representative that four seamen could be reallocated to the space now used as a hospital in the poop deckhouse and the space amidships adjacent to the room that will be occupied by the plumber, deck engineer and electrician used as a hospital it is satisfactory to the Commission. It is also noted that this rearrangement could be effected on the S.S. PRESIDENT ADAMS by the ship's personnel at no additional cost.

It, therefore, appears desirable that the same changes be made on the PRESIDENT HARRISON and that the plan submitted be modified accordingly. In this connection, it would be desirable, and no extra cost would be involved, if the quarters provided on A Deck under the poop were made symmetrical on both sides by making the following alteration on the plan:

Move the fore and aft bulkhead of the forward room designated for three oilers inboard to the door opening through the bulkhead onto the deck as shown on the port side for the room designated for four A.B.s.

Move the fore and aft bulkhead of the room designated three oilers, just aft of the room previously referred to, inboard approximately two feet forward thus providing additional space in this room.

Move the fore and aft bulkhead of the corresponding room on the port side outboard so as to make this room the same size and symmetrical with the three oilers' on the starboard side.

By moving four of the deck crew into the poop deckhouse, three men each may be allocated to the four rooms on the port side under the poop.

The suggestion that the deck engineer, plumber and electrician be assigned the same space on the PRESIDENT HARRISON as was allocated to these ratings on the PRESIDENT ADAMS is approved, and it is noted that this will necessitate moving the doctor to a room on the starboard side the same as was done on the PRESIDENT ADAMS in order to vacate the necessary space for these men and also for the hospital, which it is assumed will be moved from the poop deckhouse to the midship house as suggested for the PRESIDENT ADAMS.

It is noted that the present messrooms for the unlicensed personnel do not have sufficient space to seat the entire personnel at one seating. This, of course, is not a desirable arrangement and, if practicable, additional space should be provided, possibly by reducing the size of the petty officers' mess or by eliminating part of the steam table equipment, or both.

The plans and specifications as submitted are approved, subject to the modifications above referred to, and it is requested that, when these modifications have been made, revised plans showing the final arrangement be submitted for our records. We are returning herewith one approved print modified in red as indicated above. There is no objection on the part of the Commission to deferring the suggested changes enumerated above until the vessel reaches San Francisco.

It will now be in order for you to advise the Dollar Steamship Lines, Inc., to proceed with the rearrangement of crew's quarters on this vessel, the cost of which to be chargeable to maintenance or repair expenditure.[12]

Because money was so tight, the Technical Division of the Maritime

---

[12]Copy of the letter from Admiral Land in the ship's 901 file in RG178 at Maritime Administration.

Commission considered deferring any underwater work until her next dry-dock period, but that idea occurred too late. Since all underwater work relating to permitting the ship to retain her certificate of seaworthiness was already in hand when it was suggested, such work was performed. At a cost of $49,056.00, it proved to be the most expensive item on the yard's bill, for items like cleaning the boilers cost only $300.00, electrical repairs came to $980.00., gyro repairs $210.00 and bottom paint $1,600.00. With $6,580.00 repairs to the vessel's muff couplings connecting the tail shafts and replacing older condemned ones, refitting the PRESIDENT HARRISON cost $120,096.00, money Dollar Line really did not have. Worse, expenses involved with refits and repairs soon totalled $125,013.66. Lawsuits and threatened libels became reality, prompting the Maritime Commission to step in. Troy Marine, for one, was so incensed at Dollar Line's inability to pay their bill that they libelled the ship and only direct Maritime Commission action allowed the ship to return to service after all scheduled work was finished on Saturday, March 19th. The ship sailed up to Boston and back to New York in order to sail on March 24th for her usual ports. With 3,388 tons of cargo in her holds, the ship made her Panama Canal passage on April 1st. On April 10th the ship tied up at San Pedro on her way to San Francisco.

Additional work on their quarters was done between April 12th and her departure on the 15th while the ship lay at her San Francisco pier. At a cost of $210.00, two 7 feet long oak tables and four oak benches were made and installed in the crew's lobby under the poop. Four more oak benches, costing a total of $124.00, were fitted in the Steward's quarters in the forward section of B Deck. Two such benches were placed in each ten man cabin. Blanking off two air ducts in the after Steward's quarters on B Deck cost all of $8.00 dollars. For $7.00 a new section of aid duct connecting to the main header in the after Steward's quarters on B Deck was installed. Fitting two lockers and two hardwood hinged tables and one bench in the four berth room at the extreme after end of the poop deck house cost $68.00. From the Bos'n's room an old steel locker was removed and a new wooden one fitted in the corner, as was a new hinged wooden table and a 30 inch long wooden settee at a cost of $116.00. In the Bos'n's Mates' room, a locker and shelf plus cutting a drawer under the bunk to clear the drain pipe from the wash basin cost $55.00. Adding two drinking fountains in the after crew's quarters cost $110.00. Pricier was the $300.00 installation of foot and head boards on 54 new berths in the after crew section. Though the original order called for 82 berths to be so fitted, time allowed only 54 to be done before the ship sailed, and upon her return the job would be completed. At a total cost of $40.00, one berth was added in four crew cabins. A 5 foot long oak table and two oak benches were installed in rooms 3 and 4, the first two rooms aft of bulkhead door #14. That cost $334.00. Relocated in the quartermaster's room was one steel locker. Two such lockers were removed, as was one standee berth and a built in wooden berth complete with drawers below fitted instead, at a cost of $318.00. Installing forty gratings in the Steward's quarters aft on B Deck cost $280.00 and cleaning all steel decks and placing a composition floor over them in all rooms in the poop deck house cost $311.00. These extras added a total of $2,275.00 to the cost of improving the ship's crew quarters.

The remainder of the voyage yielded no more unusual paperwork and on June 22, 1938 the PRESIDENT HARRISON sailed from Marseilles for New York where she arrived on July 5th. That was her last arrival from Europe as a Dollar Liner. The company was moribund and in death throes. The ship's July 14, 1938 sailing from New York was cancelled and the ship laid up there. Dollar Lines went out of business on October 31, 1938 to be succeeded the following day by American President Lines. The PRESIDENT HARRISON joined that company while still laid up at New York. On November 3, 1938 her net tonnage was reduced from 6,185 to 5,952 net tons but her gross tonnage was slightly increased, boosted from 10,504.22 to 10,509.535. Similar minor tonnage adjustments were made to the other three improved "502"s on the same date. After her months of idleness, the ship sailed on November 27th from New York for Boston. Further paperwork about the PRESIDENT HARRISON in November had been prepared in relation to her change of owners. The last time Dollar Steamship Lines appeared as owners of this ship was on a Certificate of Ownership issued at San Francisco on November 22nd. It was surrendered the same day and a new one issued in the name of American President Lines. Dated November 25th, Order # C-483 called for the surrender of her marine document.

Her next sailing was Voyage 46 and it was the second round the world sailing of the Maritime Commission's new American President Lines. At 5:00PM on Friday, December 2, 1938, the PRESIDENT HARRISON cast off from Pier 9 in Jersey City and sailed out of New York harbor. The black of her funnel was now a dark blue and gone was the big white dollar sign. Now the red band of her tall funnel sported a white eagle surrounded by four white stars. Sentimental favorite of the old Dollar Line, the PRESIDENT HARRISON steamed into San Francisco for the first time with her new funnel markings at 7:00PM on December 21st and took her first APL sailing from there with her Christmas Eve departure at noon. Before she returned to New York on March 19, 1939, she made her usual calls at Havana, Panama, Los Angeles, San Francisco, Honolulu, Yokohama, Kobe, Hong Kong, Manila, Singapore, Penang, Colombo, Bombay, Suez, Port Said, Alexandria, Naples, Genoa and Marseilles.

Dropping off cargo at Boston and loading more for ports around the world, the PRESIDENT HARRISON sailed from New England's chief port on March 21st for New York. Outbound for her world journey Voyage 47, this "502" sailed on March 24, 1939. Some of the 3,857 tons of general cargo in her holds destined for Colombo when the ship made her Panama Canal transit on April 1st, the ship sailed from San Francisco on April 15th. The ship missed Cherry Blossom time in Japan that year, for she was not outbound from Yokohama until May 5th and from Kobe on May 7th. Shanghai was still "off limits" so the ship made for Hong Kong from whence she sailed on May 12th. Consider her June 3rd sailing from Bombay a sufficient marker to follow the liner's movements at that volatile time.

Tensions were rising in Europe and elsewhere when the PRESIDENT HARRISON sailed from Boston on July 11th and from New York on July 14, 1939. In her holds when she transited the Panama Canal on July 22nd were 3,183 tons of general cargo, some of it for India. Steaming for California the liner arrived at Los Angeles on July 31st and at San Francisco on August 2nd. She sailed three days later on August 5th. Her screws beating their path around the world, the PRESIDENT HARRISON called at both Yokohama and Kobe but omitted Shanghai on her way to Hong Kong. Sailing from the Crown Colony on August 31st, she arrived at Manila on September 1, 1939. Not sailing until the 3rd, her stay there coincided with the date German troops invaded Poland and the day the British and French declared war on Germany. For the time being, that European war would not have much effect on this neutral American steamer.

On her next voyage the PRESIDENT HARRISON was back in the Mediterranean about a month after the Allies declared war on Nazi Germany. Sailing from Port Said for Naples and Genoa, United States diplomatic officials in Italy had already prepared emergency certificates allowing the ship to carry as many passengers as she could reasonably accommodate, a number dependent upon the space in life saving gear. Hordes of Americans were rushing to European port cities hoping for a ride home. Before the ship sailed from Marseilles on October 11th, American President Lines bought insurance for the crew in the amount of $1,344,000.00. That first trip through a wartime North Atlantic saw her enter New York on October 31, 1939. A spot check inventory was undertaken on the following day.

While at her Jersey City pier on November 4, 1939 the ship was inventoried. On the list of items belonging to the Deck Department were 7 pistols stored in the Captain's safe. Far more prosaic were 9 used bathing suits kept by the Steward's Department for the use of passengers who had neglected to pack any. Maybe some of them were used in the Caribbean or during the ship's November 11th canal transit.

The PRESIDENT HARRISON was the first of the improved "502"s to sail from New York in 1940, taking her scheduled February 23rd departure. Captain H. J. Ehman was again her Master. By the winter of 1940 American President Lines expected trouble in the Mediterranean, suspecting Italian involvement in the European war. Under American neutrality laws, that would close off the Mediterranean to U.S. flag shipping. Before they lost their ability to carry goods and people in and out of the Mediterranean, the Line cabled their Genoa office to refuse any currency but American dollars for passage or shipment. Someone at the State Department must have suspected an imminent act of war by Italy, for Secretary of State Cordell Hull cabled American President Lines for information about the ship's current capacity. Chairman of the Board of American President Lines William Mc-

Adoo[13] cabled the Secretary of State on May 22nd: "HARRISON en route from Orient to New York via Mediterranean—inspection certificate allows 325 people—170 crew 155 passengers. Present complement 167 crew 158 passengers. Life boat capacity 347 + buoyant craft 120 325 adult lifebelts 53 child lifebelts."[14] Considering the ship easily capable of carrying additional passengers, the State Department cabled the U.S. Consulate General in Genoa to prepare a certificate permitting the PRESIDENT HARRISON to carry more than her usual number of passengers. This time all paperwork was in order before the ship even arrived. There were plenty of applicants for passage out of Italy that time. Maybe the most grateful of the 187 passengers who embarked the ship at Genoa for a ride home to the United States was a group of 31 American priests and students who had been studying in Italy. Imagine the tension among her newly embarked passengers at the moment the ship began to ease away from her berth at the Maritime Station at Genoa on June 4, 1940. Minutes later the PRESIDENT HARRISON steamed past Genoa's landmark Lanterna at the exit of the port on her way to sea. She was the last American passenger ship to sail from an Italian port before Italy entered World War II six days later. The Kingdom of Italy declared war against France on June 10, 1940, prompting Winston Churchill to go on the radio to publicly denounce Italy for her decision to attack France.[15]

Under the protection of her neutrality markings the American passenger liner crossed the Atlantic with 187 passengers and one stowaway, a Hungarian named Zsoltan Czakö, fleeing the Nazis. He had done a fairly good job of secreting himself aboard the ship. Officers and crew hadn't found him, rather, three days out of Genoa he gave himself up in a plea for food and asylum. He was put to work performing menial tasks until the arrival at New York on June 18th. There most of her passengers disembarked but the ship was busier than ever.

On her next voyage Captain Ehman had a crew of 165 officers and men. On July 17, 1940 they were 4 Deck Officers and 1 Deck Cadet, 8 Engineer Officers and 2 Cadets, 3 Radio Officers, 6 Pursers, a deck crew of 25, an engine crew of 31 and a Steward's department of 87 men.

The ship was again in the news when she began her next trip. Sailing from New York at 6:00 PM on October 23, 1940, she struck a mud bank a mere 20 feet from the pier. Quickly refloated, she was undamaged and continued on her way.

Sentimental favorite of the "502" class because she was the first of the seven ships to go out on the round the world line, the PRESIDENT HAR-

---

[13]The Social Historian will remember that a former U.S. Senator from California, Mr. McAdoo was also son-in-law to Woodrow Wilson.
[14]Copy in the ship's 901 file in RG178 at Maritime Administration.
[15]He is known to have remarked privately: "It's only fair that Germany has her as an ally this time. We had her last time." Twenty-five years earlier he had remained silent when Italy betrayed her own treaty commitments and attacked Austria, but that time Italy became an ally of the U.K.

RISON was the only one of the "502" class not renamed by American President Lines. Taking her first sailing from New York in the fateful year of 1941 the ship sailed from Pier 9 in Jersey City on February 28th and headed south towards the Caribbean. That year saw the ship's net tonnage figure reduced to 5,052 net tons. On her first Panama transit that year the liner steamed into Cristobal with 5,883 tons of cargo from New York on March 6th. She went through the Canal on the 7th. Within weeks of her March 21st sailing from San Francisco, a new schedule of passenger fares was published by American President Lines. Effective on April 15th, the day the ship arrived at Manila, the pamphlet included intercoastal fares charged for the PRESIDENT HARRISON and three sisters. The minimum rate of $185.00 per person between New York to California was charged for each of two in cabins #200, 201, 214, 216, 217, 218 and 219. A traveler going one-way to Havana could get there in one of the "502"s for just $70.00 but if he wanted a comfortable suite, and it was not taken by anyone booked for a longer journey, the traveler would pay $150.00 for the four night trip. Going in such style all the way to the Coast cost just $325.00 per person.

From Manila the PRESIDENT HARRISON continued her way westwards around the world, making a long call at Singapore between April 16th and 23rd, a regular Penang call between April 24th and 26th and a Colombo arrival on April 30th. When she sailed from there on May 2nd, Bombay was next and after three days there between May 5th and 8th, from that exotic city the PRESIDENT HARRISON sailed for Cape Town and a May 23rd call. After one night in port the liner sailed north for a June 10th call at Trinidad where she took in water before arriving at New York on June 16th. There the ship worked cargo and was repaired from earlier heavy weather during her February, March and May travels before departing on June 23rd for her side trip to Boston. There was actually a fair amount of work to do to clean her up. Eight plates were renewed, 3,000 scattered shell internal rivets were also renewed and 6,500 more rivets welded. Plate seams and tank tops as well as bilges were steam cleaned and sundry damages attended. The need for repairs delayed the ship by a few days and the ship did not meet her announced schedule for voyage #54–10, for which sailings were listed from Boston on June 16th; New York June 20th; Los Angeles July 8th, and San Francisco July 12, 1941 in the New York to Penang/Straits Settlements service.

In anticipation of an "off-subsidy" voyage to Singapore and Penang authorized that previous February 13th, the ship was inventoried at New York on June 17, 1941. This time she was at a strange pier, Pier 10, foot of 6th Street, Hoboken. She sailed from Boston on June 25th and again departed New York on June 29th. While on her way to California the Director of Operations and Traffic of the Maritime Commission recommended that effective July 1, 1941, sailings from California of the PRESIDENT HARRISON and a few other vessels on voyages approved by the Maritime Commission be subsidized no matter which of the two lines (transPacific Line A or round the world Line B) they then served. It took the busy Commission some time to approve, but with the ship's July 23rd departure from San Francisco, she was returned to subsidy participation. Similarly, Singapore was added to the itinerary of vessels running on American President Lines' transPacific run.

Prior to sailing from San Francisco on July 23, the ssPRESIDENT HARRISON was placed in Line "A" and pursuant to the Commission's action of July 29, "the current voyage will extend to Singapore."

Inasmuch as the vessel sailed from New York on June 29, 1941, on voyage to Penang and Straits Settlements, under the Commission's authorization of February 13, 1941, but was transferred to Line "A" (TransPacific) service prior to final sailing from San Francisco, the Commission's action on February 13, 1941 should be modified to the extent necessary so far as it affects this particular vessel."[16]

In command of the ship was Captain Orel A. Pierson. Veteran of several "502"s, he had had no intention of taking her out at all. In line for a job as San Francisco pilot he had a brand new command. American President Lines had appointed him Master of the new PRESIDENT POLK, last of the seven new C3 P type combiships, then still building at Newport News, Virginia. But when the PRESIDENT HARRISON arrived at San Francisco on this trip out from New York, her Master, Captain Duncan Ward, quit to take a job with Cramp's Shipyard at Philadelphia. On hand in San Francisco, Captain Pierson accepted what he expected to be an interim command. He also expected to enjoy some aspects of the trip. There were plenty of passengers aboard that time, mostly Army officers and Catholic priests heading to Manila. Out east at Penang, Singapore and Manila the ship loaded 8,000 tons of rubber and brought them to San Francisco. There the company's Marine Superintendent of the line convinced him to make one more trip in the PRESIDENT HARRISON. That was the ship's Voyage 55. It would be her last under the United States flag.

Tensions between the United States and Japan were rising daily and American shipping came more and more under military control. With increasing Japanese threats in response to a number of stimuli, with an American embargo of sales of oil to the Japanese most nettlesome of all, the United States decided the time had come to evacuate American military personnel from China and needed ships to do that. Two ships then in the area suited the Navy's requirements. Both were "502"s—the PRESIDENT MADISON and PRESIDENT HARRISON. By late autumn of 1941 these two liners came under military control on a day to day charter to the U.S. Navy, though both ships remained manned by their own civilian crews.

Sailing from San Francisco on October 17, 1941, the PRESIDENT HARRISON made her usual way west. This time, after departing Honolulu she

---

[16]From some of the pile of paperwork on that voyage in the ship's 901 file in RG178 at Maritime Administration.

diverted from her customary course and turned south for Suva and the Torres Straits before heading to Manila. Upon arrival there the Navy ordered her not to discharge any cargo but to steam immediately for Hong Kong where the ship would be fitted to carry troops. Besides berthing equipment the ship was given life saving gear for an extra 800 passengers. Payment for their passage from China to the Philippines was pegged at $95.00 per man for First Class passage and $26.40 per man in Third Class. In more obvious terms, the Navy would pay APL First Class rates for military officers and the Third Class rate for enlisted men. Also assigned to run to evacuate Marines from Shanghai was the identical PRESIDENT MADISON, which was about a day ahead of the PRESIDENT HARRISON. On her first trip to bring out the Marines from China, the PRESIDENT HARRISON embarked a contingent of some 375 Marines at Shanghai and sailed from there on November 28, 1941. Following Navy orders, the "502" set a course for the Philippines to land her Marines at Olongapoo and bring their equipment to Manila. Off Taiwan as December dawned, the PRESIDENT HARRISON picked up an escort of four American submarines. All the way south from Shanghai the crew of the PRESIDENT HARRISON noted extensive Japanese naval activity. Great numbers of transports and warships flying the "rising sun" were steaming south.

While at Manila to discharge the equipment of the Marines into a Navy barge, Captain Pierson received Captain Valdemar Nielsen of the PRESIDENT MADISON and Captain (later Admiral) Dale Collins of the American President Lines' freighter DAYSTAR. They were sitting in Pierson's cabin discussing the future when O.G. Steen, the Company's chief representative in the Far East came by with orders for all three. It was good timing for all three Captains knew that things looked bad and "all hell might break out at any time".[17] In the DAYSTAR, Captain Collins was ordered to Rangoon to deliver his cargo. For bunkering, Captain Nielsen was ordered to take the PRESIDENT MADISON to Balikpapan. They got away days before the Japanese attacked. American merchant ships with cargo for China were not going to be able to deliver their consignments. Authorities halted them at Manila. Britons, too, knew war was imminent. As of December 2nd, all British ships in North China waters were ordered to make immediately for Singapore.

With his ship on a day to day charter to the U.S. Navy commencing on December 4, 1941, Captain Pierson was ordered to run back up to Tsingdao in northern China where the Beijing and Tientsin Legation guards and 1,400 tons of their equipment awaited evacuation. Under the direct orders of Admiral Hart and in constant contact with the Naval Base at Cavite, there would not be much communication between Navy and merchant ships. The only actual order ever issued to the ship's Master, Captain Orel A. Pierson, was

---

[17]Written reminiscences of Captain Orel A. Pierson. Courtesy of Captain Warren Leback.

simple: "proceed to Tsingwangdao and bring out the Marines."[18] Unescorted and unarmed, the PRESIDENT HARRISON steamed out of Manila harbor in ballast and into history at one minute after midnight on December 4, 1941. The PRESIDENT HARRISON would be quite a lone sheep.

Besides her 154 man crew was a single passenger. He was E.S. Wise, American President Lines' Passenger Agent, aboard in connection to the evacuation of the North China Marines.

The chance of war was never far from the minds of those aboard ship. As Captain Pierson tells it: "Consider now the situation in the Far East. Tension was mounting, war or the possibility of it was on every man's tongue, the destination of the PRESIDENT HARRISON (though it was supposed to be a deep dark secret) was the talk of every hotel and bar room in Manila. The Japanese most certainly knew where we were going and for what reason or else I have formed a great misconception of their intelligence during the years I have been in contact with them. In fact, I was later informed by the Captain of a Jap destroyer that 'they knew all about our movements.' "[19]

From his bridge Captain Pierson noted more heavy Japanese shipping heading south. "On the night of the 6th just after dark we were approached by some sort of craft which flashed "stop". We stopped but as this craft did not come alongside and we were an American ship proceeding upon a peaceful mission I decided to ignore him entirely and proceed upon our way. As we were faster than this craft we soon outdistanced him."[20]

Captain Pierson knew he had only two options in the event of war between the United States and Japan. He could either try to make for Australia or attempt to break past Japan and, by the northerly route, head for home. How far he could get was moot. American President Lines had not been overly generous with a fuel delivery for the PRESIDENT HARRISON. The "502" was hardly overburdened with freight when she left Manila but she did not have full bunkers either. She left on her dangerous mission with only enough fuel for the round trip to Tsingwandao plus ten percent. A choice between destruction or interception, neither option was truly viable. The PRESIDENT HARRISON was off the Chinese coast, near the mouth of the Yang Tze when Captain Pierson heard a radio report of the attack on Pearl Harbor. Even before the order came through for him to try to run for Vladivostok Captain Pierson understood the magnitude of his ship's peril and the danger to his men. As he later told it: "The vessel was in ballast without a pound of cargo in her. We were in hostile waters surrounded on all sides by Japanese held territory or Japan proper. The vessel was completely outfitted for the carriage of troops and if she fell into Japanese hands she could

---

[18]Quoted by Captain Pierson in a postwar inter-office memorandum to the Operating Manager of American President Lines. Courtesy of Captain Warren Leback.

[19]ibid.

[20]ibid.

have been loaded and used for that purpose within a matter of hours against our forces in the Far East. I was bound and determined to use every means in my power to prevent this."[21] He gathered his officers and crew to tell them the news of the attack on Pearl Harbor. Then a few men got to work to paint out American President Lines' colors on the ship's tall funnel.

At dawn a Japanese plane, her bomb racks full, flew low overhead, ordering the American ship to stop and the Japanese flag NAGASAKI MARU, a fast mail and passenger boat on the Japan-China run, to intercept her. Then the plane opened fire sending rounds of shells into the liner's bridge. Ignoring the order, Captain Pierson maintained the ship on her course but when the NAGASAKI MARU loomed ahead and ordered the PRESIDENT HARRISON to stop, Captain Pierson hove-to. Pierson was well acquainted with the Japanese liner and knew he could not outrun his 22 knot watchdog. Whatever course he steered, the NAGASAKI MARU followed at a distance just far enough to make sure that the PRESIDENT HARRISON could not get close enough to ram her. Then the plane returned and lobbed further fire into the wheelhouse. When the plane finally disappeared from sight the Captain had to take his only chance. Aware that no escape was possible he decided to sacrifice the PRESIDENT HARRISON. Here Captain Pierson continues:

> Now the problem arose what to do next. I called all my officers together and explained the situation. I pointed out that as I thought then and still think with the vessel in a ballast condition and the system of bilge lines and drains we would never get enough water into the ship to scuttle her in the limited time we would have available. Most of the tanks we could not flood thru out the ship would give her enough buoyancy to keep her afloat and it would be a simple matter to tow her into port and pump her out. I then pointed to the chart of the China Coast and showed them the many wrecks strewn up and down it in this vicinity and pointed out that few of them when once high and dry in these waters were ever floated. My plan, to which they all agreed, was to run for the beach and send the ship up as high as possible at full speed hoping to accomplish this before any further ships made their appearance. We had nothing to worry about as far as the Nagasaki Maru was concerned (other than her following us) as she was unarmed. We started in the direction of Shaweishan as this was the nearest land and as we approached it I conceived the idea of sending the ship over the edge of it and ripping her bottom out completely. If we could achieve this the vessel would go down completely and must surely be a total loss. We had provisioned all the life boats and had them swung out and the crew standing by for any emergency that might arise.[22]

Suspecting insufficient armed force remained to prevent his plan, Captain Pierson telegraphed the engine room to give him full speed ahead. Hop-

---

[21] ibid.
[22] ibid.

ing to smash the ship onto the rocks and render her unusable to the Japanese, he ordered the helmsman to turn the ship towards the shore. As the PRESIDENT HARRISON approached the island they sighted a Japanese destroyer heading for them. Then the plane again returned over head. This time he didn't open fire or drop any bombs. Captain Pierson later learned that the Japanese wanted the ship intact. Nor did Captain Pierson yet know that the Captain of the destroyer was under orders to open fire and sink the PRESIDENT HARRISON if she did not surrender. "The loss of the Harrison was inevitable and at best all we could hope to do was to create as much damage as possible" said Pierson.[23]

Some crew were probably still daubing grey paint on exposed exterior surfaces when Captain Pierson ordered the boats swung out. The Captain continued: "It became a race as to whether we could make the island before the destroyer could intercept us. The NAGASAKI MARU had by now turned off as we were getting into shoalwater and the destroyer was approaching. Five minutes before we struck we ordered the engineers out of the engine room leaving the plant wide open. They had agreed to stay on the job until the very last minute if I would give them only time enough to get out before we crashed. The co-operation of Mr. J.C. Smith, Chief Engineer, and his engineers and men made this possible."[24]

Their efforts were good. Totally familiar with the "502" type and its construction, sturdiness and capabilities, he knew better than hitting the island head on. The "502"s had had several head-on incidents and Captain Pierson knew the ship would only bang her bow and back off. He had only to recall his own experience aboard in the ship's 1926 grounding on Bonham Island. Steaming at almost sixteen knots shortly after 1:00 PM the PRESIDENT HARRISON slammed ashore on Shewishan Island. Hitting land near Ho. 1 hatch portside, the hull was very badly damaged, but hardly destroyed. The ship was not going to co-operate in her willful destruction. With a 90 foot gash in her hull, the liner continued moving, riding along the shore of the island for a bit, then heeling over to starboard and rolled off. Unfortunately, the gash stopped far short of her engine room.

Once the ship hit the rocks, Captain Pierson gave the order to abandon ship because no one knew for sure how much damage had been wrought nor if any of the boilers would explode. He thought it wise to get everyone off the ship and make for the nearby island. All boats but his own were sent away with orders to meet up later with his on Sha Wei Shan island. As the ship hit, the radio operator transmitted Captain Pierson's message to inform American authorities of what was underfoot. As Pierson later told it, he understood his message had been received as far away as San Francisco. Once the ship began using her wireless, the plane started firing again, probably to try to silence the lone voice of the PRESIDENT HARRISON. When

---

[23]ibid.
[24]ibid.

power finally died, Captain Pierson joined his men in the last boat and made for Sha Wei Shan. As his boat pulled away, the tide was running strong ebb, the ship filling fast with water forward and listing to starboard. While the plane made no effort to fire at the boats, one boat either capsized or dropped into the water, drowning three men. Badly injured by one of the ship's propellors was Chief Steward McKay.

The rest of the crew of the American steamer reached the island as proposed by Captain Pierson. Almost in shock from an unplanned swim in the icy water and ingestion of a dose of fuel oil was the Chief Engineer. Huddled together the survivors made for the top of the island to the lighthouse. In a building turned over to them by the Chinese attendants, they planned to spend the night. At nightfall a heavily armed patrol of the Japanese Naval Landing Unit from the destroyer made its way to the lighthouse looking for the Americans. There was nothing for the men of the PRESIDENT HARRISON to do but ditch their few revolvers (into the bushes) and surrender. The Japanese were in a bad mood and wanted revenge of sorts so they smashed up the lighthouse radio station. Next they ordered the Americans to line up and then searched them for weapons. Any papers or money was taken from them and thrown onto the ground. Kept on the island under guard was all the crew but Captain Pierson, who was taken to the destroyer. A scene of jubilation greeted the American President Lines' veteran for the officers on the destroyer were in a good humor, listening to the radio in the ward room, learning of Japanese successes like the sinking of PRINCE of WALES, and the destruction at Pearl Harbor. English speaking officers happily translated

Meant to chill the American public, this photo of a scared-looking young Japanese soldier on guard aboard the captured PRESIDENT HARRISON on December 9, 1941 was widely reproduced. Frank O. Braynard collection.

for Captain Pierson whose command of Japanese was not what it would be. Joining the jubilation was the destroyer's Captain who assured Captain Pierson that Japan would soon win the war and rule the world. To share his joy, the Japanese Captain broke out a new bottle of Johnnie Walker Black Label Scotch whisky and treated all present in the ward room to a round of drinks. Captain Pierson was soon offered coffee and rice cakes before a bed was made up for him and ratings ordered to make him as comfortable as possible. The next morning brought him a typical Japanese breakfast, though for this western guest the crew somehow managed to scare up a knife and fork. At 7:00 AM Captain Pierson was ushered to the deck and told he was to be returned to the island. The boat taking him back was half way there when signalled to return to the destroyer. The boat returned to the ship and its officer went aboard. He returned soon but with a harsh, new attitude. For the next ten days Captain Pierson was held under armed guard, never to know the reason for the abrupt change in his captors' attitude. No doubt, he thought, the condition of the PRESIDENT HARRISON had a lot to do with the new Japanese mood. She was "solidly aground forward but afloat aft."[25] Once back at the island, the officer in charge ordered the Americans back to their ship. A hard row brought them to the damaged liner where No. 1 hold was partly flooded, Nos. 2, 3 and 4 flooded into the upper tween deck, No. 5 partly flooded and there were 12 feet of water in the engine room. Dry were the after holds.

Now began the work of undoing what had been wrought. To relight the fires and get steam up was their first priority. Two volunteers dove into the icy muck to get necessary valves open and closed in order to pump out the engine room. Trying to work the engines to get the ship off did not work, nor did the destroyer manage to pull the stranded liner free. To lighten the ship, the Japanese agreed to an American suggestion to strip the ship and dump it overboard. With the whispered order to sabotage everything possible, the crew of the PRESIDENT HARRISON threw at least one hundred thousand dollars worth of equipment over the side. Into the water went the ship's cinema equipment, pianos, furniture, stores, tarpaulins, furniture, hatch covers, even the stronghooks. "When we suggested unshipping the booms and putting them over they apparently decided it had gone far enough and put a stop to it."[26]

Clandestine word of the apparent destruction of the vessel and the capture of her American crew reached W. G. MacDonald, head of American President Lines' operations in Shanghai when someone slipped him a small note written by Captain Pierson. On that piece of paper were just the facts . . . the date . . . what happened and that three men had drowned.

Japanese authorities realized the job was beyond present capabilities and ordered a salvage crew to board the ship to get her afloat. At one point twelve

---

[25]ibid.
[26]ibid.

divers were busy at work patching up the damaged hull of the 12,000 ton liner. From Japan came a salvage unit from the Nippon Salvage Company replete with a crew commanded by a Japanese born and bred in Portland, Oregon, and totally familiar with his job. It took the professional salvors 43 days to get Nos. 1 and 2 holds tight enough to keep the water down. Waiting til the high tide of the month they pumped water into dry after holds. That did the trick. The ship floated off and they succeeded in getting her up the Whangpo River to dock at the Jardine wharf at Hong Kew, where another few months got her patched up. Renaming their prize KAKKO MARU, the Japanese loaded scrap metal into her and the ship sailed for Japan for final repairs. She soon turned up as a Japanese troop transport.

Taking all aboard as prisoners, Japanese military authorities used the pretext of belligerency between the two nations as an excuse to bring the case of the PRESIDENT HARRISON into court. On December 17, 1942 the Sasebo Prize Court condemned the ship as a war prize. Murky indeed is the memory of her wartime employment as KAKKO MARU, and it IS possible that she once fell victim to American attack and either very seriously damaged if not sunk in shallow water and raised. Rumors flew at the time and from some of her interned crew perhaps, that possibility was embellished into fact, though the name given for the ship when she was supposedly hit was already KACHIDOKI MARU. One cryptic notation on one of the ship's several San Francisco Marine Exchange, a record of the movements in and out of San Francisco of all ships calling there, reads: " . . . sunk by the U.S. submarine STEELHEAD between Japan and the Philippines". Other sources support that claim, for in that area on July 10, 1943, that submarine fired a brace of torpedoes at Japanese shipping. Quite a few other American vessels claimed the kill of a vessel answering the description of the former "President", yet none could prove it until the "Peaceful Pamp," the U.S.S. PAM-PANITO, now preserved at San Francisco as a museum, dispatched the fourth of the "502s". Don't overlook the probability that all of these claims were for ships rather smaller than the former PRESIDENT HARRISON. Compilers do make errors and though VERY good, the San Francisco Marine Exchange cards are not flawless. As early as February 1942, the Chief of Naval Operations was able to inform the Maritime Commission "that the ship had been salvaged and was then 'docked in the Whangpoo River' ".[27] Relying on many of the same Maritime Commission and U.S. Government documents as does this series, Captain David Grover and his daughter Cmdr. Gretchen Grover, recount the final days of the former PRESIDENT HARRISON and the fate of her crew in their important book "CAPTIVES of SHANGHAI". Father and daughter remind us that the ship was reportedly sighted by American citizens during 1942. After that the trail of the ship grows cold until her end. In any event, the ship was used to transport per-

---

[27]ibid. Pages 124–128 includes details of the ship's last movements. Grover, Capt. David H. and Grover, Cmdr. Gretchen. *CAPTIVES OF SHANGHAI*, - Napa, CA Western Maritime Press 1989

sonnel and war prisoners and was so occupied, carrying hundreds of Allied prisoners of war, when the American submarine U.S.S. PAMPANITO caught the ship in her sights off the coast of Taiwan on September 12, 1944. A torpedo fired at the captured ship found its mark. Tragically, most of those hundreds killed when the ship sank were among her Allied prisoners of war. That, of course, is the simplified version. There really is much more to tell.

Working with information gleaned from intercepted and decoded information, a small wolfpack of three American submarines went prowling for Japanese tonnage in September 1944. They had little inkling of what the convoy was, or the nature of the ships, nor cargoes and passengers. Steaming on a northeastwards course from Singapore were ten Japanese vessels—four naval escorts, two tankers, two freighters and two transports—the KACHI-DOKI MARU and the RAKUYO MARU, a 9,400 ton former Japanese passenger liner that had spent most of her career as a migrant ship in the South American trade. Aboard the former American ship were 900 British prisoners of war, soldiers on their way to perform slave labor for their captors in Japan after some 30 months of toil under conditions of utmost brutality while forced to build the railway to Burma. Aboard the RAKUYO MARU were 1,318 prisoners of war including 716 Australians, 599 British and a single American, flyer Colonel Harry Melton, who had been shot down over Burma. Both passenger ships carried hundreds of wounded Japanese soldiers and medics to look after them. For some reason Japanese authorities had not requested safe conduct for these vessels as they had occasionally done for hospital ships or those carrying Red Cross cargo. Maybe because each ship had rubber stowed in her holds, the Japanese opted to try to sneak the ships through any American naval presence. No one aboard the trio of American submarines could have known who was aboard the enemy transports.

None of those aboard the KACHIDOKI MARU and RAKUYO MARU were paying passengers and neither ship offered much in the way of accommodations, food and service. Conditions must have been hellish for all but the ships' own officers. The Japanese did not disseminate much information and as the Grovers tell it: "On the KACHIDOKI MARU, during their hours topside in pursuit of fresh air, the prisoners had noticed the ship's bell with the name PRESIDENT HARRISON on it. They were naturally curious and there was speculation as to why that name should appear on a Japanese ship, but the prisoners knew no more about the ship's past than they did about their future."[28] Little food or water found its way to the Allied prisoners, nor did the wounded Japanese fare much better. Japan at war probably could not spare much food for men who might soon die. In the prevailing attitude of the day, Allied prisoners of war were hardly considered human by the Japanese who typically lost any regard and all respect for any soldiers who allowed himself to survive defeat. Thus were the men guarding

---

[28]ibid.

the Allied prisoners harsh, though survivors later reported feeling that the Japanese wanted to get as many of their captives to Japan as they could. Life for the Allied prisoners aboard the KACHIDOKI MARU was as harsh as it was aboard other ships so employed. Regulations for nighttime steaming called for prisoners to be locked into their quarters—the ships' original cargo holds and tweendeck compartments. But those aboard the RAKUYO MARU seem to have been better organized, going as far as to develop a plan to abandon ship in time of emergency.

For the first time since they boarded, anyone with a canteen was able to get his fill of fresh water from the rains that fell on the convoy on September 10th. In the South China Sea on the following day, beyond the range of land based air cover, the Japanese convoy grew larger when three additional naval escorts and three more freighters from Manila joined them. When they came into the sights of the periscopes of the three American subs, the Japanese ships were steaming at 11 knots in three columns. First of the American boats to take action was the U.S.S. GROWLER, which fired a torpedo at 1:30 AM on September 11th. That sank the largest of the naval escorts, a destroyer. Scrambling for cover from the attack, the merchant ships moved away. "The KACHIDOKI MARU and a tanker actually collided in a glancing bow-on encounter that produced dents and scratches but miraculously neither ship was seriously damaged," the Grovers tell us, adding that the escorting naval units drove off the American attackers and the Japanese convoy regrouped.[29] It was a temporary respite for advantage remained with the wolf pack submerged below. At around 4:30 in the morning the U.S.S. SEALION fired. Taking her shots at the enemy, she sank a freighter and a tanker. Catching fire and blazing brightly, these dying Japanese vessels lit up the night scene, helping the SEALION's skipper to better aim two more torpedoes. These, discharged at a range of but 1,100 yards, hit their marks on the RAKUYO MARU. Struck by one "tin fish" forward and another aft, the former Japanese passenger liner began her death dance, taking several hours to sink.

Yet to make a kill was the PAMPANITO. Second guessing, she headed east while the convoy went west. This boat had a reputation to uphold . . . she was the "Peaceful Pamp". Her time would come . . . Looking for the convoy her master Commander Paul E. Summers ordered a new course and this time headed west. His hunch seemed to pay off for around noon he saw a smudge of smoke on the horizon. Once darkness fell he lost the trail of the Japanese ships. That night was calm and there was no moon. The PAMPANITO was on the surface about 50 miles off Hainan when Cmdr. Summers picked up the convoy on his radar. All was ripe for an all out attack on the enemy ships. From a cautious distance of 4,000 yards he fired ten torpedoes. One tube jammed so only nine got away. Two torpedoes hit Japanese tonnage. One was a freighter, the other was the KACHIDOKI MARU. Quickly

---

[29]ibid.

apparent that his ship was doomed, the Captain of the KACHIDOKI MARU shot himself. The Grovers continue: "Other Japanese officers shot wounded Japanese soldiers in No. 3 hold."[30] On deck the Japanese crew lost its composure in a frenzy to save themselves. Few of the prisoners, even those topsides, knew the ship had been torpedoed and were slow to take action to save themselves and their fellows. Those that tried to do something had little immediate success. Five minutes went by with almost no Allied prisoners taking advantage of the ladders leading to escape above. There were only ten minutes left to the former "President" liner and when the weight of water in the stern pulled the bow out of the water everyone knew the ship was lost. "By then it was too late" the Grovers wrote, "possibly a third of the prisoners never got away. The rest abandoned ship, using life jackets which had been discovered earlier in one of the holds of the ship—perhaps the extra life jackets left over from the Marine evacuation of Shanghai. At 11 o'clock at night, the KACHIDOKI MARU, ex PRESIDENT HARRISON, slid stern first into the sea in 360 feet of water, just four days short of the anniversary of her launching."[31]

Commander Summers didn't know that he had sunk a captured American passenger and cargo liner, one carrying almost a thousand Allied prisoners of war. In fact, it took about a month before Naval Intelligence learned the nature of the transport dispatched in the PAMPANITO's attack. Wanting further kills that day, the Commander ordered his tubes reloaded, firing three more torpedoes, this time at escort ships. They all missed and Summers broke off further engagement with this convoy. Diving at dawn and spending daylight hours under water, the PAMPANITO passed the next two days off Hainan. Above the American submarine all manner of Japanese craft steamed back and forth searching for survivors of the KACHIDOKI MARU. With 520 surviving prisoners and many Japanese wounded, two Japanese frigates and a trawler made for Hainan.[32] Summers called off his hunt for survivors, too. Then, in the late afternoon of September 15th, he sighted floating debris and a couple of rafts. Nearing these with the greatest of caution, Commander Summers saw men on those floats. Let the Grovers continue:

> Because they were so dark and begrimed, he could not determine their ethnicity or nationality until he heard shouting in English. On a close pass he told his crew to pick up only one man for interrogation. Once aboard, that man, an Australian named Frank Farmer, explained that the sea around them was full of others. Whether he reported that there had been a second ship in the convoy with prisoners of war was not made clear in the PAMPANITO action report.
>
> Aware for the first time of what had happened, Summers radioed Com-

---

[30] ibid.
[31] ibid.
[32] ibid.

mander, Submarine Force, Pacific, in Hawaii the news that possibly a large number of men were in the water at the scene of the RAKUYO MARU sinking. The PAMPANITO was soon joined by the SEALION in a massive rescue effort which succeeded in pulling 127 survivors from the sea, 73 by the PAMPANITO and 54 by the SEALION. Exhausted, covered with oil, and wearing little clothing to protect them from the elements, these men were brought aboard assisted by swimmers in the water and eager hands on deck.[33]

Other submarines in the area joined the hunt for survivors. Rescuing 18 of them was the U.S.S. BARB while the U.S.S. QUEENFISH saved 14 more. For their action, the skippers of the submarines won the Navy Cross, and Commander Summer's success winning the PAMPANITO many friends.

Not aboard the former PRESIDENT HARRISON when she sank as the Japanese troopship KACHIDOKI MARU was the ship's original American crew. They had remained aboard the ship through the middle of March 1942. While their ship stuck on the rocks they were at least able to eat fairly well. After arriving at Shanghai the ship's food ran out and the Japanese took over catering and proved to be very stingy hosts. Then the crew was released at Shanghai but the officers were taken to a detention camp at Hong Kew Park. "None of the officers were ever released and 16 of the crew died in Shanghai before the final end came." reported Captain Pierson.[34]

Taken to Japan on April 1, 1942 to testify at a prize court, Captain Pierson was confined with a number of veteran China Coast men in the Sasieho Hall. Through mid August not a single Japanese asked him anything about the PRESIDENT HARRISON. Then, of a sudden, one man and a single interpreter appeared, asked some routine questions, and told him that "things would go very bad for me because of the damage we had caused."[35] Some days later, a blindfolded Captain Orel A. Pierson was taken under guard to Zentsuji War Prison Camp on Shikoko Island, no doubt because he held a commission in the United States Naval Reserve. There he remained captive through June 23, 1945, when the Japanese broke up the camp and transferred the inmates to Nokoroshi Camp in mountainous western Honshu. Saying no more than "I lost 85 pounds",[36] Captain Pierson finished his narrative aboard the C3 P type passenger liner PRESIDENT POLK, his first postwar command. Liberated by American forces on September 2, 1945, Captain Pierson was quickly repatriated.

Occasional stories of the internees came through. Cleared and issued

---

[33]ibid. I am truly grateful for the kind courtesy of Captain Grover who enthusiastically gave me permission to "use any of his book I want" to disseminate the story of the CAPTIVES of SHANGHAI and the PRESIDENT HARRISON. Anyone truly interested in the story of these ships MUST read the Grover work, as should any serious scholar of the war with Japan.

[34]ibid.

[35]ibid.

[36]ibid.

through the facilities of the Office of War Information for publication in Friday afternoon papers of February 11, 1944 was this one:

> The heroism of stewardess of an American Merchant Marine vessel which resulted in maintaining morale on a liner captured by the Japanese and the saving of at least one life, that of a wounded crew member, has just come to light, the War Shipping Administration disclosed today.
>
> The woman to whom belated recognition is given is Mrs. Clara Main, who now lives at 867 East 176th Street, the Bronx, New York, N.Y. After internment by the Japanese she was repatriated on the recent voyage of the SS GRIPSHOLM. At that time she told in an interview some of the incidents attending the capture of the ship, including efforts of the captain and crew to scuttle it, but made no mention of her own brave deeds. She was the only woman aboard the captured vessel.
>
> A few days before the Japs stabbed the United States into the war, the SS PRESIDENT HARRISON was sent by the Navy from Manila to China to transport a contingent of Marines to the Philippines. The vessel, operated by American President Lines, was captured off Sha Wei Shan, in the Yellow sea, when a Japanese dive bomber dropped notes demanding surrender. The master of the liner, Capt. Orel A. Pierson, of 311 California Street, San Francisco, Calif., ignored the demand and ordered full speed ahead in an effort to beach the ship. It struck the rocky shore with a screech and almost turned on its side. The liner righted itself, however, and was carried off the rocks by currents. It then came to rest on a mudbank and the crew was ordered to abandon ship.
>
> Japanese marines took possession of the ship but it was more than a month before sufficient repairs could be made to enable the captors to take the vessel to Shanghai, where the crew was interned.
>
> 'During the capture and for some 40 days thereafter that we remained on the island and the PRESIDENT HARRISON' relates E.S. Wise, representative of the line who has just been repatriated, 'Mrs. Main displayed a courage and calmness exceeded by no member of the crew. While the bomber power-dived us, threatening the ship with bombs and actually sending several bursts of machine gun fire into the bridge, Mrs. Main remained, at least outwardly, entirely unexcited.'
>
> Before Mrs. Main could enter any lifeboat the bomber returned and again fired into the bridge, hitting very close to where the stewardess was standing. When an officer told her to take cover down in the ship her reply was: 'Why should I? I had enough trouble getting here!'
>
> Mrs. Main, anticipating the perils of exposure in the lifeboat and on the nearby island, provided herself with a bottle of medicinal whisky which was at hand when she finally left the ship. Her patient, constant care and the ministration of the whisky are credited with saving the life of Chief Steward J.L. McKay, of 814 California Street, San Francisco, Calif. He was in a lifeboat which, before it could be pushed away from the hull, was thrown by current, waves and wind into the propellor and broken in two.
>
> Three men were killed outright and several more injured. McKay suffered several broken ribs in the crash against the propellor, and before being carried clear was forced into the stern a second time and several more ribs

were broken. Picked up by another lifeboat crew, more dead than alive, McKay was taken to the top of Sha Wei Shan on a stretcher made of lifeboat oars. There he was given shelter by the Chinese lighthouse keeper.

The next day, when the Japs ordered the crew back aboard the PRESIDENT HARRISON, McKay and Mrs. Main were allowed to remain on the island. In a few days they were returned to the liner and for six weeks the stewardess nursed her patient back to health.

'It is my conviction' reports Wise, 'that without her constant and excellent care McKay would not have survived. During the time we remained aboard the half sunken ship Mrs. Main was a steadying influence on the crew and contributed toward calming those given to excitement and worry over the constant threats of the Japanese.[37]

Veterans of Japanese captivity, the survivors of the capture of the PRESIDENT HARRISON returned home to the United States in the hospital ship SANCTUARY. Arriving at San Francisco on October 22, 1945 were 127 officers and men. Heading home to Providence, Rhode Island several years late for dinner was Chester Zackiewicz. He paused long enough to tell reporters:

We never had a chance, but we gave those Japs a run for their money after being spotted and chased by a Jap fighter bomber and the NAGASAKI MARU for over seven hours.

When there was a chance of getting away, we scuttled the HARRISON by running aground near the mouth of the Whangpo River.

Three men were drowned. The rest of us were caught by the Japs.[38]

The story of a ship built as the WOLVERINE STATE but named PRESIDENT HARRISON for most of her life ended during 1945–46 when the Government credited American President Lines money towards a replacement for the lost ship. A mid July 1942 sum of $989,966.46 was diminished by the $160,377.50 outstanding on a first preferred mortgage held by the Commission. The Reconstruction Finance Corporation claimed the Line still owed $309,279.19 on monies loaned towards the rebuilding of the ship, a figure easily contested. The value of hotel equipment was reckoned at $15,551.00. That left American President waiting for a Maritime Commission payment of $680,687.31. And not until the war was over were there final totals of losses of life in the sinking of the KACHIDOKI MARU and RAKUYO MARU. Of 1,325 men aboard the latter ship, less than 300 survived. Of these, 159 were picked up by the four American submarines while the remaining 136 survivors were rescued by the Japanese naval escorts. On board the KACHIDOKI MARU were 900 Allied prisoners of war. Of those, some 520 survived. There is a "coda" to this tale. In 1946 her surviving crewmem-

---

[37] WSA press release, one of the first reports of the capture of the PRESIDENT HARRISON and the capture of her crew made public. Copy in the ship's 901 file in RG 178 at Maritime Administration.

[38] "San Francisco Chronicle" Oct. 23, 1945.

bers led by Captain Pierson initiated a lawsuit against the United States Government for benefits as war prisoners denied them by the bureaucracy. It was a suit that took years to settle, but Captain Pierson wasted little time before returning to sea. He took out the PRESIDENT POLK, commanding that C3 P & A passenger cargo ship on her first commercial voyage around the world. Then American President Lines rewarded him in early 1948 with command of one of their two new sister flagships, the PRESIDENT WILSON.

THE GRANITE STATE/PRESIDENT POLK: PRESIDENT TAYLOR

◇

Once Congress signalled its approval for the remaining emergency building projects in May 1919, workers at New York Ship treated onlookers to the favor of a double keel laying on May 22, 1919. Intended for completion as the transport or passenger and cargo liner IASSUS was hull number 245, the eventual CREOLE STATE, set onto the stocks at Camden's slipway T. The name JADWIN was planned for the other hull to grow from the keel plates of number 246, a project the Emergency Fleet Corporation knew as hull number 2587, and her keel was set onto slipway U on that same day. In November all provisional names for these big ships were dropped in favor of those "State" nicknames thought to give a certain recognition of type to the Government's passenger liners. This ship would be named GRANITE STATE. The Statistical Section of the U.S. Shipping Board took a long look at the passenger ships under construction in early December and estimated the GRANITE STATE would be 24% complete on January 1, 1920. A fair estimate, it took almost eight more months of work to get the ship ready for launching. When Hull number 246 went into the water at her launch on July 31, 1920, Miss Forsythe Patterson of Pittsburgh, daughter of a Shipping Board executive, served as sponsor. Fitting out was next, and it went a bit slowly. Fourth of the 10,000 ton liners launched, the GRANITE STATE was the fifth of the series delivered. Displacing 13,098 tons, the new ship shared all the particulars of her class. When the dust settled and the accounting department had placed its last zero on the books, the vessel's building cost had reached $4,308,694.33 or, not counting the fittings of her passenger accommodations, $4,086,027.46. Fresh in the last coat of paint applied at the Camden yard, the GRANITE STATE was delivered to the Shipping Board on March 7, 1921.

Though some writers have written that this ship sailed the London service of the United States Mail Line, she didn't. What has confused some observers was her later service on the London line for the United States Lines. First came her service on the Calcutta line under allocation to the Pacific Mail Steamship Company. Only later, when ordered returned to the Atlantic and the United States Mail Line was but a bad memory, did the ship, then named PRESIDENT POLK, work the London line under a special agreement with United States Lines. Print ads published by the United States Shipping Board announced the maiden sailing of the GRANITE STATE to Calcutta to begin from San Francisco on March 22, 1921. But further interruptions to her com-

433

Here's the GRANITE STATE pausing at San Francisco between Calcutta voyages. Howard T. Livingstone photo, courtesy of National Maritime Museum, San Francisco.

pletion delayed her delivery and the Shipping Board could do nothing more than advertise a new slate of expected departure dates for upcoming sailings to Calcutta. Now planning to send the CREOLE STATE on another Calcutta trip in May and scheduling a departure of the WOLVERINE STATE for six weeks thereafter, the GRANITE STATE was assigned to begin service on the line in July, six weeks after the sailing of the WOLVERINE STATE.

Once more the GRANITE STATE foiled the Operations Department of the Shipping Board when New York Shipbuilding Corporation managed to get her ready for service ahead of their own most recent estimates, and she was delivered to the Shipping Board during the first week of March. Before the GRANITE STATE sailed from Philadelphia on March 8, 1921 for Baltimore, the Shipping Board took the opportunity to show her off to the usual observers of new ships. At Baltimore she loaded cargo before shifting to Norfolk on the 15th to pick up the last of her freight. She finally sailed on March 17, 1921, following the wake of her sister WOLVERINE STATE south to the Panama Canal for a March 23rd transit. Once in the Pacific she turned her nose northwards towards California on her way to San Francisco. On her way there she made an unheralded, unexpected March 28th stop at Champerico, Guatemala, a regular port on Pacific Mail's Central America service, likely for additional fresh water and perhaps minor boiler repairs if not to pick up some last minute offerings of cargo. Making her maiden call at San Pedro on April 3rd, the GRANITE STATE reached her final destination, San Francisco, two days behind schedule on April 6, 1921. Before sailing for Calcutta, it is suggested that an Oriental Steerage was fitted into this ship. Since her maiden call at her home port stretched out over ten days, it is probable that the authorized 230 berths were fitted, preparatory work for a job that could have occupied a much longer period.

Ten days later, on April 16, 1921, the new American combination passenger cargo ship sailed on her maiden voyage to India. Commanding her was Captain H. Wallis. Steaming on, the GRANITE STATE called at Singapore and Colombo and then sailed up the Hooghly River to dock at Calcutta on May 26th. After landing passengers and cargo she took on new travelers and inward freight before sailing for home on June 3rd. With Colombo, Singapore, Manila and Honolulu behind her, the ship was 1,738 miles west of San Francisco on July 1st. Having completed her first round trip to Calcutta, the GRANITE STATE returned to her San Francisco pier on July 6, 1921. With the maiden voyage over, both the Pacific Mail and Shipping Board could dissect the figures turned in by the operation of three "502"s on the Calcutta line. Although the ship proved reasonably fuel efficient so far, since delivery consuming a daily average of 450 barrels of oil and steaming at an average speed of 12.5, dollar figures were of greater interest to the Shipping Board and they weren't a pretty sight, all those numbers written in red ink! So discouraging were they, that though no one knew it as the ship lay at San Francisco awaiting her next departure, only two more Calcutta trips remained for the GRANITE STATE.

Sailing from San Francisco on July 14th, Voyage 2 took the ship back to the same ports she had previously seen. After a week at sea, the ship called at Honolulu where a few passengers landed while those in transit were able to enjoy a day at Waikiki. It was August 6th when she made a call at Manila, the 11th when she stopped at Singapore, and then another ten days before her August 21st/22nd Colombo call. Arriving Calcutta a few days later she remained working cargo until her September 5th sailing for the same ports, San Francisco bound. The long trip was over when she pulled into her home port on October 10th. Plans approved that summer to install the same type of Oriental Steerage for 230 passengers in the GRANITE STATE as had been approved for her sisters CREOLE STATE and WOLVERINE STATE don't seem to have gotten very far in this ship. Expected to take three weeks to install, she was never in the port of San Francisco longer than a week. It IS possible, though, that such spaces were added piecemeal, but again, documentary evidence stating such was the case is missing. Always concerned with money, Shipping Board accountants dissected everything concerning the ship's performance and expenses. Issuing a chart comparing fuel and speed performances turned in by the "502"s, they discovered that since her delivery the GRANITE STATE had steamed at an average of 12.1 knots and consumed an average of 450 barrels of oil a day.

By the time the GRANITE STATE began her third trip home from Calcutta on October 16, 1921, the service had lost major sums of money and further losses were projected when she sailed from San Francisco again on November 18th for Calcutta. As was the practice, she called at Honolulu a week after sailing. Then via Manila and Colombo the ship arrived at Calcutta on December 24th. After spending Christmas Day and New Year's Day at Calcutta the ship began the homeward trip, sailing for San Francisco on January 4, 1922. A day after her January 29th Honolulu call, the Trustees of the Shipping Board considered her at their regular meeting. They decided to make that eastbound transPacific trip her last, resolving on January 30, 1922 to withdraw allocation of the GRANITE STATE from the Pacific Mail Steamship Company and bring the ship back to the Atlantic. It was no surprise move. A January 24th resolution approved by the Board of Trustees read in part: "In order to lay out these passenger steamers to amply protect the projected routes in the Pacific and on the Atlantic, it will be necessary to return to the Atlantic side the ss GRANITE STATE after the discharge of her cargo at San Francisco where she is expected to arrive on February 10th" . . .[1]

Similarly, the same memo recorded the immediate future of the CREOLE STATE, expected to sail from San Francisco on March 25th, and the WOLVERINE STATE, scheduled for April 22nd. Pacific Mail was instructed to drop Calcutta from the itinerary of the "passenger boats" immediately and restrict them to an area no further west than Manila. With the Shipping

---

[1]January 31, 1922 memorandum for Chairman Lasker from Secretary Clifford W. Smith. Copy in the ship's 901 file in RG 32 at National Archives.

Board's action, the GRANITE STATE's April 12, 1922 sailing to Calcutta was cancelled. Behind schedule, the ship arrived at San Francisco on February 14th. Her cargo discharged, the GRANITE STATE was redelivered to the Shipping Board. For the ship's return to the East Coast, the Shipping Board reassigned her to the management of the Pacific Mail Steamship Company. Sailing in ballast from San Francisco on February 19, 1922, the ship headed south for her new career. Arriving at Balboa at 7:55AM on March 1st, the pilot and canal crew prepared to take the ship through and at 8:30AM the ship entered the Panama Canal. Completing her passage between the seas at 3:33PM, and without making a call at Cristobal or Colon, the ship immediately cleared for sea, was on her way to New York, where she arrived after her three week trip on March 7th. There Grace Line took over the duties as ship's agent and Pacific Mail permanently withdrew from the ship's life. In very short order Grace had plenty of work to do in conjunction with the ship's maiden stay at New York. Within hours of tying up, a very strong wind blew in and the ship broke from her moorings. Drifting upstream, the GRANITE STATE fouled the moorings of the Cornell stakeboat, dragging that boat from its anchorage. Response was quick. Tugs went out to take charge of the run-away liner and bring her to a safe spot to anchor before bringing her to Pier 1, Hoboken.

Now in addition to the $17,151.00 cost of a quick refit scheduled to downgrade First Class to Cabin Class and the expansion of cabin capacity to 156 berths at the New York Harbor Drydock Company, the ship needed a touch of external cosmetic work to retouch the paint scratches on her hull. At the same time quite a bit of electrical work was done to improve both vessel safety and expand lighting and that's why the contract with New York Harbor Drydock Company was so costly. There was more work done aboard the GRANITE STATE while she remained in New York harbor.

After these alterations the GRANITE STATE spent the next three days, 2 hours and 5 minutes preparing for her maiden sailing on the North Atlantic. Neither London nor Cherbourg, the usual destinations for "502"'s working from New York, were on the itinerary. Under the command of Captain Schofield and with 116 Cabin Class passengers, 4,315 tons of freight and 988 bags of mail, the GRANITE STATE sailed from New York at 3:05 PM on April 8, 1922 for Queenstown and Bremerhaven. After a ten day crossing the liner reached Queenstown on April 18th. Her call there lasted only an hour, enough time to land some passengers and mail before steaming on to Bremerhaven, a port rarely visited by a "502". After her April 21st arrival there, she worked cargo during her call of 4 days, 7 hours and 17 minutes. There the ship loaded a homeward cargo of 3,960 tons, one of the better westbound loads offered a "502" while in service on the North Atlantic. German postal officials directed 799 bags of mail to the American liner. In the ship's cabins were 72 Cabin Class passengers sailing for New York on April 25th. The GRANITE STATE made another technical call at Queenstown, arriving there at 2:00 AM on the morning of April 28th. Her call lasted fifty minutes. After arriving at New York on May 7th there were passengers to land and cargo to discharge before the voyage was technically concluded. That done at noon on May 10, 1922, Voyage 1 on the Atlantic, her only one as GRANITE STATE, was over. Later that day the ship sailed south to Baltimore for some substantial repair work and alterations to her accommodation spaces. Papers issued that morning authorized her name change to PRESIDENT POLK and her registry from Philadelphia to New York. Final figures showed a total voyage income of $50,297.11. Once more eastbound revenues were almost triple her homeward income. Against expenses of $56,371.57, there was a net operating deficit of over $6,000.00, but compared with some of the fantastic operating losses turned in by her kind, that figure didn't look all that bad and even gave room for optimism.

Having decided to employ the ship on the Atlantic was only part of the plan for this ship. Still not convinced that the Cabin class passenger and freight service on the London line needed additional tonnage at the moment, the Shipping Board worked out another special agreement with the Roosevelt Steamship Company and Moore & McCormack, operators of their United States Lines, and assigned this ship to U.S. Lines for the Ireland/ Germany trade. Emigrating northern Europeans and Irish no longer had to accept the open steerage of days past so the "502" ships' type of Oriental steerage was not considered acceptable on her intended trade. Before beginning service from New York, the ship needed a modern, American Third Class in order to compete with European tonnage on the Queenstown/Bremen line. The work completed at New York Harbor Drydock, the vessel shifted to the Bethlehem Shipbuilding Corp.'s Sparrows Point yard where accommodations for 246 Third Class passengers was installed at a cost of $157,680.00.[2] Once again all parties concerned gave great evidence of atrocious timing for even as the ship was refitting, the Shipping Board accepted United States Lines' application to make the London line a weekly service. Switching the PRESIDENT POLK from the Bremen line, the Shipping Board suspected Irish emigrants would occupy whatever berths could otherwise have been filled in Germany.

The refit completed, she sailed from Baltimore on June 25th for New York and her first voyage as PRESIDENT POLK. From any point of view, the ship was well booked. With 200 passengers, 107 in Cabin and 93 in Third Class, the ship began her first sailing from New York under her new name on June 28, 1922. On that trip her first port of call was Boston, where 137 more passengers, 92 of them Third Class boarded after the ship arrived on June 29th. On that trip the liner was bound not to Germany for which trade she had just been refitted but for the usual ports of the London line where across the Atlantic the ship reached Queenstown on July 8th where 28 Cabin and 145 of her Third Class passengers disembarked. Disembarking at Plym-

---

[2] So say Shipping Board records—any earlier steerage accommodations would then have been considered "Oriental Steerage", a temporary expedient for the carriage of Asian passengers.

outh on the 9th were 16 travelers, half of them had crossed in Cabin Class. At Cherbourg later that day 70 Cabin passengers landed along with 3 Third Class passengers while the remaining passengers left the ship at London after the ship's arrival on July 10th. All those passengers brought the ship $34,605.75 in passage fares, one of the highest totals thus far earned by a "502". There were only 875 tons of general cargo in her holds but that light shipment was carried at good prices, adding $17,021.75 to the ship's voyage income. Additionally, 136 bags of mail added $680.00 while excess baggage charges yielded another $12.40, canteen sales brought in $450.00 and deck chair and rug hire totalled $275.00. Grand total of these various items brought an estimated voyage revenue of $53,044.90. The ship stayed at London for five days and after sailing followed the typical homeward path of her sisters, stopping off Cherbourg some hours after sailing. Figures for the westbound sailing were not quite as impressive and the ship posted an operating loss on that voyage which ended after her July 25th arrival at New York.

The ship sailed for her second voyage as PRESIDENT POLK on August 2nd. Mystery developed towards the end of the eastbound crossing. After having last been seen on the bridge deck at about 4:00 AM on August 11, 1922, Master-at-Arms Olaf Maatson disappeared. Internal Shipping Board investigations turned up reports of serious allegations against him by other crew members. Whether or not any reports of his alleged misconduct were true, the Shipping Board felt that Maatson had either "let himself overboard and attempted to swim to the Irish coast" or had managed to conceal himself aboard the vessel and went ashore at London. Not accepted by the Board was the possibility of foul play. In fact, as late as mid October 1924, the official position of the Board held that Maatson had not perished and thus they could not oblige the Swedish Chargé d'Affaires at London with a Death Certificate. Maatson's disappearance remained the talk of the crew after the ship's August 13th arrival at London. Surely not much had been ascertained by the time the ship sailed on August 19th for home, nor did anyone know any more on August 29th when she docked at New York.

September 6th was the date of her next outbound sailing, her third as a "President liner" and her fourth trip from New York. Some 686 miles east of Ambrose Lightship on September 8th, the PRESIDENT POLK reached Queenstown on September 16th, Plymouth on the 17th and arrived at London after stopping off Cherbourg later that night. From London on September 23rd, Cherbourg on the 24th and Queenstown on the 25th, the liner made her return to New York, a ten day passage. She arrived at her home port on October 4th.

Captain Schofield next took his ship out from New York on October 11th. Once again bound for Cobh, Plymouth and London, on the 16th the ship reported herself some 1,126 miles west of Fastnet. After Queenstown and Plymouth calls on the 21st the ship reached London on the 22nd for a six day stay. Sailing from London on the 28th, November 5th saw the ship call

Because the PRESIDENT POLK could carry both Cabin and Third Class passengers while on United States Line's London line she carried a number of extra lifeboats. Notice the double banks of boats in the well between fore and aft deck structures as well as atop the aft house. This photograph was taken while she ship was at New York on June 29, 1922. Eric Johnson collection.

in to report herself at 888 miles east of Ambrose. Three days later she steamed up the Narrows to land passengers, mail and freight. As ever, there were always repair bills for her owners and operators to consider and typical was the spate of work performed aboard the liner while she lay at her New York pier between her November 8th arrival and her November 15, 1922 departure for her sixth transAtlantic voyage. At a total cost of $8,547.00 to United States Lines, and ultimately, the taxpayers, for the Shipping Board and most of its services were losing unconscionable sums of money every day, the following work was performed on the PRESIDENT POLK:

Start	Complete	Contractor	Nature of Repairs		Amount
11/08/22	11/13/22	Atlantic Basin	Jack rods for weather cloths on Lower Prom		750.00
11/08/22	11/13/22	W&A Fletcher	Extend oil fuel air escape pipes from Bridge Deck to Nav Bridge		408.00
11/08/22	11/13/22	Contract Painters	Paint Third Class cabins and corridors		2,715.00
11/09/22	11/14/22	Morse D.D. Co.	Eng. Maint.	1572.	
			Hull Maint.	832.	
			Stewd. Maint.	213.	
			Oper. Ves. Exp.	282.	
			Marine Losses	324.	
			Betterments/Alt.	636.	3,859.00
11/09/22	11/13/22	United Marine	Vessel Operating Expense		395.00
11/11/22	11/11/22	Walter Kidde	Routine Inspection of Fire Detection System		25.00
11/10/22	11/10/22	AeroAlarm	Routine Inspection of Fire Alarm system		32.00
11/13/22	11/14/22	AeroAlarm	Voyage Expense		77.50
11/13/22	11/14/22	AeroAlarm	Hull Maintenance		26.50
11/14/22	11/14/22	Consolidated	Engine		46.00
11/11/22	11/14/22	Morse D.D. Co.	Engine		211.00
					$8,545.00

Before sailing out on November 15th the PRESIDENT POLK got a new Master, Captain MacLean. Under his command she arrived via ports at London on November 25th for a six days' stay. Homeward bound, the ship sailed from London on December 2nd to arrive on time at New York ten days later.

The ship was dressed for the holidays before she began her final outbound sailing of the year from New York on December 20th. Living up to its reputation for winter storms, the North Atlantic gave the ship a tough time and following a spectacularly rough eastbound crossing, the PRESIDENT POLK arrived at Queenstown on December 29, 1922 in a somewhat battered condition. Winter storms had carried away two of her lifeboats, damaged deck fittings and caused water to leak into several tweendeck compartments. While at London after her December 31st arrival damaged equipment was repaired and new boats shipped before the ship sailed for home.

With the passing of the year, besides totalling up repair costs and tallying extensive operating losses, Shipping Board statisticians checked figures of passengers carried. In spite of an abbreviated 1922 season on the Atlantic, the ship attracted a fair number of passengers, carrying 953 eastbound and 1,386 westbound. That fewer travelers chose this cabin liner for their eastbound crossings than for their westbound sailings was probably more a factor of her sailing schedule than anything else.

The following year, 1923 brought another full calendar of London line sailings, and she took her first departure of the year with a departure from London on January 6, 1923, stopping off Cherbourg that same day. Over the course of 1923 the PRESIDENT POLK carried a total of 1,300 passengers eastbound to Queenstown, Cherbourg and London, including 102 Cabin and 3 Third Class passengers scheduled to disembark with the mails at Plymouth. Westwards, the POLK carried a total of 2,600 passengers, a total of 1,119 in Cabin and 1,481 in Third Class. Fully 977 of the Third Class passengers embarked in Queenstown, indicating that the "502"'s little known Third Class was booked primarily by Irish emigrants.

That voyage ended after the ship's January 17th arrival at New York. When she sailed again for London on her first outbound sailing of the year on January 31st, she was on her eighth transAtlantic trip from New York. She reached London on February 11th. Sailing for America on February 17th she called at Plymouth on the 19th and reached New York on March 1st. After a one week stay in port the PRESIDENT POLK was off again, sailing on her ninth Atlantic trip on March 7th. Dependably, she made a typical ten day crossing followed by the usual port call at London and stops at Queenstown, Plymouth and Cherbourg. Sailing for home on March 24th the ship reached New York on April 5th. Now, about a year after her first outing from New York, the ship was about to make her tenth trip to European waters. Sailing for London on April 11th, she docked at London on the 23rd. April 28th was sailing day for the westbound trip and after stopping at her usual ports managed to get home on time on May 9th.

Like her sisters on the London line, the PRESIDENT POLK was able to make about one round trip every four weeks. That allowed a ten day crossing in each direction and about a week in port at either end. Hoping to make better use of her modern Third Class accommodations and attract Irish-Americans making a summer visit to relatives and friends across the sea in

Ireland, United States Lines added a few outbound Boston calls to the schedule, pairing the similarly equipped PRESIDENT ADAMS for the high season with the PRESIDENT POLK to work via Boston. The PRESIDENT POLK's May 16th sailing from New York was her first high season sailing that year. This time the PRESIDENT POLK called outbound at Boston on the 17th but otherwise the ship operated the same kind of schedule she had so far worked. To maintain a weekly schedule from New York the London call was shortened to compensate for the diversion to Massachussetts. Her next departure from New York on June 19th was also via Boston. That brought the ship into London on July 2nd. Adding Boston to the return schedule as well forced an even shorter stay at London, so the PRESIDENT POLK sailed from the Thames on July 5th and the ship called inbound at Boston on July 15th and 16th before her arrival at New York on July 17th. While at New York that time the ship went for drydocking before resuming her scheduled sailings.

The eastbound high season was over and the bulk of summer tourists already on the other side when the PRESIDENT POLK sailed on her thirteenth Atlantic trip from New York on July 26th. Boston was no longer on the itinerary and the ship crossed directly to Queenstown for an August 5th arrival at London. She sailed homewards on the 11th, called Cherbourg, Plymouth and Queenstown in turn and arrived at New York on the 21st. The outbound voyage yielded one of those coveted letters of praise from a passenger. Coming in for special applause this time was Captain McLean, whose style drew accolades from W. D. Hines who was an executive in the office of tire mogul Harvey S. Firestone. Here's what he wrote to Shipping Chairman Edward P. Farley on August 23, 1923:

> My wife, who has done considerable Transatlantic travelling, has recently made a trip to Europe aboard the PRESIDENT POLK, and in writing me from England gave a very enthusiastic account of the accommodations aboard the boat and the courtesies extended to all by Captain McLean. From what she has written I feel quite sure that if all the commanders aboard the ships of the U.S. Lines show the attention for the care and comfort of the passengers that Captain McLean does the success and popularity of the American Merchant Marine is assured. The Captain and other Officers aboard the boat made the trip a most enjoyable one, and other experienced travellers aboard agreed with my wife that Captain was an exceptional commander.[3]

Still commanded by Captain McLean, the ship sailed for her fourteenth Atlantic trip from New York on August 29, 1923. She was bound once more for Queenstown, Plymouth, Cherbourg and London where she arrived on September 9th. Sailing for home on September 20th from London, she was at sea on the return leg of that voyage when sold to the Dollar Steamship Lines, Ltd., Inc. per the September 25, 1923 contract. She arrived at New York on October 1st. As with her sisters, delivery was scheduled for early

---

[3]Copy of letter in the ship's 1091 file in RG 32 at National Archives.

1924 so she still had a few more Atlantic sailings to operate before delivery to her buyer. Now under contract of sale, her stay at New York before she sailed on voyage 15 was short and on October 4th the liner sailed for London again. After her usual stops the ship arrived at London on October 15th. Sailing from London on October 20th, the ship called again at Cherbourg, Plymouth and Queenstown. During that homeward crossing the ship was diverted from her customary course and made a little known call at Portland, Maine. Arriving there late in the evening of October 31, 1923, she loaded a big shipment of potatoes for Britain and sailed from Maine on November 3rd on her way to New York for a midnight arrival on November 4th/5th. Then voyage repairs by a number of New York contractors were performed before the ship sailed again on November 14th. Following her November 27th arrival at London the ship worked cargo for a couple of days and sailed home on December 1st, calling as always at Cherbourg, Plymouth and Queenstown. She returned home ten days later.

The ship's December sailing, her seventeenth eastbound transAtlantic sailing was a voyage that took her 37 days, 18 hours and 45 minutes to complete. Beginning the voyage when she started lifting 7,325 tons of outbound cargo into her holds at 4:00PM on December 12, 1923, the PRESIDENT POLK sailed at 12:15 PM on December 19th for Cherbourg and London. Homeward bound, the ship departed London at 5:15 PM on December 29th. Making a Cherbourg call on the 30th, the ship crossed directly to New York where she arrived at 11:36 PM on January 9, 1924. Tying up at her pier the next morning, she landed 70 Cabin and 18 Third Class passengers. As usual there was not as much inward freight to offload than she had carried outbound. Longshoremen discharged 2,949 tons of it at New York. Once fully offloaded, the ship's voyage ended at 10:45 AM on January 12th.

Dollar figures show a total round trip voyage income of $62,100.88. Against total round trip expense of $80,439.27, bottom line figures from the voyage report surely supported her sale. Like her sisters, the PRESIDENT POLK steadily lost money. To date, her operation on all the voyages she had run thus far including those on the Calcutta run, two trans-Panama Canal trips and her service on the North Atlantic, had yielded a deficit of $624,282.95. Yet that figure, like comparable figures for her sisters, especially the PRESIDENT MONROE and PRESIDENT van BUREN, each credited with operating losses over $800,000.00, included voyage repair costs as well as an apportioned amount of building costs. There was truly no way these ships would ever show a profit under the present scheme of accounting.

Under contract of sale since late September of the previous year, before going to the Dollar Line, the PRESIDENT POLK made a final London voyage in 1924, departing on her last round trip transAtlantic voyage on January 23rd. In her cabins were 80 in Cabin and 23 passengers in Third Class. Homewards, on her final crossing in United States Lines' colors, she had 96 passengers aboard, 67 in Cabin and 29 in Third, who all disembarked after the ship returned to New York on February 19, 1924.

Over the course of about a score of Atlantic voyages the PRESIDENT POLK had attracted a decent number of passengers for her capacity but like her sisters, this ship had suffered financially because of the small westward cargoes she had been offered. With neither heavy cargoes nor enough passengers to pay their bills, the "502"S showed such poor financial returns on most of their voyages on the London line. Again, it was all a matter of accounting, since the expenses of construction could be figured in against any voyage revenue, should the Board so instruct the accounting department. As for her speed, the PRESIDENT POLK averaged 13.88 knots over the course of all her Atlantic voyages, hardly enough to attract much of the regular Atlantic trade.

The moment of delivery was at hand. Captain MacLean signed off and was replaced by Captain O. O'Brien, the third man to command her since the beginning of her Atlantic service in the spring of 1922. Before a gathering of interested parties the PRESIDENT POLK was delivered to the Dollar Line at her New York pier at noon on February 26, 1924. Now, before beginning her career on the round the world service, her Cabin Class accommodation was restored to First Class and the ship underwent a spate of repairs before joining the round the world line. Like the PRESIDENT ADAMS, the PRESIDENT POLK had some bottom damage to be repaired at the time of her delivery to her buyer. Before beginning service on the round the world line, she was drydocked at Robin's Dry Dock & Repair Company at Brooklyn where among sundry work, forepeak rivets and 20 keel plate rivets were repaired; her bilge keel faired, tap bolts in 3 strainer plates were renewed; both propellor shafts were repaired; and one keel block was removed for repairs to the ship's keel plate and was then returned. For her long distance voyages, her fore peak tanks, thus far filled with ballast, were fitted for carrying oil, something done on all seven ships. Topsides, workmen repaired two broken laycock windows at the after end of the Promenade Deck and fixed a leak in the overhead panelling of the Third Class lounge. An ink stain in the carpet of the Cabin Class social hall attracted a fair bit of attention as did repair of some 180 broken or cracked tiles throughout the ship. A section of veneer in the Veranda Cafe was replaced and leaks in the ceilings of a few cabins and one bathroom were repaired. The ship was also thoroughly cleaned and then painted in Dollar Line colors before sailing for Havana and ports around the world on March 6th. After calling at Havana on March 10th the fifth "502" in the round the world parade of Dollar Liners arrived at Colon at 2:10AM on March 14, 1924. By Panama Canal rules the ship measured 12,031 gross and 8,443 net tons and on those figures tolls were assessed for her transit of the Canal, which began when she entered the passage between the seas that morning at 7:30. She was through at 3:54PM and at 8:15 that evening with 2,089 tons of general cargo, cleared for sea. After the scheduled ten day passage the ship called at San Pedro en route to San Francisco, where she arrived for the first time as PRESIDENT POLK on March 27, 1924. Two days later, on March 29th, the former GRANITE STATE sailed from

San Francisco on her first voyage around the world. Following her earlier path across the Pacific, the ship made her first port of call at Honolulu. After a day there, Captain O'Brien set a course for Kobe. Then it was on to Shanghai, Hong Kong and her previous haunts of Singapore and Colombo. India was not on the itinerary now . . . it wouldn't be for some five years. Then the "502" sailed for the Suez Canal. After a May 26th/27th transit, the ship headed for Alexandria, Naples and Marseilles, before sailing non-stop for Boston and New York on the last leg of her maiden around the world voyage. After arriving at New York as scheduled at 7:00 AM on Thursday, June 19th, the POLK spent a week there working cargo and preparing for round the world voyage #2. Adhering to Dollar Line's printed schedule, the ship sailed on time from New York at 2:00PM on Thursday, June 26th. As before and as she always would on future voyages, she called at Havana, Colon, Balboa and San Francisco before arriving at San Francisco on time at 6:00 AM on Thursday, July 17th. Two days later at 5:00 on Saturday July 19th, the PRESIDENT POLK cast off from Dollar Line's Pier 42. Exactly one month had passed since she arrived at New York at the end of her first global voyage. Within an hour of sailing she steamed through the Golden Gate on her second, and rather eventful round the world trip.

All went well at every port along the way until the PRESIDENT POLK headed into her last foreign port, Marseilles. Entering the harbor there on September 24, 1924, the PRESIDENT POLK stranded on the breakwater at the entrance to the port. Damage was slight, but maybe everyone connected with the ship should have become increasingly vigilant, for once across the Atlantic, worse was in store for her. Relatively incident free was the westbound transAtlantic voyage. Arriving at New York on October 8th, the ship tied up at her usual pier at Bush Terminal's Pier 6 at the foot of 42nd Street in Brooklyn. As was the practice at New York, all passengers disembarked, those bound for ports further west lodging in hotels until sailing day. The ship was still discharging freight like spices, syrups, fruit and nuts towards midnight on October 11, 1924 when a serious fire broke out in her passenger spaces. Taking immediate alarm were Chinese crew awakened from sleep by the ringing of alarm bells. Hero among them was John Zane, a cartoonist on the staff of the *China Press* of Shanghai. Working his way around the world, Zane kept his cool and helped calm his rattled compatriots whose alternate cries for help from the firemen to escape the burning ship alternated with their cries to be saved from drowning after they jumped into the water. Once fished out of the harbor, they gathered on the pier with other men of the burning steamer.

Within minutes after it ignited, the fire ate its way through the alleyways and upwards to the bridge where its heat burst the windows in the wheelhouse. As flames shot forth from the upperworks, fireboats arrived on the scene and joined land based firefighting gear. The fire burned through the night, destroying most of the ship's superstructure, laying waste to all the ship's accommodation spaces, before being brought under control around noon. Onlookers felt that every tug in New York harbor came by to shoot streams of water into the burning liner, or at least to establish a claim for having helped, but it was the New York Fire Department that put out the fire.

If there was any humor in this near tragedy, it was played out on the dock. Afraid of fire, the Chinese in the ship's crew who had not jumped into the water made a beeline for the gangway and streamed ashore as fast as the guard would let them off. They were further discomforted when part of the pier caught fire, too. Lucky for all concerned, that fire was quickly put out. Ship's officers lined them and started counting heads, expecting the number of men in line to equal the number of Chinese signed on as crew and those carried home from an American ship sold in Europe to China. Those men were being repatriated. When they reached that number there was a "string of them (Chinese) as long as the length of the pier."[4] Unable to make good their landing when the fire started, some sixty of them were stowaways, and the fire had forced them ashore where they fell in line with the "legals". Such a large number of illegal passengers in a single ship could be no coincidence. Several shoreside personnel and ship's officers had been doing a little business on the side, selling passage to undocumented Chinese, hopeful of entering the United States. This fire put a screeching halt to this enterprise, and quite a few people found themselves pounding the pavement in search of a new job. Of the officers who had brought the PRESIDENT POLK back to New York, only Fourth Officer Orel Pierson retained his job.

Daylight revealed a badly charred combination passenger and cargo liner. Heavily listing, the ship's bridge and superstructure had been burned away and part of her midships structure fire damaged all the way to her keel. Instant damage assessment suggested a repair job in the neighborhood of half a million dollars, almost as much as the Dollar Line had paid for the ship a year earlier. That day brought more sobering news. After the blaze was extinguished and the ship searched, investigators looking through the lower decks discovered the charred body of Louis Johnson, boss of one of the stevedore gangs. No one could hazard a guess about why Johnson was in a cabin aboard the burning liner, for when the fire started he had been seen above decks. Speculation considered that he either went below to retrieve valuables or to help evacuate people from the burning ship. His was the only life lost to the fire, though once the presence of a large number of Chinese was learned, officials feared a heavy toll among them, some of whom were feared drowned.

The fire out, the ship was shifted to 59th Street, Brooklyn. There, Fourth Officer Orel Pierson remained in charge as ship keeper for the next few months. While Dollar Line went through damage reports and studied plans for new accommodations to be built, they called for bids for the repair job. Dollar Line took advantage of the ship's sorry state to substantially alter the

---

[4]From a reminiscence of Captain Orel A. Pierson. Courtesy of Captain Warren Leback.

living spaces aboard the vessel and at the same time increase the ship's passenger capacity by about fifty percent. Giving the ship a new look by joining the two separate houses of the split superstructure, naval architect Theodore Ferris was given charge of the reconstruction of the burned liner. Those plans came in handy four years later when three "502" class sisters were extensively improved.

Low bid for the repair job came from the Newport News Shipbuilding & Drydock Company and that company won the contract. For an investment of about half a million dollars, the PRESIDENT POLK was nearly a new ship when she was redelivered to Dollar Line on April 9, 1925. Ferris' ideas played well in this case and the former "ugly duckling" now presented quite a handsome appearance. Topped with a cowl to deflect smoke, a new, thicker, taller funnel stood in place of the original, drawing the attention of the eye from other parts of the ship that NO amount of cosmetic refitting would much improve. In the single midships superstructure, now connected on Upper Promenade and Promenade Decks, were enlarged public rooms, improved cabins and two long covered promenade decks on each side of the ship, glassed in for up to 50% of their length.

Within were vastly improved accommodations for 150 First Class passengers and even now they are worth a look. Highest graded was a quartette of suites at the forward end of Upper Promenade Deck. Situated behind the thwartship promenade, with views out over the bows, there were two suites outboard and two on the centerline. Each provided with the usual bedroom, sitting room and bathroom, these suites featured panelled walls and were quite comfortably furnished for the long-haul voyages on the ship's schedule. Below, on Promenade Deck forward was a similar arrangement, but here, the suites were only on the centerline while outboard were two double cabins, each equipped with private facilities. On Upper Promenade Deck, whatever cabins that had been gutted by fire had been rearranged and new cabins built in the new midships section. These included six rooms of some 200 square feet each, two bedded rooms sharing a bath between every two cabins. Further aft, twelve other cabins without private facilities were built.

The newly configured Promenade Deck featured innovations beyond the deluxe cabins forward. Midships, in place of the lobby that had been furnished as a lounge, a real Lounge, a separate apartment, no longer open to the stairs, presided over all spaces. A further ten cabins had been built while further aft, only the Veranda Cafe remained as before.

Relocated half a deck below its original location was the passengers' Dining Saloon. Now entered from the Foyer by means of a prominent central staircase, workers had enlarged the dining room to allow seats for 142 persons at a time. This new dining room was made possible by filling in the well between the separate houses of the superstructure. Further aft, several more cabins were built abaft the original ten cabins on either side. Returned to his original cabin on portside aft was the ship's Doctor. On starboard side, forward, a new pair of cabins with a bathroom between them were reserved

No doubt that dapper passenger sent greetings from the writing room of the PRESIDENT POLK to loved ones at home. Author's collection.

for the Chief Purser and Chief Steward. All upper berths installed just before the ship had begun service as a Cabin ship on the London line were reportedly removed during this time of repairs and reconditioning.

Other than some water damage, the engine spaces had come through the fire unscathed. With a crew of yard workers, Orel Pierson and some of the ship's crew cleaned and painted the engine room and cargo spaces and unloaded about 800 tons of remaining steel billets put aboard to help ballast the ship in the stormy North Atlantic.

Actually, some 2,000 gross tons larger than she had been before the fire, the PRESIDENT POLK was reregistered at only 10,500 gross tons, slightly less than her original gross tonnage figure. A typical move for a shipowner,

In a suite aboard the newly refitted PRESIDENT POLK. Author's collection.

this saves money on registry fees and port charges. Perhaps more telling was the fact that port officials in most countries accepted a net tonnage figure of 6,904 net tons for her. In March, Captain K.A. Ahlin arrived at the yard to take command of the ship. Leaving the Newport News yards for New York on April 9, 1925, the PRESIDENT POLK arrived at New York on the following day. There she passed the next week loading for her outbound trip. She

Here's the Main Lounge aboard the PRESIDENT POLK, rebuilt after her October 1924 fire. Author's collection.

returned to service with her April 16th sailing. For the most part, she managed to steer clear of major difficulties, though occasionally, smaller fires broke out aboard.

The rebuilt liner could not help but invite comparison with her former sisters. Once at San Francisco, she spent three days receiving visitors and cargo before embarking passengers and sailing on May 9, 1925 on her round the world voyage. A trip made without untoward incident, she arrived at New York on July 21st. She made her Boston side trip and sailed again for San Francisco on August 6th.

Her August 29th sailing from San Francisco was another round the world sailing. Delayed on the Atlantic crossing on the homeward leg of that trip, she called Boston on November 21st and after an abbreviated New York call, began voyage 5 on November 26th. With her December 19th sailing from San Francisco the PRESIDENT POLK spent Christmas Day at sea, the 26th at Honolulu and was again at sea en route to China and Japan when 1925 gave way to 1926. The Dollar liner sailed from Kobe on January 10, 1926 for her next round of ports, sailing from Singapore on the 28th and from Penang on January 29th.

Her first New York call in 1926 was in mid March and while at Pier 23, Brooklyn on March 14th, a small fire broke out in No. 9 compartment, burning a steward's room and NO. 6 hatch. There was no cargo aboard the ship, but some freight on the pier was damaged by water used to extinguish the fire aboard the ship. The ship was otherwise undamaged and got away on schedule enabling her to take her first sailing of the year from San Francisco on April 10th. Captain Ahlin continued to command this ship and he took her out from New York on subsequent voyages that year on July 9th and October 29th and from San Francisco on July 31st and November 20th.

The ship was admeasured at 6,304 net tons during 1927, a year that she began in the waters near Malaya. By January 26, 1927 she was on her way from Marseilles to Boston and a mid February arrival. She next sailed from New York for foreign ports on February 21st with her sailing for Havana and Cristobal. From San Francisco the PRESIDENT POLK continued on March 12th with her sailing for Honolulu and Kobe. Her voyaging that year proved happily uneventful and when she returned to New York she tied up at Jersey City's Pier 9 for the first time. The ship sailed from New York again on another round the world trip on June 10th and from San Francisco on July 2nd. The time had come for Captain Ahlin to take a break and he was replaced by Captain K.B. Lowry, who took the ship around the world. It seems he stayed only that one voyage, for Captain H.S. Bauer was listed as Master for the ship on her September 29, 1927 sailing from New York. That time the ship continued her voyage from San Francisco on October 21st.

One of the lesser fires she suffered broke out on January 11, 1928 as the ship lay at her Jersey City pier. She had docked on Tuesday, January 10th after another uneventful Atlantic crossing. All passengers had left her, either terminating their voyage there or putting up in hotels before continuing on to the West Coast. Discharging an inward cargo of oil and crude rubber valued at $1,500,000.00, fire broke out in holds 1 and 2. Dense clouds of black smoke issued forth from the handsome liner, obscuring the confused scene at the dock where, in an improvised stockade, about one hundred Chinese crewmembers had been herded by ship's Captain Lowry after they had nearly rioted in their attempt to get themselves and their possessions ashore. What was touchier, the fire or the attempt of the Chinese to quit their ship and gain entry into the United States? But for Quartermaster A.A. Arthway, who, while awaiting the arrival of the local police, vigilantly fought off any crewmember who tried to run, any number of them might have made good an illegal entry into the country, leaving Dollar line liable to a fine of $1,000.00 per head. As for the fire, it was brought under control without any loss of life, but not before it had devoured thirty thousand bales of crude rubber and a large amount of oil. The ship was nearly flooded by water pumped in to fight the fire, but only those constant streams of water kept the fire confined to the hold and actual damage to the ship was light. Once the fire was under control, the ship was towed to Pier 16, Staten Island, where damaged cargo was discharged. On January 15th the ship sailed for Boston, returning to New York on the 17th. Anti-union men as well as anti-foreigners were quick to point out how often fires occurred in Dollar ships in American ports, suggesting a way someone smuggling Chinese into the United States could cause a diversion to get those men ashore. Facts spoke otherwise, but there HAD been a number of small fires in port.

The PRESIDENT POLK sailed from San Francisco on January 19, 1928 under the command of Captain Lowry. By the time the ship arrived at Honolulu on February 17th, it was announced that upon her return to New York she would be drydocked for shaft survey and repair of three shell and eight deck plates. Captain Lowry came back to the ship for the next sailing, a trip with a number of festive moments, none of them as nerve- racking or dangerous as a major fire. For starters it marked the 100th sailing of a Dollar Liner on the Round the World line. At Alexandria, Egypt, the ship's Master, Captain Kenneth B. Lowry got married, but he hurried back aboard to take his ship home. His bride made her own way to San Francisco where they were re-united. Other good news was shared while the liner operated that trip. The deficits of the first few years of the round the world service seemed to be history and when the PRESIDENT POLK cast off from New York on May 10, 1928, the liner more than made her owners proud, she was making money! That 100th round the world trip of a "502" class liner brought the ship and her complement of officers and passengers many good wishes and congratulations all along the way. The big celebration was held after the PRESIDENT POLK docked at San Francisco on May 29, 1928. While the ship was in port she hosted guests of the Dollar Line at a number of functions organized in celebration of the ships and the service. With Captain Robert Dollar away on his fourth round the world trip, Stanley Dollar hosted the festivities, commenting for the occasion: "Not only has the service proven a success, but it is a huge success . . ."[5] One can only imagine his pride when he reported to the assembled that in four years his company's ships had steamed almost 2,900,000 miles in the round the world trade, and the Company had to date bought $4,000,000.00 worth of all manner of supplies for the ships, mainly Californian products. Before the PRESIDENT POLK got underway again, Captain Lowry signed off in order to enjoy a belated honeymoon. Captain W.A. Ross came aboard to replace the honeymooning Captain Lowry. There was more to the ship's stay at San Francisco that time and it was not widely publicized at all. The line was pretty lucky that invitees didn't notice that there had been a slight fire that broke out in No. 4 hold a short while before the parties began on May 23rd. Considerably damaging No. 3, 4 and 5 hatches and causing a declaration of 15% general average to the ship's cargo, damage was repaired and external areas repainted before the ship sailed on June 1st.

Late that summer the PRESIDENT POLK left New York as usual on her way to San Francisco. There, passengers booked on one of James Boring's three specially arranged trips to Japan in conjunction with the November coronation of Emperor Hirohito boarded. Those taking the PRESIDENT POLK sailed from San Francisco on September 21st for an October 10th arrival at Kobe. One of the two other groups Boring organized sailed from there on October 12th in the Dollar Line "535" PRESIDENT McKINLEY while the other group sailed from Seattle aboard the PRESIDENT JEFFERSON on October 20th.

After her gala trip to Japan, life aboard the ship resumed its routine character until the ship reached Naples where a mishap cost a life. At Naples, Italy late in the night of November 24, 1928, Cadet W.O. Wiedman of Los Angeles was killed when he fell into an open hatch. Things aboard the PRESIDENT POLK were back to normal when she steamed out of Boston on December 16th and New York on December 20, 1928 on her way to Havana, Panama and California. From San Francisco this "502" took her first sailing of the year on January 11, 1929. Ahead were her usual ports around the world and to remind us of her progress, she sailed from Kobe on February 1st and from Singapore on February 21, 1929.

Her minor travails continued as the decade ended. She sailed again from New York on April 11th. While at sea on April 15, 1929 a fire broke out in one of the ship's holds. Not until her Master ordered the space flooded was the blaze extinguished. That of course saved the ship but severely damaged the cargo stored there.

The PRESIDENT POLK sailed from Boston on November 16, 1929 and from New York on the 21st. December 8th saw her arrive at Los Angeles and on the 13th she sailed from San Francisco on another world voyage that would result in her first notice in casualty lists that year. Sailing from Kobe on January 2, 1930, the liner got as far as Egypt before any trouble marred

---

[5]May 28, 1928 edition of the *San Francisco Chronicle*.

the way. First was a February 11, 1930 collision at Alexandria, Egypt with the Greek steamer RITA. Hardly damaged was the "President" liner, but the RITA had suffered considerably, requiring among many other incidental items, repair of five starboard shell plates. That was not the ship's last travail during the first half of that year. On voyage from Boston and New York, a fire broke out in one of the holds of the PRESIDENT POLK on April 15, 1930. Extinguished after the ship's crew flooded the hold, the ship herself remained undamaged but both cotton and general goods stowed in the affected area were badly damaged.

At least the following voyage was uneventful, but that summer, while lying at Pier 42 at San Francisco on July 23, 1930, another fire erupted, this one in the ship's boiler room. Extinguished by 8:30 PM, damage was limited to No. 5 deep tank bulkhead, warping of channels over boilers, the buckling of some deck under a portion of her crew's quarters, slight damage to some electric leads and piping and the destruction of some ship's stores. Temporary repairs were made before the ship sailed from California on the following day, while permanent repairs were deferred until her arrival at New York at the completion of the liner's present trip. During 1930 Captain Lokstad relieved Captain Ross when vacation time came. Then Captain J.J. Cadogan took command of this Dollar Liner. He would remain with her for several years.

Following the PRESIDENT ADAMS in the sailing order at the time, the PRESIDENT POLK sailed from Kobe on November 6, 1931. From Marseilles, her final leg of the trip began with her December 23rd sailing and she docked at New York after another uneventful passage on January 4, 1932. Then came the usual Boston sidetrip followed on January 14th by her departure on her first trip of the year. Through the Panama Canal on January 22, 1932, the PRESIDENT POLK came into San Francisco on February 2nd and sailed on February 5th for the Far East. From Kobe on February 25th the liner continued on to her usual ports, sailing this time from Manila, for example, on March 7th. Then it was on to Singapore, Penang and Colombo. From there the ship deviated from her usual course towards the Gulf of Aden and made a course for Bombay. A recent addition to Dollar Line's round the world itinerary, the PRESIDENT POLK made her first twenty-four hour call there on March 24th. Sailing from Marseilles on April 13th for New York, the ship tied up at her Jersey City pier on April 26th. After her Boston side trip she returned to New York to sail out again on May 5th. With the PRESIDENT HARRISON and PRESIDENT HAYES taking June 1932 sailings from New York, the PRESIDENT POLK was half way around the world, working cargo at Kobe in mid June before sailing on June 17th for Shanghai. Two months later, on August 3rd the ship sailed from Marseilles for an August 15th arrival at New York. A late summer departure from New York is always something special for the days are long and though it can be quite warm during the day, nights are often very pleasant. Day is still long but the sun in late August slants in the late afternoon and early evening, casting a golden hue on a deep blue sea. Add a ship to those factors and you'll understand why so many who can do so choose to sail around Labor Day. The ship was well patronized when she departed from New York on August 25th on her following outbound voyage which continued from San Francisco with a September 16th departure. The ship spent the bulk of autumn in the Far East, sailing from Kobe on October 7th, Shanghai on October 11th and Penang on October 26th. Through the Suez Canal on November 15th the ship sailed further, departing Marseilles on November 23rd for New York. It was already cold there when she steamed back up past the Statue of Liberty on December 6th at the end of that trip. Sailing from New York on December 15, 1932 the PRESIDENT POLK and her passengers were in warm weather three days later. After a Havana call on December 19th it was on to Panama where the liner arrived at 6:20 AM on December 23rd. With her moderate cargo of 2,787 tons of general merchandise, the ship began her canal transit at 7:25 AM. By 3:50 PM she was through and soon tied up at Balboa. She cleared for sea at 9:00 PM and arrived at Los Angeles on New Year's Day, January 1, 1933. She continued her voyage with her January 6th sailing for Honolulu and Kobe.

On her second trip that year she sailed from Kobe on May 19th and from Singapore on June 6th. By June 26th the liner had reached Suez on her way into the Mediterranean and her last ports before heading home to the United States from Marseilles on July 5th. After a twelve day passage she reached New York on July 17th. As always before sailing away again on her outbound trip, the PRESIDENT POLK ran up to Boston to work cargo. Sailing from New York on Voyage 30 on July 27, 1933, the ship steamed south for Havana and an August 4th Panama Canal transit. In her holds were 3,368 tons of general cargo. On her August 18th sailing from San Francisco she had a new Master. Captain W.H. Weaver relieved the ships long serving Master, Captain J.J. Cadogan. Having had hardly any vacation time since he joined the ship in 1930, Captain Cadogan was certainly entitled to a rest. He was also due for a promotion. When he signed off the PRESIDENT POLK for his vacation he knew he would not be back, for after his sabbatical, he would take command of one of the "535"'s. Under Captain Weaver the PRESIDENT POLK continued her round the world voyage. Milestones along the way that time were the ship's August 8th sailing from Kobe, September 25th sailing from Singapore and September 22nd from Bombay. Through the Suez Canal on October 16/17, the PRESIDENT POLK sailed from Marseilles on October 25th. The ship made a somewhat quicker passage than usual, for she arrived at New York on Monday, November 6th instead of 10:00AM on Tuesday the 7th, the expected time of her arrival. Resuming the line's printed schedule on Thursday, the ship sailed at Noon for Boston. Back at New York on Monday, November 13th, the ship sailed out again on Voyage 31 on November 16th. When she made her way through the Panama Canal on November 24th, she took 3,806 tons of cargo with her. From San Francisco the ship continued her voyage on December 8th. Across the Pacific, she departed Kobe on December 29th for a January 1, 1934 arrival at Shanghai. Other sailing dates that time were January 6th from Hong Kong and January 16th from Singapore. On January 26th the ship departed Bombay for Suez and her February 5th transit into the Mediterranean. On February 14, 1934 the PRESIDENT POLK sailed from Marseilles on her way back to the United States. She pulled into New York on February 27th and sailed for Boston on March 1st. Back at New York after her overnight call at the New England port, the "502" docked at Jersey City at 8:00AM on March 5th to finish loading for Voyage 32. March 8, 1934 was sailing day for that trip. With 3,464 tons of general cargo the PRESIDENT POLK cut through the "big ditch" on March 16th. She continued her voyage, sailing from San Francisco on March 30th. Out from Kobe on April 23rd, she called her usual ports, sailing this time from Manila on April 30th, from Penang on May 10th and Colombo on May 14th. By then ports on the West Coast of the United States were paralyzed by strikers in the maritime industry, but the crew of the PRESIDENT POLK could not go out on strike while the ship was underway. In the Mediterranean the ship called Naples on June 2nd and reached Genoa on June 4th for an overnight call. Sailing on June 6th from Marseilles, the PRESIDENT POLK reached New York on June 19th. After her usual Boston side trip, the ship tied up again at Jersey City on June 25th. Sailing from New York on June 28th on Voyage 33, the PRESIDENT POLK had 4,679 tons of general cargo stowed in her holds. That was one of the heaviest cargoes any Dollar passenger liner had yet carried through the Canal. By the time the ship reached Los Angeles on July 15th, the port of San Francisco was still nearly fully shut down by strikers so like several of her fleetmates, the PRESIDENT POLK worked San Francisco cargo there. Instead of joining the ship in the city by the Bay, Dollar Line provided complimentary train tickets to Los Angeles and embarked passengers at San Pedro. The ship omitted her homeport and began her transPacific crossing from Los Angeles on July 20th. Her next port was Honolulu and the ship docked there after her 6:00AM arrival on the morning of July 27th. When the Big Strike ended with scarcely a whimper four days later on July 31st, the PRESIDENT POLK was in midocean, her clunky bows pointing towards Kobe, Japan, where she arrived on August 9th. Further dates for the ship's Voyage 33 included an August 28th sailing from Singapore and a September 7th sailing from Bombay. Ten days steaming was Suez and then calls at the Mediterranean ports of Port Said, Alexandria, Naples, Genoa and Marseilles. New York bound, the ship departed that last port on September 26th. As usual it took the ship thirteen days to complete the crossing to New York and on October 9, 1934, the steamer sailed up the Hudson to dock at Pier 9, Jersey City. There was some delay that time for the liner did not sail from Boston until October 16th. She arrived the following day. Instead of a three day hiatus before resuming her voyage, the ship remained overnight, so whatever cargo there was for her had to be worked quickly. Passengers boarded as scheduled and on time

The PRESIDENT POLK never looked lovelier than she did in this photo taken at San Francisco during another routine voyage around the world. While the ship lay at her pier crew tested their ship's lifesaving gear. Mike McGarvey photo.

before the PRESIDENT POLK sailed on Voyage 34 at 4:00PM on Thursday, October 18th.

Her propellors beating the water, the ship steamed south to Havana and through the sunny Caribbean to Panama where on October 26th the liner made her way through the "Big Ditch". After her Los Angeles call the PRESIDENT POLK arrived at San Francisco on November 6th. It was her first call there since March 27th. Right on time the liner cast off all lines and slipped away from her berth at Pier 42 at 4:00PM on Friday, November 9, 1934. Across the Pacific again the steamer sailed from Kobe on November 30th, from Singapore on December 18th and from Bombay on December 27th. After her ten day passage through the Indian Ocean and Red Sea the ship transited the Suez Canal on January 7, 1935. From Marseilles on January 16th the ship set her course for New York and a January 29th arrival. As usual she spent two days at her pier before sailing for Boston and the weekend side trip.

Voyage 35 was the ship's first outbound voyage of 1935 and on that trip the ship sailed from New York on February 7th. Eight days later she cut through the Canal on her way to California. At Colombo, Ceylon, on the evening of April 12, 1935 a lighter belonging to the Wharf Lighterage Company was loaded with 84,224 pounds of rubber for the American liner's roomy holds. Sitting in fresh water in Colombo Lake awaiting the PRESIDENT POLK's arrival, the lighter caught fire. Soon the rubber was afire, causing a real stinking mess. By the time firefighters extinguished the fire, some three fourths of the rubber was destroyed. The ship's next voyage around the world from New York on June 1st and San Francisco on June 31st brought her name again into the casualty lists. The ship also had another man in command. He was Captain Carl Hawkins, who came aboard in mid/ late 1935 and would long continue in the service of both Dollar Line and successor American President Lines. Five years later he was the first to command the brand new C3 P type combination passenger and cargo liner PRESIDENT JACKSON. Hardly a highlight of the career of the PRESIDENT POLK was her somewhat smashing July 19, 1935 arrival at Hong Kong. Docking as usual at Dollar Line's pier there, the liner hit the wharf sustaining some damage but not enough to delay her from her scheduled arrivals and departures. On the 30th of that month the ship departed Singapore for Colombo and Bombay, sailing from there on August 9th for Suez. From Marseilles on August 26th the PRESIDENT POLK continued her westward voyage for New York and Boston before beginning yet another circuit of the world from her Jersey City pier on September 20th. That time the voyage from San Francisco continued on October 11th. On that voyage the liner sailed from Hong Kong on November 9th, from Manila on November 12th and from Bombay on November 29th. Heading for home the PRESIDENT POLK sailed from Marseilles on December 18th. It turned out to be a rough, slow crossing. So slow was her passage that the ship ran short of fuel. In order to get some oil to make it back to New York, the PRESIDENT POLK made an unscheduled stop at Halifax, Nova Scotia. That call for fuel marked the first Dollar Line visit to that port in eight years. With enough fuel to continue, the ship left Halifax as the old year faded away.

Taking her first New York departure of the year the PRESIDENT POLK sailed from Pier 9, Jersey City, on January 9th. With a gratifyingly heavy cargo of 6,580 tons the ship made her transit through the Panama Canal on January 17th to make her scheduled departure from San Francisco on January 31st. That trip brought her to Japan and China in February, the Philippines, Malaya, Ceylon and India in March, and to Italy and France in April. From Marseilles on April 8th the liner sailed for New York and an April 21st arrival.

Exacerbating the animus against organized labor was a fairly successful effort to tar all union militants as "Communists". That theme, which later became tragically familiar, easily scared Americans, many of whom were convinced that lurking "Reds" everywhere stood (or crouched behind the hedges), ready to overthrow the American government, establish communism and imprison the American mind. Many naturally suspicious, Americans were taught to suspect that any woodwork might harbor these inhuman monsters, waiting for the moment to subvert and overtake us should our vigilance but momentarily waver. So it was that three hapless union men among the POLK's crew, members of the Sailors' Union of the Pacific, found themselves accused of mutiny and murder. Once at Naples, all three, Joseph Sedemo of San Francisco, John Millard and Benny Polanski of New York, were put ashore and charged with being "red agitators involved with marine engineers in San Francisco and Alameda." Adding another smear against them, the press reported that the "three reds repeatedly insulted passengers aboard the PRESIDENT POLK."[6] Fascist Italy had no truck with them and all three were returned to the ship at Genoa. Slapped into the brig, the men were put into irons and so bound, completed the voyage in captivity. Taking testimony from travelers that all three had repeatedly insulted passengers seemed to mollify the paying guests and keep them from asking many questions about men linked with murders of two marine engineers, one in Alameda, the other in San Francisco, where local papers introduced readers to the three sailors in an April 6th article called "Cruise in Terror of Reds". Now the Dollar Line "502" stayed only two days before sailing for Boston. Back at New York the ship sailed on her outbound voyage on May 1st. The 3,920 tons of general cargo that she took through the Panama Canal on May 8th was more typical in weight for one of these Dollar liners than the freight she had shipped last time she went through. May 23rd was sailing day from San Francisco and much of that voyage was spent in some very warm places during the height of the summer heat. Late June saw her in the Philippines, July saw her in both India and Egypt, and when she sailed from Marseilles on July 29th, it was midsummer. Then came the heat and humidity of sum-

---

[6] April 8, 1936 edition of the *San Francisco Call*.

mer in New York and Boston, where she worked cargo between her arrival and sailing from Boston on August 17th and her August 20, 1936 sailing from New York for the Pacific. After an August 28th transit of the Panama Canal the PRESIDENT POLK headed for a September 6th arrival at Los Angeles and a September 8th entrance at San Francisco. Outbound from her home port she sailed on September 11th for Hawaii and Japan. From Kobe she sailed on October 2nd for Shanghai and her other East Asian ports. From Bombay on October 31st the ship sailed for the Suez Canal and her November 9th transit into the Mediterranean. Back home at San Francisco the maritime industry was in the throes of a strike to rival the big one of 1934. For the time being the ship's crew remained on the job, unwilling to come up against charges of mutiny. From Genoa on the 18th the ship reached Marseilles later that day and for a change, overnighted there before sailing for New York on November 19, 1936. Across the Atlantic the PRESIDENT POLK arrived at New York on December 2nd. Listed in arrival columns "for Boston", the West Coast strike had grown so serious that Dollar ships ceased operations, and after tying up at Pier 9, Jersey City, the ship was idled for the duration of the strike. With a bleak monetary forecast in sight the PRESIDENT POLK resumed service after the strike with her February 27th departure for Boston to finish whatever cargo work she could not do when held at New York by the strike. The Boston loop completed with the ship's March 2nd return to Jersey City, the ship still had a couple of days to work cargo before sailing out on her voyage from New York on March 4, 1937. Through the Panama Canal on March 12th, she was at Los Angeles by the 21st on her way to a March 24th arrival at San Francisco. Back on a typical Dollar round the world schedule, she remained for three days and sailed at 5:00PM on Saturday, March 27th. After Honolulu on April 3rd the liner continued on her way to Japan and an April 16th arrival at Kobe. Then in turn the American liner called at Shanghai, Hong Kong, Manila and Singapore on her way to Penang, Colombo and Bombay. She arrived back at New York on June 15th and made her Boston trip between the 19th and 22nd of June. That was her final trip under the terms of the mail contract the Dollars had signed in 1928, for the new Maritime Commission had recently cancelled it along with all the others.

Worse than the labor tensions and the great strike of 1936/1937 was Dollar Line's financial condition. Once the walkout ended on February 5, 1937, the Dollar fleet began to resume suspended services, but don't lose sight of the line's further woes. Their already shaky financial stature had grown worse during the strike and was getting less tenable by the month. A Maritime Commission promise to cancel all extant mail contracts and substitute operating differential subsidies did nothing to foster faith in Dollar Line's recovery, for no other reason than a very open animosity towards the staunchly Republican management of the financially troubled steamship line. The Maritime Commission gave the Dollar Line little reason to expect any help after June 30, 1937, the effective date of the expiration of the mail contract.

A special arrangement between the Dollar Steamship Lines, Ltd., Inc. and the Maritime Commission was able to keep the PRESIDENT POLK in service and on schedule. On June 25th she sailed again from New York, five days before her mail subsidy ran out. Machinery made up a substantial part of the 3,497 tons of general cargo she carried with her through the Panama Canal on July 2nd. As an unsubsidized liner the PRESIDENT POLK took her scheduled sailing on July 17th. Calls that time included an August 7th sailing from Kobe and August 24th from Singapore. She sailed on September 22nd from Marseilles for New York. The around the world voyage completed, she made her next outbound departure from New York on October 17th. Arriving at San Pedro on November 2nd, authorities there ordered the immediate installation of an automatic fire detection system. With her cargo for Southern California offloaded by the afternoon of the 3rd, the ship sailed with local and San Francisco workers so the delay to the ship's schedule could be minimized. Remaining work was done while the ship lay at Pier 44 and was finished on November 9th. This time there were hints of federal financial help with the mandated system's $25,000.00 cost and Dollar Line refused all comment on expenditures. With her new equipment in place, the ship headed out to sea on November 10th.

The Maritime Commission had said it would help the Dollar Line stay afloat financially but the Dollars knew a different story and operated the sailing under their own sole economic responsibility. It was January 16, 1938 before Captain Carl Hawkins gave the order for his deck crew to cast off all lines at sailing time from Marseilles. After the Atlantic crossing the ship arrived at New York on January 29th.

That was as far as she got, for Dollar Steamship Lines' financial condition was too bad to allow her to continue further. In the company of her sister PRESIDENT GARFIELD at Pier 9 in Jersey City, a few miles away lay the old PRESIDENT FILLMORE, idle at Brooklyn's Clinton Drydock for the last five years. The PRESIDENT POLK remained idle at New York through her April 16th sailing for Boston. Returned to New York, the ship sailed out again on April 21st for Havana and Panama. With a cargo of 5,808 tons of general merchandise and automobiles, she made her way through the Canal on April 29th and arrived at Los Angeles on May 8th for a two night call. Then it was on to San Francisco where she arrived on May 11, 1938. Under an agreement between the Maritime Commission and the Dollar Line for emergency assistance to the Dollars, that trip was her first directly subsidized voyage. That voyage turned out to be her final one as a Dollar Liner.

Maybe it was a good thing that her owners had decided to comply with new fire safety rules. This ship which had suffered several fires in the past was destined to burn once again. After tying up the ship at Pier 42, San Francisco on May 11th, Captain Hawkins went ashore to visit his family. He had but two nights to enjoy his house, as sailing was scheduled for the afternoon of Friday the 13th. By Thursday night only 50 of her own crew remained aboard to see to the ship and her 6 sleeping passengers. Working cargo in hold No. 8 were twelve longshoreman at 3:50 AM on Friday, May 13, 1938, when a fire broke out in the lower hold and lower tweendecks of that hold. In the words of one San Francisco newspaper: "It began with a muffled blast below decks and a puff of acrid smoke." The longshoremen were nearly trapped below and were lucky to escape with their lives. The fire instantly spread, engulfing much of the ship in smoke, threatening her with serious damage. For a while it looked serious enough to menace the waterfront. A two alarm fire, twenty pieces of equipment arrived dockside to fight the blaze which burned for two and a half hours before coming under control, but not before it had damaged her Kobe-bound cargo of baled cotton, resin and tin plate in the amount of $100,000.00. Though the fire wasn't finally extinguished until 10:00 AM, the ship was but slightly damaged, a testimony of the skill of the 108 men fighting the fire. Despite the confusion on the after decks of the ship, unmindful of the water played into their ship by the fireboats DENNIS SULLIVAN and DAVID SCANNELL, some passengers slept through the dangerous excitement of fire aboard. One passenger, retired seventy-four year old banker James Imrie of London, England remarked: "I've crossed the Atlantic twenty-three times and this is my first experience of a fire aboard ship. And then I had to miss this. I was most surprised when I woke up this morning to find all the engines here." Awakened by the excitement, one passenger bound for Bombay to meet her husband, Mrs. Dagmar Bila, hurriedly dressed and ran to an open deck, ready to get off the ship at a moment's notice. Overcome by smoke, San Francisco fireman Jim Conlon was revived on the dock. Immediately repaired at a cost of only $1,200.00, the PRESIDENT POLK sailed on time on the 14th. Number 8 hold remained empty.

If ever there had been an auspicious time for a ship to suffer a minor fire, maybe May 1938 was it. With extensive rearrangements of her crew quarters and a general overhaul in the works, even as the fire raged, men were at work on the subject of the ship's most important renovation since her 1925 rebuilding after fire had almost destroyed her. Working on behalf of Dollar Steamship Lines, Ltd., Inc., the Maritime Commission sent out specifications for bids for the job to six major East Coast shipbuilding firms in mid March. Allowing just a short time to study the specifications and blueprints, the Maritime Commission noted that bids would be opened at 11:00 AM on March 25th. Using one set of plans to renew crew spaces in all seven sisters, one item stands out, if only because in light of the course of the past half century it seems something so elementary it should have been an original feature. Not until this spring 1938 refit did all of the ship's crew spaces have inside access to toilet and shower rooms. Many were the seamen of all departments who braved extremes of weather, wind, rain, snow and heavy seas to scamper over open deck while on their way to answer nature's calls or to bathe. The contract specified completion by noon on April 16th. That meant all conversion work covered by specifications, voyage repairs and two days of drydocking had to be finished by then or the yard would have to pay a penalty. Now came a flurry of letters and memos regarding the site where the bids would be opened. Trying to extend its influence, the young Maritime Commission wanted bids opened in their Washington office. The New York office struck most players as a more likely site but most logical of all was Dollar Line's New York office. Three of the six yards invited to bid for the job sent no bid. Bethlehem Shipbuilding Company, Maryland Shipbuilding Company and Newport News Shipbuilding & Drydock Company sat on the sidelines. In other circumstances, lack of interest from the three most important yards invited to bid might have raised eyebrows, but not this time. When none of those yards offered a bid, the Maritime Commission delayed a decision on awarding the contract until the morning of March 28th when they received a telegram from Dollar Line's San Francisco head office:

> NY representative advises award on POLK **MUST** be made 1:00 PM today
> to complete in contract time—else needs overtime at additional cost.[7]

There were three bids, all from leading New York area yards. Costliest of them was United Shipyard's $72,000.00 tender. Not much less was the asked $70,550.00 by the Atlantic Basin Iron Works. Much easier on the eyes of Dollar Line's accounting department was the $57,000.00 bid from Todd Shipyards. That brought Todd the lightly contested contract. Further information about the ship's actual condition soon leaked out. Most worrysome of all was the poor condition of the ship's starboard engine. The Maritime Commission did not really wonder why the Maryland and Virginia yards passed up the chance to win the contract. Time to perform the work was limited. Indeed, yards outside New York waters were handicapped by the need to get the work done faster than New York firms because the ship had a sailing schedule to meet. There was another reason supporting the lack of overriding interest in bidding for Dollar Line work. In a telegram to their Long Range Subsidy Committee, Houlihan & Wilcox of the office of the Director of Finance of the Maritime Commission explained:

> As mentioned in phone conversation do not see advisability bids being opened in Maritime Commission office NY for work on Dollar vessels. These ships are still being run by Dollar Line and there is no reason for the intervention of the Maritime Commission to the extent we have apparently assumed control already. We have informed Dollar Line officials they are still responsible for their own operations and repairs and the Maritime Commission will be glad to advise and assist.

---

[7]March 25, 1938 telegram from Dollar Steamship Lines, Inc., Ltd. to Maritime Commission Chairman Admiral Emory Land. Copy in the ship's 901 file in RG 178 at Maritime Commission.

Requests for bids for Dollar Line work to be done by New York handled by Dollar Line and bids opened in Dollar office with the understanding that Maritime Commission will advise and assist all possible. Please discuss this with Commissioners and have appropriate instructions issued.[8]

Based on their moderate bid, Todd Shipyards got the contract to alter the ship's crew accommodations, perform voyage repairs and drydock the PRESIDENT POLK. But the final dollar figure for the ship's visit to their yard far exceeded anything in the contract, as did the scope of work performed on the ship. Years of little and deferred maintenance while she rode the seas during the Depression had left their toll. Not until $110,282.71 was spent was the ship ready to return to take her next scheduled sailing. Of that total, the sum of $41,981.60 was spent to refit, reconfigure, recondition and rebuild crew quarters.

There was a voyage to complete and on that one, the liner cleared Kobe on June 2nd, Hong Kong on June 9th, Singapore on June 18th and Penang on June 21st. Back from her ports around the world, the PRESIDENT POLK returned to New York on August 3, 1938 where she ended her first subsidy voyage under the Maritime Commissions latest scheme. It was also the end of that round of voyages, for the Dollar Line was in collapse and the ship was once more indolent at New York.

At least some of the ship's passengers enjoyed themselves during that last Dollar Line trip. Welcome was the August 11, 1938 letter written on Department of State stationery to Glenn F. Weymueller, Dollar Line passenger agent at Washington. A respite from the usual grousing so often addressed to the company by former passengers and present crew, it's the kind of letter a passenger department lives for:

> I have for your acknowledgement your letter of August 5, 1938 concerning my recent voyage from Singapore to New York on the PRESIDENT POLK, having docked at New York on August 3, 1938.
>
> Mrs. Foote and I were so pleased with the trip that we unhesitatingly told Captain Hawkins that we were sorry it was ended. We went aboard at Singapore tired out after nearly four years in Java and we needed a rest and a change of food. There never was an uncomfortable moment and the food on the PRESIDENT POLK was better than any other I have ever had in my 32 years of sea-going experience. The Chef on the PRESIDENT POLK was a master and an artist; the Purser's staff was made up of fine, polite and helpful men and we cannot say enough about Captain Hawkins. I have never met a finer and more conscientious seaman, a more thorough gentleman and an all around good fellow who endeared himself to all the passengers. With more masters like Captain Hawkins the Dollar Line would never be lacking for passengers.

---

[8]March 25, 1938 telegram from the Office of the Director of Finance of the Maritime Commission to William Radner of the Long Range Subsidy Committee. Copy in ship's 901 file in RG 178 at the Maritime Administration.

It is a genuine pleasure to me to be able to write the above; and I certainly
would not do it if I did not mean it.[9]

Maybe it was but a crumb against a flood tide of criticism against the
Dollar Line and its operation, but that letter made its way right to the top.
President of the new American President Lines, Joseph Sheehan read the
original on August 23rd, and a copy was sent to Maritime Commission
Chairman Admiral Land.

When next heard of in the general press, it was for the demise of the
Dollar steamship empire. Technically that corporate name lived on through
October 31, 1938 to be superseded on November 1st by American President
Lines. It really didn't matter because the ships were idle. Like her San Francisco based fleetmates, the PRESIDENT POLK was taken into the fleet of the
successor firm American President Lines. In Delaware on November 21,
1938, the name of the registered owners of the ship was changed from the
Dollar Steamship Lines to American President Lines, Ltd. Further to that
end, the ship's marine document had to be surrendered for a new one, and
orders to that effect, Order C-494, were written during the autumn of 1938.
A new Certificate of Ownership was issued on November 22, 1938, but to
the consternation of both the Maritime Commission and American President
Lines, the new certificate listed the Dollar Steamship Lines, Ltd., Inc. as the
ship's owner.

The PRESIDENT POLK's next sailing from New York for the West Coast
had long been scheduled for December 30, 1938. Pursuant to preparations
for that departure, she went to the Morse Drydock Company for voyage
repairs as well as her annual inspection, survey and inventory. A December
20th cable from one of the Maritime Commission's lawyers to the Commission's New York office advised: "PRESIDENT POLK and PRESIDENT GAR-
FIELD in New York together. GARFIELD scheduled to sail 12/24 and POLK
on or before 12/30. Prepare documents change corporate owner to American
President Lines."[10]

Delays in preparing to get the PRESIDENT GARFIELD underway and
the PRESIDENT POLK's documents in order drew a December 22nd response to Bon Geaslin, Maritime Commission's General Counsel, New
York's District. Counsel William Collins wrote:

> I am informed that GARFIELD not to sail til 1/14 but POLK to go to Boston
> 12/24. GARFIELD will be done in time. As to POLK, I am informed that
> her annual inspection by Steamboat Inspection Service has not yet been
> completed, and that the Collector of Customs, in accordance with his usual
> practice as required by law, will not issue a new document until this has
> been done.

---

[9]August 11, 1938 letter from Walter A. Foote, U.S. Consular Service to Dollar Line passenger
agent in Washington, D.C. Copy in the ship's 901 file in RG 178 at Maritime Administration.
[10]Copy in the ship's 901 file in RG 178 at Maritime Administration.

It is at present contemplated, however, that that will be accomplished tomorrow, whereupon we shall attend to the necessary transactions at the Customs House in accordance with your letter.[11]

Things then moved pretty much according to the Commission's time-table. The new registry certificate was issued, as suggested, on December 23, 1938. Resulting from recent admeasurement at New York, her first since before she sailed from Newport News after her rebuilding in 1925, tonnage figures for the ship were modified. At 10,508.39 gross, 6,563.59 net and 8,805.21 tons capacity between deck above tonnage deck, the PRESIDENT POLK was registered at the Port of San Francisco. Further figures from her registry papers included the capacities of enclosures on upper deck. The forecastle was 48.75, bridge deck was 826.31 and the poop measured 104.90 gross tons.

Of great interest to both Maritime Commission and American President Lines were mortgages on the ships. A preferred mortgage on this one was reduced to $220,000.00 and its maturity extended to March 31, 1943.

As late as December 21, 1938 the PRESIDENT POLK had been carried on lay up lists. Quite some time in the works, her return to service was now at hand. Ending a period of almost five months of lay up, on December 24, 1938, the PRESIDENT POLK sailed from New York for Boston where she arrived on the following day. Because of the Christmas holiday no one worked any cargo that day and the ship only got away from Boston on December 27th, but that was enough time to get back to New York in order to sail on Voyage 45 as scheduled at 6:00PM on Friday, December 30th. That sailing is also noted on San Francisco's Marine Exchange cards as is a net tonnage of 6,309 net tons, somewhat at odds with latest figures but close enough for purposes of fees and tolls. Now, on January 7, 1939 carrying 7,490 tons of general cargo, one of the best totals of her career, the PRESIDENT POLK made her first transit of the Panama Canal as an American President Liner. Ten days later the ship showed her new colors at San Pedro and on January 18th arrived at San Francisco. Taking her first American President Lines' sailing from there, the PRESIDENT POLK departed on January 22, 1939 for her usual ports around the world. There was the usual Kobe call but none at Shanghai, for tensions between Japan and China suggested to American shipping officials that passenger ships stay clear whenever possible. On February 9th the PRESIDENT POLK made her first call at Yokohama, fifth of the "502"'s to call at that port so recently added to the round the world line. The ship sailed from Kobe on February 12th for Hong Kong, from whence she sailed on the 17th. March 6th saw the ship call at Colombo and sail that evening for Bombay. From Genoa on March 27th and Marseilles on the following day, the PRESIDENT POLK headed home. Arriving at New

---

[11]December 22, 1938 letter from District Counsel to Bon Geaslin. Copy in the ship's 901 file in RG 178 at Maritime Administration.

York on April 10, 1939 she completed her first round the world trip as an American President Liner. Next was Voyage 46 and her scheduled April 21st sailing. She got off a few hours late, sailing in the early hours of April 22nd. That's how it went for much of the voyage, with arrivals and departures varying by as much as two days from American President Line's sailing schedule #1, issued November 4, 1938. The ship was a day behind schedule when she went through the Panama Canal on April 30th with 4,491 tons of general freight in her holds, none of it consigned for points further west than San Francisco. Due into San Francisco on May 10th for a May 13th departure, that second APL voyage continued from San Francisco with her May 15th sailing. A Yokohama call was made that time, and she sailed from there on June 2nd for Hong Kong and Manila.

That spring a special report on labor conditions aboard the PRESIDENT POLK and PRESIDENT HAYES circulated among upper levels of both Maritime Commission and American President Lines. Relative to an April 14, 1939 visit to the ship before her sailing from New York for California at the start of APL voyage #2, Mr. Corriveau ascertained that cadets, who had already been serving aboard the ship for the past six months, were still obliged to do cleaning work despite Section 30 of the Regulations. Corriveau took up the matter with the Chief Officer who said something like this:

> . . . the hostility of the Unions to cadets—there was no work cadets could do in which union men would participate. When a cadet seeks information in splicing or other seaman's duties, crew attitude is to ignore or refuse aid. They even refuse to rig or tie up if cadets are present because they fear loss of overtime pay—so we keep them (cadets) on the bridge. What else is there for them to do? We know the cadets do not like this situation.[12]

By the time the ship headed into the Atlantic she was four days behind APL's initial timetable. That was not much of a problem. In the meanwhile later sailing schedules had been issued. Those correctly reflected the ship's schedule. Coming into New York at the end of round the world voyage 46 on August 5, 1939, the ship scraped heavily against her pier. Damaging both herself and shoreside structure more than slightly, the accident was blamed on her tugs and the Maritime Commission instructed American President Lines to have the insurance companies slug it out. On August 7th the ship sailed for Boston and returned to Pier 9, Jersey City on the 9th. Another round the world sailing was at hand. When the PRESIDENT POLK sailed on Voyage 47 from New York on August 11, 1939 no one suspected that she was sailing into a changing world. Though political tensions in Europe were high, cargo bookings for this "502" had been average and when she went through the Panama Canal on August 19th, she had 4,329 tons of general

---

[12]from documents in the ship's 1091 file in RG 178 at Maritime Administration.

Something of a publicity picture, this retouched photo of the PRESIDENT POLK is one of the few clearly showing a "502" wearing the white eagle of American President Lines. Author's collection.

cargo in her holds. Talk of war was in the air while the ship steamed north past the coasts of the Central American republics and Mexico. By the time of her August 28th arrival at Los Angeles everyone knew it was a question of when.

The Maritime Commission found that it had time for other than routine paper work regarding this ship, and on September 1, 1939, as German troops slammed into Poland, Philip King of the Maritime Commission ordered James Mullen of the Puget Sound Orient Line to fly from Seattle to San Francisco telling him: "Imperative inspect PRESIDENT POLK. Proceed to San Francisco next plane."[13] King knew what was up in Europe and the chance that the PRESIDENT POLK was about to assume an importance unheard of since her design as a troopship over twenty years earlier. Even though it was half a world away from California, outbreak of war in Europe put everyone on edge. Labor sensed a chance to hold up the shipping men for money and they were right. With the added risks occasioned by the outbreak of war, American seaman balked at serving their trade under existing pay scales. Walkouts delayed quite a few outbound ships in American ports, so it became imperative to mollify seamen with both emergency increases and war risk bonuses. Significant pay increases for the men of the PRESIDENT POLK meant that monthly pay increased from $55.00 for the lowest rated seamen to $72.50. Quartermasters pay was raised from a monthly stipend of $82.50 to an even $100.00 while in the Engine Department, wipers' earlier $60.00 monthly pay increased to $77.50 and oilers, whose wages equalled that of quartermasters, also received $17.50 a month

---

[13]Copy of telegram in ship's 1091 file in RG 178 at Maritime Administration.

more. Working for "private terms" were ship captains, but the pay of the Chief Engineer for instance jumped from $315.00 to $362.50, and that of the Chief Officer from $215.00 to $247.25.[14] Those raises kept the PRESIDENT POLK from further labor trouble for the moment. In from San Pedro the ship arrived at San Francisco on August 31. On the following day Germany invaded Poland and on the 3rd Britain and France declared war on Germany. Before sailing again, big American flags were painted on both sides of the ship's hull to warn belligerents of her neutral American nationality. With no further precautions, the PRESIDENT POLK steamed out of San Francisco Bay on September 4, 1939, the day after World War II began. Six days later the ship reached Honolulu on her way to Kobe where she arrived on September 25th. October 16th saw her at Colombo where every available bit of rubber was loaded into her holds for the voyage to the United States. As before the ship worked a two day call at Bombay and then made for Suez and an October 30th transit. European belligerency wrought another American neutrality Act, the so-called Pittman Act, the most far-reaching of the several neutrality Acts passed by America's isolationist Congress during the 1930's. The law's provision forbidding American merchant ships to call at harbors in belligerent countries came into effect around the time the ship would be heading into Marseilles, but the homebound "502" beat the cutoff date, and after her November 5th sailing from Genoa shifted to Marseilles before French ports went off limits to American ships that month. She sailed from there on November 8, 1939. In the coming months exceptions to the law were quietly made before many provisions of the law itself were overridden by new legislation called for by President Roosevelt, and Marseilles reappeared on the itinerary of the PRESIDENT POLK. But that was in the future and the liner steamed through the Mediterranean and past the British checkpoints at Gibraltar as she began her first war time crossing of the Atlantic. She reached New York without incident on November 21st. Still following the old Dollar Line sailing plan, she shifted up to Boston to work cargo before sailing out again from New York in early December.

If a war in Europe was too abstract for California in 1939, labor trouble was not and another waterfront walkup paralyzed most of San Francisco harbor late in 1939, forcing the outbound PRESIDENT POLK to once again bypass her home port. With a capacity passenger list and full holds, the PRESIDENT POLK sailed on Voyage 48 from Los Angeles on December 29, 1939. Among those aboard was William Tyrell, her Chief Officer and the man then reputed to be the most travelled man in the world. Already a veteran of forty complete circuits of the globe, this was his 41st time around, and as 1940 began, he had logged well over one million miles at sea. Asked by a local wag if perpetual motion around the world ever got dreary, Tyrell

---

[14]see appendices for Manning Authority & Wage Scale, Issue 33, September 9, 1941, a complete table of wages and increases.

answered: "Not at all. I look forward to each voyage as a new adventure, and I am never disappointed. There are always new and exciting experiences and new friends to be made. Going around the world is not like riding a merry-go-round, you know."

That time there was no Kobe call and the ship made Manila the center-piece of her calls in the Far East. By the time she reached the Mediterranean, the provision in the Pittman Act forbidding American ships to use belligerent ports had been breached and the PRESIDENT POLK was listed for Marseilles. First American ship to call there since the provisions of the Neutrality Act had gone into effect, the PRESIDENT POLK was scheduled to call there on February 28, 1940. In any event, she was late and called there on March 10th.

She continued on from there, heading back to New York and a March 24th arrival. Another voyage round the world voyage followed. On April 25, 1940, the PRESIDENT POLK was at San Francisco, preparing to sail again. Besides her Master, her crew then comprised four deck officers, 8 engine officers, 25 deck, 29 engine ratings, 3 radio officers, 6 pursers and 91 stewards for a total of 167 souls. With a full load of passengers the ship sailed for the Far East. While she was en route to Japan on May 10th, Italy declared war on the Allies. With all her Asian ports still ahead of her, the import of the closure of the Mediterranean to American shipping had no immediate impact other than proposing new courses be set up. The ship sailed on to Japan and sailed from Kobe on May 18th after an overnight call. With Italy at war the APL ships had to come home via the Cape of Good Hope, so when the PRESIDENT POLK sailed from Bombay on June 19, 1940, her Master ordered a course for Cape Town. Because of the way the American shipping business was then conducted, American President Lines sought and received permission to embark some 100 paying passengers from the two American flag lines then operating between the United States and South Africa. Well before the ship's July 4th arrival in South African waters, and both the American South African Line and Seas Shipping Company, trading as the Robin Line, telegraphed their consent. As the ship neared the South African coast a message regarding the amount of water a full ship would need was sent to American President Lines in San Francisco. That authorized a call for water at the Caribbean island of Trinidad.

Expecting to sail for New York on July 5th, the PRESIDENT POLK was detained by South African authorities who ordered ashore all rubber originally consigned to Italy. That spurred instant action from both American and Empire diplomats resulting in the ship's release the following day under the orders of the Minister of Commerce of the Union of South Africa. The ship's release was conditional, and based on the American promise that the USA would use its good offices to the end that neither the cargo of rubber nor the proceeds render any assistance to Italy during the war. With that rubber still aboard, the PRESIDENT POLK sailed from Cape Town on July

8th and arrived at New York on July 28, 1940. The rubber was offloaded at the ship's Jersey City pier.

Late August saw the ship nearing San Francisco. Before she sailed out again, most of her bedding in deck, engine and stewards' department cabins was replaced. On August 30, 1940 an item in the *"San Francisco Morning Call"* mentioned this "502" class vessel. "Two President Liners Sail Sunday." From Pier 46 the PRESIDENT POLK set off on another round the world trip—this one via South Africa instead of Suez and the Mediterranean— while on the same day, the one-time Baltimore Mail Liner CITY OF NEW-PORT NEWS sailed on charter to American President Lines from Pier 35 for Manila, Hong Kong, Singapore and Penang. Passenger lists for each ship, while not quite to capacity, were gratifying. Moreover, both ships had loaded quite a lot of cargo before sailing.

Paperwork to rename six of the seven "502"'s was in full swing on November 4, 1940, five days before the ship's second homeward departure from Cape Town. On the following day the Maritime Commission authorized surrender of the ship's marine documents, issuing Order C-771 that same day. In exchange for a new set of documents in the name PRESIDENT TAYLOR, her papers as PRESIDENT POLK were turned in to the Collector of Customs at the Port of New York at the Customs House on December 4, 1940. Atop the bridge, crewmembers removed the ship's old nameboard, replacing it with one bearing the ship's new name. "POLK" was removed from the ship's bows and stern, lifeboats and life rings and "TAYLOR" inscribed instead. After the PRESIDENT POLK arrived at New York at the conclusion of that trip, she was renamed PRESIDENT TAYLOR to allow her old name to go to the last of seven new C3 P type combination passenger and cargo ships then building at Newport News.

Her first trip as PRESIDENT TAYLOR was a special voyage, for it was also her 50th voyage since beginning service for Dollar Line in 1924. It was also her seventh voyage subsidized by the Maritime Commission. That trip began at New York with her sailing on December 13, 1940. On that trip she was ordered to skip her customary Shanghai call, off limits to American President Line passenger ships since October. After her Canal transit and New Year's Day call at Los Angeles, the PRESIDENT TAYLOR arrived at San Francisco on January 2, 1941. For her master, Captain W.S. Tyrell, the arrival was a special event, the completion of his forty-fourth complete trip round the world as an Officer and then as Master in the American Merchant Marine. Thus a gala event was the ship's January 5, 1941 departure from San Francisco, a sailing that marked the seventeenth anniversary of the sailing of the PRESIDENT HARRISON's first sailing on the round the world line. It was also another milestone for the PRESIDENT TAYLOR herself, as it was her fifty-first world trip.

Before sailing from New York again the ship underwent voyage repairs and was then inventoried and inspected at Pier 57, 8th Street Hoboken. She sailed for her second trip as PRESIDENT TAYLOR with her April 11, 1941 departure from New York. Arriving at San Francisco on April 29th, paperwork reported crew totals of 34 Deck, 38 Engine, 82 Stewards and 6 Pursers for a total of 160, of which 5 were Deck and 8 were Engine Officers. She sailed out again on May 3rd on her way around the world, on a voyage that brought her back to New York on July 30, 1941. At that time Navy officials ordered installation of defense features be carried out at the conclusion of the liner's following voyage.

After her Boston trip from New York between August 9th and 12th, this "502" took what proved to be her last peacetime sailing from New York on August 15, 1941. As before, she would be unsubsidized for the intercoastal portion of the run, but once she touched San Pedro, subsidies would kick in. The outbound from San Francisco would be operated not on Line B, the round the world line, but on Line A, the transPacific service. Coming in from New York, the PRESIDENT TAYLOR made her last civilian appearance on the West Coast with her September 1, 1941 arrival at Los Angeles and her subsequent stay, days later, at San Francisco. It was while the ship was on that trip that the Navy issued orders to American merchant ships to avoid Japanese and Japanese-controlled ports for the time being. Never mind that the ship had passengers for China, she would not go to Shanghai nor to Japan. Instead she steamed out of San Francisco on September 9th for Honolulu on her way to Manila and Hong Kong, where she turned around and began her trip back to the United States. While the PRESIDENT TAYLOR worked her way back to California, and a November 29, 1941 arrival at San Francisco, the Navy made overtures to the Maritime Commission about her possible acquisition. At the end of October, the various Naval Chiefs agreed to try to acquire the PRESIDENT TAYLOR for conversion to and employment as an evacuation transport. They had a long road ahead of them.

Taken over by the Los Angeles office of the Maritime Commission on November 24, 1941, the ship was technically delivered to the United States Government on December 6, 1941. She had sailed from San Francisco on December 1st for San Pedro. From the port of Los Angeles the PRESIDENT TAYLOR departed on December 4th for arrival on December 6th at San Francisco. With the Japanese attack on Pearl Harbor on December 7, 1941, the outbound sailing was postponed and the PRESIDENT TAYLOR passed under the control of the brand-new War Shipping Administration (actually the Maritime Commission in war paint) on a Voluntary charter basis and then allocated back to American President Lines under the terms of a July 1941 service agreement, WSA 224.

Aboard were 21,907 barrels of fuel and 300 tons of water. For recording purposes, that began the ship's WSA Voyage 1, owner's Voyage 55.

The Navy thought she would make a dandy evacuation transport. One thing this ship was not though, was fast, and because of her limited speed and several wooden deckhouses, the Maritime Commission could not agree that the ship was suited to such conversion. Regarding the Navy's plan to fit her as an evacuation transport, Maritime Commission Chairman Admiral Emory Land wrote to Chief of Naval Operations Admiral Harold Stark on December 8, 1941. Addressing his old friend as "Betty" probably his Annapolis plebe year nickname, Land said: "I do not see how at this time we can consistently agree to turn over the PRESIDENT TAYLOR to the Navy for conversion to evacuation transport with a full appreciation of the desirability from the Navy's standpoint of obtaining the vessel for such use, I am convinced that in consideration of all the factors at this juncture the priority of the overall picture points in other directions"[15].

By January 1, 1942 the Navy had passed over the PRESIDENT TAYLOR and she was delivered to the United States Army for their Quartermaster General's Army Transportation Service, Water Division. Bareboat charter was pegged at a daily rate of hire of $1,086.93.

The Navy did not give up all that easily so on April 11, 1942 Admiral Land wrote to Admiral Forrestal:

My dear Admiral,

In order to meet the demand for two transports fitted for evacuation of wounded it had been planned to acquire and convert the PRESIDENT TAYLOR and PRESIDENT MADISON.

Arrangements were made last October with Newport News for the PRESIDENT TAYLOR but conversion was withheld due to the urgent demand for employment of this vessel in other services. It now appears those demands continue.

It has recently been found by inspection that the material condition of the PRESIDENT MADISON will not justify the large expense of government funds required to convert these vessels into transports for the evacuation of wounded.

Under present conditions it is not deemed advisable to either tie up the conversion facilities ashore or the services of United States Army transports or passenger vessels for the long period to effect the conversion.

It is understood that the C2-S1-A1 transport vessels. namely the ALCOA COURIER, ALCOA CORSAIR and ALCOA CLIPPER now being built at the Moore Dry Dock Company will, upon completion have certain hospital accommodations which with very little conversion will make those vessels ideal for transports fitted for the evacuation of wounded.

It is therefore requested that two of these Alcoa C + P vessels be transferred to the Navy upon their completion.

Your immediate attention to this urgent request will be greatly appreciated.[16]

---

[15]Copy of the letter in the ship's 901 file in RG178 at Maritime Administration.
[16]Copy of letter is in ship's 901 file in RG 178 at Maritime Administration.

Approving of Admiral Land's proposal, Admiral Forrestal replied on April 21st. In relinquishing requests for the two "502"'s, the Navy accepted far superior tonnage, the ALCOA COURIER and ALCOA CORSAIR, then building to modified C2 hulls. Designed to employ standard C3 type machinery in place of the usual steam engines fitted in standard C2 ships, these Alcoa liners were designed to be fast and powerful ships, valuable items in the Navy's eyes. In short order they took the third sister, the ALCOA CRUISER, too, and entered them into service as the first and only specifically designated evacuation transports.

So the old "President" liner remained with the Army under contract WSA-113. Converted to accommodate up to 1,742 troops, the PRESIDENT TAYLOR had one of the briefest trooping careers of any American troopships. Her first wartime voyage, listed as both American President Lines' voyage number 55 and WSA voyage 1 began on December 7th, when workers began a hasty conversion for war service. Days later she began loading at San Francisco for Honolulu. She sailed from San Francisco under the command of Captain A.W. Aitken on December 27, 1941 for Hawaii where she arrived in her grey war dress on January 7, 1942. After landing her troops and other passengers there she turned around and made her way back to San Francisco, returning on January 24, 1942 to end her first wartime voyage that day. Owner's Voyage 56, WSA Voyage 2 began at San Francisco on January 25th. With a total of 1,334 souls aboard, she sailed from San Francisco on her second wartime sailing on January 31st, this time bound for the Philippines. She never completed that trip. Under Navy orders a ludicrous grounding at Canton Island on February 14, 1942 ended her career.[17]

Let Captain A. W. Aitken's March 17th, 1942 report to American President Lines Director of Operations, Mr. H. E. Frick tell the story:

The S.S. PRESIDENT TAYLOR arrived at Canton Island on Friday, Feb. 13, 1942 in convoy of the submarine destroyer U. S. S. 'PORTER'. On Feb.12th we had been warned of an enemy submarine 60 miles north of our course.

The only anchorage at Canton Island is on a 300 foot ledge at the mouth of the lagoon in approximately 7 fathoms. On coming to an anchorage on the prescribed bearings at 09–48 of the 13th, we commenced discharge of troops and deck cargo. On the flood tide the vessel swung in dangerously close to shore so we hove up and stood outside. A heavy swell prevented handling the only large lighter available while offshore, it therefore being impossible to discharge rapidly. The Island and all ships were blacked out.

---

[17]Now spelled Kanton and an atoll in the Phoenix Islands, now part of the Republic of Kiribati, American interest in Canton Island began during what Professor Jimmy Skaggs calls "the Great Guano Rush" of the 19th Century. At first called Mary Island by American mariners, it was renamed Canton Island. Much later it was developed as a staging area and for its potential for a serviceable airstrip. At first American activity was contested by Britain but the situation was soon resolved and the atoll came under joint Anglo-American administration prior to and during World War II.

At daylight of the 14th of February, being approximately eight miles offshore, we were severely reprimanded by Capt. H. E. Overesch, Squadron Commander of the Naval Task Force in charge of operations, who was aboard the U.S.S. 'PORTER', and were informed that our action in cruising offshore would not be tolerated.

I had on the previous day expressed myself to Capt. Overesch, upon his boarding the vessel at the anchorage, that while there, if we experienced a sharp change of wind on the flood tide, we would probably ground the ship In spite of using the engines to prevent this, I considered this vessel too large and with too much wind surface to be safe in such an anchorage. Captain Overesch assured me that it was necessary to take that chance or to lie not over 2000 yards offshore, as otherwise he could not give me adequate protection, and that if I did not do so we stood an excellent chance of losing the 1200 men still aboard and the ship by submarine action.

As the Island was blacked out and currents inshore set on to the beach, we could not lie in safety within 2000 yards, I therefore remained in the best anchorage we could find by careful soundings and bearings, and hold the ship in position until 18–20 of the 14th, when we experienced a quick change of wind in a sharp squall which, combined with the tidal currents, forced the ship aground, starboard side to, in spite of all engine efforts to prevent this.

We endeavored to pass a towline to the U.S.S. "PORTER", but due to rain, darkness, falling tide and heavy swell, that vessel was afraid to approach close to us. During the night the wind hauled to W.6 with heavy rain squalls forcing the vessel hard aground. It was impossible to contact the "PORTER" the following morning due to weather conditions.

I endeavored to inform our Honolulu Agent of the stranding but was refused permission by the Navy Department, Captain Overesch notifying the 14th Naval District and sending for salvage help.

In spite of bad weather, we disembarked all troops but a working party on Feb, 15th. On this date I obtained 3 heavy kedge anchors and wires, and with the ship's kedge had out four good kedges on the port side.

Lighten ship in any way until arrival of their salvage expert.

Lt. Comdr. Leb Curtis, Salvage Engineer, arrived on the afternoon of Feb. 16th from Pearl Harbor. The wind settled in from W of N. for ten days with accompanying long heavy W'ly swells caused by a hurricane moving south of us. No salvage operations could be commenced until Feb. 24th. Holds #3, #4, & #9 were filled with sea water to hold ship down and prevent pounding as far as possible.

Severe damage to the hull, engine and fire room was sustained during the heavy working of the ship on the bottom, we losing all steam on Feb. 28th. On this date we felt the effect of a mountainous sea and swell, the two after beach gear anchors having dragged home and the ship's stern swung further up the bank. Fire and Engine Room filled to sea level this date.

Salvage work was carried out from the Navy towboat 'SEMINOLE', she placing aboard us all gear used.

Great delay and handicap was exised after the heavy weather, moderated by frozen pumps, lack of towboats, lighters, diesel oil, electricity, and principally power. We obtained an additional air compressor from the Civilian Engineer Camp ashore which, with one from the 'SEMINOLE' has constituted our only power.

All perishable stores were removed as soon as possible, the bulk having been turned over to the Army ashore; some to the Naval vessels present and a quantity condemned. The only fuel oil available was pumped to the U.S. towboat 'SONOMA', this vessel having arrived at Canton Island on Feb. 27th. A total of approximately 2500 barrels was discharged into her.

On March 14th we sent 57 members of the crew, the bulk of the Stewards Department, to Honolulu on the M.V. 'JAPARA'. We had this number and 19 of the Engine Room crew ashore in an Army Camp from March 1st to 14th in order to relieve congestion aboard.

The crew now aboard, consisting of 110 men all told, is for the most part unnecessary and incompetent for advanced salvage operations. As the Navy has taken complete charge of operations, this crew will doubtless be returned as soon as transportation is available, to Honolulu.

Due to strict Naval censorship, I have not been able to communicate with you directly before this report, except for the original notification sent to the Commandant of the 14th Naval District at Pearl Harbor, who in turn, was to notify our Honolulu Agent.

To sum up, the grounding of the vessel was due to a hazard which we had to accept on account of war conditions. In peace times, such an anchorage would never have been used. The extreme, adverse heavy weather forcing the ship high on the beach prevented immediate effort at release, and the consequent very heavy damage to the entire vessel resulted from this.

The long drawn out attempt to float the ship was unsuccessful due to lack of sufficient salvage gear and salvage operators provided by the Navy Department, it being, under the working conditions, impossible to sufficiently lighten the ship.

The first attempt, actually 21 days of concentrated effort in fine weather, was finally given up on March 18th. On this date, Captain J.M. Steel, U.S.N., in charge of salvage operations, and Lt. Comdr, Leb Curtis, U.S.N., Salvage Engineer, radioed CINCUS at Pearl Harbor for additional equipment of salvage gear and personnel, or for other orders.

Capt. H.E. Overesch, U.S.N., assured me before his departure for Pearl Harbor on Feb. 28th, that he would be willing, at any time to testify that it his order and advice that sent us into the anchorage at Canton Island, and he so made his report to the Commander in Chief of Pacific Operations.

In event the vessel is eventually floated and brought to Pearl Harbor, the present estimated time for repairs is approximately four months. Lt. Comdr. Curtis now estimates a total of two months required here before a possible successful removal of the ship.

Due to censorship and Naval restrictions, no report has been made by me to date to our Insurance Department. A resume of apparent damage sustained, has been compiled by the Chief Engineer and is herewith enclosed.

We have at present secured the vessel as far as possible and again allowed her to fill up throughout all compartments to sea level, the ship lying flat on the bottom hard aground amidships with a 10 deg. port list.

We would appreciate receiving, at the earliest opportunity, any specific instructions that you may wish to pass along to us thru the Navy Department, and will keep you informed of developments as far as possible.[18]

The weather never let up and salvage efforts were abandoned on March 2nd. All aboard were rescued and some cargo was salvaged by the time the PRESIDENT TAYLOR was written off as American President Line's fourth war loss. The elements were cheated of their prize, for the wreck of the PRESIDENT TAYLOR was eventually destroyed by Japanese air attacks.

That's the short version of what happened. The WSA/Maritime Commission didn't give up so easily. Hoping to salvage the ship, they refused or neglected to declare the ship lost. By that time, American President Line's application to abandon the ship to the underwriters on June 26, 1942 was a mere formality. The Commission did, though, stonewall American President Lines' requests for payment, leading the line to write a letter in the most explicit terms to the San Francisco District Auditor, chiding him for his failure to pass on the Company's vouchers and effect payment on June and July hire. Reminding the District Auditor of the terms of WSA Contract 113 by quoting Article 3 of the pact, the charter of the PRESIDENT TAYLOR, APL Vice President Poole went on to say:

> The SS PRESIDENT TAYLOR has not been redelivered to the Company, nor has she been lost, nor has the War Shipping Administration declared her a constructive total loss as provided in Article 14 of the Contract. It is clear that the charter hire for that vessel has accrued to us through July 31st, the date through which vouchers have been submitted to you, and is still accruing. We request that the respective vouchers be forwarded promptly to the War Shipping Administration for payment as provided in the contract, and that you advise us of the date of the forwarding.[19]

The Matson "Sub Boat" MAKUA picked up 87 crewmembers of the PRESIDENT TAYLOR under Second Officer Robert Walton, at Canton Island on April 3, 1942. For carrying them to Honolulu where they disembarked after an eight day run on April 11th, Matson sent American President Lines a bill for 87 tickets reckoning First Class fares at $80.00 per man, for a total of $6,960.00. American President and Matson battled it out for months until the WSA could decide what should be done.

Authorities finally declared the ship lost some time later. After that mat-

---

[18]March 17, 1942 inter-office memo of Captain A.W. Aitken to American President Lines Director of Operations H.E. Frick. Copy in the ship's 901 file in RG178 at Maritime Administration.

[19]August 4, 1942 letter from APL Vicepresident Arthur B. Poole to Maritime Commission District Auditor Kenneth S. Patten. Copy in the ship's 901 file in RG 178 at Maritime Administration.

As PRESIDENT TAYLOR the former PRESIDENT POLK and GRANITE STATE is shown aground on Canton Island. Her wreck was scrapped on that lonely spot in 1954. Courtesy of Hawaii Maritime Center.

ter was finally settled, it was time to put a dollar value on the ship and begin working on getting paid for the lost vessel. Predicated on the bareboat charter agreement with the Maritime Commission, American President Lines put in a claim with the War Shipping Administration for the sum of $1,260,000.00 to cover the loss of their vessel from war risk. Assuming liability for deprivations of war, the Commission had earlier agreed to pay $1,260,906.00 in case of loss of the vessel. When the various government agencies involved made their recommendations to Congress, the amount requested for the PRESIDENT TAYLOR was found acceptable, particularly as her value had been assessed in terms of freighters. Seemingly her 31,320 cubic feet of refrigerated space were of greater value than her 136 passenger beds. The replacement cost of the ship was reckoned in December 1944 at between 4 and 5 million dollars. The War Shipping Administration agreed to pay the amount claimed. The ship was replaced of course, but not by a new passenger cargo vessel. After the war the PRESIDENT TAYLOR's place on the round the world line was taken by a C-3 type freighter with limited passenger accommodation. Long hopeful of her salvage, the hulk of the PRESI-

DENT TAYLOR was never really abandoned by the Maritime Commission. Title to the hulk passed to the new Maritime Administration in 1952. During the following year that agency actually got a positive response to its "as is, where is" offer of sale of the hulk of the PRESIDENT TAYLOR. The North Coast Corporation bought the wreck and began scrapping it on the spot during the winter of 1954.

The Centenial State/
President Adams:
President Grant

◇

At Camden, New Jersey, workers at the New York Shipbuilding Corporation continued the job of building ships for the Government as well as for their employer's own account during most of 1919. There was so much work to do that for several months after the thrill of the dual keel layings of two "502"'s on May 22, 1919, New York Ship could lay down no more of these important sisters until autumn. There just wasn't a slipway to spare. Never mind that a scrap of steel had yet to rise on a stock, the sixth intended "502" already had a provisional name. Mrs. Woodrow Wilson and her two cohorts had long since chosen the name IDAS for the Emergency Fleet Corporation's projected hull #2590. Assigning her hull number 249, New York Shipbuilding Corporation set the first keelplates of this ship onto slipway T at their Camden plant on October 1, 1919. Hardly six weeks later the Fleet Corporation discarded provisional names then intended for "502"'s and "535"'s and settled on a slate of nicknames of the states instead. The name IDAS was dropped and in honor of the state of Colorado this sixth "502" was assigned the name CENTENNIAL STATE. Work on her went smoothly enough at first and by January 1, 1920 the ship was deemed 15% complete. That was before the Shipping Board modified and altered plan after plan for this ship and her remaining sister, the eventual BLUE HEN STATE. Though scheduled for delivery in December 1920, the CENTENNIAL STATE was not even launched until December 11, 1920, her construction schedule a frequent unwitting victim of manpower and materiele shortages, delays of every kind, bureaucratic interferences and the thousand and one things that can plague any government project. Whatever glamour the launch of this project might have had was swamped on the very day when Mrs. D.S. Edmonds christened hull #249 CENTENNIAL STATE, for a couple hundred miles to the south at Newport News, Virginia, the Newport News Shipbuilding & Drydock Company was putting over the SILVER STATE, the second of their two larger and more impressive "535" class liners.

Where the CENTENNIAL STATE would go to work was a subject that began to truly occupy the minds of a good number of Shipping Board and steamship men as early as August 1920. It didn't matter that there were more than eight months to go before the ship was delivered, the Shipping Board was ready to hear pleas for her allocation. Rushing an application for her employment into the offices of the Division of Operations was the United

481

That's the CENTENNIAL STATE heading into the waters of the Delaware River at her launch on December 11, 1920. New York Shipbuilding Collection. Courtesy of Independence Seaport Museum Library.

Carried by her own momentum towards the Pennsylvania side of the river, tugs took the ship to the fitting out pier. New York Shipbuilding Collection. Courtesy of Independence Seaport Museum Library.

States Mail Steamship Company which plead the need of a third sister to the PANHANDLE STATE and OLD NORTH STATE in order to maintain a fortnightly service. Crusty and savvy, U.S. Mail's chief, Judge Mayer, knew he had the inside track on winning the award of this vessel because he knew he could rely on the Shipping Board's commitment to its policy of supporting the expansion of resident operators. Mayer, also variously referred to as "Colonel" Mayer, had plenty of friends in the Shipping Board and on August 14th one of them, Paul Foley, Director of Operations, sent Chairman Benson memorandum #331 supporting US Mail's request. Noting that assignment of the CENTENNIAL STATE would indeed interfere with the Board's tentative plans for allocation of these steamers to a projected new line, likely an intercoastal service, assignment of the CENTENNIAL STATE should nonetheless not unduly disrupt development of that idea, and another ship could be substituted. From the vantage point of the end of the century it may appear that perhaps Foley was sticking his neck out just a bit, but at the time US Mail was riding high, performing some of the few American flag transAtlantic passenger services, and arguably the only one not doing it with British partners. So in keeping with both the spirit of the times and the letters of the law Foley recommended speedy approval of U.S. Mail's request adding that the CENTENNIAL STATE need serve that company only until such time as "larger and better ex-German ships becomes available to displace them (the "502"s)."[1] A decision to assign the unfinished CENTENNIAL STATE was speedy. On August 18, 1920 Admiral Benson informed Captain Foley: "Answering your memorandum of the 14th instant re assignment of the ss CENTENNIAL STATE to the U.S. Mail Steamship Company:

> The assignment of this vessel to the above named company is approved. Before definitely notifying them of the assignment, a statement in writing should be obtained by you from the officials of that company advising them of the services in which the 15 vessels chartered by them are to be placed. This statement should show specifically the trade in which each particular vessel covered by the agreement already entered into is to be operated.
>
> The CENTENNIAL STATE, the PANHANDLE STATE and the OLD NORTH STATE can be assigned to them for operation in the trade routes prescribed by them as above. They should definitely state what trade routes these three new vessels are to be operated in, and it will be understood that these three vessels covered by the original agreement which have not as yet been turned over to them. Just as soon as the vessels to be operated in the trade routes on which these three vessels will be engaged, in whose places they are assigned, are turned over to that company and reconditioned and ready for service, the CENTENNIAL STATE, the PANHANDLE STATE and the OLD NORTH STATE will be recalled, if, in the opinion of the Board, this is advisable.

---

[1] Memorandum 331 August 14, 1920 from Captain Foley to Admiral Benson in the 1091 file for the ssPRESIDENT ADAMS in RG32 National Archives.

> Please have the U.S. Mail Steamship Company understand thoroughly
> that these vessels are turned over to them under the above conditions.[2]

Mayer had further "dibs" on a new "502", one that could not become apparent for many months. At the time of Foley's memorandum, everyone expected allocation of the CREOLE STATE to US Mail Line's London line. When the Division of Operations made a late in the day assignment to Pacific Mail within days of the ship's scheduled departure from New York for London, executives at U.S. Mail were thrown for a loop. That ship's maiden sailing had long been advertised and the line had already accepted bookings for it. Scrambling to get the PANHANDLE STATE to cover for the CREOLE STATE, U.S. Mail was soon mollified when the Shipping Board agreed to allocate a later "502" to them. Long since forgotten is another item, the fact that the Shipping Board really had not intended the "502"'s to serve long on the London line anyway and concerns about the viability of several of the "502" type steamers on the London Line led the Board to reconsider its planned assignment of both the incomplete CENTENNIAL STATE and the similarly unfinished BLUE HEN STATE. On October 5th the question of employment of the new passenger carriers came up at a meeting of the Board, but action was deferred until a later date. There was already talk of using the CENTENNIAL STATE and BLUE HEN STATE to the New York & Cuba Mail Steamship Company, also known as the Ward Line, for that company's triangular transAtlantic trade linking New York with Cuba, Mexico and Spain. Later that month the Manager of the Traffic Department then got busy and urged the Commissioners of the Board to make a decision about the ships, especially the CENTENNIAL STATE and BLUE HEN STATE. The reason for the rush to decide the future of the incomplete ships was simple: "These assignments will make it necessary to provide for steerage passengers, and in order to obtain the most satisfactory result in the arrangements of these quarters at minimum expense, modifications should be undertaken before the vessels are too far advanced on lines of original plans to have the necessary modifications effected while the ships are still in the builders' yards. This will save expense and avoid the necessity of making extensive interior changes."[3] Flaherty took up the matter with the Chairman's secretary on the following day. November 1920 saw a great many memos regarding the ships' future employment. Nothing anyone suggested brought any definitive action, not even the Shipping Board's November 30th meeting during which the planned assignment of the two ships to the Spanish trade was again discussed. A backer of the plan, Secretary John J. Flaherty did all he could to bring about definitive assignment of the pair of ships to the Ward Line. A mailman in downtown Philadelphia on December 1st brought Com-

---

[2]Memo from Adm. Benson to Capt. Foley in the 1091 file for the ssPRESIDENT ADAMS in RG32 in National Archives.

[3]Nov. 2, 1920 memo from Asst. Director of Operations W.B. Keene to Shipping Board Secretary John J. Flaherty in 1091 file for the ssPRESIDENT ADAMS in RG 32 National Archives.

mander R.D. Gatewood, Director of Construction and Repairs, the following letter from Secretary Flaherty:

> At a meeting on November 30, 1920, the Shipping Board considered the recommendation of Mr. Keene, contained in memorandum dated November 2, 1920, that the ss CENTENNIAL STATE and ss BLUE HEN STATE be assigned to the New York & Cuba Mail Steamship Company for service between New York and Spanish ports, and directed that the question of the proposed change of cargo space into steerage passenger accommodations be referred to you for report as to the estimated expenses that would be incurred by reason of making such changes. Will you kindly give this matter your early attention.[4]

Losing no more time Secretary Flaherty addressed Mr. Keene on the same date in a memorandum informing Keene of the letter to Commander Gatewood and asking the Assistant Director of Operations to let the Commander in on any new information that might affect the proposed changes in the ships' accommodation. When Flaherty next wrote about the presumptive allocation on December 7th, he replied to Keene's boss, the Director of Operations. From that letter we learn that the Director was also interested in the possibility of using the ships on the Spanish trade and had asked Flaherty about it by memo on November 30th, after the meeting of the Shipping Board Commissioners. Still awaiting Commander Gatewood's detailed response, Flaherty told him:

"As soon as this report is received the matter will again be presented to the Board for consideration, and you will be promptly informed of any action taken in the premises."[5] Gatewood decided that the ships could be altered in the builder's yard at reasonable cost. If that idea held, dropped would be the idea of their service for the United States Mail Steamship Company and the two youngest "502"s would go to work for Ward Line where expectations of thousands clamoring for third class passengers lit the eyes of all concerned with dollar signs. This time it was a busy New York Shipbuilding Corporation itself that would not oblige Commander Gatewood. Doing its best to scuttle any further changes in the outfitting of these last two "502"s and to get them out of the yard in order to allow the company to get on with other building projects, New York Ship put a hefty pricetag on the desired work, pegging the latest round of alterations at a price of about half a million dollars per ship. Questioned by Shipping Board personnel about the extortionate bid, shipyard officials were frank. Admitting the bid represented quite a lot of money, they explained a hefty chunk of that amount would be their compensation for altering their construction schedules again to install steerage spaces which had heretofore never been mentioned for these ships.

---

[4]Dec. 1, 1920 letter from Secretary Flaherty to Cmdr. Gatewood in 1091 file. RG 32 National Archives.

[5]December 7, 1920 memo from Flaherty to Director of Operations. 1091 file for ss PRESIDENT ADAMS in RG32 National Archives.

The yard just did not want the job for at very least, they hadn't the manpower to assign to the installation of any steerage spaces in these last two "502s". New York Ship's hesitant reception of this latest Shipping Board desire was one reason why the Board remained so sluggish on a decision on the question of definitive assignment for the CENTENNIAL STATE and BLUE HEN STATE. That was on John Flaherty's mind when he gave Chairman Benson the text of a telegram from Commander Gatewood on February 19, 1921:

> Referring your letter December First regarding proposed change cargo space into steerage passenger accommodations steamers CENTENNIAL STATE and BLUE HEN STATE and referring also Commissioner Teal's letter to me February seventh delay in submission estimates of cost due inability obtain from builders this estimate Stop Builders estimate finally obtained and considered grossly excessive probably because they do not desire work but prefer complete vessels in accordance original plans and get them away from their yard which is already overcrowded Stop Consider it essential before vessels can be Profitably operated by Cuba Mail Company to which understand they are tentatively assigned and consider it entirely possible to advertise this work on competitive bids to be proceeded with immediately upon delivery and obtain prices for it at a saving of at least one hundred fifty thousand dollars total under builders present estimate and without undue delay to vessels Stop Specifications for this now being prepared and the whole matter will be presented to the Board for approval Stop Please furnish copy this wire to Commissioner Teal and Captain Foley.[6]

Nothing seemed to move them to make an allocation. From his Philadelphia office in the building of the Emergency Fleet Corporation, Construction Manager Thomas D. Pitts wrote Shipping Board Secretary John Flaherty on April 2nd:

1. It is our understanding, from information obtained through the Division of Operations, that the Board has taken no final action relative to the assignment of the above vessels for operation.
2. The "Centennial State" is scheduled for delivery may lst, and the "Blue Hen State" June 15th. Construction has now progressed to the stage where it becomes necessary to know what colors are to be adopted in painting these vessels.
3. You will readily appreciate the fact that if these ships are painted in Shipping Board colors, as would be the procedure in the absence of an assignment, and then later be assigned to a private company, that such company will no doubt desire the vessels painted in their colors, which would involve considerable expense, whereas if an assignment is made now this could be obviated.
4. Will you kindly bring, this matter to the attention of the board, with the

---

[6]February 19, 1921 telegram from Commander Gatewood to John J. Flaherty as presented by memo to Chairman Benson in the 1091 file for ssCENTENNIAL STATE in RG32 National Archives.

view to obtaining if possible the assignment of these ships to an operating management.[7]

Like most others in the Board's hierarchy Chairman W.S. Benson then seemed more interested in the prospect of saving a few dollars on paint than on who would actually run these ships, answering Pitts on April 5, 1921 with another memorandum on the Ward Line idea:

> Answering your memorandum of April 2nd re steamships CENTENNIAL STATE and BLUE HEN STATE:
>
>   There has been no tentative or definite allocation or assignment of these two steamers to any particular trade or shipping company. The Division of Operations has recommended that the vessels be fitted for carrying steerage passengers and be turned over to the New York and Cuba Steamship Company for operation between New York, Spanish Ports and Cuba. I understand the Construction Division is preparing estimates covering the cost of fitting these two steamers with steerage accommodations, and that such estimates will be submitted within a short time In view of the fact that nothing definite has been decided as to the allocation or assignment of these two vessels, you are directed to have them painted a Shipping Board color.[8]

Yet at Camden, workers continued to bring the pair nearer to completion, bringing them closer to delivery with every passing day. Now, as those dates neared, the subject of color schemes continued to occupy men's minds and this time the New York Shipbuilding Company called for instructions, asking for orders to paint the CENTENNIAL STATE and BLUE HEN STATE as well as the larger "535" type sisters then nearing completion, the SEA GIRT (soon to be renamed SOUTHERN CROSS) and AMERICAN LEGION. Construction and Repair Division Thomas Pitts finally got some action from Washington. In an April 4, 1921 memorandum signed by John J. Jones, the Shipping Board at least answered the question of livery. In reference to the sister "502"s he said:

> The CENTENNIAL STATE and BLUE HEN STATE were recommended by the Division of Operations to be assigned to the Ward Line, but no tentative or permanent allocation thereof has yet been made. This recommendation for the assignment of these vessels was subject to their being equipped to handle steerage passengers. . . . As the CENTENNIAL STATE and the BLUE HEN STATE have not been tentatively or permanently assigned to any company, it would appear that these ships should be painted a standard Shipping Board color.[9]

---

[7]April 2, 1921 memo from Pitts to Flaherty in 1091 file for ssCENTENNIAL STATE in RG 32 National Archives.

[8]April 5, 1921 memo from Admiral W.S. Benson to Mr. Pitts in 1091 file for ssCENTENNIAL STATE in RG32 National Archives.

[9]April 4, 1921 memos from Jones to Pitts and to New York Shipbuilding Company in the 1091 file for the ssCENTENNIAL STATE in RG32 in National Archives.

The CENTENNIAL STATE spent the winter of 1921 fitting out at Camden. Beyond her is the "535" type steamer LONE STAR STATE, then completing for allocation to Pacific Mail Steamship Company. New York Shipbuilding Collection. Courtesy of Independence Seaport Museum Library.

Beyond a hesitant Shipping Board there were a couple of other factors holding up definite assignment of the two "502"s. One was the worldwide shipping slump of 1920. By 1921 the downturn in freight offerings had become a Depression severe enough to occasion the lay up of over 900 Shipping Board steamers. Relative to the trade depression was the end of Spain's war related economic boom. Neutral at war, Spain had enjoyed a flowering of trade and economic influence not seen since the loss of her American empire almost a hundred years earlier. Spanish steamship companies, which had flocked to American trades during the war withdrew to waters nearer home until only the biggest firms remained in the transAtlantic trade. Soto Aznar and Compañía Trasatlántica rode out the financial storm. Against them operated many other steamship companies of several nations, all competing for an ever dwindling trade. Among them were a number of American firms working to or via Spanish ports with varying degrees of success. One of those whose results made withdrawal from the Spanish trade a good move was the New York and Cuba Mail Steamship Company. Even at that, it was a complex parcel of protectionist Spanish tax laws that forced Ward Line's hand. Otherwise hungry for Shipping Board tonnage, and eventual operator of a hundred or so Emergency Fleet Corporation steamers on any number of routes between 1917 and 1922, the company probably wanted to operate the two new prestigious ships but found no other line they then handled could gainfully employ them. Labor unrest in the maritime industry occupied the Shipping Board as did ever reddening figures in voyage reports on almost every Shipping Board route. The future of the two ships needed less attention than other matters. Assignment could wait until the ships were finished. Experience had showed the Board that preliminary allocations had often been superseded upon delivery of a ship. The assignment of these two ships could wait a while longer and maybe the players themselves would allow matters to sort themselves out. For the CENTENNIAL STATE, matters did and did not do that. Towards the third week of April the Shipping Board apparently decided to assign both the CENTENNIAL STATE and BLUE HEN STATE to the London Line and withdraw the older pair, PANHANDLE STATE and OLD NORTH STATE. All four would need to have steerage spaces fitted so it struck the Board to do this. Assign the new ships to London service. They could begin work once a Third Class was installed. First to enter service would be the CENTENNIAL STATE. She would take not only the place of the PANHANDLE STATE, she would take that ship's crew as well. Replacing the OLD NORTH STATE, the BLUE HEN STATE would take her sister's crew. Then that pair would go to have steerage installed. That is what the Board thought should happen. They did not expect New York and Cuba Mail's precipitous decision to abandon the triangular transAtlantic trade.

No matter the latest and continuing developments, the CENTENNIAL STATE, and the last of the "502"s, the BLUE HEN STATE, were painted in Shipping Board colors when they ran their trials. The CENTENNIAL STATE was so painted when she was shifted to the Philadelphia Navy Yard for installation of her wireless apparatus on April 20th. On the following morning, April 21st, the spanking new CENTENNIAL STATE steamed out into the Delaware and out to sea to show her stuff to her builders and to officialdom of the Emergency Fleet Corporation and the Shipping Board. She performed well enough on her trials to be accepted without any further modifications by New York Shipbuilding Corporation and the new ship was delivered to the Shipping Board on April 23, 1921. Built at a cost of $4,231,534.19, (or, without her passenger fittings and steerage accommodations, $4,088,466.49), her measurements differed slightly from those of her older sisters. Gross tonnage for this ship was 10,558 tons, net was 6,200 tons and the liner displaced 13,000 tons.

New York Shipbuilding Corporation fitted the new ship with accommodations for 78 First Class passengers. But the newest of the "502"'s left her builder's yards at Camden with as many steerage berths as had the other members of the class—NONE. She could well have begun commercial service on the London line without such accommodations but the Shipping Board refused to approve a voyage without the ability to carry Third Class, so her maiden departure had to wait. Nor did the question of "502" ships for allocation to Ward Line go away, and it died a very slow death. As April drew to a close the Shipping Board still thought to send two of those sister ships to work for the New York and Cuba Mail Steamship Company. An April 26th memo from Commander Gatewood to the Chairman's special assistant R.H. Bailey proves it:

> With reference to your memorandum of April 23rd, you are advised that it has been decided to install steerage quarters in the CENTENNIAL STATE and BLUE HEN STATE, and these vessels have been allocated to the U.S. Mail Steamship Co. in place of the OLD NORTH STATE and PANHANDLE STATE, which latter vessels are to be assigned to the Ward Line? In pen he added "Specifications are out and work will proceed soon."[10]

Even at that, definitive assignment to the United States Mail Steamship Company was not made final until May 21, 1921 when the new CENTENNIAL STATE, registered to the United States Shipping Board Emergency Fleet Corporation at Philadelphia, was allocated to the U.S. Mail Line. Before the CENTENNIAL STATE was delivered to U.S. Mail Line in June 1921 she was sent to the Robin's Drydock Company's Brooklyn shipyards where Third Class passenger spaces for about 150 passengers were fitted at a contract cost of $128,000.00. Beyond a dining room, Third Class was given a small smoking room and an equally small Lounge. Her arrival at the yard was something of a spectacle. Entering Erie Basin on May 7th under the control of seven Moran Towing Company tugs, no one was in the liner's

---

[10]April 26, 1921 memo from Commander R.D. Gatewood to R.H. Bailey in 1091 file for the ssCENTENNIAL STATE in RG 32 National Archives.

engine room. The tide at ebb, it was a calm, clear noon. Before anyone could do anything about it, the ship started for the concrete breakwater and hit it, denting several plates on the starboard side opposite No. 2 hatch. Damage repairs added to the cost of this repair contract and the Shipping Board looked to Moran to make good on the difference.

One facet of the Shipping Board's old "502" swap did go through. Under the command of Captain J. Pendlebury, the CENTENNIAL STATE entered service with an experienced crew, most of them veterans of the PANHAN-DLE STATE. The Board made that move under hazard of protest, and it came this time from Nellie Bly, now President of the American Seaman's Association. She stirred the cauldron while the ship was on her maiden voyage by writing Shipping Board Chairman Albert Lasker on June 29th: "Every one of these men were British from the mate down."[11] Such an exaggeration it was laughable, Lasker suggested the ship was very heavily manned by Americans and directed her to copies of the ship's articles. It turns out that neither correspondent stood on very firm ground as the ship's articles showed more than a dozen nationalities. All nine officers were United States citizens, six born in the country, the other three naturalized. Of the 148 un-licensed personnel of the CENTENNIAL STATE, forty-four were native born U.S. citizens and nineteen were naturalized U.S. citizens. The remainder comprised sixty British subjects, one Norwegian, two Swedes, two Danes, two Spaniards, six Russians, three Italians, one Dutch, one German, one French and one Central American. Five others were listed as of "other" na-tionality, presumably Hong Kong Chinese laundrymen.[12]

Shortly after they delivered the CENTENNIAL STATE to the United States Mail Steamship Company for service on the London passenger and cargo service, the Shipping Board awarded the Line an MO-4 operating agreement to cover her operation. Hoping to attract passengers to her Third Class accommodations, this ship would feature calls at Queenstown (later Cobh) Ireland in both directions, so to fit her into a schedule with her sisters, for now at least there would be no calls at French ports. Flying US Mail's houseflag and sporting the Shipping Board's shield on her tall funnel, the CENTENNIAL STATE began her first voyage at New York when she began loading the first of her outward freight on June 24th, the day her sister PAN-HANDLE STATE came in from London on Voyage 8. They would meet at New York a few more times over the following months for the PANHAN-DLE STATE was summarily withdrawn and in the waning days of summer went for the installation of Third Class passenger accommodations. Placing great faith in profits from the transport of migrants, the Shipping Board hoped for good results with the newer CENTENNIAL STATE and watched

---

[11]Quoted in Chairman Lasker's reply July 6, 1921 in 1091R file for the ssCENTENNIAL STATE in RG 32 National Archives.
[12]August 5, 1921 list provided to Chairman Lasker by Nellie Bly in 1091 files for ssCENTENNIAL STATE in RG 32 National Archives.

carefully as the ship sailed on Voyage 1, for London with 84 First and 12 Third Class passengers on June 28, 1921. Following an arcane Shipping Board practice, that inaugural trip was listed as Voyage 50. Calling Queenstown and Plymouth on July 7th, the CENTENNIAL STATE arrived at London on the 8th. The ship worked cargo at her British terminal and sailed for home on July 14th. Two days later America's newest liner called at Queenstown but few Irish were aboard when the ship sailed for New York. At the end of her westbound crossing the CENTENNIAL STATE came into New York on July 24th with 50 First Class passengers. Her travelers landed and her light inward freight ashore, Voyage 1 ended at New York on July 27, 1921.

Voyage 2, or Shipping Board Voyage 51 began at New York on July 28th. During her last night in the port of New York, 23 men were employed aboard, ten had been assigned to do nothing more than guard the wine-room! The oft-visited subject of Prohibition had yet to be finally settled and when it was soon thereafter, American ships had to run "dry". With cargo, mail and 40 passengers in First Class and 23 in Third Class, the CENTEN-NIAL STATE sailed for London again on July 30, 1921. A stop off the roads at Boulogne to land or embark passengers was on both her eastbound and westbound itinerary that time which would also be her last crossing under the operation of the United States Mail Steamship Company. Inbound to London the liner called at Plymouth on August 8th and Boulogne on August 9th. Making a quick Channel crossing the ship sailed up the Thames to dock at London later that same day. With the collapse of United States Mail Line the CENTENNIAL STATE was momentarily stranded while the Shipping Board figured out its next move in the struggle against a defiant United States Mail Line. The ship sailed from London on August 15th for Boulogne, where she stopped that evening and Queenstown on August 17th where she boarded additional passengers on the following day before setting a course for New York. She tied up on time on August 25th.

The Commissioners of the Shipping Board paid special attention to the success of the Third Class fitted in this ship. The only "502" on the Atlantic so far able to carry steerage passengers, westbound calls at Ireland were scheduled in order to allow the CENTENNIAL STATE to take advantage of the demand for steerage passage to America. Admittedly experimental, both Shipping Board and operator could determine the viability of these new steamers in the Irish emigrant trade. An undated, unattributed clipping in the files of the Shipping Board tells a story:

ss CENTENNIAL STATE AT COVE

The successful inauguration on Monday last of the call for passengers at Cove by the S.S. AMERICA, of the United States Mail Steamship Company, Inc., was quickly followed by the coming of another ship of that enterprising line, the S.S. CENTENNIAL STATE, to Cork Harbour on Saturday morning to embark passengers for New York.

It is palpable evidence of the fixed determination of that company to carry out their expressed intention to seriously enter into competition with the existing liners that make Cove a port of call for whatever there is of Transatlantic passenger traffic to be picked up at the well-known Southern Irish port.

It is not suggested that the CENTENNIAL STATE is in all respects equal to the SS AMERICA, but she is undoubtedly a ship which will gain much favour amongst the class of passengers whose needs she is intended to cater for, and will, when the passenger traffic to the United States begins to flow normally, there is reason to believe, be extended a large share of patronage by Irish travellers.

The CENTENNIAL STATE has also been adapted to carry cargo, and, no doubt, when the move now being developed has progressed somewhat, she will get her share of Irish produce at the Cove Deepwater Quay, now, thanks to the initiative of the U. S. Navy during the war, well equipped for dealing with such traffic.

At one time there were no less than six lines of passenger steamers using Cove as a port of call, and there is no reason for assuming that three cannot do a paying trade by calling at that port in the future, when the country's affairs have righted themselves and eastbound as well as westbound ships are free to enter the Cove of Cork.[13]

The end of the feisty United States Mail Steamship Company was at hand and the ship was on her way home from London when the line collapsed. While receivers began examining the company's books, the new ship returned to New York and docked at Pier 74, North River with 45 passengers in First Class and 26 in Third Class on August 25th. The end of US Mail mattered almost not at all to ship and crew, for the new United States Lines immediately stepped in to replace the fallen firm. Nearly all marine personnel employed aboard the ship remained and the new operators went so far as to accept their defunct predecessor's passage tickets. The only discernable difference was the loss of the Shipping Board shields from former US Mail steamers's funnels. That device was ordered removed by the Shipping Board as a means to distance ships and Shipping Board from the failed Line.

US Mail Line was now out of business, but the possibility of filling the "502"s on the London line with America-bound Irish immigrants acted on the Shipping Board like a drug. After the ship returned from her second voyage she went into the Brooklyn yards of the Morse Dry Dock Company where several more tweendeck compartments were quickly given over to steerage accommodations. By the time that yard redelivered the vessel, they had increased her Third Class capacity to 596. The timing of the project could hardly have been worse, for that same year the first new immigration quotas came into effect to put quite a damper on a once unchecked immigration into the United States. But for new American quota rules there might well have been a steady stream of willing Irish passengers to fill many ships' steerage spaces on westbound crossings. The deleterious effect of such pro-

---

[13]1091 file for ssCENTENNIAL STATE in RG32 National Archives.

tectionist legislation on North Atlantic steamers is too well known to delve further into it here. Suffice it to say that the Third Class on the CENTENNIAL STATE was little patronized in either direction and lead to great hesitation about fitting such spaces in sister ships running on the North Atlantic.

Service on the London line was uninterrupted by the change in management and new United States Lines also retained the old United States Mail Lines' schedule of sailings for the London service. Going to work for her new operators, the CENTENNIAL STATE sailed again from New York on September 6th. Now there was no eastbound call in Ireland. The CENTENNIAL STATE would only call at Queenstown westbound. Via Plymouth on September 15th she pulled into London on the 16th. Turning around there after an six day call the ship sailed on September 22nd for New York. On that third voyage the CENTENNIAL STATE was better booked than on her earlier sailings. Landing at New York after her October 2nd arrival were 95 First and 50 Third Class passengers, her highest totals so far.

Four more Atlantic sailings remained for the CENTENNIAL STATE to operate before the end of 1921. On the first of those the ship departed New York on October 11th to arrive at London on October 22nd. Her next outbound departure from New York took her out past the Statue of Liberty on November 14th. Across the Atlantic she arrived at London on November 25th. Five days later on November 30th the ship sailed for Boulogne. On December 2nd the liner called at Queenstown to embark passengers for New York where she arrived on December 10th. A few days later the ship sailed out again on her sixth crossing to London.

On her last few eastbound sailings that year passenger totals continued to disappoint. On no sailing that season did the vessel depart New York with more than 27 First Class passengers eastbound. Blame her low bookings on sailing dates more than on anything else. A preference for any particular member of the class could not yet account for any sister's better or lesser passenger numbers. One source listed 1921 totals for this ship, whose average transatlantic speed was listed at 14.09 knots, at 431 passengers. Of great concern to the Shipping Board was the percentage of Americans in her crew and in November statistics were provided through the courtesy of United States Lines. Over the course of her September-October 1921 Voyage 4, the ship counted 36 Americans and 5 aliens in the deck department and 35 Americans and 1 alien in the Engine Department, but the overwhelming national character of the crew was lessened in the Steward's Department, which numbered 35 Americans and 23 aliens among its personnel. In terms of percentages, Americans were 88% of the Deck, 97% of the Engine and 60% of the Steward's Department, or a total of 78% of the entire 134 man crew. At the end of that voyage the CENTENNIAL STATE went into the yards for installation of additional berths in her Third Class. When the ship departed from New York on Voyage 5 on November 14, 1921, 82.7% of the 127 man crew were American citizens.

On Voyage 6, the CENTENNIAL STATE sailed from New York on December 14th. Her schedule brought her into Queenstown and Plymouth in time for disembarking passengers to spend Christmas in Britain. Because of the holiday the ship did not tie up at her London pier until Boxing Day, December 26th. Homeward bound for New York she sailed on December 30, calling at Boulogne in the early hours of the 31st, so the ship was at sea when calendar year 1922 began. She arrived at New York on January 7, 1922. During that year she carried a total of 1958 westbound passengers. Voyage 7 was her first outbound sailing that year and on the eastbound leg she sailed for Queenstown on January 17th. After completing her usual itinerary she arrived at London on January 28th. This time her stay lasted only three days and she departed for home on January 31st. After calling at her usual westbound ports the CENTENNIAL STATE completed her voyage at New York on February 17, 1922. There was no lay up for her that winter and she kept working all season. By March 23rd she completed Voyage 8, her second voyage of the year. Then Shipping Board accountants began poring over her latest dollar figures.

Before sailing again the liner was held at New York long enough to permit her First Class accommodation to be downgraded into Cabin Class, a job that was accomplished in under four days in time for the CENTENNIAL STATE to sail on March 28, 1922 for London. On that first crossing as a Cabin liner she took out only 81 passengers, 49 in Cabin and 32 in Third Class. On that voyage, 73 adult, 7 child and 1 infant fare brought in $9,143.10. Cargo offerings weren't very gratifying either. The ship took out only 1,449 tons of general cargo. It was mail that earned the real revenue that time. Before sailing the ship had loaded 3,497 sacks of mail for Britain and Europe. With revenues of just over $41,000.00, the ship posted another hefty deficit. Only her homeward Atlantic crossing from London beginning on April 13th remained for the ship to operate as CENTENNIAL STATE before she became PRESIDENT ADAMS on April 27th three days after her arrival at New York. As with her renamed sisters, her registry was transferred from Philadelphia to New York. She sailed out on her first trip, voyage 10, under her "President" name on April 29th. That journey called for a May 16th departure from London and she was back at her New York pier again on May 27th.

The high season of heavy eastbound passenger movement was just beginning and to capitalize on her Third Class and the Queenstown call, United States Lines added an outbound Boston call to make it even more convenient for Irish-Americans living there to get back to Ireland for a summer visit with relatives and friends across the sea. That decision had a lot to do with an earlier one to further increase the ship's Third Class passenger capacity. Only the timing, at the start of the summer rush, was odd. At a time when the ship could best have been employed at sea, she spent 18 days at New York and did not sail for Ireland and Britain on Voyage 11 until June 14th. She called at Boston on the following day and arrived at Queenstown on June 24th. On the next day she stopped at Plymouth and Cherbourg and arrived at London on June 26th. After a typical six day call the ship cast off her lines on July 2nd and sailed for New York where she arrived to complete her voyage on July 11th.

Schedules were not quite as rigid as they would become nor was the world in the hurry that ours seems to revel in. Between arrival on Voyage 11 and her departure on Voyage 12 the PRESIDENT ADAMS remained in port for eight days. She sailed again on July 19th. Two days later her wireless reported her in a position 661 miles east of Ambrose Light. From London she sailed on August 5th on her homeward trip and arrived at New York ten days later on the 15th.

Now the reverse migrations of Americans in Europe was on and the ship was not full when she sailed from New York on Voyage 13 on August 23rd for a September 2nd arrival at London. But she was booked nearly to capacity for the westbound trip. She sailed from London on September 9, 1922 to arrive back at New York on the 19th with 137 Cabin and 429 Third Class. She had been so overbooked in Cabin Class that some passengers holding tickets for that class of accommodations had to be berthed in Third Class cabins. Though they ate in the Cabin Class Dining Room and otherwise used Cabin Class spaces, it was the only time any of the "502"'s carried over 500 passengers on any single commercial voyage. Even more notable was the ship's arrival. Steaming into New York harbor on schedule, her docking was delayed by five hours by a near "mutiny" in Third Class. Off Quarantine, steerage passengers balked when U.S. Public Health Service officers instructed them to pass an inspection occasioned by the presence of a passenger requiring delousing. Though the ship's doctor suggested that four passengers boarding at Queenstown (Cobh) be deloused prior to taking passage, they were embarked nonetheless. During the crossing they allegedly came into contact with seven others with whom they shared their "little pets". At New York, U.S. Health Inspectors ruled that all eleven would have to go to Hoffman Island for delousing. Ten of the afflicted were quickly found and separated from the rest of the Third Class passengers but the identity of the eleventh remained a mystery. Unwilling to take the chance that the man transmit lice to others on these shores, authorities ordered all 429 steerage passengers to Hoffman Island for examination unless the eleventh be turned over. But the mystery man could not be found and disembarkation of Third Class passengers into the tender for the island began. Unwilling to comply were 56 passengers who felt that the Cabin Class passengers who were berthed in Third Class cabins also be required to undergo inspection on Hoffman Island. When the authorities disagreed, those 56 passengers still refused to board the boat for Hoffman Island. With that, Captain J. Pendlebury ran up the police flag and radioed for help. A squad headed by Acting Police Inspector Falconer, an Acting Captain, Acting Sergeant and several other oversized officers came out in the police tug MANHATTAN. Facing the recalcitrants, the Acting Inspector gave them a choice: "Go peacefully into the Hoffman Island boat or my men will put you there." That did the trick and after a delay of five hours, the PRESIDENT ADAMS sailed upriver

Recently renamed PRESIDENT ADAMS, the ship was photographed during her June 15, 1922 Boston call. Richard Hildebrand photo. Eric Johnson collection.

to her pier. That seems to have been the only time Third Class in the "502"s ever made the pages of the general press.

Far quieter than her arrival was her September 27th sailing on Voyage 14 from New York for Britain and France. The uneventful eastbound passage was but a prelude to a quiet incidence of racial prejudice. Actions and sentiments so typical of the times, mention of it was not carried in the general press and it remained ignored by all but the principals. It occurred aboard the PRESIDENT ADAMS on the ship's homeward crossing. After sailing from London on October 14th she shifted as always to Cherbourg where she stopped off the roads in the early hours of the morning of the 15th. A rather heavily booked westbound trip, berths could be had, but, alas, for whites only, so a "colored" maid boarding there in the company of her employers had difficulty finding cabin space in the PRESIDENT ADAMS. With a notation of the inclusion of a colored maid on the passage ticket, the Delatour family of Brooklyn Heights had bought passage home in the New York bound vessel. With no spare cabin for her, the Purser attempted to place her in a cabin with two white women who refused to have her in the room. A Cabin Class room for the maid was never really found and she spent the trip in a crew cabin. For his efforts to accommodate the maid, the Purser was fired, for in the words of United States Lines General Manager Thomas Rossbottom, "because we realize that no self-respecting white American woman would for one minute consider occupying a berth in a room with a strange colored woman. A Purser of the transatlantic passenger steamer service is expected to use better judgement than that."[14] Explaining the berthing problems on that particular sailing to Mrs. Delatour, he admitted that the Paris office had informed the Delatours that if they waited until sailing day to arrange actual accommodation for the maid there would be no need to pay for the exclusive use of a cabin for her. Rossbottom also faulted that office for issuing a ticket calling for such an arrangement before ascertaining availability of cabins. The Purser came in for further blame, this time for his delay of 36 hours in persuading the nurse to give up her room and share the cabin of one of the stewardesses. But what of the feelings of that poor human being, the maid, sad in the knowledge that for the hue of her skin alone, she was a creature unwelcome in such company? Disembarking the PRESIDENT ADAMS after the ship's October 24th arrival at New York, she likely had few kind thoughts about her crossing in the American liner.

Now came Voyage 15 and it was quite a routine journey evincing neither the passion nor the tensions aroused on the previous inbound trip. With a new Purser the PRESIDENT ADAMS departed New York on November 1st for a November 12th arrival at London via her quick stops in her usual ports. After six days in port, the homeward trip began on November 18th. The ship got home on November 28th.

---

[14] Nov. 4, 1922 letter from T. Rossbottom to Mrs. Delatour in the 1091 file for the ssPRESIDENT ADAMS in RG 32 National Archives.

The PRESIDENT ADAMS took a final sailing from New York that year. With 87 passengers in Cabin and 32 in Third Class and a total of 3,769 tons of general cargo including 2,568 tons of grain and 4,617 sacks of mail plus on board sales of $119.00 for deck chair and rug rental, $60.00 for canteen sales and $8.60 for excess baggage charges for a combined voyage revenue of $63,048.33, the ship steamed out from New York on Voyage 16 on December 6, 1922 for Plymouth, Cherbourg and London, a voyage that brought her into London on December 17th. Sailing for New York on December 21st, the ship spent both Christmas and New Year's Days at sea. On January 1, 1923 the PRESIDENT ADAMS reported herself in a position some 450 miles east of Ambrose. She docked in New York on the following day, January 2, 1923.

Westbound figures for 1923 showed that the PRESIDENT ADAMS carried 2,638 passengers. Outbound from New York again on January 10, 1923 the ship was on Voyage 17. The ship ran that trip on an amended itinerary. Rather than run another regular London trip she would skip both London and Cherbourg on the eastbound leg of the trip to turn around at Bremen.[15] In her cabins were a total of 86 passengers, all but 4 in Cabin Class. Stowed in her holds were 3,775 tons of cargo and 4,901 sacks of mail for Ireland, Britain and Germany which she offloaded at Queenstown and Plymouth on January 19th before her January 21st arrival at Bremen. Unclear are the dates of her departure as well as her arrival at London but in any event the ship sailed from there on January 27th, stopped to receive passengers off Cherbourg that same day and proceeded to both Plymouth and Queenstown where after sailing on January 29th headed into the Atlantic again on her way back to a February 8, 1923 arrival at New York. There was no diversion to Bremen on Voyage 18. Another routine London line trip, the ship sailed from New York on February 14th. Her passage was quick and by January 25th she had reached London. She remained there until sailing time on March 3rd. After calling at her usual homeward ports the ship made her way back across the wintry North Atlantic to arrive at New York on March 15th. After a ten day stay in port where regular maintenance and some voyage repairs were effected the liner headed back out to sea on Voyage 19 on March 25th. Less than a month later she was back at her home port, getting ready for her next sailing.

Voyage 20 called for the ship to depart New York on April 24th and she did, heading for Queenstown, Plymouth, Cherbourg and a May 7th arrival at London. The homeward sailing began with her May 12th departure for Cherbourg. Across the Atlantic once more the ship arrived at New York on May 22nd. The annual high season was upon her and to take advantage of the eastbound peregrinations of American travelers, United States Lines once more added Boston to the ship's outbound schedule. The next trip was Voyage 21, and after sailing from New York on May 31st the PRESIDENT ADAMS diverted to Boston to embark passengers, cargo and mail on June 1st

---

[15]Per *The New York Maritime Register*. February 7, 1923 edition.

before sailing on June 2nd. On the other side of the Atlantic the liner stopped at Queenstown on June 11th and reached London on the 12th. Migration of Americans was still eastbound so when the ship sailed from London on June 20th there was no high season surcharge to the tariff. The PRESIDENT ADAMS stopped at Queenstown on June 22nd and then sailed directly for New York to arrive on July 2nd. Then came Voyage 22, her second high season crossing of 1923. On that trip the "502" departed New York on July 5th. Once again she detoured up to Boston for a June 6th call before beginning her Atlantic crossing to Queenstown, Plymouth, Cherbourg and a July 15th arrival at London. From there her July 23rd sailing was on the early side of the homeward movements of the bulk of American travelers so it was not sold as a real high season sailing. At the end of the crossing the ship steamed into New York on August 1st. By then the eastbound high season was over and Voyage 23 was a regular trip, meaning that there would be no Boston call that time. Sailing from New York on August 8th the PRESIDENT ADAMS headed out into the Atlantic for Queenstown and an August 19th arrival at London. She was still under the command of Captain Pittman when she sailed from London on August 25, 1923 for New York and a September 4th arrival. The summer rush over, there was time in the schedule for some upgrades. At New York in mid September 1923, just before the contract of her sale to Dollar Line was signed, a Sperry automatic pilot, a "metal mike", was installed as part of a Shipping Board program to upgrade navigation equipment aboard the more important Fleet Corporation ships then operating. Two days before the date of her sale the PRESIDENT ADAMS sailed on September 23, 1923 on Voyage 24 from New York to Plymouth, Cherbourg and London. Already under contract of sale when she returned, the ship sailed from New York again on October 17th. Aboard for Voyage 25 were a total of 117 passengers, 82 in Cabin and 35 in Third Class. In her holds were 2,783 tons of grain, 1,613 tons of general and 387 tons of refrigerated cargo and 337 sacks of mail. Outbound revenue came to an estimated $63,575.00. Westbound, she sailed from London on October 31st and Queenstown on November 2, 1923 on her way back to New York. There ten days later, Captain Pittman went ashore and was relieved by a new Master, Captain Look, who had come to the ship after his vacation following months commanding the PRESIDENT GARFIELD. On Voyage 25 the ship sailed out again from New York on November 21, 1923 on one of her last trips from New York as a member of the fleet of United States Lines. In her cabins were 47 Cabin and 10 Third Class passengers. Besides the $6,480 their combined fares brought in, there was cargo in her holds to add to voyage revenue. Though cargo booked that time was more than she had carried in early December 1922, the ship garnered consistently lower cargo bookings. Probably chagrined by the PRESIDENT ADAMS's generally poorer cargo performances, US Lines' managing director reminded Shipping Board Commissioners T.V. O'Connor, W.S. Benson and E.C. Plummer: "The freight list amounts to $37,000, which I consider a very good showing in view of the fact that this steamer, like the ssPRESIDENT POLK about which I wrote to you last week has less cubic capacity for cargo than the other ships of the Fleet on account of steerage fittings."[16] Somehow he managed to ignore a chart of comparisons between the ship's late November 1923 sailing with her December 6, 1922 departure. In any case it was not a pretty sight. With 122 passengers aboard when she sailed in December 1922 the ship took in $13,788.89, more than twice what her 57 passengers paid for the November 1923 sailing. Loaded with 5,317 tons on Voyage 25[17] for an income of $37,000.00, that was the only dollar figure that looked better than the previous late autumn sailing. A year earlier the ship left the United States with 4,617 sacks of mail for a revenue of $27,117.02. November 1923 brought her only 552 mail bags for an income of $2,760.00. Final figures made all concerned happy the ship had been sold. She had brought in revenues $67,246.43 on her autumn 1922 sailing but this time had managed to earn just $46,359.50. Whatever her dollar earnings or losses, her screws turned the required revolutions and she sailed from London once again on December 8th for a December 17th arrival at New York.

Scheduled for delivery to Dollar Line in the winter of 1924, the PRESIDENT ADAMS had time for a final winter round trip on the London line. On her bridge was another Master, Captain J.J. Pendlebury, former Master of the PRESIDENT MONROE. That was voyage 26 and it began when she started loading cargo at 3:00 PM on December 20, 1923. With 5,491 tons of cargo, 899 tons of it general, 3,857 tons of it grain and 483 tons of it refrigerated produce and 252 tons of provisions for other American ships, 5,240 sacks of mail and 21 Cabin and 12 Third Class passengers, the ship sailed from New York at 12:41 PM on December 26, 1923. In light of the figures above, estimated earnings of a total of $84,340.00, weren't bad for a late December eastbound crossing. The voyage report shows an income of $3,569.01 for passage fares, $32,511.95 for ocean freight and $34,368.00 in mail revenue. Added to that during the crossing were $21.77 canteen income, $6.00 earned for chair and rug hire and another $25.04 in miscellaneous income, so the voyage revenue totalled $70,501.85. After steaming nine days, 14 hours and 50 minutes, the PRESIDENT ADAMS reached Plymouth, England to land mail, 2 Cabin and 2 Third Class at 10:35 PM on January 4, 1924. She remained only two hours and twenty minutes, sailing again at 12:55 AM on the morning of January 5th. After seven hours and 25 minutes steaming she arrived at Cherbourg at 8:20 that morning. Her call there was characteristically short, lasting but an hour and ten minutes to land more mail, 6 Cabin and 5 Third Class passengers. Then she headed back across to Britain, logging one day, three hours and fifteen minutes steaming before tying up at London at 12:45 PM on January 6th. Landing 12 Cabin and 5

---

[16]Nov. 21, 1923 memo to Commissioners. Copy in ship's 1091 file in RG 32 at National Archives.
[17]For some reason the Shipping Board called it Voyage 45 but that may have been an error in this case.

Third Class passengers[18] took no time at all but discharging her cargo kept her busy until 9:15 PM on January 11th. Loading began before the ship's freight was fully offloaded. First of her westbound cargo went onto the ship at 2:00 PM on January 9th. It didn't take very long since she had only 608 tons of general merchandise, 198 tons of straw hats, 322 tons of rubber, 15 tons of refrigerated freight to total 1,143 tons of cargo and 10 sacks of mail to bring to New York. It was all stowed by 7:20 PM on the 11th, about two hours before the last of her cargo from New York went onto the dock. Forty-one Cabin and 10 Third Class Passengers joined the ship early the next afternoon and the PRESIDENT ADAMS sailed for Cherbourg at 3:00 PM on January 12th. There, after a 55 minute call on January 13th the last of 61 Cabin and 11 Third Class New York bound passengers boarded and at 9:00 AM the ship sailed. After a ten day, four hour and twenty-one minute crossing, the PRESIDENT ADAMS made her final entrance to New York in United States Lines' colors at 6:21 PM on January 23, 1924. After discharging the last of her cargo at 4:10 PM on January 25, 1924, Voyage 26 of 36 days, 1 hour and 10 minutes, was over. What were the dollar figures of her westbound crossing? Ocean freight rates yielded $9,471.37, mail income was $94.30 and ocean fares totalled $7,288.83. With more passengers aboard expected income from canteen sales did rise. That added $43.55 to the balance sheet as chair and rug hire brought in another $40.50 and miscellaneous charges brought another $50.07. Westbound, the ship earned $16,988.62, much less than she had brought in for her eastbound crossing. Added together, income for Voyage 26 was $87,490.47. That might have allowed a small profit since expenses totalled $75,675.01, but maintenance and major repair charges of $16,693.90 against that trip's books wiped any surplus income out and left an operating loss. With net operating expenses reckoned at $4,878.44 and overhead expenses totalling $19,452.75, the net voyage result was calculated as a $24,331.20 loss. That was nothing unusual for the "502"'s in United States Lines service on the London line. The bottom figure for voyages to date showed that the PRESIDENT ADAMS had turned in an operating loss of $613,954.08 over the course of her service on the Atlantic.

Now the machinations of transfer of the ship to her purchasers went into action. Per a January 21st request from Shipping Board Assistant Admiralty Counsel A.M. Beal, the Collector of Customs of the Port of New York sent the Shipping Board the needed papers to effect delivery. These included "the ship's original outstanding document for the vessel, the complete abstract and certificate of record of title for the ship which gave full data particularly concerning the Master Carpenter's or Builder's certificate for the vessel, and the bill for the abstract of title"[19]. After the ship was redelivered by United

---

[18]There's no word about where the Cabin passenger unaccounted for in port disembarkation totals got off.

[19]See January 21, 1924 letter regarding sale of ssPRESIDENT ADAMS. Copy in ship's 1091 file in RG32 at National Archives.

States Lines to the Shipping Board, the PRESIDENT ADAMS was delivered to the Dollar Line in New York at Noon on February 1, 1924. Next came a few repairs. As covered in agreements between buyer and seller, anything awry after September 25, 1923 was for the account of the Shipping Board. In rather fine shape, the PRESIDENT ADAMS needed little work but among the repair work in her engine department were these items: Clean away the dirt on the sides of her six 3-furnace Scotch boilers; repair the high pressure ahead slipper of the port engine; supply new piston rings; and repair damaged legging in fire and engine rooms and pump up two furnaces (#5 and 12). For hull repairs some anchor chain links were replaced. For the Steward's department, workers replaced broken grating strips in refrigerating space and repaired galley fire boxes in both the Cabin Class and Third Class galleys. There was minor bottom damage to this ship, but whose responsibility to pay for their repairs was under debate. Not requiring drydocking to fix, those repairs included fairing first and sixth starboard bilge keels; renewal of port and starboard propellor rope guards; renewal of starboard propellor cone nut; renewal of the inspection plate of the starboard and port sides of the rudder; renewal of some 20 rudder rivets; fair two blades of the port propellor and weld some 20 feet of the rudder. With little else besides putting in some new equipment like a "metal mike", the first of its kind installed aboard a "502", replacing a broken flushometer in an officers' toilet and repairing some broken cargo battens, cleaning the ship top to bottom and painting her in Dollar Line colors, the PRESIDENT ADAMS was ready to go to work within a week of her delivery to her buyers.

Captain J. J. Pendlebury accepted a Dollar Steamship Lines, Ltd., Inc. job offer and stayed with his command. Now a prominent white dollar sign stood on a red band about midway up her black funnel. The first of the five Atlantic sisters to begin her Dollar Line career sailed from New York on February 7, 1924 with a capacity passenger list on her first Dollar Line voyage. Ahead of her lay a course of 25,619 miles to be covered in 78 sea days. Among the department heads aboard on that inaugural trip were Chief Purser F.C. Charman, Chief Steward J. Ronan and ship's Doctor S.R. Titworth, M.D.. Overnighting at Havana on the 11th she sailed on February 12th for Colon and her February 15th maiden Panama Canal transit. Ordered from the Panama Canal Commissary Division was a garden of exotica, most of it for the ship's Chinese crew. Loaded at Colon were Chinese cabbage, dried white cabbage, white lily root, dried lily flower, bamboo shoots, green beans, salted black beans, bean sticks, salted eggs, seaweed, dried scallops, salted ginger, pickled lemons, pea oil, dried oysters, dried shrimp, curb beans, bean sauce, plum sauce and flat fish. Ordered but unavailable there at the time were fresh lily root and 24 cans of okra.[20] Arriving on her maiden call at San Pedro, the port for Los Angeles on February 25th, the PRESIDENT ADAMS spent one night before heading up the coast to her new home port

---

[20]Panama Canal Record, February 16, 1924.

Taking the first sailing from New York on the round the world service on February 7, 1924, the departing PRESIDENT ADAMS sails past the flag of the ssAMERICA. Frank O. Braynard collection.

of San Francisco and her February 28th maiden arrival. There, the papers forwarded from New York were replaced by new ones issued by the Collector of Customs of the Port of San Francisco.

The first of the "New York" boats to join the fleet was now the third of the sisterships to sail on the round the world line from San Francisco, sailing from Dollar Line's China Basin pier at 5:00PM on Saturday, March 1, 1924. Her ports of call were the same already visited by her two sisters. Honolulu was first. The PRESIDENT ADAMS made a one day call there on March 8th. From there she set her course for Kobe and a March 21st arrival. She sailed the next day for Shanghai where she remained until the 26th. Then it was on to Hong Kong and a March 31st arrival. Manila, Singapore, Penang and Colombo were next as the ship's screws beat their path around the world. When the ship docked at Alexandria on April 30th, the end of the voyage was in sight. The ship departed Marseilles on May 7th to begin the last leg of her inaugural round the world voyage. For counting purposes, though a Mediterranean port, her Marseilles departures always heralded the beginnings of her Atlantic crossings. After an uneventful voyage the PRESIDENT ADAMS steamed into New York at the end of her first world trip on May 19, 1924. It took ten days to get her ready for her next departure. Sailing again from New York on Voyage 2 on May 29, the PRESIDENT ADAMS made a stop at San Juan, Puerto Rico en route to Havana and the Panama Canal. For statistical purposes the ship's June 21st sailing from San Juan was also considered the beginning of an outbound trip. At the end of that trip, the ship called at Boston on September 10th while inbound to New York. Eight days later the ship sailed from New York and on October 11th from San Francisco on her third round the world trip, a voyage that kept her busy through Christmas time that year.

This "502" began 1925 with a January 2nd departure from New York. Captain Wilbur C. Ross replaced Captain Pendlebury on her bridge early that year. She sailed from Los Angeles for San Francisco on January 27th, arriving the next day for her usual three day stay in her home port. Aboard the ship that time when she sailed for Japan was a group of 38 passengers booked by well known Los Angeles steamship agent D.F. Robertson. On March 11, 1925 Robertson cabled Commissioner Meyer Lissner:

> Have this day received letter from Japan my party thirty eight passengers including Ernest Rivers VanNuys and others who left Los Angeles January 27th around world on Dollar Line PRESIDENT ADAMS. All express wonderful satisfaction food and service throughout. Have booked hundred of passengers Dollar Line around world and not one kick. Old Robert Dollar sure knows how to operate American steamships.[21]

Robertson may have had a better reason to send in an unsolicited pat on Dollar's back . . . the Seattle based Admiral Line "535"'s would be sold

---

[21]Copy of March 11, 1925 telegram in the ship's 1091 file in RG 32 at National Archives.

that year and fearing monopoly, Fleet Corporation President Elmer Crowley opposed their sale to Dollar interests. Accolades like Robertson's could only help the Dollar cause. April 24th of that year saw the ship sailing out of New York on her fifth round the world sailing, a voyage she ended with an August 11 call at Boston. Then came a week at New York between August 13th and 20th before getting underway on voyage 6. While at Brooklyn's Pier 22 on August 19th a fire broke out in a hold. A city owned fireboat and two tugs belonging to Dalzell Towing came to help out. After causing only slight damage the fire was extinguished and the ship was able to depart on time on August 20th. That trip was of course also marked from San Francisco and her September 12th sailing. As the PRESIDENT ADAMS carried passengers and cargo around the world she posted operating losses every trip so far and the eighth one was no different. That was the ship's December 10, 1925 departure from New York and January 2, 1926 sailing from San Francisco.

She took the last of her four 1926 departures from New York on November 11th. Through the Panama Canal on November 19th the ship made San Pedro on the 29th and arrived at San Francisco on December 1st and sailed on December 4th. At the end of that year the ship was in Japanese waters, sailing from Kobe on December 27th for her usual ports in Asia and Europe. She began her homewards Atlantic crossing from Marseilles on February 9, 1927.

Seemingly uneventful was her first full trip in 1927. After a Boston visit she sailed February 24th to continue loading cargo at New York before her March 3rd departure. That trip took her out of Kobe on April 16, 1927 for a May 30th New York arrival. It was her last time at Dollar's Brooklyn piers. When she returned from that voyage she tied up at Pier 9, Jersey City. From there longshoremen worked her inbound cargo and loaded her for her following voyage. The ship next sailed from New York on June 23, 1927. Taking her last sailing of the year from New York on October 6th, the ship was a day out of Havana on her way to the Panama Canal when the lookout spotted a sailing vessel in the haze on the horizon. Suspecting distress, Captain Ross put the PRESIDENT ADAMS about and went to investigate. Soon, Captain, crew and ship came upon the schooner WILLIAM A. BURNHAM of Mobile and her crew had quite a story to tell. Caught in a fierce tropical storm just after leaving Trinidad in September, the BURNHAM sprang a leak and began filling with water. Her crew tried to convince Captain A. Ryan to abandon ship but he would not enter a lifeboat as long as his schooner floated. For the next two weeks, all aboard the leaky sailer, including Captain Ryan, his wife and three children took turns at the pumps working them day and night in a fulsome effort to triumph over the sea and keep the schooner afloat. In spare moments they tried to attract the attention of passing ships but had no luck until the eagle-eyed lookout on the PRESIDENT ADAMS alerted the Captain. Coming alongside the schooner, the liner sent a boat to take off the schooner's weary men, woman and children. Last to leave was the BURNHAM's Captain. The ADAMS landed the survivors at

At Boston on August 11, 1925 during her fifth trip around the world, the PRESIDENT ADAMS showed off modifications to her bridge front. Richard Hildebrand photo. Eric Johnson collection.

The PRESIDENT ADAMS on her way around the world. Eric Johnson collection.

Panama on October 21st from where they made their way back to Alabama. The voyage continued from San Francisco with the ship's November 1st sailing. The ship got another Master that year, Captain William C. Morris. He would remain with her until 1929 except when he was shoreside on vacation.

She began 1928 in the Red Sea, and arrived at Suez on January 2, 1928. Her first outbound sailing of 1928 took her from New York on February 2nd. A tough year for West Coast based American shipowners, who suffered a spate of inexplicable incidents that began without warning and stopped just as suddenly, the PRESIDENT ADAMS steamed through the first three quarters of that year without incident serious enough to put her name on the casualty lists. By mid March she was back in Japan, and sailed from Kobe on St. Patrick's Day, March 17th. Beginning her way back to New York she called at Manila on the 27th. On the final leg of that trip she sailed from Genoa on May 1st and Marseilles on May 2nd on her way to New York. Midsummer saw her again in Japan and she departed Kobe on July 6th. She was at Colombo loading tea and rubber on August 1st. When she went through the Suez Canal on August 14th any American passengers aboard and most of her crew no doubt could begin to think of getting home.

Due into San Francisco on October 1, 1928, the PRESIDENT ADAMS sailed for Havana with about 100 passengers from New York on September

S. S. " President Adams "

W.A. Ross, Commander   Tuesday, December 29, 1925

All Perishable Supplies Purchased in Los Angeles

DINNER

MESS ROOM

Queen Olives   Spring Onions   Chilled Celery

Soup

Consomme Vermicelli   Duck a-la Parisienne

Fish

Filet of Fresh Fish, Hollandaise

Entree

Calf's Feet a-la Vinegrette

Chicken Saute Marengo

Raisin Fritters, Vanilla Sauce

Roast

Prime Sirloin of Beef au Jus, Browned Potataes

Roast Lamb with Mint Sauce

Vegetables

Fried Egg Plant   Cauliflower en Cream   Steamed Rice

Potatoes: Roast   Mashed   Boiled

Salad

Lettuce and Tomato, Roquefort Dressing

Pastry & Dessert

Sponge Pudding, Strawberry Sauce

Fruit Jelly   Ice Cream, Nabiscos

Soda Scones   Cake

Cheese: American   Swiss

Fresh Fruit

Author's collection.

A small Lounge in the PRESIDENT ADAMS. Beamed ceilings, dental moldings and a softly carpeted floor set a classic tone in this room. Author's collection.

13, 1928. On the night of the 16th the PRESIDENT ADAMS ran into the most severe hurricane to hit Florida in years.

She came through all right but not before San Francisco papers had the story of her rough passage in print. After her October 5, 1928 sailing from San Francisco, it looked like the fates had set her up for a tough time. It was too bad, for on the occasion of her sailing from her home port she shipped a 100% American crew. The first American steamer in service across the Pacific to replace Chinese with Americans, there was no altruistic patriotism on the part of the Dollars. The fifty some odd Chinese sailors and firemen were replaced by Americans in order for the PRESIDENT ADAMS to be in compliance with a new Shipping Board ruling calling for crews of American nationals in ships handling the U.S. Mail at new, higher rates. Nonetheless, the departure of an American passenger ship crewed wholly by Americans was news. Apparently Stewards were unaffected by such rulings nor did they seem to be counted as crew, a fact publicized widely in the shipping press and an item in the general press around the country. As usual, most

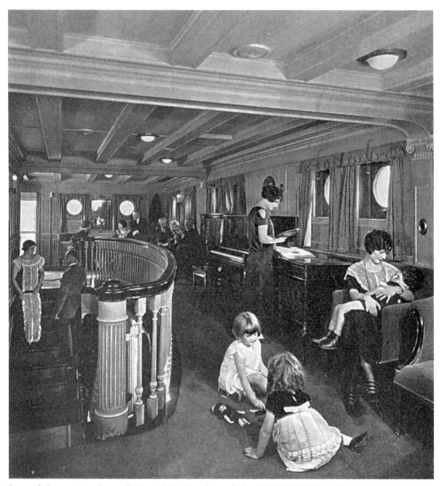

One of the original small Social Halls aboard the PRESIDENT ADAMS. None of its fittings, a piano, Victrola, arm chairs and curtained port holes could disguise the fact that it was little more than an enlarged stair lobby. Author's collection.

of the voyage was routine and on October 26th she sailed from Kobe for Shanghai. After working cargo at Hong Kong she sailed on November 4th on her way south to Manila where she worked cargo during her two days there on November 6th and 7th. From Penang on the 17th and Colombo on November 21st, the PRESIDENT ADAMS continued her voyage, reaching Suez on December 3rd. The remainder of the trip would have its moments, for before completing that voyage the PRESIDENT ADAMS went aground on two separate occasions. At Port Said, Egypt on December 6, 1928 the ship hit a reef, damaging about 200 feet of bilge plating on her port side. The ship wounded herself badly enough for the engine room and some of her fuel tanks to leak. At Alexandria on December 7, 1928 the ship's bilges were damaged but she was able to continue her voyage.

Adding to her embarrassment, much worse was to come. On the inter-coastal leg of the following outbound trip from New York the PRESIDENT ADAMS made her mark among the seven sisters for a spectacular grounding. California bound, the ship ended the year with a December 30th sailing from Boston to New York where her last freight was loaded. With 3,561 tons of cargo, 89 passengers and a crew of 78 officers and men the ADAMS departed New York on January 3, 1929. Inbound into Panama on her way to the Pacific just before 6:00 AM on January 11th, she ran hard aground on a reef outside the West Breakwater at the entrance to Cristobal, Panama Canal Zone on the Atlantic side of the isthmus. Inbound to Cristobal with 90 passengers from New York and Havana (apparently one traveler embarked there), the liner made so spectacular a bump that her Master, Captain W.C. Morris, lost his balance and fell from the bridge into the water. Keeping his wits about him, Captain Morris swam to shore and returned to his ship by tender. All tugs at the Atlantic end of the Canal were sent to the stranded ship's side to try to assist her off the rocks but the liner stayed fast. A few of the tugs took on the stranded liner's passengers and brought them to shore where they were transferred to the big Panama Pacific Line steamer CALIFORNIA for their passage to San Francisco. Other tugs continued their efforts to pull the ship free. At about 9:30 PM that evening the ship was refloated and towed into Cristobal and tied up at Pier 6. Initial damage reports indicated plenty of trouble. Crashing ashore, the ship's fuel oil feed pipes broke and some of her boilers were unseated. Each passing day brought further news of the ship's condition. On the next day the ship's deep tank and holds were reported dry, five boiler space flooring and five boilers set up, and steam was up in the sixth. Divers had a look at the ship's bottom on the 13th. They discovered bottom damage running a length of 167 feet and many bottom plates very badly corrugated. Luckily, none of the ship's bottom plates was holed so surveyors pronounced the ship fit for towing to drydock at Balboa where loose rivets and plugs could be tightened. On orders from the head office not to try to make it under her own power, the PRESIDENT ADAMS was under tow when she began her canal transit at 6:15AM on the 14th on the way to a Balboa repair yard for drydocking. Through the canal at 8:45PM that evening, the ship was tied up at Balboa where a complete survey began on the 17th once a drydock became available for her.

Quick examination revealed bottom damage so extensive that repairs would keep the PRESIDENT ADAMS out of service for four months. The PRESIDENT ADAMS was at first supposed to be towed to Newport News where she would not only be repaired but substantially refitted under the terms of the recent Jones—White Act, but since the ship was westbound, Dollar Line allowed San Francisco firms to bid for the job. Able to proceed under her own steam, the PRESIDENT ADAMS left Balboa on January 23rd and after an overnight call at San Pedro on February 2nd, reached her San Francisco homeport on February 4th. Survey was made while the ship was in dry dock on the 8th. A local yard made an attractive offer in terms of both money and time. They promised to have the ship back in service after ninety-five days. The Union yard of the Bethlehem Shipbuilding Company did the work after winning the contract on February 15th. Damage to the ship's hull was severe. As many as 123 bottom plates had to be removed and 67 of them, nine of those on the keel, replaced. Hard hit in the grounding were the ship's propellor shafts. While trying to free the ship, machinery had been strained and that had to be made good again. Also considerably damaged had been auxiliary machinery, refrigerating machinery and piping. Repairing the PRESIDENT ADAMS was a big job . . . and so was remodelling her. Before spending a penny to rebuild the ship's accommodation spaces, the cost of repairs and alterations came to $375,000.00. The Dollar Line took a loan from the Construction Loan Fund, in the amount of $300,000.00 and refitted the passenger accommodation aboard the 10,558 gross ton ship using as their guide the blueprints used in the reconditioning of the PRESIDENT POLK. Naturally, no increase in tonnage was registered once the ship was rebuilt. On the contrary, she now registered 10,516 tons. Steamship companies always need to economize, after all.

Repaired and rejuvenated, the PRESIDENT ADAMS left the yard on May 2nd. The *"San Francisco Chronicle"* thought her refit worth a story on May 7th:

> After a layup of practically three months, during which time the steamer has undergone repairs and reconditioning amounting to approximately $1,000,000, the Dollar Liner PRESIDENT ADAMS is due to sail from San Francisco next Friday for Los Angeles harbor to take up her schedule on the company's round the world service.
>
> The job on the PRESIDENT ADAMS, which was carried out by the local yards of the Bethlehem Shipbuilding Corporation, is said to be the largest job of its kind to be executed at any Pacific Coast yard in the past ten years, and was accomplished in eighty days.
>
> . . . Heretofore the PRESIDENT ADAMS had accommodations for but eighty passengers but when she goes back into commission she will have accommodations for 182 passengers. The smoking and dining saloons and social halls have all been enlarged and rebuilt, new carpets, beds and mattresses have been installed, and the interior decoration of the liner has all been done over. Hot and cold water has been put into each cabin.[22]

Even before these repairs and rebuilding began, it was apparent that the ship would miss an entire round the world voyage. Unwilling to forfeit either their mail pay nor disappoint shippers and passengers, the Dollar Line hastily chartered the Pacific coastal liner RUTH ALEXANDER from their associated Admiral Line to take the place of the injured PRESIDENT ADAMS on

---

[22]May 7, 1929 *"San Francisco Chronicle"*

San Francisco's A.F. Marten Company designed and executed the rebuilding and redecoration of the public rooms of the PRESIDENT ADAMS. Retaining its early American flavor despite its larger size to accommodate all passengers at a single leisurely seating was the Dining Room of the PRESIDENT ADAMS after her 1929 rebuild. Walls were painted a light tan, drapes were aquamarine taffeta. Crispy linens were snow white. Author's collection. Author's collection.

the advertised January 23rd sailing from San Francisco. Smaller than the "502", the RUTH ALEXANDER was nonetheless well equipped to handle a trip on that line. Her holds adequate to the demands of the trade, her passenger accommodations found great approval among her passengers. After her thorough rebuilding the PRESIDENT ADAMS made a trial run. In San Francisco Bay she met the RUTH ALEXANDER. Passengers, baggage and cargo joined the ship's newest Master, Captain William Kohlmeister, and transferred to the Dollar Liner. The PRESIDENT ADAMS returned to service with her sailing on May 10 from San Francisco to San Pedro where she made an overnight call. She was back at her home port on the 14th and resumed her place on the round the world line with her May 17, 1929 sailing. From there, the voyage operated as it had in the past, with the ship calling at her usual ports around the world. Let her Marseilles departure on July 25, 1929 serve once more as a marker for the ship's progress as she steamed on around the world. At the end of her first trip since her rebuild the PRESIDENT

No longer a stair lobby, the Main Lounge after the refit. Decorated in a modified French style with walls of café au lait highlighted in gold leaf with drapes in peach damask hung from cornices finished in gold leaf. Author's collection.

ADAMS entered New York on August 6, 1929. Two days later she sailed for Boston, sailing on August 11th on her way back to New York. For recording purposes, the ship's date of redelivery under the terms of her Reconstruction Loan was given by the Shipping Board as August 12, 1929. Her second post rebuild sailing from New York was on August 15th and from San Francisco on September 6th.

Taking her third sailing after her repairs and refit she sailed from Boston on December 1, 1929 for New York and her next outbound trip. She left New York on December 5th for Havana, Panama, California and the world. That year her crew had Christmas in port—the ship's home port. The PRESIDENT ADAMS steamed into San Francisco Bay on December 24th for her usual three day stay at San Francisco. She sailed away on December 27, 1929.

Again a Kobe departure serves as a convenient milepost to track the movements of a round the world Dollar Liner so note the ship's January 16, 1930 sailing from there for her customary calls. Captain Maynard Griffith was appointed to command the ship during that year. Heading into the final days of the long voyage the PRESIDENT ADAMS sailed from Marseilles on March 5th for New York and Boston. In 1930 the steamer made her usual

Enlarged and fitted with sliding doors which could be
closed in unpleasant weather, the Veranda Cafe
retained its feeling of light airiness. Author's collection.

circumnavigations of the globe, sailing from New York on outbound voyages
on March 27th, July 17th and November 6, 1930.

The following year was ordinary as far as regular sailings of this Dollar
Liner was concerned. Captain Charles Jokstad relieved Captain Griffith that
year and San Francisco port officials began listing the ship's net tonnage at
6,345 tons. At sea when that year began she arrived at Singapore for her
usual three day call on January 5, 1931. Sailing from Marseilles on February
4th for New York, the ship came into New York on February 17th. The next
outbound sailing took the ship from New York on February 26th and San
Francisco on March 20th. About a month later the ship was in Japanese and
Chinese waters. In usual rotation, the PRESIDENT ADAMS began another
homeward crossing from Marseilles on May 27th and arrived back at New
York on June 8th. After a quick Boston sidetrip, the next sailing began a
week later. July 10, 1931 saw the ship clear the Golden Gate once more for
Honolulu and Kobe. On the following outbound sailing the liner departed

Much lightened and more welcoming to women passengers was the Smoking Room aboard the PRESIDENT ADAMS, redecorated during the 1929 rebuild. Author's collection.

New York on October 8th and by mid autumn the ship was in the north west Pacific. She sailed from Kobe again on November 20, 1931. After Christmas in the Red Sea the ship arrived at Suez on December 26th. At Naples on January 3, 1932 the ship followed the usual course to Genoa and Marseilles before heading back to New York and Boston, sailing from the French port on January 6th. By the 11th her radio reported her 1,477 miles east of Ambrose light.

Like clockwork the ship steamed on, though economics were not at all in her favor. The ship returned to New York from her autumn 1931 round the world trip on January 20, 1932. As always there was the Boston side trip followed by the January 28th sailing for Havana and Panama. From San Francisco that time the ship sailed on February 19th and from Kobe the liner cast off on March 10th. On this trip around the world the PRESIDENT ADAMS had a new port to call and after sailing from Colombo, Ceylon at 8:00PM on April 4th, her Master set a course for Bombay. After a passage of three nights and two and a half days she arrived at Bombay at 1:00PM on Thursday, April 7, 1932. Scheduled for a call of 24 hours, the ship sailed at 1:00PM on the following day. Ten days later she was at Suez. May 12th saw

One of the new double cabins in the PRESIDENT ADAMS. Author's collection.

the ship back at New York where the process of getting the ship up to Boston and back and loaded for another round the world trip went on without a hitch. May 19, 1932 was sailing day from New York. That trip kept her busy until September when she sailed out again.

A hint of the financial troubles that would eventually culminate in the collapse of Dollar Steamship Lines hit in 1932 when Dollar Line defaulted on its expected August 20th payment of $20,000.00 on her construction loan note. At the time the Line missed that payment the PRESIDENT ADAMS was on a routine voyage, on her way back to New York.

Around the time of her November 8, 1932 call at Penang everyone aboard the PRESIDENT ADAMS learned that President Herbert Hoover had been turned out of office, losing a landslide to Franklin D. Roosevelt. The election of that Democrat presaging a return to those "happy days" did not please everyone—especially those in responsible positions aboard a Dollar Liner, a company that owed not a little of its fortune to Republicans in government. There would be time to think about that later. There was a voyage to continue to operate now and the ship kept working her way west, sailing again from Marseilles on December 7th for New York. From Boston on December 26, 1932 the liner made her way back to New York where her usual overnight call lasted through December 29th. That morning passengers for points south and west embarked and early that evening the ship sailed out

The PRESIDENT ADAMS in a stern quarter view taken before she grounded and was rebuilt in 1929. Frank O. Braynard collection.

again to begin both a new voyage, Number 30, and a new year. Minimum rates then in effect for the full round the world trip were $749.00 per person in a B-3 type cabin, an outside room without private facilities.

Touching all her ports in their customary sequence on that trip, the ship returned to New York on April 10, 1933. Boston was next and before sailing for California again at the beginning of Voyage 31, the PRESIDENT ADAMS returned to New York to load her last parcels of freight and embark a complement of passengers at Pier 9, Jersey City. Bound for points west, the ship sailed down the Hudson River on April 20th. It was probably during the ship's San Francisco call between May 9th and 12th that Captain H.S. Bauer assumed command.[23] Working her way around the world again the PRESIDENT ADAMS sailed from Kobe on June 2nd, Hong Kong on June 10th, from Singapore on June 20th, from Bombay on June 30th and from Marseilles on July 19th. After her usual thirteen day passage, she steamed up through the Narrows into New York harbor on August 1st. Fifty hours after tying up at her Jersey City pier she sailed at Noon on August 3rd for Boston. Back at New York again on August 7th, her three day stay was put to good use. Stevedores worked cargo, crew at liberty enjoyed New York and passengers turned up at Pier 9 around midday on Thursday, August 10th. Lines were let go at 4:00PM and the ship sailed on Voyage 32. That trip continued from San Francisco on September 1st and the ship was back at New York on November 21st. The ship's last trip that year was Voyage 33 and she sailed from New York for ports around the world on that trip on November 30th.

---

[23]If not then, Captain Bauer would have taken command during the ship's next call.

The extensive refits given four of the "502"s were not as externally drastic when viewed from the stern quarter as these two views prove. This one was taken by Richard Hildebrand at Boston on November 2, 1930. Eric Johnson collection.

Next was Havana on December 4th. Through the Panama Canal four days later the ship headed north to California and a December 17th arrival at San Pedro. Into San Francisco at 4:00PM on December 19th the ship docked at Pier 42. With a Christmas tree above her crow's nest and assorted holiday decorations adorning her living spaces, the PRESIDENT ADAMS sailed from San Francisco at 4:00PM on Friday, December 23rd, for Honolulu and the Far East.

There was a real holiday atmosphere aboard ship and a few passengers who embarked at San Francisco had booked passage only as far as Hawaii. After Christmas at sea they disembarked once the ship reached Honolulu on December 29th to enjoy a stay in the islands. Continuing on from Oahu later that same day the PRESIDENT ADAMS greeted 1934 at sea. No one knew that the world had reached the worst year of the Depression. Ships by the hundreds lay up all over the world but somehow the Dollars managed to keep a lot of their ships at sea and the PRESIDENT ADAMS reached Kobe on January 11th. She sailed from that Japanese port on January 12th, Manila on the 22nd, Singapore on the 26th and arrived at Suez on February 19th. Departing Marseilles on February 28th the PRESIDENT ADAMS came into New York harbor on March 13th. Over the following ten days the ship spent two of them working cargo at New York before sailing on her Boston side trip. Back at New York on March 19th, there were still three days to work cargo before sailing out from New York on March 22nd. The PRESIDENT ADAMS was then on Voyage 34, a trip she continued from San Francisco on April 13, 1934. Across the Pacific, the PRESIDENT ADAMS sailed from Kobe on May 4th. Five days later the Big Strike broke out among maritime industry workers on the West Coast of the United States. Agitators aboard ship wanted to walk out as soon as the ship made her next port, but Hong Kong didn't seem the place to prove their point and the pro-strike voice was soon drowned out by voices of reason suggesting starvation or worse might be the benefit of such unsanctioned union activity. At very least strikers aboard a ship underway could be charged with mutiny. Union agitators, assorted hot heads and malcontents then enjoyed plenty of chances to disrupt and obstruct the peaceful atmosphere of an American passenger liner at sea. With their history of antipathy to their bosses it was a sure bet to the onlooker that militant voices aboard the Dollar Liner called for a walkout to show solidarity with the striking folks back home. But such talk remained only talk until the ship neared American waters and hotheads forced a vote aboard ship in the hope they might force the ship to tie up at New York until the strike ended. Knowing the extremes of financial hardship all over the world, the more rational among the men aboard the PRESIDENT ADAMS knew that no benefactor waited in the wings to provide striking sailors their daily bread so the majority voted their stomachs rather than any "big picture" or solidarity with strikers on the San Francisco waterfront.

The ship's crew brought their vessel around the world pretty much on schedule during that anxious season. When the PRESIDENT ADAMS reached Marseilles on June 20th the strike was still on but her crew continued to work. When the PRESIDENT ADAMS arrived at New York on July 3, 1934, labor was still out and the West Coast was still paralyzed. No matter how sour their faces or sullen their disposition, the crew of the PRESIDENT ADAMS remained at their posts to see their ship out from New York on the Boston side trip between July 5th and 9th.

By the time agitators could have made movement difficult for the PRESIDENT ADAMS, the ship was underway again. When the PRESIDENT ADAMS sailed from Boston for New York and her next outbound sailing on Voyage 35 at 4:00PM on Thursday, July 12th, tempers were short and a general strike was brewing in both San Francisco and Oakland. But the "502" sailed for California anyway, her owners confident that should San Francisco still be closed by strikers, they could handle the ship's business and cargo during her San Pedro call, and send her on her way to Japan without bringing her into San Francisco at all. So it was with some uncertainty that the ship made her way to Havana. Back in the San Francisco Bay area, the threatened general strike became a reality on July 16th. Luckily for everyone, those at the very top of the union hierarchy were pretty square and conservative so they had the matters at hand settled within four days. By the time the PRESIDENT ADAMS completed her July 20th Panama Canal transit, only the original die-hard maritime strikers were still out. When the PRESIDENT

ADAMS reached San Pedro late on July 29th there was still no word about strike's end, but when sailing time approached on July 31st the strike was over. Eighty three days after it began the Big Strike was over, issues largely unsettled, awaiting arbitration that took until October to come through. A pyrrhic victory was labor's which won the right to operate hiring halls but won little of the real power it sought. Dollar Line management ordered the ship to sail from San Pedro and make for San Francisco where no visible traces of the recent violent labor unrest reminded those aboard ship that some had died brutally defending their perceived rights.

First of the "502"'s to come home since the strike began, the PRESIDENT ADAMS pulled into San Francisco on August 1st. No one protested the workings of the liner this time and she got away on time on August 3rd. With her sailing that day Dollar Line resumed regular weekly sailings for points across the Pacific and fortnightly sailings on the round the world service. From Kobe the liner sailed on August 24th, from Singapore on September 11th, from Bombay on September 21st to reach Suez on October 1st. Sailing from Marseilles on October 10th the ship crossed the Atlantic to end Voyage 35 after her October 22nd arrival at New York. Two days later saw the ship steam out of New York harbor at Noon on Friday on her way up to Boston, a twenty-four hour passage. Departing from that Massachussetts port on Sunday at 8:00AM, another twenty-four hours at sea brought the liner back to New York.

Rounding out that difficult year, the ship sailed from New York again on Voyage 36 on November 1st and on November 22, 1934 from San Francisco. She ended that year in the Far East. From Kobe the ship sailed on December 14th. From Manila on Christmas Eve, 1934 the PRESIDENT AD-AMS made her way to Singapore. On New Year's Day, 1935 the liner sailed on to Penang. From Bombay she sailed on January 11th and made her way through the Suez Canal on January 21st. From Marseilles on January 30th the ship was due at New York on Feb 12, 1935.

Sandwiched between two years of exceptional labor trouble in the American maritime industry and of amazing shipping news in the latter year, 1935 was much quieter in the shipping business so it is less studied a year than the others. Captain H.S. Bauer was still on the bridge as the ship took her first sailing of the year at the start of Voyage 36 from New York on February 21st. That was the first of three outbound sailings from New York in 1935 and compared to 1934, things were looking up for they had loaded 4,510 tons of miscellaneous freight before sailing. She took her canal transit on March 1st on her way to California. A spring departure was on the bill for the beginning of her next trip and she sailed from New York on June 13th on her way around the world. Again on her way to the Pacific, the PRESI-DENT ADAMS made her way through the Panama Canal on June 21st with 4,126 tons of freight. Following that uneventful trip came another routine trip and she began that one at New York in time to sail on October 3rd. On that third and last 1935 passage through the "Big Ditch" on October 11 the ship carried 4,593 tons of general cargo with her.

Beginning the fascinating year of 1936 with a sailing from Marseilles on January 1st, the PRESIDENT ADAMS arrived at New York on January 15th. After her Boston side trip the steamer headed out on a new voyage on January 21st. Suggesting a slowdown for the economy she had only 3,232 tons of cargo. That trip was Voyage 40 and continued with her February 14th sailing from San Francisco. From Kobe she sailed on March 5th, from Bombay on April 3rd and from Marseilles on April 23rd. She reached New York on May 4th. After landing passengers and putting ashore New York bound freight, the PRESIDENT ADAMS was ready to begin Voyage 41. She sailed for Boston on May 9, 1936. Working quickly through her Boston cargo the ship was back at New York on May 12th to take on her final consignments of outbound cargo and embark passengers before sailing for Havana and the Panama Canal. The ship cast off from her Jersey City pier as scheduled at 4:00PM on May 15, 1936. After calling at Havana the ship steamed through the Caribbean for her May 22nd Panama Canal transit. She went through with 3,050 tons of freight in her holds. Up from Panama the PRESIDENT ADAMS made her Los Angeles call, arriving there on May 31st. Instead of a single night there the ship stayed for two nights overnighting there on June 1st as well and sailing on June 2nd for San Francisco. Without undue delay the ship worked cargo and sailed on schedule on June 5, 1936. As routine as usual she made her way west, stopping at Honolulu en route to Japan. The ship sailed from Kobe on June 26th and with her August 13th sailing from Marseilles, the final leg of the voyage was underway. The ship came into New York on September 1st.

Voyage 42 began at New York on September 3, 1936 and between cargo loaded at New York and Havana, she took 4,612 tons of cargo through to California that time. After a typical three weeks passage the ship was on the West Coast in time to sail from San Francisco on September 26th, less than two weeks before shipping up and down America's Pacific Coast was tied up by a massive, violent strike of seamen and dock workers. Making a usual Honolulu call the PRESIDENT ADAMS continued her way around the world reaching Kobe on October 17th. Shanghai, Hong Kong, Manila and Singapore all saw her work cargo and land and embark passengers before November 1st. The liner was in Italy one month later and sailed from Genoa for Marseilles and New York on December 2nd. The winter North Atlantic lived up to its reputation, tossing the "502" about for the bulk of her crossing. An entry in her log from the 4:00 PM to 8:00 PM watch on December 9th recorded: "cloudy, rough seas . . . wind from the north, northeast . . . heavy swells . . . Ship rolling heavily and shipping water fore and aft." More such motion was reported by the following watch. The next day was little better but as Friday rolled around, the weather improved. The Midnight to 4:00 AM watch on Friday morning, December 10th logged: "rolling and pitching normally." Using between 590 and 600 barrels of fuel oil daily, the ship had some 6,470 barrels left on board. An entry written later that night is a siren call to the shiplover: "calm sea, low swell, pitching gently." Fog set in a few hours later. The next two watches reported the whistle blowing. Thickening fog Sunday morning won a notation from the officer on the 8:00 AM to noon watch. Noting "dense fog between 9:26—10:02 AM," the watch noted adherence to Rules of the Road. The sea was moderate letting the ship roll gently and yaw lightly. The afternoon watch that Saturday, December 13th wrote: "rolling easily." A fire and boat drill was held at 3:30 PM . . . hoses were led out. Water pressure was good. The engine in the motor boat was tested and found in good working order. Also tested and found in good order were watertight doors. As the drill came to its conclusion, the fog thickened. Winds blew stronger, causing the liner to ship heavy water during the evening watch. By 10:00 PM a squall had blown up. Two days later the ship was in no better weather. The report of the Midnight to 4:00 AM for Monday, December 14th: "overcast and passing rain squalls to partly cloudy and clear. Shipping seas over forward decks and hatches. Rough sea, shipping water fore and aft. pitching easily." In red ink was an entry written by the morning watch: "10:00 AM SHIP SEARCHED FOR CONTRABAND, STOWAWAYS and DRUGS by department heads. NOTHING FOUND."

Fine, though chilly was the weather noted by the 4:00 PM watch as the ship neared the American coast. Nothing more of note filled the ship's log before her arrival at New York where she arrived from Alexandria, Naples, Genoa and Marseilles on Wednesday, December 16, 1936. Passing through the Narrows and steaming up to the Bay, the PRESIDENT ADAMS dropped anchor at noon. The mail boat came alongside at 1:25 PM and took on the first sacks of the liner's incoming mail while the ADAMS awaited completion of formalities. Pratique was granted at 1:30 PM. Nine minutes later all mail was off the ship. Eleven minutes later, at 1:50 PM, she raised anchor and began her slow passage up the Bay and into the river to her Jersey City pier. At 2:50 she passed the Statue of Liberty. Off the pier head at 3:09 PM, the tugs DALZELLEA, BRITTANIA and DALZELLITE met her and took over charge of maneuvering the PRESIDENT ADAMS alongside. They worked pretty fast. The first lines were ashore at 3:15 and at 3:50 PM the ship was made fast to the pier.

There was cargo to handle but the West Coast strike factored heavily into what happened next, and delaying her next sailing for nearly two months. With uncertainty over the extent of East Coast sympathy for the strikers, the Boston call was postponed. Since no one was sure when the strike would end nor when the PRESIDENT ADAMS might be able to deliver it to California, the Line ordered most of the cargo to be landed at New York. First off from the liner's holds on December 21st was New York reefer cargo. All New York cargo was ashore by the 29th, a fact Captain Bauer's oversized, florid script attested. As called for by consignees, Boston and West Coast cargo was landed until only scattered shipments of cargo for those ports remained in the ship's many holds. January 11, 1937 saw New York's stevedores unload the ship's Los Angeles bound cargo for transhipment to Cristobal.

All cargo work occurred while the ship was technically in lay up. Not until February 5, 1937 did the fleet begin sailing again, and when it did the first of the Dollar Line ships to move was the PRESIDENT ADAMS. While idled in ports during the strike, Dollar Line ships had not been totally dormant. Aboard the PRESIDENT ADAMS at New York, Captain H.S. Bauer and his men had not been idle. They had had plenty to do all along.

Reporting on their progress, Captain Bauer addressed Dollar Line Marine Superintendent Captain Westdahl after the end of the workday on January 23rd. Commenting on the situation during his ship's voyage 47, here is how Captain Bauer saw things:

I herewith submit a summary of work accomplished and conditions aboard from January 9th to January 24th inclusive:

Stevedores at various discharging special consignments called for and loading wines for storage.

All white and Chinese crew fine. Men working well and appreciating the opportunity to make money. Peace and good will reign/ Since last report, January 8th, we have been having mild weather and at no time has temperature dropped below freezing and so has been ideal for painting and working.

In the Steward's Department, three painters finished staterooms starting Jan. 12th, 215 and bath, 211, 209 and all baths, showers and toilets on upper deck and lower promenade decks and saloon deck portside. An average of seven men were engaged in the ice boxes. In all stewards boxes the coil piping was scraped, wire-brushed and one coat aluminum primer and paint applied. Galvanized sides wire-brushed and gratings repaired and renewed. Floors and gratings scrubbed. All steward's boxes in first class condition.

Cargo reefer hatches were finished in starboard upper 'tween decks as work done above and now working in port lower 'tween deck chamber, which needs attention. The starboard lower 'tween deck chamber and port lower chamber is in rusty condition. The starboard lower chamber needs little work except gratings and side strips for prevention of cargo against same. Plenty of carpenter work in all chambers. All this will be attended to if time permits.

Cargo holds: Various times after cargo was removed or shifted the holds were cleaned and dirt and dunnage removed. Still handicapped by cargo in nearby decks. Finished chipping decks in #1 upper and lower 'tween decks and applied one coat of everjet black. The overhead and sides were given one coat hold white over the old red paint. This paint needs little sealing except at rivets overhead and near decks. Hatch combings and hatch strongbacks were painted. #2 upper 'tween decks finished all over except port side where Boston cargo is. Crew shifting cargo to complete same. #9 upper 'tween decks, except on port side where cargo is, and lower hold decks were chipped and painted. Strongbacks, combings and sides and overhead in #9 are finished in upper tween decks, lower 'tween decks, and lower hold. Crew now working in #7 & 8 lower 'tween decks and lower hold. Paint used to date: 120 gallons hold white, 20 gallons red lead and 60 gallons everjet black.

Carpenter and helper renewing cargo battens and reefer gratings and strippings from coil pipes. Lumber for cargo battens used to the present time: 2,000 feet. Grating lumber: 1,500 feet. Ordered 50 rungs for ladders and requisitioned for removal of the ladders in #2,3 & 4 lower holds. #3 upper 'tween decks and #2 upper and lower 'tween decks to straighten angle irons and straighten or renew rungs where necessary and secure ladders. All in bad shape.[24]

Here is his next report to Captain L.H. Westdahl, the Line's Marine Superintendent at San Francisco. Under the heading of "Adams. Voyage #42, Jersey City, Feb. 2/37" he wrote:

I herewith submit a summary report on work accomplished and conditions aboard from Jan. 24th to Feb. 2nd inclusive.

White and Chinese crew fine . . . Men worked well & appreciated the opportunity to make money . . . Ceased all work due to stevedores commenced discharging & loading cargo.

Holds & reefer hatches . . . the lower between decks starboard & port chambers refinished. In port reefer . . . all old shellac was removed from the wood and one coat of shellac applied. Coil piping was thoroughly scraped . . . wire scraped and one coat of primer & one coat aluminum applied . . . Grating & side walls repaired & renewed . . . Decks chipped & one coat shellac applied . . . decks chipped & one coat everjet applied . . . Gratings renewed or repaired . . . All boxes in first class condition . . . In Starboard and lower port reefers gratings were repaired or renewed & also side battens to coils . . . The forward reefer is in good condition . . . The port reefer the coils are in rusty condition & need attention . . . All Strainers in boxes . . . Stewards used to move boxes and these were cleared and are free.

All the holds are in good condition approximately 230 feet renewed . . . Two ladders. 52 rungs were repaired of renewed . . . Five ladders, # 2 lower between decks & lower hold . . . #3. Lower between decks & lower hold . . . #4. Lower hold were taken ashore and repaired and replaced . . . All ladders and rungs to all holds in good condition . . . All ladders were cleared except one the # 2 upper between deck starboard side blocked. mechanics unable to finish this due to cargo . . . Precautions will be taken to dunnage high . . . had to have two scuppers cleared from buildup. 21 scuppers have no bars or screens over . . . Hatches are in good condition, except for replacements which are 2 hatches short.

All hold decks . . . All hold decks were chipped. wire brushed & one coat of everjet applied except #3 & 4. Lower between decks . . . #7. Lower between decks on starboard side forward. . . .#9, Upper between decks port side lack if men to move freights here prevented same being finished.[25]

---

[24]Captain H.S. Bauer's January 24, 1937 report to Dollar Line Marine Superintendent Westdahl of work done aboard the PRESIDENT ADAMS during the ship's lay up at New York. Copy in National Maritime Library, San Francisco.

[25]Captain Bauer's February 2, 1937 report to Dollar Line Marine Superintendent. Copy in the National Maritime Library. San Francisco.

The PRESIDENT ADAMS, one of five round the world ships laid up at New York, was the first returned to service, leaving New York on February 5th with 2,471 tons of general cargo and a few passengers. Written in the hasty hands of ship's officers delighted to get back underway and out to sea, the ship's log for Friday, February 5, 1937 tells the story:

> 3:00 PM tried out all navigating gear, whistles, telegraphs to engine room, telephones, running lights, all in order.
> 4:00 PM weather cleared.
> 6:00 PM finished loading, covered #4.
> 6:45 PM finished # 7 & 8 and covered up.
> 6:50 PM finished #2,3 and covered up.
> 6:55 PM finished and closed #5. All cargo aboard. crew engaged in securing hatches and cargo gear for sea.
> 7:34 PM stand by engines. Dock Pilot J. Hanson on bridge.
> 7:40 PM gangway ashore. singled up fore and aft.
> 7:51 PM let go fore and aft. proceeded out from dock assisted by tugs DALZELLEA, DALZELLITE and F.B. DALZELL.
> 8:01 PM clear of dock.
> 8:08 PM tugs left. Sea pilot W.A. Mitchell on bridge.
> 8:12 PM various courses and speeds proceeding to sea under Pilot W.A. Mitchell.
> 8:30 PM Statue of Liberty off starboard.
> 8:41 PM off Robbins Reef Light House.
> 9:41 PM off Fort Wadsworth.
> 10:07 PM stand by Sea Buoy approached Pilot Boat.
> 10:09 PM stop.
> 10:20 PM Pilot away.
> 10:20 PM Departure New York. Full ahead.
> 10:43 PM Ambrose Light Vessel. Fine, clear weather, moderate heavy northerly sea and swell. Vessel rolling moderately. Night watchmen making hourly reports. all secure and quiet. Draft leaving New York: Fwd: 21'8'' Aft: 29'2''.[26]

It was cold when the ship sailed and for the next few days she worked her way south through wintry weather. Once she rounded the tip of Florida, the weather warmed considerably. After her February 13th Canal transit, she had no calls scheduled before Los Angeles, almost 3,000 miles away. Passengers and off-duty crew alike lined the rails at 10:30 on the morning of December 19th in anticipation of passing the southbound PRESIDENT LINCOLN. The ships passed each other at 10:42 at a distance of four miles. There were still three more days' steaming to California. The PRESIDENT ADAMS arrived at San Pedro late in the night of February 22nd, approaching the breakwater at 12:17 AM. She remained outside the harbor until daybreak. It was very foggy at 7:18 AM when the pilot boat came alongside and put a

---

[26]From the log of the ss PRESIDENT ADAMS held in the collection of the National Maritime Library. San Francisco.

Pilot aboard to take the liner to her berth. The ship had enough cargo to work at Los Angeles to keep her in port for one day, 16 hours and 9 minutes. Getting ready to sail on Wednesday, February 24th, the gangway was put ashore at 3:34 PM. Eleven minutes later lines were let go and at 3:50 the PRESIDENT ADAMS was clear of the dock. The California coastal water was typically moody, the ship's officers reporting: "vessel pitching and rolling heavily" during the 4:00 AM to 8:00 AM watch on Thursday, the 25th. The seas picked up that afternoon and by dinnertime, the vessel was once again shipping water forward.

Once more coming in at night, the PRESIDENT ADAMS was off the San Francisco light ship at 9:56 PM that night. She took on the pilot at 10:08. At 11:30 PM she was under the Bay Bridge. Clocks struck midnight as the "502" approached Pier 42. Twenty eight minutes later she was made fast and at 12:35 AM on Friday, February 26, 1937, the gangway was ashore. The PRESIDENT ADAMS was home for the first time since she had sailed on September 26, 1936.

If nothing else her arrival meant to the port and to Dollar Line that things were getting back to normal, if that word can ever really apply to any facet of the shipping business! After daybreak began the ship's three day long annual inspection by a three man team.

Her departure for her around the world voyage quite delayed by the strike, the PRESIDENT ADAMS departed Pier 42 for ports around the world at noon on Monday, March 1, 1937. Honolulu bound once more, she ran into typical North Pacific weather. Wednesday's report recalled "rolling, pitching, laboring heavily and shipping seas over forward decks and hatches." Now a note of mechanical trouble showed up when No. 2 boiler went out at 7:00 PM. That furnace was back in operation by the time the ship arrived at Honolulu on March 8th. And so went the ship around the world once more, her officers duly noting weather, speed, fuel consumption, arrivals and departures of another uneventful voyage, the kind of trip best loved by sailors. After missing a scheduled call while idled by the strike, the PRESIDENT ADAMS returned to Kobe in time for a March 23rd sailing to Shanghai. Her earlier absence notwithstanding, she made her usual two day visit there between March 25 and 27th. Right on her revised schedule she pulled into Hong Kong on March 30th, sailing again on April 1st. Manila saw her during her overnight call on April 2nd and 3rd. Then it was on to Singapore and Penang where she took a heavy cargo of rubber. As ever in the past, Colombo, Bombay, the Suez Canal, Alexandria, Naples, Genoa and Marseilles lay ahead and then there was the Atlantic on the way to New York. Those last ports were called in early May, maybe the loveliest time in the Mediterranean. On May 22nd the PRESIDENT ADAMS sailed into New York harbor at the end of her second voyage since the end of the strike.

The next trip out began with a Boston sailing on May 27th. From New York the liner sailed on May 30th for Havana and a June 7th transit of the Panama Canal. After calling at Los Angeles the ship steamed north to San

Francisco and her usual three day call before sailing out again at 5:00PM on Monday, June 21st. Two items stand out on that voyage. With the greatest implications for a hard pressed Dollar Line was the first of them, the end of subsidy payments with the Maritime Commission's cancellation of mail contracts. As of July 1, 1937 the ship was on her own to earn her keep while the Dollar Line management and Maritime Commission haggled over future assistance. In the Mediterranean weeks later, the testiness of some of her crew nearly provoked a major diplomatic episode. When mail payments ran out the PRESIDENT ADAMS was on her way to Japan and was half a world away from the East Coast of the United States when she sailed from Kobe on July 12th. On she sailed, calling at her usual ports in order, taking sailings from Shanghai on July 15th, Hong Kong on July 19th, Manila on July 22nd, Singapore on July 28th, Penang on July 29th, Colombo on August 4th, Bombay on August 9th, Alexandria on August 19th and Naples on August 24th. Perhaps fueled by local wine, some crewmembers were rowdy as the PRESIDENT ADAMS made ready to sail from the Maritime Station at Naples that evening. It was the departure that almost wasn't. A dozen crewmembers were not aboard and refused to rejoin the ship before the ship's scheduled 7:00 PM departure. Eleven of them drunk, another man, maybe drunk, maybe not . . . records don't say. In vain the Captain tried to get the recalcitrant aboard but they would have none of it. As the ship was pulling away from the pier twenty minutes later, two men jumped overboard into the waters of the Bay of Naples. Shouting obscene anti-Fascist epithets at *Carabinieri* (one of the branches of police in Italy) standing on the dock, a few other crewmembers lining the rails abaft the superstructure began throwing potatoes at the hapless Italian policemen below. Enraged, one of the *Carabinieri*[27] fired his gun into the air. Curiously, local officials took no action to impede the ship's departure and allowed her to sail unimpeded. Nine of the eleven intoxicated crewmembers were hauled off to a nearby jail to sober up during the night before being packed onto a train with their comrades to rejoin their ship at Genoa. Inexplicable was the lack of newspapermen to cover the incident. Not one word appeared in the Italian press nor did officials at Naples do more than wire their opposite numbers at Genoa that an unruly crowd of Americans was on the way by land and sea.[28]

But there was a lot more and it was played out privately. Alerting their colleagues up north, the Neapolitan Questura (Police) telegraphed the Questura of Genoa shortly after the ship sailed:

At 7.20 p.m, today at the time of sailing of the American steamship PRESIDENT ADAMS for Genoa—New York a sailor stood on the pier with the

---

[27](Author's note.) Telegram from Naples Questura to Genoa Questura states the man who fired the gun into the air was the Customs Agent Biagio Crudele.

[28]From a number of dispatches and letters in the 901–438 file of the Maritime Commission for the PRESIDENT GRANT (exPRESIDENT ADAMS) in RG 178 in the custody of the Office of Records Management of the Maritime Administration.

deliberate intention of refusing to join the ship. The Captain of the vessel who in vain asked the seaman to get on board withdrew the gangway, and loosed the moorings. Just then another seaman jumped from the vessel into the water to reach the pier and join the other sailor already on the pier but as he reached same, he was stopped by the Carabiniere Ferrara Pietro who wanted to accompany him to his superior officer for further action. But the seaman with a push succeeded in getting free and jumped again into the sea succeeding to reach a line and got on board again. At this moment a score of seamen who were on deck started shouting epithets evidently against Italy and Fascism as one of them clearly pronounced the word "Mussolini" stretching his right arm and holding it with the left a gesture intended to show the greatest contempt. At the same time from the ship they threw potatoes. Giarrusso Stanislao, a waiter of the Steamship CITTÀ DI NAPOLI who was on the pier and knows English, stated to have heard from the vessel the following expressions which translated in Italian are "disgraziato cornuto Mussolini, agli Abissini avete potuto vincere ma noi americani vi fassiamo . . . così". The Customs guard, Crudele Biagio, who was present for the purpose of stopping the throwing of bottles and potatoes, fired a revolver in the air, and succeeded in his object. Steamer proceeded without further incident.[29]

Congruently, this incident garnered considerable State Department interest. From the American Consulate at Genoa on August 28, 1937 went the following report to the Secretary of State:

SUBJECT: S. S. PRESIDENT ADAMS

SIR:
   I have the honor to inform the Department that on the morning of Tuesday, August 24, 1937, I received a call from the director (Cav. Nuzzolesi) of the Foreign Section of the Questura (Police Department) of Genoa, who asked me to read an urgent telegram just received from Naples. A copy of a translation of this telegram is Encl. No. 1 enclosed herewith.
   When I had read the telegram he told me that the Chief of Police and other officials at Naples and Genoa took a very serious view of what had occurred when the S.S. PRESIDENT ADAMS was in Naples on Monday and that some consideration had been given to the idea of closing the Port of Genoa to the ship, but that they had decided merely to forbid the landing of any of the crew at this Port. They had therefore requested the Agent of the Dollar Line to inform the Captain to this effect. In addition it was the

---

[29]SNo.50788 File. Enclosure No.1 to State Department Despatch 6, August 28, 1937 to the American Consulate at Genoa, it bore in small print an edited translation of the epithetical Italian: "Disgraceful (swear-word) Mussolini, you have been able to conquer the Abyssinians but we Americans will do to you like this (probably indicating with a gesture). But don't take much time on this point—in these days of rampant lewdness and obscenity it is easy enough to translate what the sailor screamed: "F**ing disgraceful Mussolini, you might be able to beat the (racial epithet implied) Abyssinians but we Americans know how to F** you (that's where the man stretched his right arm and held it with his left). (From the ship's 901 file in RG 178 at Maritime Administration.)

desire of the Chief of Police, whom Cav. Nuzzolesi represented, to have me hold an inquiry on board the ship, in order to discover who were the offenders and ringleaders among the crew. If I would do this they would themselves keep off the ship entirely, merely placing a guard of Carabinieri on the dock to see no member of the crew landed.

I pointed out to Cav. Nuzzolesi that due to labor unrest on the Pacific Coast, the crews of these ships were at times unruly and that it should be kept in mind that this crew had just passed through Indian waters and the heat of the Red Sea to have their first shore leave in a long time at Naples, and that a certain amount of rough conduct, although it might be deplorable, was almost to be expected. I also said to him, without stressing the point, that the alleged insulting remarks of the American sailors were patently impossible and that there therefore must be some fabrication in the story of the Italian witnesses. I had to explain to him in some detail that, although the American sailor is armed with sufficient vocabulary to take care of any situation, the expression "disgraziato cornuto" or its English equivalent is not part of that vocabulary. I told him, however, that I would willingly agree to his request and go on board as soon as the ship docked, meeting him on the Pier.

At 8 o'clock in the evening the S. S. PRESIDENT ADAMS docked at Ponte del Mille and I went on board accompanied by Messrs. Ramsay and Moss of the Consulate General. I was immediately received by the Captain in his cabin. He gave me a good deal of information, mostly of a negative and useless character. He did not know who the men were who had caused the trouble at Naples and although he had carried out an investigation during the day directly and through his officers, he did not find out which men had used the filthy language and had insulted the Italian Government. He was willing to do anything in his power to help and if he knew the men he would throw them in the brig but he did not know them. Eleven of the men, he said, had remained at Naples, apparently too drunk to get on board but he did not think them permanent deserters. They did turn up next day.

I questioned in turn the Chief officer, Mr. James Phelan, the Second Mate, Mr. George Veitch, the Chief Engineer, Mr. A. Pittman, the Chief Steward, Mr. Frank Kennedy, the Boatswain's mate, Herman Strauss, the Quartermaster, James E. Ashford, and two Cadets, Dean V. Hanscom and Donald J. Hanscom. None of these officers or seamen could give any information leading to the punishment of the ringleaders, although they all admitted there were ringleaders and trouble-makers—principally, Patrick Lutz and John or James Kelly of the fire room. For the most part they insisted that they were so busy with their own jobs getting the ship out of harbor that they did not see what took place. Even the Captain "did not see" much although he had already informed me that he had conducted an investigation during the day.

I did my best to impress the Captain and Officers with the seriousness of what had taken place, at least with the fact that the Italian officials took the thing seriously. The Captain's reply was that the seamens' unions made it impossible for him to have things as they should be on board his ship and that he was entirely helpless in the matter. He offered to let me speak with the "delegate" but I refused.

As a result of the cancelled shore leaves and my semiofficial inquiry in the Captain's cabin, the behavior of the crew in Genoa was as exemplary as could have been expected. The ship left the harbor without a sound and, according to the representative of the Dollar Line, Mr. Sokall, the men were in an humble mood, even the toughest of them. The eleven men who had stayed ashore at Naples had re-joined the ship, which, in Mr. Sokall's opinion, indicated that the ship was not so bad after all and that the men in Naples had not been so much disloyal and grumbly as they had been under the influence of strong drink.

Before going on to a description of conditions on board the S. S. PRESIDENT ADAMS, which I think it my duty to give to the Department, I wish in fairness to quote the statement made to Mr. Ramsay by one of the passengers, Mr. David Orkow, of 960 East 12th Street, Brooklyn, New York. I had asked Mr. Ramsay to obtain the statements of as many passengers as possible but except for general remarks concerning the complete lack of discipline on board, he was unable to obtain any story except from Mr. Orkow. His statement puts the story of the American sailors in a somewhat better light than that of the Italian witnesses. It is as follows:

'There had been a good deal of drinking on shore in Naples by the crew. Just before casting-off the lines there was some argument on the pierhead apparently about waiting for someone. When the lines were actually cast off, a man, apparently pretty drunk, dived off the pier and started to swim towards the vessel. A man standing in a group of seamen on the after-well deck jumped into the water from the ship, apparently in the belief that the man already in the water would not be able to make the ship and would be drowned. In the meantime, however, people on shore had cast a line to the man and had dragged him from the water. The rescuer, however, swam on to the pier and in his turn was hauled up. Then an argument developed between him and a gendarme. In the meantime, a short fat man, whom I believe is the Dollar Line agent in Naples, shouted something at the man loafing in the midships of the vessel about "two weeks in the brig if they did not behave". This angered the men on the ship and the sailor who was brawling with the gendarme having again jumped into the water and been hauled aboard, some of the crew shouted insultingly about the Italians and Italy. Other members of the crew tried to shut them up, telling them that there would be serious trouble if they did not. While this tumult was going on, a couple of shots were fired and the ship rapidly gained way, and the racket stopped.

In so far as the Naples' incident is concerned, the Italian authorities are apparently satisfied, realizing as they do that the identification of the guilty men would be next to impossible. Cav. Nuzzolesi thanked me on behalf of the Questura for the action taken by the Consulate General and the good results obtained. He did not, however, fail to make a remark or two which I thought fully justified and one of which I will quote as I think it pertinent— 'it seems to me that your Government makes a mistake in allowing American citizens to travel on ships where there is no discipline, for in time of peril such ships would be very dangerous.

Consul General Chas. L. Hoover, recently in Hong Kong, came on the S. S. PRESIDENT ADAMS from Naples. He told me that there was absolutely no discipline on board the ship which was in a filthy condition due to this lack of discipline. The head waiter of the dining room, Michael Goller, spoke to Mr. Ramsay voluntarily and asked what penalty there would be if be deserted the ship at Marseilles, saying that he could no longer stand conditions on board ship and that it was an absolute hell-hole, without any discipline, where the decent elements had no protection. He said that he had decided, although he would lose his gear by desertion and would have to pay his way home, to leave the ship at Marseille. In addition to this, the chief steward, Mr. Frank Kennedy, spoke to me and asked me how long the American Government was going to allow such outrageous conditions in American ships.

I wish to add to these items an account of what took place when I went on board accompanied by Mr. Ramsay and Mr. Moss, on arrival of the ship in port. I will give Mr. Ramsay's description rather than my own. It is as follows:

'I went on board the S. S. PRESIDENT ADAMS of the Dollar Line at approximately 8 p.m. with Consul General Wilson and Mr. Moss. The Chief Officer who was standing on deck put us in the hands of a steward to take us up to the Captain's cabin. The steward took us as far as the companionway and attempted to turn us over to a Chinese cabin boy. The cabin boy refused to have anything to do with us and told the steward to 'go to hell—why can't you take the Consul up'. The Captain welcomed us on the bridge and took us into his cabin. He had hardly been seated a moment before he excused himself and dashed at full speed on to the roof of the cabin to see if any spies were listening through the open hatch window. He returned with the remark that he had caught several of the crew there recently.

'Mr. Wilson told him of the complaint of the Italian officials in Naples, against his ship and his crew, and asked him to read a copy of the telegram received by the local Chief of the Police. The Captain then, after denying that he had seen much that had happened, admitted that he had been making inquires but without result and that he simply could not name any of the men who were guilty although there were some bad characters on board the ship. He constantly referred to the "delegate" with him who had talked during the day and said that the ship was so Unionized that it was impossible for him to have real discipline; that the trouble-makers insulted the officers of the ship including himself, openly, and that on the previous night three of them had come up on the bridge and said to him "You old ____ we run this ship". However, he could not identify any of the three who had done this nor could the others who had been on the bridge at the time. During the questioning of the various officers and members of the crew by Mr. Wilson it was obvious that the Captain did not wish any of them to talk. At one time it looked as if the Second Officer, Mr. George Veitch, wanted to speak up and tell the truth but received a glance from the captain which stopped him. At another time, an attempt on the part of the Captain to put some blame on the Chief Officer, resulted in a very strong rejoinder from this officer. All the officers, apparently, were in a state of rebellion against existing conditions but were afraid to speak. It was apparent that while the Captain was pretending to be heedful to the Consul General, he had actually already arranged that little testimony of any kind should be given. He was strong enough in his denunciation of the unions and said that he had filled a log book with complaints but that the authorities in San Francisco and New York paid no attention to them. He gave the impression of being pitiful and helpless and at the same time Mr. Wilson and I had the feeling that his sympathies might be on the side of the undisciplined crew, or that he was afraid of them.'

It is entirely possible that both Mr. Ramsay and I got a wrong impression of the Captain, but Mr. Moss, the consular clerk who accompanied us, agrees that things looked as they have been reported. However, it is not my intention in this despatch to make trouble for the Captain, who was probably a victim of circumstances and in an especially nervous state due to events of the last year or so. The important and undeniable fact is that the crews of many American ships, particularly those sailing in Eastern waters, are being stampeded and bullied by paid agitators and that the result may be little short of disastrous for the American Merchant Marine. The Captain, his officers, and the local agent of the Dollar Line all shrugged their shoulders and said 'What can we do?' Of course, the Captain's job is to bring his ship home and it might be that rigid disciplinary measures might be followed by wholesale desertions or a strike of the entire crew, but I fail to see how a 'what can we do?' policy can improve matters. The travelling public is beginning to talk about the scandal of these undisciplined American ships and of the unethical familiarity of the crews and officers, with resulting lack of discipline. I do not believe we can permit such conditions to continue if, in accordance with the President's program, we are about to build up our Merchant Marine on a large scale. I am departing a little from the essentials in this despatch in the hope that its contents may be shown to Government offices concerned with the Merchant Marine.[30]

With copies to the Consulate in Naples, the written record against organized maritime labor grew. The Secretary of State sent Admiral Land a copy of the report in September, inviting him to take all appropriate action. More immediately, American officials questioned crewmembers at length once the ship docked at New York after completing her Atlantic crossing on September 9, 1937.

Her next outbound sailing from New York was on September 12th when she sailed for Boston, and October 9th from San Francisco. Through the Canal on the 24th of September she had 3,910 of freight in her. Continuing on that trip the PRESIDENT ADAMS departed Kobe on October 30th. Then came her Shanghai call even though tensions between China and Japan were so high. Hong Kong was of course next and the ship was there between November 4th and 7th. By December 9, 1937 the ship was at Suez ready to head into the Mediterranean and the final leg of the trip. When the PRESIDENT ADAMS returned to New York from that round the world voyage on December 31, 1937, she was ready for her winter 1938 refit. Before that, though, she worked cargo for the better part of a week and sailed for Boston

---

[30]Consular Report by Warden McK. Wilson, American Consul General at Genoa. Copy in the 901 file for the PRESIDENT ADAMS in RG 178 at Maritime Administration.

on January 7, 1938. She arrived on the following day and remained there until the 17th. Then it was once more back to New York where she tied up at her owner's Jersey City pier on the 18th. A few days later on February 23rd the ship went to the Atlantic Basin Iron Works in Brooklyn, there to undergo her part of a major overhaul costing $96,000.00 including upgrading the ship to comply with the latest safety standards for passenger vessels and the rearrangement of much of the ship's crew quarters. Uncertain is the extent of the work performed by Atlantic Iron but whatever they did towards refitting the ship cost $47,200.00. When the PRESIDENT ADAMS was discharged by the yard at 3:55 PM on February 25, 1938, her voyage #47 technically began and new operating subsidy payments began once again. Sailing from Brooklyn that afternoon at 4:22 PM she headed for Boston once again. There overnight between the 26th and 27th, the PRESIDENT ADAMS returned to New York to really begin her round the world voyage with her sailing on March 1, 1938. With only 2,545 tons of cargo aboard, her weakest outbound booking in several years, she made her way through the Panama Canal on March 9th. Reviewing the ship's recent whereabouts, Maritime Commission executive Sheehan asked in effect: "Why two trips to Boston?"[31] Restive labor once more played with the ship's schedule. Due to arrive at Los Angeles on March 20th, the ship had to omit her call. Striking longshoremen had the port closed.

First of the newly refitted Dollar liners to call at San Francisco, local newspapers announced her arrival some two weeks before her scheduled return. On March 21, 1938, the PRESIDENT ADAMS arrived back at San Francisco to a warm reception. Three days later, on March 24th, the liner began what proved to be her last Dollar Line passenger cargo sailing from California. Dollar Line called it Voyage #47. After calling at Honolulu on March 31st, she set her course for the usual ports, calling this time at Kobe on April 13th, Hong Kong on the 18th and 19th, Manila on April 21st. She sailed from Boston on June 15th and from New York the ship headed out to sea again with 3,611 tons of freight on the 18th. On that sailing the PRESIDENT ADAMS was required to sail with no more than 12 passengers. One of them, Ellen L. Goebel of Tulsa, Oklahoma, was so upset by her perception of the crew's attitude and conditions aboard that she put pen to Dollar Steamship Lines' stationery on July 4th, the day before the ship arrived at Los Angeles, and wrote directly to the Maritime Commission: "Some sort of investigation should be made of conditions on the PRESIDENT ADAMS. This is about the tenth ocean vessel that I have travelled on and I am sorry to say that it is the only one on which I have ever felt such an utter lack of discipline and an unruly spirit of insubordination. Whether this condition is the fault of the officers, the steamship company or the crew I hesitate to say. All I know is that they do not seem to work together harmoniously. As a result the vessel is not clean and the meals are not served properly, due to

---

[31] Memo from Sheehan in 901 file for PRESIDENT ADAMS. RG 178 Marad custody.

lack of dishes, napkins and other necessary articles. Source of this was due to sabotage or rather lead to it, I am not prepared to say. I hope you will investigate this matter at your earliest convenience as I do not think it fair that innocent passengers should be made to suffer inconvenience due to misunderstandings between labor and capital." One can only imagine what her letter to Dollar Line said and what the Maritime Commission said in their response to her (the file for the ship contains no direct response), but the letter touched off a flurry of letters between the Maritime Commission and Dollar Steamship Lines.

When she sailed again from San Francisco on July 12th no passengers were aboard but records of her arrivals and departures at her ports of calls for that trip certainly exist. On that trip the PRESIDENT ADAMS sailed on August 3rd from Kobe and was at Manila on August 11th, Bombay on August 28th, Suez on September 9th, and Marseilles on September 17th. The ship was on her way to New York when Dollar Line collapsed. Almost every writer concerning himself with the aftermath of the failure of the Dollar Line unequivocally places the entire fleet in lay up but things were not quite that simple. Ships abroad had to come home and under special arrangements made by the Maritime Commission the PRESIDENT ADAMS had been able to continue on her voyage and come home to the United States, arriving at New York on October 1st. While Dollar Line ships caught in port when the axe fell remained idle in whatever harbors they lay and those at sea were

The PRESIDENT ADAMS shows off her fine lines in this shot taken by Captain Hildebrand on November 2, 1930. Eric Johnson collection.

idled once they made an American port, the "idle" PRESIDENT ADAMS of a dead company moved around quite a bit. With her return to the United States placing her officially in lay up, those special arrangements permitted her to continue her voyage up to Boston and back to New York.

The PRESIDENT ADAMS first laid up at Boston but didn't stay put for long. This is because she was only technically laid up, a situation that can indeed permit a vessel to move, albeit without passengers or cargo. She sailed on October 9th for New York where she was laid up until the end of the month, as things turned out. For recording purposes, Voyage #47 ended at New York at Noon on October 11, 1938 and lay up began one minute later. October 27, 1938 brought the ship new marine documents to replace her previous papers which Order C-473 cancelled as a result of a tonnage change. When the ship sailed as a freighter without passengers from New York for Boston three days later on October 30th, she was still technically in lay up, and remained so until she arrived at Boston on October 31st. One minute after she tied up there, Voyage #48 began.

The failed Dollar Line was immediately succeeded by American President Lines. Ninety per cent of its stock held by the Maritime Commission, the new firm quickly picked up the most important Dollar Line trade routes. The important round the world service quickly resumed under the white eagle of the American President Lines. The successor firm technically resumed the round the world line with the sailing of the PRESIDENT ADAMS for Boston. Before sending the ship out the new owners had her accommodation spaces quickly upgraded to meet the latest standards, and authorities issued her a new passenger certificate before she departed the East Coast for the Caribbean Sea. After loading cargo at Boston, the PRESIDENT ADAMS sailed from there on November 1st to return to New York to begin her first American President Lines voyage. That was the ship's Voyage 48 and it continued with her sailing for California on November 4, 1938. Still under the command of Captain Gregory Cullen, the ship began the latest phase of her career with 2,300 tons of cargo in her ten holds. News of that sailing was carried in "The New York Times" which headlined their story "Round-World Line Resumes Service". Smaller headlines continued: "PRESIDENT ADAMS leaves today on passenger run to West Coast and Far East". Continuing headlines told more of the story: "Sailings every four weeks". And before going into detail, a final headline told of a fleetmate: "PRESIDENT MONROE starts from San Francisco Tomorrow on Way to this Port." Future sailings from New York were announced. The PRESIDENT GARFIELD was expected to sail on December 2nd, the PRESIDENT POLK was to go out on December 30th. Taking the new Line's first scheduled New York sailing in 1939, the PRESIDENT HARRISON was listed for January 27th. These ships were all to sail with passengers but the other "502"s, the unmodified PRESIDENT HAYES, PRESIDENT MONROE and PRESIDENT van BUREN as well as the "535" type PRESIDENT PIERCE, then also attached to the round the world service,would work as freighters with passenger accommodations limited to 12 beds.

Just as she had been the first Dollar Liner to sail from San Francisco in 1934 at the conclusion of the Big Strike, now she was the first ex-Dollar ship to sail on an American President Lines' voyage. With the colors of the new company atop the masthead, the PRESIDENT ADAMS introduced her new American President Lines flag and funnel colors in Havana on November 8th, the Panama Canal on the 12th. Averaging 14.4 knots on the run to Los Angeles, the ship arrived at San Pedro pilot station at 5:00 AM on November 21st. Embarking before sailing on the 22nd was Mrs. Wm. Morris Furlong, widow of a PRESIDENT COOLIDGE steward. With her were the ashes of her late husband who wanted them spread from the taffrail of a Dollar Liner. Before a gathering of ship's officers and men and Mrs. Furlong at 10:58 AM on Wednesday, November 23rd, the vessel stopped and the ashes of the deceased were consigned to the sea. Two minutes later the bridge signalled the engine room "Full Ahead" and the ship steamed on to arrive at San Francisco at 4:40 that afternoon. At 6:50 that evening she was made fast at Pier 42. On time and on schedule the PRESIDENT ADAMS sailed on November 26th. On the next day another memorial was held when the ship stopped at 11AM. With her flag at half staff a ceremony commemorated Lt. Larry Warvis, USNR, a former Dollar Line Chief Officer. During the appropriate service his ashes were strewn over the side and at 11:08 the ship resumed her course under full power. The weather got rough that day, becoming so fierce that on the following morning the Captain was unable to make his routine inspection. Plowing through storms and winds, the ship reached Honolulu on December 3rd. Other departure dates that time were as follows: Yokohama on December 16th, Kobe overnight on the 17th, Hong Kong on the 22nd and 23rd, Manila on Christmas Day through her December 27th departure for her New Year's Eve arrival and three night call at Singapore, a January 5, 1939 call at Penang, her Colombo transit on January 9th, her Bombay visit between January 12th and 14th and her January 23rd arrival at Suez for her canal transit. Then came Port Said on January 24th, Alexandria on the next day, Naples on January 29th before Genoa on February 1st and Marseilles, the last port of call on that inaugural American President Lines voyage. She sailed from that French port on February 2nd for New York where she arrived on February 15th.

On her second American President Lines voyage, Voyage number 49, the PRESIDENT ADAMS sailed from New York at 6:00PM on Friday, February 24, 1939. With a number of automobiles aboard, she listed the biggest freight of her career, a whopping 8,233 tons. At San Francisco between March 16th and 19th she sailed into yet another labor dispute and with the "535" type liner PRESIDENT TAFT, she was nearly idled there after her March 16th arrival. This time aggrieved members of the Sailors' Union of the Pacific walked out and picketed both ships on March 16th charging that instead of A.F.L. members, C.I.O. men were scaling the ships' hulls. American President Lines quickly cancelled their old contract with the C.I.O. union and signed one with the A.F.L.. Pickets cleared off and cargo loading resumed. Scheduled for a March 19th departure, the PRESIDENT ADAMS sailed on time. Milestones again: departure from Yokohama on April 6th, Kobe on April 9th.

The ship was at Bombay on May 4, 1939 when a court at San Francisco charged her a $7,500.00 libel for littering, accusing the liner of "cluttering the Golden Gate with some 40 old mattresses, ten pillows and unmeasured quantities of oil and sludge" during her November 23–26, 1938 call. Asking for the maximum $2,500.00 penalty on each count, U.S. District Attorney Frank J. Hennessy filed three counts against the ship and one against her Master, Captain Gregory Cullen. "The liner started to dump sludge while moored at Pier 44, Her Master was warned and moved out into the stream and started to dump again. Again she was warned, and then moved out into the Golden Gate, and apparently, undergoing a house cleaning, there dumped all the refuse on the ship, from old mattresses to bilge sweepings."[32] The line claimed no knowledge of any of this.

Nor did crew discipline much improve since the ship passed back under Government ownership. On her third APL voyage the ship sailed from New York on June 18th with 3,811 tons of cargo. Through the canal on June 25th she sailed from San Francisco on July 9th. Excerpts from the log of the PRESIDENT ADAMS for the period between July 30th and September 20th provide examples of the constant frustrations ships' officers lived with. The liner was at Kobe at the end of July. On the 30th, suffering from appendicitis, the Assistant Laundryman was sent to a shoreside hospital. Another patient was the painter. Unable to perform his duties because of venereal disease (don't ask ME how not), he was confined to the ship's hospital and his wages stopped for the duration of his recuperation. Enroute to Manila on August 5th a bellboy, harried by frequent calls for his services, lost his cool and spoke too loudly. He was logged and fined two days' pay for using profane language. At Singapore on the 15th a waiter didn't watch his mouth and when told to stop using boisterous language in passenger quarters, refused. Twice warned previously for his conduct, that outburst cost him three days' pay. While en route to Bombay, not admitting the Third Steward was his superior officer, a messman refused to obey one of the Third Steward's orders, topping his insolence by calling the Third an obscene name. Two days' pay was the pricetag for that violation, too. At Bombay on the night of August 25th the night bellboy was caught napping on a sofa in the foyer instead of his post near the bell indicator board in the pantry. Beyond reporting hourly to the officer on watch, he, too, forfeited two days' pay. On the 26th an assistant laundryman either fell or jumped into the water between the ship and the dock below the gangway just as the crew was being mustered before sailing. This hapless soul was admitted to a local hospital for observation and his

---

[32] Item in the *San Francisco Chronicle* May 4, 1939

pay was forwarded to him. On the way to Genoa on September 13th after drinking too heavily a fireman took up the advocacy of an injured colleague. Storming into the Doctor's office he addressed the Surgeon in abusive and surly terms, warning him that if his friend were not all right, harm would come to the Doctor. Admitting intoxication the fireman gave up two days' pay. Another fireman repeated the performance on the following day but this one thought the passenger quarters would be a dandy spot to voice his concerns. He, too, lost two days' pay. Not many quick learners among them, another fireman did the same thing again on the 15th and lost two more days' pay. At 9:30 PM that evening he went to the pantry and demanded a steak be cooked for him. The Chief Steward told him that everything was closed but he could get sandwiches from the night pantryman in the mess room. Angered, the fireman then insulted the Chief in obscene terms. Calling a bellboy to fetch the 1st Asst. Engineer, the fireman invited the Chief Steward to the mess room where he would beat the Chief Steward to a pulp. Never daunted, the fireman called uninvited on the Captain and created a further disturbance. When the Captain told him to return to his quarters, the man refused so the brig was where he slept that night. Sober in the morning, he claimed to have been unaware of his actions. Because he had already been fined, the Master added no more financial penalty but did report the man to the Maritime Commission.

When German troops invaded Poland on the morning of September 1, 1939, the PRESIDENT ADAMS was in the Red Sea on her way to a September 4th transit of the Suez canal. From their offices in San Francisco, American President Lines wired the Maritime Commission's Washington offices, answering some of the Commission's most recent questions:

> PRESIDENT MONROE insurance your telegram 31st we believe we can get regular war risk insurance same amount and have not contracted for such insurance. please advise Commission's judgement as to reasonableness of rate quoted. You are probably interested to know ADAMS due Port Said September 5. To sail from Marseilles September 13 after calls Alexandria, Naples and Genoa. We have instructed our agent Genoa prepare to take up to 250 passengers provided American want passage, necessary lifesaving equipment available and appropriate consular certification issued.[33]

The figure of 250 was discussed in a memo explaining that American President Lines had decided to limit accommodation in the PRESIDENT ADAMS to that figure because provision to carry any more than that would have made them obtain an amended passenger certificate, fit extra lifeboats and rafts and overextend housekeeping abilities. No matter the emergency, crew did not appreciate stops in a belligerent port and with the ship's September 15, 1939 call at Marseilles, entered a protest of breach of contract with the American Consulate. Five days later that particular cycle of crew annoyance

---

[33]Sept. 5, 1939 Cable from American President Lines to Maritime Commission in RG 178 Maritime Administration custody.

came full circle when the night bellboy was found asleep on duty once more. This time his snooze could have had further implications for when awakened he was asked by the Second Officer why he did not investigate the smell of smoke coming from the pantry. Abusively replying that what occurred on lower decks were not his affair, the sleeping bellboy lost another two days' wages.

Her emergency passengers breathed a collective sigh of relief once their ship steamed past the Statue of Liberty on September 27, 1939. They were landed into the safety of America. But for the ship Europe's war meant much more. Voyage 50 ended at Boston at midnight on October 2, 1939 and before the ship returned to New York at 10:46 AM on October 4th increasing security measures had followed higher crew wages, war risk bonuses and higher insurance premiums. Compensating for those quickly spiraling costs, freight offerings boomed and revenues multiplied. The ship had plenty of work to do. Now wearing American flags on both sides of her hull to remind belligerents of her nation's neutrality, she sailed on her fourth APL voyage from New York on October 6, 1939. There were 4,312 tons of freight on her manifest when she cleared Balboa a week later. The ship had gotten as far as the California coast on October 25, 1939 when Captain Cullen spotted a submarine some fourteen and a half miles off Point Pinion lighthouse. Making an immediate report of his sighting, his news made quite a stir in the California press, even when it turned out that the submarine had been the U.S.S. SWORDFISH which had passed out of the Golden Gate at 9:15 AM that morning. It also led to a request from Captain Cullen that the Navy provide merchantmen with descriptive details and silhouette drawings of American submarines, reminding the Navy that flags flown by submarines were usually small and often very dirty, thus making identification difficult.

Just how much the war in Europe increased American President Lines' operating costs for the ship was immediately apparent. Not only was war risk insurance costly, the war risk bonus the crew had won amounted to a cool 25% of their normal wages. To that would be added an extra emergency wage bonus of 25% for the crew of any ship returning to the United States via the Mediterranean. Those bonuses would kick in once the ship came through the Suez Canal and called at Port Said on her way to Alexandria. That extra wage to crew as much as any threat of hostility from warring nations led to American President Lines' spring 1940 decision to amend the itinerary of the round the world service and omit Egyptian, Italian and French ports. Japanese ports were still regular features of the line's itinerary, though they would be soon enough dropped, but nothing out of the ordinary recalls her November 19th Kobe call. En route to Hong Kong on November 22, 1939 scullery worker Elmer Price stabbed oiler W. Erikson during a fight on the after deck at 6:05AM. The fight broken up by others, Chief Officer Wilson confined Price to the Brig. Less eventful was the rest of the voyage and the ship made her subsequent calls in her usual range of ports along the line. With her January 21, 1940 arrival at New York, she completed her first full voyage since Europe went to war on September 3rd previous. Working quickly, stevedores had her inward freight discharged and loaded 5,718 tons of outbound cargo in time for the PRESIDENT ADAMS to sail from New York on January 30th. She took 5,718 tons of cargo with her through the canal. That trip continued with her outbound sailing from San Francisco on February 22nd. There was a Shanghai call that time, seemingly the ship's last, and she was at that Chinese port on March 20th. Again omitting Marseilles because of French belligerency, the ship once more began the homeward leg of the trip from Genoa, sailing from there on May 5, 1940 for her Atlantic crossing. That was the ship's last call at Genoa because when Italy entered the war five days later, the Pittman (or Neutrality) Act of November 1939 closed Italian ports to American commercial shipping for the duration of hostilities. When the PRESIDENT ADAMS returned to New York from her final Italy calls on May 19, 1940, Captain Cullen counted 4 deck officers and one deck cadet, 11 engineer officers and 2 engineer cadets, 3 radio officers, 6 pursers, 25 sailors, 29 engine room personnel, and 91 stewards among his officers and crew.

The liner sailed up to Boston from New York on May 21st. This "502" then began her next round the world trip with her sailing from New York for California on May 30, 1940. The ship had rarely, if ever before, been so heavily laden. With 7,035 tons of general cargo in her holds and on deck, she arrived at Cristobal on the evening of June 6th for her Canal transit. Clearing Balboa after midnight on June 7th she steamed on to California, arriving at San Pedro on June 16th and San Francisco on the 18th. Four days later the PRESIDENT ADAMS continued her outbound voyage when she steamed out past the Golden Gate on June 22nd. On this voyage Shanghai was once more on the itinerary and in connection with the ship's mid-July call there, Captain Cullen penned the following notice in the ship's log: "Keep a lookout for narcotics, in this port particularly."[34] With Italy and the Mediterranean now closed to American merchant ships, homeward sailings on the round the world route were now made via the Cape of Good Hope. One overriding concern for American President Lines was the attitude of the American South African Line towards calls by APL ships, so there was relief in the San Francisco office of American President Lines on August 13, 1940 when the Farrell owned company agreed in writing to allow American President to carry passengers from South Africa to New York. With a full load of paying guests the ship arrived at New York at 1:00PM on the afternoon of September 30, 1940. While at her pier on the next afternoon another incident of crew strife near the C Deck crew mess found its way into the ship's log. Messman C. Newall was assaulted and injured by 4th Cook C. Mullen. An ambulance was called to take Newall to a local hospital for treatment but police who arrived at the scene to arrest Mullen had no luck finding him.

---

[34]July 18, 1940 notation by Captain Cullen in the ship's log. Many Dollar/APL ships logs are held at National Maritime Library.

Immediately after the incident the man bolted from the ship and didn't return by sailing time.

Long buried in musty old newspaper morgue files was the story of Viennese born Dr. Hermann Frederic Erben. A specialist in brain and tropical diseases, he had years earlier migrated to the United States and acquired citizenship in 1940. Once in a while he signed on Dollar Line steamers in the capacity of surgeon. With tensions between the United States and Germany running high (and of course, Austria had been absorbed by Germany in 1938), questions about prominent Germans resident in or citizens of the United States sometimes came under scrutiny. So it was with Dr. Erben, who tried several times to prove his loyalty to the stars and stripes, attempting to enlist variously in the United States Army, Navy and Marine Corps. Rejected by each branch, he signed on the PRESIDENT ADAMS as an ordinary seaman on September 15, 1940. After serving for two days, he was discharged, as the Government preferred he remain in the country and wanted to be able to keep an eye on him. When the ship began another outbound voyage from New York on October 2, 1940 the war in Europe was thirteen months old. That trip continued from San Francisco on October 25th.

Even with a war on in Europe, the "502"'s were approaching retirement age and with a replacement building program underway, a new PRESIDENT ADAMS was to take her name. After nearly nineteen years as the PRESIDENT ADAMS, the aging ship made her final arrival under that name at New York on January 27, 1941. Her complement was smaller then. Reduced had been the engine and steward's departments. Now there were only 5 engineering officers and 3 cadets in the engine department and the steward's department shrank from 91 to 85 men. Authorization to rename her dated from January 16th and Government records support the claim that she was renamed on that date, but the shipping press reported her arrival eleven days later under her old name. Official documents issued on January 29th, when she sailed to Boston on the 28th, name her as PRESIDENT GRANT, so the exact date the ship was renamed is uncertain. Under either name she sailed from Boston on February 1, 1941 for New York and her next sailing on the round the world line. Her net tonnage was now given as a reduced 5,954 tons. What can be said with a degree of certainty is that as PRESIDENT GRANT, the former PRESIDENT ADAMS and CENTENNIAL STATE sailed from New York on her first round the world trip under her new name on February 7, 1941. She cleared Balboa after her February 15th canal transit with 6,845 tons of cargo. The old liner took her first sailing under her new name from San Francisco on March 2nd. Leaving Manila on April 3rd she made her way via Penang to Bombay and thence to Cape Town where she called on May 11th. New York bound this "502" made a stop at Trinidad on May 28th before steaming past Ambrose lightship on her way into New York harbor on June 3, 1941.

Over the months preceding that departure, through the Quartermaster, United States Army Transportation Service Water Division, the Army had been trying to buy both the former PRESIDENT ADAMS and her sister the former PRESIDENT GARFIELD, then renamed PRESIDENT MADISON. On the day of the PRESIDENT GRANT's first departure from New York, American President Lines wrote a letter about the proposed purchase of the two "502"s to Maritime Commission Chairman Admiral Emory Land. The Line's position was quite clear. They stood willing to sell both ships to the Army at a price of $800,00.00 each with delivery of each vessel at the conclusion of her present voyage. The PRESIDENT MADISON would be free for delivery to the Army after her New York arrival on April 25, 1941 and the PRESIDENT GRANT would be available for delivery to her prospective purchaser about a month later. There was a "catch" - in order to proceed with the sale, the Maritime Commission, which was the actual holder of at least 90% of the shares in American President Lines at the time, would be obliged to provide at minimum or no cost, tonnage until the place of the "502"s could be taken by two new C3 P type ships.

Into this proposed sale stepped the members of the Maritime Commission who declined permission for the sale to occur, issuing a resolution to that effect on April 2nd when the ship was once again at Manila. Their reasoning was quite simple and had everything to do with the American defense build-up. They noted that cargo bookings for the PRESIDENT GRANT were strong and that for July she had firm commitments to lift 4,000 tons of vitally needed rubber with further commitments for another 5,000 tons scheduled in mid December. In his comment to American President Lines' President Joseph Grady, Admiral Land wrote in effect on April 5th: "because the Army has just taken the WASHINGTON, the PRESIDENT GRANT could best serve the national defense effort now underway by remaining in commercial service for the time being."[35]

A world away from war and paperwork the PRESIDENT GRANT steamed on, her propellors beating the water to take her to her accustomed ports and she sailed from Manila on April 3rd, Bombay on April 30th and Cape Town on May 11th for a June 3rd arrival at New York. American President Lines took a good look at the physical condition of the PRESIDENT GRANT in early June 1941. Finding the ship clean, the inspection team prepared a list of things to do. It ran to six pages and included every imaginable area. Heading their June 6th list was "Quarters". The Master's room needed painting as did those of the Chief Officer, Chief Radio Operator, 3rd Radio Operator, 1st Assistant Engineer, 4th Asst. Engineer, Carpenter and Bos'n's mate. Mattresses and pillows in Deck department cabins were found unsatisfactory and bed springs needed repair. Untouched since the mid 1938 refit, all deck department crew cabins needed paint and inspectors called for all portholes to be checked and repaired where needed. Aft, Engineering quarters needed resurfacing. Bedding in those cabins was marginally better but

---

[35] April 5, 1941 letter from Admiral Land to Joseph Grady in 901 file for the PRESIDENT GRANT in RG 178 at Maritime Administration.

the inspectors called for renewal of those items. Also in need of painting were the cabins for the Steward's Department personnel. In poor shape was their bedding, too, and in some cabins cracked port lights were listed for replacement. Inspectors found overhead leaks in several Steward's Department rooms. Bathrooms in all officer and crew areas were also listed for painting and some minor renewal, as were crew recreation and mess rooms and the galley, while tiles in the butcher shop needed repairs. Responding to the Chief Steward's request the entire ship was fumigated and his requests that the Line investigate the source of leaks into crew rooms taken seriously. There were several items requested for the Steward's Department. Thought desirable was a drinking water line to supply crew with drinking water at night time during the long haul between Bombay and New York, when fresh water would often be shut off. For the stewards' passageway aft, the Chief asked for the installation of a bookshelf with lock to function as a library of 150 books for his men. For the long stay at New York, the Chief wanted the Company to provide an adequate supply of light and water. Calling for the Line to revamp the entire ventilation system in galley and pantry, he asked that they further arrange to ventilate the dry store room and offices of the storekeeper and Second Steward. Turning to his crew's wash and shower rooms, the Chief Steward asked for installation of doorknobs on doors, chains and stoppers for basins, repair of faulty water faucets before moving on to more expensive items like thorough scraping of those rooms before painting, installation of fresh water outlet for laundry purposes and for janitors' convenience, installation of soap trays in shower stalls and replacement of worn shower heads. For both crew and passengers, the Chief Steward called for more ice trays, ash trays, ice pitchers, more crew silverware for stewards' mess, a butter cutting machine, paper drinking cups and bags for disposal of waste from passenger cabins. Requests such as the call to repair the desk in the butcher's shop; repair broken steam lines and radiators in the bedroom stewards' rooms; repair the broken locker in the scullion's room reflected poor maintenance over the years. The Chief Steward wanted more men, too, at least once it became obvious that military preparedness would come one day to affect the "502"s. On his "want list", the Chief Steward listed the 10 more needed men, one steward's yeoman, one steward's messman, one galley scullion, one hospital attendant, one saloonman, two laundrymen, one painter, one officer's bedroom steward and one stewardess. Both Deck and Engine Departments had wish lists, too, specifically 25 new cots, new mattresses and pillows, new bed springs, a separate line for a new drinking fountain aft, wind shoots and screens where needed, and a better way to control water temperature in showers. Besides wanting forecastle decks smoothed over where needed, the Chief Officer wanted the slop chest moved to a cooler place so cigarettes and tobacco could be kept fresh for longer periods of time. Other items such as fixing the steam radiator in the bos'ns' mates and carpenter's room and installation of an outdoor faucet for longshoremen's use would require some labor. So, too, would installation of a screen door at the entrance to the crews' quarters aft and overhaul of some portholes. Simplest to fulfill was the Deck Department's request for four new coffee pots. Not to be left out, the Engine Department submitted a wishlist, too. They not only wanted new bedsprings in all beds in all cabins used by members of the Engine Department, they asked for beds of the newest type. Engineers wanted replacement of porthole glass wherever needed, oscillating fans and a clock in their messroom and paint for messrooms and all toilets used by their department. Going past the Deck's request about forecastle decks, the Engineers asked for resurfacing of decks where the oilers and watertenders lived. They also wanted the installation of writing desks and benches in the after recreation area, a drinking water line and cots. Calling for 30 cots for use on deck in hot weather, the Engineers outdid the Deck Department, requesting to have the name of their department stencilled on each. Like the Deck Officers, the Engineers wanted better temperature control for showers and a new location for the slop chest.

Beating summer heat in North America and heat in general in tropical climes continued to concern everyone. Throughout the ship's career thus far, reports of uncomfortably warm temperatures within many sections of the ship appeared in countless reports and comments. Additional items appeared on the Chief Steward's want list. High on the want list were more electric fans for many areas of the ship. "Through the tropics the dining room is uninhabitable" stated Item 17, the Dining Room, in this six page report. Perhaps the Chief Steward's request for the installation of two to four fans on each of the 6 stanchions in that room might help. He also asked for wind chutes for the room's air ports. Without calling the owners stingy the Chief Steward remarked of "an unnecessary shortage of working gear", asking for an adequate supply of trays for waiters, bedroom stewards and bellboys; linens; napkins; large tea and coffee pots; silverware for passengers and crew; tablecloths; poultry bags (for waste disposal from passenger quarters; paper drinking cups; ice pitchers; ash trays; coats for waiters and cooks; better side towels; more hickory pants, especially smaller sizes—this last because of limited laundry facilities and shortage of water during long laps of voyages.

June 7, 1941 saw her begin Voyage 2 under the name PRESIDENT GRANT. Six days later she sailed from New York on her way around the world. Sailing from San Francisco on July 8th, the ship was two days into her Pacific crossing when on July 10, 1941 the War Shipping Administration and the American President Lines signed an agreement, WSA 224,[36] regarding the employment of American President Lines' ships by the Government. Not yet directly affected, the ship sailed on, her cargo carrying abilities much appreciated by the Maritime Commission. A charter specified in WSA 224

---

[36] Never mind that technically there was no War Shipping Administration. An agreement signed that day was later rewritten to include the name of the WSA and backdated to the date of the original.

to the War Shipping Administration was already in the works. Months later war would make that charter necessary. In fact, the agreement signed that summer included eventual Government service by the entire APL fleet. A schedule worked out and dated September 6, 1941 gave a date for delivery to the WSA as charterer of each "President" liner. The ship completed her present voyage after her October 2nd New York arrival.

Now, unknown to anyone at the time, came the final commercial peace-time sailing for the sixth of the "502"'s built twenty years earlier at Camden, New Jersey. The PRESIDENT GRANT left New York on Voyage 57[37] on October 17, 1941 for a round the world voyage. Whatever the real voyage number, it was the ship's ninth voyage under the subsidy arrangement worked out in mid 1938. She called at Havana on October 20th, transited the Panama Canal on the 24th and made San Pedro on November 2nd. As was customary, she spent that night at her pier before steaming up the California coast to San Francisco where she docked at Pier 42 on November 5th and immediately came under the direct control of the Maritime Commission, which classified her a Class A-1 vessel.

At San Francisco the PRESIDENT GRANT was assigned to the Army but prior agreements left her operation in the hands of American President Lines. Sailing under a Class A Emergency Ship Warrant # 915, issued September 18, 1941 to cover cargo labelled "Government—Strategic—Critical—General", the PRESIDENT GRANT passed under the Golden Gate Bridge on November 9th under the command of Captain Emmett Tyrell. Under secret orders she had commercial passengers and cargo including a shipment of wool for Calcutta. On her itinerary were Honolulu, Hong Kong, Manila, Penang, Singapore, Colombo, Bombay, Cape Town, Trinidad and New York. She would get no further than Manila before events caught up with her and changed the course of her career. Crossing the Pacific the PRESIDENT GRANT arrived at Honolulu on November 16th. She sailed two days later in convoy for Manila.

Back at home, more and more shipping men were well aware of the increasing likelihood of American belligerency. In the Washington headquarters of the War Shipping Administration (Maritime Commission), officials directed naval architects on their staff to draw plans for the accommodation of a Naval Armed Guard in a number of American merchant vessels including the PRESIDENT GRANT and her sisters PRESIDENT FILLMORE and PRESIDENT TAYLOR. On November 27, 1941 the Navy Department issued a list of merchant vessels they wanted armed. Three of those ships were "502"'s, the PRESIDENT FILLMORE, PRESIDENT TYLER and PRESIDENT GRANT, each of which was to be defensively armed during her next Boston call. Two days later a little noticed memo from the Director of Maintenance

---

[37]Some Maritime Commission paperwork refer to this sailing as Voyage 54. Researching American merchant ships I find that actual voyage numbers are often at odds with the calendar. I don't know why.

and Repairs to the Bureau of Ordnance of the Navy informed that service that all three "President" liners would need to be armed not at Boston but at New York. The first two ships would get their guns in December, but not until her expected February 8, 1942 arrival was the PRESIDENT GRANT scheduled to receive hers. Plans for their armed guard's quarters were ready on December 17, 1941, ten days after America entered the war.

The group of ships entered Manila harbor on December 4, 1941. As the PRESIDENT GRANT steamed into port, she may well have passed close enough for her passengers and crew to see her identical sister PRESIDENT HARRISON, outbound that morning for North China and a date with fate. Also in Manila waters that day was another sister, the PRESIDENT MADISON. As if the world were not coming apart at the seams, local stevedores and the ship's crew worked cargo, even loading cargo like hemp for discharge at points further west.

The PRESIDENT GRANT was at her Manila pier on December 8th as Japanese planes were bombing Pearl Harbor (Manila, of course, is on the other side of the International Date Line). After Japanese planes flew over Manila that day, precautions were taken against air attack. The ship was shifted late that night to an anchorage in Manila Bay and cargo worked only when it was thought safe to do so. She was expected to return to her pier the following day to continue offloading. On the 9th, aware of the imminent danger of Japanese attacks, the PRESIDENT GRANT was shifted to a safer location in the harbor. At 6:00 PM on December 11, 1941, a United States Navy officer went aboard the PRESIDENT GRANT and told her Master: "it is not safe here and if you wish to go within 30 minutes you may go if you like."[38] The liner's Captain took up the Navy's offer. Leaving all of his passengers and 57 of his crew ashore at Manila, he ordered his ship to proceed to sea.

Some of her crew managed an early departure but any of her men still in Manila when Japanese forces invaded were eventually interned in Japanese prisoner of war camps. One man was quite unlucky. Arriving at Honolulu aboard another ship on December 16th, a former PRESIDENT GRANT crewmember, Lorin O. Smith of Chicago, died in an accident while helping to moor the ship. After the war some of those left behind or their survivors challenged American President Lines in court. Alleging their abandonment led to their deaths, the families of seamen Sergei Olferieff and Joseph Weisman, late of San Francisco, sued the Line for $700,000.00. Captured by the Japanese, the two men died in Japanese hands when, as passengers in a prison transport, their ship was torpedoed and sunk on October 24, 1944. Ten other crewmembers left behind at Manila eventually filed suit against American President Lines, asking damage awards of a million dollars. Survivors of over three and a half years in Japanese prison camps, the claimants

---

[38]Full text in the 901 file for the ship in RG 178 at Maritime Administration.

each wanted $100,000.00 plus $30,334.00 for unpaid war bonuses and an additional $43,245.00 per man.

No doubt American President Lines could justify Captain Tyrell's decision to get away but it would be tough to answer the questions raised by the families of crewmembers left behind. Certainly the father of Quartermaster Sergei Olferieff raised many a valid point in his letter to U.S. Senator Hiram Johnson.

To lose one's son is hard but to lose him the way we might have lost ours is simply unbearable. This letter is a respectful request of your cooperation in investigating the case presented below, punishing those responsible and clearing the name of our good son. To this my wife and I decided to devote all the remaining days of our life.

You probably know that at the outbreak of the war two American President Liners were caught in Manila: The PRESIDENT GRANT and the RUTH ALEXANDER. One of these is still safe, and the other—the RUTH ALEXANDER although sunk, did not lose her crew.

Our son Sergei Olferieff was Quartermaster on the PRESIDENT GRANT, which sailed from Manila on December 11, leaving behind more than half of her crew (57) and all the passengers. Our son is among the missing.

Since then all our attempts to learn his whereabouts were in vain. The company simply answered that sailors who miss their ship automatically break relations with the Company and the Company is not interested in their fate.

A few weeks ago, as the next of kin to Sergei Olferieff, I was notified by the President Lines to inform them as to how I wish to dispose of his effects. When the effects were delivered to me by a friend I found them all labelled: 'Deserter'. No official explanation followed, and the Company insulted my wife over the telephone, when she attempted to ask them as to why they kept his effects for eight months and now at a sudden decided to send them to us. It was only natural to think that they have learned recently something new of him.

The name 'deserter' in application to a seaman means the one who abandons his ship without leave and with the intention not to return.

In view of the fact that Sergei Olferieff could not defend himself, I felt it my duty to intervene in the case. Here are the facts, which I discovered, and which were given to me mostly in form of written testimonies.

According to the words of most of the witnesses the situation on the ship since the outbreak of war became so confusing, that none can exactly establish the time of my son's departure from the pier. Most, however are inclined to believe that he left in the morning of the day the ship moved from the harbor and anchored in the middle of the bay to avoid being destroyed by bombs. It was understood then, that she would return to the pier the next day for unloading.

As we learned, the Captain claims that he issued order forbidding the shore leaves. This order according to some of the crew members has been issued in the afternoon during the bombardment. It was issued by the first mate over the loudspeaker and understood by those who heard it that it concerned the time of the bombardment only. In any case my son was ashore at that time and the Company pretends of not knowing anything of his whereabouts ever since.

The next day Dec 11 instead of returning to the harbor the Captain called the officers and declared to them his decision to flee Manila immediately. After a mild objection on the part of the officers and suggestion to send a boat to bring the men left ashore (private boats being forbidden in the bay by military authorities) the Captain sailed without making a slight attempt to rescue his men.

When the sailors noticed that the boat is leaving Manila they demanded to return, but this demand was overruled and the ship proceeded to Australia.

According to one of the witnesses, not long before the PRESIDENT GRANT arrived to San Francisco, her Master received an inquiry from San Francisco office as to why he calls his missing men deserters, because Manila has informed them that all 57 men including the Chief Purser reported to the Agent. This information was given to me confidentially, because the man is still working for the Company.

In the effects which were delivered to us, we found all our son's clothes and even some cash in the suit case, which definitely indicate the boy's intention to return. The only thing missing is his honorable discharge paper from the Coast Guard.

The question arose to me: why none of the missing men sailed for America on RUTH ALEXANDER, which left Manila on the 26th of December?

The Company insists upon stating that they were offered to sail by a Navy officer, but the speaker for the group presented certain demands, which were not acceptable.

According to my information this officer was a company employee.

A former sailor from RUTH ALEXANDER reported as follows: On December 23 he met my son in Manila and learned from him that as long as he was abandoned by the GRANT, his duty is to return to the Navy in which reserve he is registered and that he "sticks around Cavite" awaiting enlistment. He was penniless and the witness gave him a few dollars.

Another boy, by the name of Weisman, left by PRESIDENT GRANT, was on board of RUTH ALEXANDER when the gangway was being removed in order to sail. When the witness suggested to him to remain on board, Weisman replied: 'They do not want to take me as a regular employee, I cannot pay my passage, and I would not want to run away from here as a stowaway.' With these words he jumped off the boat. His father a resident of San Francisco received a letter from him dated February 20, in which he states that he is driving a truck for the Army. The Company considers him a deserter also.

When my son was leaving San Francisco for the Orient, I asked him how does he like his new ship? His answer was: 'I like it very much-all people there are very nice except the Captain. He is afraid even of light houses.'

Two women, who recently returned from the imprisonment camp in Santo Thomas University in Manila, where they resided for six months, have not heard the name of my son among the prisoners, and do not recognize his picture.

All the above facts do not give a single hint which would allow to name my son a deserter.

On the other hand how could be called the behavior of the skippers of both liners?

They were not ordered to leave Manila, as the Company wanted us to believe, but merely not prevented from sailing. There is no doubt that most of the Americans who now suffer humiliation in the prison camps would have been rescued if the President Lines had Captains who would realize that a skipper of a boat which flies the American Flag must know better how to meet this kind of situation. Did they make an honest effort to take on board all those who overcrowded hotels and did not know how to escape? NO they even forced all their passengers to go ashore.

If the skipper of PRESIDENT GRANT insists upon stating that he issued an order forbidding shore leaves did he try to enforce it? Did he gather all the crew to tell them, that he assumes emergency powers being on the field of battle and under menace of a drastic punishment he orders everyone to remain on board? He is a longtimer with the Merchant Marine and knows well that the sailors obey him only at sea. Ashore everyone is a king.

He tries to make us believe that those left behind were cowards, Let us suppose some of them were cowards, In a situation of the kind which developed at Manila, the cowards are usually looking for authority, and the authority ones found, they immediately surrender to it their weak will power and become obedient sheep, and later on some of them quite often become heroes. This is my own experience from the last war, and not a philosophical conclusion based on theory.

There is a testimony of a sailor from the RUTH ALEXANDER, that while their ship was anchored near Corregidor, an officer came from the fortress asking to share with them some of his water. The water was not given and the ship sailed immediately. This however I do not want to believe, and having no way of checking it I give it to you for what it's worth.

To the opinion of one officer who witnessed all the above incidents, those Masters have written the darkest pages in the history of the merchant marine.

And it is not all: In order to clear themselves, they are throwing now accusations upon their minor sailing companions who cannot even defend themselves.

Who deserted who and what? This question must be answered now because, as far as I know, Captain Tyrell remains to be commander of PRESIDENT GRANT and some hundreds of American souls remain to be entrusted to him.

Our personal desire is to receive a written recognition by the Company of the fact that my son is not a deserter. An assurance of their active participation in the attempts to locate him.

To you our fearless defender of the truth I address my letter, and I know that if I allow myself to tell you all what I think not making efforts to choose expressions, you would forgive the form, because here speaks the father who is a soldier himself.[39]

---

[39]October 4, 1942 letter from Theodore Olferieff, father of Quartermaster Sergei Olferieff to Senator Hiram Johnson. Copy in ship's 901 file in RG 178 at Maritime Administration.

Maritime Commission records contain no American President Lines' response. No doubt any direct comments to the Olferieff family repose among the papers of the Olferieff's case against the line.

Now the round the world service was suspended and the PRESIDENT GRANT steered a course for the Macassar Straits, and the relative safety of Australia. Darwin was her next port. Then orders came directing her to proceed to Sydney. She arrived at Sydney at 2:48 PM on January 14, 1942. Now, during the emergency of war, legal technicalities and commercial niceties took second place to exigency. There, except hemp for Singapore loaded at Manila, all cargo bound for her ports of call along the way was offloaded there for transport on the next available ship. Onto the dock went all sorts of merchandise including reefer cargo and Hong Kong banknotes. As for the hemp, U.S. Government officials considered it a strategic material and ordered that to remain aboard for delivery at San Francisco. Responding to the inquirer of a shipment to Calcutta, the War Shipping Administration said only: "The PRESIDENT GRANT is not to return to a United States port at this time. Cargo for Calcutta is at Sydney . . ."[40] Not yet legally under charter, just under the authority of the War Shipping Administration, the PRESIDENT GRANT was assigned to the sub-agency of Matson Navigation Company's subsidiary Oceanic Steamship Company for her return voyage from Sydney to San Francisco. Among the first war cargo loaded in Australia were 12,820 bales of wool for California. Of that cargo, 6,485 bales of wool were for Chicago based commercial accounts. All the rest of the wool was for the government and would go into uniforms for the military. With cargo in her holds and passengers in her cabins, the ship sailed across the Pacific observing all wartime precautions and black outs on her way to Los Angeles, where she arrived on February 18, 1942. Two days later she made her first call in her wartime dress at her home port, San Francisco.

Three days later greetings came to American President Lines from Ralph Keating of the War Shipping Administration. His telegram said:

> WSA on behalf of the United States of America hereby offers to charter your passenger vessel PRESIDENT GRANT on time or bareboat charter basis as may be mutually agreed upon which vessel is required for war purposes for period about one year with option to either party to cancel at termination of voyage on thirty day prior written notice. stop. Charter hire and other terms and conditions to be agreed upon as soon as practicable. Valuation for total loss purposes to be not less than minimum provided for in Maritime General Order 53. stop. Risks to be assumed by United States of America pending completion charter arrangements as per letter from administration to be furnished or prior to delivery of vessel. Deliver upon completion of discharge at San Francisco expected 24th hire to commence upon completion of numerous voyage repairs and redelivery at a California port.
>
> In absence of mutual agreement within 60 days with respect to hire val-

---

[40] A letter in the ship's 901 file in RG 178 at the Maritime Administration.

uation and other charter terms and conditions, vessel will be requisitioned under Section 902 of Merchant Marine Act of 1936 effect bareboat charter basis effective as of time of delivery.[41]

Financial details were quickly sorted out. Against loss the United States of America agreed on $1,265,280.00 plus 3.5% annual interest against total loss. All costs incurred in the modification of the ship to suit defense purposes, equipment and installation of armament and degaussing was paid by the United States which further undertook to absorb the costs of reconversion of the ship at the end of hostilities. Finally, the charterer agreed to pay American President Lines a daily rate of $1,086.93 for each and every day the United States of America held possession of the PRESIDENT GRANT. Further to the remuneration to American President Lines, the daily charter hire price was broken down to show a daily price of $108.02 for depreciation, $403.91 for overhead allowance and $575.00 daily profit allowance. At 8:00 AM on March 4, 1942 the War Shipping Administration and American President Lines signed a Service Agreement Form General Agency Agreement, giving the line operation of the vessel subject to further military considerations. The mechanics of her immediate future resolved, the transition from commercial vessel to an Army long range passenger transport began with the termination of Voyage Number 57 at San Francisco at 7:59 AM on March 4, 1942. All papers in order, Voyage Number 58, or WSA Voyage 1 began one minute later at 8:00 AM when the ship was delivered to the United States Army Transportation Service under WSA Contract-109, the charter arrangements between the War Shipping Administration for the United States of America and American President Lines. Reimbursement for the cost of the 27,566.83 barrels of fuel oil in her bunkers at $0.93 per barrel brought the ship's owners $25,637.15. The charterer paid the owner a further $75.65 for the 511 tons of fresh water in the ship's fresh water tank. In turn, the WSA handed her back to American President Lines for operation but before sailing anywhere, authorities wanted the ship provided with defense features. Installation of such things occupied workers aboard ship for the remainder of the month—a period of time recorded on her books as Voyage No. 59. San Francisco port records indicate a March 8th departure and a March 20th return, with an undated call at Honolulu. Conversion into a troopship began upon her return. In terms of milage, it was not much of a trip, comprising nothing more than the passage across San Francisco Bay to the Oakland yards of the Moore Dry Dock Company where she was converted into a long range passenger transport with accommodations for 244 officers and 1,468 troops. Much cargo space was sacrificed to build troop spaces. During that refit her cargo capacity was reduced from 445,800 to 166,000 cubic feet. Characteristically, the Army fudged a bit on her size and registered the 12,000 gross ton liner at only 6,214 gross tons. Under American President Lines'

---

[41] February 23, 1942 telegram from Keating to APL in 901 file in RG 178 at Maritime Administration.

management the ship served Pacific routes during the war. At least two of her voyages were shuttle trips to Honolulu, one of them apparently performed before her conversion, and two other trips which took her to Australia. On April 8th the ship steamed out of San Francisco for Honolulu with a ship full of military men and supplies. She was back at her home port on April 30th.

After investing so heavily in preparing the old ship for transport services, authorities decided to take advantage of her and sent her to Australia. Whenever the PRESIDENT GRANT was dispatched to Australia, the Oceanic Steamship Company handled her as agents there, as American President Lines had no Australian offices. Before she sailed on May 9th she was once again appraised. This time her market value was listed as $1,040,292.00. Sydney was again her destination on Voyage 61.[42]

Perhaps it was the altered financial arrangements that precipitated a change in voyage numbers, for when the PRESIDENT GRANT sailed from Sydney on Voyage 61 on August 25, 1942 she was on Voyage 62. While in Sydney she loaded 1,000 tons of lead and 25 tons of naval stores and embarked New Zealand Air Force personnel for the northbound voyage. Bound for San Francisco, she called at Suva to load sugar for the United States. Once again, Matson served as sub-agent for the homeward trip.

When the PRESIDENT GRANT returned to San Francisco on September 14th, the wines and spirits every passenger liner carries in peacetime produced a flurry of paperwork. On an oversight, perhaps, or maybe consciously squirrelled away during her refit at Moore Dry Dock were her stores of alcoholic beverages. Not to worry, military personnel attended to that matter with warrant SW-1 issued on September 18, 1942 to cover the order issued on the previous day for all wines and spirits to be removed from the U.S.A.T. PRESIDENT GRANT.

The ship's following voyage, numbered owner's voyage No.63, began when her crew signed articles on September 17th. There was surprisingly little hurry to get her underway. Many decades have passed since the PRESIDENT GRANT next sailed on November 10, 1942, nearly two months after her voyage began. While at San Francisco she was converted for the needs of war.

Included in Maritime Commission files for the ship is the text of a telegram about her departure: "Nov. 10, 1942 sailed without cargo from San Francisco white poppy."[43] "White poppy" was either an Australian or New Zealand port. The next telegram referring to her whereabouts was a January 18, 1943 telegram from the War Shipping Administration's San Francisco office to WSA headquarters in Washington, D.C.: "PRESIDENT GRANT departed Fantan January 15 cumberland following casuals 81 marines 55 sailors

---

[42] New voyage designations crop up often in maritime history. It is rarely a safe bet to trace a career by following voyage numbers only.
[43] The copy of the telegram is in the ship's 901 file in RG 178 at Maritime Administration.

11 naval officers 8 merchant officers 6 merchant seamen 12 army officers (12 patients) 184 soldiers (163 patients) 66 bags of mail."[44] Perhaps the ports might not be recognizable in their coded form, but even a casual observer would recognize the makeup of her passenger list. Cumberland was the code name for San Francisco, where the 140 day Voyage No. 63 ended on February 3rd.

American President Lines had been informed of her arrival, having received a letter from the local office of the War Shipping Administration advising them:

Subject: ss PRESIDENT GRANT

The above vessel, allocated to you for operation under Service Agreement Form GAA, has just returned from the South Pacific and is now available at San Francisco.

This vessel has been assigned to the Army for her next outbound voyage and it is requested that you contact United States Army Transportation Service, Fort Mason for further instructions.[45]

The War Shipping Administration dealt further with the Line in regard to the ship, advising the company's accounting department that some $11,616.04 of consumable stores had been used. More on the subject of money came later when American President Lines wrote to the Fiscal Affairs section of the WSA to advise them that by conversion of results over the course of her last three commercial voyages, the annual earning power of the PRESIDENT GRANT was $771,781.55.[46]

Before sailing out on Voyage No. 64, the PRESIDENT GRANT was repaired at San Francisco. During that time her six 50mm guns were removed and eight new 20mm guns installed in their stead. That occurred during Voyage No. 64 while her charter to the War Shipping Administration was still in effect. The ship would come under requisition charter as per Section 902 of the Merchant Marine Act of 1936, the famous Bland Act. Once again American President Lines received a telegram from the War Shipping Administration. This March 1, 1943 cable advised them that upon completion of discharge of cargo on her current inbound voyage, the ship would fall under requisition. Six days later the WSA sent American President Lines a letter ordering the PRESIDENT GRANT to Sydney in ballast and that the Government would pay for the requisitioned ship on a bareboat charter basis. Later, officials changed their minds and assigned the ship once more to the sub-agency of the Oceanic Steamship Company.

Another coded telegram between WSA offices on April 15th advised that

---

[44]ibid.

[45]February 1, 1943 letter from War Shipping Administration to American President Line. Copy in the ship's 901 file in RG 178 at Maritime Administration.

[46]October 15, 1943 letter from APL Vicepresident & Secretary to R.W. Seabury, Asst. Deputy Administrator for Fiscal Affairs. WSA. Copy in the ship's 901 file in RG 178 at Maritime Administration.

the PRESIDENT GRANT: "departed Acacia on April 14th loaded wool private bales 9,465 rabbit skins 1,240 tons 10 sacks of mail 50 passengers one
four four[47] RAAF 238 Army 138 22 civilians one child 3 women." "Acacia"
was the wartime code name for Sydney. Before clearing for home, the ship
had 16,000 barrels of oil in her bunkers and 950 tons of fresh water. This
time the WSA asked American President Lines to appoint the Matson Navigation Company as sub-agent for the northbound trip. Handled once more
by the Oceanic Steamship Company, the PRESIDENT GRANT arrived at
San Francisco on May 11, 1943. At 12:01 AM Pacific War Time on May 12th
the charter expired and the ship was formally delivered to the War Shipping
Administration under requisition charter and simultaneously turned over to
American President Lines for operation under a new General Agency Allocation agreement. She soon sailed out again. Some weeks later the War Shipping Administration advised American President Lines that the ship should
be available at Noumea, New Caledonia on June 15th. From there the ship
came home, arriving at San Francisco on July 3rd. While inbound to San
Francisco on June 30th, the War Shipping Administration increased the daily
payments to American President Lines to the sum of $1,120.35.

Before the voyage was technically over on July 5th, the ship shifted into
one of the yards of the Bethlehem Steel Company, Shipbuilding Division for
the authorities were not yet satisfied with the ship. Bethlehem worked on
her between July 4th and July 22nd. It was after the ship arrived at Bethlehem's yard that authorization came through from Washington to pay the
$129,429.49 bill incurred to convert the ship into an Army transport over a
year earlier. There would be another big bill for this visit and as late as
August 12th the expense involved was yet to be approved by the bean coun-
ters in Washington. One necessary item on the ship's shopping list was a
pair of two 60 kilowatt generators. Her respite from the war lasted until
August 18th. Before any costs of the current refit were detailed, a further
$13,000.00 spent for materials for her first wartime refit in 1942 was soon
added to the original cost which covered installation of troop accommodations, degaussing, armament and defense features. That brought the total
expense of this refit to $142,429.49. Early 1944 was to bring a further round
of bills for modifications and repairs.

Next came Voyage 66 and it began on August 18, 1943. A 77 day voyage,
it was operated for the account of the Army and took her to the Southwest
Pacific. American President Lines was once more advised by letter on September 3rd that on completion of her present outbound voyage the ship was
scheduled to return to San Francisco from the Southwest Pacific, and that
for any but Army or Navy cargo, Matson would act as agent. That voyage
ended once the last of her inbound cargo was discharged at San Francisco
on November 3, 1943.

Wherever she had been, she arrived at San Francisco around November

---

[47] ibid.

1st. Voyage articles ended on the 2nd. Between November 4 and November 25, 1943 the PRESIDENT GRANT went nowhere and was carried on lay up lists. It is true that she did not leave the waters of San Francisco Bay, but the PRESIDENT GRANT was far from idle. During her stay in the area she was again overhauled, repaired and cleaned. Discharged from the repair yards on the 25th, she began voyage 67 on November 26th, a one day trial run which brought her back into San Francisco on the 27th.

This time the ship went into the United Engineering Company yards at San Francisco where work started on January 22, 1944. Before workmen finished their last task on February 2nd, general repairs, alterations, defense installations and fulfillment of military requirements racked up total charges of $172,500.00. Under the heading of General Repairs and Alterations, $90,000.00 of that sum covered overhaul to high and intermediate pressure cylinders, main engine condensers, feed pump, evaporator, steam valves, boiler valves, #2 boiler, fuel oil pumps, heating system, capstan engine, crew's quarters, galley equipment, installation of escape panels, boiler cleaning and general painting. By then she was armed with one Navy 4"/50 caliber surface gun, four Navy 3"/50 caliber dual purpose guns and eight Navy 20mm guns, all stocked with requisite ammunition. Defense installations, including the repair of gun crew quarters, replacement of broken sections of hand rails between 20mm gun tubs, replacement of deteriorated portions of the port side ammunition trunk, and the provision of necessary installations in gun crew quarters came to $7,500.00. Unspecified work costing $75,000.00 covered needed additions and repairs to all existing military accommodations. Aware that unforeseen items frequently cropped up and increased overhaul costs, the War Shipping Administration prepared for any such extras and authorized an additional $15,000.00 for this job.

January 28, 1944 brought American President Lines another standard letter from the War Shipping Administration advising them that the ship was completing repairs and was now available at San Francisco. Crew signed articles on January 31st for a period of twelve months. Once again the PRESIDENT GRANT was assigned to the Army for her next outbound voyage. The WSA told American President to take the ship on February 2nd.

The PRESIDENT GRANT's last trip was at hand and it came quite by accident. It was owner's voyage 68 and Captain J.D. Ryan was in command. Once more acting as agents in the Southern Hemisphere was Matson Navigation Company's Oceanic Steamship Company, and their local offices handled the ship in several ports. New Guinea was again on the ship's homeward itinerary when she sailed from Sydney on February 20, 1944. Steaming at 13.5 knots at 0510 hours on the morning of February 26, 1944, in position 11°07'S, 150°58'E[48], she stranded on the southwest corner of Uluma Reef, only

---

[48]The position where she struck the reef was also given as 11°15'South, 150°55'East, at least according to the report from the Commanding General, Army Service Forces, Washington, DC as per copy in the ship's 901 file in RG 178 in the custody of the Maritime Administration.

70 miles from her destination of Milne Bay. Two attempts to get the vessel off the rocks by the use of her own engines failed. Under the command of Captain Fant of the Australian Commonwealth Salvage Board, salvage operations began on the following day. The ship refused to budge and it was soon evident that she would remain fast for quite some time. The order to abandon ship was given on February 28th and no lives were lost in an orderly disembarkation from the stranded vessel. One company of the ship's complement remained aboard but they abandoned the ship on March 1st. By the 15th all cargo and ballast was off the ship and efforts to free the ship from her precarious perch began in earnest.

Officials near the salvage efforts requested the WSA to inform American President Lines of the situation. March 16, 1944 brought the War Shipping Administration further news of the condition of the stranded PRESIDENT GRANT. By then all permanent ballast had been removed. Two boilers were slack in their saddles. Twenty-five frames at Number eight hatch were loose and probably broken under the tank tops. The shell plating at Number 8 was known to be broken as well as were both condensers. At least, according to her Master, her engines were in good shape. An attempt to refloat the ship was made on March 18th. It failed as did every subsequent attempt and six weeks later, giving in to the facts of life as well as the expected high cost of repairs should the ship be freed, the War Shipping Administration gave up on April 26th and declared the wreck of the PRESIDENT GRANT a constructive total loss under charter as of 12:00 noon on February 26, 1944. Declaring all charter hire payments to American President Lines ceased as of that moment, on May 3rd they asked the Line to pay back money received from charter hire and send them a check in the amount of $17,672.63, reckoning 34–1/2 days at a rate of $512.25 per day. The Line did not consider the request at all amusing and sent the WSA a strong reply on May 5th. They were in no mood to play the backdate game this time:

> We are in receipt of your letter of May 3rd, requesting return of charter hire alleged to be overpaid to us in the amount of $17,672.63, exactly.
>
> You overlooked the fact that under Clause 18, Paragraph C of the Charter Party, we are entitled to receive additional charter hire equal to 3–1/2% per annum of the just compensation value of the vessel—or the agreed value, as the case may be—for the period between the date of the last casualty resulting in or causing or contributing to the loss of the vessel and the date of declaration of a constructive total loss, and as the declaration of the constructive total loss was not made until April 26, we are entitled to a considerable amount for charter hire for the period between February 26 and April 26.
>
> As the value of the vessel—either as just compensation of the vessel, or agreed value—has not been determined, it is impossible to calculate the amount of charter hire refundable to you, we suggest that the matter be held in abeyance until the value of the vessel is determined.[49]

---

[49] May 5, 1944 from APL Comptroller D.T. Buckley to U.S. maritime Commission. Copy in the ship's 901 file in RG 178 at Maritime Administration.

The WSA was not prepared to abandon the wreck while the Army considered the wrecked liner a no cost bazaar and cast a covetous gaze at the bounty aboard her. Somewhere along the line, someone had a go at the stranded ship's stores, for several communications refer to extensive pilferage of them. On May 5th, while APL's comptroller let the WSA know he was writing no check to them, the Chief Transportation Officer USASOS made the following request:

> If PRESIDENT GRANT abandoned, Army desired to take possession of all salvageable gear, equipment and stores . . .

Wasting no time in letting the WSA know that in the event the ship were declared abandoned, the Army quickly turned up with a shopping list. Going a step further they told the Administration that they wanted EVERYTHING that could be removed from the ship. Top of their list was all salvageable cargo gear including booms, winches and tackle. Next came mention of all Steward's, Engine, Deck and Purser's Department stores. Not neglected were all removable furniture; all navigation equipment including degaussing cables and generators; all engine room equipment and any other salvageable items. The army went so far as to instruct their local Base Commander to arrange delivery of all those things with the WSA representative in New Guinea. Short of the manpower to inventory items removed from the ship, and prodded by local Army officers, WSA locals suggested to their bosses in Washington that the ship be turned over to the Army. On May 23rd the ship was turned ninety degrees, but still remained fast aground. The Army continued lobbying for possession of whatever usable gear could be removed from the stranded "502", but continued to balk at the WSA suggestion that they charter the now useless ship. By May 30th the WSA was ready to give in and allow the Army to take what they could.

Of course it was a long leap between authorization to strip the ship of anything useful and getting the material off the stricken vessel. Men, tugs and barges were needed but the Army simply hadn't enough of any of these to devote to that purpose so they turned to the Australian Commonwealth Salvage Board for help but that group hadn't the equipment nor personnel either to accomplish this work. Worse, in the eyes of the Army, through an unfortunate misunderstanding, the War Shipping Administration representatives at Milne Bay informed the Navy that the Army was no longer interested in retrieving equipment and gear from the ship and turned the wreck of the PRESIDENT GRANT over to them for stripping with no reservations. So the Army received no salvage material from the transport at all, as the Navy salvaged only material desired by that service, and even that wasn't much more than the 4"/50caliber surface gun, removed soon after the ship slammed onto the reef. Turned over to the Commander, United States Naval Base, Milne Bay, where there was no equipment to handle it, the 4"/50 caliber gun was eventually abandoned with the ship. Other ordnance fared better. Less one mount lost during salvage, the Navy reconditioned all eight 20 mm guns as well as one 3"/50 caliber dual purpose gun. All of those were turned over to the Army which stored the 20 mm guns at Milne Bay until needed. The 3"/50 caliber gun was also reconditioned by the Navy and was returned to the Army for storage until needed. Except for those guns, the United States Army declared itself in no way accountable or responsible for any salvaged material from the PRESIDENT GRANT.

Through it all, salvage crews and American President Lines' volunteers continued to work tirelessly to float the ship through June 3rd and they nearly succeeded but nature defeated them. As if for spite, a severe gale blew up on June 1st. Striking the PRESIDENT GRANT, a huge wave broke her back, flooding her engine and fire rooms. All lighting and cooking facilities were lost. Throwing in the towel after almost one hundred days of herculean efforts, all remaining crew abandoned ship, taking with them whatever salvage equipment they could carry on June 3rd. The Army officially abandoned her on that day but not the War Shipping Administration or the Navy.

Those were the simple facts of the loss by stranding of the steamship PRESIDENT GRANT, sixth of the "502" class ships. Of course there is much more to the story than that and Government documents provide great insight into the affair. Before she was wrecked the steamer was a fully equipped, fully fitted transport and the bounty of her provisions, furnishings and fittings sorely tempted both Army and Navy. It began like this around the 5th of May when the Chief Transportation Officer, USASOS asked the Regional Director of the War Shipping Administration for permission for the Army to take possession of all salvageable gear, equipment and stores if the PRESIDENT GRANT were to be abandoned. A reasonable request under war time conditions, to be sure, the WSA had no objection, further suggesting to the Army through several discussions and communications that the Army take over the vessel on bareboat "as-is where-in" charter basis. Even General MacArthur got into the act wiring the War Department in Washington from Brisbane on June 1, 1944:

> War Shipping Administration offering PRESIDENT GRANT to Army on a bareboat charter basis as is where is without officially abandoning vessel further reference V 23587. Not understood is necessity to take vessel over on any charter basis for a simple exchange of equipment between 2 government agencies. Request matter be referred to War Shipping Administration and if possible authority be granted for Army to take possession of usable furnishings, equipment and gear aboard this vessel on a basis of exchange of property between 2 government agencies otherwise do not desire property.[50]

Bureaucratic, yes, but stupid, no, the Army politely declined the chance to pay for this bonanza of a wreck, and she remained under charter to the War Shipping Administration. On June 2nd the Washington office of the

---

[50] June 1, 1944 telegram from General MacArthur to War Department. Copy in ship's 901 file in RG 178 at Maritime Administration.

WSA instructed their Regional Director in Australia that the Army had been authorized to remove such furnishings, equipment and gear as desired as long as they gave him a receipt for anything they took.

Back at San Francisco the general public was apprised of the ship's loss on July 8th when local newspapers ran stories of the ship's end. Simpler than any of the attendant stories running through the files of War Shipping Administration, Army and American President Lines' offices were the words of Chief Engineer John Hanson. In the engine room when a huge wave hit his stranded ship broadside almost a hundred days after the liner ran aground: "Rivets popped like bullets. Engines and boilers toppled, steam and water filled the air." He and his men were truly lucky to get away with their lives.

Plenty more paperwork attended the end of the ship's life. There were also PRESIDENT GRANT crew to bring home. Covered by Warship ticket #3693, twenty six of them got a ride home in Matson's MONTEREY. Two days after the ship's April 15, 1944 arrival at San Francisco, Matson Lines billed American President Lines $7,150.00 for 26 First Class fares at $250.00 each. Hoping for reimbursement, American President Lines paid that bill and then sent a receipted copy of it to the Marine Section of the Vessel Operations Section in Washington asking for further instructions. Under the provisions of their War Risk P & I insurance, these repatriation expenses weren't covered, for the ship was not lost by act of war, rather this was a case of marine peril and the insurance company was not going to pay. July 4th brought the American President Lines the desired withdrawal of the General Agency Allocation of the PRESIDENT GRANT, backdated to be in effect as of February 26th. Somehow the WSA conned American President Lines into accepting the backdating. APL would certainly not have taken kindly to any WSA suggestion that any further charter hire payments be returned. In a December 5, 1944 interoffice memo reproduced for the benefit of Congress, the War Shipping Administration took up the matter of compensation to American President Lines for the loss of the vessel. Noted were her 10,533 gross and 3,050 deadweight tonnages as well as a reefer capacity of 32,320 cubic feet and 144 passenger beds. The Administration mentioned that like the PRESIDENT TAYLOR, the PRESIDENT GRANT had been under charter and according to the contract with the owners, it was the War Shipping Administration that was responsible for assumption of risks of loss. Basing an assessment of her value at a speed of 13 knots, the Administration accepted a figure on the date of her loss of $887,966.00 but at 14 knots, a value of $925,560.00. Moving on, the Administration's report discussed depreciated reproduction costs, allowing three different figures. First was their own, on a one ship replacement basis—for the one-time CENTENNIAL STATE, best known as PRESIDENT ADAMS, her replacement on that basis would run about $4,594,000.00. Her owners estimated a cost of $5,156,000.00 while on a five ship basis—the number of "502"s and "535"s under discussion at the time, cost of replacement would run only $3,920,000.00.Not greater than 25% higher than 1939 estimates, the Administration reported a 1940 assessment on the GRANT of $900,000.00. Next considered were estimates of value tendered by ship appraisers Frank Martin who allowed the PRESIDENT GRANT a value of $1,054,000.00 on February 26, 1944 and Captain Pilsbury, who allowed $1,400,000.00 for the old "502". Amazingly, the Administration recommended approval of the settlement with American President Lines without reducing assessed values to absurdly low figures as they had in other cases. When taken over, war risk insurance against loss in the amount of $1,344,000.00 had been taken out on this ship, and payment was made in 1945.

The Blue Hen State/ President Garfield: President Madison/Kenmore/Refuge

Finally there was EFC contract 2591, last of the seven known orders for "502" class ships. Shipping Board Statistical Section records included her hull number and name in a December 4, 1919 estimate of building progress. Appraisers listed her state of completion on January 1, 1920 at 0%, and they were right, of course, as the ship had not yet been laid down. Bearing Emergency Fleet Corporation hull number 2591, she was supposed to be named IDMAN, a name she lost well before her keel was laid down as hull number 250 on slipway U at New York Shipbuilding Corporation's Camden yards on March 4, 1920. Talk about eventual disposition and potential employment on the Ward Line's Spanish trade of the BLUE HEN STATE and her sister CENTENNIAL STATE was in full force as early as September 30, 1920. At a meeting of the Shipping Board five days later, action on a decision was deferred until construction of the ships was further along. By early November all indications pointed to an assignment to the New York and Cuba Mail Steamship Company for service to Spanish ports. A memorandum from Assistant Director of Operations W.B. Keene to Board Secretary John Flaherty quoted the Board's Memorandum No. 339 suggesting assignments for both "502" and "535" type ships when mentioning these last two "502" class ships. In the interim, the Manager of the Traffic Department continued to lobby for assignment to the New York and Cuba Mail Steamship Company of the CENTENNIAL STATE and BLUE HEN STATE. Accordingly, late that year, at the urging of the Traffic Department, the Division of Operations requested Board Secretary Flaherty to ask the Commissioners to settle the matter soon. Pointing out that assignment on that line would precipitate the need for steerage accommodations, the Division of Operations suggested that "in order to obtain the most satisfactory results in the arrangements of these quarters at minimum expense, modifications should be undertaken before the vessels are too far advanced on lines of original plans to have the necessary modifications effected while the ships are still in the builders yards."[1] More than a month passed with no decision. Then, on December 7, 1920, John Flaherty advised the Division of Operations that the Commissioners had deferred a decision on the disposition of the last two "502"'s, concurrently referring the question of fitting steerage to Commander Gate-

---

[1]Nov 2 1920 letter from Asst. Director of Operations to Secy. J.J. Flaherty. Copy in Shipping Board General Files in RG 32 at National Archives.

An impressive 33 feet of waterline dwarfs the men on the foredeck of the BLUE
HEN STATE in this dramatic photo snapped by the official photographer of New
York Shipbuilding Corp. as the new ship ran down the ways. New York
Shipbuilding Collection. Courtesy of the Independence Seaport Museum Library.

wood of the Construction Division. The year ended and no decision had been made.

Working to complete the last two "502"'s, the Shipping Board's Technical Department forwarded plans of the desired steerage spaces to New York Shipbuilding Corporation on January 6, 1921. Busy with many other projects and well tired of the often changing "502" project, the yard wanted no further part of design changes on these ships and replied immediately. Their January 7th answer informed the Shipping Board that construction of the last two ships was too far along to permit further conversion at Camden. By no means would that be the last words heard on that subject. As February 1921 dawned, the question of the ships' employment was still open. When the subject was next broached, in a February 19th memorandum quoting a telegram from Gatewood for the Chairman, the builders, the New York Shipbuilding Corp., were blamed for the long delay in providing estimates of the cost of the installation of steerage accommodations. By then some employees of the Shipping Board accepted the fact that New York Ship simply had no interest in fitting steerage in these sisters. It was true—New York Ship wanted nothing more to do with the "502"'s at that point than to complete these long delayed ships to "original" plans and get them out of their crowded yard. Gatewood again intimated the future assignment of the ships to the Ward Line, mentioning a tentative allocation, suggesting at the same time advertising for bids from yards interested in installing Third Class in the new ships. If such work were to be undertaken at another yard immediately upon delivery by New York Ship, the Board could save up to $150,000 according to the builders' estimates.

Four days later, on February 23, 1921, Clara Bolling, sister-in-law of Edith Wilson, second wife of President Woodrow Wilson, sponsored the vessel's launching, christening the ship BLUE HEN STATE. It seemed that the ship could be delivered on June 15th and have steerage spaces installed before going to work for Ward Line on the triangular trade connecting New York with Spain, Cuba and Mexico. Based on Shipping Board "leaks" and press releases during the winter and spring of 1921, stories in the shipping press regarded their ultimate disposition to Ward Line as a "done deal". Imagine everyone's surprise when it next appeared that the CENTENNIAL STATE and the BLUE HEN STATE would not go to Ward Line after all, but were to be completed for allocation to the United States Mail Steamship Company, and in an even exchange, the PANHANDLE STATE and OLD NORTH STATE would go to Ward Line.

Ink went onto more paper and pleas for the installation of steerage accommodations crossed the desks of leading executives of both Shipping Board and New York Ship. March 15th brought the yard a new booklet of specifications covering changes in building plans desired for the CENTENNIAL STATE and BLUE HEN STATE. With the specs came instructions that the yard "leave loose such work as would be effected by these modifications."[2] Included in these latest modifications to the oft changed set of building plans was steel work like divisional bulkheads, ventilators, boom rests and riveting of rigging pads, any or all of which could have interfered with the proposed conversion to two class ships. At least the yard was cooperative enough not to do any but the most essential work on the ships after their receipt of the Shipping Board's latest instructions.

As late as April 2nd, when construction had proceeded far enough for the yard to prepare to paint them, no final disposition towards the ultimate operation of either new ship had been made and Construction Manager Pitts called on the Commissioners of the Shipping Board for orders. On April 5th, Pitts had his answer directly from Chairman Benson, who noted that nothing definite had been decided. "Paint them in Shipping Board colors," he said. By June, the ship was not yet ready. Delivery to Ward Line, originally planned for May 1st in the case of the CENTENNIAL STATE and early July for the BLUE HEN STATE, was now reported delayed by the definite decision to allocate them for London service, and fit them for 176 Cabin and 400 Third Class rather than some fewer Cabin and 450—650 in "open steerage". Remember the events that changed the course planned for the four ships. Slumping cargo bookings and dwindling passenger demand on the Spanish service combined with complicated Spanish tax laws led Ward Line to drop the run. The United States Mail Line won allocation of both the CENTENNIAL STATE and BLUE HEN STATE on May 21, 1921. Even then the Shipping Board still thought they could entice New York and Cuba Mail back into the Spanish trade and when they announced assignment of the CENTENNIAL STATE and BLUE HEN STATE to US Mail, the Shipping Board stated their intention that this pair replace the PANHANDLE STATE and OLD NORTH STATE on the London line. With this definitive assignment, officials ordered further changes in accommodations in the newest "502"s.

If nothing else, delays in her construction allowed New York Shipbuilding to fit her with a funnel of proper height so with a rather tall stack painted in the colors of the United States Mail Steamship Company, the only part of the ship painted in that firm's colors, she greeted everyone boarding to witness her river and sea trials. With the grey hull for passenger ships chosen by the Emergency Fleet Corporation,[3] the BLUE HEN STATE ran trials off the Delaware Breakwater on June 25, 1921. She measured 10,596 gross, 6,233 net and 12,862 deadweight tons and displaced 21,300 tons of water. Including refrigerated spaces, the ship had a (bale) cargo capacity of 445,800 cubic

---

[2] April 19, 1921 memorandum from District Manager G.K. Nichols to Construction Division Manager Thomas Pitts. Copy in both ships' 1091 files in RG 32 at National Archives.

[3] Passenger ships owned by the EFC assigned to specific operators were painted in the operator's colors but by the time the BLUE HEN STATE was ready for delivery, US Mail was clearly in trouble. The Shipping Board ordered her hull painted in EFC's grey. When Government passenger ships were allocated to an operator for an assignment of short duration they were generally not repainted.

Because there was no work for her anytime soon, the brand new BLUE HEN STATE carried very few lifeboats when she left the yard on her way to New York. Her EFC livery was amended when she was painted grey all over soon after her arrival at Hoboken. With the coming of spring 1922, workmen painted her hull black to conform to the livery of United States Lines. New York Shipbuilding Collection. Courtesy of the Independence Seaport Museum Library.

feet. The seventh and last of her type, the BLUE HEN STATE cost $4,115,137.70. Delivered to the United States Shipping Board Emergency Fleet Corporation at Camden, New Jersey on July 6, 1921, the ship left the yard under the command of Captain Deery who set a course for New York. There on the following day, July 7th, the ship was handed over to the United States Mail Steamship Company for operation. After such a long time in gestation and under construction, the ship was finally completed and ready for service.

This was the fourth "502" sister to wear US Mail Line funnel colors. Some writers for the shipping press reported that once fitted with steerage accommodations at a New York area yard the ship would be allocated to Ward Line for the Spanish trade. Never mind that though no US flag operator remained in the Spanish passenger trade . . . those same sources reporting the decision to allocate these two ships noted that the additional cost of fitting a "502" class ship with "closed" steerage was estimated at between $200,000.00 and $300,000.00 above the cost of the vessel, reported in June 1922 as $4,088,274.71, a figure which did not include the cost of her First Class passenger spaces.

Some at the Shipping Board saw the allocation to US Mail to be a temporary expedient and it would be quite a while before the spanking new BLUE HEN STATE went anywhere. Scheduled for mid June 1921, her maiden voyage was cancelled. United States Mail Line was about to collapse and business was bad all around. There seemed little point in sending the new ship out with little cargo and very few passengers. There was simply no work for her under the American flag and upon arrival at New York the BLUE HEN STATE went into lay up. The BLUE HEN STATE immediately became a ship in search of a career as all offices in the Shipping Board and Emergency Fleet Corporation welcomed solid suggestions for the ship's future. Before the end of June, the Acting Director of Operations had called for the PANHANDLE STATE to replace her on the London service. Actually, he recommended LEAVING that ship on her accustomed service, but since the Board had altered its own papers and announced that the BLUE HEN STATE was replacing the PANHANDLE STATE, they had to reverse themselves and have the PANHANDLE STATE replace the BLUE HEN STATE! This seventh "502" would eventually enter service on the London line, and with two classes of passenger accommodation at that, but just as her gestation and construction was a long, drawn out affair, it would be a long time before the ship sailed for London. Since arriving at New York from the builders' yard the BLUE HEN STATE got no further from her pier than an anchorage off Staten Island.

So far it seemed that nothing about getting this ship ready to work had been easy. Nor was it a very easy matter to decide just what kind of Third Class accommodations to install in the BLUE HEN STATE. Still toying with the thought of equipping the PANHANDLE STATE with 650 (!) "closed steerage" berths, the Shipping Board approved that idea on July 5, 1921.

They also decided to keep her under allocation to the US Mail Line as a replacement for the BLUE HEN STATE, a ship which had yet to sail for that firm. That left the Board the option to withdraw allocation from US Mail of both the new BLUE HEN STATE and the OLD NORTH STATE.[4]

Witness this JULY 12, 1921 letter:

MEMORANDUM FOR THE ACTING DIRECTOR OF OPERATIONS

The Shipping Board, at a meeting today, considered the recommendations contained in your memorandum to the Board dated July 5, 1921, with reference to the installation of open steerage quarters on the SS. BLUE HEN STATE, and authorized and directed the Director of Construction and Repairs, prior approval thereof having been first obtained from Messrs. Smull and Love, to take the necessary steps to have open steerage quarters installed on said vessel.

The Board further directed the Division of Operations to submit to the Board as soon as practicable definite recommendations for the employment of said vessel upon the completion of said installation.[5]

At a cost of $170,000, the Robins Repair Company in Brooklyn fitted the ship with a Third Class able to accommodate up to 450 passengers. She would never fill all of those berths.

From her refit at Robins, the BLUE HEN STATE went into lay up in Hoboken where she was eventually photographed among a number of ex-German passenger liners. When the United States Mail Steamship Company collapsed, the idle BLUE HEN STATE passed directly into the fleet of the new United States Lines. She had a few months more to lay up at Hoboken. On November 30, 1921, under the command of Captain Deery, the BLUE HEN STATE moved from her Hoboken pier for the first time. Europe was not on her itinerary for she wasn't going very far at all. In company with her sister OLD NORTH STATE, the BLUE HEN STATE sailed that day for lay up at New London, Connecticut. Though a December 20, 1921 Shipping Board order awarded her or the OLD NORTH STATE, at the assignee's choice, to United States Lines for operation, a meeting of the Commissioners of the Shipping Board that same day decided the ship's immediate fate. Acting Secretary J.P. James' memorandum for USSB vice president Love tells it:

---

[4]Secretary John J. Flaherty wrote the following July 5, 1921 memorandum for the Director of Operations:
"The United States Shipping Board, at its meeting today, approved the recommendation contained in your memorandum of June 28th, 1921, and authorized and directed that the SS PANHANDLE STATE be equipped with closed steerage quarters and retained in her present assignment to the United States Mail Steamship Company for New York/Boulogne/London service, instead of the BLUE HEN STATE, leaving the SS. OLD NORTH STATE and BLUE HEN STATE, when withdrawn from said United States Mail Steamship Company, available for other employment." Copy in 1091 file/RG 32

[5]July 12, 1921 memorandum from Board Secretary Clifford W. Smith. Copy in the ship's 1091 file in RG 32 at National Archives.

The United States Shipping Board at a meeting on December 20, 1921, deferred action on your recommendations, approved by the Trustees, E.F.C., on December 19, 1921 that the steamers BLUE HEN STATE or OLD NORTH STATE be immediately assigned to United States Lines for operation in their New York-London service and that authority be granted to make such changes in the third cabin accommodations of the steamers CENTENNIAL STATE, PANHANDLE STATE and either the BLUE HEN STATE or OLD NORTH STATE as may be necessary to meet the requirements of the said trade, pending discussion with General Manager Rossbottom of United States Lines on Wednesday, December 28, 1921, at 9:00 A.M.[6]

Through the end of February 1922 the BLUE HEN STATE remained laid up at that Connecticut port where pier rental charges were substantially less than in busy Hoboken.

There were several reasons for the decision to bring the BLUE HEN STATE into service. During the ship's winter of indolence the Shipping Board considered several alternatives to the ship's lack of work. With the resolution to withdraw the three "502"s on the Pacific from the Calcutta service and restrict them to the area east of Manila came the return to the Division of Operations of the two big "535"s from Matson. Once they proved unable to draw enough business on the Baltimore—San Francisco—Honolulu run to earn their keep, the ships had no further appeal to pragmatic Matson Navigation Company and the two ships were handed back to the Government with many thanks. Since the Pacific Steamship Company's Admiral Line already had allocation of five such units for their transPacific line from Seattle, San Francisco's Pacific Mail Steamship Company had a good claim for two more such ships for their own California—Orient service. Once the Shipping Board made arrangements to allocate the HAWKEYE STATE and BUCKEYE STATE to them, the question of the three "502"s under allocation to Pacific Mail was tackled. In fact neither parent company W.R. Grace in New York nor the San Francisco office of Pacific Mail wanted to retain operation of the CREOLE STATE, WOLVERINE STATE and GRANITE STATE. Curtailing the itinerary made one of the three sisters instantly redundant and with her return to San Francisco in February 1922 her Pacific Mail career came to an end. Leaving the CREOLE STATE and WOLVERINE STATE on the abbreviated Manila line was a convenient short term expedient giving Shipping Board and Pacific Mail time to resolve the question of those ships' future.

Another factor affecting the debut of the BLUE HEN STATE came with the decision to downgrade the cabin accommodation spaces of the Atlantic based "502"s to Cabin Class. Returning the GRANITE STATE to the Atlantic for service from New York was coupled with the decision to finally enter the BLUE HEN STATE into transAtlantic passenger and cargo service.

---

[6]December 20, 1921 memorandum from James to Love. Copy in 1091 for BLUE HEN STATE. RG 32 National Archives.

Though the GRANITE STATE was ostensibly sent to New York to be placed into service alongside her sisters on the London line, that ship was instead sent to work on the Ireland/Germany run. Around the time the GRANITE STATE was on her way to New York from San Francisco, on her first such Atlantic trip or even while undergoing repairs upon its conclusion, someone at United States Lines won Shipping Board approval to offer a weekly sailing on the London line. That gave the BLUE HEN STATE a place on the Cabin service, so the Shipping Board made arrangements for her long delayed debut. Under tow she left New London on March 1st for New York, arriving there on the following day. Still to sail under her own power for more than a day, the ship went into the Brooklyn yards of the Robins Dry Dock & Repair Company in early May 1922 as the BLUE HEN STATE. She would emerge some weeks later as the PRESIDENT GARFIELD. Among the work to be performed by Robins that May was the installation of 24 additional berths, "Bachelor's Quarters." At the same time upper berths were installed to increase the ship's Cabin Class passenger capacity. Similarly, authority had been granted to alter her Third Class spaces as necessary for the London trade so that quarters for that class were fitted. There at about 3:40 PM on May 11th a small fire broke out in the pantry of the beverage room. Aboard were a skeleton crew and a number of shipyard laborers. Near hatch #10 was Chief Officer Kenneth B. Lowry, a man who would spend a few years with the ship, many of them as her Master. He later deposed that while supervising work towards the ship's stern, he noticed smoke issuing forth from the Smoking Room. He immediately went up there to check out what he knew would be a fire. Recalling that he had seen some of the yard's workmen working with torches there half an hour previously, he felt the yard responsible for the blaze. Maybe Kenneth Lowry's quick thinking saved the ship from greater damage. Under his orders the fire was fought and extinguished by 4:00 PM. It seems that one of the yard's workers was careless with an acetylene torch though neither United States Lines nor the Shipping Board had an easy time of proving that point. Damage to the ship was slight but the Shipping Board jumped to charge Robins Dry Dock & Repair Company with negligence. Repairs, reduced by the shipyard's offer of $1,000.00 credit in settlement of the matter, cost $1,741.12. On the advice of General Counsel, the Shipping Board accepted. For the record, the cost to prepare the ship for service at Robins was $32,000.00, less the credit offered by the shipyard.

Belatedly ready for service on the London line, she now had 50 Cabin class cabins fitted with a total of 176 berths. Thirty seven original cabins were fitted for four, there were "Bachelor" cabins and two more original rooms were still doubles. The last "502" class ship never sailed commercially under the name of BLUE HEN STATE, for as the refit ended the ship was renamed PRESIDENT GARFIELD. From the shipyard the ship went to a United States Lines Hoboken pier to load passengers and cargo for her maiden voyage. During her transAtlantic career for the United States Lines, she seems to have enjoyed as much popularity as any of the class, but just like her sisters, her operation lost a lot of money. At 2:20 PM on May 31, 1922 Captain Lock ordered lines to be cast off and the ship backed out of the slip and into the river on her maiden sailing for London and Boulogne, Cobh (Queenstown), and Plymouth. Aboard ship on that maiden voyage were 116 Cabin Class passengers whose combined fares yielded $16,080.50 plus 4,516 tons of general cargo and 74 sacks of mail. With $125.00 paid by passengers for deck chair rentals and another $400.00 brought in from beverage sales, total voyage revenues from that first trip amounted to $45,872.97. Across the Atlantic, the PRESIDENT GARFIELD arrived for a 40 minute call at Queenstown at 9:40 PM on June 9th where 35 adults and three children landed; Plymouth for a 30 minute call at 12:30 PM on June 10th where another 12 passengers disembarked before the ship crossed over to land 38 more adults and one child at Cherbourg during another 40 minute call at 10:00 PM that evening. At 2:30 PM on the 11th she docked at London where her remaining 26 adult and single child passengers got off. She remained at London working her 3,084 tons of grain and 1,432 tons of general cargo for 5 days and 23 hours. Sailing for New York at 1:30 PM on June 17th, the GARFIELD again made a quick one hour stop at Cherbourg at 7:05 AM on the morning of the 18th before sailing westbound across the Atlantic with a total of 107 passengers and a measly 122 tons of cargo. With passage fares amounting to $13,673.62 and ocean freight bringing in $1,324.90, the homeward trip was a financial burden, turning the $10,000+ profit earned on the eastbound trip into a $23,398.00 loss for the round trip. At 9:00 AM on June 27th her maiden voyage was over.

If her maiden voyage had been a financial disappointment, her second sailing gave even less room for optimism. Sailing on July 5th, she had a good passenger load, 118 passengers bound for Queenstown, Plymouth, Cherbourg and London, but besides a decent cargo of 4,140 tons, she took out only 38 sacks of mail. With miscellaneous on board revenue, her outbound income amounted to $41,393.50. She arrived at London on July 16th for a six days' stay before sailing for home on July 22 via Cherbourg and an August 1st arrival. Voyage 3, of course, began at New York and she sailed for the usual ports on the London line on August 9, 1922. Six days were allotted to her London call and on August 26th the PRESIDENT GARFIELD sailed for New York and a September 5th arrival. On her fourth outing the youngest of the "502"s departed New York on September 13th to arrive ten days later at London. Again she remained in port for six days working cargo and getting ready for her westbound return trip. Captain Lock took her out from the Thames on September 30th. Stopping as usual at Cherbourg on her way to Plymouth, Queenstown and New York, the ship took on passengers and some mail and headed out to sea for a lovely autumn crossing and an October 10th arrival at New York.

While in port there the ship underwent some voyage repairs. Longer to complete than expected, the ship's next sailing was delayed by about a day.

The tug GEORGE M. BARRETT helps maneuver an outbound
PRESIDENT GARFIELD sailing for London. Frank O. Braynard
Collection.

By the time she sailed from New York on Voyage 5 on October 18th the ship
had comfortably settled down to the routine of the United States Lines Cabin
service to London. On the 29th she tied up at London where she worked
cargo through November 4th, when she sailed for Cherbourg. Some 702
miles east of Ambrose Lightship on November 13th the ship reached New
York two days later. Next was voyage 6 and a November 22nd departure
for London. Across the Atlantic the ship stopped at Queenstown late in the
evening of December 1st, Plymouth on the 2nd and after her Cherbourg stop,
reached London in the early hours of the morning of December 3rd. Sailing
for home, the PRESIDENT GARFIELD departed London on the evening of
December 9th for her stop off Cherbourg. After calling at Plymouth the ship
sailed from Queenstown on the 11th for another ten day crossing to New
York and her December 19th arrival. That gave her crew Christmas at New
York before the vessel sailed on Voyage 7 on December 27th.

When 1923 dawned on January 1st the ship was at sea on her way to
Queenstown where she stopped on January 6th. Then came her Plymouth
and Cherbourg stops before her January 7th London arrival. On the 13th she
sailed for New York, arriving there on January 24th. Before sailing again on
her subsequent voyage the ship underwent various repair work and then
began loading for Voyage 8 and a February 7th departure for Britain. Via

ports, she arrived at London on February 17th. Homeward that time the ship sailed for New York on February 24th and though scheduled for another ten day crossing which should had seen her steam up the Hudson on March 6th or 7th, she was badly delayed by heavy weather and did not get in until March 9th. Then came Voyage 9, another generally uneventful trip. On that one the PRESIDENT GARFIELD sailed out of New York on March 14th. Typically ten days in either direction across the Atlantic and about a week in port on either end brought her to Voyage 10.

Operating that tenth transAtlantic trip between April 12th and May 16th, 1923, her passenger bookings were gratifying. She left New York on April 18th with 109 passengers and by the time she had made her last overseas stop after sailing from London on May 5th she had 114 passengers aboard. She landed them at New York on May 15th. She hadn't much cargo to discharge so the voyage ended on the following day. Then Shipping Board accountants took over, at least as far as her receipts and cash drawers were concerned. Once more they pored over voyage results and sad to say, there was nothing but disappointment in store for them. Reflecting the general pattern of nearly every Shipping Board vessel and every operator of Shipping Board tonnage, net results were negative. Over the course of those first ten trips the PRESIDENT GARFIELD posted a net loss of $344,513.08. To put these figures into perspective, crew meals were reckoned at a cost of $0.43 per man per meal! There was no way around a simple truth. Operating this ship cost a lot of money. Recalling that her entry into service was not until June 28, 1922, near the end of the "high season" eastbound, it was no surprise that lower loss figures than those of the other sister cabin liners were recorded. The PRESIDENT GARFIELD carried only 640 passengers eastbound during her months of service in 1922, and had only a marginally better westbound total of 671. During 1923, her eastbound totals, lower for all the "502s" than westbound totals, showed that she was chosen by 752 Cabin passengers sailing from America, and that 909 Cabin passengers made a westbound crossing in this ship. No record of Third Class passengers totals have ever been reported and though it is certain the ship had such spaces, it is not certain if any Third Class passengers were ever carried on any sailing.

Now began the summer rush of eastbound Americans intent on spending the summer in Europe. The demand for space carried a premium tariff and on the ship's next two sailings from New York on Voyage 11 on May 23rd and on Voyage 12 on June 27th every Cabin Class room was taken. Even when the ship was full, her Steward's Department satisfied most passengers. Not many passenger comments have survived, but so pleased was passenger William Leslie of Aberdeen, Scotland with his crossing in the PRESIDENT GARFIELD, finding the vessel, her food and service just as advertised, that he wrote the Shipping Board suggesting they place "502" type steamers in Clyde service, where they would likely garner a sizeable share of the weekly movement of the 1,000 some-odd passengers who sailed from there every week for the United States and Canada. Advising him that all such steamers were at that time employed elsewhere, they omitted word of the ship's upcoming sale.

Labor strife at London idled the docks in July 1923. Arriving at London on Voyage 12 on July 8th, the PRESIDENT GARFIELD was delayed as a result. So was her sister PRESIDENT ADAMS. Expected to sail for New York on July 14th, the PRESIDENT GARFIELD was held up for a whole extra week and did not sail from London until July 21st. That got her into New York on July 31st. Trying to recoup some of the time the delay at London had caused, United States Lines had the ship ready to sail in almost record time (for a "502") and the liner sailed from New York on Voyage 13 on August 4th for another ten day crossing to London. Now came the time to get the ship back on her printed schedule and after only two days the ship sailed for New York where she arrived on September 4th.

Captain Lock was still in command and maybe he had an inkling of the negotiations about the sale to the Dollar Steamship Lines, Ltd., Inc. then still underway between R. Stanley Dollar and the Shipping Board, but they were still considered secret. Indeed, so private were the negotiations between the Dollars and the Shipping Board, no one aboard was thought to be aware of the impending transaction when the PRESIDENT GARFIELD sailed on voyage 14 from New York on September 8, 1923 with 109 passengers, 2,194 tons of cargo and 970 sacks of mail. Four days later San Francisco newspapers published reports of the sale, so when the ship reached London on September 18th, every man aboard learned of the ship's upcoming transfer to private hands. The time lost to strikers was still not fully made up though this time the ship was able to remain at London for four days. She arrived back at New York on October 3rd. Under the terms of the September 25, 1923 sales contract, delivery of the ship was scheduled for early 1924. Meanwhile, the PRESIDENT GARFIELD still had several more London line voyages to operate. Figures for voyage 15 showed that when the ship sailed on October 31, 1923 from New York she had 83 passengers and a freight list that brought in just over $40,000.00. They reached Queenstown on November 9th, Plymouth and Cherbourg on the 10th and London in the earliest hours of the morning of November 12th. That time the ship had a five day stay in port. She sailed for New York on November 17th for a November 26th arrival.

At 6:20 PM on November 30, 1923, the PRESIDENT GARFIELD began voyage sixteen. Over the next few days stevedores worked long shifts to load 1,438 tons of general merchandise, 4,494 tons of grain and 469 tons of refrigerated products. Beyond those 6,402 tons of cargo, the ship took 44 sacks of mail. Embarking 88 passengers on December 5th, the ship sailed from New York. Outbound revenues amounted to $48,743.00. Once across the Atlantic the liner arrived at Cherbourg for a six and a half hour call at 1:20AM on December 15th. The ship reached London at 6:30 AM on December 17th. The westbound crossing began at London when all lines were cast off at 12:50PM on December 22nd. When she discharged the last of her inbound freight at New York at 2:55 PM on January 3, 1924, she had turned in a cumulative operating loss of $555,770.24, a figure closely approximating her sales price. No wonder the Shipping Board was relieved to get rid of these ships. Yet before the taxpayer could bid her adieu, she had more money to lose operating a final transAtlantic round voyage.

That was her Voyage 17 and for the last time in United States Lines' colors, the PRESIDENT GARFIELD sailed on January 9th for London via Plymouth and Cherbourg with 59 passengers, 6,344 tons of cargo and 2,752 sacks of mail providing a total eastbound income of $59,836.76. She arrived at London for the last time on January 19th. That final call was a long one and not until January 27th did she sail for home, a passage once more marked by heavy weather. While she was at sea, homeward bound, on January 31st, an abstract of the record of her title was mailed from New York to the Collector of Customs of the port of San Francisco. The PRESIDENT GARFIELD ended her transAtlantic career when she landed her 65 passengers at New York at the end of her seventeenth westbound trip on February 5, 1924. After discharging her cargo, the stage was set for the transfer to take place.

All paperwork was finally in order and all inbound freight and mail was off the ship. The moment of delivery to her buyers was at hand. Abstracts of title to the ship were mailed on January 31st by Customs officials at New York to their opposite numbers at San Francisco. At her New York pier the PRESIDENT GARFIELD was delivered to the Dollar Line at Midnight on February 12, 1924. The new owners wasted no time getting her ready to run in their service. First order of business was to repair any damages as per agreements between buyer and seller. A result of the recent heavy weather and requiring quick attention, the PRESIDENT GARFIELD's forepeak was leaking badly in the way of the stem. The Shipping Board paid for that one. The ship was otherwise in excellent condition and other than sundry repair or replacement of very minor items and a general cleaning of living spaces, she was painted in the livery of the Dollar Line whose big white dollar sign was affixed to either side of the ship's funnel. Prepared for her career under private owners, the youngest of the "502"'s left New York on Voyage 1 at 2:00PM on Thursday, February 21st. California bound under the command of Captain Kenneth B. Lowry, the ship called at Havana on February 25th and at 6:20AM on February 29, 1924 made her maiden arrival at Colon, Panama Canal Zone. An hour and a half later at 7:50AM she entered the Canal to make her maiden transit and at 3:17PM was through the last of the locks and in the Pacific. With 1,800 tons of general cargo, the 12,057 gross and 8,509 net ton (by Panama Canal rules) liner cleared for sea at 9:05PM on February 29th. Right on time on March 10th the new Dollar Liner arrived at Los Angeles and on March 13, 1924 the ship made her first arrival at San Francisco.

The fourth ship to enter the round the world service, the PRESIDENT GARFIELD was the second of the New York ships to reach San Francisco, home port of the Dollar Line. She sailed from San Francisco at 5:00PM on Saturday, March 15, 1924 on her first circuit of the world. The next "502" to sail out was the PRESIDENT POLK which followed two weeks later. On the PRESIDENT GARFIELD's first trip around the world the vessel called at Honolulu on March 22nd en route to Kobe. When she sailed from there she headed for Shanghai, Hong Kong and Manila from which port the voyage continued on April 19th for Singapore, Penang and Colombo. Sailing from Ceylon on May 2nd the ship arrived at Suez for her transit from the Red Sea into the Mediterranean on May 12nd. Then came maiden calls at Alexandria, Naples, Genoa and Marseilles. From there the homeward portion of the trip began with the ship's May 21st departure for Boston and New York. Steaming past the Statue of Liberty on June 5, 1924 the ship completed her first round the world voyage. She would take over fifty more such circumnavigations of the globe before a war more terrible than that which called her into existence disrupted her service. On Voyage 2 the PRESIDENT GARFIELD sailed from New York on June 12th and from San Francisco on July 5th. That brought the ship back to New York as summer gave way to fall and Voyage 3 started as scheduled on October 3, 1924. From San Francisco on that trip the ship sailed on October 25th and from Kobe on November 14th. December 6th was sailing day from Penang. At Naples on December 28th the ship touched bottom but did not remain fast for very long. Without needing any repairs for her minor grounding the ship continued on her way and completed her third circuit of the globe at New York in January 1925. First, though, came the Boston call. She left there for New York on January 13th. Arriving at New York in the early morning of January 15th the liner passed Quarantine at 5:40AM and anchored off Red Hook with steering gear trouble. Tugs saw her to her Brooklyn pier where workers boarded the ship to correct her steering gear problems.

In her first full year on the round the world service, this "502" sailed from New York on January 22nd and from San Francisco on February 14, 1925. On voyage 4, that trip saw her in the Far East by mid March and at Suez by mid April. The liner concluded her voyage at New York on May 6th. Out on voyage five, the PRESIDENT GARFIELD sailed from New York on May 14th and heading to East Asia clearing the Golden Gate on June 6th. She sailed from Kobe on June 26th for Shanghai, Hong Kong and Manila and then steamed on to Singapore, Penang and Colombo on her way to the Mediterranean. Through the Suez Canal on August 2nd, the ship docked that day at Port Said before heading to Naples, Genoa and Marseilles where Captain and Mrs. Dollar boarded the ship on August 12th for the trip back to New York. Across the Atlantic the PRESIDENT GARFIELD arrived at Boston in time to run aground on Half Moon Shoal off Cape Cod on August 26, 1925. One can only imagine Captain Dollar's reaction and his attitude towards the ship's Master, even when the ship was refloated without damage at 5:10PM that same day and proceeded on her way to New York where she arrived on the 27th.

Voyage 6 began at New York and she sailed on September 4th which got her to San Francisco in time to begin the voyage from there on September

Now in Dollar Line colors, the PRESIDENT GARFIELD arrives at San Francisco with her booms swung out to work cargo. Mike McGarvey photo.

26th. Late October saw the ship at Hong Kong and by the end of November she was at Genoa. Coming into Boston from Marseilles on December 15th, the voyage was nearly over. After her December 15th arrival at New York, passengers disembarked, the ship was off-loaded and the voyage accounts from New York closed out. Sailing out again on December 24, 1925 the PRESIDENT GARFIELD was on voyage 7. Through the Panama Canal on January 2, 1926, the ship was at San Francisco in time to sail on January 16, 1926. In turn she visited her usual ports, sailing from Kobe on February 7th and from Port Said on March 16th. From New York the ship departed on voyage 8 on April 12th and from San Francisco on May 8th. The rest of the voyage was routine and by midsummer the ship was back at New York.

There, on August 4, 1926, the ship suffered trifling damage in a small fire that broke out and was quickly extinguished. It was certainly not enough to delay the ship's announced sailing on August 5th on voyage 9. Once more around the world she steamed, sailing from San Francisco on August 28th and from Suez on October 25, 1926. From Boston towards the end of that trip on November 18, 1926, the PRESIDENT GARFIELD steamed back to New York, from whence with a moderate cargo and newly embarked passengers, she sailed on voyage 10 on November 25th for Havana, the Panama Canal and California. From San Francisco she sailed on December 18th on her way to Honolulu and the Far East. Late that year Captain Lowry left the ship and was relieved by Captain Wilson.

Greeting 1927 a day out of Kobe, the PRESIDENT GARFIELD called at Kobe to land passengers and work cargo before embarking a few more travelers and sailing on January 3rd. February 15th saw her steam through the Suez Canal and on February 23rd she sailed out of Marseilles on her way to voyage's end at New York after her March 8th arrival. The PRESIDENT GARFIELD began her next routine round the world voyage at New York, sailing for her usual ports on March 17, 1927. She was in the Pacific on her way to Los Angeles when fire broke out in No. 5 tweendecks during the night of March 26/27, 1927. Not until some damage had been done to the cargo and some to the ship herself at Number 5 tweendecks could the crew extinguish the fire. At least scorched if not crackled or buckled were decks, deckheads and bulkheads in ten passenger cabins, the Steward's store room, the Saloon passageway, the specie room, special cargo locker and the mail room. Hold No. 5 was flooded during the fight to control the fire. For a while it appeared that the blaze and its congruent smoke had been serious enough to damage some of the freight stowed in holds Nos. 3 and 4. It would take quite a long while before claims could be sorted out, but early evidence suggested $150,000.00 damage to $1,200,000.00 worth of cargo. Surveyors had a look at the ship while she was at her San Pedro pier overnight between April 3rd and 4th. Damage was minor enough for them to allow the ship to proceed. From San Francisco the PRESIDENT GARFIELD continued her voyage on April 9th. Sailing from Kobe on April 29th the ship was back at New York to end that trip in late June 1927.

Like clockwork the ship departed on her thirteenth trip on July 1, 1927. From San Francisco the voyage continued with the ship's July 30th sailing. Late August saw the ship sail from Shanghai and work cargo during the typical three day Hong Kong call. On September 28th the ship was at Alexandria, Egypt. It seems that Captain Wilson was relieved by Captain J.P. Quinn before the ship sailed from New York on voyage 14, her last voyage of the year, on October 27, 1927. Through the Panama Canal on November 4th she arrived at San Francisco on November 16th for her usual three day call and sailed out again on November 19th. From Chinese waters the ship cleared Shanghai on December 11th and continued on, stopping as always at Hong Kong and Manila on her way to Singapore and Penang, from which port the voyage continued with a December 31st sailing for exotic Ceylon. Passengers and crew of the PRESIDENT GARFIELD celebrated the arrival of the new year as the ship steamed in the Indian Ocean en route to Colombo, where she arrived on January 4, 1928. It was 12 days' sailing for her from Ceylon to the Suez Canal and with calls at her usual ports in the Mediterranean, the PRESIDENT GARFIELD began another Atlantic crossing on January 28th. After dropping off her passengers at Pier 9, Jersey City on February 7th, she sailed for Boston again on the 10th. After overnighting there between February 12th and 13th, the liner steamed back to New York where she began another of her customary circuits of the world from New York on February 16th. On that trip the voyage from San Francisco began with her sailing on March 9th. She sailed from Kobe on March 31st. It was probably at that time that Captain Quinn relinquished command of the PRESIDENT

In a lock of the Panama Canal during one of her many transits, the PRESIDENT GARFIELD had her picture taken. Author's collection.

GARFIELD to Captain Gregory Cullen, a man who spent much of the following decade on the bridge of that Dollar Liner.

The spotlight of publicity shined on the PRESIDENT GARFIELD after a collision in Massachussetts waters. Inbound in calm, clear weather for Boston at 14 knots in the early hours of June 1, 1928, the PRESIDENT GARFIELD slammed into the 2,599 gross ton coastal freighter KERSHAW, an old Merchant and Miners steamer built in 1899, at 12:20 AM while a few miles off East Chop Island of Vineyard Sound, Massachussetts. Sailing as a coastal freighter during her last years, the KERSHAW had served for over 20 years as a coastal passenger ship and was bound for Norfolk, Virginia when the PRESIDENT GARFIELD hit her portside, just forward of the bridge. For a short while the PRESIDENT GARFIELD remained fast inside the KERSHAW, which rolled over. Then she broke apart and within 19 minutes had sunk. Losing their lives in the sinking of their ship were seven members of the KERSHAW's crew while the PRESIDENT GARFIELD and Coast Guardsmen from nearby Woods Hole station fished the surviving thirty men from the sea, including all the KERSHAW'S officers except the 2nd Assistant Engineer. Delaying for four hours to hunt for survivors, the PRESIDENT GARFIELD marked the spot of the crash with a buoy and at 7:00 AM proceeded on her way into Boston where she arrived that afternoon. After an inquest into the cause of the accident, the licenses of two Captains were suspended for one year. Losing his privilege to command American vessels for twelve months was Captain E.S. Brooks, Master of the KERSHAW. Captain Ralph W.C. Smith, a New York based pilot licensed for the waters between New York and Boston on the PRESIDENT GARFIELD at the time of the collision, was suspended for one year by the local supervising inspector. Feeling unfairly penalized, Captain Smith appealed and his suspension was reduced to two months. So, too did Captain Brooks appeal. This was one of three rather notable incidents involving a member of the "502" class in the waters of Massachussetts.

No further incident brought her either into the press or into casualty lists that year except for a minor fire that broke out in a forward hold and slightly damaged some of her cargo of hemp while the ship was at the port of New York during the night of September 24, 1928. The ship was undamaged and ready to sail on her last trip of the year. With passengers, mail and cargo, the PRESIDENT GARFIELD sailed from New York on September 30th. After calling once again at Havana it was on to the Canal and an October 7th transit on her way to San Pedro and her October 19th arrival at San Francisco. On her way to the Far East the ship made her very popular Honolulu call on October 26th. Across the Pacific, the liner was at Kobe on November 8th and 9th, Shanghai between November 12th and 14th, Hong Kong on the 17th and 18th and arrived at Manila on the 20th. She sailed the following day for her calls at Singapore, Penang, Colombo and Suez where she arrived on December 17th for her transit of the Suez Canal. After passing Christmas holidays in Italian waters, the ship began the last leg of her world voyage to arrive at Boston in early January 1929.

With a very respectable total of 89 passengers aboard, the PRESIDENT GARFIELD left New York under the command of Captain Quinn on the wintry evening of January 17, 1929. Inbound to Havana on the morning of January 20th, she was some sixty miles off the Florida coast and steaming through fog at 7:10 AM when she went aground on the hidden Mantanilla Reef in the middle shoals of the Bahamas. The second time the ship made a real landfall, it was her third incident. Lucky this time, the ship was not much damaged, just stuck. Early reports to the Dollar Line informed the home office that the ship was fast and safe, not leaking and in no great danger. For about a day passengers waited aboard their idled PRESIDENT GARFIELD before Captain Quinn and Dollar Line officials decided what to do with them. Breakfast and lunch were served as usual and then some passengers joined a number of Chinese stewards and mess boys in an afternoon of fishing from the ship's railings. Ninety miles away, the Munson Line's PAN AMERICA, then working on a New York—Nassau run, altered course and came to help out. Dollar Line arranged to transfer the PRESIDENT GARFIELD's passengers, their baggage and the ship's mail to the PAN AMERICA for passage to nearby Nassau. There they remained and enjoyed an unscheduled stopover while Dollar Line sorted out the problem of the stranded PRESIDENT GARFIELD. Freed from her perch by the Merritt, Chapman and Scott wrecking steamer WARBLER at 6:10 AM on the morning of January 23rd, the "502" made her way to Miami where a diver examined her hull. A certificate of seaworthiness was granted and on the 23th, the PRESIDENT GARFIELD sailed for the short passage over to Nassau where she picked up her passengers and steamed out again on January 24th. Resuming her itinerary, the liner called at Havana on the 26th on her way to Panama. After her February 9th arrival at San Francisco, she was dry-docked where the full extent of her damage revealed the need to renew and or fair a total of 74 plates including fourteen bottom plates, replace one propellor blade and some incidental repairs. Declaring the ship nonetheless seaworthy, officials granted Dollar Line's request to defer permanent repairs, and make only temporary repairs like making good slack rivets and caulking, so the ship could return to her schedule. That done, three days later, on February 12th, the PRESIDENT GARFIELD sailed for Kobe. She sailed from that major Japanese port on March 1st. Coming in from Marseilles and Boston as usual, the liner arrived at New York on April 29, 1929.

Now came a hiatus from her usual globe-girdling. It was time for the PRESIDENT GARFIELD to be upgraded. With $225,000.00 in funds made available from the Construction Loan Fund, the PRESIDENT GARFIELD was improved internally and externally according to the formula used for the PRESIDENT POLK. Winning the contract to improve three "502"s was the Newport News Shipbuilding and DryDock Company and the PRESIDENT GARFIELD arrived at their yards on May 4, 1929 to be reconditioned.

Using a variation of Theodore Ferris' 1925 repair and refit plan for the fire damaged PRESIDENT POLK as a guide, Newport News rebuilt the bulk of the PRESIDENT GARFIELD's passenger accommodations much as they had in her sister during 1925. Such a refit was also done that season on the PRESIDENT ADAMS and PRESIDENT HARRISON. During ten weeks of work at Newport News the separate houses of the PRESIDENT GARFIELD's superstructure were joined together under a new boat deck, new public rooms and cabins were built and a new funnel casing erected in place of her original thin stack. When the work was done the liner was practically a new ship with much improved passenger accommodation for some 150 First Class passengers. Though the 10,495 gross ton ship was actually enlarged by about 2,000 gross tons by the work just accomplished, the Dollar Steamship Lines, Ltd. Inc. registered her at the lower figure to save money on registry fees and port charges. The job done, the PRESIDENT GARFIELD was redelivered to her owners by Newport News Shipbuilding and Drydock Company on July 13, 1929. Back on the bridge once more was Captain Gregory Cullen, now in command of a crew of 20 officers and 128 men. The rebuilt liner sailed for New York to rejoin her sisters and other fleetmates like the PRESIDENT FILLMORE and PRESIDENT JOHNSON on the round the world service. Fresh from the yards, the newly refitted ship proved an instant magnet for passengers and was full when she sailed from New York for foreign ports on July 17, 1929. Paperwork regarding her redelivery was entered with the proper officials on the 18th. On August 6th the newly refitted vessel steamed past the Golden Gate on her way to Dollar Lines piers 42 and 44 where she showed off her new looks to admiring visitors. On that trip the ship sailed from San Francisco on August 9th for her usual ports. That time she sailed from Shanghai on September 4th and Hong Kong on the 7th. From Manila on September 9th the PRESIDENT GARFIELD sailed for Singapore and Penang. On September 25th the liner sailed from Colombo for Suez and the Mediterranean. At every port along the way the ship's new look and new accommodation spaces caused comment, all of it favorable. Even Genoa, home to some of the world's finest liners, had kind words for the American ship. So, too, did Marseilles when she called there on October 16th for New York.

The ship was two days out of New York on October 29th when the New York stock market crashed. By the time the ship tied up at her Jersey City pier on October 31st, several men had already jumped from their office windows in lower Manhattan but the Wall Street implosion had not yet sobered the nation. Even though fortunes were instantly swept away, the PRESIDENT GARFIELD had work to do and she continued as usual, sailing again from New York on November 7, 1929 for ports around the world. Through the Canal on November 15th the PRESIDENT GARFIELD called at San Pedro on the 24th on her way to her November 26th arrival at San Francisco. The ship spent three days there before heading out once again across the Pacific. From Kobe that time the ship sailed on December 20, 1929. January 1, 1930 saw this "502" sail from Singapore as she continued her westwards course

Here's how the PRESIDENT GARFIELD looked on April 16, 1932 as John Lochhead photographed her. Courtesy of SSHSA.

around the world, a voyage that took her into New York on February 20, 1930. Tied up to her Jersey City pier that same day, a fire broke out among cases of oil stored in a hold. Fire fighting tugs and the local fire department raced to the scene but before they could extinguish the blaze, 548 cases of rubber stored in the same hold for discharge at Boston were damaged. Other than the acrid smell of smoke and a lingering aroma of scorched rubber, there was no damage to the ship that her own crew and a few dollars worth of paint couldn't remedy. She was cleaned up by the time she took out passengers again on February 27th. On that voyage the ship called at Havana on March 3rd, Panama on March 8th and San Pedro on March 16th before arriving at San Francisco again on March 18th. Advising readers of passenger ship movements, local newspapers noting the arrival of the PRESIDENT GARFIELD reported the landing there of 37 passengers including Wallace Alexander of the important Honolulu firm of Alexander and Baldwin. Records also show that the ship landed 461 tons of cargo and 400 bags of mail before she loaded more of the same, greeted some new passengers and sailed again on March 21st. Round the world like clockwork she went once more, sailing from Kobe on April 8th, Shanghai on April 16th, Colombo on May 7th, Naples on May 24th and Marseilles on May 28th. Across the Atlantic the PRESIDENT GARFIELD steamed past the Statue of Liberty on her way to her Jersey City pier on June 10, 1930.

   Captain Cullen was still aboard when the PRESIDENT GARFIELD left New York on her next sailing on June 19th. That voyage took her from San

Francisco on July 11, 1930 and as usual en route to the Far East, she made her call at Honolulu seven days later. Other sailing dates for that voyage were August 13th when she left Manila, August 22nd when she sailed from Penang, August 27th when she steamed out of Colombo and September 17th when she cast off from Marseilles on her way to New York where she arrived on September 30th. After her Boston side trip the liner sailed for her next outbound voyage with her October 9, 1930 departure from New York. As always, Havana, Balboa and San Pedro were ports of call on the three week trip to San Francisco where the ship arrived on October 28th. Three days later, on Halloween, 1930, Captain Cullen took his ship back out to sea. Across the Pacific the liner visited usual ports of call, sailing, for instance, from Hong Kong on November 29th. December 13th was the day she worked at Penang and with a shipment of tea loaded on December 17th the Dollar Liner sailed from Colombo for Suez. Transiting de Lesseps' monumental canal on December 29th, the ship made fast at Port Said on December 30th. That time the Alexandria call coincided with New Year's Eve, after which the ship headed to Naples and a January 3rd arrival. At last calls at that picturesque and important Southern Italian port had been lengthened both to allow more time for passengers to make interesting shore excursions and to work cargo. The ship sailed on January 4th for Genoa and Marseilles. Her calls on that world circuit complete, on January 7th the PRESIDENT GAR-FIELD sailed from Marseilles on her way to New York. At her usual speed of 14.5–15 knots it always took a "502" almost two weeks to get back to New York and on that voyage there was no exception. The ship arrived at New York on January 20th. Boston was next, called on January 23rd. Away the following day for New York, the PRESIDENT GARFIELD sailed again from her Jersey City pier on January 29, 1931.

On that first round the world voyage for 1931 the ship called at Havana on February 2nd and made her canal transit on February 6th. Ten days later the liner was at San Pedro. Sailing day from San Francisco was February 20th and the ship sailed on time. Meeting her scheduled ports in sequence, her March 15th sailing from Shanghai, March 21st sailing from Hong Kong, March 25th sailing from Manila, April 4th from Penang, April 20th from Suez and April 29th sailing from Marseilles serve as mile markers for that trip which ended after her May 12th arrival at New York. Surely, many documents refer to the actual start of the next trip as the moment the voyage ended at Boston, but informally and usually, starts to round the world voyages were counted by the company and personnel as beginning with outbound sailings from New York and San Francisco and voyage endings were usually thought to coincide with the moment the last inbound freight was offloaded at New York, with the Boston visit a nebulous area.

For the record the ship sailed for Boston on May 14th and two days later was again back on the way to New York. Off again on Voyage 25, another round the world trip, Captain Cullen took his ship through the Narrows on May 21st. Continuing on from San Francisco that time, another routine voyage lay ahead with departures from Shanghai on July 7th, Penang on July 23rd and August 19th from Marseilles. Autumn was on the way when the PRESIDENT GARFIELD sailed again from New York for her twenty-sixth round the world trip on September 10, 1931. Nineteen days later the liner sailed past the Golden Gate on her way into San Francisco. After her usual three day stay at her home port the ship sailed on October 2nd for Honolulu. Calling overnight at Kobe on October 21st the ship next went to Shanghai. She sailed from there on October 28th on her way to Hong Kong and a November 1st sailing. From Colombo on November 18th the ship made her way to the Suez Canal and the last leg of that voyage. From Marseilles on December 9th Captain Cullen pointed his ship's bow into the Mediterranean and set a course for Gibraltar.

Sailing from Boston on December 28, 1931 the PRESIDENT GARFIELD headed back to New York and her next sailing for her customary ports. Overnighting at New York on December 30th, she sailed on Voyage 27 on the 31st. On January 8, 1932 she steamed through the Canal on her way to Los Angeles. Two days later at noon her radio operator reported her 537 miles north of Balboa. She continued to make good time and after her Los Angeles call continued on to San Francisco for her January 22nd sailing from the Bay. Now on her itinerary was a call at Bombay and she made her first call there on March 10th. On the ship's second trip of the year, she sailed on Voyage 28 from New York on April 21st for Havana and an April 29th transit of the Panama Canal. Arriving at Los Angeles on May 8th, the ship continued her voyage with her May 13th sailing from San Francisco. She sailed from Kobe on June 3rd, called at Shanghai between June 6th and 8th, Hong Kong overnight on the 10th and 11th and arrived at Manila on June 13th. Sailing out on June 15th, the PRESIDENT GARFIELD made for Colombo to load tea and rubber before beginning her ten day passage through summer heat en route to Suez and her scheduled July 11th canal transit. After her Alexandria, Naples and Genoa calls the ship sailed from Marseilles on July 20th on her way to New York.

She ended that classic year of major economic Depression with her December 1, 1932 sailing from New York on Voyage 29 on her way to her usual ports of call. After a quick Havana visit she steamed on to Colon where she arrived at 5:55 AM on December 9th. With 3,327 tons of machinery and general cargo, she began her canal transit at 7:20 AM. Her passage through the big ditch complete at 2:37, she docked at Balboa and at 9:21 that evening cleared for sea. Captain Gregory Cullen had stayed with her all the while.

During the awful Depression year of 1933 when so many vessels lay idle, the PRESIDENT GARFIELD managed to remain in service, making her usual circuits of the world. As is so often the case for any ship, her first voyage of a new year began in the old. Taking her last sailing of 1932 from San Francisco on December 23rd, the ship called at Honolulu on December 30th. At sea on New Year's Day, the ship headed for Kobe and a January 11, 1933 arrival. From Shanghai on January 23rd came reports of trouble. Casting off from Pai Lien Chen Wharf on January 17th, one of the ship's propellors hit the fender piling of the wharf, breaking several pilings. Curiously, the PRESIDENT GARFIELD dealt herself no apparent damage, but Dollar Line ordered the ship drydocked at Hong Kong where the bent propellor blades were repaired. Not more than a bit delayed, the ship sailed from Singapore on January 27th.

The ship pulled into Cristobal, Canal Zone at 6:45AM on March 31, 1933. At 8:25AM she entered the canal. With 2,853 tons of general cargo in her holds the PRESIDENT GARFIELD was through the canal at 4:41PM. Five hours and nine minutes later, at 9:50PM the ship cleared for sea on Voyage 30.

To save money on registry and port fees, Dollar Line decided to reregister all their ships at slightly lower gross tonnage figures. That correspondingly raised net tonnage figures and the PRESIDENT GARFIELD, thus far listed at 6,233 net tons by San Francisco port authorities, was listed at 6,253 net tons after her March 31st, 1933 Panama Canal transit. Of course Panama Canal tonnage rules differed greatly from other accepted schedules and canal officials then listed the ship at 12,583 gross and 9,207 net tons. The ship took her next outbound sailing from San Francisco on April 14th. At Japan in the spring of 1933 the PRESIDENT GARFIELD sailed from Kobe on May 5th and from Marseilles on June 21st, continuing toward New York. After her slow, sunny run the ship arrived at New York on July 4th. Right on schedule the ship sailed at Noon on Friday, July 6th for Boston and her weekend call. This time she sailed from there a day late and instead of an 8:00AM arrival on Monday, July 10th, the PRESIDENT GARFIELD reached New York on Tuesday the 11th as she began Voyage 31.

There was no delay in her outbound sailing from New York and on July 13th the ship quit her Jersey City pier for her usual ports around the world. With 3,380 tons of general cargo stowed aboard her, the ship made her Panama Canal transit on July 21st. From San Francisco the youngest of the "502"s sailed on August 4th on her way to the Far East. Before the ship sailed, a "cosmic ray" electroscope was installed on the ship's bridge. Considered quite a feather in the Dollar Line cap for the honor of having been chosen to participate in the scientific experiments, this "delicate and intricate" device for recording the intensity of cosmic rays at various points of the globe would make, Dollar Line publicists gave Captain Cullen of the PRESIDENT GARFIELD a special pat on the back, noting that operation of the instrument would be under his personal observation. August 25th was sailing day from Kobe and on September 22nd she sailed from Bombay for an October 2nd Suez Canal transit. Sailing day from Marseilles was October 11th. That trip brought her back to New York on time on Tuesday, October 24th. After two days at her Jersey City pier the ship sailed on October 26th for Boston. Her work there done, the steamer tied up again at Pier 9, Jersey

City at 8:00AM on Monday, October 30th. From New York the ship sailed on Voyage 32 on November 2nd. Taking 3,748 tons of cargo through the Panama Canal on November 10th the ship sailed north to California to continue her voyage from San Francisco on November 24, 1933. This time the sturdy PRESIDENT GARFIELD sailed from Kobe on December 14th. With the company's schedule calling for a tighter Manila call, the crew of the PRESIDENT GARFIELD had little rest on Christmas Day for that was the day of the ship's call there and there was much to do before the ship's midnight sailing for Singapore. From that ever more important port on January 2, 1934 the ship sailed for Penang and Colombo on her way to India. From Bombay at 1:00PM on Friday, January 12th this "502" class liner sailed for Suez. Ten days later she had reached Suez. After her canal transit on the 23rd the ship docked at Port Said, Egypt before going on to Alexandria. A week later the ship was ready to begin the final leg of that voyage and on January 31st sailed from Marseilles for New York.

Murder on the high seas now brought the PRESIDENT GARFIELD into the news again after two passengers argued and only one survived. On the transAtlantic leg of Voyage 32 from Marseilles to New York during early February 1934, antique weapons collector Andrew D. Kirwan quarrelled with 52 year old fellow passenger Gillman Sessoms of Seattle. Kirwan was the "forgotten son" of socialite Jean Nash, then called the "best dressed woman in Europe" and at the time married to French distiller Paul Dubonnet. No one aboard saw a murder committed on February 10th after a drinking bout, but after Sessoms died of stab wounds to his abdomen and shoulders, suspicion quickly fastened upon Kirwan, whose baggage contained "a startling assortment of weapons—knives, dueling blades, stilettos . . ." Asserting crime of that type to be the province of federal officials, Jersey City police did not detain Mr. Kirwan once the PRESIDENT GARFIELD docked on February 13th, but Customs did hold his baggage while Department of Justice officials looked for him. To his defense came eminent attorney Frederick Coudert, Jr., a former U.S. Assistant District Attorney. That brought public attention to the strange case. Coudert admitted that he was Kirwan's grandfather and Mrs. Dubonnet's father.

Newsmen awaited the arriving ship at Pier 9, Jersey City on the morning of Tuesday February 13, 1934. Unrelated to the felony aboard the liner, a new Master was appointed to command the PRESIDENT GARFIELD. Captain J.E. Murphy, one of the youngest men to command a Dollar Liner, took command of the ship at New York. He took his ship out on Voyage 33 on February 22nd. Taking 4,592 of general cargo and drugs through the Panama Canal on March 2nd, it was one of the ship's best bookings so far. When Captain Murphy brought his ship into San Francisco on his first voyage as Master on March 13, 1934 local newspapers outdid each other in publishing their greetings to him and wished him well when he took his ship out across the Pacific on March 16th. A week later on March 23rd Honolulu papers

Lochhead caught the ship in his lens on August 7, 1932 when she returned on another round the world voyage. Courtesy of SSHSA.

welcomed him, running his photo alongside the news of his first arrival there as Master. Taking his ship around the world, Captain Murphy took his ship out of Shanghai on April 9th, from Hong Kong on April 13th, and Penang on April 26th. When unionized workers walked off their jobs in West Coast port cities on May 9th, the PRESIDENT GARFIELD was on her way from Bombay to Suez. That was no place for an American crew to walk out and though the occasional malcontent disrupted the mood aboard the ship and the ship's officers reported less co-operation than usual, the men stayed at their posts. May 23rd was sailing day from Marseilles and after the usual 13 nights, the ship reached New York on June 5th. For Boston the liner sailed on June 7th and was back at her Jersey City pier to finish loading for Voyage 34 on June 11th.

The ship sailed out again from New York on Voyage 34 on June 14, 1934. On schedule on June 22nd the liner took her 2,567 tons of general cargo including a few automobiles through the Panama Canal on her passage to California. San Francisco was still shut down by the strike, but the strong arm of Los Angeles anti-union activists had kept their port open, so the PRESIDENT GARFIELD worked San Francisco cargo there. She also landed San Francisco bound passengers at San Pedro after her July 2nd arrival. Omitting her home port she sailed out for Honolulu. That summer saw her working the waters of the Far East and Asia. From Shanghai on July 31st

Considerably lighter in tone than the same room aboard some of her sisters was the Smoking Room aboard the PRESIDENT GARFIELD, as this photo taken after her 1929 refit shows. Author's collection.

and Bombay on August 24th the PRESIDENT GARFIELD sailed ever west-wards. From Marseilles on September 12th the liner began the final leg of her round the world voyage and arrived at New York on September 25th. Then came her weekend sidetrip to Boston. From New York she sailed on Voyage 35 on October 4, 1934 for Havana and an October 12th transit of the Panama Canal. After sailing from Los Angeles on October 22nd the ship headed for her first call at San Francisco since mid March. After her usual three day call there she took her scheduled October 26th departure. From Kobe on November 16th the ship continued on her way around the world calling at Shanghai on November 19th and 20th, Hong Kong on November 23rd and 24th, Manila on November 26 and Singapore on Saturday, December 1st. Sailing at Noon on Tuesday, December 4th, the ship crossed over to Penang where she arrived on the following day. Taking on her allotted con-signments of rubber, the ship sailed on December 5th for Colombo, Ceylon, a four days passage. The call there was still a one day affair with an 8:00PM sailing time. Next, of course, was Bombay, and the ship reached that port on time at 1:00PM on Thursday, December 13th. Now bound for Suez, she sailed twenty-four hours later at 1:00PM on Friday, December 14th. Then came ten days steaming through some of the warmest waters of the world and it was Christmas Eve, December 24th when the steamer reached Suez. Ships know few holidays and Christmas means but little to Islamic Egypt, so at least Dollar Line faced no holiday overtime charges from Egyptians working on December 25th while the ship worked cargo at Port Said and Alexandria. Then the ship made her way across to Naples and a December 29th call. Taking a day to sail up the Tyrrhenian Sea, the ship reached Genoa on the last day of that dismal year and sailed for Marseilles on January 1, 1935. Scheduled for a nine hour call at that busy French port between 8:00AM and 5:00PM on January 2nd, for some reason the ship remained there over-night and began her passage to New York with her January 3rd sailing. Scheduled for a New York arrival on January 15th, the ship was delayed by storms. Following her customary practice she sailed for Boston two days after tying up at Pier 9.

The ship returned to New York on January 23rd. Replacing Captain Mur-phy around that time, Captain Gregory Cullen returned to command his ship. With the Statue of Liberty on her starboard side, the PRESIDENT GAR-FIELD was off to a late start for Voyage 36. Scheduled to sail on Thursday the 24th, she didn't get underway again until January 26th. Sailing for Cuba, Panama, California and the world the ship was on Voyage 36 and of course it was her first trip of that year. By the time she reached the Pacific she was back on schedule and was able to sail from San Francisco on time at 5:00PM on Friday, February 15th. From Kobe on March 8th and Shanghai on March 12th the liner worked her way through her itinerary to return to New York in May. Then she underwent her annual survey and was found to be in good condition all over. Off again on another voyage she went, sailing from her Jersey City pier on May 16th and sailing again from San

Francisco on June 7th. Records show her next sailing from her home port that year was the September 27th departure for a trip that brought her back to New York in mid December. In from Marseilles on the 17th she sailed on December 21st for her Boston side trip. Then she was back at New York on the 24th. That was one of the few times a Dollar Liner passed Christmas at New York. On December 26, 1935 the PRESIDENT GARFIELD sailed on another round the world voyage.

That winter 1936 trip saw the liner sail from San Francisco on January 17th and from Kobe on February 7th. On March 22nd the ship left Singapore and after her March 15th Suez Canal transit called at Port Said on the 16th, Alexandria on the 17th and Naples on March 21st. After sailing from Genoa on March 25th the PRESIDENT GARFIELD returned to Marseilles and then began her homeward passage to New York where she arrived on April 7th. The biggest news to come from the ship during that first 1936 voyage were complaints from passengers. Forwarded by irate, patriotic citizens patronizing the American flag line, to both the San Francisco office of the Dollar Line and the Washington headquarters of the Shipping Board, aggrieved letters spoke in horrified tones that the crew was circulating communist literature aboard ship. It seems that there was not much union sympathy among Dollar Line travellers!

Neither a condition survey which found her in good condition all over nor past passenger ire could delay the ship's April 11, 1936 departure from New York for California. After her Havana call the ship continued on to transit the Panama Canal on April 24th. From San Pedro on May 4th the ship headed into San Francisco on May 5th to spend her usual three days before continuing on her way around the world. There, union strife again troubled the career of a Dollar Liner. In response to violence against crew members by militant unionists on the morning of May 8, 1936, San Francisco police took swift action. Here's what happened—as the ship lay at San Francisco's Pier 42 that morning, two crew members were beaten and others threatened. Before a significant police presence showed up, two trouble-making crewmembers were in irons while Dollar Line personnel awaited the arrival of all available local police who rushed to the pier to prevent further trouble. Nothing else untoward happened while stevedores loaded the last of a cargo into the ship's holds. The PRESIDENT GARFIELD sailed that afternoon. On June 6th she was at Hong Kong. Next was Singapore, from whence she called at nearby Penang on her way to Colombo and Bombay. From that Indian port the "502" headed for the Red Sea and a July 5th transit through the Suez Canal. The Atlantic crossing began at Marseilles on July 17 when the PRESIDENT GARFIELD left for New York. She steamed up the Hudson River to dock at Jersey City's Pier 9 on July 28th. Outbound again the liner sailed out of New York on another global trip on August 6, 1936. She arrived at her home port San Francisco on August 26th and continued her round the world trip from there three days later on the 29th.

Working her way around the world the PRESIDENT GARFIELD arrived at Kobe on September 18th. On schedule as usual she sailed from Shanghai on September 22nd, Penang on October 8th and Marseilles on November 6th. By the time she completed her Atlantic crossing and arrived at New York on November 20, 1936, the West Coast maritime industry was at a standstill caused by striking trade unions. When her outbound voyage was postponed pending settlement of the strike, Dollar Line had no idea it would be a long wait. With the coming of the New Year the PRESIDENT GARFIELD was still idle at New York, the acrimonious West Coast strike not yet settled. She had plenty of fleetmates for company. With her at New York were temporarily idled the PRESIDENT ADAMS, PRESIDENT POLK, PRESIDENT TAFT and PRESIDENT van BUREN. The PRESIDENT HARRISON came in at the end of December and joined them. These Dollar sisters would not move again for months. With the arrival of her sisters and fleetmates the PRESIDENT GARFIELD saw herself crowded out of Dollar Line's Pier 9. Her owner ordered her to shift out into an anchorage in the river with the PRESIDENT van BUREN until a more suitable spot could be found for her. It took several weeks before Dollar Line sent the ship to a local shipyard. Once the strike was settled, the yard made voyage repairs and otherwise got the ship ready for sea. The PRESIDENT GARFIELD did not quit New York until April 18, 1937. When she sailed she had quite a good cargo aboard, going through the Panama Canal April 23rd with 5,009 tons of general cargo and scrap iron for Japan. Nearly half a year after pulling into New York from her last round the world voyage of 1936 did the ship get home to San Francisco. Arriving at her home port on May 5th she remained there for the customary three days before sailing away again on May 8th for Honolulu. Next, of course, was Kobe and the ship sailed from there on May 29th after an overnight call. Then in quick succession the PRESIDENT GARFIELD showed herself in the East Asian ports of Shanghai, Hong Kong, Manila, Singapore and Penang, sailing from that last on June 17th for Colombo and Bombay. Federal subsidies came to an end while the ship was on her way to the Red Sea. With Dollar Line's mail contracts cancelled by the Maritime Commission on June 30, 1937, the ships were on their own financially after July 1st. Coming into the Mediterranean on July 7th after sailing through the Suez Canal, this "502" arrived at Alexandria on July 8th. Then the ship called at her usual European ports of Naples, Genoa and Marseilles. The ship's first trip around the world since the end of the debilitating ninety-nine day strike ended at New York on July 31st.

Here's a quick list of most of her port arrivals and departures for the next few trips. From New York on August 5, 1937 and San Francisco on August 28th the PRESIDENT GARFIELD called at Honolulu on September 4, Kobe for an overnight between September 17/18, Hong Kong between September 23 and 28, Manila for September 30/October 1, Singapore between October 5 and 8, Penang on October 11, Colombo on October 15, Bombay on October 18, Marseilles for a November 3 departure and a November 20, New York arrival. After 8 days working cargo at Pier 9 Jersey City, the ship shifted to

Boston. Arriving there on November 29th, she sailed the next day for New York and a December 2nd outbound sailing for Havana. Then she once again made her way to the Panama Canal where she transited on December 10th. Nine days steaming brought her to San Pedro. She stayed there until Christmas Day when she sailed for San Francisco. Outbound through the Golden Gate on December 29th, the PRESIDENT GARFIELD beat her usual course for Honolulu. She was on that trip when her first emergency Maritime Commission voyage subsidy kicked in at Hong Kong on January 29, 1938. That month ended with an emergency subsidy granted by the Maritime Commission. So for subsidy purposes the trip ended at Boston on April 4th. Two days later the ship steamed into New York where the voyage ended. That was her last arrival as a Dollar Liner, for unable to obtain further financing or operating subsidy, the Line could no longer afford to operate the ship.

At New York she laid up through January 21, 1939 though during the course of those ten months, she was the scene of a good bit of activity and quite a lot of expense. There was also a major refit and a fire as well as many repairs during those months she spent at New York. With the latest suspension of mail contract payments, the Dollar Line sent the PRESIDENT GARFIELD into lay up at the Bethlehem Shipbuilding Company yard at 56th Street in Brooklyn. There she would be begin a period of lay up lasting many months. Before sending her out to sea again, Dollar Line wanted the ship to meet the new safety requirements for American passenger ships so they decided to invest a large sum of money they didn't really have to upgrade the vessel. Calling for plans to be drawn for a major overhaul of her crew quarters and many improvements and renewals to her machinery, the company called for bids. Plans ready, Dollar Steamship Lines had specifications for the job ready to distribute to interested contractors in early April. It was a long list, one running to 9 pages, most of it in small type.

So many who love ships give no thought of the thousands of mechanical details in each vessel nor of what it takes to make a ship move. A shipowner does and the Dollar firm certainly did, too. For the important refit awaiting machinery and crew spaces in the PRESIDENT GARFIELD, they omitted nothing from their consideration. Extracted from those pages, a list of much of the desired work is reproduced below.

Dollar Line wanted the successful bidder to "furnish all labor, material and/or equipment to complete the following items of work, unless otherwise specifically directed:

ALTERATIONS TO POOP DECK HOUSE

This space to be torn out in its entirety and rearranged as shown on plan, building new steel bulkhead of 3/16″ material, forming shower and toilet spaces.

Berths for Boatswain, Carpenter and Boatswain's Mate rooms to be built in with drawers under berths, also desks. Lockers to be of metal. Quartermasters room, watchmen, A.B.s rooms to be fitted with standee berths and metal lockers.

Doors to be altered and cut in as shown on plan of new arrangement also portlights, are to be supplied and installed.

Each door also to be fitted with glass solid deadlight.

Hot and cold running water to be installed in washbasins and shower spaces. Also toilets to be provided with flushometers.

Rooms to be provided with radiators and berth lights, also electric fans of the twelve inch oscillating type.

All rooms to be sheathed in plywood panels against the steel forming these quarters.

All alterations to blower ducts to be taken care of by the contractor.

All floor covering in way of these spaces, also shower spaces, to be removed and where found corroded through, to have suitable doublers installed or plates renewed as necessary.

Bathroom to be tiled. Room floors to be covered with asbestolith.

ALTERATIONS TO SEAMEN'S QUARTERS "A" DECK AFT

Existing bulkheads, steel and T & G to be altered and replaced with T & G 1 1/8" x 3 forming eight (8) rooms to conform with the plan. Existing sheathing in deckheads of rooms to remain. In all other rooms, sheathed in deck-head with the same material as rooms on port side. Ship's sides and forward bulkheads to be sheathed with plywood panels. Wooden doors to be fitted in steel existing bulkheads and all doors to be renewed. Rooms to be fitted with standee berths, lockers and settees as shown on plan. Existing electric wiring where rooms are not sheathed, to be brought below sheathing.

Existing room in centerline to be removed. Hatchway enclosure to remain. Stairway leading down to "B" Deck enclosed with pipe railings. Starting box for blowers to be installed on rails.

Washrooms serving these quarters to remain. Cement floors to be removed and tiled, including shower spaces. Plumbing repaired and placed in good order. Toilet bowls to be provided with balance seats. Door frames and doors leading into toilets to be renewed. Floors in the way of these spaces to be covered with Asbestolith.

Oil skin and boot locker to be built in between doors of baths 36" deep of T & G, with two doors; also coat hanger rack.

"B" DECK AFT

Existing arrangement to be removed. New rooms built in with 1 1/8" x 3 T & G as outlined in plans. Ship's sides to be sheathed with plywood panels. Rooms to be fitted with standee berths, lockers and settees as shown on plan. Forward end of this compartment, center line, telemotor lines, steam and water lines and fire pump to be removed and relocated. Watertight door to be supplied 21" x 65". Bulkhead to be cut through for same and door installed.

Toilets serving these quarters to be removed and rebuilt as shown . . .

No. 9 CARGO SPACE

Steel booby hatch 4' x 5'6'' x 6'6'' to be made and installed with watertight door, properly dogged. 10'' port lights to be fitted forward and after ends. Sill of watertight door to be 24'' above the deck. Ladder to be installed 40'' x 14' to be of white pine, fitted with suitable treads and 1'' pipe hand rails, leading into compartment.

Holes to be cut into ship's side for port holes and a total of 8 ports to be supplied and installed in this compartment, with proper backers, to American Bureau Requirements.

Bathroom and toilet to be built in as outlined on plan in the after end of the Steward's room . . .

Six (6) rooms to be built as shown on plan. . . . rooms to be fitted with standee berths, lockers and settees as shown.

WASH ROOM

Washroom to be built in the center line of this compartment . . .

No. 9 hatch to be trunked with 2'' x 10'' Oregon pine. Hatchway in way of cargo space to be sheathed with 1/16'' galvanized iron. . . .

No. 8 HATCH, AFTER END

Steel bulkhead to be installed, ship' side, 1/4'' material fitted with angle stiffened, spaced 30'' in its entirety. . . . Shower spaces to be built. . . . Steel bulkhead separating cargo from quarters to be watertight 9'' from deck. Holes to be cut in ship's side for port holes and a total of 8 port lights to be supplied . . .

Four rooms to be built in this compartment as shown . . .

PRESENT WAITERS' QUARTERS—AMIDSHIPS

Same to be divided into two rooms as shown on plan, providing hospital which is to be fitted out with standee berths as shown. Bathroom to be provided with tub, washbasin and toilet bowl. Bulkhead to be closed up between rooms. Bulkhead to be built in bathroom now forming shower spaces. Bulkhead to be cut through and door furnished and installed forming room for Deck Engineer, Plumber and Machinist as shown. Room to be fitted with standee berths, lockers, settees and berth lights. Bathroom space to be sheet metal lined.

PRESENT OILER'S AND FIREMEN'S QUARTERS ''B'' DECK

Rooms to be rearranged as shown on plan. All floor covering to be removed and floor to be recovered with Asbestolith. Where decks are corroded same to have suitable welded doublers installed. All bulkhead bearers to be removed and renewed. Doors and frames to be removed and repaired where necessary and put in good condition.

Ship's side in way of rooms to be sheathed with plywood panels, fitting same with standee berths, lockers and settees as shown on plan.

Existing toilet to be lowered in order to give sufficient headroom. Fitting one new shower and one urinal.

Present cement to be removed from floor and floor to be tiled. Plumbing to be repaired and put into good condition.

One room to be fitted with half-lockers for work clothes as shown on plan.

SAILORS' AND FIREMEN'S MESSROOM

Present floor covering to be removed and where deck is corroded same to have suitable welded doublers installed. Bulkhead bearers to be removed and renewed. Floors to be covered with Asbestolith. Door in after messroom to be closed up. Passage ways in way of engine room casing, port and starboard passage way in way of machine shop spaces to be covered with asbestolith.

Deckheads over dynamo flats in way of messrooms and crew quarters to be insulated with mineral wool, sheathed with 1/32" galvanized iron.

All plywood sheathing installed on ship's side to be secured with round head screws for easy removal and preserving steel work. Full sized panels to be used where possible.

All berths to be fitted with berth lights and shades. Room lights to be provided with switch at door; also fan connections for each room. All rooms to be supplied with 12" fans in new accommodations and two fans to be supplied in each big room. All existing rooms where fans now in use, same to be taken down, cleaned and replaced. All settees to be made of white pine or fir with stripped top, stained, tables of white pine or fir.

All lockers to be renewed, size to be 15 x 21 x 6" fitted with coat hanger rods. New berths to be supplied, standee type, 30" x 76" with bed rail fitted at head only, in all rooms.

Radiators of suitable size to be installed in all new rooms, lobbies, alleyways and old insulation altered to conform with new arrangements. Also rooms not now fitted with radiators to be so fitted.

New ventilating systems to be provided for rooms in new locations with suitable mechanical blowers and air ducts leading into new rooms.

New quarters to be provided with fire lines and hydrants and alarm bells as required by local inspectors.

Fire detecting system to be extended to cover new quarters.

All washrooms to be equipped with mirrors, soap trays and toilet paper rolls and racks provided under mirrors for toilet articles.

All rooms to be provided with door hooks and ajar hooks, port hole hangers and coat and hat hooks.

All new quarters to be given two coats of paint. All existing quarters, including bathrooms and messrooms and passageways to be given one coat of paint. This includes poop deck quarters, "A" Deck and "B" Deck quarters, aft, new hospital space and one room, firemen's quarters, Chinese quarters, bathrooms and all messrooms, and dynamo floats.

Big rooms in stewards' quarters to be fitted with two tables, one in each room, 84" long x 36" wide and four benches, same length as table.

Suitable locker to be installed on "B" Deck, aft, for library books.

All berths to be fitted with racks for stowing small articles, to be installed at foot of berth, two shelf type.

Contractor to remove all obsolete pipe lines, flush tanks, in all crew toilet spaces which are being reconditioned, also to remove all old bunks, lockers and equipment. All loose electric wire ends to be properly taped and secured in all locations where new crew quarters are being installed.

By no means overlooked was the ship's main machinery:

ENGINE MAINTENANCE

Remove all plain tubes in No. 5 boiler, consisting of 312 tubes, also two sway tubes, and renew. Tubes are 7' 9–7/8" long 1/4" added to each and for rolling and bending. Tubes are No. 10 BWG. Stay tubes are #2 BWG. Center box has 37 plain tubes in lower section that are 1 1/16" longer. Contractor to furnish tube with certificate of origin. After all tubes are cut, all tube shafts are to be thoroughly sealed inside before putting in new tubes. Contractor to take his own measure of tubes before ordering.

Open up water end of port circulator, remove and renew impeller shaft. Shaft of bronze, approximately 4" x 40". New lignum vitae bushings to be made and installed and circulator closed up in good order.

Remove the following valves from six boilers, overhaul valves, reseat and renew bonnet studs, yoke studs and shell studs, with the exception of six safety valves which have only to be lifted and shell studs renewed.

6—3.5"	Safety valves	studs 7/8 × 3 3/4"	— 72 studs
6—2.5"	Main feed valves	studs 7/8 × 3 1/2"	— 48 studs
6—2.5"	Auxiliary Feed checks	studs 7/8 × 3 1/2"	— 48 studs
6—1.25"	Surface Blow valves	studs 5/8 × 3"	— 36 studs
6—1.5"	Bottom Blow valves	studs 5/8 × 3"	— 36 studs
6—1.5"	Water column valves, top	studs 5/8 × 3"	— 36 studs
6—1.5"	Water column valves including spoon pce., bottom	studs 5/8 × 3"	— 36 studs
6—1.5"	Bottom blow cocks	studs 5/8x 2.5"	— 24 studs
18—Tri-cocks to be removed and overhauled.			

Supply and install one new Worthington horizontal duplex pump, size 7–1/2 x 6 x 6 for ice machine circulator, making all necessary alterations to foundation, suction and discharge lines, steam and exhaust lines, and prove in good order.

Remove to shop and remetal with 4X new Babbitt three main engine eccentric straps, size 27–7/8" x 4". Ship's crew to remove and assemble same.

Remove from ship and remetal with 4X Babbitt, one main engine slipper, machine to size 7–7/8", face to face and replace on board.

Make and supply one main engine crankpin parting piece.

Disconnect and remove from ship one section 4" x 12" copper exhaust line in port shaft alley. Bronze in way of flange, anneal, install and recover with asbestos, canvas sewn.

DECK DEPARTMENT—MAINTENANCE

Supply right and left hand frames, also right and left hand cylinders for Lidgerwood winch 8–1/4" x 8". Assemble same, using new throttle valve supplied by vessel making all alterations to pistons, valves and making new rings, and remetalling bearings, and prove same in good working order.

Remove and renew loader section of 4″ air vent in way of door frames stuffing box in No. 9 hold from No. 11 fresh water tank.

Remove and renew one section of air vent in No. 1 cofferdam No. 2 hold, pipe 3.5″ by approximately 16′, bent to suit, flanged at both ends.

Cut away deteriorated sections of six channel frames in way of Chinese toilet, removing two brackets, and fitting reverse bars in frames by welding top and bottom. Re-rivet brackets back in place.

Cut away deteriorated sections of channel frames, two port and two starboard, in way of "A" Deck toilets, and fit reverse bars on same, welding top and bottom.

Remove and renew port and starboard shaft alley escape doors and install new doors with watertight gaskets and proper dogs.

Remove old by burning off and welding on new channel iron stiffeners top and bottom, using old clips for hatch fittings, riveting on same as original on the following hatches:

Hatch No. 3	Forward end
Hatch No. 4	Forward end
Port reefer hatch	After end
Hatch No. 7	Starboard side
Hatch No. 8	Starboard side

FORECASTLE DECK

Scale thoroughly 14 welded doublers (as specified on list).
Steam and exhaust lines to capstan to be removed and replaced.

POOP DECK

Scale thoroughly and install the following 15 welded doublers, 6 on starboard, 9 on port side. Lockers in way of same to be removed and replaced.

CLEANING CARGO HOLD

No. 1 cargo hold: No 1 tanks, port and starboard, to be cleaned and proven gas free.

No. 2 cargo hold: clean out cofferdam, forward end. clean sumps port and starboard in after end. #2 tanks—port and starboard to be cleaned and proven gas free.

No. 4 cargo hold: Sumps on the after end, port and starboard to be cleaned.

No. 5 cargo hold: ceiling to be raised in its entirety. Tanks to be cleaned. Deep tanks to be opened up, steam and cleaned and proved gas free; also sumps port and starboard after end to be cleaned. No. 4 tanks, port and starboard, to be cleaned and proven gas free.

No.6 cargo hold: ceiling to be raised in its entirety, including all storeroom spaces. Deep tanks to be opened up, steam and cleaned and proved gas free; also sumps port and starboard after end to be cleaned. No. 5 tanks, port and starboard, to be cleaned and proven gas free.

No. 6 tank tops under boilers to be thoroughly cleaned. Port and starboard settling tanks to be steamed, cleaned and proven gas free.

Cofferdam in after end of engine room to be opened up, thoroughly cleaned out.

Cofferdam in after end of refrigerator spaces to be opened up, thoroughly cleaned out.

Nos. 7 and 8 cargo holds: ceiling to be raised in its entirety, tank tops in way of same to be thoroughly cleaned of fuel oil; also under fresh water tanks.

All manhole covers of double bottom tanks, settling tanks, sumps, cofferdams, to be removed by contractor and replaced after completion of survey.

All ceilings to be replaced as originally, after completion of survey.

Contractor to supply all barrels and remove dirt, refuse, etc. and dispose of same from ship.

CONTRACTOR TO SUBMIT SEPARATE PRICE OF EACH ITEM[7]

Limiting bids to contractors in New York, Boston, Baltimore and Norfolk, Dollar Line advised that bids would be opened at 11:00 AM on April 22, 1938 in the office of the Port Engineer on the Line's Pier 9 in Jersey City. In bold print, interested New York bidders were told that all work had to be completed by noon on May 14th, but contractors located elsewhere, in Boston, for instance, would have two days' less in order that the ship be at her Jersey City pier in time to sail on time.

Winning the contract was the United Drydock Company which signed a $64,000.00 contract with an $8,000.00 side contract for extras with Dollar Steamship Line. Once the ship was at their yards her boilers were opened up and found to be in much worse condition than expected. Asking how much worse, Dollar Line was informed "$40,000.00 worse", meaning that a good deal more work and seven extra days would be required to put the ship into good shape. By then the Dollars were already behind in their payments to the shipyard. Not in a position to pay the extra money, which soon grew to $60,000.00 worth of extras, at 4:30 PM on Friday, on May 6th, all work on the ship stopped. Informing the Commissioners of an upcoming debacle, Maritime Commission Director of Operations and Traffic M.L. Wilcox wrote:

In view of the financial condition of the Dollar Line, we are informed that United Drydock are suspending all work to be done on the PRESIDENT GARFIELD and will hold the ship until some money is forthcoming. The PRESIDENT GARFIELD is scheduled to sail from New York on May 16th for Boston, thence return to New York for an intercoastal voyage as the first leg of her round the world voyage. She will be unable to make this schedule.[8]

---

[7] April 18th SPECIFICATION No. 430 for the PRESIDENT GARFIELD issued at Jersey City, New Jersey. Copy in the ship's 901 file in Maritime Commission files, RG 178, held by the Maritime Administration.

[8] M.L. Wilcox May 6, 1938 letter in the 901 file for PRESIDENT GARFIELD. RG 178 held by Maritime Administration.

Meanwhile, the ship remained laid up at the Bethlehem Shipbuilding Company yard at 56th Street in Brooklyn where Captain Gregory Cullen was eventually relieved by Captain A.W. Aitken. At the Bethlehem's 56th Street Brooklyn plant on October 11, 1938, a fire broke out at 5:20 PM in the ship's boiler room when fuel oil in the service pump strainer joint blew out. Quickly enough extinguished, there was some damage. Both forward and after bulkheads were badly buckled, and the forward bulkhead portside needed four new stiffeners between the Upper Deck and the tank tops. Also badly buckled were a steward's storeroom and the alleyway near the butcher shop. The *New York Maritime Register* printed a blurb describing the range of repairs: "Deck bulkhead coamings, beams, stringers and brackets bent and buckled. Renew two feed pumps, two feed heaters, renew 600 feet of steam auxiliary piping, renew boilers and piping relay, steam clean tanks and test as well as repair sundry fire and smoke damage".

After the slow collapse of the Dollar Line, the PRESIDENT GARFIELD passed into the fleet of the new American President Lines. Other than new people in top management, much of the staff was the same and everyone hoped to send the ship out from New York on Voyage 45 on December 24, 1938. Unfortunately, the recent fire scotched those plans and her sailing was postponed to January 24, 1939 while Bethlehem Shipbuilding repaired the latest damage at a cost of $39,975.00. Costs from the intended May 1938 refit by then had mounted greatly, prompting a wire from the San Francisco head office of American President Lines to the Maritime Commission on January 19th:

> Increase of $123,232.00 over original estimate for GARFIELD repair (does) not include October 11th fire damage. Bethlehem's Morse plant did that. No disbursement for repair fire damage yet approved.

Meanwhile, under the watchful eye of Captain Aitken, an inventory of the ship began on December 30, 1938. All repairs and modernization work completed at a cost of about a quarter of a million dollars, the PRESIDENT GARFIELD was redelivered to American President Lines at the Morse yard on January 21, 1939. Then began Voyage 45/46 and the ship shifted back to Pier 9, Jersey City where she loaded cargo and took on passengers, baggage and mail before sailing at 6:00PM on Friday, January 27th on her first passenger sailing as an American President Liner. Recorded as the ship's Voyage 45, Captain Aitken was still in command. Notables among her passengers this time were L. R. Blanchard, managing editor of the Rochester, New York *"Times Union"* and his wife, San Francisco bound to attend a fair. They left the ship after her 7:00PM arrival there on Wednesday, February 15, 1939. Though the PRESIDENT GARFIELD now met the strict new safety standards for passenger ships, her crew still left much to be desired. Labor trouble and frequent grousings continued unabated, bothersome as hundreds of pinpricks, and interfered with many aspects of life at sea. Even renewed quarters, a new houseflag and operating company did nothing to quench the malcontent's thirst for trouble. Several infuriating incidents during that trip prompted letters from Captain Aitken and one from Chief Steward C. Martin. Word of the refitted liner's February 15th San Francisco arrival was carried in the local press, but word of her feisty unionists was not mentioned. Captain Aitken must have been pretty steamed when he typed the following letter to American President Lines' Honolulu agent after sailing from San Francisco on February 18, 1939:

> Dear Sirs:
>
> At 9:00 AM of the above date (February 22) I was informed by the Chief Steward of the Vessel that his galley crew were holding a passive sit down strike. In other words working at very slow speed and also refusing to carry the food as heretofore, up to pantry for the waiters service to the dining saloon.
>
> I understand that this condition was directly brought about by the stewards union delegate coming aboard on sailing day and instructing the cooks and scullions as to exactly what they were or were not to do in carrying on their respective duties.
>
> The Chief Steward of the vessel and also the acting assistant Port Steward assured me on sailing day from San Francisco that all these difficulties had been satisfactorily settled.
>
> I called all cooks and scullions together and told them in no uncertain terms that they were now at sea and beyond jurisdiction of their union delegates and would take orders from the Chief Steward under myself or be placed in the brig. They were also brought to realize that they were aboard a *government owned and operated vessel* and any further such insubordination on their part would be instrumental in severing all connections with their unions and they would all be on the beach.
>
> No requests or complaints have been voiced to date by other departments or delegates.
>
> I am informing you of this condition aboard the vessel so you will be conversant with the facts should further controversy arise at your port.
>
> Kindly forward this report, as per instructions, to the Vice President, Operations, San Francisco.[9]

Food and unions, matters at the heart of so much labor trouble in the American maritime industry for so many years had much to do with the problem. No one on the union side ever seemed to suspect that sustained action on their part could lead to unemployment and begging for food, but no matter. One can almost see the Captain in a white fury when he wrote from Genoa on April 24th to American President Lines' President Joseph Sheehan in San Francisco. Here is what Captain Aitkens next reported about his ship's labor woes:

---

[9]Feb. 22, 1939 letter from Capt. Aitken to Honolulu agent. Copy in the general files for the PRESIDENT MADISON in the files of the Maritime Commission in RG 178 in the possession of the Maritime Administration.

On Saturday April 9, 1939 while this vessel was at the port of Bombay, India, ten members of the deck crew walked ashore before 8:00 AM, and were not aboard to take orders from the Bos'n. These men were all sober and stood inspection before the British Port Doctor with myself present at 1:00 PM of the same date, after which inspection they turned to securing cargo gear, the vessel leaving the berth at 2:00 PM.

On the following morning 10:00 AM at sea, the Chief Officer, Boatswain and deck delegate were summoned before me and interrogated as to the above insubordinate action. The excuse put forth by the deck crew delegate on behalf of the insubordinate seamen was to the effect that they had contracted with shoreside coolie labor to do their work for them . This statement was clearly and substantially refuted by the Chief Officer and the Boatswain.

The names of these insubordinate seamen were duly entered in the official Log Book as a record for further and subsequent disciplinary action.

At 9:30 PM of Saturday, April 8, 1939, I was waited upon by the crew delegate of each department comprising the Deck, Engineers and Stewards and informed that a joint meeting of all the unlicensed personnel had been held and that they had decided to demand to be put on the lawful rations or "whack" as it is called.

I have personally investigated and observed the fact that during the entire voyage from San Francisco, where the present agreed menu went into effect, up to this date that the menu has been adhered to as closely as humanly possible.

It has come to my attention that the entire unlicensed white crew has, since departure from San Francisco, attempted to bring discredit in every way on the Chief Steward, partially because he did not attempt to discharge the colored cooks and scullerymen now aboard the vessel at San Francisco as requested by the crew, but principally because this Steward has no Union affiliation. This Steward has been openly cursed and maligned before passengers and otherwise by crew members, principally the Engineer's department and his own department at every opportunity.

As previously observed the Steward has strictly adhered to the menu as agreed upon by the operating company and the unions and has at times given them more than is strictly called for. In addition he is in my opinion a first class passenger ship steward.

One statement made to me by the stewards' delegate was to the effect that he and some of the crew had been aboard the PRESIDENT PIERCE while in Manila and were told that the Steward of that ship 'used the company menu as merely a guide to a better one'.

As in some crews of the past two years there appears to be a distinctly radical, trouble making element aboard this ship at this particular period set on disrupting the service.

At 4:30 AM on April 10, 1939 on the day which I granted the crew permission to go on their "whack" the Chief Steward and the Storekeeper were ready in the storeroom to apportion the rations as per the ship's articles. Whereupon the crew delegates refused to accept their legalized 'Whack unless it was doled out to each man separately in individual containers, and they demanded the privilege of each man's cooking his own food on the galley range.'

On being informed on this farcical demand I summoned the aforesaid crew delegates and informed them that they were on the verge of mutiny and would give up their ridiculous demands at once and return to the ship's menu and their respective duties or suffer the consequences. Having thrown a considerable scare into them, they about faced and returned to work.

The gist of this whole occurrence was plainly nothing more than a demonstration of their Union activities and power, it being their sole object to impress on me the fact that the Chief Steward of the ship was not a member of any Union and therefor what he did or did not do was entirely wrong. In view of the present policy of the American President Line management in employment of strictly Union crews it is clearly seen that the present Chief Steward of this vessel, although he is a competent man, will be unable to continue aboard this ship and maintain proper service and discipline in his department.

Since the above mentioned episode it has been necessary upon several occasions for me to personally settle disputes and arguments among several members of the stewards department in regards to their respective duties, the whole department being most antagonistic and insubordinate to the Chief Steward's orders.

It was brought to my attention shortly after the unlicensed personnel held their mass meetings, that the Chief Wireless Operator and one of his assistants were attending them. On summoning this Chief Radio Operator, one Donald Mealy, he readily admitted his action and in defense stated he felt his Union and the seaman's, firemen's and steward's unions all stood together. I reminded him of the fact that the ship was at sea on a foreign voyage and he was supposedly one of the ship's officers, although a minor one and also that recognition as such had been a long fought for endeavor of the wireless operators, but that his actions certainly did not entitle him to such consideration. He admitted that "probably" he had made a slight error in judgement.

During the passage from Bombay to European ports we had among our passengers several high ranking Naval, Marine and Army officers accompanied by their wives and families, among them Captain Harold McKittrick, just relieved from duty as Commissioner of our Asiatic flagship, the AUGUSTA. The crew mass meetings and general unionized conduct of the crew, especially the steward's department came, unavoidably under present conditions, directly under their observation, creating a decidedly unfavorable impression.

To sum up, the present manning of vessels with radical unionized crews is not conducive to the best service that may be offered to the travelling public in our American ships.[10]

Captain Aitken's whiny letter to the home office set the stage for the more inclusive May 9th missive penned by Chief Steward Martin to the line's Port Steward in San Francisco. American passenger ships long enjoyed a reputation for poor, if not surly, passenger service. If nothing else, Chief Martin's letter suggests that unhappy reputation was not undeserved nor

---

[10]Captain Aitken's April 24, 1939 letter to APL president Sheehan. Copy in ship's Maritime Commission 901 General File in RG 178 in custody of the Maritime Administration.

will this letter fill the ranks of union sympathizers, candid as was its observation of the deleterious effect union activities could wreak on a single ship during a single voyage. Unquestionably the bane of the American steamship operator since the early 1920's, American maritime unions always proved shortsighted. Usually taking a sledgehammer approach to their employers, their fanatic interest in short term gains did so much to chip away at the shaky economic base of American steamship companies. Long derided as a leading factor in the demise of the United States Merchant Marine, perhaps such types well deserve to be "on the beach" in a nation without ships.

Subject: Insubordinate Crew Conduct Voyage 43

Dear Sir:

Herewith enclosed is a report of crew conduct and activity encountered during this voyage between San Francisco and New York:

Passengers during this voyage have been continually subjected to mis-inconvenience due to crew conduct and Union activities. On sailing day service was continually disrupted by Union Patrolmen aboard the vessel collecting dues, issuing instructions, etc. to crew members already signed on the vessel. These delegates were found in the galley, pantry, dining saloon and about the vessel soliciting the men, this procedure was constantly an annoyance and interference with the normal functioning of the ship and the rendering of an efficient service.

Two of the patrolmen on board this ship, names—Cayton and Sneddon, were stationed in the galley and pantry were particularly irritating the cooks telling them to the following effect: 'that the starvation wages they were receiving were just enough to ride on the ship, never mind the work. No work of any kind should be performed outside the galley and the men were absolutely forbidden to go into the pantry at any time.'

Due to the activities of the patrolmen mentioned above, as soon as the ship sailed the galley staff pulled a 'passive sit down strike', by slowing up their work and refusing to bring food up from the galley to the pantry. It was necessary to call the Master, who threatened to take drastic action if these men did not 'snap out of it' and tend to their work properly. Their work improved for the time being but gradually slipped back into a state of lazy indifference until it may be said that the Chief, Second and Third Cooks carried the ship around the world. The Scullerymen even going so far as to refuse to get up in the morning to light the fires for the preparation of breakfast.

Shortly before sailing time I was handed an envelope containing the newly approved crew bill of fare with a letter enclosed advising me to live up to this menu as closely as possible and signed by Mr. Smith. The Engine and Sailor's delegate also presented me with copies of this menu the following day at sea telling me that it should be lived up to as specified. This menu was upheld as closely as possible.

Upon arrival at Singapore I was again approached by the delegates requesting a change of menu, this request I refused on the grounds that the menu had been specified by the Port Steward and accepted by the Union. Following this action the men appealed to the Captain for permission to go on their legal ration otherwise known as 'whack'. On April 10th the Master advised me that this permission had been granted. The men were duly notified to secure their rations beginning at 5:00 AM.

On the following morning the Storekeeper and myself were on hand with the rations weighed out for each department; the delegates and the handful of men who were on hand refused to accept their "whack" in this form demanding that they be doled out individually. This of course was a fantastic and impossible request, meaning that each man would have his portion of supplies weighed out and would have the individual use of the galley range for preparation of the food, which would entirely disrupt passenger service. This brought to light the fact that the entire idea was to assert power and use the nuisance value of the legal right to 'whack'. The Master was notified of the refusal and called the delegates warning them that they were on the verge of mutiny and that they had better give up the whole idea and return to the regular menu, this the men did.

Following departure from San Francisco, the Steward's Department elected as its representative one, Americo Zapponi, sculleryman (eleven months sea experience as a messman), who attempted to fill the position, however upon sailing from Honolulu, the position appeared too much for him, so three sub-delegates were appointed. Representing the Galley, Bernard Stuart, 4th cook; representing the waiters, Vincent Butler; and representing the Room Stewards, Harry Walker. These sub-delegates immediately informed all those under them that they must not turn to, five or ten minutes ahead of time or render any form of service of any nature prior to the specified working time. (Due to this arrangement many passengers were subjected to rank insolence and inconvenience by men in passenger quarters refusing service prior to the appointed time by a matter of as little as five minutes or less, i.e.—filling a water bottle). These delegates have rigidly enforced this regulation throughout the entire voyage, even though men knock off work continually before the scheduled hour and defied those in authority who suggest they remain.

Shortly before the ship's April 22nd arrival at Naples, Elias Weiss, Room Steward, was informed that he should stop preparing trays a few minutes early for passengers desiring an 8:00 AM breakfast or else suffer the consequence. This notice was served by Walker. Upon arrival at Naples, while most of the men were ashore Weiss was beaten up by Walker and another Room Steward, Lee Shaul. This was reported to me by Weiss.

Fred Hauptman and Edwin Gibson also reported having been threatened by Walker and admit these men have been carrying on in 'beef squad' fashion with accomplices whose names cannot be directly attacked. Undoubtedly there are other men who have been similarly threatened or attacked but who are afraid to report these activities.

Throughout the voyage continual trouble has been experienced with the observance of work hours as posted, this has at times resulted in more passenger inconvenience. The pantrymen have continually persisted in closing the steam table at 8:00 o'clock, the close of the dinner hour even though the work schedule calls for the men to be on duty until 8:30 PM. Waiters leave the dining room almost before the passengers and are rude and sarcastic to passengers who enter the dining room a few minutes after the appointed dinner hours. The waiters should be on duty until 9:00 PM.

Upon arrival at a port the situation becomes even more aggravated. The Pantrymen do not show up until the latest possible moment and the waiters show up late often intoxicated or with liquor on their breath. Every meal in port is a nerve wracking experience, I never know whether or not the cooks, pantrymen or waiters will be on hand. The waiters think nothing of boldly inquiring of passengers whether or not they will be back to the ship for the next meal. Passengers services is wholly disrupted while the vessel is in port.

Waiters apparently have little interest in their work and make every effort to make it easy for themselves even though this may mean cold food for or other discomfort for their passengers. Trays are overloaded in the galley with courses to save themselves an extra trip to the galley thus causing some of the food to get cold.

Upon arrival at port, crew members are often the first ones ashore often appearing on the dock in trunks or other unsightly garb presenting a very bad picture and to passengers and visitors to the ship. Often times the men are intoxicated and use foul and abusive language in the presence of passengers.

In Singapore, Oiler Smith, returning to the ship saw me talking to passenger Mr. Minnock, upon seeing me he let forth a barrage of language not fit to print. This scene was witnessed by Mr. Balkunas, First Officer. That same night while uptown I was encountered by Mr. Parker, Ordinary Seaman, who told me to the effect—that I had a lot of nerve coming uptown alone as the 'bunch' were after me.

The conduct of the Stewards Department towards passengers is deplorable and is a discredit to the company. In regard to the matter of gratuities the Stewards are telling the passengers how much they shall give and as here pointed out have even returned the offerings of passengers.

Lieut. W. Kirvan, U.S.N., a passenger SF/Manila was told by his waiter that he had been served a given number of meals since sailing from San Francisco and was entitled to more than he had been given.

Mrs. E. Romain, SF/Naples, reports similar treatment from Room Steward, Mr. H. Walters, SF/Naples, reports similar treatment by Room steward. Mr. & Mrs. W. Effinger, SF/Singapore, Standard Oil Co. employees, report similar treatment from stewards.

Regarding appointed work hours: at sea the men are lax about observing hours particularly about knocking off, the men leave their stations at their own discretion regardless of orders entirely ignoring any reprimand. Upon arrival in port members of this department are to be found on all sides conspicuously soliciting gratuities from passengers.

A great amount of gambling is going on in crew quarters and in consequence the men are tired and inefficient or late for work in the morning, those that have been losing are disinterested in their work, causing a degrading effect upon the morale of the men.

There is absolutely no regard for company property in fact there are deliberate attempts to destroy crockery, silver and linen. The men appear to delight in seeing broken crockery.[11] Linen is treated as if it were "rags" and no attempt is made to preserve it for future use. The cooks may be classified as a group of food destroyers due to the lack of interest in their work. The waste in preparation of such things as spinach, string beans and potatoes is appalling.[12]

Referring to the department as a whole, there is a complete lack of co-operation and harmony among the men themselves. A good deal of this difficulty is due to the fact that some of the men are N.M.U.[13] and others are from the West Coast Union. Further than this all the men are antagonistic to the colored galley staff. The radical element on board is another factor doing its best to disrupt the staff and undermine the men.

A good deal of inter-departmental difficulty is caused by the 'tipping' procedure in vogue in the department. It is necessary, in order that a waiter secure edible servings for the waiters to tip the pantrymen; failure to comply results in the waiter getting poor cuts, small servings or being told that there is none of the desired item. It is also customary for crew members to tip the "glory hole" janitors, failure to do this is liable to result in a shortage of towels or soap, or the forgetting by the janitor to make up the bed, or in a locker being broken into or a suitcase mysteriously destroyed. This results in a great amount of departmental antagonism and strife. This attitude is carried to the passengers thru dissatisfied and grumbling stewards.

Considerable trouble has been experienced in having passenger baggage moved from rooms to appointed places for baggage on deck and in moving trunks between the baggageroom and staterooms. The men have on occa-sion refused to do this work and dispute the fact that it is part of their work to move such baggage.

A continual cry of "overtime" is heard on all sides, even though the men show up late and knock off early, or it is necessary for them to work during regular hours for a fellow department member who is sick, drunk, or oth-erwise indisposed. This cry should loom large again due to the fact that overtime refused by me at San Francisco was awarded by patrolmen Shed-don and Cayton with the attitude that the patrolmen and delegates are run-ning the ship.

On this voyage it is hard for me to see how this voyage could have been successfully completed without the invaluable service of Mr. John Marshall, Second Steward and Mr. Peter van Dusen, Storekeeper, whose loyalty and assistance was unfailing. It might also be said at this time that there are a good many men in this department whose desire is to do the job well but these men are unable or afraid to do so because of the radical element ex-isting in this department. This element has done everything in its power to disrupt the men and discredit the company.

The offenders have been subjected to every possible kind of reprimand, I have endeavored to talk to them appealing to their reason, they have been placed in the log book, fined and where necessary have been locked in the brig but such punishment does not even appear to phase them. Time and

---

[11] (Collectors of steamship china now know why some of it is so difficult to find!)
[12] And maybe this is why American passenger ships consistently won low marks for food.
[13] National Maritime Union, based on the East Coast.

again passengers have expressed sentiments of pity for me that I must endure such conditions as they have witnessed and have offered to write to
the company on my behalf. They feel it is beyond reason to see how we in
authority on board are able to contend with such conduct and such trying
conditions and abuse.

No doubt similar troubles are existing on other ships and it is my desire
to point out some of the difficulties which are being encountered at sea at
the present time in the hope that some action will be taken to protect the
position and standing of the Chief Steward, who at the present time is subjected to unwarranted insults and criticism by crew members who have
absolutely no respect for his position of authority.[14]

Chief Steward Martin correctly intuited (or knew from his colleagues)
that other American ships suffered the frequent indignities of "pipsqueak"
union members blighting peaceful operations but the volume of paper written about labor woes of the PRESIDENT GARFIELD suggests she may have
had some of the worst crewmembers of all. These were among his many
concerns as the PRESIDENT GARFIELD steamed around the world and
made her calls at Yokohama on March 9th, Kobe on the 11th and 12th, Hong
Kong on the 16th and 17th, Manila between March 19th and 21st, Singapore
between the 25th and 28th, Penang on the 29th and 30th, Colombo on April
3rd and 4th, Bombay between April 6th and 9th, Suez on the 17th, Suez on
the 18th, Alexandria on the 19th, Naples on the 22nd and 23rd, Genoa on
the 24th and 25th and Marseilles on the 26th. Concluding her first American
President Lines' round the world voyage, the PRESIDENT GARFIELD
steamed into New York harbor on schedule on Tuesday, May 9, 1939.

More about the PRESIDENT GARFIELD came from American President
Lines' Port Captain E. McCarthy's May 23, 1939 Vessel Movement Report to
the company's San Francisco based Marine Superintendent H.L. Foshee.
What a beehive of activity she was for much of her New York stay:

Tuesday May 9th 7:50 AM—steamer arrived at New York from Marseilles,
her last port of departure, anchored in Quarantine to await pratique.

8:30 AM—granted Pratique, hove up anchor and proceeded to berth,
docking at Pier 9, Jersey City, N.J., southside, at 9:50 AM. Three tugs assisted
ship to berth.

10:00 AM—U.S. inspectors of Hulls and Boilers aboard.

10:25 AM—passengers ashore.

10:30 AM—signals for fire and boat stations sounded.

11:00 AM—fire drill completed. Signal for crew to assemble at boat stations.

11:15 AM—signal to swing all lifeboats, port and starboard side.

11:30 AM—signal to man and lower all portside lifeboats. Port lifeboats

---

[14]Chief Steward C. Martin's May 9, 1939 letter to the company's Port Steward. I have reproduced
his text as he wrote it, not correcting any irregularities in capitalization and punctuation. This
copy is in the 901 file for the PRESIDENT MADISON in the Maritime Commission's RG 178 in
the custody of the Maritime Administration.

lowered to water and crew exercised in handling and rowing lifeboats up and down the slip.

11:50 AM—boat drill completed, boats hoisted and secured.

11:30 AM—mail and baggage ashore.

12:00 Noon—crew dismissed.

12:00 Noon—porters handling baggage and stevedores getting ship ready for discharge.

Stopped for lunch. Watchmen in No. 4 and No. 5 where gold and silver stored remained on duty.

1:00 PM—stevedores aboard and commenced taking off beams and hatches.

1:15 PM—commenced discharging cargo from No. 1,2,3,4,7,8,9 and reefer hatches. No. 5 hatch, discharged 55 cases of gold from specie tank and delivered same to armored truck, finishing at 1:30 PM, then commenced discharging cashew nuts from No. 5 upper tweendecks.

All hatches continued discharging until 5:00 PM, when stevedores closed down all hatches and secured tarpaulins and finished all work for the day. Shipyard workers aboard making repairs in engine room.

Wednesday May 10th 8:00 AM—stevedores aboard and resumed discharging cargo from hatches No. 1,2,3,4,5,8 and 9—and two gangs in the reefer hatch.

10:00 AM—Reefer X gang stopped discharging and gang shifted to No. 7 and resumed discharging there.

12:00 Noon—all gangs stopped for lunch

1:00 PM—Resumed discharging from hatches No. 1,2,3,4,5,7,8,9 and reefer and continued discharging from all hatches until 5PM, when stevedores closed down and secured all hatches and tarpaulins and finished work for the day.

Shipyard workers making repairs in engine room throughout the day and night; also deck steam lines, winches, painting ship's hull from water line up, also boat, upper and lower promenade decks, including crew quarters, pantry, galley and all messrooms. Crew engaged in painting and overhauling lifeboats.

Thursday May 11th 8:00 AM—Stevedores aboard and resumed discharging from hatches Nos. 1,2,3,4,5,7,8,9 and reefer.

9:00 AM—fuel oil barge came alongside with 9,300 barrels of fuel oil.

10:50 AM—No.9 finished discharging New York cargo. Stevedores put on beams and hatches in LTD.[15], and commenced loading Boston cargo diverted from New York.

11:50 AM—finished and then put on beams and hatches and checked out. All other gangs stopped for lunch.

12:45 PM—commenced pumping fuel oil from barge to ship.

1:00 PM—resumed discharging cargo from hatches No. 1,2,3,4,5,7,8 and reefer.

4:00 PM—No. 1 hatch finished discharge and commenced loading Boston diverted cargo.

---

[15]LTD = lower tween deck

5:00 PM—all other gangs put on beams and hatches and finished all work for the day.

12:00 Midnight—finished and barge towed away.

Shipyard workers making repairs in engine room throughout the day and night. Crew throughout the day overhauling and painting lifeboats; also contractors painting ship's hull from water line up; also promenade deck and quarters.

Friday May 12th 8:00 AM—Stevedores discharging cargo from hatches No. 2,3,4,5,7,8 and reefer. Shipyard workers aboard making repairs in engine room cleaning boilers, repairing deck steam lines, scraping and cleaning No. 10 and 11 fresh water tanks, cleaning holds, painting exterior of ship's hull, promenade decks, crew quarters and "C" deck alleyways.

12:00 Noon—Stevedores stopped for lunch.

1:00 PM—resumed discharging from hatches No. 2,3,4,57,8 and reefer.

3:00 PM—No 8 finished discharging New York cargo, then put on beams and hatches and checked out.

3:30 PM—No. 7 finished discharging New York cargo, then put on beams and hatches and gang shifted to Port reefer and resumed discharging over No. 7 hatch to pier.

4:00 PM—No 3 finished discharging New York cargo, then put on beams and hatches, LTD and UTD and commenced loading Boston diverted cargo.

4:40 PM—finished, stevedores put on beams and hatches and checked out.

5:00 PM—No 5 finished discharging New York cargo, then put on beams and hatches and gang checked out. Hatches No. 3,4 and reefer continued discharging until 6:00 PM when No. 3 and 4 closed down for the day and gangs checked out.

6:00 PM—reefer finished discharging New York cargo, then put on beams and hatches and gangs checked out.

OVERTIME—5:00—6:00 PM 3 gangs

5:00—5:30 PM 3 gangs 1/2 hr

8:00 PM to 12:00 Midnight—ship shut down for engine repairs. Lights and fire protection furnished from Pier during the shut down period.

12:00 Midnight—repairs completed engine room, winches and deck lines.

Saturday May 13th 8:00 AM—stevedores resumed discharging cargo from No. 3 and 4 hatches and continued discharging until 11:30 AM, when all New York cargo was discharged.

8:00 AM—11:30 AM ship undergoing dock trial.

12:00 Noon—gangway ashore, let go lines, vessel sailed Pier 9 Jersey City and proceeded to sea for Boston, Three tugs assisted ship leaving berth. Draft forward 20'06" Aft 27'00".

Detention in New York discharging and undergoing repairs four days, four hours—ten minutes.

Sunday May 14th 9:42 AM—vessel arrived at Boston from New York docking at Pier 44, Charlestown, Mass. at 11:20 AM.

Draft—Forward—19'03" Aft 27'00"

No discharging—no loading. Sunday observed.

Monday May 15th 8:00 AM—gang of stevedores aboard getting ship ready for discharging and loading.

8:30 AM—commenced discharging cargo from No. 1,2,5 and reefer hatches. Loading cargo commenced in hatches No. 4 and 8.

9:30 AM—all Boston reefer cargo discharged and gang shifted into No. 7 and commenced discharge.

10:00 AM—commenced loading frozen cargo in reefer chamber.

12:00 Noon—gangs stopped for lunch.

1:00 PM—stevedores resumed discharging and loading operations from and to hatches as above and continued discharging and loading until 5:00 PM when all gangs stopped for dinner.

7:00 PM—stevedores aboard loading cargo into hatches No. 1,2,5,7,8 and reefer and discharging from No. 3 and 5.

9:20 PM—reefer stopped loading and gangs shifted into No. 9 and resumed loading.

10:50 PM—No. 2 hatch stopped loading and resumed discharging.

11:50 PM—stevedores closed down all hatches and stopped work for the night.

OVERTIME—7:00 PM to 11:00 PM—6 gangs.

Tuesday May 16th 8:00 AM—stevedores aboard and resumed discharging from hatches No. 2 and 4—and resumed loading cargo in hatches 1,3,5,7 and 9.

10:00 AM—No 9 gang finished and gang shifted into reefer and resumed loading.

10:50 AM—finished discharging in No.2 and 4 and commenced loading.

12:00 Noon—all gangs stopped for lunch.

1:00 PM—resumed loading in hatches No. 2,3,47,8 and reefer.

3:00 PM—finished loading and gang checked out.

3:30 PM—finished loading and discharging all cargo. Ship ready for sea.

3:48 PM—gangway ashore, let go lines and vessel sailed from Pier 44 Boston and proceeded to sea bound for New York via Nantucket Shoals.

Draft—Forward 19'00" - Aft—28'00"

Detention at Boston discharging and loading cargo—2 days, 5 hours, 6 minutes,

Cargo discharged at Boston— 700 tons,

Cargo loaded at Boston—1168 weight tons—measurement 2,235 including reefer cargo.

Wednesday May 17th 1:00 PM—vessel arrived at New York from Boston, docking at Pier 9, Jersey City, N.J. southside at 2:00 PM. Three tugs assisted ship to berth.

Draft Forward 19'00" Aft 28'00"

2:00 PM—stevedores aboard—7 gangs rigging up and getting ship ready for loading.

3:00 PM—commenced loading in hatches No. 1,2,3,4,5,7 and 8 and continued loading until 8:00 PM—then closed down hatches for the night.

OVERTIME—156 men—9 foremen

Thursday May 18th 8:00 AM—stevedores aboard—9 gangs and resumed loading in hatches No. 1,2,3,4,5,7 and 8, and commenced loading No 2X and reefer.

10:50 AM—reefer stopped loading and gang shifted into No. 9 and commenced loading.

12:00 Noon—all gangs stopped loading except No 2X,4,5 and 7.

OVERTIME Noon—1:00 PM—89 men—6 foremen.

1:00 PM—resumed loading in hatches No. 2,3,4,5 and 7.

2:00 PM—resumed loading in hatches No. 1, 2X,8,9 and reefer.

6:00 PM—all gangs stopped for dinner.

OVERTIME—5:00 PM to 6:00 PM—gangs 1,2,3,4,5,7,8,9 and reefer. 200 men—12 foremen. Gangs No. 4,5 and 7 continued until 7:00 PM—OVERTIME 67 Men—5 foremen.

7:00 PM—resumed loading cargo in hatches No. 2,3,4,5 and 7. OVERTIME—112 men—8 foremen.

7:00 PM—9:30 PM—Gangs 1,2,3,4,5,7,8,9 and reefer. 178 men—11 foremen.

9:30 PM—11:30 PM OVERTIME gangs 2,3,4,5,7 and 8—134 men—8 foremen.

Friday May 19th 8:00 AM—stevedores aboard and loading in hatches No. 1,2,3,4,5,7,8,9 and reefer.

8:00 AM—repairs completed.

10:00 AM—ship undergoing dock trial.

12:00 Noon—all gangs stopped for lunch except No. 1 and 7 continued to 1:00 PM—OVERTIME 46 men—4 foremen.

1:00 PM—resumed loading cargo in hatches No. 1,2,3,4,7 and 8.

2:00 PM—full complement of officers and seagoing personnel on board.

2:00 PM—No.9 and reefer hatches resumed loading.

4:00 PM—No 3 hatch finished loading and gang checked out.

4:30 PM—No. 2,7,8 and reefer finished loading and checked out.

5:00 PM—ship cleared from Customs House.

5:00 PM—Hatches 1,4 and 8 finished loading all cargo.

5:30 PM—hatches, booms and all cargo gear made secure.

5:40 PM—passengers and baggage aboard. Ship ready for sea.

6:00 PM—gangway ashore, let go lines and vessel sailed from Pier 9 Jersey City, N.J. and proceeded to sea Around-the-World via Havana, Canal Zone, West Coast ports, Honolulu and Far East ports.

Three tugs assisted ship leaving dock.

Draft—Forward—24'08" - Aft—30'00".

Weather clear and fine—light southerly wind. Flood tide.

DETENTION IN PORT—2 days, 5 hours, 0 minutes.

Cargo loaded at New York—Weight tons—3,254—Meas. Tons—5,313.

Several members of the crew in the various departments were paid off by mutual consent while ship was at New York.

Overtime for porters handling baggage, gangway and ship's lines, 5:30 PM to 6:00 PM—18 men and 2 foremen.[16]

---

[16]This copy of the ship's Vessel Movement Report came from the ship's 901 general file held in the Maritime Commissions RG 178 files held by the Maritime Administration.

Like a sleeping giant, the American Merchant Marine stood helpless against cancerous recurrent disruption by recalcitrant unionists. Even full passenger lists did nothing to deter determined union trouble-makers. It didn't on this voyage either, when every cabin in the ship was taken when the PRESIDENT GARFIELD steamed out of New York on May 19th. None of the words of either Captain Aitken nor Chief Steward Martin had much impact on the ship's feisty crew who continued to assert their "rights" during the course of the following voyage, her last before Europe plunged into the darkness of World War II. This time Captain Aitken took his frustrations to the top, copying excerpts from the ship's log and sent them on to the Maritime Commission. Showing strength in their limited numbers, other senior officers affixed their signatures to a number of these. Besides Captain Aitken, Chief Officer James Phelan, Chief Engineer William Henry and First Assistant Engineer Edward Hill all signed copies of extracts of the ship's log included in a packet of information sent to the Maritime Commission.

A shipment of tires figured prominently among the 4,757 tons of general cargo the ship had in her holds when she made her May 27th transit of the Panama Canal. Under the white eagle on her funnel, things seemed in order and the ship arrived at San Pedro on schedule on June 5th. No items record frustrations suffered on the intercoastal segment of that voyage from New York but irritations by the crew continued before the ship sailed from San Francisco on the early evening of June 11, 1939. A scullery worker deserted and the ship sailed with a new man signed on at the last moment. At sea that night it was very dark, the sky overcast with patches of fog. Before midnight on June 11, 1939 fireman A. Carlson of the 8:00 PM to 12:00 midnight watch called for an oiler named Whitman to get ready to stand the 12:00—4:00 AM watch. The oiler didn't show up. Still absent at 12:40, the engine crew notified the First Assistant Engineer. After notifying Second Officer Abernathy, the officer on watch, of a missing crewman, at 1:20 AM a search party began looking for him. Five minutes later the Chief Engineer joined the group. When no trace of the oiler had been found by 2:20 AM, the party notified Captain Aitken. Ten minutes later the Captain broadcast "man missing" over the wireless, logging the incident at 08:30 G.C.T. June 12 Lat 37 degrees 15'N. 134 degrees 30'W on 251 degrees true course. That day and the next, San Francisco newspapers carried an item about a man missing from the liner as all ships nearby were asked to scour a stretch of water for about 150 miles west of Santa Cruz.

Since no one had seen the man go over the side, the Captain decided to hold the ship on course. Now questions were being asked. Some crewmembers remembered a drinking party in the oilers quarters during the preceding night. Whitman had been there, they said. An Electrician recalled seeing the oiler at 7:30 PM, volunteering that Whitman had had a bottle of whiskey in one pocket, a beer in the other. The mystery grew deeper when it was recalled that Whitman had not stood his 12:00 AM—4:00 AM watch before the ship sailed either but that he had been seen by another oiler at 11:25 PM.

What to do in such a case? No oiler, no body, only recollections of his absence from the engine room during his watch and the presence of his belongings. Those were gathered up and put under seal for transfer at Honolulu to the PRESIDENT COOLIDGE and transportation back to the U.S. Shipping Commissioner at San Francisco. Back aboard the ship, Captain Aitken and Chief Engineer Henry continued to have trouble with engine room personnel. By mutual consent, two men were signed off on June 18th just before the ship made landfall at Honolulu. Later that day, just before sailing, the failure of a wiper to return to the ship was entered in the log. That same day an oiler who had signed on at Honolulu was demoted to wiper.

At "7:52 PM with engines on standby, vessel signalled ready for departure, Roy McCarthy, shore delegate for the fireman's union M.O.F.W., rushed into the master's room and in the presence of the company's agent, Mr. Jay Murphy; Pilot, Captain Jennings, and ship's Master, in a loud and threatening voice demanded the immediate retraction of a statement printed in the *Honolulu Advertiser* or he would "pull off the entire engine room crew". He accused the Master of giving a statement to the newspaper to the effect that Whitman, the oiler who disappeared during the voyage from San Francisco to Honolulu, jumped overboard during a fit of drunken despondency. This accusation was denied by the Master and McCarthy was ordered out of the room. Whereupon McCarthy went to the after deck and ordered all unlicensed engine crew members to leave the vessel. This they did with the exception of the watch on duty.

At 8:00 PM, the sailing hour at hand, the Master sent the Chief Officer to the after gangway to order the engine crew aboard and they refused to do so. Captain T.K. Whitelow, U.S. local steamboat inspector, was notified of this situation but replied there was nothing he could do and that he could not become involved in the matter.

At 10:30 PM McCarthy appeared in the Master's quarters with two affidavits which he requested the Master to sign, whereupon he said that he would order the crew aboard and we might proceed to sea. One statement was to the effect that the Master would retract the statement he allegedly made to the newspapers, the other that the Master would take no discriminatory action against any of the men who had walked off the ship. Both of these requests were refused by the Master.

Mr. Ray Coll, editor of the *Honolulu Advertiser*, being present, assured McCarthy that he would publish a retraction of the newspaper account. The Master made the statement that no discriminatory action would be taken against these men on proceeding to sea, whereupon McCarthy went on the pier at 10:55 PM and ordered the men aboard. Vessel sailed at 11:00 PM delayed three hours by crew action. The names and ratings of the members of the engine room crew who walked off the vessel and refused to come aboard and proceed to sea when ordered to do so were logged.[17]

---

[17] Report of Chief Officer to American President Lines Port Captain.

Crew trouble did not stop with the ship's delayed departure from Honolulu. On July 4th and 5th, an A.B. failed to show up for two of his watches. He was fined two days' pay. Another seaman was found drunk that afternoon and confined to the brig for the rest of the day and that night. Leaving Hong Kong on July 8th, a laundryman failed to rejoin the ship. At Manila three days later the Assistant Fourth Engineer deserted the ship. So, too, did a watertender and an able bodied seaman. The chief baker was so drunk on the afternoon of the 13th after a two day drinking binge since the ship left Manila, that he was unable to work. Captain Aitken had a dandy rest cure for him, sending him off to the ship's brig for the night. Driving home his displeasure with the baker's antics, Captain Aitken logged the man four days' pay. At Singapore on the 17th, a watertender was carted off the ship and hospitalized. Three days later on July 20th, a fireman was promoted to watertender and a wiper stepped up to fireman. Next on the list of recalcitrant crewmembers was a dining room waiter. After several admonitions following insubordinate behavior to the chief and second steward, his waiter's jacket was removed on August 7th and he was put on a clean up detail. The PRESIDENT GARFIELD was at Naples on August 10th. There, soaking up the rays of the Neapolitan moon and drinking in the delights of that hospitable Italian city, two oilers were arrested for "cohabiting with unlicensed prostitutes". Unable to spring themselves from jail in time, they were logged as "AWOL" during the time of the ship's passage to Genoa. The pleasures of the shore attracted those of higher rank, too. Absent without leave during the ship's August 16th-17th transit from Genoa to Marseilles was the Third reefer Engineer. So, too, was a dining room waiter similarly absent. Each lost one days' pay for his prank. Unable to stand watch at sea on August 18th because he was drunk, an A.B. went to jail, spending a night in the PRESIDENT GARFIELD's increasingly popular brig. Released from detention on the 19th, he was logged four days' pay because he had been tipsy during four previous watches.

The transAtlantic portion of that difficult ride around the world ended at New York with her August 29, 1939 arrival. Even as the ship lay at her Jersey City pier at the end of that month, notations about the crew dotted the ship's log. On the 30th an ordinary seaman had to be hospitalized. He was joined the next day by the Second Steward and a wiper.

Europe fell into war and the PRESIDENT GARFIELD started another voyage. Once again the ship's log notes another absence without leave. An able bodied seaman failed to sail with the ship when the liner left New York on September 2nd on her way to Boston. That prank cost him two days' pay. The ship sailed from New York again on September 8th. The chief baker paid a return visit to the brig on September 10th, this time for absences from duty without leave. In exchange for his freedom on the morn, he accepted a demotion to third baker as his two former subordinates each increased one rank. When the PRESIDENT GARFIELD sailed from Havana on September

13, 1939, she was short one waiter, a man reported as failing to join the ship before sailing.

Add crew troubles to the factors combining to the demise of the Dollar Line. The outbreak of the European war made life just as tough for new American President Lines, though before long they would reap tremendous profits from skyrocketing freight rates. But first, American mariners of all ranks took their justified fear of sailing to and through war zones to new wage heights, refusing to sail from American ports until shipowners granted hefty concessional wage hikes. Just before the ship's scheduled October 1st San Francisco departure, the men walked out, refusing to sail unless their demands were met. Passengers were landed on the 3rd and put up at local hotels at company expense. Hit by the possibility of a long delay in getting the PRESIDENT GARFIELD away from San Francisco, American President Lines finally agreed to many of the seamen's wage demands and signed agreements with all six of their unions. Company president Joseph Sheehan wired the Maritime Commission Chairman Admiral Emory Land on October 4, 1939: "crew agree sign on PRESIDENT GARFIELD 5 PM today and ship will sail at 9 PM. crew finally accepted 25% wage increase + $2,000 war risk insurance. This culminates 2 days whole negotiations. hope following ships be dispatched without difficulty."[18] Under darkening world conditions the PRESIDENT GARFIELD seems to have omitted both Kobe and Shanghai that time, steaming directly from Honolulu to Hong Kong and sailing from there on October 30th on her way to Manila. From there on November 3rd the ship called at all other customary ports until her December 8th sailing from Genoa. With ports in belligerent countries now about to shut to neutral American vessels, her December 10th call at Marseilles was one of the last legal calls an American vessel would make at that port for some time, as American operators complied with the law once the Pittman (neutrality) Act took effect. Sailing from France on December 10th, the PRESIDENT GARFIELD made a course for the United States. No reported difficulty delayed her passage and she steamed back into New York on December 24, 1939.

The PRESIDENT GARFIELD began 1940 manned by 119 officers and men under the command of Captain Aitken. Into the uncertain waters of a world dominated by news of a European war, she sailed once more for a customary voyage around the world. Through the Panama Canal on January 8, 1940 she had 5,336 tons of cotton and general cargo in her holds. She began her first sailing from San Francisco since the start of the European war on January 25, 1940. Back at New York again on April 19, 1940, she went back to the 56th Street Brooklyn yards of the Bethlehem Shipbuilding Company for nine days of repairs between April 18th and the 26th. She sailed again from New York on April 27, 1940 for her ports around the world, but this time, from Bombay on July 19th, she made a course not for Suez but for Cape

---

[18]Sheehan's October 4, 1939 telegram. Copy in ship's 901 files in RG 178 held by the Maritime Administration.

Town, from whence she sailed for American waters on July 28th. Next outbound again on August 25th the PRESIDENT GARFIELD was on her final voyage under the name by which it seemed an entire world knew her. She was an old ship by then and due for replacement by a new ship which would carry her name. Another "President" name was found for this old one and she would change names at the end of her voyage. Meanwhile there was a schedule to keep and she did pretty well. The European war was a year old when the ship went through the Panama Canal again with 4,320 tons of machinery and general cargo on September 2nd on her way to California and a September 14th sailing from San Francisco. October 10th saw her sail from Kobe. It was one of the last visits she would make there. The PRESIDENT GARFIELD sailed from Singapore on October 28th for Penang and Bombay, and sailed from there with her holds full of rubber, tea and other cargo useful to the defense effort on November 13th. From there she made a non-stop passage to Cape Town before beginning the final leg of her round the world voyage with her November 29th sailing.

Approval to surrender the marine documents of the PRESIDENT GARFIELD in preparation for her renaming came in Maritime Commission Order C-768 issued while the ship was in the Indian Ocean on November 5, 1940. She would perpetuate the name long worn by the old Admiral Line "535" type steamer, PRESIDENT MADISON, which had been sold to Philippine buyers in 1940 after years in layup following a devastating accident at her pier. And though the Maritime Commission approved the ship's new name on December 15th, she was still named PRESIDENT GARFIELD when she made the casualty lists a few days later. The date was December 19, 1940. Frustration must have been the feeling of everyone aboard as the ship attempted to dock at New York from Marseilles. Nearing Pier 9 in Jersey City, the ship's bow stuck in the mud and lodged there. Not until three hours later was she freed and able to dock. Beyond the embarrassment and time lost in the process, the ship was not at all damaged. Passengers landed, cargo was worked and the ship resumed her services. Two nights later, at 11:10 PM on December 21st, a new certificate for her in the name PRESIDENT MADISON was issued and the ship was officially renamed.

Captain Valdemar Nielsen was now in command and January 4, 1941 saw her make her departure from Boston for another New York call. There, on January 10th, she began her first commercial round the world voyage under her new name. The PRESIDENT MADISON called Havana on the 14th and after calling Cristobal on the 18th, transited the Canal with 5,116 tons of general cargo and cotton on the 19th. After overnighting in San Pedro on January 27th she sailed on the 28th for San Francisco and a January 29th arrival. On February 1st she began her transPacific crossing. After sailing from Singapore on March 5th, she made her way to India. From there she sailed once again to Cape Town for an April 2nd call. Sailing from there on April 3rd she made her way to New York and her April 23rd arrival.

Offering American President Lines the sum of $800,000.00 per ship, that winter the Army tried to buy the PRESIDENT MADISON and one sister for conversion to and employment as troop transports. That was a very fair price for a ship whose October 1939 appraisal came in at a depreciated value of $758,451.08, a figure inflated by omission of the estimated $310,855.00 in repairs and betterments the ship should have had. The Army was willing to pay twice her real value. Postwar records show that the ship was taken in May 1941 for military service under the service agreement WSA 224 that was finalized and formally signed in June 1941. But that agreement was back-dated because at the time the War Shipping Administration was not yet extant and the need to move cargo was still heavier than defense require-ments. Military authorities did not acquire the ship at that time and she was instead allowed to remain with American President Lines to operate what was her final commercial sailing. That was an unsubsidized voyage to Sin-gapore and Penang, one of four authorized for APL "502" type steamers permitted by the Maritime Commission at their February 13, 1941 meeting. Pursuant to a request from American President Lines, the Maritime Com-mission granted the company permission to divert the PRESIDENT MADI-SON from her planned round the world itinerary on her next voyage and allow her to make a trip from New York on May 5th to Singapore and back. At the time, that route was called Line A, the Atlantic/Straits service, as opposed to Line B, the round the world service. So important did American President Lines consider that trip to the Straits that they offered to operate the ship as a freighter west of San Francisco. The Maritime Commission wouldn't hear of it. Fully manned as a passenger ship, the ship departed New York on May 6th for the Canal Zone. Lucky she was to have a full complement in the stewards department because at Panama she embarked 175 Chinese passengers booked for a June departure in the PRESIDENT PIERCE. But when the military took that ship they were landed, there to await the next westbound "President" liner.

The PRESIDENT MADISON departed San Francisco on May 29th bound for the Far East. Partly to relieve the monotony of the long voyage, she called at Honolulu on June 5th her way west. There she took on fuel, water and stores. Hong Kong was next followed by Manila, Singapore, Penang and Singapore before heading back across the Pacific to Honolulu where she stopped on August 2nd en route to San Francisco, Los Angeles and Panama. From San Francisco on August 12th she sailed for New York, thus making one of her few eastbound trips through the Panama Canal. She arrived at New York on August 31, 1941.

Because the Army and Navy had taken over six American President Lines ships, the Maritime Commission considered assignment of the PRES-IDENT MADISON to Line "A" along with her sisters PRESIDENT HAR-RISON and PRESIDENT TAYLOR and the yet unrenamed PRESIDENT POLK. When the PRESIDENT MADISON began Voyage 53 from New York on September 5, 1941, her voyage would also eventually be referred to as WSA voyage 1. From New York the ship made her usual tracks for Boston where she arrived on September 6th. There, before sailing, she was delivered to the Maritime Commission for national service under bareboat charter at a rate of $1,086.93 per day and allocated to American President Lines. Despite an announcement by the Commissioners that the ship would be assigned to the Navy once they had taken possession, plans changed. The cargo and passenger lift capabilities of the ship were more important at that moment than any possible use as a Navy auxiliary and the movement of strategic defense cargoes was the reason the Maritime Commission kept the PRESIDENT MADISON and her sisters in commercial service as far as they were able to at that time. All parties agreed to allow the ship to continue commercial operations and operate at least one more subsidized round the world voyage. The United States needed rubber more than the Army or Navy needed another troopship. As things turned out, it would be her final trip on that prestigious peacetime service, the last such voyage completed by any of the "502" sisters. At least before sailing it appeared that the ship would operate another voyage on Line B, the round the world service. In fact the ship did make another circumnavigation of the globe on that voyage, but by the time she was ready to depart from San Francisco, the Maritime Commission had decided to authorize American President Lines to utilize the ship on transPacific service Line A. That's not quite what happened.

Still in command of the ship and her crew of 168 officers and men was Captain Valdemar Nielsen. Danish born veteran of the "502"'s, he had been with these ships since the early 1920s and was thoroughly familiar with all aspects of the Line's operation. In his capable hands the PRESIDENT MADISON sailed from Boston that September 6, 1941. His officers were:

Chief Officer ....Young Biggs
First Officer ....Arthur Henrikson
Second Officer ....Arnold Erickson
Third Officer ....Walter Nilson

Chief Engineer ....Andy Bennett
First Asst. Engineer ....Harry Breen
Second Asst. Engineer ....Albert Wilson
Third Asst. Engineer ....Dmetri Yesnick
Fourth Asst. Engineer ....Patrick Kane

Chief Purser ....Edward Seeley
Surgeon ....Bernard Mark, M.D.
Chief Steward ....Albert Bissel

On the day after sailing from Boston the liner arrived at New York where she followed her typical pattern of loading cargo and preparing for her September 12, 1941 departure on another subsidized voyage. She was again a ship with the world on her itinerary. Captain Nielsen took his ship into Havana on the 16th and through the Panama Canal on the 20th. On the 29th the ship made San Pedro and on October 1st the youngest of the "502"'s steamed out on her way to her San Francisco home port. It would be her last arrival there as a commercial passenger and cargo liner. The frenzied exigencies of the day brought another change in official plans almost three weeks after sailing. As San Francisco bound cargo and mail were being offloaded shortly after her October 2, 1941 arrival, the ship was transferred back to Line A and diverted to the transPacific service. Then covering the route since the sale of the "535"'s were some of the "502"'s assisted by four of the CITY OF BALTIMORE class, chartered by American President Lines from the Baltimore Mail Line/Panama Pacific Line for a California to the Philippines route. Because of worsening tensions with Japan, no Kobe or Yokohama calls were scheduled but the ship was able to load cargo and mails and embark passengers for Shanghai. American President Lines had already closed their passenger offices in both countries.

Now the ship was under orders from American President Lines to make for Singapore via Honolulu, Shanghai, Hong Kong and Manila, from whence the ship was to turn around and sail home. Before sailing for the Far East the PRESIDENT MADISON embarked 1 passenger for Shanghai and 174 for Hong Kong. In the ship's holds were 8,544 tons of freight and 4,537 bags of mail, one of her best totals ever. Broken down by destination, there were 675 tons of cargo and 122 bags of mail for Honolulu, 1,294 tons of cargo and 3,057 bags of mail for Shanghai, 2,052 tons of cargo and 1,185 bags of mail for Hong Kong, 3,368 tons of cargo for Manila and 1,155 tons of cargo and 183 bags of mail for Singapore. Maybe it did take a war to fill her!

Into uncertain waters the PRESIDENT MADISON sailed out past the Golden Gate on October 4th for Honolulu. After a few hours there she sailed, only to return there ten days later. Captain Nielsen's report tells why:

SS PRESIDENT MADISON . . . . Voyage 53–10 . . . . MASTER'S REPORT

10/12/41 ....Arrived Honolulu—0621
10/12/41 ....Sailed Honolulu —1849

ORDERS
American President Lines to proceed to Shanghai next port of call.

10/17/41 ....At 0130 received radio message from the
                             United States Navy Dept. addressed to ALL
                             U.S. MERCHANT SHIPS to return to nearest
                             friendly port. Honolulu was the nearest port
                             from my position (Lat. 30–14 N., Long. 176–
                             43E). Thereupon set course immediately for
                             return to Honolulu.
10/21/41 ....Arrived Honolulu (return)
10/22/41 ....Sailed Honolulu

ORDERS
Confidential orders received from the Navy Department to proceed to Manila via Torres Strait—calling at Port Moresby, New Guinea, for Pilot to take me thru Torres Strait. Thence via Banda Sea, Ambon Island thru Manila

Strait, Molucca Passage, Banca Island passage, Celebes Sea, Basilan Strait, and Mindora Strait to Manila.[19]

Preparing for the war they felt was near, the Navy needed suitable ships to bring remaining units of the 4th Marines and their equipment out of China. Ignoring the September visit of their own transport HENDERSON, which came and went without embarking a single man stationed there, that ship was long gone. Scouting around for tonnage available in the area, only the "502" class ships looked suitable for this special mission. Three of them would be at or near Manila around the time the Marines HAD to evacuate. Near enough for consideration were two sisters, the PRESIDENT HARRISON and PRESIDENT MADISON—both flew the pennants of the United States Naval Reserve, for their masters and most officers held commissions in the U.S. Naval Reserve. Not that that technicality much mattered, all merchant ships would become subject to requisition for war use by the Government should hostilities start. Going over the heads of the ships' owners, the Emergency Shipping Controller made the ships available to the United States Navy for special services. Now the movements of those two ships were directed by a November 11th agreement between the Navy and the Maritime Commission. The actual paperwork came later. The PRESIDENT MADISON was then one day out of Manila.

At Manila the needs of the Navy intervened and brought the PRESIDENT MADISON close to danger. After the liner anchored at the Quarantine anchorage, on November 12, 1941 Captain Nielsen took one of his ship's boats to shore in order to report to American President Lines' office and the United States Naval Control Office. With no passengers for Manila, none was landed there. Nor was any freight or mail discharged while the ship called there that time.

The Navy issued orders to Captain Nielsen on the morning of November l3th: " . . . sail that day via Hong Kong and thence proceed to Shanghai". Before sailing the PRESIDENT MADISON took on fresh water and provisions, but no additional fuel.

Executed on November 17, 1941 with American President Lines by Captain (SC) E.G. Morsell, Supply Officer of the United States Navy, Navy Contract Number N 321 s 8393 was a day to day charter of both the PRESIDENT HARRISON and PRESIDENT MADISON. Needed to evacuate Navy and Marine Corps personnel from China, the agreement included a rate of $2,675.47 per day for excess time these ships lost from their normal voyages. Months later brought a decision from the Maritime Commission that the dollar figures in that Navy contract could be disregarded as a bareboat charter to the Maritime Commission and the Service Agreement of September 6, 1941 superseded any subsequent Navy commitment on this score to American President Lines.

---

[19]Copy of the Master's Report for Voyage 53–10 is in the ship's 901 file in RG 178 at Maritime Administration.

Both ships would go to Hong Kong where the PRESIDENT MADISON would load the materials required to fit the ship for the emergency carriage troops and the PRESIDENT HARRISON would be hastily converted. Neither ship would have an escort for any of her northbound passage to Chinese waters but for her passage southbound from Shanghai, each ship was promised the escort of a pair of American submarines. No matter the missed opportunities to get men and material out of China thus far, authorities thought of everything this time, even planning the number of hours it would take to fit both ships for the carriage of troops. The Master of each ship was assured that in keeping with the common practice when large numbers of passengers could be carried in emergency situations, the American Consul at Shanghai would have the certificates each ship needed to allow her to carry more than the usual permissible number.

First of the two "502"s into Hong Kong was the PRESIDENT MADISON. After her November 15th arrival there her 174 passengers ticketed to that port disembarked. While the ship was there all cargo for that port was discharged. That was more work than it should have been because when the ship had been loaded in North America everyone expected the ship to call at Shanghai en route to Hong Kong instead of the other way around. A considerable amount of Shanghai cargo had to be moved in order to discharge Hong Kong cargo. Then the PRESIDENT MADISON took on Shanghai cargo from the SS PRESIDENT van BUREN, earlier discharged at Hong Kong. There was also room for the ship to load some Honolulu and San Francisco transshipment cargo from India.

While working cargo at Hong Kong on November 17th, instructions came in from American President Lines' Manila Office. The Marines that the SS PRESIDENT MADISON would evacuate were to be brought directly from Shanghai directly to Manila. For that reason Captain Nielsen was instructed to take on sufficient stores at Hong Kong to bring his ship all the way back to Manila. APL also told him to take on some lumber for the construction of the Marines' accommodations. Taken ill, one crew member was brought to the Kowloon General Hospital for medical care. The ship would sail without him.

On the ship's third day there, November 18th, the local American President Lines' office brought Captain Nielsen orders to leave immediately for Shanghai, where men from the Shanghai Engineering Company would use the lumber recently brought aboard and construct emergency accommodations for up to 800 troops in the record time of three days. Then the PRESIDENT MADISON would evacuate 400 Marines. Without all the requisite lifesaving equipment she would need, off she went and headed for Shanghai, a three days sail. Whatever had not arrived at Hong Kong in time to be placed aboard her would be brought up to Shanghai in the PRESIDENT HARRISON. Any uncompleted work towards her conversion would have to be finished with the help of her Marine passengers while the ship was underway. On November 18,1941 the PRESIDENT MADISON sailed from

Hong Kong. Aboard were now 23 passengers and 2,795 tons of cargo and 1,405 bags of mail (all of it had been censored while the ship lay at Hong Kong)for Shanghai. For Manila was one bag of mail and 3,401 tons of cargo, for Singapore were the same 1,155 tons of freight the ship had taken from North America. Added to the cargo manifest were 267 tons for Honolulu and 175 tons for San Francisco.

Passengers, cargo and mail for Shanghai were finally landed there after the PRESIDENT MADISON arrived on November 21, 1941. The ship's lines were hardly ashore when stevedores started to work. Besides offloading Shanghai cargo, a lot of the Singapore and Manila cargo was shifted in order to allow workmen to construct the emergency quarters for her expected Marines. Hers was one of the last Shanghai calls made by an American passenger ship at a Chinese port before America went to war. A way of life was fast coming to an end in that city, where in the International Settlement, the crews and passengers of American vessels had been welcome fixtures for years. On taking leave of the citizenry, the Marines had planned a parade for the 27th. At the American Club on November 26th a farewell party was held for them. Heading the guest list were Captain Valdemar Nielsen of the PRESIDENT MADISON, Admiral William A. Glassford, commander of U.S. Naval Forces, Shanghai, and Colonel Samuel L. Howard, Commanding Officer of the 4th Marine Regiment. Sending his regrets was Captain Pierson of the PRESIDENT HARRISON. Years later Captain Nielsen recalled the event and Captain David Grover and his daughter Gretchen G. Grover recorded it in their excellent book, *CAPTIVES OF SHANGHAI*:

> During my conversation with the Admiral he asked me when my ship would finish discharging her cargo. I informed him we had finished some time earlier, and now we were waiting to complete the Marine accommodations, otherwise we were ready to sail.
>
> I thought the Admiral was going to blow his top. 'I have been misinformed,' he said. Then he hollered 'Sam, come over here.' When the Colonel appeared the Admiral said 'Captain Nielsen has just informed me his ship is ready to embark. Are you ready?'
>
> The Colonel replied, 'Accommodations on the ship are not quite complete,' to which the Admiral said, 'The Marines are very handy men; they can complete the unfinished work on the way. Forget about the parade. I suggest you commence embarkation at 0800 tomorrow, and we will set a sailing time on the afternoon high water tide. I can see the handwriting on the wall. It is later than we think.'
>
> The Colonel hesitated, and then replied, 'Yes sir. Can do. Will do.'[20]

The following morning was Thanksgiving Day. In Shanghai that November 27th it was a bleak, miserable day, not the kind of weather conducive to parades of any sort, so the Marine officers could thank the climate that

---

[20]Grover, Capt. David and Grover, Commander Gretchen G., U.S.N.R., CAPTIVES OF SHANGHAI. Pages 31,32. Reproduced here by kind permission of Captain David Grover.

their men would not parade out of town. Double-decker buses carried the men to the docks where the Danish owned MERRY MOLLER and other small vessels tendered them out to the waiting PRESIDENT MADISON. Loading priorities had been worked out in advance. Topping the list was ammunition. Then field equipment, medical supplies, rations, motor transport, clothing, miscellaneous and household effects. The PRESIDENT MADISON had room for all 2,224 tons of it. Now in her holds were 5,625 tons of freight and 1 mail bag for Manila, 1,156 tons of freight and 13 mail bags for Singapore, 267 tons and 2 bags of mail for Honolulu and 180 tons of freight and 9 bags of mail for San Francisco. There were also PLENTY of passengers—72 civilians and 396 officers and men of the United States Marines Corps.

At just before 4:00 PM the liner was ready to sail. Off The Saddles, where she expected to meet her submarine escorts, four Japanese destroyers awaiting her lined up behind her and escorted her downriver.

Radioed instructions from the Commander-in-Chief Asiatic Fleet came in on November 30th. These ordered the PRESIDENT MADISON to "proceed to Subic Bay to land all Marines and part of their equipment and sail for Manila at 1400 December 1st."[21] Thus the PRESIDENT MADISON altered course and made for the Naval Station at Olangapo to disembark her Marines before returning to Manila to offload the rest of their equipment. Even with that freight ashore, the ship still had plenty of commercial cargo for Singapore and the United States.

Captain Nielsen brought the PRESIDENT MADISON into Subic Bay at 1:45PM on December 1st. Later that day the ship arrived at Manila where she anchored at Quarantine at 6:41PM.

Pratique was granted the next morning at 6:45AM and the PRESIDENT MADISON proceeded to dock at Pier 7 south side. By 7:40 AM she was all fast. Five minutes later a Naval Officer came down to the ship and instructed Captain Nielsen to shift to the north side of the pier. One hour and two minutes later the ship was all fast on the north side of the pier. Then began discharge of all remaining Marine equipment, emergency accommodations for the Marines and Manila cargo. While in port that day the PRESIDENT HARRISON caught up with her again. Captain Nielsen went over to that ship to visit his old friends and colleagues Captain Pierson of the PRESIDENT HARRISON and Captain Dale Collins of the freighter DAYSTAR. They were in Captain Pierson's cabin discussing the probable war when American President Lines Far East section chief Steen dropped in around 6:00 PM with orders for the three men. To North China to evacuate Marines were the orders for the PRESIDENT HARRISON. "Deliver your cargo of fuel to Rangoon, Burma" went the orders to Captain Ward and the DAYSTAR. "Make for Balikpapan for bunkers" were the first words for Captain Nielsen. Running low on fuel was the PRESIDENT MADISON and whatever fuel

---

[21] From the Master's Report for Voyage 53–10.

was stored at Manila was for the Navy's immediate use. The service was not really in a position to share with a fuel thirsty passenger liner. The ship was free to go. The Navy had no further need of her at the moment. That order no doubt saved the ship and her crew from the fate in store for the PRESIDENT HARRISON and her men.

With 69 passengers bound for Singapore as well as 1,478 tons of cargo for that port in addition to freight for the same shipments for American ports loaded at Hong Kong, the PRESIDENT MADISON sailed from Manila on December 5th. War broke out between Japan and the United States on December 7th, of course, and it was December 8th in the Dutch East Indies when the PRESIDENT MADISON arrived for fuel at Balikpapan, Borneo. To make way for the U.S.S. MARBLEHEAD, the "502" was forced to shift from the pier and anchor in the roads, but on December 10th the PRESIDENT MADISON again tied up and had her fuel tanks topped off. Shortly after the ship's arrival at Balikpapan, Captain Nielsen reported to the Dutch Naval Control Office. Officers there asked the American Captain to await instructions they would receive once they were able to report the ship's arrival to the Colonial government at Batavia (now Djakarta).

On December 15th, while still awaiting instructions to be forwarded by the Balikpapan Naval Control Station, the American submarine tender U.S.S. HOLLAND[22] hit the PRESIDENT MADISON as the liner lay at anchor in Balikpapan Bay. Damage was slight and repaired by workmen of the local BPM Engineering Company. On the evening of December 16, 1941 orders from Batavia finally came for the PRESIDENT MADISON. Before leaving there on December 18th, three passengers who had embarked at Manila disembarked. Beyond the 60 remaining passengers, 60 more civilian passengers, civilian Dutch women and children embarked for a ride to Soerabaja, Sumatra. Between the two Dutch colonial ports, Captain Nielsen followed secret routing instructions from Dutch officials. On the 19th the American liner arrived at Soerabaja where all the Dutch and eight other passengers disembarked. Now "Wait for instructions from the United States Naval Observers at Batavia" were the orders for Captain Nielsen and wait he did. The PRESIDENT MADISON rode at anchor in Soerabaja Bay through December 28, 1941, when orders came for the ship to make for Colombo, Ceylon as soon as the ship could be made ready for sea. The ship would have sailed immediately but for the request from the ship's local agent who asked Captain Nielsen to delay departure until the next day in order to permit a number of additional passengers, American women and children among them, to embark.

The ship sailed on December 30th. Those orders were in effect a message to Captain Nielsen to resume his ship's usual round the world itinerary on

---

[22]That ship, like a well-known tunnel linking New York and New Jersey, honored John P. Holland, the man credited with the development of the modern submarine. The name has nothing to do with the colloquial name for the Kingdom of the Netherlands.

his trip back to New York via Bombay, Cape Town and Trinidad. With 108 passengers and 29 bags of mail for Ceylon, the liner arrived at Colombo on January 8, 1942. Once the ship's agents informed Captain Nielsen that they had no orders for him, he reported to the U.S. Naval Observer for instructions. Now during wartime, that office at Ceylon had the power to direct American ships despite orders from owners. Commander Lammers of that office gave Captain Nielsen written orders to proceed to Calcutta to discharge all Singapore cargo and to load ore and gunnies for the United States. Thirteen passengers bound for Bombay disembarked before the liner sailed from Colombo on January 9th.

Off Calcutta Pilot Station on January 13, 1942 the ship anchored off Saga Island to await high water. At around 1:30PM the liner received a radio message from the U.S. Naval Observer at Colombo: "Calcutta call cancelled. Proceed Madras." On receipt of that news Captain Nielsen broke radio silence and asked Colombo for confirmation. That came at 1:00AM on January 14th and soon after that the PRESIDENT MADISON sailed for Madras.

Imagine Captain Nielsen's frustration and feel what contempt he must have had for the United States Naval Observer at Colombo when the Madras agent told him after the ship's January 16th arrival that he had no definite news or assignment for the ship and showed him a message from Colombo: "IF THE MADISON CALLS AT MADRAS INSTRUCT CAPTAIN TO PROCEED TO COLOMBO TO LOAD. ALL SINGAPORE CARGO IS TO BE LANDED AT BOMBAY AND ABANDONED THERE."[23] Not a word was said about the ship's passengers so Captain Nielsen insisted that all India and Burma passengers be landed at Madras. That afternoon the American Consul at Madras informed Captain Nielsen that the ship's Colombo agents were instructing him to land Singapore cargo at Madras. That prompted Captain Nielsen to request confirmation from both the Colombo agent and the Naval Observer. He received no answer for quite some time. Finally a message came: "INSTRUCT NIELSEN TO LAND PASSENGERS RETAIN CARGO ON BOARD AND PROCEED TO COLOMBO"[24] Ashore went his India and Burma bound passengers and aboard came water and some fresh provisions. On January 17th the PRESIDENT MADISON sailed from Madras for Colombo.

Two days later the ship arrived back at Colombo, ten days after beginning her odyssey to Naval nonsense. There, the local agent told Captain Nielsen that he had definite instructions from American President Lines' San Francisco office. The ship was to load a maximum cargo at Colombo and steam to Bombay to unload all cargo for Singapore and Penang there. At Bombay the ship would load 4,000 tons of manganese ore. Imagine now, if you can, Captain Nielsen's meeting that day with the United States Naval

---

[23]From Master's Report. ibid.
[24]ibid.

Observer who told him he had had instructions from the Navy Department to turn the ship over to American President Lines' agents. Loading began in earnest and before sailing from Colombo on January 27, 1942 the ship took on 6,155 tons of cargo and three passengers.

Three days later the American liner arrived at Bombay where she waited for a berth inside the Alexandria dock until January 31st. At 3:02PM she tied up. There all Singapore cargo, much of it loaded at Boston and New York and aboard since September, was discharged. Taking on 3,050 tons of manganese ore and 670 tons of general cargo, the ship embarked 141 passengers trying to get home, or as close to home as the ship could take them. Among them were the crew of the Navy gunboat TUTUILLA, who had just been flown out of China. With orders to proceed for bunkers and water to Durban, South Africa, the PRESIDENT MADISON sailed from Bombay on February 6, 1942. Aboard were 178 passengers, 40 bags of mail, a crew of 169 officers and men (a deck cadet signed on at Bombay) and 9,359 tons of cargo. Bound either for Trinidad or New York were 139 tons of freight. Boston bound were another 477 tons but by far the lion's share was the 6,825 tons of freight consigned to New York. For carriage to Baltimore were 1,447 tons of freight, most of it ore. For Los Angeles were 5 tons and the cargoes for both San Francisco and Honolulu was still aboard. After a 12 day run the ship arrived at Durban.

In the aftermath of the Japanese attacks on Pearl Harbor, Singapore and Hong Kong, Japanese radio broadcasts gleefully broadcasts news of the destruction of the PRESIDENT MADISON, trumpeting her capture off Shanghai (they must have meant the PRESIDENT HARRISON), her sinking by torpedo in the South China Sea and her loss by torpedo in the Bay of Bengal. Happy to say they were wrong every time, though Captain Nielsen admitted that had he followed Navy orders ("Stupid Navy operations orders" he called them) to the letter, there was no doubt in his mind that the Japanese would have sunk his vessel. Quite a few people had begun to suspect her loss for the ship was expected to arrive at New York sometime during the first week of March 1942. She neither showed up nor did she alert anyone to her presence by using her radio.

Arriving at Durban the Naval Examination office ordered the ship to wait for a berth inside the harbor. At a few minutes after 6:00 PM on the 19th of February the PRESIDENT MADISON docked at oil wharf. It had been a long time since the ship had had maintenance and her engines needed some 40 hours of repairs as well as to load fuel, water and provisions. Bunkering was completed by the morning of the 20th and the ship was shifted to another berth where repairs were completed and the stores and provisions brought on. Sailing time was called for noon on February 21st. At the appointed hour Captain Nielsen mustered the crew. Not all were present and since two of the missing men were radio operators, the ship could not sail. Four hours later all save one A.B. and the radiomen were aboard. Captain Nielsen took his ship out into the harbor to anchor in the roads to both await the return of his errant men and prevent others from going back ashore where they had obviously enjoyed too many cocktails. Because the port closed at night, the PRESIDENT MADISON could not sail until after 6:00 AM on February 22nd. She was still short one A.B.

Cape Town was next and the ship arrived there at 8:02PM on February 22nd. With permission from the Naval Examination Officer the American liner entered the port and anchored. Granted pratique at 7:30 the next morning, Captain Nielsen obtained a copy of the amended Naval Code. A new man was signed on to replace the man left behind at Durban and the ship sailed that same day for Trinidad where she arrived on March 14th after an uneventful passage. Before sailing for New York, Captain Nielsen asked for 18,000 barrels of fuel and 600 tons of water. The Captain and local agents hoped to have everything completed in time for the ship to join a New York bound convoy scheduled to depart on March 16th. Topping off bunkers at 5:30 PM and finishing taking on water at 10:20 PM that day, the ship was entered in the convoy to leave on the following morning. Escorted by bomber plane until they reached the Gulf of Paria, they sailed at 7:00 AM. Later that day the convoy scattered.

Much to the delight of American President Lines' officials, some of whom had come to accept Japanese reports of the loss of their old vessel, the ship arrived at Quarantine station off New York at 6:58 AM on March 28, 1942. Pratique was granted at 9:05 and the ship tied up at her old New York harbor home, Pier 9, Erie Basin, Jersey City at 11:12 AM. There, Owners' Voyage 53, WSA Voyage 1 technically ended on April 2, 1942 with an offer American President Lines could not refuse. As they had done in the case of the PRESIDENT GRANT, the Maritime Commission wired American President Lines ordering them to charter the ship to the government "or we will seize her." From Washington, A.E. King telegraphed the Line: "PRESIDENT MADISON in interest of national defense and for safety of vessel personnel and cargo you are directed to discharge entire cargo at New York."[25]

On March 31st the ship was bareboat chartered at New York to the War Shipping Administration. There was still cargo aboard and some of it was for New York. After that freight was off the ship on April 2nd, voyage 53, also called WSA voyage 1, ended. Then the ship was ordered to Baltimore on April 4th and to discharge any remaining cargo there. That order was a "CYA[26]" technicality. In fact the PRESIDENT MADISON was already on her way there. She had sailed from her Jersey City pier at 8:00 AM on April 3rd and arrived at Baltimore on the 4th.

With paperwork for hundreds of ships flying about in many directions, proper channels could well be backed up had there been many more questions like those posed on April 9th by J.A. Bouslog of the United States

---

[25] March 28, 1942 telegram from A. E. King to San Francisco office of American President Lines in 901 file for the ship in RG 178 held by the Maritime Administration.
[26] Excuse the vulgarity, CYA means simply "cover your ass."

Maritime Commission. In a cable to Chief of Vessel Operation Section Paul A Sullivan, then in Baltimore, Bouslog asked: "Would appreciate definite instructions as to proper steps to be taken regarding ss PRESIDENT MADISON. Advise how vessel can be placed on bareboat charter to the War Shipping Administration effective September six nineteen forty one if War Shipping Administration did not come into being until February seven nineteen forty two."[27] It would all be moot days later when the Navy took the ship.

On April 7th the Navy decided they wanted to convert the ship for service as a convoy loaded transport. Virtually hours later they changed their minds and thought she would make a dandy evacuation transport. They called for her quick delivery and the PRESIDENT MADISON was handed over to them under allocation for duty as the first evacuation transport on April 11, 1942. The Navy then took another good look at their new vessel and found her not to be the prize they expected, though the ship's stock of wines and liquor went so far unnoticed. Indeed they were not much impressed with the twenty-one year old passenger and cargo liner. Admiral Forrestal wrote to Admiral Land: " . . . It has recently been found by inspection that the material condition of the PRESIDENT MADISON will not justify the large expenditure of government funds required to convert this vessel into a transport for evacuation of wounded. Under present conditions it is not deemed advisable to either tie up conversion facilities ashore or the services of any troop transports or passenger ships for any period necessary to affect the conversion."[28] Nonetheless, the Navy needed troop transports and on the same day decided to so fit the ship. To smooth over paperwork, her bareboat charter was simultaneously revised to a requisition for title purchase by the War Shipping Administration from American President Lines and from the WSA to the United States Navy as purchaser. Indicative of the confusion wrought by the frequent changes of mind, plan and order, consider the following telegram:

GH BALTIMORE, MD APR 9 354P

Paul A Sullivan Chief Vessel Operations Section

War Shipping Administration

Would appreciate definite instructions as to proper steps to be taken regarding SS PRESIDENT MADISON stop. Advise how vessel can be placed on bareboat charter to the War Shipping Administration effective September six nineteen forty one if War Shipping Administration did not come into being until February seven nineteen forty two.

J A Bouslog US Maritime Commission[29]

---

[27] Copy in ship's 901 file at Maritime Administration.
[28] From Admiral Forrestal to Admiral Land April 11, 1942 in 901 file for the ship in RG 178 held by the Maritime Administration.
[29] Copy of that telegram in the ship's 901 file in RG 178 at Maritime Administration.

At least one official was troubled by glaring discrepancies in paperwork. Maybe he had his eye on future historians. And who can deny that what happened on the bridge of the ship on April 11, 1942 was not in the classic comedic mode of a scene in the Marx Brothers' classic comedy *A Night at the Opera*? Meeting his brother Harpo backstage in an Italian opera house, Chico announces: "Hey, I brought you something!" and then asks: "You got something for me?" As Harpo affirmatively shakes his head, he begins to extract from within his coat a salami to hand to Chico just as his brother hands him one. It went something like that at noon on April 11th aboard the PRESIDENT MADISON when American President Lines delivered the ship to the Maritime Commission. The Commission's representative then handed her back to the Line under a service agreement and simultaneously delivered to the line under the terms of the September 6, 1941 bareboat charter agreement. Then the Navy took her. A daily rate of hire for the ship was reckoned at $1,086.93. At the same time American President Lines delivered the ship to the War Shipping Administration under purchase agreement WSA-106. None of that paperwork really mattered, for the Navy got the ship a minute later when the WSA handed her over to them at the conclusion of a four step process. At the time of the sale, there was no pricetag, nor would the ship's marine documents be surrendered, not even as late as February 7, 1944.

On April 12, 1942, the day after the four step swap, American President Lines received an arcane message from the authorities. The jist of it was: "We intend to buy her. Figure out the price or we will requisition her." [30]

From his desk in American President Lines' San Francisco home office, T.E. Cuffe wired Ralph Keating on April 14th: "not clear from your wire whether you are instructing us to turn vessel over to USN for purchase or whether will continue under our present bareboat charter but under Navy operations. would you please give us clarifying instructions."[31]

The ship was sent to the yards of the Maryland Drydock Company for limited conversion to Navy requirements. That work lasted a few weeks for the Navy was initially unsure if they would man the ship themselves or let her civilian crew operate her. In the end they decided to man her themselves and assigned her a crew of 543 officers and men. Her name was changed to KENMORE at her commissioning at Baltimore on August 5, 1942. Designated number AP-62, the KENMORE was under the command of Commander Myron T. Richardson. Now the KENMORE began a "shakedown" cruise of about a month's duration. The ship's new crew trained long and hard as the ship cruised in the sheltered waters of the Chesapeake. That peaceful mission accomplished, the ship called at Norfolk on September 6th where she embarked an important contingent of men, the 13th Marine De-

---

[30] A directive from the WSA's Ralph Keating 901 file in RG178 held by Maritime Administration.
[31] April 14, 1942 telegram from Cuffe to Keating in 901 file. RG 178 held by Maritime Administration.

fense Battalion and both the 18th and 19th Naval Construction Battalions. The KENMORE steamed out to sea on September 19, 1942. Bound for the South Pacific, her first stop was a call at the Naval base at Guantanamo Bay, Cuba where she was ordered to await the other ships assigned to steam to the Pacific with her. Her convoy took five nights passage to reach the Panama Canal and on October 4th the collection of merchantmen steamed out for the Pacific. The convoy arrived at Noumea, New Caledonia five weeks later, on November llth. During eight days there her troops were finally landed. No matter what lay in store for them, they must have been relieved to finally get off the ship. After discharging her cargo the KENMORE joined Rear Admiral R.K. Turner, Commander, Amphibious Forces, South Pacific.

Joining Task Force 62, the KENMORE sailed out of Noumea on November 28, 1942. Her destination was Guadalcanal. After arriving there on December 3rd, she spent 2 days disembarking her troops and cargo. Then she was ordered to return to Noumea where she arrived by December llth. Next was a voyage to San Francisco, a trip made without cover of escort. Alone and but lightly armed, the KENMORE arrived on January 4, 1943 and went to the yards of the General Engineering & Drydock Company for improvements, repairs and maintenance. A month later she was back in service, this time shuttling back and forth between the West Coast and Hawaii. In mid June, she was ordered to return to Noumea from whence authorities sent her back to the United States, but this time to the East Coast. She sailed for Norfolk on July 20, 1943, and after an uneventful passage via Cristobal, Panama Canal Zone and Guantanamo, arrived at the Virginia port on September 2nd.

Shortly after her Norfolk arrival, the ship was sent back across the Chesapeake to Baltimore where she was decommissioned on September 16, 1943. Another career awaited her. Perhaps not suited for conversion to the once desired evacuation transport, the "502" was of a good size and with sufficient power and capabilities to be a dandy hospital ship. Once more the Maryland Drydock Company won a contract to convert this ship. At their Baltimore yards conversion to a hospital ship began in October. All armament of any kind was removed. A five-foot wide green stripe interrupted by red crosses was painted around her hull, now painted white. Further red crosses as specified by Geneva conventions were painted on her decks and affixed to her funnel. Before the job was done, the ship was renamed REFUGE and designated AH 11 when commissioned at Baltimore on February 24, 1944. Proud commanding officer of the ship was Commander M.A. Jurkops, U.S.N.R. whose crew included 22 line and staff officers and more than 200 enlisted men. Senior Medical Officer was Captain C.R. Wilcox, Medical Corps, U.S.N. who had charge of medical facilities as modern and up-to-date as those in the newest shoreside hospital. The ship's medical department comprised 20 physicians, three dentists, five Hospital Corps officers, 29 Navy nurses, an American Red Cross representative, 14 Chief Pharmacist's Mates and 200 hospital corpsmen. Working alongside them was a Volunteer Specialist officer as head of the first optical repair unit ever put aboard a ship. Equipment as far reaching as a mobile field hospital comprising 72 cots, the REFUGE further boasted a laboratory furnished with the newest equipment like autoclaves, bacteriological incubator and refrigerator. The ship had X-ray equipment and all necessary medical and surgical equipment and supplies. Twelve wards provided beds for 630 patients and a few private rooms could be utilized for patients of high rank. Each ward was fitted with a surgical dressing room, diet pantry, utility room, linen locker, toilet and shower facilities. An elevator connected the ship's six deck hospital. On the library's shelves were all kinds of medical books while a complete physiotherapy department and an eye, ear and nose clinic rounded out the gleaming medical facilities installed at Baltimore.

On March 10, 1944 she steamed over to Norfolk where remaining conversion work was undertaken at the Norfolk Navy Yard. By late March she was assigned to the Service Force, Atlantic, ready to begin her mercy work. Irreverent crewmembers called her USS REFUSE—a double entendre to be pronounced as the reader wishes, for after all, the crew used both pronunciations. Her first assignment took her across the Atlantic and through the Mediterranean to Algeria. That first voyage ended at Charleston, South Carolina, principal port for military hospital ships. Two voyages to Britain with returns to Newport News followed. Another Mediterranean trip followed those runs. The REFUGE sailed from Naples for New York with a load of wounded passenger-patients on September 16th. More casualties were embarked at Oran.

On October 6, 1944 the REFUGE came into New York for the first time since she sailed for Baltimore on April 3, 1942. She was drydocked and quickly reconditioned there before returning to duty, this time in the South Pacific. Beginning another long voyage the ship steamed out through the Narrows on her way out of New York on November 1st. Some six weeks later the ship reached her destination where she was assigned to Service Force, 7th Fleet. Records show the ship called at Humboldt Bay, New Guinea on December 16th on her way to the Philippines. Arriving at Leyte on Christmas Eve, she put her boats into the water to help small craft bring patients out to her. The REFUGE served the remainder of the war in the Pacific, making at least six round trips across the Pacific by June 1945, usually between Leyte and New Guinea, often calling other places now mostly memories to veterans and spots on the map to war historians. On July 1, 1945 the REFUGE sailed from Seeadler Harbor for Manila. Stationary there through the end of August, the ship took patients from various other ships of the U.S. Fleet.

With the war winding down, studies were made regarding the costs of reconverting the ship for postwar commercial service. May 11, 1945 brought the figure of $1,170,000.00, a figure that would be billed to the United States Navy. Nobody made any quick plans to do that job for no one evinced great enthusiasm in pouring additional money into this old ship. All she got were reasonable periodic overhauls. On August 31, 1945 the ship was ordered to proceed to Jinsen, Korea. After ten days there she sailed for Shanghai and after a call at Okinawa was sent to Tsingtao, China. At Shanghai on September 27, 1945 a rather special group of men were embarked. Recently freed from harsh years of Japanese captivity, they were the unlicensed personnel of the PRESIDENT HARRISON. They rode the REFUGE to Okinawa, where they transferred to the new, modern C4 type hospital ship SANCTUARY for the trip back home. Four years and five days after they sailed out of San Francisco in the PRESIDENT HARRISON, her crew sailed back into the Bay.

The REFUGE had a few weeks of work to do in East Asia before it became time to send her back across the Pacific. Besides wounded personnel, she took a load of troops aboard and sailed from Okinawa on October 22, 1945. Almost one month passed before she steamed into San Francisco on November 18th. There, she was overhauled again before departing on December 10th for another Pacific crossing. At Yokosuka, Japan the REFUGE embarked Army personnel for repatriation. She sailed for Seattle on January 7, 1946.

Her war duties ended when the last of her soldiers trooped down her gangways after her arrival at Seattle on January 28th. She was the only one of the four "502"'s improved in the 1920s to survive the war. Idleness followed. With one battle star to her name, the REFUGE was again decommissioned at Seattle, this time permanently, on April 2,1946. Declared surplus on May 6, 1946, she was described on a standard Navy surplus personal property form as such that day, with a figure of $6,000,000.00 listed as the total cost of Navy money invested in her. Her name was stricken from the Navy List on May 8th. On June 19, 1946 a check from the American President Lines to the Maritime Commission in the amount of $7,079.00 covered her final mortgage payment. Her immediate future had been decided. She would lay up with the Reserve Fleet at Olympia, Washington. At 3:00 PM on June 29, 1946 the ship was delivered by the Navy to the War Shipping Administration and simultaneously handed over to the Reserve Fleet of the Maritime Commission at her moorage at Olympia, Washington. Then and there the ship was technically renamed PRESIDENT MADISON but no one seems to remember if anyone bothered to restore that name to the ship's bows and stern, boats and other equipment and the ship was usually referred to as REFUGE in Maritime Commission documents of that period. Later that year a Mr. R.J. Wilson of Long Beach, California offered to buy her for use as inexpensive housing but the Maritime Commission would not allow her sale for such a purpose. So there at the anchorage she lay as property of the government until 11:30 AM on February 2, 1948, when the Puget Sound Tug & Bridge Company, agent for her purchaser, took delivery of the ship when one of their tugboats came to take her to her new owners. Recently buying her for scrap was Consolidated Builders of Vancouver, Washington.

Appendices

Among other things, changing the name of a documented American merchant vessel required plenty of paperwork. Here is the text of the standard form authorizing the surrender of the marine document of the PRESIDENT MONROE pursuant to her change of name to PRESIDENT BUCHANAN. Identically worded resolutions covered her "502" class sister ships.

RESOLUTION

WHEREAS an application has been filed by American President Lines, Ltd., San Francisco, California, for the approval required by Sec. 30, subsection C (a), Merchant Marine Act of 1920 (46 U.S.C.961) of the surrender of the marine document of the S.S. PRESIDENT MONROE, Official No. 220325, incident to the change in the name of the said vessel to PRESIDENT BUCHANAN;

WHEREAS the PRESIDENT MONROE is covered by an individual preferred mortgage and a blanket preferred mortgage, both in favor of the United States of America, represented by the U.S. Maritime Commission, and a blanket preferred mortgage given jointly to the United States of America, represented by the U.S. Maritime Commission, and to the Reconstruction Finance Corporation; and

WHEREAS the Reconstruction Finance Corporation has given its consent as mortgagee to the surrender of the marine document of the S.S. PRESIDENT MONROE incident to the change in the name thereof;

RESOLVED, that the Commission hereby consents as mortgagee to the surrender of the marine document of said vessel incident to the change in name thereof;

RESOLVED FURTHER, That the approval required by Section 30, subsection C (a), Merchant Marine Act (46 U.S.C. 961) of the surrender of the marine document of the S.S. PRESIDENT MONROE, Official No. 220325, for the purpose set forth, be, and it is hereby granted upon condition that, concurrently with the surrender of the outstanding marine document, that the vessel shall be redocumented under the laws of the United States, and that all endorsements necessary and proper to preserve the status of all preferred mortgages thereon, of any, be made upon the new document, when issued, with particular reference to that certain individual preferred mortgage and blanket preferred mortgage in favor of the United States of America, represented by the U.S. Maritime Commission, and that certain blanket preferred mortgage given jointly to the United States of America, represented by the Maritime Commission, and to the Reconstruction Finance Corporation; all recorded in the office of the Collector of Customs at San Francisco, California.

RESOLVED FURTHER, That this approval shall be null and void unless the surrender of the marine document of the S.S. PRESIDENT MONROE, Official No/ 220325, hereby approved, is effected within six months of the date of such approval.

APPROVED AS TO FORM

E. Russel Lutz
Assistant General Counsel

RIDER FOR THE SS PRESIDENT VAN BUREN V-50
ROUND THE WORLD

The American President Lines agrees to pay an emergency wage increase to the crew of the SS PRESIDENT VAN BUREN of 25% of the base wages earned by the ship's personnel between arrival at Manila and departure from Singapore. Should the vessel be routed through the Mediterranean Sea, the company further agrees to pay an emergency wage increase of 25% of the base wages earned by ship's personnel between point of departure from Singapore until arrival at Port Said. From departure Port Said until arrival New York the unlicensed personnel will be paid an emergency wage increase of 30% of their base wages. In the event the vessel does not proceed through the Mediterranean Sea, but is rerouted and returns to the United States via the Pacific Ocean, the 25% increase in base wages will apply between arrival at the first Japanese port westbound and departure from the last port in the Orient eastbound. If the vessel proceeds to New York via the Cape of Good Hope the 25% increase in base wages will apply between arrival at Manila and arrival at New York.

In the event the vessel be interned and for that reason be unable to continue her voyage, the company agrees to pay wages including emergency wage increases, to the date members of the crew arrive in a continental United States port.

In the event of loss of personal effects by any member of the crew due to necessity of abandoning ship resulting from torpedoing, mining or bombing of the vessel, the company agrees to reimburse each man so affected by the amount of $150.00.

The company agrees further to furnish, through the medium of private insurance companies, war risk insurance in the amount of $2,000.00 for each member of the crew of the SS PRESIDENT VAN BUREN V-50 for the voyage from San Francisco to New York in accordance with insurance policy or certificate to be made available at the company's head office within forty-eight hours after departure of the vessel from the Pacific Coast.

6/29/40

Included here for illustrative purposes is a copy of the standard form for REQUISITION BAREBOAT CHARTER used by the War Shipping Administration during 1943. This one is for the PRESIDENT TYLER, the former PRESIDENT HAYES and CREOLE STATE.

Form No. 110   Contract No. WSA-5229
6/11/43
WARSHIP
(Passenger Form)

WAR SHIPPING ADMINISTRATION

REQUISITION BAREBOAT CHARTER
FOR COMBINATION CARGO AND PASSENGER VESSELS
Part 1

REQUISITION BAREBOAT CHARTER, dated as of May 12, 1943, between AMERI-CAN PRESIDENT LINES, LTD. Address 311 California St., San Francisco, California OWNER of the SS PRESIDENT GRANT (herein called the "Vessel"), UNITED STATES OF AMERICA, CHARTERER:
WHEREAS, pursuant to Section 902 of the Merchant Marine Act, 1936, as amended, and the President's Executive Orders Nos. 9054 and 9244, the Administrator, War Shipping Administration, has requisitioned the use of the Vessel.

NOW, THEREFORE, pursuant,to said Section 902., the Administrator, War Shipping Administration, hereby transmits to the owner this Charter, consisting of Part I and Part II, setting forth the terms which, in the Administrator's judgment, should govern the relations between the Charterer and the owner and a statement of the rate of hire which, in the Administrators judgment, will be just compensation for the use of the Vessel under the terms of this Charter:

CLAUSE A. PERIOD OF CHARTER: From the time of delivery to the time of expi-ration of the voyage current at the end of the emergency proclaimed by the President of the United States on May 27, 1941; provided, however, that either party may sooner terminate this Charter upon not less than thirty (30) days' written or telegraphic notice to the other. In either case the Vessel shall be redelivered as hereinafter pro-vided.

CLAUSE B. TRADING LIMITS: As and where the Charterer may from time to time determine.

CLAUSE C. HIRE: The owner is hereby given an election either (I) to accept the rate of hire hereinafter set forth in Option I, which states the rate which in the Adminis-trator's judgment will compensation for the, use of the Vessel under the terms Char-ter; or (II) to reject such rate of hire and to of just compensation judicially determined. If the Owner selects Option I, hire at the rate therein stated shall be paid by the Charterer to the Owner in the manner provided in Part II. If the owner does not accept the rate of hire set forth in Option 1, but elects Option II, the right of the Owner to pursue whatever legal remedy it may have to recover just compensation under the laws and Constitution of the United States shall not be impaired or prejudiced either by the execution and delivery of this Charter, or by the acceptance of 75 per cent, of the rate of hire set forth in Option I, and this Charter in any such event shall then be deemed an agreement governing only the relations between the Owner and the United States in respect to matters other than the amount of just compensation for the use of the Vessel under the terms of this Charter.

PART I

Option I—The rate of hire shall be $_____ per day and pro rata for any portion thereof.

Option II—The Charterer shall pay to the Owner just compensation, to be judicially determined, for the use of the Vessel, and shall pay on account of just compensation a sum equal to 75 per centum of the rate of hire set forth in Option I above, as the same may from time to time be, due under the terms of this Charter, and the Owner shall be entitled to sue the United States to recover such further sum as added to such 75per centum will make up such amount as will be just compensation for the use of the Vessel under the terms of this Charter. The term "just compensation" as used in this Clause C and elsewhere in this Charter shall be deemed to include interest, if any, to which the owner would be entitled under the laws and Constitution of the United States if the Owner had rejected this Charter.

TIME OF ELECTION BETWEEN OPTIONS—The Owner shall elect between Option I and Option II on the execution of this Charter, unless a rate has not then been inserted in Option 1. In the latter case, such election shall be made by the Owner in writing within thirty (30) days after receipt of written notice from the Charterer of the rate to be so inserted. In the event of the owner's failure to elect Option I at the time of execution, or within such 30-day period, as the case may be, Option II shall apply; provided, however, that at any time after election has been made of either Option I or option II, but before redelivery and before commencement of suit for just compensation, the Owner may change such election to the other Option in such manner and under such conditions as the Charterer may determine.
PAYMENT ON ACCOUNT—Prior to initial election as between Option I and Option II above, the Charterer, upon application of the Owner, shall pay at least once in each month on account of hire $512..25 per day, and the Owner may accept such payments on account without prejudice to the rights of either party under this Charter or otherwise.

RATE REVISION (Option I only): At any time after October 1, 1943, but not more often than once every 120 days, either party may request a redetermination of the rate of charter hire upon thirty (30) days' written or telegraphic notice to the other. If a revised rate is determined and agreed upon within sue 30-day period, it shall become effective as of the date specified in the determination and shall continue for the balance of the period of this Charter, subject to further redetermination in accordance with the provisions of this paragraph. If a revised rate is not determined and agreed upon within such 30-day period, then the rate of hire in effect at the time of such notice shall apply only until noon (EWT) of the day after the end of such 30-day period, and the Charterer shall make a redetermination of the rate of hire as to which the provisions of Option II of this Clause C shall apply for the balance of the period of this Charter. A change in the rate of charter hire under this paragraph shall not terminate the period of or otherwise modify the provisions of this Charter, and any such charge shall be without prejudice to the rights of either party to terminate this Charter as provided in Clause A, Part I.

CLAUSE D. TOTAL LOSS LIABILITY: In the event of the actual or constructive total loss of the Vessel as provided in Part II of this Charter, the Charterer shall pay to the Owner a sum to be mutually agreed upon but failing such agreement, shall pay just compensation for the loss of the Vessel. In the latter event, the Owner may accept 75 per centum of the sum determined and tendered by the Charterer and. shall be entitled to sue the United States to recover such further sum as added to such 75 per centum will make up such further amount as will be just compensation under the laws and Constitution of the United States.

CLAUSE E. PORT OF DELIVERY: San Francisco, California

CLAUSE F. TIME AND DATE OF DELIVERY: 12:01 A.M. (P.W.T.) on May 12, 1943

CLAUSE G. PORT OF REDELIVERY: Not less favorable to either party than the port of delivery, unless otherwise agreed provided however, that at Owner's option, redelivery shall be made at the U. S. continental port where the Owner maintains its principal operating headquarters.

CLAUSE H. NOTICE OF REDELIVERY: Not less than twenty (20) days' written or telegraphic notice.

CLAUSE I. UNIFORM TERMS: This Charter consists of this Part I and Part II, conforming to the Requisition Bareboat Charter for Combination Cargo and Passenger Vessels, published in the Federal Register of July 1, 1943.

Unless in this Part I otherwise expressly provided, all of the provisions of said Part II shall be part of this Charter as though fully set forth herein.

CLAUSE J. PRIOR CHARTER OR REQUISITION: Execution and delivery of this Charter by the Owner shall not impair any rights or obligations of either the Charterer or the Owner existing at the time of delivery of the Vessel under this Charter and In connection with the use or operation of the Vessel or any services related thereto under any prior Charter or requisition of the Vessel or otherwise, but with respect to any rights or obligations in connection with the use or operation of the Vessel or notices relating thereto after delivery of the Vessel under this Charter, the terms of this Charter shall govern.

CLAUSE K. SPECIAL PROVISIONS: 1. In the event that the surveys and inventories of the Vessel required upon delivery hereunder be waived, the parties hereto agree that the condition surveys and inventories of the Vessel upon delivery as required in Part II of this Charter shall be the condition surveys and inventories taken of the Vessel upon her delivery under a prior charter between the parties dated March 4, 1942 (Contract No. WSA-109). In the event that surveys and inventories of the Vessel under such prior charter were waived, the parties hereto agree, for the purposes of this Charter to be bound by the provisions of such prior charter respecting their mutual obligations when surveys and inventories under such charter are waived. Whenever reference is made In Part II of this Charter to the condition or class of the Vessel upon delivery, or to surveys and inventories of the Vessel upon delivery, such references shall be deemed to be the condition and class and inventories of the vessel upon her delivery under the above mentioned prior Charter and shall be governed by the provisions of such prior Charter relating to surveys and inventories upon delivery.

IN WITNESS WHEREOF, the Owner has executed this Charter quadruplicate the 13th day of January, 1944, and has elected Hire Option (election to be deferred if rate not inserted in Part 1), and the Charterer has executed this Charter in quadruplicate the 21st day of January, 1944.

As to execution for OWNER	AMERICAN PRESIDENT LINES, LTD.
D. T. BUCKLEY	M. J. BUCKLEY
Secretary	Vice Presidant

or if not incorporated

In the presence of:

Witness

witness   BY: UNITED STATES OF AMERICA
                                       E.S. LAND, ADMINISTRATOR
                                       WAR SHIPPING ADMINISTRATION

Approval as to form: BY: T.M. Torrey
                                       For the Administrator

FRANK J. ZITO
Assistant General Counsel

BIBLIOGRAPHY

REGISTERS and SHIP LISTS

Dictionary of American Naval Fighting Ships—eight volumes, Superintendent of Documents U.S. Government Printing Office Washington, D.C.

Johnson's Steam Vessels Annual—1921 ed. Eads Johnson, N.Y., N.Y.

Johnson's Steam Vessels and Motor Ships Annual—1927, 1931 eds. Eads Johnson, N.Y., N.Y.

Lloyd's Register of Shipping—Various editions (1918–1960), published annually by Lloyd's of London, London, U.K.

Merchant Marine Statistics—1930, 1931, 1932—published by the Bureau of Navigation, U.S. Dept. of Commerce Washington, D.C.

Merchant Ships—1942—E.C. Talbot-Booth, published by the Macmillan Co., Ltd. London & New York

Merchant Ships of the World—1923—Frank C. Bowen & F. N. Wedge, published by Sampson Low Muston & Co., London 1923

Merchant Vessels of the United States—U.S. Treasury Department, Bureau of Customs, later by Commerce Department. Various Editions (1919—1950)

Register of Ships Belonging to the United States Shipping Board, First Edition, February 1919

Register of Ships Belonging to the United States Shipping Board, Fourth Edition, January 1920

Register of Ships Belonging to the United States Shipping Board, Fifth Edition, August 1920

Supplement to the Register of Ships, (5th Edition) No.2-Feb. 1921, No.3-May 1921, No.4-Nov. 1921

Seagoing Vessels of the United States—Various Editions (1920–1940) published annually by the Steamboat Inspection Service, Bureau of Navigation, Department of Commerce, Washington, D.C.

PERIODICALS, NEWSPAPERS and ANNUAL REPORTS

American Shipping—November/December 1924

Belgian Shiplover, The—*various issues*—*this publication included invaluable ship lists compiled by the late Norman McKellar of Tamworth, Australia*

Daily Freight Record—New York—various 1930's editions

Los Angeles Times—various issues 1920's, 1930's

Marine Engineering—various issues 1920's–1940's, (this magazine took over *Shipping Review* in 1935, adding that late publication's name to its own)

Marine News—(American periodical-not the organ of the World Ship Society) various issues 1920's-1938

Marine Review—various issues through 1960

New York Herald Tribune—various issues 1920's–1940's

New York Maritime Register—various issues 1919–1949

New York Times, The—various issues 1917–1960

OUR YARD—House organ of the Sun Shipbuilding Corporation, Chester, PA.

Pacific Marine Review—various issues through 1951

Philadelphia INQUIRER—various issues 1920 through 1927

Report to Congress of the Federal Maritime Commission—1937, 1938, 1940, 1941, 1944

San Francisco Chronicle—various issues 1916–1946

San Francisco Examiner—various issues 1916–1946

San Francisco Morning Call—various issues through 1946

San Francisco Morning Call-Bulletin—various issues

*Seabreezes*various issues

Seattle POST-INTELLIGENCER—various issues 1923

Shipping Illustrated—various issues 1917–1932

Shipping Magazine—various issues 1917–1933

Steamboat Bill—the quarterly journal of the Steamship Historical Society of America—various issues 1970–1990

ANNUAL REPORTS

Second Annual Report of the United States Shipping Board, 1918

Third Annual Report of the United States Shipping Board, 1919

Fourth Annual Report of the United States Shipping Board, 1920

Fifth Annual Report of the United States Shipping Board, 1921

Sixth Annual Report of the United States Shipping Board, 1922

Ninth Annual Report of the United States Shipping Board, 1925

Thirteenth Annual Report of United States Shipping Board, 1929

Maritime Commission Reports to Congress . . . annually 1937—1945

BOOKS

The American Merchant Marine—American Bureau of Shipping (1933)

Brown, Prof. Giles T.—*Ships that Sail No More*, University of Kentucky Press Lexington 1966

Charles, Roland W.—*Troopships of World War II*, Army Transportation Association, Washington, D.C. 1947

Clephane, Lewis—*History of the Naval Overseas Transportation Service in World War I*, Dept. of the Navy, Naval History Division Washington, D.C. 1969

Dollar, Capt. Robert—*Memoirs*, Four volumes privately printed. San Francisco 1918–1928

Dollar, Capt. Robert—*130 Years of Steam Navigation* privately printed San Francisco 1931

Grover, Capt. David H. and Grover, Cmdr. Gretchen G.—*Captives of Shanghai*, Western Maritime Press, Napa, California, 1989

Hurley, Edward N.—*The New Merchant Marine*, The Century Foreign Trade Series, The Century Press, 1922

Hurley, Edward N.—*The Bridge to France*, J.B. Lippincott & Co. Philadelphia & London, 1927

Marine Progress.—*Merchant Marine Laws* Enacted by the 74th Congress 1936

Mattox,W.C.—*Building the Emergency Fleet*, The Penton Publishing Co., Cleveland 1920

Mitchell, W.H. & Sawyer,L.A.—*The Empire Ships*, Second Edition, Lloyd's of London Press, London 1990

Nelson, Prof. Bruce—*Workers on the Waterfront, Seamen, Longshoremen and Unionism in the 1930's*, University of Illinois Press Urbana and Chicago, 1990

Newell, Gordon & Williamson, Joe.—*Pacific Coastal Liners*, Seattle, Superior Publishing 1959

Niven, Prof. John—*The American President Lines And Its Forebears*, University of Delaware Press 1987

Skaggs, Professor Jimmy M.—*The Great Guano Rush*, St.Martin's Griffin, New York 1994

Skalley, Michael—*A Medal for MARIGOLD*, Seattle, Superior Publishing 1982

Society of Naval Architects and Marine Engineers—*Transactions*—Volume 29— 1921, New York

Stindt, Fred A.—*Matson's Century of Ships* Privately published at Modesto, California, April 1982

Swazey, Edward Scott,—*New York Shipbuilding Corp.* Privately published Camden, NJ 1921

Time, Inc.,—*Our Ships,* An Analysis of the United States Merchant Marine, reprinted and expanded special 1937 edition of FORTUNE magazine devoted to American shipping.

United States Maritime Commission—*Financial Readjustments in Dollar Steamship Lines Inc., Ltd.* Feb. 17, 1938 Washington, DC..

Weiss, George—*America's Maritime Progress,* The Marine News, 1920

Worden, William L.—*CARGOES Matson's First Century in the Pacific,* University Press of Hawaii Honolulu 1981

UNPUBLISHED SOURCES

Movement Cards of vessels of the port of San Francisco, 1926–1950

Assorted Notes and/or pamphlets of the Admiral Line (Pacific Steamship Company), Charles Nelson Company, Matson Navigation Company, Swayne & Hoyt

Dissertation: Gregory C. O'Brien "The Life of ROBERT DOLLAR" presented to the General Faculty of the Claremont School 1968

PRINTED PUBLICITY MATTER

Booklets, brochures, plans, sailing schedules, rate sheets, menus and programs printed by/for United States Mail Steamship Company, United States Lines and Dollar Steamship Lines, and American President Lines, all held in the author's collection